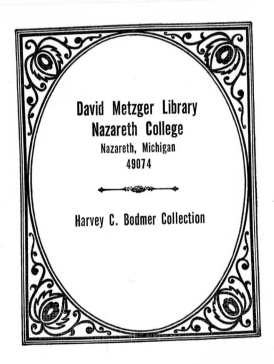

To Lose a Battle
France 1940

To Lose a Battle
France 1940

by ALISTAIR HORNE

LITTLE, BROWN AND COMPANY · BOSTON · TORONTO

Grateful acknowledgment is made for permission to re-
print the following copyrighted material:

Excerpts from the book *Panzer Leader* by General Heinz
Guderian, translated by Constantine FitzGibbon. Published
1952 by E. P. Dutton & Co., Inc. and reprinted with their
permission.

Excerpts from *The Rommel Papers,* Copyright 1953 by
B. H. Liddell Hart. Reprinted by permission of Harcourt,
Brace & World, Inc.

The poems "Spring Song" (or, "Crocus Time") and "Baku,
or the Map Game" from *Siren Song* by A. P. Herbert,
published by Methuen & Co. Ltd. and Doubleday & Company, Inc. Copyright 1940 by Alan Patrick Herbert. Reprinted by permission of Sir Alan Herbert, his agents A. P.
Watt & Son, and Doubleday & Company, Inc.

Excerpts from *The Second World War* by Winston
Churchill, published by Houghton Mifflin Company.

Excerpts from *Berlin Diary* by William Shirer. Copyright
1940, 1941 by William Shirer. Reprinted by permission of
Alfred A. Knopf, Inc.

ILLUSTRATION CREDITS
Front Endleaf: Newsphoto
Back Endleaf: United Press International
Title Page: Wide World Photos

For Alexandra

La France a perdu une bataille!
Mais la France n'a pas perdu la guerre!

(France has lost a battle!
But France has not lost the war!)

> —General de Gaulle's proclamation in
> London after the Fall of France

When at last . . . the will-to-live of the German nation—instead of continuing to be wasted away in purely passive defence—can be summoned together for a final, active showdown with France, and thrown into this in one last decisive battle with the very highest objectives for Germany; then, and only then, will it be possible to bring to a close the perpetual and so fruitless struggle between ourselves and France.

> —ADOLF HITLER, *Mein Kampf,* 1925

Preface

IT IS now roughly one hundred years since the Franco-Prussian War began, fifty since Versailles concluded World War I, and thirty since the first act of World War II, the Fall of France. This book endeavours to tell the story of the last of these episodes. Although it was designed to stand firmly on its own, it represents the third panel of a triptych of which the other two were *The Fall of Paris: The Siege and the Commune, 1870–1871* and *The Price of Glory: Verdun 1916,* and is therefore closely linked to the theme of the earlier books. During most of this past hundred years —at least until 1945—the seminal issue in Europe was Franco-German rivalry. Now it is no longer so. As I explained in the Preface to *The Fall of Paris,* the original ambition of the triptych was to deal with this important chunk of modern European history, woven around three great Franco-German battles, each decisive in its own war and in wider contexts as well. They are not, essentially, military studies. As the reader will discover from the present book, there are various aftereffects from both 1870–71 and 1916 that have an important bearing on the French defeat of 1940. And so much that has happened since then—is still happening—can find an explanation in the debacle of 1940.

In a number of ways, *To Lose a Battle* has been the most difficult to write of the three books. It was not easy to decide when the story begins and ends; to start in with the crushing superiority of the German Stukas and Panzers on May 13th leaves a lot unexplained; and the *decisive* battle was over long before Pétain asked for armistice—even before the British Expeditionary Force embarked at Dunkirk. After I had finished my researches I decided to begin with France's moment of supreme power, as seen at the Victory Parade of 1919; to deal with only those factors in the interwar world which seemed relevant to France's weakness and Germany's strength in 1940; and to end the main account with

the failure of the last Allied counterattacks in northern France—
May 21st to May 24th, 1940. After this date, for the Germans
the campaign was little more than a matter of marching.

The greatest difficulty of all concerned source material. The
Siege of Paris and the Commune together continued, in the same
setting, for nine months; Verdun, ten. Thus in both battles a multitude of chroniclers on either side had the leisure to provide detailed day-by-day accounts of what went on—often of superb
quality. The historian is additionally aided by the presence in Paris
in 1870–71 of many "neutral" British and American observers
whose accounts provide a special dimension of objectivity; while,
for 1916, the official war histories of both sides have long been
open to scrutiny. In contrast, the decisive battle for France in 1940
lasted less than two weeks, but covered over two hundred miles
in depth alone. Many war diarists, especially on the French side,
had no opportunity to write up their diaries or even scribble a
letter home.

As to the German side, the Allied capture of all Nazi archives
provided historians with an unprecedented treasure-trove. The
French, on the other hand, have not yet published an official history of 1940* and the archives at Vincennes are not open to inspection. It is easy to understand French reticence; yet one feels
it may be prompted less by what is there than by what is not there.
However, the lack of any French official history is in part compensated for by the plentiful personal accounts of participants
granted access to the archives—such as Generals Doumenc
(*Major-Général* of the French General Staff), Roton (General
Georges's Chief of Staff) and Ruby (Chief of Staff to the French
Second Army); not to mention the lengthy memoirs by the leaders
themselves, Reynaud, Gamelin, and Weygand. But because of
the pressure and speed of events—if for no other reason—such
accounts often disagree, and it is not easy to determine what happened and when.

For example, recording General Weygand's crucial visit to the
northern commanders on May 21st,† both Baudouin and Churchill—neither of whom was there—write that Weygand's plane was

---

* The findings of such enquiries as the Serre Commission are at best only partially satisfactory.
† See Chapter 18.

attacked and forced to land at Calais. Weygand himself says he landed unchallenged at Norrent-Fontès and then flew on to Calais. After the meeting, Baudouin says Weygand left from Ypres at 4 P.M. by torpedo boat from Dunkirk to Cherbourg; Churchill says 7 P.M., by submarine to Dieppe; while Colonel Goutard puts the time at "between 5 and 6 P.M." Churchill and others state that Lord Gort arrived, too late, at the Ypres meeting at 8 P.M.; Bénoist-Méchin, "about 9 P.M."* These may seem like hair-splitting points, but they make the historian cautious about accuracy on the bigger issues.

Napoleon once warned: "Above all, be distrustful of eyewitnesses . . . the only thing my Grenadiers saw of Russia was the pack of the man in front." Obviously the advice can be taken too far, and Napoleon's Grenadiers certainly saw more of the Russian campaign than he would have liked. But one has to be cautious about the fallibility of human memory; with one or two notable exceptions (such as the late Air Chief Marshal Sir Arthur Barratt, whose reminiscences proved invaluable to me) I have restricted myself to what was written at the time, or very soon afterwards. Even here, one has to exercise caution. For reasons suggested earlier, I found myself forced to lean heavily on German eyewitness accounts of battle operations—such as the crossing of the Meuse. Some, such as Rommel, seldom let one down, even though at times he stole perhaps more than his fair share of the glory. But all too often the National Socialist overtones of the moment, the vaunting of Teutonic deeds and depreciation of the enemy's—never a reverse, never the sight of a burnt-out German tank—make one recoil in distrust. On the other hand many of the memoirs of French leaders are but one long apologia; although, set against each other, they too can be revealing.

Inevitably, there is much in this book that will be hurtful to French *amour-propre*. Although many of the studies emanating from France herself could scarcely be more scorching, the French —perhaps more than most nations and particularly at this time of resurgent nationalism—tend to regard outsiders writing about their history as *voyeurs* who peep through other people's bathroom

---

* Paul Baudouin, *Private Diaries. March 1940–January 1941;* J. Bénoist-Méchin, *60 Days That Shook the West;* W. S. Churchill, *The Second World War,* Vol. II; Col. A. Goutard, *The Battle of France, 1940;* Gen. M. Weygand, *Recalled to Service.*

keyholes. And it is indeed almost impossible for any outsider fully to comprehend the lingering wounds left by invasion and defeat in a nation as proud as France.

Again, Dutchmen and Belgians and my own countrymen may criticise me for dealing too briefly with their roles in the Battle of France; Americans may feel that I should have said more of their role in the interwar period, and of the 1940 exchange of communications between Reynaud, Churchill and Roosevelt. I can only excuse myself by repeating that this is, like *The Fall of Paris* and *The Price of Glory,* primarily a story about France and Germany.

Acknowledgments

DURING MY researches on this book, I was—once again—accorded much indispensable help, with utmost courtesy, by Dr. Rohwer and Herr Haupt of the Bibliothek für zeitgeschichte in Stuttgart and by M. Hornung of the Bibliothèque de Documentation Internationale Contemporaine of the University of Paris. Of the libraries and archives in England, the vast collection of books and periodicals owned by the Imperial War Museum proved invaluable, and I am additionally most grateful for access to other collections granted me by the Ministry of Defence Library, Professor Michael Howard of King's College, London, Captain Sir Basil Liddell Hart, the Royal United Services Institute, and the London Library. In Germany, the Bundesarchiv proved a source of much vital material; and in France, I am grateful to Colonel le Goyet of the Service Historique de l'Armée at Vincennes for his answers on certain specific points. Among the people who have helped in various ways, given advice, or the benefit of their own memories, I particularly wish to record my thanks to Major-General Sir E. L. Spears (who, in his classical reminiscences on the French scene in two World Wars, deserves to rate as the Suetonius of our times), Captain Sir Basil Liddell Hart, Colonel A. Goutard, Mrs. Clare Boothe Luce, the late Air Chief Marshal Sir Arthur Barratt, M. Gaston Palewski, M. Édouard Leng, Constantine Fitzgibbon, Colonel G. B. Jarrett.

For illustrations and their collation, I am beholden to Colonel Jarrett, to the Bibliothek für Zeitgeschichte, the Musée de la Guerre (Vincennes), Radio Times Hulton Library, the Imperial War Museum, and to the Honorable Mrs. Anne Money-Coutts and Mrs. C. M. James; and for maps to Mr. K. C. Jordan, F.R.G.S.

Throughout the sifting of research material, I was enormously helped by the painstakng and critical diligence of Mr. Peter Bradley. Among those who read the manuscript and offered valuable suggestions, I am particularly grateful to Major-General the Honorable Miles Fitzalan-Howard, who scrutinised it with a professional eye, and also to Mr. Philip Whitting; as well as to my editors in London and New York, Mr. Alan Maclean, Mr. Richard Garnett, and Mr. Harry Sions, to whom I am indebted not only for their arduous work done on the manuscript but also for their sustaining encouragement over the past many months. I owe a special debt of thanks to Mrs. Angus Nicol for typing the manuscript, several times, in addition to providing invaluable assistance in a multitude of other ways—often at impossible hours. I am deeply appreciative of the unfailing kindness of my old friend, William F. Buckley, Jr., who at a critical moment in production provided a haven of peace; and finally my wife deserves special mention both for acting as map-reader during tours of the battlefields and, above all, for putting up with nearly a decade of battles.

Unlike some of the principals in this story, however, the author recognises that for any disasters in the end result he has nobody but himself to blame.

London, Ashington, Château de Rougemont, 1967–68.

Contents

List of Illustrations

Giraud and Corap

Winston Churchill with Generals Ironside, Gamelin, Gort and Georges

Rommel, Keitel, Kleist and Manstein

Halder, Brauchitsch, Rundstedt, Balck and Reichenau

(Between pages 300 and 301)

Barricaded Dutch road is no barrier to Germans

German engineers swarm over Belgian roadblock

Rotterdam after Nazi air raids

German paratroopers land in the Netherlands

Germans storm Belgian fortified bunker

Germans penetrate the "impenetrable" Ardennes

Crossing the Meuse near Dinant

German motorcycle reconnaissance unit

German tanks pass demolished French column

The end for a French B tank

The end for a German motorcyclist

(Between pages 396 and 397)

German troops on the move—panzer column and infantry-men

Refugees on the western front

Gort and Barratt

War comes to England

A couple of French soldiers surrender

German victors jeering at French prisoners

German infantry on the march, singing

Germans in Berlin follow progress of war

Lebrun and de Gaulle

Weygand, Baudouin, Reynaud and Pétain

Truck pulling armistice railroad car to Compiègne

Ribbentrop, Keitel, Goering, Hess, Hitler and Brauchitsch at Compiègne

(Between pages 492 and 493)

List of Maps

DIAGRAMS

Abbreviations

AASF	Advanced Air Striking Force
BEF	British Expeditionary Force
CGT	Confédération Générale du Travail
CGTU	Confédération Général du Travail Unitaire
CIGS	Chief of the Imperial General Staff
DINA	Division d'Infanterie Nord Africaine
DAT	Défense Aérienne du Territoire
DLC	Division Légère Cavalier (Light Cavalry Division)
DLM	Division Légère Mécanique (Light Mechanized Division)
GHQ	General Headquarters
GQG	Grand Quartier Général (French G.H.Q.)
OKH	Oberkommando des Heeres (Army High Command)
OKL	Oberkommando der Luftwaffe (Air Force High Command)
OKM	Oberkommando der Kriegsmarine (Navy High Command)
OKW	Oberkommando der Wehrmacht (Armed Forces High Command)
PC	Poste de Commandement (Command Post)
PCF	Parti Communiste Français
SFIO	Section Française de la IIe Internationale Ouvrière
ZOAN	Zone d'Opérations Aériennes Nord (Air Operations Zone North)

Part I

1

Grandeur and Misery of Victory*
(1919−1930)

Victory was to be bought so dear as to be almost indistinguishable from defeat.
　　　　　　　　−WINSTON CHURCHILL, *The World Crisis*

Youth could win, but had not learned to keep; and was pitiably weak against age. We stammered that we had worked for a new heaven and a new earth, and they thanked us kindly and made their peace.
　　　　　　　　−T. E. LAWRENCE, on Versailles

Sunday, July 13, 1919

EVEN ON the afternoon preceding the next day's great event, the crowds had begun to form along the Champs Élysées. By 3 A.M. that night an estimated one hundred thousand people had already taken up positions there. The Arc de Triomphe was unapproachable. A tone of restrained—almost sober—jubilation dominated, tempered by the presence of so many women still clad in mourning for a son or a husband. It was all very different from the August day five years earlier when frenetic Parisians had swarmed through the city singing the "Chant du Départ" and shouting "*À Berlin!*"

The janitors and charwomen had barely finished sweeping away the debris of diplomacy from Versailles's great Hall of Mirrors, where in 1871 a victorious Prussian king had proclaimed himself Kaiser and which, half a century later, France with an unsurpassable sense of theatre had selected as the fitting stage for the

---

* The title of Clemenceau's memoirs.

final act in the tragedy entitled Revenge. After more than four
years of the most terrible war humanity had ever known, peace
was a fact. In London, as the guns boomed out the news that the
treaty had at last been signed, loyal Britons had thronged outside
Buckingham Palace to hear King George V say, "I join you in
thanking God." But somehow—the discussions having dragged on
so tediously—details of the treaty itself had fallen a bit flat. The
British public was as glad as the press to get back to more immediate and appealing topics; there were the first postwar Wimble-
don and Henley, even though the *Illustrated London News*
mourned that the latter was "not quite itself this year."

In Paris especially the signature of the treaty had swiftly become eclipsed by the imminence of this other, tangibly more magnificent occasion. July 14, 1919, was the day of the Victory Parade,
France's moment of supreme triumph—to many Frenchmen, possibly the greatest triumph in all her long history. Certainly never
was there to be an occasion more fitting of *le jour de gloire* celebrated by "The Marseillaise" than this first Quatorze Juillet since
Alsace-Lorraine had returned to the fold from the forty-eight
years of bondage.

On the eve of the procession, a temporary cenotaph* almost
filled the mighty vault of the Arc de Triomphe. Each of the four
sides of the cenotaph was guarded by a Victory, the wings of
which had been fashioned from the fabric of warplanes. On the
surfaces of its plinth could be read: *Aux Morts pour la Patrie.*
Throughout the night, flames of Greek fire smouldered and flickered from urns mounted at its angles, while powerful searchlights
transformed its gilt plaster to gold. Surrounding the cenotaph,
soldiers of all arms of the French Army kept vigil with rifles
reversed.

July 14, 1919

Shortly after midnight the massive pylon was towed out from
under the arch by tractors, to enable the triumphal procession to
pass through it, and established a short distance away. As the
dawn prefacing a day of silver and blue broke (it recalled to some
of the more romantic-minded French journalists the day of Aus-

---

* The idea of burying under the Arc de Triomphe an Unknown Warrior, selected from the remains of eight fallen at Verdun, was not conceived until later.

terlitz), a remarkable spectacle greeted those lucky enough to have gained access to balconies high up on buildings flanking the Champs Élysées. As far as the eye could see, down the green line of the Avenue de la Grande Armée, and all the way along the five miles of the processional route, fluttered the flags and pennants of the Allied nations from an endless forest of white masts. On either side of the Rond Point was heaped a huge mound of captured German guns, surmounted on one side by the Gallic cock of 1914, preening himself for the fight, and on the other by the victorious cock of 1918, crowing his ascendancy to the world. Down at the Porte-Maillot, the resplendent masses of the Allied contingents were forming up behind their leaders, greeted by members of the Municipal Council, who, like the aediles of antiquity, were opening the city to the conquering armies.

At 7:45, a car arrived at the Étoile bringing Clemenceau, the dread "tiger" who had flogged France from the brink of defeat on to victory through the last desperate year of the war. Occasionally shooting fierce glances to right and left, the old tiger—followed by his inseparable lieutenant, a serious and pasty-faced young man named Georges Mandel—shambled slowly up to the official stand. Shortly after eight appeared the President of the Republic himself: Raymond Poincaré, the man of Lorraine, a symbol of all that France had fought so gallantly to regain, his open car cheered along the length of the Champs Élysées. Accompanied by France's two glorious Marshals, Joffre and Foch, the President laid a wreath at the base of the cenotaph. The Marshals then drove off to take up their positions at the head of the parade. As the President resumed his position on the tribune, cannon began to speak out in the distance; from the Bois de Boulogne, from Mont Valérien, from all the forts which, during the bitter winter of 1870, had endeavoured to save the city when besieged by the now humbled enemy. Rockets soared up and exploded over the Arc de Triomphe. Down at the Porte-Maillot, a captain took out his watch and gave the order heard at so many lethal dawns during the preceding four years: "*Avancez!*" The drums rolled, the trumpets sounded out their fanfares in those peculiarly Gallic, almost querulously high-pitched notes, and approaching the Arc de Triomphe was soon heard the music of the regimental bands playing out the stirring strains of "Vous n'aurez pas l'Alsace et la

Lorraine." A sense of expectancy rippled through the crowd. The fatigue of the long wait evaporated.

The chains had been removed, the ones which had encircled the Arc ever since the day, forty-eight years ago, the Prussians had engraved hatred in French hearts by insisting on their rights to a triumphal march through the prostrate city. Now, for the first time since that day of shame, marching men appeared through the sacred arch. But those who led the way across the threshold in this historic moment were not Joffre nor Foch; nor the cavalry, nor the Zouaves, nor any Allied detachment. They were the three young men, or what remained of them; unspeakably crippled by war, still in uniform, and trundled by their nurses in primitive chariots like the prams of deprived children. Immediately behind them came a large contingent of more *grands mutilés*. Officers and men of all ranks mixed together, many already in mufti, they marched—or hobbled—without precedence or any semblance of military order, twelve abreast. Hardly one had not lost an eye or a limb, and many bore on their chests France's most coveted decoration, the Médaille Militaire. The totally blind—some accorded the privilege of being ensign-bearers—came led by the one-legged or the armless; men with their destroyed faces mercifully hidden behind bandages; men with no hands; men with their complexions still tinted green from the effects of chlorine; men with mad eyes staring out from beneath the skullcaps which concealed some appalling head injury. Some were famous heroes, easily recognised by the crowd; among them, identifiable by his immense stature, limped Sergeant André Maginot, already a well-known figure in the National Assembly, who had been badly wounded at Verdun.

With a painful, halting pace the column moved by, down the Champs Élysées to the stands specially set apart for them. As they passed a stand filled with a hundred and fifty young Alsatian girls in national costumes, flowers rained down upon them. For a moment the spectacle of the broken men was met with a stunned silence. Then, "an immense cry, which seemed to spring from the very entrails of the race, arose from the vast crowd, a cry which was both a salute and a pledge."

No one who watched the *mutilés* pass that day could be unaware of what they represented: the many thousands more, hopelessly maimed, lodged in hospitals across the country which they would never leave; the hundreds of thousands of other war casualties, only relatively more fortunate, to whom the future could hardly offer much—and who in turn would be able to contribute little toward the reconstruction of their exhausted nation; but above all, the lost legions of men who had not returned at all from the martyrdom of the western front, either whole or crippled. From metropolitan France alone, these numbered 1,315,000, or 27 percent of all men of the ages eighteen to twenty-seven. No combatant nation except little Serbia had a higher mortality rate; higher than Russia, higher than Germany or her allies. It was a fact which, so brutally brought home on this luminous day of victory celebrations, would never cease to haunt the nation.

There was a long pause in the procession, "as if to permit us to breathe—or to dry our tears." Then came *la gloire* itself. Accompanied by a thunderous roll of drums and blast of trumpets a squadron of the magnificent Gardes Républicains rode through the Arc de Triomphe, and just forty yards behind them appeared Joffre and Foch. Up to the eleventh hour there had been some discussion as to whether Joffre, fallen from grace during the Battle of Verdun, should take part in the parade at all, but Foch had settled matters by declaring that unless Joffre rode with him, *inter pares,* he would not march either. So here they both were, riding abreast, the man who had saved France on the Marne in 1914, and the man who had brought her to final victory in 1918; France resisting, France attacking. Each of the two leaders was wearing the uniform with which he had so long been associated: Foch all in grey, with a kepi bearing three rows of oak leaves; Joffre in black dolman and scarlet breeches. Joffre, a portly figure showing his age, seemed to be much moved by the vast crowds, which he repeatedly pointed out to Foch as if surprised they should still recognise him; Foch, rigidly upright in the saddle of his famous charger, Emir, his Marshal's baton with its seven gold stars firmly grasped in his right hand, resembled all that a victorious general should be. A few discreet paces behind—a position that had long become habitual—rode the neat and dapper General Maxime Weygand, Foch's Chief of Staff. Then came the rest of the Allied Generalissimo's staff, including a Colonel Georges who, like Weygand, would be called upon to fill a role of dreadful responsibility twenty years later.

Now it was the turn of the Allies. First, in alphabetical order, appeared the Americans with General Pershing at their head. Swinging along the route, they struck a *Times* correspondent as "the finest American troops Paris has yet seen, and their marching is really perfect." As the bandsmen strummed out "Over There," something about the lilt of it reminded excited French ears of the jazz that was now all the rage in Paris. Next came the Belgians, followed after a five-minute interval by the British, led by Sir Douglas Haig. As they bore past the colours of two hundred regiments that had fought and bled in Flanders or along the Somme, the crowd showed its enthusiasm by taking up the refrain of "Tipperary" that France had got to know so well. Then followed Italians in slate-coloured uniforms, little Japanese in khaki, Portuguese, Rumanians, Serbs and Siamese, and men wearing French tunics of *bleu horizon;* men from the "new" nations who owed their existence to the Allied victory and who would in turn be abandoned by these same Allies within the next two decades: Czechoslovaks and Poles. So many armies it had required to overthrow the might of the German Empire. Yet one army was missing, one without whose aid the "miracle of the Marne" could never have occurred and without whose bottomless reserves of men there would not this day be any victory celebrations: Russia, now sealed off from her former allies by revolution and civil war, and apparently—forgotten!

Once the initial restraint imposed by the sombre overture to the parade had passed, the crowd allowed itself to go wild. As each national detachment marched by, a fresh gust of cheering broke loose. Against all orders, cavalrymen closing intersections hoisted girls onto their saddles to provide them with a better view. Children and young women flung basketfuls of flowers onto the triumphal way and garlanded the bayonets of the soldiers with green and gilded paper crowns, so that as the morning went on it seemed as if they were marching on a carpet of blossoms. On this day at least there was nothing grudging in France's gratitude to her allies. But, understandably, it was the mighty French contingent bringing up the rear of the parade for which the spectators had preserved the power of their lungs. A solitary figure riding through the Arc de Triomphe on a white horse, gravely majestic, tall and magnificent in a uniform of *bleu horizon,* the austere face even paler than usual, provided the signal for the opening of the day's great climax: Marshal Pétain, the Commander-in-Chief.

Behind him followed the poilus he had led through the ten months' hell of Verdun, had doctored through the mutinies which so nearly broke the French Army the following year. From each of France's twenty-one army corps, a company of the regiment bearing the highest battle honours for gallantry had been selected to march in the parade. What a spectacle of triumphant glory they presented as they marched past with the regimental music thundering out "Sambre-et-Meuse" and the "Marche Lorraine," the battle hymns that had so stirred French hearts during the years of agony! There came the little chasseurs with their rapid pace and large floppy berets, men who had borne the brunt of the first German onslaught at Verdun; resplendent-looking hussars and cuirassiers in their glittering breastplates, who had not really had much of a chance in this war, after the first mad carnage during the Battle of the Frontiers; marvelous-looking men from France's overseas empire, Foreign Legionnaires, ferocious Moroccan Goums in turbans and flowing white robes, Algerian and Indo-Chinese Tirailleurs, coal-black Senegalese with an alarming reputation for not taking prisoners; artillerymen drawing a battery of the famous 75s that had halted the Germans on the Marne, and a battery of the less elegant, stubby 155s that had played so vital a role in the defence of Verdun; airmen, led by one of the few survivors of the legendary aces, René Fonck, bearing an ensign; marines in navy blue, who, cheek by jowl with the Belgians and British, had anchored the line in the muddy swamp of Flanders.

At various intervals came the victorious commanders, whom the crowd instantly recognised and applauded. Gouraud, the one-armed hero; Pau, also bearing an empty sleeve, but from 1870; Fayolle and Debeney; Maistre and Mangin, once nicknamed by his troops "the butcher"; and Castelnau, whose black brassard recalling that he had lost three sons in the war seemed to draw particularly warm acclaim from the stands. All famous warrior names, and in the recognition each received those angry memories of the futile costly offensives, the frightful reverses, the reproaches that the generals were wantonly throwing away the lives of their men—all these had been submerged in this moment of sublime thanksgiving. But it was the men, not the chiefs, that the crowd were chiefly saluting; and particularly the infantry that made up the vast bulk of the procession. Wave upon wave they came, the cutting edge and very substance of the French Army, men who

had fought and endured, suffered and died, all through the war
from the first murderous clash on the frontiers, through Verdun
and the Somme and Chemin des Dames, to the Second Marne and
the final glorious advance of October 1918. As the crowd watched
the tattered *drapeaux* of the infantry regiments go by, a kind of
delirium overtook it. There were many who began, instinctively,
to sing "La Madelon," with tears streaming down their faces.
What thoughts, what memories were passing through the minds of
the troops as they marched by the statue of Strasbourg in the Place
de la Concorde, now disburdened of its mourning crepe for the
first summer since 1870! For in all French hearts this Quatorze
Juillet was a day of destiny that had been dreamed about, not
merely over the past agonising five years, but for another forty-
three beyond them. Enough Frenchmen, both watching and marching, were old enough to recall the shame of that defeat. Pétain
(who, alas, would live on to act as caretaker for France under a
new and still more humiliating defeat) had been a schoolboy,
but Foch as a youth had witnessed Louis Napoleon retreat sick and
defeated through Metz, and Joffre had manned a cannon on the
ramparts of Paris during the four-month siege; Clemenceau had
been one of the deputies to protest against the surrender of Alsace-
Lorraine in 1871, and had narrowly escaped being lynched in
the civil war that followed with the Commune. But now, as President Poincaré had declared to him in a special message: "In the
light of this glorious morning, the last traces of the painful past
have just been removed forever."

For more than an hour the march-past of the French contingent continued. Finally, to close the procession, nine of General
Estienne's assault tanks rumbled through the Arc de Triomphe.
The sulphurous smell of burning oil and the deafening roar and
clatter that reverberated with their passage under the great arch-
way seemed more a token of the potency of the French Army of
that day than a harbinger of the battles of tomorrow. Who could
have any doubts that France, emerging triumphant from the inferno, now possessed the world's most powerful instrument of
war on land? What a day! What a spectacle! As the dust from
tanks settled and the golden cenotaph was dragged slowly back
under the arch, the thought impressed itself on one onlooker that
"a sight like this will never be seen again. Because there will never
again be a war. . . ."

Light and shadows

All through the night of July 14, 1919, revellers danced through the streets of a dazzlingly illuminated Paris, turning it (as *The Times* remarked) into "one vast ballroom," hoping, believing, that the euphoric *vie douce* of pre-'14 would return, had returned. But sombre spectres were already casting their deep shadows. For anyone who read the small print in the newspapers, they were apparent even before the feast began. On the previous Friday there had been a disagreeable little incident at the Café de la Paix. It had been thronged with gay, chattering customers—including many Allied officers and their ladies—when a group of waiters on strike suddenly appeared on the scene, upsetting tables, breaking crockery and spilling drinks. Blows were exchanged between patrons and strikers, but the arrival of some hundred reserve police quickly restored order. The disgruntled waiters, it appeared, were striking for an eight-hour day and better food and working conditions—demands similar to those which, on the very day of the signature of the Peace Treaty a fortnight before, had brought about a metro and bus strike, paralysing the city. That spring, inflation and the growing restiveness of the workers—*la vie chère* instead of *la vie douce*—had been the main topic of conversation in many a French household. Fortunately, or so it seemed to Parisian property-owners, the government was being tough with these left-Wing demonstrators. But its toughness was only embittering the atmosphere. It was clear that France, in giving her all for victory, had gravely neglected some aspects of her internal health. The Union Sacrée, that miraculous wartime truce between all parties and all classes, had barely survived the Armistice!

Then, on the very day of the Victory Parade, there had been disquieting reports from Berlin in the papers, telling of a street fight between wounded German ex-soldiers and some French officers. The affray had ended in the killing, by some unknown hand, of a French serviceman. It was a nasty reminder that the "Beast" was still not quite dead. And meanwhile, from Washington where the Senate was beginning its deliberations on the Peace Treaty, rumours were coming that President Wilson might yet have difficulty in persuading the American Congress to ratify the instrument that was to guarantee France, once and for all, against the menace of the "Beast." Four months later the dreadful rumours became reality.

Left-wing dissent

One important group had boycotted the victory celebrations in Paris, the political constellation of the far left: Communists, internationalists, extreme Socialists. The recent war, in their eyes, had been but a criminal affair between the capitalist classes. The workers in millions had died in it, but it had been no concern of theirs; and the war had not ended in a holy revolution, bringing the overthrow of the existing order, as had happened in Russia. Therefore there was no cause whatever for rejoicing. Instead, the extremists had decided to stage their own show. Together with some disabled ex-servicemen, about a hundred strong* they gathered near the Place de la Trinité. As a macabre demonstration against militarism, they had intended to roll several of the *mutilés* in their invalid carriages in front of Foch's horse as he rode past the Opera. But they were forestalled by the police and dispersed. Re-forming on the exterior boulevards, they then marched through the east end of Paris to pay tribute to the Communard martyrs enshrined at Père Lachaise Cemetery. There was a scuffle at the cemetery, and some twenty arrests were made. The next day, Marcel Cachin, editor of *L'Humanité* blazed forth in vituperation against the Victory Parade:

Bitterness! Disgust! I have recognised the crowd. It is not the crowd that took the Bastille and sang for the first time of liberty in the streets. It is not the crowd that religiously followed the bier of Zola or Jaurès. . . . It is the brutish elemental crowd which does not change, which slavishly acclaims Caesar and Boulanger, which yells at the vanquished, which chooses indifferently its heroes among boxers, gladiators and captains.

Cachin's ire may well have been fanned by the poor turnout of his supporters on the 14th, but their small numbers that day were deceptively irrelevant to the intrinsic, let alone the potential strength of the new left in France. For in no other of the victorious nations had Russia's October Revolution evoked stronger

---

* Despite exhortations the vast majority of the left appear to have been lured away by the greater attraction of the Victory Parade.

sympathies than among the workers of France—France the home of revolution itself. It struck powerful chords with the ancient and deep-rooted revolutionary mystique of 1793, 1848, but above all with the Commune of 1871; the Commune, the brutal repression of which remained stamped in the minds of the French left wing and whose failure Lenin had now used as a textbook to perfect his own revolution. The foundation in March 1919 of the Third International in Moscow had revived hopes of successful revolution in the hearts of the spiritual heirs of the martyred Communards, while it was no accident that among the interventionist forces in Russia it was the French at Odessa who had raised the flag of mutiny. At home, there was already abundant fuel on the economic and social scene for the flames of revolution to feed upon. From the earliest postwar days the presence of a potent new force on the French political scene was increasingly apparent, and the bourgeois, property-owning classes closed their ranks accordingly.

French illusions

With the Armistice of 1918, a series of insidious illusions had pervaded France. Falling back on the eternal, rather arrogant dogma of it being civilisation's implicit duty to come to the rescue, when necessary, of its fountainhead, she automatically presupposed that her Anglo-Saxon allies would henceforth never abandon her; that they (particularly America) would maintain their interest in reshaping Europe. But when President Wilson had come over to France to address the victorious doughboys about "peace upon the . . . foundation of right," they had shown themselves frankly bored. They wanted to get home, and the American electorate showed that it wanted to keep them there—forever. As the idealism of 1918 evaporated, so the Anglo-Saxon nations would retreat further and further into their shells. Even more than France, they would become preoccupied with their own pressing internal problems. Feelings would grow (particularly in Britain) that Germany had been treated with excessive harshness at Versailles; feelings generated partly by honest altruism, partly by the dictates of commerce, but partly by instinctive concern at a victorious France's apparently annexationist tendencies—as revealed by her reaching out for the Saar and her sending troops into Germany's bankrupt and defaulting Ruhr.

Another illusion, one to which the glory of the Victory Parade doubtless added impetus, was that France felt she had won the war largely by her own superlative exertions. But the British and Americans *knew* that it could not have been won without them, and they would soon feel that the price paid, both in men and gold, had been too high. They would do almost anything rather than risk having to save France a second time, let alone regain Alsace-Lorraine for her. Hand in hand with this illusion went France's belief that, primarily through the supremacy of her army, she could enforce the peace by herself. But she could not, because morally, numerically and economically the war had left her feebler than she realised.

As the true state of France's economy became more widely apparent, it became popular to cherish the happy, simple illusion that "the Boche will pay." But Germany could not pay, would not pay. The Allies would not make her, and the effort to do so was to cost France herself too much. Finally, there was the mortal illusion (although Foch, for one, certainly did not share it) that vanquished, ruined, truncated, revolution-torn Germany could never again be a military menace. But had Frenchmen forgotten already how the harsh settlement imposed by Prussia in 1871 had kept alight France's own fire of revenge for the best part of half a century? Would France indeed have been so ready to rush to the aid of her ally Russia, in 1914, had the amputation of Alsace-Lorraine not weighed heavily upon the balances? Now France's supreme grievance had been erased, but Versailles had simply transferred its burden to Germany, mourning her lost territories in the east.

Financial stresses

Of all the sources of her illusions, probably the most consequential was France's overestimation of her powers to mould the postwar world. The bare economic facts were daunting. France had expended some 25 percent of her national fortune; almost 7 percent of her territory had been devastated by war, including some of the richest industrial areas; 3.25 million hectares (12,500 square miles, or roughly the area of Belgium) of fertile soil had been ravaged, 3,500 miles of railroads and over 30,000 miles of roads destroyed; coal production was down by 37 percent, compared with 1914, steel down 60 percent; the trade deficit had risen from 1.5 to 17.5 millions. France's Ministry of Finances estimated the material damage caused by the Germans, and which should be the basis for reparations, at 134 milliard gold francs; a staggering figure compared with the 5 milliard which Germany had demanded, and got, from France in 1871. Yet, showing the same extraordinary recuperative capacity that had amazed the world in 1871, France after 1918 repaired her shattered industries, and her courageous peasants got her raddled fields back under the plough far quicker than anyone could have imagined. It was to her financial structure, however, that the really lasting damage had been done. To pay for the war, France had brought on inflation by issuing a flood of paper money. By the Armistice, the franc had lost nearly two-thirds of its value. This was only a beginning; whereas then it exchanged at 26 to the pound sterling (5.50 to the dollar), already by the time of the Victory Parade it had depreciated to 51 to the pound. By May 1926 its value had sunk to 178 to the pound, and finally, two months later, with a hostile mob beating on the gates of the Palais Bourbon, to 220.

The causes were not hard to find. Fanned by the new virulence of the revolutionary left, the French workers' justifiable demands for better conditions and higher wages to offset this wartime inflation gave the spiral an extra spin. Then there were the additional millions which had to be spent in paying the pensions of the legions of ex-servicemen, notably the *mutilés*. But the most pernicious influences here harked back to the two illusions that France's allies would always be ready to help her, and that *le Boche payera*. By the end of the war the public debt had reached 156 milliards, of which 32 milliards were owed to the United States and Britain. The budget of 1919 had been postponed more than seven months, during which time further vast loans had been launched, so that when the budget was finally agreed it showed an enormous deficit of 27 milliards. Nobody viewed this too tragically. First, it was automatically assumed that the Allies would be accommodating, and generous, in the recovery of France's war debts; it was widely thought that the Allies could not possibly—to use a cynical expression popular at the time—expect France to repay "the cost of overcoats in which her soldiers had got themselves killed." But Britain for one, nearly a million of her own men lying dead in Flanders' fields and with equally grave internal problems, did not quite see things that way.

Hopes for reparations

When the budget had been postponed in December 1918, the Minister of Finance, Lucien Klotz (according to Clemenceau, "the only Jew who knows nothing about money"), indicated clearly that he expected France's budgetary deficits to be made good by German reparations. At the Peace Conference, France had estimated her total war damages at 209 milliard gold francs, while the overall claims of the Allies amounted to some 400 milliard. But British treasury experts reckoned that the most that could be squeezed out of Germany would be 75 milliards. With the British showing marked distaste for the whole subject from the outset, most bitter discord had surrounded the talks on reparations at Versailles, a discord that certainly did not go unobserved beyond the Rhine. Finally—and fatally—the sum to be paid by Germany was left open for future negotiation. The issue of reparations indeed remained open, an open sore, gaining little for France but ill-will. In 1923, Germany defaulted on her payments, and France occupied the Ruhr to force her to pay. Britain, seeing political ambition behind the financial pretexts, dissociated herself. From the ensuing industrial breakdown resulted the final collapse of the German mark. Down in Bavaria an angry unknown Austrian acquired his first national publicity. Throughout Germany a lasting resentment was created, as well as a few martyrs of whom Hitler would later make excellent capital. Relations with Britain became chronically estranged and would hardly regain their former cordiality before the eve of the second world crisis; while in France herself the franc threatened to run after the Reichsmark. When France was forced to retreat from the Ruhr, the illusion of her power in the postwar world received its first serious shock.

Reparations undoubtedly helped to clear the way for the Second World War. They certainly did not result in balancing France's budget, as Klotz and his successors had hoped. In fact, out of all the international transactions intertwining reparations with the repayment of war debts in the twenties, Germany gained more than France. During the first half of the 1920s, seven different Ministers of Finance, following on each other's heels, failed to put France's house in order. Although the return of Raymond Poincaré in 1926 brought France an almost miraculous three-year period of quasi-stability—as well as prosperity—in the seventeen months after his retirement in 1929 another five governments came and went. France's financial dilemma extended itself into the 1930s, bringing down government after government, rendering impossible any consistent foreign policy—let alone any policy of reconciliation with Germany; bedevilling the Third Republic throughout the remainder of its existence, and finally hamstringing it when the necessity to rearm confronted France with desperate urgency.

Lack of men and ideas

"The means by which Providence raises a nation to greatness are the virtues infused into her great men." So said Burke in his memorial to Pitt. By the end of the 1920s it was painfully apparent that the Third Republic was suffering from a deficit of great men as much as it was of great ideas. Clemenceau had been rapidly dispatched, in much the same manner as the British nation was to deal with its war lord in 1945—*"passé le péril, maudit le saint."* Briand was tottering, Painlevé aging; and in the same year that both Clemenceau and Foch died, 1929, ill-health forced Poincaré from the political scene. After the ceremony solemnising the liberation of Strasbourg in 1918, he had been heard to sigh, *"Now I can die."* Despite his resurrection in 1926, the overtones of Poincaré's remark were loaded with a double significance. With the return of Alsace-Lorraine, the supreme motivating and uniting ideal had been removed from French politics. Where was there now a Holy Grail worth questing and fighting for? Balancing the budget was hardly a substitute. At the same time, Poincaré's suspiration echoed the psychological lassitude that was increasingly to beset French politics, later to be compounded with the physical consequences of France's terrible war losses; for among these, the category bled whiter than all the rest (of the total mobilised, 23 percent killed) comprised the liberal professions, the source which should have supplied the new Clemenceaus and Poincarés. In her autobiography, *The Prime of Life,* Simone de Beauvoir tells of a Dr. Lemaire who, on returning from the front where he had operated on hundreds of wounded under the most sickening conditions, "took to his bed and never got up again." How many of France's young intellectuals lucky enough to survive the trenches, and who should now be taking over the reins of government, had—like Dr. Lemaire—slumped within themselves, mentally and morally drained?

The left-wing challenge immediately following the end of the war was succeeded in France by a brief phase of deceptive parliamentary stability. Thoroughly alarmed by fears of the Bolshevik menace, the bourgeois parties rallied to form a right-of-centre Bloc National Républicain. At the elections of November 1919, the Bloc swept into power, winning nearly three-quarters of the seats in the Assembly and furnishing France with the most strongly right-wing parliament she had known since 1876. Meanwhile, the left wing seemed to be tearing itself apart by internal divisions. During their congress at Tours in December 1920, the Socialist Party had split into the new Parti Communiste Français— uncompromising devotees of the Soviet Revolution—and the more moderate Socialists calling themselves the Section Française de la IIe Internationale Ouvrière (SFIO). This was followed, in 1921, by a similar split within the trades unions from which emerged the dissident Communist Confédération Générale du Travail Unitaire (CGTU), obedient to every instruction from Moscow and pledged to total war against management, in contrast to the more moderate line pursued by the old Socialist Confédération Générale du Travail (CGT). Until the great reunion under the Front Populaire of 1936, Communist would chastise Socialist. Employers and bourgeois rejoiced at this rift in the left-wing camp, and were encouraged by its apparent weakness to backtrack on essential social reforms, thereby building up for the future an explosive reserve of grievances and ill-will.

Expressing his fundamental mistrust for the League of Nations, Clemenceau once remarked, "If you want to have a new spirit between nations, start by introducing a new spirit at home." In fact, postwar French politicians swiftly showed an instinct to return to the old spirit of the Third Republic—only worse. Before the war, issues had at least been relatively clear-cut and simple; hardy perennials such as anticlericalism and the Dreyfus Case helped define boundaries between parties, and there was always the supreme polarising force of Alsace-Lorraine. Now *la Revanche*—Revenge—was fulfilled, anticlericalism virtually a dead duck; issues were blurred and complex, and there was the mounting shortage of strong wills and clear minds capable of guiding their parties in the search for a coherent programme. Parties divided and redivided. Politicians became subject to the pull of the rapidly growing number of pressure groups all acting upon parliament, and for many self-interest came—in the absence of any other grander motive—to be their guiding star. With the collapse of each successive government, it proved just that much harder (especially after Poincaré had gone) to create a majority with any promise of stability. A mad game of musical chairs ensued, to be played at a giddier and giddier rate until Hitler's panzers finally stopped the music.

Though France's governmental instability in the 1920s was principally provoked by discord over internal matters, such as the budget, it was upon her external policy—particularly towards Germany—that this had the most baneful effects. The overriding practical purpose of the Versailles Treaty had been to guarantee the security of France, to prevent her ever again being swamped by the Teutonic hordes. To this end the Germans were required by the treaty to disband their General Staff and to reduce their awesome army in perpetuity to a militia of only a hundred thousand men—forbidden tanks, heavy artillery or aircraft. Under the separate treaties of St. Germain and Trianon, the Hapsburg Empire had been broken up into a row of small nations, so as to deprive Germany of any powerful potential ally in Central Europe; and it was hoped that these Poles, Czechs, Yugoslavs, Hungarians and Rumanians would all show their gratitude by remaining constant allies of France. By augmenting French industry at the cost of Germany's, it was reckoned that reparations would help erase the traditional disparity between the economic power of the two countries. Finally, to secure her vulnerable eastern frontier France had been granted a footing in Germany's Rhineland. But here she had got less than she wanted. Foch had declared, "If we do not hold the Rhine permanently, no neutralisation, nor disarmament, nor any kind of written clause can prevent Germany . . . from sallying out of it at will." In the future, he added prophetically, there would not be time for the arrival of Anglo-American aid to save France from military defeat. But Lloyd George and President Wilson had thrown up their hands in horror, exclaiming that they could not countenance annexations by France that would only create another Alsace-Lorraine. In the end, France had to be satisfied with the permanent demilitarisation and a temporary occupation of the left bank of the Rhine.* Foch boycotted the signature of the treaty, grumbling in disgust and with some accuracy, "This is not peace. It is an armistice for twenty years."

As the realities of the postwar world proceeded to destroy France's illusion that she by herself was capable of maintaining the peace of Europe, so her leaders were beset by mounting anxiety that the provisions of Versailles could offer only partial and temporary security. In the background was the one unalterable fact of life: even with the addition of Alsace-Lorraine's 1.8 million inhabitants and Germany's population losses, there were still only 39 million Frenchmen† compared to 59 million Germans. And Germany sustained a vigorously expanding birth rate, whereas that of France was static, so that even by 1931 she had still barely made good her war casualties. This was the one fundamental, constant factor at the back of France's European policy through the 1920s and into the thirties. But because of her chronic governmental instability, she found herself incapable of facing this problem with any consistent strategy. One moment she would show herself bent on grinding down the Germans by marching into the Ruhr; the next, she was offering the olive branch of reconciliation. She would vaunt the supremacy afforded by the offensive might of the French Army, then hide herself behind a twentieth-century Great Wall of China. She would appear to place her faith in the League of Nations, but she also endeavoured to hem Germany about by alliances with the new East European buffer states (although it was doubtful that any combination of these could ever replace the weight of the Russian behemoth, France's defaulting ally now engrossed in the dream of Marxism and the nightmare of civil war). Even during the most hopeful postwar period of the Briand-Stresemann entente, which stretched intermittently from 1925 to 1929, attacks from the right and lack of support on the left forced Briand again and again to renege on his declared aim of Franco-German *rapprochement*. Finally, in 1929, when Premier for the eleventh time, Briand proposed from the tribune of the League of Nations a European Federation embracing Germany. It was a grandiose ideal a generation, alas, ahead of its time, and Briand was

---

* The last French soldier left the Rhineland in June 1930.
† As of 1919.

promptly overthrown by the French nationalists. Almost simultaneously came the death of Stresemann, Weimar's most inspiring and inspired leader, and possibly the one man capable of stemming the rising tide of Nazism. Shortly before he died, exhausted and disillusioned, Stresemann summed up his dealings with France: "I gave and gave and gave until my followers turned against me. . . . If they could have granted me just one concession, I would have won my people. But they gave nothing. . . . That is my tragedy and their crime."

By the end of the first postwar decade France had made substantial concessions; she agreed, for instance, to withdraw her troops from the Rhineland five years ahead of the specified time. But her concessions were so hedged about with the reservations imposed by the waverings of her divers governments that, in German eyes, they bore no signs of genuine magnanimity or forward-looking statesmanship; rather they seemed acts of weakness and irresolution, forced upon France by her dissident allies or by the *force majeure* of external events. As the 1930s opened, Briand lamented with bitterness that despite all recent concessions made on reparations, nothing had diminished Germany's ill-will. By 1931 Germany was like the genie in the bottle who, instead of showing gratitude to his innocent liberator, slew him in requital for his prolonged sufferings.

Now, in the midst of France's perennial legislative games there burst the malignant, irreconcilable genie figure of Hitler.

2

Thank God for the French Army

Against an army sailing through the clouds neither walls
nor mountains nor seas could afford any security.
—SAMUEL JOHNSON, *Rasselas*

"THANK GOD for the French Army," cried Winston Churchill
before the House of Commons on March 23, 1933. It was two
months after Hitler's coming to power. Few statements by
Churchill outraged even Tory opinion more than this one. All
round the House, he observed looks "of pain and aversion." For
it was also the year that Britain, having reduced her arms ex-
penditure to its all-time low for the interwar period, was urging
France to follow suit. Preoccupied with the yo-yo craze, trunk
murders and the amorous successes of the Rector of Stiffkey,*
Britain had assumed a progressively detached attitude towards
Europe's problems. The emotional view of the Great War as a
glorious crusade had been widely replaced by the doubts voiced
by Lloyd George when he declared, "We all blundered into war,"
and France's role in leading Britain into this supreme blunder
seemed to be illuminated with ever-increasing clarity. British public opinion, shocked at accounts by the Spenders and Isherwoods
of starving, rickets-ridden children growing up in a Germany apparently broken by France's avarice for reparations, had, unlike

---

* Throughout most of 1932, the middle-aged Rector of Stiffkey (pronounced
"Stewky" locally) had provided the British press with an unending source of anti-
clerical entertainment through his escapades with battalions of teen-age waitresses
in London teashops. Defrocked, he ended his career in a lion's cage in 1937, where
he was billed to give a lecture. The lion objected.

the French, ceased to regard Germans as the eternal enemy.* By and large it had lapsed back into that normal, healthy Anglo-Saxon *status quo ante* of mistrusting all French designs—a spirit of the age which as late as July 1934 *The Times* epitomised with its forecast, "In the years that are coming, there is more reason to fear for Germany than to fear Germany." It was the vision of the huge French Army, still presumptively the most powerful in the world, constantly poised over Europe which alarmed Britons; Winston Churchill stood for only a dissident minority.

But as Hitler began to make it abundantly plain that he would not rest until the *Diktat of Versailles* was overthrown and Germany returned to her former ascendancy, what in fact was the state of the French Army? Was it still the superlative weapon of 1919?

Influences of Verdun

The training and morale of an army, and even its weapons, are transient factors that can alter the balance between opposing forces within the course of one campaign. It is the more immutable matters of doctrine and fundamental strategy that require to be considered here. That a victorious army should, in its subsequent peacetime development, be strongly influenced by the experiences of the past war is a historical platitude and only too natural; but, to quote Frederick the Great, "experience is useless unless the right conclusions are drawn from it." France having borne so much of the brunt of the fighting on the western front, experiences there came to weigh with particular gravity upon French military minds.

Predominant were those of Verdun, 1916, whence arose three separate influences, in many ways self-conflicting, but each vitally affecting the postwar French Army. The first related to the psychological consequences of Verdun's emerging as the symbol and legend of ultimate glory. In most of the great Allied undertakings of the war, the glory had been shared, but Verdun—the longest and most terrible struggle of all—had belonged solely to France. For ten agonising months, and at a cost of over 400,000 men, she had measured herself in single combat against the full power of the German Army and won. As well as stylising the very nature

---

* The inverted attitudes of post-1945 make an interesting comparison.

of the war itself, Verdun proved to be a kind of watershed in it, "the walls upon which broke the supreme hopes of Imperial Germany," declared President Poincaré. With every justification, Verdun at once became a legend of national heroism and virility. In the passage of years it grew to be enshrined with the holy qualities of a miracle.

It was France's Battle of Britain, symbolising just as much though perhaps imbued with even greater emotive force—and bearing the same kind of latent peril. Just as post-1945 Britons, perplexed by imperial disintegration and adversities of trade, found (and still find) unreasoned comfort in the belief that whatever divinity had presided over Dunkirk and in the London skies would always, in the end, sally forth to save them, so Frenchmen came to regard Verdun as a touchstone of faith in the jungle of the interwar world. In the Army, as recurrent financial crises rendered the replacement of obsolescent equipment a constant nightmare, it was always agreeable to recall the fundamental superiority which the French warrior race had displayed over the (now disarmed) enemy in 1916. Just as the British Navy ossified after Trafalgar, a kind of conservative complacency was bred in France: "What was good enough in 1916 is good enough now." To challenge it hardly guaranteed popularity in Army circles.

Yet, parallel to the first influence, a second contained the awareness of just how much warfare like Verdun had cost France. More regular officers and men of the French Army had gone through the inferno of Verdun than of any other battle, and the frequent postwar commemorations ensured that their minds retained the full horror of those ten months: the ceaseless shelling from an enemy whom one rarely saw, the wounded men agonising untended, the hideous mutilations, the reliefs and ration parties never arriving, the senseless counterattacks to recapture at impossible cost a few yards of shell holes; the thirst, the hunger, the stench, the misery, the fear; above all, always the shells. A young lieutenant killed at Verdun scrawled in his journal: "They will not be able to make us do it again another day; that would be to misconstrue the price of our effort. They will have to resort to those who have not lived these days." Privately the men of France's postwar army wondered if they could do Verdun again, if any other Frenchman, if any other human being could. In the lassitude left by the war, they felt the answer, morally, was "No!" There was indeed no doubt that, numerically, Verdun was the kind of battle that France with her depleted population could never, never fight again. But what kind of battle could she fight?

Certainly, whatever those British critics of Churchill might have feared, it seemed increasingly improbable that France could ever herself engage in offensive warfare. Defensively, her interests were protected by the Versailles Treaty—for the time being. But the function of military staffs is to plan for contingency. France *might* be attacked once again by the traditional enemy; in this event, how could she fight a defensive battle without suffering a Verdun? What new strategy, what new technique could be evolved to avoid it? In their pursuit of an alternative, the footsteps of France's military thinkers led them back towards Verdun itself. The lessons gained there, and the conclusions drawn from them, constitute the third and most portentous influence emanating from that hideous battlefield.

Most of the siege warfare of 1914–18 had surged back and forth over an amorphous line of trenches. What was peculiar about Verdun was the presence of concentric clusters of powerful, underground forts. Although, for various reasons, France had grossly neglected these at the beginning of the battle, the subsequent course of the struggle seemed to indicate that Verdun owed its survival to them. The mightiest of these forts, Douaumont, had been captured early in an extraordinary, bloodless coup by a small group of Germans; its loss was later estimated to have cost the French the equivalent of 100,000 men. Its neighbour, Fort Vaux, with a garrison of only 250 men, heroically stood up to a whole German army corps and delayed the advance on Verdun one vital week. Others, like Souville, proved invaluable by furnishing shellproof shelters from which infantry could sally forth to repulse the attacking Germans, while supporting them with fire from artillery mounted beneath almost indestructible carapaces of thick steel. Only the very heaviest enemy shells could penetrate them. When a French Army Commission led by Marshal Joffre visited Verdun in 1922, it was astonished at the way in which the forts had absorbed the pounding of the German "Big Berthas"—an impression reinforced by the nigh-impenetrable strength which their scrutiny of Germany's deep-dug Hindenburg Line revealed. If only the French High Command could have utilised those forts properly in 1916, think how many valuable poilu lives might have been saved, all the while assuring the integrity of Verdun! Let these lessons not be ignored, the Commission warned itself.

The Maginot Line

There was an additional factor. From the days of the barbarians onwards, France had constantly lain open to invasion through her vulnerable eastern frontier. With the new rapidity of movement afforded by railways it had twice been proved, in 1870 as in 1914, that a battle lost in the east could bring the Germans to the very doors of Paris itself within a matter of weeks. In Lorraine and the Nord, France's most vital industrial centres lay particularly exposed to German aggression, and deprivation of them had nearly brought defeat in the Great War. Among a nation where the peasant voice still predominated, the soil of France —every square yard of it—assumed sacred qualities; it was the unyielding defence of this which had persuaded the French High Command to adopt such rigid and costly tactics at Verdun. After the stabilisation of the fronts in 1914, the French infantry had paid out a steady and prodigious rent in blood just to hold on to that continuous line of ill-protected trenches, stretching from Switzerland to the North Sea. But at least they had held, and by doing so had ensured the inviolability of France's sacred soil. Supposing now, the Army Commission of 1922 asked itself, France should prepare to defend herself behind—not shallow, hastily dug trenches—but a continuous and permanent line of forts even deeper and more sophisticated than those of Verdun? In the event of another German war, would not such a line surely save both lives and the ravaging of French territory? Might not its mere existence pose a formidable deterrent to any aggressive-minded German rulers in the future?

For seven years the Battle of Verdun was refought in the higher councils of French military thought, as argument swayed back and forth over the blueprints for France's new fortress line. On one premise the majority were agreed from the start: the line must represent a "continuous front." Above all, this was the view of Pétain, appointed Inspector General of the Army after the war and, as age removed Joffre and Foch from the scene, for many successive years her most influential soldier. He was also the man who had been more closely concerned in the immortal defence of Verdun than any other. But although Pétain, in the years following his trial and disgrace, has come to be regarded in France as a scapegoat for all that was faulty about interwar military thinking, it is entirely unjust to suggest that he singlehandedly laced his army into a kind of intellectual strait jacket. The French Army donned it all too willingly. For during the past war its officer corps had no contact with the great fluid movements of the campaign in the east in which so many Germans had taken part; nor had they any direct knowledge of the highly mobile campaigns fought by Allenby and the British in Palestine. "We had been haunted," wrote a distinguished subsequent Army leader, General Beaufre,* "by the tenacity of the German machine guns, and the impossibility in which we found ourselves of breaking the enemy front." From the lessons of their four years of static warfare, which even the introduction of tanks did disappointingly little to alter, had emerged the doctrine of the "continuous front," espoused by French military thought, with its experience of no other form of strategy. This must prove to be the shape of future warfare; moreover, as shown above, it was a shape peculiarly expedient for the defence of the fort of France. But expediency usually turns out to be a poor strategic guide.

On January 4, 1930, a vast majority in both chambers of the National Assembly voted for a law accepting the Army's long-debated plans for a Great Wall on the eastern frontier. André Maginot, become one of the Third Republic's most honourable politicians, happened to be Minister of War at the time; thus it was his name that the fortress line would bear henceforth. For the first phase of its construction, the Assembly voted the immense sum of 3,000 million francs,† to be spread over four years. Work on the Maginot Line began at once; as Maginot himself stressed, it *had* to be completed by 1935, the date appointed by the Versailles Treaty for France finally to withdraw her troops from the Rhineland. It was to run from Basle on the borders of Switzerland to Longwy close to where the Belgian, Luxembourg and French frontiers meet; why it was not intended to continue

---

* Andre Beaufre, a junior staff officer at the Ministry of War after World War I, later became a full general and one of France's leading military intellects after World War II. He led the French contingent at Suez in 1956.

† 120 million dollars.

to Dunkirk, thus covering Belgium, will be seen later. The strength and depth of line varied, but for 87 miles it consisted of "fortified regions," guarding two major invasion avenues. One covered a potential assault aimed at Metz and Nancy, while the other faced north to guard the plain of Lower Alsace. Facing directly east, a chain of lesser fortifications stood along the wide river barrier of the Rhine. Just behind the frontier, the defences of the fortified regions began with a series of antitank obstacles, and barbed wire, backed up by reinforced barracks, known as *maisons fortes,* and pillboxes. The object of these advance posts was to provide warning of an attack and delay it. At their rear was a deep antitank ditch and then came the subterranean casemates and forts which comprised the backbone of the Line. Protected by up to 10 feet of concrete, each casemate contained rapid-firing antitank guns and machine guns firing out of underground slits with a 50-degree arc, as well as grenade throwers to dislodge any enemy infantry approaching by means of dead ground. Their 25-man garrison lived and slept on a floor still deeper under the earth. Superbly blended into their environment, about all that an enemy could see of these concrete casemates were two small nipples formed by the observation cupolas surmounting them.

The real pride of the Maginot Line, however, lay in its forts which backed up the casemates at intervals of three to five miles. Ever since Vauban, French engineers have been without rivals in the art of fortifications, and the Verdun forts were masterpieces of their time, but these new concrete and steel monsters were veritable wonders of the modern world. When troops passed through their cavernous gates placed discreetly at the base of some hill, they entered a Wellsian civilisation in which they could live, sleep, eat, work and exercise for many weeks without ever seeing the surface of the earth—not unlike nuclear submariners of today embarking on a voyage under the Pole. Electric trains whisked them from their underground barracks and canteens to their gun turrets; vast power stations, equally underground, provided them with heat and light; powerful compressor plants supplied them with air and ensured that the forts were proof from poison gas; immense subterranean food stores, reservoirs, and fuel tanks would enable them to remain cut off from the rest of the French Army for up to three months. There were three differ-

ent types of forts, the biggest of which—Category 1—housed a garrison of up to 1,200 officers and men, and contained from 15 to
18 concrete "blocks," each bristling with guns mounted in disap-
pearing turrets and of calibres that ranged from 37 mm to 135
mm. Each fort was divided into two sections, connected by deep
subterranean galleries lying beyond the penetration of any bomb
or shell, and varying from 400 yards to a mile and a half in
length. Thus, even if one half of the fort should be knocked out
the other half could continue to fight; and each half was so located that it could bring down supporting fire on its twin, its
neighbouring forts or casemates.

At Verdun the greatest danger experienced by the French
forts had been from infantry infiltrating onto their superstruc-
tures and working their way underground. Both Douaumont
and Vaux had been lost this way. To prevent a repetition, the
Maginot Line plan incorporated "interval troops," infantry complete with field artillery, which could be moved up to counter any
threat to a particular fort or group of forts. These were intended
to compensate for what, by definition, the Line lacked: mobility.*

Much has been said about why the Maginot Line failed to save
France in 1940—though not always the right reasons have been
given. It was enormously costly. Partly owing to errors of construction brought about by bureaucratic jealousies, the 87 miles
of "fortified regions" completed by 1935 had already cost 7,000
million francs, a sum far in excess of the parliamentary estimates.
In addition to its construction, the maintenance of the Maginot
Line represented a considerable financial burden. For a country
plagued by budgetary difficulties and with a powerful left wing
opposed to rearmament in any form, this overall costliness meant
that inevitably the French Army would be forced to accept econ-
omies elsewhere. The Maginot Line also lacked depth, with its
four successive positions never occupying, even in their most advanced state, a belt larger than 12 miles deep. This too was a
consequence of expense.

But the mortal defect of the Line lay not in its depth but its
length. Romantically, it came to be dubbed "the shield of
France." The essence of a shield, however, is that it can be ma-

---

* Ironically, when the supreme test came, the drain imposed by maintaining the
interval troops was to be one of the leading factors in depriving the French Army
of the mobility it so sadly lacked.

nipulated to protect any portion of its owner's body. The Maginot Line obviously was incapable of motion, yet it did not extend to cover what Clausewitz called "the pit of the French stomach," the classical invasion route across the Belgian plains, over which the Schlieffen Plan had so nearly brought total calamity in 1914. By as late as 1935, the motives for not fortifying the remaining 400 kilometres along the Belgian frontier were only partially related to problems of cost. This extension would have to run right through the heavily industrialized Lille-Valenciennes area which straddles the frontier, and it would be immeasurably disruptive as well as costly. A factor carrying even greater weight, however, was that Belgium, mindful of how her neutrality had been outraged by Germany in 1914, remained France's close ally, so that a fortified line on the French side of her frontier would leave her out in the cold, abandoned on the wrong side of the ramparts. She would then have no option but to return to her former neutrality and rely upon German morals. Pétain, despite his reputation for defensive-mindedness, made it clear when Minister of War in 1934 that, in the event of German aggression, it was part and parcel of French strategy to "go into Belgium" and to fight an offensive war of movement against the enemy there.* As the French Army stood in 1934, still with its crushing superiority over the Germans, who had not yet invented the Panzerkorps, this strategy made excellent sense—as long as Belgium remained within the alliance. It was also clearly in France's interest (though she could hardly explain this to the Belgians) to protect her soil by fighting the battle, with all its destructiveness, as far forward of her frontiers as possible.

With the construction of the Maginot Line, the wheel of French military thought, which had started spinning in 1870, performed a fatal full cycle. In 1870—in simplest terms—France had lost a war through adopting too defensive a posture and relying too much on permanent fortifications. Fortress cities such as Strasbourg, Metz and Paris had been simply enveloped by Moltke's Prussians and besieged one by one. In reaction against this calamitous defeat, France had nearly lost the next war by being

---

* Both in 1927 and 1932, Pétain, the President of the Army Council, had stressed the importance of having "a mobile force near the frontier and to make sure of its swift advance into Belgium."

too aggressive-minded. Now, once again she was seeking safety under concrete and steel. Rapidly the Maginot Line came to be not just a component of strategy, but a way of life. Feeling secure behind it, like the lotus-eating mandarins of Cathay behind their Great Wall, the French Army allowed itself to atrophy, to lapse into desuetude. A massive combination of factors— complacency, lassitude, deficiencies of manpower and finance— conspired to rust the superb weapon which the world had so admired that Quatorze Juillet of 1919.

The French Army: Men and arms

By the end of 1935, the eve of France's first major confrontation with Hitler, the Army was below par in numbers and quality of manpower. The call-up was just beginning to suffer the full effect of the "hollow classes," caused by the drop in births during the Great War; in Germany, the 1915 class available for conscription amounted to 464,000 men; in France only 184,000; and it was a ratio that would continue right through to World War II. Yet politics had forced a reduction in the length of military service from three years to one, and hopes that the population deficit of metropolitan France could be made good by a vast colonial army were never quite fulfilled. Thus, instead of a total strength of over 300,000 men, about two-thirds of this was the most the French Army could muster. As for the hard core of professionals, there was certainly little inducement for good men to stay on. With a captain paid approximately £11 a month, and a major in command of a whole battalion paid only £16,* officers without private incomes lived in desperate straits; they had no vote; and now that the supreme goal, *la Revanche,* had been achieved, wherein resided the glory of an Army career?

Composed of all too many officers whom the previous war had left drained of *élan vital,* the French General Staff allowed itself to become bogged down in bureaucratic methods; *paperasserie* as the French call it, the blight to which all armies are susceptible, flourished. It was difficult to see where the power of decision lay. The once omnipotent and cohesive Conseil Supérieur de la Guerre, from whose members would be designated France's senior

---

* Even in the underpaid British Army at this time, a captain (unmarried) received a basic pay of £38 a month, a major £53.

commanders in time of war, no longer filled anything but a consultative role. Divided by mutual antipathy and jealousies, its generals had little contact with each other; their staffs followed suit, each existing in its own watertight compartment. There was not much discussion on a higher strategic and tactical plane, and what there was tended to follow abstractly intellectual paths from which little practical ever emerged.

At the Ministry of War, [writes General Beaufre of his own experiences at that time] the General Staff commanded in theory, but had not the money, the administration, the personnel nor the matériel; the Permanent Secretary had the money and the administration, without the responsibility of command; the various departments had personnel and matériel, but neither money nor command. The Minister stood at the head of all this, but could achieve nothing without obtaining unison from the whole orchestra, the complexity of which helped to paralyse all initiatives. The ensemble possessed only one force; that of inertia.

In this state of inertia, the Army tended to rest content with the techniques and equipment of 1918. To a large extent the financial strain imposed on successive military budgets by the Maginot Line provided it with little alternative.* Although, with the "taxis of the Marne" and later by her victualling of Verdun along the *voie sacrée,* the French Army had pioneered warfare by road, as its postwar mechanical transport aged and was not replaced it regressed to relying for mobility once more on railways —and horses. While other armies, notably the German, were experimenting with radio communications, the French clung to the telephone, despite the lessons gained from 1914–18 when operations had so often failed after the severing of lines by artillery barrages, and regardless of the new threat to land communications which modern airpower and tanks posed. In 1924 the Army decided to replace its automatic rifle and to modify the standard infantry cartridge; the new weapon came into service by 1932, but the rifle intended to utilise the same cartridge was not selected until 1936. As late as 1939, only a few hundred thousand had been issued. General Weygand, before he retired as Inspector

---

* Arms credits for 1936 totalled 1,492 million francs, roughly a fifth of what had already been spent on the Maginot Line.

General of the Army in 1935, had prescribed that five infantry divisions be motorised and a cavalry division be converted into a Division Legère Mécanique (DLM),* but otherwise the Army showed little advance on that which had paraded so resplendently through Paris in 1919.

Tanks and doctrine

There is no weightier problem, common to the General Staffs of all peaceable countries in modern times, than the decision for what year to plan the re-equipment of military forces with a new armoury.† Weapons designed too long before the moment of crisis, becoming speedily obsolete, are almost as useless as those that arrive too late. In its tank production policy, the French Army had remained for many years a prisoner of the mass of machines left over from 1918. With the rise of Hitler, it adopted the expedient of building prototypes but year by year postponing their mass production until such time as the threat of war seemed imminent—a national date which self-deception and appeasement would constantly defer. So long as Germany obeyed the Treaty of Versailles, binding her not to build tanks, France's obsolete armour was sufficient for her purposes. In any case, she could hardly afford to replace it. But the most insidious long-term consequences—and it would be hard to find any single military factor contributing more directly to the defeat of 1940—of this residuum lay in the shadow it cast over the development of France's doctrines of armoured warfare. The bulk of the tanks inherited from the war consisted of the Renault FT model, lightly armoured, slow and strictly limited in operational radius. It was useless against concrete fortifications or in battle against other tanks; it was predominantly an instrument of infantry support. In the culminating battles of 1918, the FTs moved up with the infantry after the usual heavy bombardment. When the infantry had advanced beyond the range of their artillery—and the tanks had run out of petrol—the attackers would consolidate and wait for the guns, drawn by horses, to move up and prepare for the next laborious step forward. At each pause, the hard-pressed Germans were given a respite in which to repair their defences. Never

---

* A mechanised division equipped with lightly armoured vehicles.

† In Britain, for instance, up to 1932, the services worked on the simple assumption each year of not having to anticipate a major war for at least another ten.

was the rhythm of attack maintained; never were the French tanks, numbering over 4,000 but spread out all along the front, concentrated for a break-through; and never did any deep penetration occur. Again and again in the French communiqués there appeared sentences like the following: "The tanks put to flight the defenders, but the infantry did not reach the objective." Against an enemy that was already beaten, losses in both tanks and infantry were disheartening, the conclusions drawn discouraging.

In his postwar Instruction of 1921, Marshal Pétain—then Supreme Commander—dismissed the future role of armour in two lines: "Tanks assist the advance of the infantry, by breaking static obstacles and active resistance put up by the enemy." For the next fourteen years this was to remain the accepted creed of the French Army. As at Verdun, the plodding infantrymen dominated. But meanwhile, in England, a prophet had arisen with a new and revolutionary concept of warfare. A twenty-four-year-old former regular officer invalided out of the Army as a result of gassing on the Somme, Captain Basil Liddell Hart, was invited to help draft the British Army's postwar infantry training manual. The manual gave him a first opportunity to propound his "expanding torrent" theory of deep, swift penetration as an antidote to the static warfare of 1914–18. As his thoughts evolved, Liddell Hart saw offensive operations being spearheaded by powerful concentrations of fast-moving, wide-ranging tanks, no longer mere adjuncts of foot soldiery, and backed by equally mobile self-propelled guns and infantrymen transported in armoured carriers. Instead of battering away along a wide sector with the old, methodical siege techniques, the attacker, having probed out a weak spot in the enemy's defences, would pour through it at top speed with his "expanding torrent" of mobile firepower, creating vulnerable new fronts deep in the defender's rear. If Liddell Hart's theories should be proved viable, it obviously meant the death of the "continuous front" school of thought, on which the whole of France's interwar strategy was based.

Harried by this awkward and gangly guru and his small band of supporters within the walls, the British Army decided in 1926 to lead the way by establishing an experimental mechanised force. Within two years, however, the conservative factions of the Army "Establishment" reasserted themselves and this force was disbanded. In France, there was an even smaller body of youthful and bright officers who considered Liddell Hart's doctrine—in Beaufre's words—"as dazzling a discovery as the rediscovery of antiquity must have seemed to the men of the Renaissance after the conformist sterilities of medieval scholasticism." But otherwise his teachings went ignored by the shapers of French military policy, comforted by the unreceptiveness of orthodoxy in England. Only elsewhere, in Germany, was their full import grasped. In an attack upon proposals for the creation of an armoured corps, Pétain's successor as Minister of War, General Maurin, summed up French attitudes prevailing in 1935 when he asked the Chamber of Deputies, amidst loud applause: "How can we still believe in the offensive when we have spent milliards to establish a fortified barrier? Would we be mad enough to advance beyond this barrier upon goodness knows what adventure?" Yet, if the offensive was damned and its mechanical requisites neglected, how then was the French Army to carry out that essential component of Maginot Line strategy, the march into Belgium, against a presumably rearmed and re-equipped Germany?

Alliances undermined

The significance of the defensive posture the French Army had adopted by the end of 1935 far exceeded simple military considerations of protecting France's own soil. Most important, it gravely impinged upon the system of alliances painfully constructed since 1919 as breakwaters against possible German aggression. From the very beginning, the Quai d'Orsay had realised they could no longer count on the traditional ally of 1914, Russia, to contain Germany by means of the deterrent which the threat of a two-front war imposed. The Allies' policy of intervention, their subsequent instinctive mistrust of Bolshevism, and Russia's multitudinous internal problems all made this clear. As a substitute, France had to rely on diplomatic accords with the small nations of Eastern Europe, which had been carved out of the rump of Austria-Hungary, Germany and Russia. On paper, the combined sum of their military forces seemed impressive enough, and the Poles, for instance, under General Weygand, had proved themselves doughty warriors against the Red Army; but, as the aftermath of Munich was to prove, they would never be combined insofar as they would just as soon cut each other's throats as form a coherent front against Hitler's Germany. In 1914, as the Germans surged through Belgium to the Marne, it was Russia who came to France's aid by taking the offensive. Now, as should have been obvious to any amateur strategist, France was faced with a reversal of the situation, and in the event of war she would in all probability have to rush to the aid of her weaker eastern allies. Yet, with that all too typical Gallic arrogance, all she asked was "How can they help us?" and never "How can we help them?" And France's defensive posture of the 1930s made it increasingly doubtful whether she could effectively help her allies at all. Ironically, the creation of Poland was to benefit Germany more than the Allies; instead of providing a *cordon sanitaire* to protect Russia from the Germans, it meant that, when the crucial moment came in 1939, Russia (even if she had wanted to) could not help France because a mistrustful Poland lay in the way. For France the only hope of helping her eastern allies, threatened by Hitler's Germany, was for her to replay 1923 (and how unpopular that had been!) by marching into the Rhineland, the one part of Germany directly vulnerable to her. Yet, as General Maurin had revealed with painful clarity, the Maginot Line strategy virtually discounted this possibility. So, as with Poland in the east, in the west the Maginot Line indirectly came to be a *cordon sanitaire* protecting Germany as well as France.

Herein lay a fatal contradiction between France's diplomatic and military policies. And, exploiting this contradiction, Hitler was soon to slam the door to the Rhineland in France's face by one swift, brutal act.

Reoccupation of the Rhineland

On March 5, 1936, William Shirer, the Columbia Broadcasting System correspondent in Berlin, noted in his diary: "Very ugly atmosphere in the Wilhelmstrasse today, but difficult to get to the bottom of it." Two days later, the mystery solved itself and Shirer could add, melodramatically: "Tonight for the first time since 1870 grey-clad German soldiers and blue-clad French troops face each other across the Upper Rhine." Acting with the lightning speed which was to characterise all his subsequent actions, Hitler had moved into the demilitarised Rhineland. Although rearmament had already been overtly under way for the past year, the new Wehrmacht could only afford three battalions with which to make the initial crossing of the Rhine, and these had orders to withdraw immediately in the event of any French reaction. As yet unarmed planes of the Luftwaffe flew from airfield to airfield to create an impression, and (so some German sources allege) as soon as they landed new identity marks were painted on them. Three battalions and a handful of planes cocking a snook at what was still rated as the world's most powerful land force! It was one of the most remarkable gambles in history. Would it come off? Desperate nervousness gripped the German Army. During the crisis, Shirer met General von Blomberg, the Minister of War, "walking along with two dogs on the leash. His face was white, his cheeks twitching. 'Has something gone wrong?' I wondered." Later even Hitler admitted that "the forty-eight hours after the march into the Rhineland were the most nerve-racking in my life." All the world looked at France to see how she would meet this gross breach of the Versailles Treaty.

In her turn, France looked towards Britain. But Britain was preoccupied with Italy and Abyssinia; besides, had not France declared impatiently, just two years previously, thereby killing the Disarmament Conference, that "Henceforth France will guarantee her security by her own means"?* In any case, a large portion of Englishmen agreed with Lord Lothian's historic comment about the Germans "only going into their own back-garden." So Britain told France that this was her problem. The French Government called in General Gamelin, Weygand's successor as Army Commander-in-Chief. Gamelin, already revealing himself a master of political if not military manoeuvre, temporised and equivocated in the style that was to prove fatal to France four years later. Of course the Army was ready for instant action; but did the government realise that the Germans had nearly a million men under arms, 300,000 of them already in the Rhineland? It was an absurd exaggeration deliberately intended to avoid action and pass the responsibility to the politicians. Without conceding that the Army might in any way be unfit for a swift offensive operation, Gamelin pointed out that it was numerically under strength

---

* For sheer arrogant folly, the Barthou declaration of April 17, 1934, is hard to beat. Yet it had its parallel in more recent times when in 1966 de Gaulle informed the North Atlantic Alliance that he felt strong enough to dispense henceforth with its benefits. There are moments when one feels that—like the Bourbons, only worse —France has learned nothing and forgotten everything.

owing to the reduction in military service (the fault of the politicians, he implied). Then he dropped the bombshell that, if it were to act over the Rhineland, the government would have to face up to the prospect of general mobilisation.* The French ministers looked at each other in horror. Mobilisation! And six weeks before an election? It was madness. The electorate would never stand for it. Parliamentary defeat would be certain; why, their very jobs were at stake! It was impossible. Now both the military and the politicians had their excuses. It remained to blame Britain for their joint paralysis of will. This was, however, said Churchill, "an explanation, but no excuse"; and indeed, at least in the opinion of Paul Reynaud, had France acted alone, in defence of her vital interests, Britain would have been bound to back her up.

Belgium opts out

So France did nothing, and Hitler got away with his first and most desperate gamble. The consequences were not long delayed. The most immediate followed with the reaction of France's ally, Belgium. That gallant sovereign who signed the Franco-Belgian Alliance of 1920, King Albert, had alas died tragically in 1934 and his son, Leopold III, did not inherit his wisdom and moral courage. Instead of the protective belt of the demilitarised Rhineland, the new king now saw armed German soldiers once again on Belgium's frontier, while behind him he saw an apparently impotent France. Wherein lay the security of Belgium? On October 14, 1936, Leopold III revoked the Franco-Belgian Treaty, thereby opting for a return to the neutral status of pre-1914. Said the king, with the optimism of the imprudent little pigs, "This policy should aim resolutely at keeping us apart from the quarrels of our neighbours." For France it meant that, in the event of war, she could not enter Belgium until Hitler had already invaded. In one stroke, the whole of her Maginot Line strategy lay in fragments. Belgium's neutrality now confronted France with two fearful alternatives.

---

* In retrospect, Gamelin's torpor becomes all the more criminal since it now appears that, as long as two months in advance of the reoccupation of the Rhineland, he had predicted to a French general (Armengaud) the likelihood of Hitler's move. Flandin, too, is purported to have raised the possibility in a Cabinet meeting of January 1935. Why then did the French Army allow itself to be taken by surprise?

No longer could there be any "rush into Belgium" carefully co-ordinated with the army of an ally; instead, she would either have to meet the invading Germans somewhere on the defenceless Flemish plains, in a hastily improvised battle of encounter, which her defensive-minded army was least suited for; or prepare to meet them once again on French soil, the prospect dreaded above all others. The only way to certain safety now lay in prolonging the Maginot Line to the sea. But the 87 existing miles of the "fortified regions" had already cost 7,000 million francs, and it was obvious that to extend the Line all the way to the sea, through the industrialised north, would prove infinitely more expensive. So the politicians of the Third Republic resorted to that time-honoured expedient of deceiving their constituents—and their al-lies—by *pretending* to do something which they recognised to be beyond their powers.

Meanwhile, in the reoccupied Rhineland itself, Hitler hastened the construction of his own powerful line of concrete forts, op-posing the Maginot Line: the West Wall, or Siegfried Line. As Churchill predicted in a remarkable prophecy on April 6, 1936, those fortifications would

enable the German troops to be economised on that line, and . . . enable the main forces to swing round through Belgium and Holland. Then look East. There the consequences of the Rhineland fortification may be more immediate. . . . Poland and Czechoslovakia, with which must be associated Yugoslavia, Roumania, Austria and some other countries, are all affected very decisively the moment that this great work of construction has been completed.

Indeed, its completion would make it virtually impossible for France to render any effective aid to her eastern allies. Hitler could henceforth mop up in the east at will, and then, with his rear secured, deal with an isolated France when the moment came.

The reoccupation of the Rhineland marked the watershed be-tween 1919 and 1939. No other single event in this period was more loaded with dire significance. From March 1936, the road to France's doom ran downhill all the way. And in Germany Hit-ler was rearming with terrifying speed.

3

Fortune Changes Sides

Before the year was out it seemed as if Fortune, recognising her masters, was changing sides.
—WINSTON S. CHURCHILL, *A History of the English Speaking Peoples*, Vol. III (on the coming of Pitt)

There are only two powers in the world . . . the sword and the spirit. In the long run, the sword is always defeated by the spirit.
—NAPOLEON

SUNDAY, MARCH 17th of 1935, was Heroes' Remembrance Day in Germany. At a ceremony in Berlin's State Opera House, Hitler presided, flanked on the right by the veteran Mackensen, Germany's last surviving field marshal, and on the left by Crown Prince Wilhelm, the heir to the deposed Kaiser and one-time commander of the army attacking Verdun. The whole of the stalls was a sea of military uniforms. Far from being one of sober commemoration of the Great War dead, the atmosphere was charged with jubilation and thanksgiving. Amidst powerful acclaim, Blomberg declared: "The world has been made to realise that Germany did not die of its defeat." It was a fact; for the previous day Hitler, in full defiance of Versailles, had announced to the world his intention to rearm, and to do so by introducing conscription.

Hitler rearms

The sequence of events which led to the nightmarish rise of the Third Reich lies still too close to us for anything new to be added here. But, the decline of the French Army up to the Rhineland crisis of 1936 having been sketched in, one needs to examine briefly the awe-inspiring process by which Hitler, within the following four short years, was to create a force not only crushingly superior to the combined might of France and Britain, but indeed the most dazzling instrument of war the world had yet seen. By the end of his first year in power, Hitler had already secretly ordered the Army to treble its statutory strength of 100,000 men, imposed by Versailles, before October 1934. During that year, the defence budget was drastically raised from 172 million Reichsmarks to 654 million. Then, on March 10, 1935, Hitler deliberately leaked to the British press the news that he already possessed an air force in the shape of the infant Luftwaffe.

His pretext was that France had just "expanded" her army by retaining a class of conscripts (done, in fact, simply to mitigate the consequences of the "hollow classes"). No more than a blast of protest was registered by either France or Britain, so on March 16th Hitler went ahead and published his brief decree announcing the creation of a new German Army, based on compulsory military service. In peacetime alone, it would have the imposing total of thirty-six divisions. This was many more than was wanted by even the grateful generals congregated in the State Opera the next day, who realised the mountainous difficulties that digesting this fivefold expansion would present to the small regular cadres. In fact, as has already been seen, by the time of the reoccupation of the Rhineland, the new Wehrmacht was still a relatively feeble, small and lightly armed force; up to that moment still no more than 5 percent of Germany's national product was being spent on rearmament. But then, as later, what Hitler lacked in hardware he made up by the loudness and terrorising effect of his boasting. After 1936, there followed the "quiet" two years of semirespectability, the years of no territorial adventures, during which the expanding Wehrmacht assumed its definitive shape. By the beginning of 1937, its army divisions numbered thirty-nine; by 1939, fifty-one.* By 1939 it had also added to its potential the manpower of both Austria and the Sudeten Germans.

Seeckt's bequest

When Hitler began the task of rearming Germany, daunting though it was, he was presented with a number of advantages de-

---

* Upon mobilisation in August 1939, this number was doubled.

nied to the French. In the first place, as the vanquished party, the German Army was not saddled with the victor's impediments of obsolescent ideas and equipment. Secondly, Hitler inherited some remarkably solid groundwork in the shape of Colonel General Hans von Seeckt's Reichswehr. As Mackensen's Chief of Staff on the Russian front, Seeckt had been responsible for the spectacular break-through at Gorlice in 1915. His monocle and hard features, making him seem like a traditional, rigid Prussian Junker, in fact concealed a remarkable elasticity and breadth of vision. From the moment of taking over command of the Reichswehr on the morrow of defeat, his guiding principle had been "to neutralise the poison" in the clauses of the Versailles Treaty by which the German Army had been disarmed, and to create a nucleus from which a new, greater army could one day be formed. When the Allied terms had forced the Reichswehr to purge some 20,000 of its officers, Seeckt made sure that it was the elite who remained. Every subaltern was trained to command a battalion, and every field officer a division. At one moment, of the 100,000 men permitted by Versailles, 40,000 were NCO's, and each of these was regarded as potential officer material. Mistrustful of the unwieldy mass armies of conscripts of '14–'18, so lacking in mobility, Seeckt selected the rank and file of the Reichswehr all from carefully vetted volunteers. Determined to safeguard traditional values, at the same time he introduced a new, closer and more comradely relationship between officers and men, based on mutual confidence. Gone was the stiff social segregation, which to a large extent still afflicted the French Army, and gone too was much of the harsh bullying, or *Kommiss,* of the old days. The result was a remarkably professional, technically efficient force in miniature.

Considerable ingenuity was employed to surmount the Allied restrictions imposed on heavy equipment. In Reichswehr manoeuvres right up to 1932, soldiers could be seen trundling along "dummy tanks" mounted on bicycle wheels. After protracted arguments with the Allies, the Germans were permitted to construct a small armoured vehicle with a revolving turret; although barred from carrying any weapon, it was of great use in teaching officers the art of armoured warfare. Barred from producing any tracked vehicles,* the Germans ingeniously developed eight- and ten-wheeled armoured cars—forerunners of the famous eight-wheeled reconnaissance vehicle which did such good service during the Second World War. Short of transport, Seeckt began experimenting with motorcycle companies, later an essential component of the Wehrmacht's *Blitzkrieg* technique. But Seeckt's greatest contribution lay in guiding German military thought onto the correct lines. He insisted, wrote Churchill, "that false doctrines, springing from personal experiences of the Great War, should be avoided. All the lessons of that war were thoroughly and systematically studied. New principles of training and instructional courses of all kinds were introduced. All the existing manuals were rewritten." Unlike the French with their vision fixed upon the static warfare of the western front, too gratified by the fact of final victory to study the military mistakes which had come so close to compromising it, Seeckt, together with many other German staff officers who had fought on the Russian front, enjoyed the advantage of having seen that there were other ways of waging war. He had helped devise the tactics of the great sweeping operations in the east, had directed the break-through at Gorlice, leading to a depth of penetration such as was never to occur in the west. From these wartime experiences, he concluded as early as 1921: "The whole future of warfare appears to me to be in the employment of mobile armies, relatively small but of high quality, and rendered distinctly more effective by the addition of aircraft."

Guderian and the Panzerkorps

Seeckt retired for political reasons in 1926, and died ten years later. But he left solid foundations for his successors to build upon. In 1922, a thirty-four-year-old staff captain called Heinz Guderian was appointed to the staff of the Army's Motor Transport; a signals specialist, it was the first time he had anything to do with mechanisation. During the Great War, Guderian, as an intelligence officer on the Crown Prince's Headquarters, had been at Verdun throughout the German offensive of 1916. What he had seen there had been enough to convince him that the sense-

---

* Within a year of the departure of the Allied Control Commission in 1927, Krupp was producing the first tanks, and under the strange, secret alliance with the Soviet Union these were shipped in pieces to Kazan on the Volga, to be put through their paces there.

less carnage of this kind of static warfare should never again be indulged in. Encouraged by the ideas of Seeckt, he began ardently to study the effect of motorisation on mobility, and at an early stage fell under the profound influence of the writings of the British military thinkers Liddell Hart, Fuller and Martel. After eighteen months in the Inspectorate of Transport, Guderian was selected to assist Lieutenant Colonel von Brauchitsch* at exercises in cooperation between motorised troops and aircraft. He did so well that he was next given a job lecturing on tactics and military history, which provided him with an admirable opportunity to develop his ideas further. Guderian himself claims that by 1929 he had become "convinced" of the fundamental importance of integrated armoured divisions, in which tanks would assume the primary role, instead of being subordinate to the infantry. In 1931, he received his first motorised command—of a battalion equipped with dummy tanks and dummy antitank guns. Meanwhile, in Britain, during 1934 some advanced experiments on deep penetration had been carried out by General Hobart's 1st Tank Brigade. Guderian kept abreast of these manoeuvres by employing at his own expense a local tutor to translate Liddell Hart's articles about them the moment they appeared in England. By the following year his own thinking had reached the point where he could both give utterance to it in an astoundingly prophetic book† and put it into practice. As has often been the humiliating story with British inventions and discoveries, the development of armour was now left to another, unfriendly country.

Guderian began his book, *Achtung—Panzer!*, by examining the causes underlying the success and failure of Allied tank operations (the Germans hardly employed any tanks at all) during the First War. He listed the following fundamental errors: the Allies did not attack in sufficient depth, and were never backed up by sufficiently powerful mobile reserves, so that they broke *into* the enemy front, but never *through*—where they would have been able "to knock out his batteries, his reserves, his staffs, all at the same time"; the full potential of the tanks was sacrificed by their being yoked to two such slow-moving components as foot in-

---

* Later Field Marshal, and Hitler's Army C-in-C in 1940.
† *Achtung—Panzer!*, Stuttgart, 1937.

fantry and horse-drawn artillery; they were thrown in by "penny packets" instead of powerful concentrations; and they were the wrong kind of tanks.

Guderian saw the remedy to all this in the fully mechanised panzer divisions, the components of which would collaborate closely, and which had to be capable of moving at equal speeds. The panzer division was to be built around the tank itself; not the slow, short-range "infantry escort" tank to which the French Army was still wedded,* but a medium "break-through" tank possessing "armour sufficient to protect it against the mass of enemy antitank weapons, a higher speed and greater cruising range than the infantry escort tank, and an armament of machine-guns and cannon up to 75 mm." From the beginning, commanders of these tanks would be trained to "fight in large units," thus providing maximum concentration of firepower. Close behind the "break-through," tanks would follow motorised infantry with the role of mopping up and exploiting the successes of the armour, and interspersed with them would be mobile antitank guns. These were to be rushed offensively forward, to hold the vulnerable flanks of the panzer salient against any counterattack by enemy tanks. The unwieldy horse-drawn artillery of '14–'18 would be replaced by self-propelled guns mounted on tracks. But here Guderian, writing in 1936, was able to provide a solution which he admitted to be only partially satisfactory. The essence of the panzer thrust, he stressed, must be surprise. Yet a prolonged softening-up bombardment, even from highly mobile artillery, was always liable to give the game away, as happened repeatedly during the set-piece offensives of the Great War. The full answer was to come only with the development of the Stuka dive bomber.

Guderian stressed the advantage of tanks attacking in mass and, if possible, at early dawn, on account of the difficult targets they would present to the defender's antitank guns. He also stressed the need to strike with such speed that the tanks would get into the enemy's main defence zone before these guns could be properly sited. But he regarded "the most dangerous opponent" of the panzer division to be the enemy tank. If the attacker "cannot succeed in beating them, then the breakthrough can be

---

* It was significant that the infant Panzerkorps chose to base its procedure on the British Army manual on the use of armour rather than on the French—because of the rigidity of the French links between tanks and infantry.

considered as having failed, because neither the infantry nor the artillery will be able to get through any longer. Everything depends on delaying intervention of enemy antitank reserves and tanks and encountering them as early as possible with powerful units, i.e., panzer units capable of taking part in a tank battle in the full depths of the battlefield, in the area of the enemy reserves and command centres." The intervention of the defender's reserves was to be delayed by the tactical air force, which Guderian already saw as working in close cooperation with the panzers; this delaying task would be one of airpower's principal functions in the battle. He also mentions the employment of airborne troops in capturing important points in the enemy rear to open routes for the oncoming panzer thrust.

Once the attacker has succeeded in breaking through into the enemy's defence area,

the crushing of the enemy batteries and the mopping up of the infantry battle zone can be achieved with relatively weak panzer units. The infantry can then exploit the successes of the tanks. . . .

The endeavour to strike the enemy defence simultaneously in its whole depth [continues Guderian] must therefore be regarded as highly justified. This lofty goal is only to be achieved with numerous tanks in the necessary deep deployment, with panzer units and panzer leaders who have been taught to fight in large units and to break any unforeseen resistance rapidly and decisively. Apart from its depth, the breakthrough attack must also be on so great a width that the outflanking of a centre of the attack is made difficult. . . . We thus sum up our demands for a decision-seeking panzer attack in these terms: suitable terrain, surprise and mass deployment in the necessary width and depth.

Here lay an astonishingly accurate blueprint of how, four years later, Guderian himself would effect the break-through at Sedan. In *Mein Kampf* Hitler had already broadcast to the world his intentions to obtain *Lebensraum* by conquest in Europe; now, in finer detail, Guderian revealed the technique by which these conquests were to be made. Despite the admonition contained in its very title, *Achtung—Panzer!* was ignored by French and British leaders even more completely than *Mein Kampf* had been. It was never translated into French or English, and appears never to have been properly studied by anyone in a key position in the

General Staffs of either country. Yet already by February 1935, the Deuxième Bureau (so its chief, General Gauché, tells us) had warned the French High Command of the potential of Germany's embryo panzer divisions; moreover, by the time of the publication of *Achtung—Panzer!*, Guderian was already a well-known military figure who had published his theories in professional magazines for all to read, and who was now commanding Hitler's 2nd Panzer Division.

As early as 1933, when Hitler had attended a demonstration of Germany's earliest tank prototype, he exclaimed repeatedly to Guderian, "That's what I need! That's what I want to have!" Hitler's own technical grasp was a constant source of astonishment to his advisers; mechanical details fascinated him, and among other things it was reputedly he who first suggested (in 1938) that the 88 mm antiaircraft gun be used in an antitank role, thereby giving birth to a weapon which was perhaps the most successful to be used on either side in World War II. But above all, Guderian and his theories were just what Hitler needed to execute his policy of lightning conquests effected with minimum force. With that visionary intuition of his, he had remarked to Hermann Rauschning shortly after coming to power: "The next war will be quite different from the last world war. Infantry attacks and mass formations are obsolete. Interlocked frontal struggles lasting for years on petrified fronts will not return. I guarantee that. They were a degenerate form of war"; and later, even more prophetically: "I shall manoeuvre France right out of her Maginot Line without losing a single soldier." Although Guderian had to face opposition from conservative elements in the German Army, almost as tough as anything encountered by the French and British reformers, under Hitler's patronage he received the utmost support. In October 1935, the first three panzer divisions were formed, with Guderian, still only a colonel, receiving command of one of them. By the beginning of 1938, Guderian was promoted lieutenant general and placed in command of the mobile corps which played a lead role in the march into Austria. At the end of that year, now a full general, he received the key post of Chief of Mobile Troops on the General Staff. Guderian and the philosophy of *Blitzkrieg* had arrived.

The revolutionary Wehrmacht

In *Achtung—Panzer!* Guderian describes the highest human quality called for by the Panzer Corps as being "a fanatical will to move forward." It was this very quality which the strange and terrible creed of National Socialism was instilling into the new Wehrmacht as a whole. How difficult it is at this range to recapture, let alone explain, the instant magic that, in the 1930s, Hitler wielded over German youth—sublimely unaware as it was of the dark tunnel of unprecedented horror into which he would eventually lead them and all Europe! Onto the fertile stock of German childhoods cast over by the miseries of hunger, crazy inflation, followed by depression and mass unemployment, the humiliations of defeat and occupation, the apparent injustices of Versailles and the seeming pointlessness of life under Weimar, Hitler was able to graft the bud of intoxication. As Nietzsche said of the Germans, "Intoxication means more to them than nourishment. That is the hook they will always bite on. A popular leader must hold up before them the prospect of conquests and splendour; then he will be believed." Hitler was believed and his early bloodless conquests confirmed and reconfirmed that belief. Satisfying some elemental need for mysticism in the German soul, the gigantic Nuremberg Rallies with their pageantry and colour, their hysterical, chanting masses of assenting humanity, filled young Germans with a revolutionary fervour which they carried with them into the Wehrmacht. Among the older generation, for all those whose nightmare memories of the shell holes on the western front, implanted as deeply as in French minds, caused them to wonder fearfully where Hitler's rearmament would lead, there were many who could only think of one word: Revenge! Visiting Germany in 1934, Jean-Paul Sartre was deeply shocked by the fanaticism of an ex-sergeant of the Great War: "If there's another war," the man said, "we shall not be defeated this time. We shall retrieve our honour." Sartre replied that there was no need for a war; everyone ought to want peace. "Honour comes first," the sergeant said. "First we must retrieve our honour." As Hitler's successes brought his promises to reverse the *Diktat* of Versailles ever closer to fulfilment, so did the numbers of those sharing the views of Sartre's ex-sergeant multiply. Patriotism rekindled, the Army became imbued with a new glory.

A military career satisfied the young German's inherent yearn-
ing for *Kameradschaft,* as well as his passion for mechanical
matters, canalising all that tremendous fund of technical skill and
imagination latent in Germany in the 1920s and early thirties. At
the same time, the Wehrmacht's programme of expansion promised swift promotion. Here, at last, was something that imparted
to life a new meaning! Seeckt and Guderian had provided the
Wehrmacht with a revolutionary doctrine; Hitler and Nazism a
revolutionary spirit to go with it.

The training of German youth, both within the new Wehrmacht
and, earlier, in various paramilitary organisations, was in itself
revolutionary. Already at the tender age of six, their regimented
education began. At ten they entered the *Jungvolk,* pledging "to
devote all my energies and my strength to the saviour of our
country, Adolf Hitler. I am willing and ready to give up my life
for him so help me God." At twelve, the most outstanding members of the *Jungvolk* were picked out to be dispatched to special
schools for the instruction of elite cadres. The most select of these
were called *Ordensburgen.** The emphasis here, as everywhere
else under the Nazis' educational system, was strongly on physical
culture and disciplined teamwork; among other preliminary military training, the boys also received courses in parachute jumping. At fourteen young Germans became eligible to join the vast
body of the Hitler Youth itself. In 1936, a law was passed closely
coordinating the Hitler Youth with the Wehrmacht; from local
units, its members received instruction in marksmanship and on
leadership, visited army barracks and were taken to watch manoeuvres. One of the liaison officers later organising these programmes was a certain Lieutenant Colonel Erwin Rommel. At
eighteen, youths became of age for conscription into the Wehrmacht or the Arbeitsdienst, the Labour Service. Inside the
Arbeitsdienst, while young Germans served their country by building roads and barracks, the work of inseminating corporate
consciousness and paramilitary discipline and of preaching the essential classlessness of the New Order continued. Then, for vaca-
tion times, there was the Nazi "Strength through Joy" welfare
organisation to provide still further regimented *Kameradschaft.*
There was no mistaking the enthusiasm of the recipients of this

---

* Roughly translatable as "Citadels of Chivalry."

massive indoctrination; even a dispassionate British journalist*
studying "these young Germans of 1933" was deeply impressed
(as indeed were so many other observers at the time) by the
"tremendous sense of comradeship amongst themselves. They
were happy to learn together, play together, march together and
to learn to fight together. They loved the open air and they flung
away clothes from them with an abandon which would have horrified the Victorian generation. . . . Their animal energy was
gigantic." By the time they reached the Wehrmacht, these Spartan,
dedicated youths were already superlative material for a "revolutionary" force, instinctively versed in the one craft which was to
pay off in Germany's early military operations more than any
other: teamwork.

Antimilitarism in France

By comparison, what contrast one may glimpse in the spirit of
France of the mid-thirties! The last of those rosy postwar illusions
had been roughly swept aside by the revelation of her impotence
during the Rhineland crisis, the urge for national *grandeur,* the
desire for supremacy in Europe replaced by a deep longing simply to be left in peace. It was a longing widely diffused through
all strata of French society, though, of course, the symptoms were
paralleled in and stimulated by the mood prevailing in the England of Cliveden and Lansbury, the Peace Ballot and the Peace
Pledge Union. But in France particularly the instinct for peace,
or for what was later to become stigmatised as "appeasement,"
remained strongly rooted in the dread memories of the Great
War; memories which, perhaps perversely, had become more potent with the passage of the years. This was to a large extent a
consequence of the spate of antiwar literature which had swept
Europe in the late twenties, all telling basically the same tale of
the horror and wastefulness of war, combined with the cynical cal-
lousness and sheer incompetence of the war leaders. In Germany, Hitler had been swift to stifle such books as Remarque's
All Quiet on the Western Front, but in France the terrifying
novel of Henri Barbusse, *Le Feu,* had an immeasurable impact:
for the Verdun generation, here indeed was an indelible re-

---

* Terence Prittie, *Germans Against Hitler,* p. 154.

minder of what it had really been like; for their juniors, a nightmare fantasy the re-enactment of which must be avoided at all costs. Wielding enormous intellectual influence were various antiwar associations formed by such giants of France's literary left wing as André Gide, Paul Éluard, Louis Aragon and Romain Rolland. But Barbusse was the torchbearer; when he died in 1935 more than three hundred thousand persons followed his coffin to Père Lachaise Cemetery in Paris.

With his instinctive genius, Hitler knew well how to play on French fears and hopes, accompanying each new adventure with barrages of peace propaganda and repeated pledges of renunciation of any claim to Alsace-Lorraine, aimed at making Frenchmen sleep all the more comfortably at night behind the safety of their Maginot Line. With the vileness of the concentration camps yet to come, the full menace of the New Order only apparent when it would already be too late to check it, Hitler did not seem especially malignant to the average Frenchman. Besides, as will be seen shortly, there were other dangers much closer to home. What hatred and fear of the Nazis existed were roughly balanced out by equal hatred and fear of war itself.

So often in history when the unpleasantness of reality induces emotional confusion, societies are tempted to bury themselves in imaginary pleasures and distractions. The louder the barbarians outside hammered at the walls of Rome, the wilder grew the public diversions in the Colosseum and the private orgies within the walls. At many levels of French life during the late twenties and thirties, escapism reveals itself as the ruling factor. Dadaism and surrealism in art are matched by the *fantaisiste,* fairy-tale world of Cocteau and Giraudoux. The frenzy of the fox-trot *dansomanie* of the twenties marches with the stage extravaganzas of Diaghilev; the Ballet Russe, Ballet Suédois; Josephine Baker, the Revue Nègre. Anything for *spectacle.* The circus is rediscovered. Then France suddenly finds she can play tennis and rugger; to be able to beat England provides a welcome sop to the Quai d'Orsay's growing dependence upon the Foreign Office. The sporting pages of *Paris-Soir* make it overnight the journalistic success story of the decade. Bicycling is all the rage; for the masses, the Tour de France supplies the nearest emotional equivalent to Germany's Nuremberg rallies. In the cabarets, even the sacred fetishes of pre-1914 can be made mock of, with bearded ladies from Alsace chanting melodramatically:

> "No, no, a thousand times no! My breast is French,
> I shall never give suck to a German child."

In literature, the passion for romantic travel, so powerful in the twenties, gives way to an equal fascination in the personal "heroic quest" of the agonising man-of-action, as represented by such adventurers as Saint-Exupéry and Malraux.

Despite its philosophy of "engagement," no form of literature demonstrated a greater revolt from reality than the existentialism of young Jean-Paul Sartre and his fellow inmates of the Café Flore in the latter 1930s. In her autobiography, Sartre's mistress, Simone de Beauvoir, furnishes a revealingly honest chronicle of the attitude of French left-wing intellectuals. The autumn of 1929 had made her feel she was living in a new "Golden Age": "Peace seemed finally assured; the expansion of the German Nazi party was a mere fringe phenomenon, without any serious significance. . . . It would not be long before colonialism folded up." Of Hitler's coming to power in 1933, she writes: "Like everyone else on the French left, we watched these developments quite calmly," and in the same breath that she records, in passing, Einstein's flight from Germany she deplores the closing down of the German "Institute of Sexology." Still, "there was no threat to peace; the only danger was the panic that the Right was attempting to spread in France, with the aim of dragging us into war." To the "elders" of the left, as to so many of that generation, "the memory of the 1914–18 war stuck in their throats. . . . In 1914 the whole of the intellectual elite, Socialists, writers, and all—no wonder Jaurès was assassinated—toed a wholly chauvinistic line. . . . Our elders, then, forbade us to envisage the very possibility of a war." In their filmgoing, this dread of war led Sartre and Beauvoir to miss Renoir's classic *La Grande Illusion,* by preference seeking escapism in such American farces as *My Man Godfrey* and *Mr. Deeds Goes to Town.*

Political scandals

At the important elections of 1935, after Hitler's occupation of the Rhineland, Sartre had refused to vote: "The political aspirations of left-wing intellectuals made him shrug his shoulders." Yet, while regarding the French political scene with "disengaged" aversion, and finding nothing "to stir my interest" in the assassination of King Alexander of Yugoslavia and French Foreign Minister Barthou, Simone de Beauvoir concedes at the same time that "Sartre and I read every word" of the latest turn in the Stavisky scandal. This duality of attitudes extended far beyond the narrow circle of the Café Flore. Upon the futility of the Third Republic's political jungle had now become superimposed (though perhaps "grafted" is the better word) a miasma of corruption cases. The first big shock came in 1928 with the arrest of Klotz, the former Minister of Finance about whom Clemenceau had been so scathing, on charges of issuing dud cheques. Two years later there followed the Oustric scandal. Oustric had built up a bogus banking empire largely propped up on vast loans somehow obtained from the Bank of France; when his empire crashed, the involvement of the second Tardieu Government was sufficient to bring about its fall too.

But the greatest furor was caused by Serge Stavisky, the son of a Ukrainian-Jewish dentist and a seductive young man with an apparently limitless number of useful contacts in politics, the press and the judiciary. Already by 1933 his financial operations had come under official scrutiny, but he appeared to be immune from police interference and a criminal case against him had actually been postponed nineteen times. It so happened that the public prosecutor who was failing to bring Stavisky to justice was the brother-in-law of the current Prime Minister, Camille Chautemps. Then suddenly, on December 30, a major fraud, concerning the issue of millions of francs based on the assets of a municipal pawnshop in the small town of Bayonne, was pinned on Stavisky. The Mayor of Bayonne, Garat, who was also a Radical deputy, was arrested, but the indications were that much bigger game was involved. How else had Stavisky managed to pull off such swindles, and how had he evaded justice for so long? Before any answers could be provided, the police found Stavisky dead in a house in Chamonix where he had been hiding with his mistress. Suicide was alleged, but it was widely believed that he had been shot by a policeman—conveniently, it seemed, for Chautemps. Overnight Stavisky became the best known name in France since Dreyfus. Crowds appeared outside the National As-

sembly shouting "Down with the thieves!" and spitting on deputies. On January 27, 1934, the Chautemps Government fell—after
just two months and four days.

In common with Sartre and Beauvoir, the great mass of
Frenchmen indulged themselves heartily in the "spectacle" of
political scandals as part of the nation's pursuit of escapism.
Hand in hand with this indulgence went a deep disgust and disillusion with politicians and government, which were about to
create a grave split in France just at the moment when the Nazi
jackboots were striding out. By 1934 the reputation of politicians
in France had sunk to a record low; but it was to sink still lower,
and with it all efficacity of government. Constantly there was
some new scandal and, however distantly, some minister in what
the cynics dubbed "the Republic of Pals" always seemed to be implicated. French politicians had assumed the habit of "dealing
with their country as if it were a commercial company going into
liquidation." In a typical scene of the Third Republic, Georges
Bonnet and Camille Chautemps at a lunch party are pictured as
having "vied with one another to succeed a Premier whose ministry had just fallen. 'It's my turn!' 'No, Georges, it's mine.'" Dizzier and dizzier became the game of musical chairs played by the
little men unaware of the proportions of the tragedy moving in on
them; in the eighteen months preceding 1934, there had been five
different governments but with virtually the same faces in each;
from mid-1932 to the outbreak of war in 1939, France's score of
governments was to total nineteen, including eleven different
Premiers, eight Ministers of Finance, seven Ministers of Foreign
Affairs, and eight Ministers of War. A favourite insult with
Parisian taxi drivers became *"Espèce de Député."* The populace
loathed the politicians; the politicians loathed each other.

Beginnings of civil war

On February 6, 1934, passions overflowed. This was the date
marking the beginning of what approximated civil war in France,
which was to have so insidious and powerful an influence on the
events of 1940 that its background needs to be carefully understood. Since Armistice Day, 1918, two major ideological streams,
distinct and opposing, had flowed through the political life of
France. One was revolutionary, the other patriotic; or, simplified
in terms of the two historic events which supplied each with its

most potent, fundamental inspiration, they might well be called, respectively, the streams of the Commune and of Verdun. The revolutionary, Commune stream traces its source back to the Great Revolution of 1789, whose spiritual heirs fought against the "Establishment" on the barricades of 1830 and 1848; while, as has already been suggested, its main motivating force in the post-1918 world was derived from the Russian Revolution. But it was the Paris Commune of 1871 in which resided the numen of France's left wing, and especially of that important section comprised by the Parisian proletariat. For it was the Commune which, though unsuccessful, had first pointed the way to the possibility of a government by the proletariat, based on revolution and the destruction of the bourgeois monopoly; moreover, it was upon the achievements and errors of the Commune (as interpreted by Karl Marx) that Lenin had based his own triumphant revolution of 1917. Above all, in France it was the savage memories of the 20,000 Communards so brutally massacred by Thiers's forces of order which kept alight the flame of revolution, making the gulf between bourgeois and proletarian wider and more unbridgeable than in any other nation of the western world. The link with the Commune has never been severed; in the thirties (and today), every Whitsun the leaders of France's left wing make a solemn pilgrimage to the Mur des Fédérés at Père Lachaise Cemetery, to commemorate the summary execution there on May 28, 1871, of 147 Communards. The "internationale" was their marching song, but the Mur was the shrine to which they marched.

The Verdun stream, on the other hand, drew its main impetus from the middle-class, conservative forces which had repressed the Commune. It believed in the fundamental, indestructible *grandeur* of France (in a more contemporary setting, it might be rated as essentially Gaullist); it hankered after *la gloire* as embodied by the military triumphs of Louis XIV and Napoleon. While the heirs of the Commune marched to the Mur des Fédérés, it was to the tragic glories of Verdun that this second stream turned for its inspiration. It felt that France should not renounce benefit from all the blood gloriously shed in her numerous wars; especially in this last and most terrible (though it was torn when, like the left wing, it reflected upon the realities on the reverse of the Verdun coin). Still clinging to many of the illusions left over from the Quatorze Juillet of 1919, it was sickened by France's subsequent retreat from *grandeur,* sickened by the corrupt ineptness of her politicians. At the same time, it too had its memories of the Commune which the new strength infused into the French left by the Russian Revolution had revivified. The spectre of Bolshevism, teeth clamped upon a bloody knife, was constantly breathing down its neck.

By the thirties, the most vocal and extreme of those Frenchmen borne along in the Verdun stream had banded themselves together in various right-wing "leagues." There were the Camelots du Roi, shock troops of the monarchist, Catholic anti-Semitic Action Française of Charles Maurras,* which had led the assault on Stavisky and his "pals" highly placed in the Radical Party. There were also the Jeunesses Patriotes, nationalist and violently anti-Communist, who had assumed the mantle of the fire-eating Paul Déroulède's Ligue des Patriotes founded to avenge the defeat of 1870. But now with the grievance of Alsace-Lorraine eradicated, the patriotism of the Jeunesses was as defensive as that of any other section of the country for whom the Maginot Line had become a way of life, and their energies were directed largely towards the protection of private property against real or imagined threats of "Bolshevism." In 1932, the Solidarité Française was created by funds from the perfumery fortune of François Coty, its members wearing a paramilitary uniform of black beret and blue shirt. Their motto was *La France aux Français!* and a newspaper also founded by Coty, *L'Ami du Peuple,* bore at its masthead the slogan "With Hitler against Bolshevism." In 1933, the Françistes were formed, adopting a uniform not dissimilar to that of the Nazi storm troopers.

Less extreme politically, though still well right of centre, were various veterans' associations, whose members came largely from the *petite bourgeoisie.* But the most activist and significant of the "Leagues" was the Croix de Feu, founded in 1928 originally as an association of ex-soldiers decorated for bravery. Its leader, Colonel Casimir de la Rocque, who had served on the staffs of both Foch and Lyautey, was now dedicated to the purgation of all that was corrupt in the institutions of the Third Republic. Under his impulse the Croix de Feu assumed a distinct political

---

* In 1945, Maurras was sentenced to life imprisonment as a collaborator.

orientation. "Honesty" and "Order" were its twin battle cries, and, though it could not strictly be described as fascist (unlike some of the more right-wing leagues) it shared their admiration for the vigour and efficiency that Mussolini had instilled into Italian youth; in addition, as the scandals multiplied, the Croix de Feu had adopted a more blatantly anti-Republican attitude. The patrician colonel himself was certainly no rabble-rouser like Hitler. A British journalist* says of him: "His head was too narrow and unimpressive, his voice was too high, his diction too elaborate for mass appeal. His gestures were those of a romantic actor not a tribune. He was too genteel." Nevertheless, to the left wing in France Colonel de la Rocque had come to epitomise everything that it understood, loathed and feared in the meaning of the word *Fascism.*

During the week that followed the fall of the Chautemps Government on January 27, 1934, tension had been rising in Paris. Enraged by the revelations of the Stavisky case, de la Rocque met with leaders of the other right-wing leagues to coordinate a march upon the Assembly. On February 5th, there were demonstrations and various collisions with the police. The next morning, *L'Action Française* printed in the most provocative headlines: THE THIEVES ARE BARRICADING THEMSELVES IN THEIR CAVE. AGAINST THIS ABJECT REGIME, EVERYONE IN FRONT OF THE CHAMBRE DE DÉPUTÉS THIS EVENING. At about 6 P.M., the first shock troops—consisting largely of the Camelots du Roi, with a number of *grands mutilés* veterans placed conspicuously to the fore—attempted to force their way through police barriers drawn up on the Pont de la Concorde. They hurled bottles, stones and sections of lead piping at the police, and when the mounted police charged, the hocks of their horses were slashed with razors tied to sticks. Meanwhile, inside the Chamber the new government, headed by Édouard Daladier, was still struggling to get a vote of confidence. By 7:30, the police were becoming increasingly hard pressed, and after three warnings to the crowd they received the order to fire. Seven demonstrators were killed and a large number wounded. Though driven back as far as the Opera, a counterattack brought them once more to the Concorde. The police opened fire a second time; but it was not until midnight that the deputies could con-

---

* Sefton Delmer, *Trail Sinister.*

clude they were safe from a repetition of September 3, 1870, when the Palais Bourbon had been stormed and the government overthrown by a Paris mob outraged by news of Louis Napoleon's defeat at Sedan. Out of 40,000 demonstrators, 16 had been killed and at least 655 were known to be wounded; well over a thousand policemen received injuries.

Nevertheless, the next day Colonel de la Rocque proclaimed from his secret battle headquarters: "The Croix de Feu has surrounded the Chamber and forced the deputies to flee." The proclamation infuriated the leaders of the other leagues, who considered that de la Rocque's men had played only the most prudent of parts in the battle. But the impact that the colonel's braggadocio had upon the *left wing* was even more dramatic. Suddenly, in the heated atmosphere of the moment, it seemed as if a new General Boulanger had arisen. Fears were greatly exacerbated on the afternoon of the 7th when, quite unexpectedly, Daladier resigned. Ex-President Gaston Doumergue, aged seventy, took his place at the head of a "National Government" with—as a special sop to the *anciens combattants* of the right-wing leagues—seventy-seven-year-old Marshal Pétain, the "Hero of Verdun," as its Minister of National Defence. It was the first time since 1870 that the mob had brought about the fall of a French government; but, alas, not the last time that a disastrous display of weakness by Daladier would bely his nickname, "the bull of Vaucluse." Discussing his resignation, Daladier explained feebly, "Otherwise we should have had to shoot."

On February 6th, the Communists, sharing de la Rocque's detestation of corrupt Republican politicians, had also taken up cudgels against the government. One eyewitness actually saw a Camelot du Roi and a Communist, each recognisable by his badge, jointly pulling down a lamppost—just about the last occasion in time of peace, before de Gaulle, that the two extremes of French political life would be able to find common cause. But now, with the shock administered by the fall of the Daladier Government, the entire left wing thought in terror that it saw the imminence of a right-wing *coup d'état*, along the lines taken in Germany and Italy, with Colonel de la Rocque playing the role of Louis Napoleon—or Mussolini. Abruptly it reversed its position. On the morning of February 9th, the Communist *L'Humanité* called a mass meeting for that evening in the Place de la République, to demand the dissolution of both the Chamber and its ephemeral allies, the right-wing leagues. That night an event of major importance occurred. Near the République, two rival columns approached each other, one of Communists, the other of Jeunesses Socialistes, representing the two principal left-wing parties, which had hardly been on speaking terms ever since the great schism of 1920–21. At first it looked as if there would be conflict. However, amid cries of "We're not clashing, we're fraternising . . . we're all here to defend the Republic," the heads of the two columns mingled and clasped hands, then marched together chanting "Unity of action!" On February 12th, the CGT called a general strike in protest against the "fascist peril," and for the first time since its breakaway thirteen years before, the Communist CGTU collaborated fully. In the course of that day the new pact was sealed in blood when, amid the Old Communard strongholds of eastern Paris, three-cornered melees between strikers, right-wing layabouts and the police resulted in four deaths. "United as at the front!" had been on the lips of Colonel de la Rocque's *anciens combattants* on February 6th; "Unity of action!" the slogan of the heirs to the Commune three days later. But in fact both would only lead disastrously to the greater disunity of the French nation.

After February 6th, whatever chance the right wing had of pulling off a *coup d'état* vanished, but the protest march against the "corrupt politicians" drew a mass of new, young recruits to de la Rocque's standard. In response the left closed ranks more tightly to form a "common front against Fascism." That July, Blum the Socialist leader and Thorez the Communist signed a pact of unity; by October 1934, *L'Humanité* was beginning to talk about a *Fronte populaire contre le fascisme*. Meanwhile, other factors were lending further cohesive force to this new display of left-wing solidarity. France found herself still plunged deep into economic darkness by the world slump, while Britain and America were already emerging from the tunnel; between 1928 and 1934, French industrial production dropped 17 percent; between 1929 and 1936, average incomes fell 30 percent, and by the end of 1935 over 800,000 were unemployed. Fearful of the "Bolshevist" threat to private property and never quite forgetting the Commune, the steely-faced managers of French industry, the patrons had taken full advantage of the past splits between the Socialist and Communist trades unions to put the brake on essential social reforms. Now (although from mid-1935 onwards the economy did begin to show an upturn) the plight of the workers in many French industries was genuinely appalling.

On Quatorze Juillet, 1935, the Croix de Feu marched with smart military precision down the Champs Élysées; de la Rocque was seen paying homage at the Arc de Triomphe. But the day belonged to the left, demonstrating at the other end of Paris. Down from Belleville and the Faubourg Saint-Antoine they flooded to the Place de la Bastille in their thousands; some papers estimated that well over half a million turned out that day. At a mass meeting on the Bastille, beneath great red banners proclaiming *"Paix, pain, liberté!"*, the Front Populaire was officially launched. That afternoon, a vast column paraded from the Bastille to Vincennes. Daladier, the Radical-Socialist former Prime Minister whose downfall the Communists had helped bring about the previous year, marched alongside Marty, the revolutionary who had organised the postwar mutinies in France's Black Sea Fleet; arm in arm, like blood brothers, went Blum and Thorez, Herriot and Barbusse and Duclos. Such scenes of left-wing solidarity, and elation, had not been seen since the heyday of the Commune sixty-four years earlier. But, as Herriot grudgingly remarked later on, it did seem rather as if the Communists had dominated the proceedings.

At their congress that October, the French Radicals decided to throw in their lot with the Front Populaire. Then, in March 1936, came Hitler's reoccupation of the Rhineland. On May 3rd, France went to the polls and the Front Populaire was swept into power. Formerly with only 10 seats, the Communists now emerged with no less than 72; the Socialists, gaining another 49 seats, became the strongest party and accordingly it fell to Léon Blum to form a government. In a frenzy of thanksgiving, some 400,000 Parisians marched on May 24th to do homage at the Mur des Fédérés, amid cries of *"Vive le Front Populaire! Vive la Commune!"*, while a contingent of soldiers from Versailles bore a banner proclaiming: "The Versailles soldiery of 1871 assassinated the Commune. The soldiers of Versailles in 1936 will avenge it." The left had scored its greatest triumph since 1871; but how, with the clouds growing more and more sombre beyond the Rhine, was it going to exploit this victory?

4

Palinurus Nods

Lost was the nation's sense, nor could be found,
While the long solemn unison went round;
Wide and more wide, it spread o'er all the realm;
Even Palinurus nodded at the helm.
—ALEXANDER POPE, *The Dunciad*

In tragic life, God wot,
No villain need be! Passions spin the plot;
We are betrayed by what is false within.
—GEORGE MEREDITH, *Modern Love*

France on strike

ALMOST FROM the moment of his accession, things went badly
for Léon Blum. The difficulties of agreeing a programme meant
that subtle negotiations between the disparate members of the
Front Populaire coalition dragged on all through May. The French
proletariat, buoyed up with the exhilaration of victory, now
watched with impatience for efforts to implement the Front's
electoral promises and to alleviate their hardships. Within a
week of the election, strikes broke out at the Bréguet aircraft
factory in Le Havre. At a meeting of the Communist Party on
May 25th, militants began calling for the party to break with the
dilatory Blum. Thorez urged restraint, but at the same time demanded immediate economic action from the government. The
next day the Lavalette factory in the northwest suburbs of Paris
and the Nieuport aircraft works at Issy in the southwest were
paralysed by strikes. These assumed a new form, later to become
known as *grèves sur le tas*—sit-in strikes. The workers presented
their demands to the management, which rejected them. They
then sent the women home and simply occupied the factory.

Friends outside provided them with food, cigarettes and bedding, and they settled down for the night, arguing, playing cards or boules, singing and dancing. Alcohol was banned, but the general tone was one of *fête,* again evoking memories of the first jubilant days after the Commune seized Paris in 1871—but also related to the mood of mass escapism then gripping France. Day by day the bizarre situation renewed itself, the factory owners being told, forcefully, that if they attempted to break the strike, their plants would simply be burnt down.

At first, the stoppages appear to have been anarchic and spontaneous; one observer remarked that as soon as the "pressure" of management had been felt to weaken with the coming of the Front Populaire, "immediately all the suffering, the humiliations, the rancour, and bitterness silently built up over the years created a force sufficient to break all restraint." Gradually, however, the unions assumed control. Over the 27th and 28th, similar strikes smoothly took over the Farman aircraft works and the factories of Citroën, Renault, Gnome et Rhône, and Simca in the Paris area; virtually all these plants, it should be noted, happened to be vital to the French armaments industry. By the beginning of June the number of strikers reached 500,000 (eventually they were estimated to total 2 millions), affecting more than 12,000 enterprises. Parisians began to take their Sunday promenades out to the factories to gaze at the workers laughing and entertaining themselves among the dead machinery.

Blum became thoroughly alarmed by events, which he later described as this "social explosion which slapped the Government in the face," and began hastily to prepare reformative legislation. Prices on the Bourse plunged, and some *patrons* transferred their money abroad. Although at shop-floor level there were Communist agitators at work, the party leaders seem to have been taken by surprise by events—just as they were during the Paris riots of May 1968, three decades later. Then at 1 A.M. on June 8th, Blum signed the famous Matignon Agreement, named after his new official residence. Under what was undoubtedly their greatest single advance in the history of French industrial relations, the workers were guaranteed compulsory collective bargaining and annual paid holidays, a 40-hour week, and an immediate general raise in wages of 7 to 15 percent. Still the strikes continued, until on the 11th Thorez was forced to intervene by appealing to Parisian

Communists: "You must know when to end a strike!" On the
13th, the workers evacuated Renault, and on the 14th—at what
was both the high point and the swan song of the Front Populaire
—the entire left celebrated its great triumph, once more with
linked arms around the Bastille.

Simone de Beauvoir describes how the Matignon Agreement
"filled us with joy"; thanks to the 40-hour week "couples on tan-
dem bicycles could now be seen pedalling out of Paris every Saturday morning; they came back on Sunday evening with bunches
of flowers and foliage tied to their handlebars"; and Léon Blum
movingly remarks: "I had the feeling, in spite of everything, of
having brought a lull, a vista, into their dark difficult lives . . .
we had given them hope." Yet in fact he had rendered the future
for France as a whole more hopeless. A week after the Assembly
ratified the Matignon Agreement, the Spanish Civil War broke
out; in Germany, Hitler's rearmament was picking up at an alarming speed. Necessary and long overdue as were Blum's reforms,
they could not have come at a worse time for France. Far from
producing a magical panacea for all her economic ills, if anything
they aggravated them. One reasonable estimate puts the immediate additional cost of the Agreement to French employers at
between 64 and 107 percent; which in turn pushed up the cost
of living 50 percent by the end of 1937. Finding their new gains
thus whittled away, the workers at once saw the hand of the employers attempting to neutralise the new laws, and through 1937
another series of wildcat strikes was sparked off. The sharply increased costs meant that French exports became less competitive
abroad, with the result that, in September 1936, Blum was forced
to devalue (once again) the franc by 25 percent—to the fury of
the Communists.

French industry continued to stagnate. Because they assumed
it created unemployment, the Front opposed the introduction of
the assembly line—which meant that much of France's badly
needed new military equipment would continue to be turned out
laboriously by manual processes. Most insidious of all was the
impact that the 40-hour week had on French rearmament, at a
time when the Germans were toiling away in Hitler's munitions
industries an average of 52 hours a week. By the autumn of 1938,
while German production was 30 percent higher than it had been
in 1930, French industrial production was probably as much as

25 percent lower; Paul Reynaud considered that the 40-hour week "was equivalent to destroying one-sixth of French plant." Another injurious legacy from the stay-in strikes of 1936 which contributed to the enduring stagnation of French industry was the loss of power and prestige of works foremen; less visible beneath this lay a newly acquired instinct for disobedience, a disdain for authority of all forms, whether of government, management or the union, which was certainly to bear moral fruit in 1940.

France rearms—Reynaud, de Gaulle and Pétain: 1936–39

Alarmed by the rise of Hitler and his reoccupation of the Rhineland, France had begun to make tentative efforts to refurbish her armed forces. In March 1935, the period of military service had been extended to two years, although at the time the official Socialist organ, Le Populaire, complained that "as in 1913, the Chamber has capitulated to the generals." In September 1936, a mechanisation programme was laid down providing for the creation of three light mechanised divisions and two armoured divisions; but it was desperately slow in getting off the ground. Work began on the prototypes of some impressive new weapons, all of which were to prove superior on various points to their German counterparts in 1940. In 1935 came the first heavy "B" tank; in 1936, the fast, hard-hitting medium Somua; and in 1937 the 47 mm antitank gun. But hesitancy on the part of the High Command, lack of coordination between the army and the arms manufacturers, added to the inbuilt hostility of the Front Populaire towards rearmament of any kind, plus the consequence of the strikes and the 40-hour week, resulted in the first orders for even the necessary machine tools not being given until the year after the launching of the new armament programme. During 1936, 120 tanks had been leaving the factories each month, but by January 1937 the number fell to 19. The arms budget, which in 1936 amounted to 1,492 million francs, rose to 2,938 in 1937 and 5,152 in 1938; but much of it was pointlessly frittered away. In 1937, the government decided to construct a line of unconnected light pillboxes along the now unguarded northern frontier; the press immediately assumed this meant the prolongation of the Maginot Line proper, and the government wholeheartedly encouraged it in this act of self-deception.

As early as February 1935, the Deuxième Bureau had notified

the French High Command of the appearance of the first panzer division in Germany, and gave a reasonably accurate account of its intended role. But from the leaders of government right down to the patrician cavalry officers with their conservative shibboleth, "Oil is dirty, dung is not," the nation in general was disinclined to believe that any combination of tanks and aircraft could alter the existing balance of warfare. Chief among the "rebels" who dared fight against the current was that political maverick, Paul Reynaud, who as early as 1924 had been calling for a mobile and offensive army as the sole means of deterring German aggression. Later he found a useful ally in an army major, Charles de Gaulle, who had first come to notice by pleading the case of the armoured division in a review article published in 1933. Two years later de Gaulle expanded his ideas into a slender book, *Vers l'Armée de Métier*. For this audacity, de Gaulle was struck from the 1936 promotion list, just as his earlier idol and patron, Marshal Pétain, had suffered before 1914 for his unorthodox views on firepower.

In assessing de Gaulle's contribution one has to exercise extreme caution. The events of the war and the Vichy era, coupled to the growth subsequently of a potent Gaullist myth-making machine, have tended to cast de Gaulle, in peacetime, as an unhonoured prophet of original genius; in wartime, as the heroic executor of his own theories, on a plane above all other French commanders during the brief conflict of 1940. Pétain, on the other hand, emerges as the malevolent scapegoat responsible for all the military shortcomings of France in the interwar period. Both estimates err by exaggeration. This is not the place to attempt to restore the image of Pétain, but on a few specific points it may be relevant to put the record right. As has been noted earlier, Pétain with his doctrine of the "continuous front" may well be blamed for inculcating wrongheadedness in the French Army —up to 1936. But this false doctrine was shared by the vast majority of French leaders; and one might well ask, why did even Reynaud appear to challenge Pétain's errors only in the wake of 1940? The same question could be levelled with equal force at other eminent Frenchmen. Pétain is also accused of having gravely neglected the Army while Minister of National Defence under the Doumergue Government of 1934; but in fact his term of office was one long struggle with the politicians to obtain the necessary military credits—a struggle which he, already approaching eighty and with a life of antipathy to politicians behind him, was little fitted to wage. One of Pétain's utterances strongly held against him *ex post facto* was that of March 1934, when he claimed that the Ardennes Forest was "impenetrable." But this, too, was the general view of the French Army, and indeed, as Guderian's panzers had not yet been invented, at the time it made reasonably good sense. Also, Pétain had added the essential qualification: *"provided we make some special dispositions."* As will be seen, no such "special dispositions" were ever made. Further, the generalisation that de Gaulle foresaw the potentialities of the armoured *Blitzkrieg* while Pétain, in his dotage, failed to do so is also not strictly true. Speaking at the Ecole de Guerre in 1935 about the impact of airpower and armour on warfare of the future, Pétain made a prophecy that de Gaulle would not have improved upon: "Victory will belong to him who is the first to exploit to the maximum the properties of modern engines and to combine their action, on whatever level, to destroy the adversary's means of carrying on the struggle." At St. Quentin the following year he declared: "The conception of the defensive army which has had priority in France since the Treaty of Versailles has had its day . . . we must direct our activity so that we have on the ground and in the air powerful forces for immediate unleashing . . . for modern offensive techniques are alone capable of effectively collaborating with an ally in peril." But what is really important, as far as Pétain is concerned, is that during the years when the irreparable damage was done to the French military machine—1936 to 1940—the old Marshal's influence had largely been removed from the councils of war.

Although the publication of *Vers l'Armée de Métier* in 1934 provoked the final breach between Pétain and his former protégé, by his heretical unorthodoxy in the book de Gaulle showed himself to be (in the view of one of his biographers*) "the spiritual heir of the Pétain of 1914." After beginning, characteristically, with a great sweep of history, de Gaulle wrote: "Nowadays, Germany is ceaselessly marshalling the means at her disposal with a view to rapid invasion." To meet this menace, "A certain portion of our own troops must always be on the alert and capable of deploying its whole force at the first shock of attack." An inert,

---

* J. R. Tournoux, *Pétain and de Gaulle.*

passively defensive army, de Gaulle scornfully predicted, would be "surprised, immobilised and outflanked; and thus you have . . . Bazaine blocked in Metz." He heaped contempt on France's conscript army with its "provisional groupings," which, "once dispersed, are reunited with difficulty, like a pack of cards continuously shuffled and mixed up." The only hope for France, de Gaulle considered, lay in mobility—"it is therefore in manoeuvring that France is protected"—and mobile striking power could be obtained only by an efficient professional army mounted on tracks. Six Guderian-style armoured divisions backed by airpower would form the nucleus of de Gaulle's force; but the main point was that it had to be a *professional* corps, of some 100,000 elite troops. This point is hammered home repeatedly in *Vers l'Armée de Métier*.

Yet there is a certain romantic imprecision about all de Gaulle's ideas expounded here, and none of the meticulously technical blueprinting to be found in Guderian; nor, for that matter, is there any of the original thought-content produced at an earlier date by Liddell Hart or Seeckt. In fact, de Gaulle was a fairly late convert to the mechanised philosophy of the earlier apostles. He seems only incompletely to have understood the importance of air–armour cooperation; and in the postwar edition of his book there is a bad piece of *ex post facto* "fudging" where he adds an important passage on the impact of airpower written *after* the fall of France.* Nevertheless, the real significance of de Gaulle and his prewar writings was that, for France at that time, his views were as outstanding as his courage in stating them.

The Reynaud–de Gaulle heresy was assailed from every side. Pétain, his natural pessimism exacerbated by his unhappy experiences as Minister of National Defence, considered that—pragmatically—it would be impossible to obtain the additional 700 million francs per year that de Gaulle's armoured contingent would require. Weygand, the retiring Army Chief of Staff, had been so obsessed by the shortage of numbers caused by the "hollow classes" that he was prevented from giving full attention to de Gaulle's ideas. But much more consequential were the attitudes of Daladier and Gamelin, the team which would lead France into war in 1939. Even in January 1937, Daladier as Minister of

---

* *Vers l'Armée de Métier* (1946), p. 86.

National Defence was declaring to a Senate Commission that the German panzers might be all right in the vast unprotected spaces of Eastern Europe, but never against so sophisticated a defence system as France's. The Spanish Civil War, claimed Daladier, "has seen the crumbling of immense hopes based on certain machines." Outside Madrid the tanks lay "pierced like sieves." "Be reassured," Daladier added, "our fortified works are sufficiently equipped to halt a sudden attack, even on Sunday." On Whitsunday three years later, the words "even on Sunday" would acquire an historic irony.

Following Daladier's exposition, the new Chief of Staff, General Gamelin, rallied to his support with a letter in which he stressed that the development of the antitank gun now meant that tanks, unless supported by ponderous artillery, would inevitably be halted "just as infantry is by the machine gun." Thus the only conclusion was to scatter armoured divisions among the various old-style infantry corps, "that is to say, let them be melted into the *dispositif général*." Speaking to the British Chief of the Imperial General Staff, General Sir Cyril Deverell, in 1936, Gamelin echoed Daladier by dismissing the German tanks in Spain as "inadequately protected, just good for the scrap heap," adding smugly, "All our information shows that it is our doctrine which is correct." As further evidence of Gamelin's fundamental, technical miscomprehension, at another time he is quoted as having said (in response to de Gaulle): "You cannot hope to achieve real break-throughs with tanks. The tank is not independent enough. It has to go ahead, but then must return for fuel and supplies." Had Gamelin read Guderian, it seems doubtful that he could have maintained this view. Lukewarm about armour, Gamelin apparently never regarded it as his job to see even the 1936 mechanisation programme, such as it was, executed purposefully. Perhaps nothing is more revealing than his own admission in his memoirs, where feebly he regrets not having "demanded in 1935 the creation of an independent armoured force. . . . Had I known that the war would not break out before 1939, I would certainly have tackled the problem."

In the opposition to Reynaud and de Gaulle, there were also other factors which underline to what extent the political "civil war" in France blinded French leaders to all but internal developments. The immediate reaction of Léon Blum and his allies of the Front to de Gaulle's "professional army" was to see in it an *"armée de coup d'état"* by means of which the likes of Colonel de la Rocque might be able to emulate Louis Napoleon in seizing power. Daladier the Radical had also backed Blum, declaring: "We do not want any professional shock army, more dangerous than one could believe for the security of the country"; and— apart from a brief policy switch by the Communist Party during the Czechoslovak crisis of 1938—Thorez consistently opposed French military expenditures, for the same motives as Blum. "Not a *sou* for military service," he pronounced in 1935, adding in words that were to assume particular significance on the out- break of war: "We ask our followers to penetrate into the army and fulfill the task of the working-class by disrupting the army." Meanwhile, at the opposite end of the spectrum, the Catholic ultraconservative General Weygand's view of de Gaulle's "pro- fessional army" was: "What a hotbed of Communism, this troop of mechanics!"

So the Reynaud–de Gaulle doctrine received little support. At the beginning of 1937 a new Army "Instruction on the Tactical Employment of Major Units" came into force, framed by General Georges and bearing the signature of Daladier. Baldly it stated its dogma that "technical progress has not appreciably modified, in the tactical sphere, the essential rules laid down by its prede- cessors." As before, it was the infantry which was to be "entrusted with the principal duty in battle. Protected and accompanied by its own guns and by the guns of the artillery, and occasionally preceded by combat tanks and aviation, etc., it conquers the ground, occupies it, organizes, and holds it." With a nostalgic glance back to 1916, it continued that the role task of the infantry was "particularly dangerous and of outstanding glory." The In- struction gave its considered opinion that the development of antitank guns "will result in the employment of tanks only in an attack after the protection and support of a very powerful ar- tillery"—a belief that was to mislead the French High Command fatally in their assessment of the speed of the German attack in 1940.

Thus in the new Instruction France's official doctrine of war remained the mixture as before, and this was essentially the blue- print with which she would face Germany in September 1939. Still the bulk of her tanks stayed scattered among her infantry divisions; some were (reluctantly) received by the cavalry, but, as Guderian pointed out, the combination of horse and motor presented "more disadvantages than advantages." At the same time, Guderian rightly dismissed France's new light mechanised divisions (DLMs) as possessing no more striking power than reconnaissance units (though, to some extent, this deficiency would be repaired at the eleventh hour). In the remaining three years before the deluge, slow and halting attempts were made to find a formula for creating French panzer-type divisions; but when these did arrive they would be too little and much too late. Meanwhile, above it all, the cumbersome system of High Command, with its duplication of channels and dispersal of powers, continued without reform under the aegis of General Gamelin. In September 1938, when war threatened over Germany's confrontation with France's Czech allies, the Deuxième Bureau informed Gamelin that Hitler's new army had definitely gained military superiority over France.* Thus, in less than twenty years, had the European balance sheet been reversed.

The new weapon: Goering's Luftwaffe

In 1938 the horizon was further darkened by France's sudden realisation of a terrible new weapon in Hitler's armoury: the Luftwaffe—the German Air Force which won for Hitler his political victories of the late thirties and undeniably provided the ingredient essential to his lightning victories in the early part of the war.

Before Hitler came to power, the Versailles restrictions hit the building up of a German military air force harder than they did the army; in engine design Germany never made up the years that were lost between 1918 and 1933. Nevertheless, once again, what the Germans lacked in material, they made up in ingenuity and enthusiasm. Full use was made of the "Black Reichswehr" Pact, in force long before Hitler, to train pilots in Russia. Aircraft designers like Ernst Heinkel and Willy Messerschmitt managed to dodge the Versailles bans either by building planes in plants abroad or by undercover construction in Germany.† By 1933 the

---

* At the time, the equally conservative German Army High Command certainly did not agree with this appreciation; but the important thing, from Hitler's point of view, was that Gamelin did.

† An apocryphal story current in Germany told of a worker who thought that he was employed in a pram factory and was asked by his wife to steal pieces from

French were already disquieted at Professor Heinkel's production of a "postal" plane faster than their fastest fighter. Erhard Milch's Lufthansa empire provided an invaluable cadre of highly trained pilots, while all over Germany glider schools were crowded with eager young trainees. When Hitler made clear his intentions of creating an air force, the members of these schools hitched themselves to the Nazi bandwagon with passion.

The man to whom Hitler handed responsibility for creating the new Luftwaffe, Hermann Goering, had been the last commander of the famous Richthofen Squadron at the end of the Great War, and he immediately surrounded himself with other wartime flyers —men like Udet, Loerzer, and Milch. Combined with Hitler's daemonic impatience for results, the get-up-and-go attitude to life of these aces paved the way for the essential early successes of the Luftwaffe; at the same time their fundamental lack of administrative and technical experience would be the cause of its ultimate failure. One thing all agreed upon was that the Luftwaffe was primarily to be an instrument for rapid conquest in a series of short wars. Here a governing consideration was the limiting factor of Germany's industrial capacity, and as early as 1936 the Nazis adopted a policy of concentrating upon mass production of light and medium bombers at the expense of heavy four-engined machines and sophisticated fighters which required large quantities of labour and material. The function of the Luftwaffe was seen to be purely offensive, flying in support of the army in the field, rather than carrying out any long-range strategy of its own. In terms of the war to be fought in France in 1940, this philosophy was to prove ideal, though it would lose the Battle of Britain and from then on would leave Germany increasingly deficient of air cover when she would most need it. Everything was subordinated to speed in creating the new weapon. Already by 1935, when Hitler first announced its birth, the Luftwaffe mounted 1,000 front-line aircraft and 20,000 officers and men. In March that year the first fighter group, called "Richthofen No. 2," was formed. Also that year, the civil Heinkel 111 appeared, followed by its military version a year later; and by 1939, 800 of these bombers had been produced. The forerunner of Messer-

---

the plant to make her a pram. When the stolen pieces were put together under cover of darkness, he discovered he had constructed not a pram but a Messerschmitt fighter.

schmitt's Me–109, later to become Germany's standard fighter
during much of the war, was shown in 1936, and the following
year it shook Britain by winning the London–Isle of Man race.
During the summer of 1936, the Luftwaffe took part in the first
full-scale joint manoeuvre with the Army, and a young man named
Wernher von Braun persuaded Professor Heinkel to carry out
experiments in rocket propulsion.

The secret of the Luftwaffe's rapid expansion lay to a large extent in its ruthless policy of concentrating on a few types–in
marked contrast to the policy of France and Great Britain. Always the emphasis was on quantity, if necessary at the expense
of quality. New aircraft factories were opened to build machines
under license from bigger firms rather than to develop designs of
their own. Junkers was ordered, to the displeasure of both himself and Professor Heinkel, to abandon his Ju–86 and take on
construction of the He–111, which Goering wanted in vast quantities. The hard core of the Luftwaffe was formed of four basic
types: the twin-engined He–111, which (by 1938) had a top
speed of approximately 260 mph with a range of 1,200 miles,
but a bomb load of only about 4,000 pounds–supplemented in
1939 as the standard German level bomber by the Ju–88, with
a top speed of 300 mph; the Me–109 fighter, which in its 1939
version could top 350 mph with a battle endurance of about one
hour; the Ju–52 transport plane and the Ju–87 Stuka* dive
bomber. As far as France 1940 is concerned, these last two were
the secret of the Luftwaffe's success.†

The Stuka was the brain child of Ernst Udet. Udet was a cos-
mopolitan, bohemian *bon viveur,* with considerable charm, who
claimed to have shot down over sixty Allied aircraft when flying
with the Richthofen "Flying Circus," and who after the war had
become a stunt flyer for a film company, often performing hair-
raising acrobatics in a top hat and tails. In 1936 Goering appointed him Director of the Technical Department of the Air
Ministry, then probably the biggest arms concern in the world.
Udet made a point of personally testing all new prototypes, and in

---

* Abbreviated from the German *Sturzkampfflugzeug* = dive-attack plane.

† Two other front-line planes engaged in France which should be mentioned in
passing were the Dornier 17 medium bomber, nicknamed the "Flying Pencil"–
faster than the He–111 but carrying only half its bomb load–and the twin-engined
Messerschmitt 110 "destroyer" fighter, which proved highly unsuccessful.

1938 won the world speed record at over 400 mph in a Heinkel 112. In 1933, while working in America, he had flown a Curtiss Hawk at Buffalo, N.Y., and immediately saw its potential as a dive bomber. Overnight he became a single-minded convert to the technique of dive bombing, and persuaded Goering to buy two Curtiss Hawks for Germany, one of which Udet promptly crashed. At first Udet met with the same kind of doubting conservatism that had confronted Guderian and his panzers, but from the moment of his appointment as the Luftwaffe's Technical Director he threw all his weight behind his conviction. Gradually the idea caught on in Germany. At its plant in Sweden, Junkers was already at work on a dive bomber which emerged in 1935 as the Ju–87. The following autumn, a trial was held between the Ju–87 and Heinkel's rival He–118. The He–118 could not stand up to a power dive; Udet flying it himself crashed once again, but emerged safely as usual. Henceforth the Luftwaffe adopted the Ju–87, or Stuka, as its dive bomber.*

A single-engined plane whose fixed undercarriage gave it the appropriately sinister aspect of a bird of prey swooping with talons outstretched, the Stuka carried a crew of two. Its top speed was only 200 mph (later increased to 240 mph) and its normal radius of action was limited to little more than 100 miles. It carried three machine guns and a bomb load of only 1,000 pounds. But it could place its bombs on a small target with immensely greater precision than could a level bomber. Poorly armoured and slow, its vulnerability was great—both from fighters and ground antiaircraft fire, provided the gunners were not panicked. Its capacity to demoralise was quickly realised by Udet, who added a siren which he dubbed the "trumpet of Jericho"—the howling screech of which, when diving, was to become all too familiar to Allied troops in the early stages of World War II. But the principal significance of the Stuka was that it could provide the essential factor which, up to 1936, had been lacking from Guderian's panzer doctrine, mobile artillery. Here, as Guderian at once realised, was flying firepower which could be brought to bear swiftly and devastatingly on any target miles behind the battle front, and without any of the laborious preliminary concentration of

---

* Udet, unable to face the chaos into which the Luftwaffe had fallen, committed suicide in November 1941.

gun barrels so deleterious to the element of surprise. Considering that the German Condor Legion was to demonstrate in the Spanish Civil War just how effective dive bombing could be, it is once again surprising that no serious notice of the new weapon was taken by leaders of France's Army and Air Force.

Second in effectiveness only to the Stuka was that old workhorse transport, the triple-engined Ju–52. Still in service with some airlines today, the Ju–52 first appeared in 1932, and was produced in such large numbers that already by 1936 it had given Junkers the lead over de Havillands as the firm with the largest number of civil planes in operation throughout the world. As many as fifty were used in Spain, both as bombing and as transport planes, ferrying Franco's troops from Morocco. Experiments were also carried out in Spain at dropping airborne troops from the Ju–52, but the experience with the greatest relevance to France in 1940 lay in the employment of massed Ju–52s as cargo planes bringing bombs, fuel and spare parts from airfield to airfield. Probably nothing learned from the Spanish Civil War proved of greater value to Hitler's war machine. Out of it the Luftwaffe gained the true mobility which it would require to maintain its short-range combat planes always in step with the advancing ground troops—a mobility that no other air force in the world possessed at that time.

In August 1938, on the eve of the first Czech crisis, General Vuillemin, the French Chief of the Air Staff, accompanied by Brigadier General d'Astier de la Vigerie, who in 1939 would be given command of the crucial Northern Zone of Air Operations, paid an official visit to Germany. At Heinkel's Oranienburg works, Professor Heinkel, Udet and Milch did everything to impress the Frenchman—deploying the habitual Nazi technique of bluff combined with reality. After taking him up in an experimental He–100 fighter, Udet told Vuillemin that the model was already entering into service, although in fact only three test prototypes then existed. Vuillemin was then taken around workshops crammed with He–111 bombers under mass production, and was heard to murmur as he left, "I'm shattered!" On his way back to Berlin with François-Poncet, the French ambassador, he confessed despondently, "Should war break out as you expect late in September, there won't be a single French plane left in a fortnight." On his return to Paris, Vuillemin's account of the stupefying power of the Luftwaffe made a profound impression, particularly upon Georges Bonnet, France's current Foreign Minister.*

The French Air Force

André Maurois recalls meeting Churchill towards the end of 1935 who urged him "to write one article a day . . . saying the same thing, to warn France of the decline of her airforce." By that time the French Air Force had decayed for much the same reasons as the Army. The gap between it and the Luftwaffe over the next five years was to grow even greater and become irremediable. As with the tanks she inherited from the Great War, France entered the thirties with a mass of obsolete planes accumulated in the 1920s. Meanwhile, aircraft design was moving ahead at an infinitely greater rate even than that of tanks. In 1934, France was fortunate to have a farsighted and energetic Air Minister, General Denain. Realising the importance of fighters, Denain had ordered a large quantity of Dewoitine fighters, the best of their period; but by 1939 these were already outclassed. After Denain, French aircraft production was stricken with that malaise of the Third Republic, multiplicity of govern-

---

* No doubt aided by the exaggeration of Udet, both French and British experts feared the Luftwaffe for the wrong reasons in 1938. While they remained blind to the potential tactical significance of its dive bombers and fighters, they were hypnotised by the carnage that Goering's He–111s seemed poised to wreak upon the civil population. In Britain in 1938, the Imperial Defence Committee estimated that the Luftwaffe could drop 3,500 tons of bombs on London within the first twenty-four hours of an attack; while the Ministry of Health was anticipating 600,000 killed and 1,200,000 wounded in the first six months. (In fact, during the whole of the London Blitz only 18,000 tons of bombs were dropped, causing a total of 90,000 casualties over a period of seven months.) The RAF—reckoning its fighter force to be below the minimum required for the defence of Britain in 1938—misled the government (as indeed the exponents of strategic air power have been misleading governments ever since) on the capacity of carpet bombing to win wars; which in turn greatly influenced Chamberlain's determination not to face war over Czechoslovakia. No doubt, in the event of war in 1938, London (and probably Paris) would have been bombed, for which they were ill-prepared, but the damage inflicted could not have been greater than, or indeed as great as, Britain suffered during the Blitz. Furthermore, in 1938 Hitler still had neither panzers nor Stukas in sufficient quantity (nor were the crews of these yet adequately trained) to risk a decisive campaign against the French Army. On military grounds alone, the passage of time makes Munich increasingly indefensible; as Churchill remarks: "The year's breathing space said to be 'gained' by Munich left Britain and France in a much worse position compared to Hitler's Germany than they had been at the Munich crisis."

ments, which impeded the formulation of any consistent policy. The aircraft constructors wielded considerable power in the political lobbies. Successive Air Ministers found it hard to refuse their diverse propositions; thus contract for a prototype would be followed by an order for an uneconomically small number of planes. Then, as often as not, the next Air Minister would cancel the order. Typically the selection of each prototype was surrounded with an immense amount of abstract argument, so that it could well be said that the best was the constant enemy of the good so far as French air production was concerned.

As has already been noted, the French aircraft industry in particular suffered from the industrial disturbances which followed the advent of the Front Populaire in 1936. The new Air Minister, Pierre Cot, showed himself at once more concerned with vague dreams of international disarmament, and with solving the industry's problems at home by nationalisation, than with laying down any solid programme of rearmament. No doubt there were strong arguments for nationalising the French aircraft industry, but the fundamental disarray into which Cot threw it was hardly to be made good before the coming of war, and the Air Force itself suffered from his injection of politics into such matters as promotion. Under Cot, the 1936 programme (which only reached the drawing board stage the following year) resulted in two bombers, a Bréguet and a Potez. One hundred and twenty-five Potez 633s were ordered in May 1939, but the order was cancelled a short time later. Meanwhile the French press continued to delude itself and the electorate by boasting: "Our air force is the strongest in Europe!" In March 1938, the French Government attempted to implement a crash programme called "Plan V" by which priority was given to fighter and reconnaissance aircraft, but out of 864 aircraft ordered, only one-sixth consisted of attack and dive-bombing aircraft, and long indecision delayed the production of a three-seater attack bomber well into 1939. In January 1938, a vigorous new Air Minister, Guy la Chambre, took over, but by then the accumulated chaos of the past was too great for anyone to set right within a brief eighteen months. On his appointment, La Chambre reputedly found nothing but a disheartened industry of small workshops of which only one factory was equipped for mass production. As war approached and the pro-

duction gap with the Luftwaffe appeared hopelessly wide,* he
tried to fill it by large-scale purchases from the United States;
but even this measure of desperation met with intense opposition
from the French aircraft manufacturers' lobby.

Deprived of any ruthless overriding agency such as Goering's
Air Ministry, the French Air Force suffered from being treated
as a poor relation by the Army. As Chief of the Defence Staff,
General Gamelin was nominally responsible for the well-being of
the Air Force, but as a thoroughly conservative Army man, new
ideas of airpower did not commend themselves to him. His view
was that the Air Force should look after itself, and General
Vuillemin, Chief of the Air Staff, an elderly bomber pilot not
overendowed with dynamism, obliged by not pestering him. The
role of the Air Force was also clearly laid down in the Army's
"Instruction on the Tactical Employment of Major Units"; preparation for the attack was to remain the work of the artillery; only
troop concentrations, columns on the march or in retreat at the
rear of the battlefield were considered suitable targets for the Air
Force. "It is convenient," said the Instruction, "to leave to the
air force commanders the initiative for launching their attack."
Here was no question of any intimate liaison between the Army
and the Air Force such as Guderian and the Luftwaffe pioneers
were developing in Germany.

One of the most serious faults of French prewar air policy was
its inability to appreciate the importance of dive bombers. As
early as the Riff War in the 1920s French airmen had recognised
the potentialities of this weapon, and others had fully compre-
hended the importance of the German dive bombers in Spain
later; but they were in a minority. In his memoirs General Gamelin claims that the Army was in favour of dive bombers, but that
the Air Force opposed them on technical grounds; yet there is
no evidence to show that Gamelin ever actively pushed the Army's views in this instance. Worried by reports from Spain, after
much contemplation Vuillemin decided in 1938 to develop the
Loire-Nieuport as a bomber. But finally it was thought to be too
slow and only the Navy was equipped with it. Instead, the Air
Force went ahead, belatedly, with experiments in ground-level

---

* By 1939, German production of first-line aircraft was already nudging the
3,000-a-year mark, while France was producing at a rate of perhaps 600 a year.

(*vol rasant*) attack planes. As a result of this indecision, when 1940 came France possessed a total of only fifty dive bombers. The belief was that sufficient and fast enough fighters could be made available to destroy the slow dive bombers and deal with the enemy's fighter cover as well. But in 1940, France's best fighter, the Morane 406, was 50 mph slower than the Me–109, and barely able to catch up with the swifter German level bombers; yet, because of the backwardness of the French production lines, each Morane required 18,000 man-hours of labour, compared to only 5,000 for the Messerschmitt. Consequently, production of the plane was gravely low. Armed with one cannon and two machine guns, the Morane carried ammunition for only the briefest of encounters. In equipment, the French planes were also inferior in a number of ways. During 1938, some French units were unable to use their guns during any exercise that year owing to constructional defects in their aircraft. By 1939, most French bombers were still not equipped with radio communication, so that once they left the ground they were out of touch. Ground equipment for loading them with bombs was slow and cumbersome; hence, much time was wasted in getting them off the ground. And by comparison with the Luftwaffe, the French Air Force possessed no proper air transport facilities.

One further important function in which the French air defences lagged was the ground antiaircraft arm. In Germany this was fully integrated into the Luftwaffe, and the mobility and firepower—particularly of its light flak units which accompanied the panzers in the forefront of battle—were to have an important influence in the Meuse crossing of 1940. In France, antiaircraft defences came under the individual armies, with a separate detachment hived off under the Défense Aérienne du Territoire (DAT). In 1939, when the Luftwaffe possessed seventy-two antiaircraft regiments, France had only five, and was notably short in the small calibre 25 mm and 40 mm guns essential for protecting ground troops from attacking aircraft—especially Stukas.

Enter the fifth column

As the Front Populaire continued its reign, so the political chasm in France widened; Blum, like so many other thoroughly honourable European leaders of that time, remained blind to the real threat of Hitler until too late. For all its declared *raison d'être* of presenting an antifascist front, it was constantly against the French "Fascists" at home rather than those abroad that the Front Populaire concentrated its zeal. When it should feverishly have been stepping up its arms industry, it was preoccupied with social reform, its attitude encouraging and prolonging an indolent and illusory sense of ease among the French workers. On the other hand, the acts of the Front Populaire generated in its opponents passions hard for an Anglo-Saxon to comprehend at that time. On the extreme right, a terrorist group called the Cagoulards made its appearance with a series of bomb outrages. As General Spears remarked of his bourgeois friends in Paris, "these people hated the Front Populaire and all it stood for," and—though he himself could never be accused of left-wing sympathies—he was shocked by their inability "to take into account that the very violence of the socialist reaction was due to the selfish, the merciless attitude" of the *patrons*. On this subject Spears found that there simply "could be no argument." "The revolution is about to break out!" had been the rallying cry of the French conservatives ever since 1934, and the experience of the stay-in strikes had done much to aggravate their terror. In their alarm they persisted in regarding the enemy within as infinitely more menacing than the monster without. "Rather Hitler than Blum!" became their motto, and in it Hitler saw possibilities that he wasted not a minute to exploit. To the attentive Rauschning he predicted that France "in spite of her magnificent Army could, by the provocation of internal unrest and disunity in public opinion, easily be brought to the point where she would only be able to use her Army too late, or not at all."

One comes to that most elusive of factors in the fall of France: the bogey figure of Germany's prewar fifth column.* Hitler, says Rauschning, had made a thorough study of Machiavelli's *Il Principe,* from which he concluded that "a thorough knowledge of the weaknesses and vices of each one of my opponents is the first condition of success in any policy." To act upon the weaknesses and vices of the Third Republic, Hitler sent to Paris a personal envoy endowed in abundance with the talents praised by Machiavelli: Otto Abetz, who, after France's defeat, was to become Nazi

---

* The origin of the expression came from the Spanish Civil War when General Mola boasted that he had four columns outside Madrid and a fifth inside.

ambassador in Paris.* Abetz, a friend of Ribbentrop who had been won over to the Nazis in 1933, had a French wife and professed deep love and admiration for all things French. "I had a liking for the man," admitted Jules Romains, the novelist. "First, he was cheerful. . . . He might have come from French Flanders or Alsace. . . . He represented himself as a real western German who, by all his natural affinities and cultural tradition, felt a bond with the western nations. The Belgians, the northern French, the Swiss, they were his brothers. On the other hand, he felt nothing but aversion and mistrust towards the Prussians." One recognises the type.

Tall and square-shouldered, with reddish-blond hair, a pale face and blue eyes, Abetz swiftly gained acceptance by smart Parisian café society at various echelons. He was a frequent visitor to the chic political salon of Madame de Portes, Paul Reynaud's influential mistress. Skilfully he played upon the snobbishness and anti-Semitism of the ruling classes; upon the hatred of Socialism of the *nouveau riche* bourgeoisie; upon the deep-seated pacifism of the French as a whole. Principal among the Frenchmen in the circle which Abetz collected around him were Fernand de Brinon,† a journalist closely associated with Laval and Georges Bonnet, and a prime mover of the Comité France-Allemagne, which under cover of intellectual rapprochement between the two countries became an instrument of Nazi propaganda; Jean Luchaire, another journalist, who had once been Frau Abetz's boss; and Paul Ferdonnet, director of Agence Prima, who in wartime was to establish himself as France's "Lord Haw-Haw," broadcasting propaganda out of Stuttgart. Through this circle, Abetz organised flattering trips to Germany for sympathetic French intellectuals, who were also promised enticing contracts and immense German editions for their books. The Comité France-Allemagne sponsored superbly stage-managed reciprocal visits of ex-servicemen, culminating in moving pledges that there should never again be war between France and Germany. Abetz encouraged, on occasions financed, and generally exploited for his own use such newspapers as Maurras's *Action Française,* weeklies like *Gringoire, Candide* and *Je Suis Partout* which combined a running attack

---

* In 1949, a French military court sentenced him to twenty years' hard labour.
† He later became the Vichy ambassador to Paris.

on Republican statesmen and institutions with a violent Anglophobia generally guaranteed to appeal to a wide readership in France. Typical of what Abetz inspired, and France's right wing eagerly consumed, was the line that, in case of war, a French victory over Germany would only lead to the ruin of France and the civilised world—since Germany represented the chief rampart against the bolshevisation of Europe.

The direct achievements of Abetz and his circle were not great; neither he nor any other German agency succeeded in creating in prewar France any large-scale network for espionage, sabotage or subversion, and compared with what the world has since come to associate with the Kremlin, all their efforts were child's play. But what was important about Abetz's fifth column was not what it was, but what other Frenchmen thought and feared it to be. Writing in 1941, Élie Bois claimed typically: "The traitors did not show themselves, they worked in the deepest shadow, so that the eye of justice should not surprise them. From afar they pulled the strings of puppets, some of whom did not even suspect it, while others, being aware, feigned ignorance." These "traitors," claimed Bois, were held together "by a truly mystical bond." Hitler's cunning propaganda of bluff and double-bluff, just as it made his army and Luftwaffe seem even more imposing than they really were, helped inflate the sinister spectre of the fifth column. In the last years of peace, Abetz's work further widened the gulf between Frenchmen; in war, it was to foster belief in the presence of a vast, malignant, invisible machine of agents and traitors efficiently paralysing the French war effort at every remove. In fact, France had no need of villains; she was effectively enough "betrayed by what is false within."

Fall of the Front Populaire

On June 21, 1937, after the Radicals had deserted him in the Senate, Léon Blum and his government resigned. The Front Populaire lay in fragments. Blum's refusal to intervene in the Spanish Civil War (despite pressure from his Communist allies), his attempt to come to terms with the *patrons* by temporarily pegging wages, the "Clichy massacre" whereby six workers had fallen to police bullets, and finally the drab failure of the Great Exhibition of 1937, had provided the nails in the Front's coffin. Within the next fourteen months, another three cabinets came and went in

France, in what one French historian describes as "a sombre period marking perhaps the low point of French political life under the Third Republic." Although the Front Populaire had disintegrated, the most pernicious of the effects of the "civil war" associated with it remained rooted in France. Out of the wreckage, the Communist Party had emerged immeasurably strengthened, principally at the cost of the Socialists of the moderate and patriotic Léon Blum. In 1922, while the German Communist Party numbered 218,555 members, the French totalled only 60,000. After sinking to an all-time low of 29,415 in 1931 (its electoral vote representing 6.8 percent of the population), already by January 1936 the French Communist Party's membership had risen to 32,000, gaining a 12.6 percent slice of the nation's votes; and by the end of 1937 its strength had attained the fantastic figure of 340,000, making it the strongest in the western world, an ascendancy it would long retain. Not only had the party gained in numbers; it had also gained vastly in wisdom, tactical skill and striking power. These were factors that were to help the party survive the rude shock of the Nazi–Soviet Nonaggression Pact of August 1939, and to lend weight to its assault on the national war effort during the "Phoney War." Secondly, after the psychological and physical upheaval caused by the Front Populaire, the equilibrium of French industry could not be restored in time to meet the crash rearmament programme forced upon France in the wake of Munich. And though the French Communists stood alone in opposing the Munich settlement and maintained their opposition to Hitler until the new *volte-face* of August 1939, hatred of the party and mistrust of Russia—augmented by doubts as to her value as a potential ally, following the 1936 purges within the Red Army—inclined the French bourgeoisie more and more towards appeasement.

The rush towards war, 1938–39

In March 1938, after two years of deceptive passivity during which his rearmament programme had gone into top gear, Hitler resumed his march of conquest by annexing Austria. At one blow, France with her static population of 42 millions was confronted by a Reich of 76 million virile Germans. The powerful frontier defences of France's principal continental ally, Czechoslovakia, were now turned. Again Britain and France stood motionless.

Hardly had Hitler begun the work of digesting Austria than he was directing his attention against the Czechs. With ever-increasing momentum, events swept Europe again towards the abyss of war. President Beneš appealed to France to stand by her treaty obligations to her ally. The French Government, with Édouard Daladier once more at the helm and that slippery arch-apostle of appeasement, Georges Bonnet, at the Quai d'Orsay, represented a divided and thoroughly pacifist nation. Terrified by General Vuillemin's recent revelations of German air strength, and doubtful that its defensively organised army could strike effectively and without suffering enormous losses at the hands of Germans (protected by their West Wall), it cast about desperately for a way of evading its obligations. Salvation was granted in the shape of Neville Chamberlain, who was obligingly prepared to fly to Germany to offer Hitler any sacrifice of the Czechs that might avert the unspeakable prospect of a renewed war with Germany. Nervously France watched the negotiations at Munich. The Paris bourgeoisie had already fled the capital in thousands, in cars with mattresses heaped high upon the roofs—a concomitant of panic that would be all too familiar eighteen months later. Then Daladier returned from Munich. Expecting to be lynched, he was astonished to find himself besieged by an enthusiastic crowd at Le Bourget airport. Simone de Beauvoir recalls that "that evening a great wave of rejoicing swept over Paris; people sang and laughed together, lovers clung together"; she herself "was delighted, and felt not the faintest pang of conscience at my reaction. I felt I had escaped death, now and forever." The honest Léon Blum represented a wide range of French feeling when he said that he greeted Munich with a mixture of "shame and relief." In the Chamber, only Thorez's Communists, acting on the latest instruction from Moscow, voted solidly against the Munich sellout.

After Munich, France's whole interwar strategy of alliances at Germany's eastern rear lay in ruins. The great Skoda arms complex fell under Hitler's control, and the bloodless surrender of the Czechs' "Maginot Line" meant that the full weight of the Wehrmacht could now be deployed against France—if need be. But Poland was next on Hitler's timetable. In March 1939, he occupied the rump of Czechoslovakia, in flagrant breach of the Munich agreements. Though France remained mutely pacifist, an extraordinary change of heart now swept England; enraged, she at last girded herself for war against Hitler. Chamberlain extended his "guarantee" to menaced Poland, thereby jettisoning Britain's traditional policy of noninvolvement in East European affairs, and at the same time assuming direction of the Franco-British alliance. "Here," said Winston Churchill, "was decision at last, taken at the worst possible moment and on the least satisfactory grounds." France followed Britain's lead, reluctantly.

By summer of 1939, British war production was rapidly catching up with that of Germany, and at last, desperately late, a new sense of urgency began to filter through to France's stagnant industries. She had a long way to go; her share of world production had fallen from 6.6 percent in 1929 to only 4.5 percent in 1937; because of the plunge in her birth rate, the number of her workers had decreased, between 1932 and 1938, by nearly a million and a half, while the number of hours worked per year had fallen from 8 milliard in 1933 to 6 milliard in 1937. In the latter year, when Germany was producing 19 million tons of steel, France's total was 6.6 million. Although the world slump of the early thirties had hit her far less hard than it had Britain, it had also hit France later, so that she was only just shaking off its effects as war approached. In November 1938, a new, energetic and fearless Minister of Finance, Paul Reynaud, assumed office. At once he challenged the French worker's sacred inheritance from the Front Populaire, the 40-hour week. "Do you believe," he asked in a broadcast, "that in today's Europe France can maintain her standard of life, spend 25 milliards on armaments, and at the same time take two days off every week?" He followed up with forty-two decrees, largely repudiating the Front Populaire reforms, and reinstating a 48-hour week. On November 30th, a 24-hour strike, Communist inspired, gripped France in protest against Reynaud's fiats. But the protest was a failure and a remarkable new vitality began to make itself felt throughout the French economy. Unemployment fell rapidly, and in 1939 French productivity rose 17 percent compared with the previous year. Would France, however, be granted enough time to set her house in order?

In June 1939, Britain and France opened negotiations at the Kremlin in a desperate bid to put teeth into the Polish guarantee by gaining a Russian commitment. With misgiving ("I must confess to the most profound distrust of Russia," Chamberlain had declared that March) and almost incredible dilatoriness on the part of the western powers, the talks dragged on through the summer. Marshal Voroshilov, the principal Soviet negotiator, stated that his government had a "complete plan, with figures" for co-operating over Poland; but what about the others? The British and French delegates had to admit they had neither a plan nor plenipotentiary powers even to discuss one. All propositions had to be passed back to their respective governments. How many British divisions might be available for dispatch to France? asked Voroshilov. Five infantry and one motorised came the reply. Blandly Voroshilov declared that the Soviet Union would be ready to put into the field against an aggressor 120 infantry and 16 cavalry divisions; 5,000 heavy and medium cannon, and about 10,000 armoured vehicles. Then, what about Poland, the subject of the Allied guarantee? Obstinately Colonel Beck's Government declined to permit entry of the Red Army into Poland under any pretext. "With the Germans we risk losing our liberty," Marshal Smigly-Rydz told the French ambassador in Warsaw, "but with the Russians we would lose our souls." As events of post-1945 have shown, his fears were not entirely ill-founded.

In Paris that last summer season of 1939 passed with a particular frenzied brilliance. The official receptions all seemed to have a note of unreality, but nothing quite rivalled the July ball held at the Polish Embassy. It appeared as if the women had all been invited for their beauty as much as for their distinction, and the ambassador, Lukasiewicz, excited the admiration of Paris by leading his staff, barefooted, in a polonaise until three in the morning across the lawn of the embassy. The dancers were macabrely illuminated by red Bengal lights and one spectator could visualise Poland herself being consumed in front of his eyes, *"courageuse et légère, en danses, en fumée."* Ten days later came the last Quatorze Juillet, an echo full of the splendid panoply of a past age; Foreign Legionnaires, Senegalese, cuirassiers in shining breastplates—and a detachment of British grenadiers in red tunics and bearskins to reassure Frenchmen as to the reality of the entente. But there was little that offered encouragement for the immediate future. How the facts of life had changed since that *jour de gloire* of just twenty years ago!

Meanwhile, in Moscow the Russians had become exasperated by Polish intransigence and Franco-British temporising, and were

convinced that the Allies' object was to involve the Soviet Union
in a war in which she could expect little or no support from them.
On August 17th, the talks ground to a halt; but already three
days earlier Ribbentrop had started making overtures to Molotov.
On August 23rd came the shattering news that Nazi Germany
and Communist Russia, those apparently irreconcilable foes, had
signed a pact of nonaggression. It was a crushing defeat for
Anglo-French diplomacy, though at this distance it is difficult to
see that Russia had any alternative. If Britain stuck to her guarantee to Poland, war seemed inevitable. The pact sealed the fate of
Poland; and for that matter France too, because now the only
military ally she could count on in the east was the valorous but
antiquated Polish Army. As Paul Reynaud wrote later, "the Allies
had lost the game"—but he might well have added "set and
match" as well. France, on holiday, was utterly stupefied by the
news of the Russian *volte-face,* which caught even the Communists momentarily off balance, though *L'Humanité* hastened to
interpret it as a move for "peace." The full moral effects of the
shock upon France would only later become felt. In Berlin the
German nightmare of a two-front war seemed to have been removed. Surely, whatever now happened to Poland, France and
Britain would not dare intervene?

On August 28th, Berliners were watching troops packed into
moving vans, trucks, all kinds of transport driving towards the
east. Three days later, the world heard that the German Army
had attacked Poland without warning. On September 3rd, a
stricken Chamberlain announced that Britain was fulfilling her
guarantee to the unhappy Poles. In a France desperately disinclined to "die for Danzig" and even more mindful than Britain
of the unreplaced dead of 1914–18, Foreign Minister Bonnet still
tried to skate upon the slippery ice of appeasement, replying to
the outraged protests of Ambassador Lukasiewicz, "You don't
expect us to have a massacre of women and children in Paris."
But the game was up, and France too found herself in the war
she had dreaded for so long; with no allies but Britain and Poland; Belgium neutral and the Maginot Line incomplete between
Longwy and the sea; her army strong on paper but weak in fact;
her air force hopelessly outclassed; and the nation divided.

5

Queer Kind of War

We talked to many of the soldiers. They were sick of
the war before it had started . . . they wanted to go
home and did not care a bean for Danzig and the Corridor. . . . They rather liked La France, but they did
not actually love her; they rather disliked Hitler for all
the unrest he created, but they did not actually hate
him. . . . The only thing they really hated was the idea
of war.

—ARTHUR KOESTLER, *Scum of the Earth*

IN LONDON, Berlin and Paris the coming of war was accompanied
with none of the hysteria, throwing of flowers or cries of *"À Berlin!"* that had characterised August 1914. The memories of the
Great War were still too recent. The correspondent of the *Christian Science Monitor* in Berlin, Joseph Harsch, even went so far
as to claim that "the German people were nearer to real panic
on September 1st, 1939, than the people of any other European
country. No people wanted that war, but the German people ex-
hibited more real fear of it than the others. They faced it in something approaching abject terror." In France, there was no
repetition of the mad crushes outside the recruiting offices. The
slogan of the moment—though somewhat forced and accompanied with a resigned shrug of the shoulders—became "Let's get it
over with." But it carried no real conviction. Meanwhile, for the
third time in seventy years, the Venus de Milo left the Louvre for
a safer place. There were air raid false alarms in Berlin, Paris
and London on the first day of war. When the warning first
sounded in Paris, Parisians rushed panicky to shelter where
women sat stifled and half-fainting in their gas masks. Soon, as

each alarm turned out to be false, they began walking around
with their masks abandoned at home. Initially, all cinemas and
theatres closed; within ten days they were reopening.

France mobilises

Up in the forward zone beyond the Maginot Line, peasants,
women and children were hastily evacuated to the interior of
France, leaving the wretched farm animals to fend for themselves.
In the Line itself—henceforth to be known unflatteringly as *le
trou*—the reservists were arriving leisurely, with bottles of mira-
belle and kirsch in the packs. Defiant slogans from another age—
Ils ne passeront pas! and Pétain's *On les aura!*—began to appear
on the damp walls; meanwhile the tenants of *le trou* settled down
peaceably to their duties like a vast army of concierges. On the
whole, mobilisation proceeded smoothly; on the outbreak of hostilities, 67 French divisions—plus the first contingent of 5 BEF
divisions that were arriving in the north—stood on a war footing,
as opposed to an initial overall total of 107 German divisions.

If anything, French mobilisation was *too* efficient. Several vital
war industries were brought almost to a standstill by the drafting
of skilled technicians. The Bourges Arsenal, for example, was so
deprived that it was reduced temporarily to delivering only 10
percent of its monthly quota of shells. At the Renault works, the
numbers of workers fell abruptly from 30,000 to 8,000, and several plants producing the planes that France was to need more
desperately than anything else were forced to close down. There
were also some strange distortions: one large automobile factory
which might have been building tanks continued to turn out civilian cars by the thousand throughout the winter of 1939; and
when Paul Reynaud after dinner one evening in October decided,
according to André Maurois, "to make a tour of certain armament factories in the region of Paris, he was astounded to find
them closed. They did not work at night." On September 13th,
the French Government appointed Raoul Dautry, a brilliant engineer who had reorganised French Railways in the interwar period, to coordinate French arms production. But the appointment
was late; Dautry confided to Maurois that he would be unable to
provide the armies with all they required "before 1942." One of
Dautry's first actions was to bring back the conscripted technicians.

Here was one more by-product of France's bleeding-white of '14-'18, reflected in the scarcity of manpower of 1939. Although we now know that Hitler's arms industry in 1939-40 was far from being totally geared to the needs of all-out, prolonged warfare as was generally believed at the time, its shortcomings would only make themselves felt midway through the war; by comparison, as Dautry pointed out, it would not be until 1942 that French arms production would get into its stride. It was hardly an encouraging picture.

The Saar "offensive"

Fortunately it was in the east—not against France—that Hitler was meanwhile concentrating the overwhelming power of the Wehrmacht, which with terrifying swiftness was slicing into Poland in two great pincer thrusts. But what were Britain and France doing to help their solitary ally in the east?

In May 1939 Gamelin had given an undertaking to the Polish High Command* that immediately on the outbreak of war the French Army would assume the offensive against Germany and that it would throw in the full weight of "the majority of its forces" at latest by the fifteenth day after mobilisation. In session with British military leaders after the outbreak of hostilities, however, Gamelin declared with caution, "Certainly, we shall do all we can to help the Poles," but he would not countenance "discouraging" the Army by any hastily prepared offensive.† Elsewhere he was recorded as promising, "I shall not begin the war by a Battle of Verdun"—again, a revelation of how deeply the defensive mentality was ingrained in the subconscious of France's Army leaders. To his deputy, General Georges, Gamelin telephoned a message couched in terms that were hardly those of a Foch: "We have a duty to fulfil towards Poland. The method does not exclude action." On September 4th Georges signalled Gamelin: "All reconnaissance groups have reached the frontier from the Moselle to the Rhine." By September 7th French forces had advanced into German territory in the Saar. As the news filtered through the apparatus of censorship and propaganda, the

---

* Subsequently he took refuge behind the fact that this accord had never been officially ratified by the two governments.

† The project of a Saar offensive had already existed for a full year, ever since the Czech crisis of 1938.

Allied press promptly interpreted this to signify the launching of a major effort. The *Daily Mail* spoke of the "French Army Pouring over German Border," while the next day the *Daily Express* headlined: "GERMANY RUSHES MORE TROOPS TO THE WEST." On the 9th, the *Express* announced: "France last night began the first big attack on the Siegfried Line," and on the 12th: "France's secret 70-ton tanks crash through German lines." In fact, no more than nine divisions ever took part in the vaunted Saar operation, and their orders were to move up to the outposts of the Siegfried Line and no further. By the 12th, the French had advanced a maximum of five miles on a sixteen-mile front and occupied some twenty abandoned villages, including Spicheren, scene of one of the first of Louis Napoleon's defeats in 1870.

As one observer remarked, the Saar "offensive" bore a certain resemblance to an eighteenth-century campaign, where "great nations delegated a few companies to measure their arms; the rest of the nation watched and applauded." Casualties were light, principally caused by mines and booby traps, and—with memories of France's million and a half dead from '14–'18 casting its ponderous shadow, it was strict Army policy to avoid losses at all costs. One regimental diary recorded: "X Platoon tried to continue its advance; it was halted by the fire of an automatic weapon." Commenting on this entry a cavalry officer, Marcel Lerecouvreux, remarked acidly: "Imagine if in 1918, the attack of July 18th had been halted by a single machine gun!" Meanwhile, for a few minutes each day the guns in the famous Hochwald bastion of the Maginot Line fired desultory rounds; but only the 75 mm cannon had range enough to reach enemy territory, and after the first shots one of them jammed.

In the air, the Allied effort to relieve Poland was even more pathetic. Fears of Luftwaffe reprisals against Paris caused the French Government to veto any RAF bombing of Germany, as later Daladier was to bar Churchill's project "Royal Marine" to float mines down the Rhine—in case Hitler should retaliate by blowing up a Seine bridge. In Britain, when Leo Amery suggested to the House of Commons that the brutality of the German air onslaught against Poland should be countered by incendiary attacks on the Black Forest, the Secretary of State for Air, Sir Kingsley Wood, was aghast. "Are you aware it is private property?" he exclaimed. "Why, you will be asking me to bomb Essen next!" So the RAF was employed in showering tons of nonlethal leaflets on Germany—"truth raids," Sir Kingsley called them; ignominious "confetti warfare," in the view of another Member of Parliament, General Spears.

Poland abandoned

The halfhearted Allied efforts resulted in not a single German division being diverted from Poland. There, for all its bravery, the Polish Army—cavalry pitted against tanks and Stukas—was succumbing even more rapidly than the most pessimistic Allied staff officer dared imagine. For the first time the world was beginning to understand the meaning of the word *Blitzkrieg;* Guderian, now in command of the XIX Motorised Corps which provided the steel tip to one of the encircling pincers, was proving his theories in practice. On September 14th, the German pincers closed behind Warsaw, and that same day Guderian's panzers—dashing far ahead of the infantry—reached Brest-Litovsk. Visiting his protégé, Hitler expressed astonishment at the spectacle of a smashed Polish artillery regiment on the Vistula. "Our dive bombers did that?" "No," replied Guderian, "our panzers!" On September 17th, in fulfilment of the secret clauses of the Ribbentrop–Molotov Nonaggression Pact, the Red Army entered eastern Poland. On September 28th, Poland capitulated. She had resisted for twenty-eight days; Gamelin had calculated she would be able to hold out until the spring.

On September 12th, Gamelin, alarmed at the way things were going in Poland, sent a secret order to General Prétélat, the commander of the Saar "offensive," ordering him to halt and assume a defensive posture. When Poland capitulated, the French War Cabinet decided to pull back its forces to the Maginot Line; by October 4th the withdrawal had been completed without a hitch, Gamelin heaving a sigh of relief that the Germans had obliged by letting his forces go peacefully. At least France had made a gesture on behalf of the Poles; thus honour, he felt, was satisfied. Militarily, he excused the withdrawal with the comparison: "Wasn't this after all what the Germans did at the start of 1917 in withdrawing on the Hindenburg Line?" Speaking to Anthony Gibbs,* the British war correspondent, a French general dotted

---

* Anthony Gibbs, *Gibbs and a Phoney War.* Peter Dawney.

the *i*'s: "It was simply a token invasion. . . . We do not wish to fight on their territory. We did not ask for this war! . . . Now that the Polish question is liquidated . . . we have gone back to our lines. What else did you expect?" Thus ended France's first and last offensive operation of the war. During it, the morale of the French troops had been promisingly high—"We're starting to invade *them!*" wrote an infantry NCO, René Balbaud—but frustration at the subsequent withdrawal was correspondingly great. Out of the experiences gained, the Army settled down to the dubious consolation that German antitank shells had been observed to bounce off French tanks. Henceforth it would be Allied war policy to wait until their war potential matched Germany's before launching any offensive from French territory, or for a miracle; though it was hard to gauge which, in September 1939, seemed the less remote.

In Germany, the Wehrmacht leaders observed France's supineness in the west with mixed amazement and relief. Aware of their own Army's unreadiness for full-scale war, they had viewed Hitler's lunge into Poland as one more lunatic gamble; when Britain and France declared war, they were terrified that, this time, Hitler's bluff had been called and that immediately they would face a powerful break-through offensive in the west. According to General Westphal, during the whole Polish campaign the frontier from Aachen to Basle was held by no more than twenty-five reserve, militia and depot divisions, with not a single tank under their command and with enough ammunition for only three days' battle. At the Nuremberg Trials, Milch declared that the Luftwaffe stock of bombs had been so small that the Polish campaign had consumed half of it; and Jodl, the Wehrmacht Chief of Operations, claimed that, because of ammunition shortages, in Poland "we only managed solely because there was no battle in the west." The Siegfried Line, despite Hitler's boasting, was nothing like as formidable as the Maginot, and was far from complete; according to his Chief of Staff, when Rundstedt inspected it for the first time, he laughed. If the French had seriously attacked it in September 1939, their troops would at least have gained the training which was to prove so badly lacking seven months later, while many responsible German generals believed (and indeed still do) that the French could have reached the Rhine within a fortnight, and possibly have won the war. From Berlin, Joseph Harsch reckoned that German morale "was probably no better able to withstand the shock of invasion in September 1939" than French morale the following summer. Probably he exaggerated, possibly he was right; but both Harsch and the German generals ignored the fact that Gamelin's Army no longer possessed the offensive capacity of Foch's of twenty years previously, let alone the *will* of Joffre's Army of the Marne. Hitler, the amateur, alone knew, and in being right he had won his first crucial wartime round against the professional soldiers.

Queer kind of war

On the first day of war, people in France were saying "Let's get it over with!" On the twentieth day, they confined themselves to the comment, *"Drôle de guerre."* And so, for the next seven months, interpellated by periodic false alarms that Hitler was about to invade Belgium and Holland, the *drôle de guerre*—or what United States Senator William E. Borah dubbed the "Phoney War"—dragged dismally on. At sea, Britain hung her head in shame when, on October 14th, HMS *Royal Oak* was torpedoed inside Scapa Flow; two months later the score was evened with the cornering of the *Graf Spee* off the river Plate. But on the western front, action was limited to desultory patrol actions, carried out by volunteers, so-called *détachements francs,* a system hardly designed to improve the fighting qualities of the non-elite mass of the French Army. The Duke of Windsor visited Fort Hochwald, which honoured him by firing four shells into no-man's-land; later there was champagne in the officers' mess. Dorothy Thompson also came and was allowed to fire a 75; while Clare Boothe "adopted" a fort to which she sent cigarettes in exchange for a "brave flag" embroidered in gold with those evocative words, *Ils ne passeront pas!* Visitors to the front were constantly astounded by the state of truce existing there. After a trip to the German lines in October, William Shirer wrote:

Where the train ran along the Rhine, we could see the French bunkers and at many places great mats behind which the French were building fortifications. Identical picture on the German side. The troops seemed to be observing an armistice . . . one blast from a French '75 could have liquidated our train. The Germans were hauling up guns and supplies on the railroad line, but the French did not disturb them. Queer kind of war.

Some five months later, President Roosevelt's peace emissary, Sumner Welles, noted the same picture. "There was not a sound as we passed. Not even an aeroplane was seen in the sky." From the French side, the inactivity infuriated British war correspondents like Gordon Waterfield:

Across the river a young German was standing in the sun, naked to the waist, washing himself. It annoyed me that it should be possible for him to go on washing calmly there with two machine-guns on the opposite bank. I asked the French sentry why he did not fire. He seemed surprised at my bloodthirstiness. *"Ils ne sont pas méchants,"* he said; "and if we fire they will fire back."

That the enemy were *pas méchants* became the keynote of the Phoney War, and it was a notion assiduously fostered by the Germans. When Strasbourg was being evacuated on the outbreak of war, they obligingly aided by turning on searchlights from their side of the river; for several months, power plants in the German Saar continued to supply French frontier villages with electricity. On the river Lauter, where the opposing troops used to do their washing in plain view of each other, there was a typical incident when a French soldier strayed over to the German side and was captured. This was immediately followed up by a note under flag of truce from his company commander, asking for his return; first, explained the French captain, the man's capture was "against the custom"; and secondly, his sector was so wide that he simply could not do without him! It was hardly surprising that, by November 7th, a French lieutenant, Claude Jamet, should be writing in his diary: *"Et la guerre?* Frankly, one isn't interested in it. One does not think of it. Does it really exist?" When the bell of his fort sounded the warning of German aircraft, "instead of taking shelter, on the contrary one rushes out, nose in the air, dazzled by the sunshine and excited, making gestures like football supporters or race-track touts."

After the initial fear had passed of the Luftwaffe air raids which never materialised, life behind the lines in France resumed something very close to its normal course. In Paris the black-out remained sombrely effective; but once outside, "the glare and dazzle of head-lights was like returning from the Aldershot Tattoo," remarked Anthony Gibbs. "Every shop in St. Germain and in the outskirts of Paris blazed to high heaven." In Brittany and the remoter provinces, Simone de Beauvoir reported, "Chic refugees cruise around in cars and complain about the lack of entertainment; what a mad twittering world they inhabit!" Driven by their age-old dread of exile, the smart Parisians soon began to return to the capital. People were earning good money there, and spending it freely. Symbolically, the hit of the season was Maurice Chevalier's *Paris Reste Paris*. But the psychological atmosphere was far from happy. In October, Simone de Beauvoir questioned in her diary: "What does the word 'war' really mean? A month ago, when all the papers printed it boldly across their headlines, it meant a shapeless horror, something undefined but very real. Now it lacks all substance and identity."

Some outside observers felt that the canker of Munich had gnawed deeply and ineradicably into the French soul. Janet Teissier du Cros, a Scotswoman married to a Frenchman serving in the Army, reflected:

I often wonder what the outcome would have been if we had fought instead of giving in over the Czechoslovakian crisis. I think the temper of France would have been very different. After the first moment of relief, Munich left people in France with a cynical taste in their mouths. . . . There was no honour left in public life; all one could now do was to cling to what was left of private life. The door was open for the "realists" who were to do so much harm.

Arthur Koestler agreed; "the cynicism of the Munich era," he declared, "destroyed any creed worth fighting for." And the German Intelligence was well aware of this spirit.

To stave off boredom and lack of interest in the war, and to show *bon volonté,* Parisian women busied themselves in good works of varying value to the war effort. In the Ritz, chic ladies in "simple black dresses" shook tins for refugee relief and soldiers' canteens—then (if it happened to be a "spiritless day," of which there were three a week) took themselves off to a champagne lunch. The Red Cross and volunteer nursing organisations were womanned to excess; according to the cynical Fabre-Luce, much as in 1870, "twenty-thousand nurses and more were demanding the wounded. Some of them gave the impression of believing that the military authority was failing in its duties by not providing them." *Le Jour* tried once again to institute *les marraines de guerre,** the good women who in '14–'18 had each adopted a poilu, whose every need they endeavoured to fulfil. As it was, most already had their soldier "somewhere in France"—that delightful euphemism of the censor much guyed in the music halls—to whom they sent all manner of games, detective novels, drink and handkerchiefs.

Life at the front

Despite all this attention, conditions at the front were by no means brilliant for the simple soldiers. Initially, there was an acute shortage of boots and blankets among some units; in the Second Army on the Sedan front, owing to the lack of proper billets, men slept in the stables with their horses. Where they were lodged out in villages, it was often found that the contagious influences of civilian life from which so many reservists had been lately uprooted had a debilitating effect on discipline. In sharp contrast to the more democratic Wehrmacht, French officers seemed to look after themselves much better than they did their men, with whom they had deplorably little contact. Although the wearing of helmet, gas mask and belt was obligatory at the front, officers were often seen strolling around in service caps, jackets unbuttoned, hands in pockets and cigarettes dangling from their lips. An American canteen worker who had been a nurse with the French Army in 1917 was shocked by the well-groomed officers, with their "well polished nails and brilliantined hair, compared with the soldiers in their grubby barracks and the dreary canteens in which they could spend their fifty centimes a day."† Somehow the poilu's pay had improved little over the scandalous wages for which he fought and died in '14–'18, and family emoluments were equally poor; a wife with two children, for instance, though living rent free, received only 16 francs a day in the provinces and 21 francs in Paris. Soldiers would often use their ten days' leave to drive a taxicab in Paris, or run errands to make a little more

---

* Literally, "wartime godmothers."

† At comparative rates of pay, a British private received 17 francs a day—a source of friction made much use of by Goebbels.

money for their dependents. The officers, however, seemed some-how to manage to carry on their civilian business; wangle official "missions" to their hometowns; run their own cars in the pro-hibited Zone of Armies and even keep wives and mistresses in lodgings there. At least, so the stories went; and they were as implicitly believed as that hoary chestnut common to bored sol-diers in all armies of the world—namely, that men on leave from the front had it spoilt because their potency had been diminished by the bromides with which their officers laced the issue of wine. And, as the Phoney War dragged on, leave was the one thing the French soldier really cared about.

To add to the harsh conspiracy of Fate against France, the winter of 1939 turned out to be the coldest in nearly half a cen-tury. The English Channel froze at Dungeness and Folkestone. Germany suffered too; clothes rationing came into force. The bitter cold and an incipient coal shortage made Christmas in Berlin indeed bleak that year. But for France the arctic condi-tions were particularly undesirable; apart from their effect on military morale, they severely curtailed training and work on those neglected defences stretching from Longwy to the sea.

A French soldier described the lonely monotony of guard duty at an advance post of the Maginot Line during the bitter winter: "Before you, an unknown countryside, a black night. The nearest post is several hundred yards away. Your feet are frozen in their stiff boots. Your helmet weighs heavily. Your eyes are tired from looking without seeing." Night after night, the same meaningless vigil. Days turned into weeks, weeks into months. *Le Rire* printed a cartoon showing two poilus, one white-bearded and bedecked with many First War medals telling the younger: "It all began in the time of my grandfather, but no one any longer knows why." As the winter dragged on, the whole Army became chroni-cally tainted with that most pernicious of Gallic diseases, bore-dom. Commented Fabre-Luce with his customary acridity, "We're no longer fighting the Germans, we're fighting *l'Ennui*." By com-parison with the French sectors of the front, visitors to the BEF tended to remark on the constant bustle of activity even during the period of worst weather. Much of this activity may have been senseless, of the order of digging holes, then refilling them, but at least it preserved the BEF from the boredom gnawing at the

French. General Spears, so closely acquainted with the French
Army at the time of the 1917 mutinies in which neglect of the
troops' welfare had played no inconsiderable part, noted—in contrast to the BEF—the same neglect once again. He found the
scenes at the French front "horribly depressing." And the "un-
fathomable, limitless boredom" he saw there was hardly con-
ducive to maintaining good morale.

Disquieting symptoms of the state of morale in the French
Army began to reveal themselves in various ways. In many units
discipline left much to be desired; men did not salute their officers,
and the officers often failed to exact such "external marks of
respect." This seemed to be particularly the fault of the reservist
officers; "the events of 1936 had perhaps caused them to lose in
civil life the habit of being obeyed," suggested Marcel Lerecouvreux of the 2nd Cavalry Division, and—whether right or wrong
—his was a view widely shared among the French officer corps.
With horror Lerecouvreux recalled how he had observed the
sentry of a neighbouring unit, charged with guarding the demolition charges placed under a Meuse bridge, quietly abandon his
post and his rifle to assist a *copain* fishing some fifty yards
away. Another aspect of indiscipline manifested itself in the
widespread pillaging of the evacuated areas; according to Lieutenant Jamet serving with the Third Army, "the Gendarmerie
reports are overwhelming. Here, there are acts of vandalism;
wherever the Zouaves have passed, for example, not a piece of
furniture remains upright; everything that could not be drunk or
stolen has been smashed." Already by the end of September six
soldiers were reported to have been shot for pillaging villages near
the Maginot Line.

As in the Siege of Paris in 1870, alcoholism became a concomitant of boredom. General Ruby of Huntziger's Second Army
wrote: "The sight of our men in railway stations was not always
comforting . . . in the larger stations special rooms had to be
prepared, euphemistically known as 'disethylation rooms.'"
Another disturbing phenomenon was the increasing number of
young and healthy officers prepared to go to any length to get a
staff job, away from the dreariness of life in the front-line canton-
ments; whereas, in '14–'18, anyone appointed to the staff, unless
badly wounded, was in danger of being condemned as an *em-*

busqué.* With no General Staff escape hatch open to them, the simple soldiers registered their discontent in the steady growth of "French leave."† "Without permission, secretly at first, and soon almost openly, they went away Saturday at midday, sometimes in the morning, to reappear Sunday evening, Monday morning, or even Monday at mid-day," writes General Menu. Threats of discipline seemed to have little effect. Even President Lebrun, an *ancien combattant* of Verdun, shook his head sadly after his visits to the front: "I seemed to encounter slackened resolve, relaxed discipline. There one no longer breathed the pure and enlivening air of the trenches of 1914–18."

Meanwhile, Lieutenant General Alan Brooke, then commanding the BEF's II Corps and later to become Churchill's Chief of the Imperial General Staff from 1941 onwards, in whom the listlessness of the troops he had seen on the Belgian frontier had early aroused "most unpleasant apprehensions as to the fighting qualities of the French in this new war," put his finger on a different—though perhaps equally undesirable—psychological factor within the Maginot Line, complacency. The Line reminded the critical Brooke of "a battleship built on land, a masterpiece in its way. . . . And yet! It gives me but little feeling of security." Living in far greater comfort than the troops billeted outside in the mud and ice, the guardians of *le trou* maintained a higher morale; but, as Brooke noted prophetically in his diary of February 6, 1940, "the most dangerous aspect is the psychological one; a sense of false security is engendered, a feeling of sitting behind an impregnable iron fence; and should the fence perchance be broken, the French fighting spirit might well be brought crumbling with it."

Apart from boredom and the impact of winter, there were certain other readily identifiable viruses sapping military morale. There was the singularly discouraging effect of the repeated false alarms. On January 12th, for example, Major Barlone, serving in the French First Army, recorded in his diary: "All leave suspended . . . the entry of the Germans into Belgium is considered imminent. . . . All the men, roused from their sleep on an intensely cold night, are full of enthusiasm for the idea of going to

---

* A shirker.

† Or what in France is known of course as *filer à l'anglais!*

fight the Germans at long last"; but six days later: "The 'stand-by' is now at an end . . . our men are very disappointed." There was the sense of resentment that for the "civvies" behind the lines life should continue apparently unaffected by the war, while at the front the troops were suffering all the discomforts, the dislocation of their professional and private lives, that war brings, and enjoying none of its excitements or glory. And then there was bitterness at the way Britain seemed to have pushed France into the war; then while France had fully mobilised her forces Britain continued to submit herself to only partial conscription, and had sent no more than a handful of BEF divisions to hold the line, this French grievance was certainly not without justification.

Finally, what was the *point* of the war? Since the fall of Poland, no kind of declaration of war aims had been put out by either the British or the French Government. Why not? The question of why they were fighting was constantly raised by the troops, but it was never answered. In 1914, they were fighting because they were attacked and to retake Alsace and Lorraine. Yet, although the French High Command must have been well aware how much lower morale was than in 1914, and of its causes, it did absolutely nothing about it even to the extent of trying to improve the deplorable mail service, through whose inefficiency at the beginning of the war some troops had remained six weeks without news of their families. Perhaps the reason for inertia is revealed in Gamelin's subsequent mild apologia: "I realise that as I spent my time exclusively with staff officers, I was not in sufficiently close touch with the spirit of the country and the troops."

The propaganda war

In its state of boredom and malaise, the French Army was eminently susceptible to the propaganda directed at it by Goebbels and his experts. Throughout the Phoney War, each side made up for the lack of shells it fired at the other by a constant barrage of words. Across the Rhine, huge rival hoardings and loud-speakers confronted one another; French troops did not fire on the enemy's artifices by order; the Germans reciprocated, possibly because they found French propaganda so utterly risible. Its general tenor was to be found in the posters plastered all over France which contained a map of the world displaying the vast areas covered by the French and British Empires, overprinted with the slogan

"We shall win because we are the stronger." This was backed up by attributing, each month, some new project of conquest to the Germans; when nothing happened, an Allied victory was then claimed. Another popular line widely disseminated, both for internal and external consumption, was Daladier's boast at the beginning of 1940: "In 1914, we suffered 100,000 killed during the first four months. This time we have only lost 2,000"—while steady favourites were the themes that Germany was on the brink either of revolution or of starvation induced by the Royal Navy's blockade. Hardly less fantastical was the story recorded by Clare Boothe, much publicised by the French press, of a miraculous spring in Lorraine which evidently ". . . started flowing exactly three months before the end of the Franco-Prussian War of 1870. It flowed again in August 1918. On February 19th, 1940, the miraculous spring began to flow once more. 'Will Germany collapse by the end of May?' asked the papers." If most of the French propaganda seemed insulting to so intelligent a people, to Allied sympathisers among the neutrals in Germany its sheer grotesqueness was one of the most depressing features of life.

We heard over *Paris Mondiale* [wrote Joseph Harsch from Berlin] that Berlin was on the verge of starvation, and then went out and ate meals at any one of a dozen Berlin restaurants which were all a man could eat. . . . We read in copies of English newspapers which came through the American Embassy that the German army was under-trained . . . that it still employed the technique of the mass charge of herds of men with officers driving them forward from behind.

On the other hand, German propaganda was adroit, direct and immensely effective. It was based on three hypotheses: the Frenchman's lack of interest in the war, his hereditary dislike and distrust of "perfidious Albion," and the damage done to an already divided France by the Nazi-Soviet Nonaggression Pact. Again and again it pounded out the simple, torpor-inducing theme which increasingly reflected the wishes of a large portion of the French Army: "You remain in your Maginot Line. We will stay in the West Wall." Undoubtedly the most accomplished performer in the propaganda war was Otto Abetz's old ally, Ferdonnet, who had run off to Germany and whose "Lord Haw-Haw" style broadcasts earned him the sobriquet "the traitor of Stuttgart." He shocked French troops by his extraordinary knowledge of their movements. René Balbaud, an NCO in Lorraine, noted that Ferdonnet announced in December that Balbaud's division was going back to rest, and gave the identity of the division due to replace it. On another occasion, he warned a certain corps commander that the wives and mistresses of officers under his command were joining them for the weekend in nearby towns. The general's enquiries proved Ferdonnet right. Ferdonnet's slogans, such as *Les Anglais donnent leurs machines, les Français donnent leurs poitrines,* stuck easily in the mind. Over the radio and their frontier loud-speakers, the Germans played cunningly on the French love of music; Gaston Palewski, then an Air Force officer and later a leading Gaullist, admitted to the author that the programmes piped from Germany used to be far and away the best the French forces could receive. Then would come the slogans: "Don't transform France into a vast field of battle . . . Don't listen to perfidious England . . . Your feet are cold in this mud . . . *La France aux Français!*" Then some more of Tino Rossi singing "Marinella." Meanwhile, crudely pungent cartoons would flutter down from aircraft; in November, Lieutenant Claude Jamet picked up one entitled "The Bloodbath." The first picture showed a little Frenchman and a large, pipe-smoking Tommy standing on the edge of a blood-filled pond; in the second, the two were preparing to jump in, but the third revealed that the Frenchman alone had dived, leaving the Tommy standing on the bank; in the fourth, the Frenchman was up to his neck in blood while his ally walked away laughing. Another cartoon, which struck a lively chord, depicted British officers in Paris fondling half-naked women while a poilu kept watch in the Maginot Line. Occasionally this kind of meretricious appeal backfired; General Spears relates how the Germans once put up an enormous hoarding, informing "Soldiers of the Northern Provinces" that the licentious British soldiery was "sleeping with your wives, raping your daughters"; but the French regiment opposite promptly riposted: "We don't give a bugger, we're from the South!"

There was, however, no mistaking the impact made by this artful propaganda onslaught. Already by mid-November, Jamet noted in his diary that the common catchword had become "Have you seen the English?" adding that "Anglophobia seems to be almost universal in the French Army." Meanwhile, behind the lines, while the government had been prompt to ban Communist newspapers on the outbreak of war, such crypto-fascist organs as *Je Suis Partout* and the *Petit Parisien* continued to flourish with their blatantly anti-British, anti-Semitic lines. Neville Chamberlain was depicted as being in the hands of the war-lusting British Jewry, and cartoons of British soldiers philandering with French wives and sweethearts as their men drilled for ten sous a day appeared under captions identical with those showered down in German leaflets.

In all the German armoury of psychological warfare against France there was, however, no weapon of greater potency than that which—at the end of August 1939—Hitler had been presented by the Nonaggression Pact with Stalin.

To many intelligent non-Marxist Frenchmen, mindful of how vital Russia's assistance had been in 1914, hopes of victory had vanished with her defection to the Nazi camp; the leadership of the Communist Party, however, had been just as paralysed by the brutal shock of the Kremlin's *volte-face*. For a month, during which Stalin was cynically grabbing his share of the Polish booty, the Party awaited its new orders. Meanwhile, it was forced to perform, in the eyes of Arthur Koestler, like "one of those conjurers on the stage who can produce an egg from every pocket." The first consequence was the physical dissolution of the last bonds of the Front Populaire—though not its effects. On September 25th, the CGT broke once again with the Communists. Léon Blum, who, however misguided in the past, was a patriot through and through, stood squarely behind the war effort and renounced his former allies. "They are defeatists," he declared, adding sadly: "We can't deal with these people at all. I know them well—there is nobody who has been more thoroughly fooled by them than I have." From the ranks of the Communist Party itself, during the first three months of the war twenty-one deputies and one senator quit in disgust, as well as a large number of mayors, councillors and trade unionists. Into party headquarters flowed telegrams such as the following: "Since Polish invasion, consequence of Hitler-Stalin Pact, await your condemnation in vain." The party suffered a severe setback. But the great accretion of power and tactical experience gained during the Front Populaire enabled it to survive—greatly aided by the maladroitness of Daladier's Government.

On September 27th, the French Government decreed the dissolution of the Communist Party. Between October 5th and 10th, thirty-five of its deputies were locked up; Thorez (having deserted from the army to avoid arrest) was deprived of his citizenship; *L'Humanité* was closed down, and youths were sentenced to two years' imprisonment for circulating Communist pamphlets. Ilya Ehrenburg, the *Pravda* correspondent, complained that "in reality the bourgeois was taking its revenge on the workers for the fear they had inspired in 1936," and indeed the fact that throughout the Phoney War no comparable attempt was ever made to round up the right wing's pro-Nazi sympathisers, or to close down such malevolent rags as *Le Petit Parisien,* did lend force to his assertion. Measures against the Communists bore a strong resemblance to the fear-inspired "spy mania" which had swept Paris in 1870 and again in 1914. Together with the known Communists, the police in their zeal arrested thousands of non-Communist "suspicious" foreigners, many of whom—dedicated anti-Nazis—were refugees from Hitler's concentration camps. Arthur Koestler, among those rounded up, describes the French concentration camps into which these unfortunate "scum of the earth" were flung as being "even below the level" of those from which they had escaped in Germany; about the only difference was that "in Vernet people were killed for lack of medical attention; in Dachau they were killed on purpose." It took the inmates of Vernet a long time to understand "this general and puzzling outburst of hatred against those who had been the first to fight the common enemy," says Koestler, "and when we understood it, it laid bare one of the main psychological factors which finally led to the suicide of France."

Of the French Communists he met during his internment, Koestler remarks that they represented several millions of "the toughest, most active and most violently anti-Nazi part of the French working class . . . the best fitted to give an example of comradeship and reckless sacrifice in the struggle." In their state of utter bewilderment and disillusion at Stalin's *volte-face,* they could have been wooed to join in the common crusade against Nazism. "It was murderous stupidity on the part of the French Government," argues Koestler, "to start a police pogrom against the Communist rank and file, instead of seizing this unique opportunity to win them over." Oppression of the Communists

and martyrdom of its leaders did in fact only help close the ranks
of the party; nothing could have rendered it greater service than
the banning of *L'Humanité* and *Ce Soir,* as Léon Blum for one
realised. Already by the end of October 1939, *L'Humanité* was
beginning to appear illicitly, while with great effectiveness Thorez
continued to direct the party, clandestinely, from a refuge in
Belgium.

On October 1, 1939, Édouard Herriot, the Radical Socialist
president of the Assembly, received a letter from the banned
Communist deputies, urging that Hitler's "peace proposals" be
seriously examined by the government. This marked the formulation of Moscow's new policy for the French Communist Party:
all-out resistance to the continuation of the war. Later a tract by
Georgi Dimitrov, the powerful secretary of the Comintern, calling
for an end to this "war of plunder" was passed by hand from
factory to factory, as well as being widely distributed in the French
Army. On Armistice Day, 1939, Communist peace pamphlets
appeared demanding, "Who in France would want to fight to
reconstitute a Poland of reactionary and fascist colonels?"
Others found in factories at this time proclaimed in one breath,
"Vive Stalin! Vive Hitler!" Constant play was made of the theme
that, for the French proletariat, there remained but one enemy,
the bourgeoisie. "Away with this government of misery and ser-
vility to the bankers of the City of London!" cried another
pamphlet. For Communist propaganda—as for Goebbels'—Britain
provided target No. 1. Always trying to create hostility between
French and British troops, it harped upon the differences in pay
between the two armies. As late as May Day, 1940, when the
German *Blitzkrieg* was posed for its lunge into the Low Countries,
the Communists launched a last offensive against the "imperialist
war," in which—among other things—they charged France with
having descended to the rank of a "British Dominion."

Although there was not much to choose in the content of Communist and Nazi propaganda, the former was considerably more
effective. As well as its striking a more responsive chord within
the nation as a whole, its means of dissemination were vastly superior. Pamphlets seemed to be in circulation everywhere, chain
letters made the rounds at the front, soldiers coming on leave
were approached outside the Gare de l'Est, and there was even a
special underground edition of *L'Humanité* (called *Les Soldats*

Contre la Guerre) expressly designed for Army consumption. Quick to realise the immense value of this ready-made propaganda machine, the Germans did all they could both to aid and cash in on its efforts; Luftwaffe planes were employed to drop pamphlets reporting Molotov's speech of October 31, 1939, in which he had identified himself with Hitler's peace proposals. In the progressive boredom of the Phoney War, the Communist propaganda slowly began to poison and win back even adherents of the former parties of the Front Populaire which had broken with the Communists. More and more the Army was divided as the ranks inclined towards the Communist line while, for the officer corps, the principal enemy remained "the enemy within"— Communism. It was all very well for Somerset Maugham to write a tract from the azure and gold of Cap Ferrat claiming (for British consumption) German "ignorance of the French temper" when they thought that "they were fighting a house divided against itself," but there was no mistaking just how effectively joint Nazi-Communist propaganda was widening the rifts left by the Front Populaire era.

Equally depressing upon French war morale were the more tangible results of that close concomitant of Communist subversion, sabotage. During the Phoney War, numerous slowdowns of mysterious origin struck at France's war production. Most of the worst cases of sabotage appear to have taken place at the Renault (tanks) and Farman (aircraft) works, those old hotbeds of trouble in Paris. A report on the damage wreaked upon Renault's production of the "B. 1," France's gravely needed new heavy tank, itemised: "nuts, bolts, various bits of old iron put in the gear-boxes and transmissions; . . . filings and emery-dust in the crank-cases; saw-strokes producing incipient rupture of the oil and petrol ducts, intended to make them fall to bits after several hours running." In April 1940, a number of fatal flying accidents led investigators to the Farman factory. Here it was found that on engines ready for delivery a brass wire acting as a lock on the nut which held the petrol feed nozzle in position had been severed. After a number of hours' flying, the nut, stripped of its lock, unscrewed itself with the engine vibration and allowed the petrol to drip onto the white-hot exhaust pipe, which eventually led to a lethal explosion. It was claimed that, under the very eyes of Sûreté investigators a young Communist, Roger

Rambaud, was caught in the act after having snipped the locking wires on seventeen out of twenty engines on the test bed. Elsewhere, at a factory producing the 25 mm antiaircraft gun—which the army was to need at least as badly as the "B. 1" tank—one act of sabotage wrote off some two hundred barrels, the normal equipment of four divisions. In the chaos that followed the Fall of France, purported acts of sabotage went either unverified or unpunished. Undoubtedly many allegations were exaggerated; but—as with the shadowy German fifth column—the constant *fear* of Communist-sponsored espionage and sabotage was to prove almost as effective as the weapon itself.

How many Russian lives, one might well ask in retrospect, were to be forfeited from June 1941 onwards as a direct consequence of the success of the Kremlin's whole dingy policy towards France in 1939–40?

6

Gamelin

What kind of a nation will they make of us tomorrow,
these exhausted creatures emptied of blood, emptied of
thought, crushed by superhuman fatigue?
—Marc Boasson,* *At the Evening of a World*

One of Napoleon's marshals once brought him a plan of
campaign in which the French Army was neatly and
evenly lined up from one end of the frontier to the
other. "Are you trying to stop smuggling?" Napoleon
asked heartlessly.
—Theodore Draper, *The Six Weeks War*

As the spring of 1940 approached, French eyes—military and
civilian—turned instinctively towards the Château de Vincennes,
as the nation wondered what new Allied strategy was being
evolved behind its grim walls. Here Henry V of England had
died, and as one of France's favourite execution grounds it was
against these walls that the Duc d'Enghien, Mata Hari and the
last of the Communards had died. One of the most forbidding
castles in all France, to Spears it "seemed to drip with blood."
Despite its sombre historical associations, Vincennes on the eastern outskirts of Paris was now the home for the Grand Quartier
Général (GQG) of General Maurice Gamelin, Chief of the General Staff of National Defence and—since the outbreak of war—
Supreme Commander of all French land forces. Descended on
his mother's side from an old military family of Alsace-Lorraine,
Gamelin had passed first out of St. Cyr in 1891, and entered
the Algerian Tirailleurs. In 1914 he had been on Joffre's opera-

---

* Killed in Flanders, 1918. The passage related to the fighting at Verdun in the
summer of 1916.

Allied Victory Parade in Paris, July 14, 1919, Marshals Foch and Joffre
at the head.

Antitank obstacles
on the Maginot Line

Sun-ray treatment for the soldiers of the Maginot Line

Contemporary sketch of a cross-section of the Maginot Line, the underground fortress stretching from Belgium to the Swiss border, the most elaborate defense system the world had ever known.

A gun in a Maginot Line emplacement "speaks"

French 13-ton Renault tanks

German troops enter Düsseldorf with fanfare, March 1936

Hitler's elite: new officers of the army, navy and air force assembled to meet their Führer

Seeckt

Guderian

Ilya Ehrenburg *(second from left)* at a peace meeting in Paris, 1935

André Malraux

Romain Rolland

André Gide *(right)*
with American
Communist writer
Mike Gold, Paris, 1936

Parisian right-wing mob demonstrates against government handling
of Stavisky affair, January 29, 1934

"Sit-in strike," Paris, June 6, 1936

tions staff and had drawn up the orders on which rested the victory of the Marne; in 1916 (then aged forty-four) he became both one of the youngest and most competent French divisional commanders; by 1918 he had generally come to be regarded as the outstanding officer of his "promotion." A small sandy-haired man usually clad in tight tunic and high-laced boots, he had already reached the age limit of sixty-eight at the beginning of 1940. To André Maurois, "his short, stiff moustache, his small eyes and thin-lipped mouth gave him an indecipherable aspect, which no spontaneous gesture served to clarify. He had neither the sparkling vivacity of Foch nor the massive geniality of Joffre." Nor was Gamelin, he might have added, adorned with the coldly imposing presence of Pétain. Britain's six-foot-four CIGS, General Ironside, rather patronisingly regarded his opposite number as a nice little man in well-cut breeches; in less polite terms, Air Chief Marshal Sir Arthur Barratt, the former commander of the Advanced Air Striking Force, described Gamelin* as "a button-eyed, button-booted, pot-bellied little grocer." Modest and unassuming, Gamelin's ideal inconspicuousness as Joffre's Chief of Operations had led Jules Romains in his famous novel *Verdun* to base upon him his characterisation of "Lt.-Col. G . . . ," a model staff officer. General Spears recalls him from 1914, following Joffre "like a shadow," and it was upon his former master that Gamelin seemed to model himself. His blue eyes certainly gave an impression of calm serenity, but he possessed none of the solid basis for Joffre's legendary imperturbability—and in any case this attribute, carried to excess, had cost Joffre his job, and had nearly cost France the war, in 1916. Like Joffre, Gamelin was taciturn; but whereas the explication often given for Joffre's silence was that he simply had nothing in his mind, this was certainly not the case with the cerebral Gamelin. When Gamelin did speak, he had a habit of clasping his hands and moving them as if giving a benediction—indeed there was something faintly monkish about him, which could never have been said of Joffre.

A senior French diplomat dining with Gamelin at the French Embassy on one of his visits to London was amazed to hear the Generalissimo discourse on nothing but philosophy and Italian

* To the author.

painting. Joffre, he thought, would have been much discountenanced by the tenor of the conversation, while, listening to Gamelin, "I felt a cold draught at my back." Unashamedly, Gamelin
was an intellectual who felt ill at ease in front of the troops (with
whom his contacts were certainly kept to a minimum), much pre-
ferring the company of his fifteen adulatory staff officers with
whom he could discuss books and painting. According to de
Gaulle, after a visit to the gloomy vaults at Vincennes tenanted
by the Supreme Commander, Gamelin "dwelt in an atmosphere
very akin to that of a convent, surrounded by only a few officers,
working and meditating, completely insulated from current
events. . . . In his *Thébaïde** at Vincennes, General Gamelin
gave me the impression of a savant, testing the chemical reactions of his strategy in a laboratory." Adding to this isolation
from the outside world there was the extraordinary fact that
Vincennes possessed no radio communications centre.†

Gamelin considered experience to be everything, ignoring Frederick the Great's sally that if this quality "were all a great general
needs, the greatest would be Prince Eugen's mules." To Jules
Romains he dwelt upon the grave disadvantage of the Wehrmacht, because "I can think of very few of their present generals
who fought in responsible posts in 1914–18. Here we are almost
all former 1918 divisional commanders." The tragedy of Gamelin
was not that he misconstrued modern trends through stupidity;
certainly, his very luminous mind had *thought* deeply about tanks
and their possible effect on warfare, but in a kind of abstract intellectual vacuum, and his private lucubrations had hardly helped
provide the French Army with more and better tanks. When
Gamelin gave orders, they sounded less like the words of a
fighting man calling for vigorous action than topics for academic
discussion. Worried about defects in training at the end of 1939,
he had simply indicated to his subordinate, General Georges, "a
few ideas" phrased in a style which the Quai d'Orsay would have

---

* Literally an "Ivory Tower."

† In a letter to the press after the war (*L'Aurore* of November 8, 1949) defending this deficiency, Gamelin challenged: "What would we, at this level, have done
with a transmitter?" He added that, in any case, there had been one at the General
Staff Headquarters some twenty-two miles away; "but we avoided using it so as not
to give our position away."

admired—instead of issuing clear-cut instructions. It was hardly surprising that the Army took no notice of these "ideas." Even Daladier, Gamelin's political protector, once remarked to General Weygand, "When you speak, one has something; as for Gamelin, it is like sand running through one's fingers"; while the final damning remark about Gamelin, made by Reynaud, was: "He might be all right as a prefect or a bishop, but he is not a leader of men."

Indeed, as Georges Mandel described him, Gamelin was a kind of "military prefect" who tailored his decisions closely to the whim of the politicians. One of his officers at GQG recalled how "when he had to take a decision in the domain which interested me, I often saw him hesitate, postpone his decision to another moment, so as to weigh up all the consequences, and finally take that which would not expose him to a subsequent conflict with the civilian powers." It was for the express purpose of keeping a close feel on the political pulse that Gamelin selected Vincennes in spite of its grim historical associations. But because he was too close to his political masters, too remote from the zone of operations, Gamelin fatally compromised his authority over the fighting forces.

The whole French chain of command was anomalous and hardly satisfactory. The Minister of National Defence (which role Daladier filled, besides being Premier) wielded only nominal power over the Navy and Air Force, and Gamelin as the Chief of Staff possessed no more authority than his political boss. So the French Air Force, under the depressed General Vuillemin, tended to go its own way. Vuillemin had his HQ at Coulommiers, outside Paris. Under him came General Têtu, with the title of "Officer Commanding the Air Co-operation Forces," who was supposed to coordinate air activities with the Army's Northeast Front HQ. This front was divided into "Zones of Air Operations," corresponding to the various Army Groups. In theory the arrangement was adequate, but in practice it meant that the individual Army Commanders found it impossible to obtain a sufficient concentration of air power at the right moment. The fundamental trouble, of course, was the sheer numerical shortage of French aircraft. Of the RAF in France, Air Marshal Barratt's Advanced Air Striking Force came directly under Bomber Command in England, the

Royal Air Force Component of the BEF under the Army Commander, Lord Gort.*

As Supreme Commander of all French land forces, Gamelin gave direct orders to the armies in the Alps, in Syria and in North Africa. But to the great bulk of the forces grouped together under the Armies of the Northeast, Gamelin issued his orders through the intermediary of his deputy, General Georges, who initially bore the indefinite title (which had originated under Napoleon and, in the First War had been held, under Joffre, by General de Castelnau) of *Major-Général des Armées*. On the next level came the commanders of the various Army Groups. No. 1 Army Group, which, stretching from the Channel to the beginning of the Maginot Line, would play the predominant role in the Battle of France, was commanded by General Billotte. Among the five armies on Billotte's front was the BEF; Lord Gort, however, received his orders not from Billotte but from Gamelin, via Georges.†

It soon became apparent to Gamelin that he could not effectively control overall war strategy *and* exercise specific command over the Zone of the Armies of the Northeast all from one inflated headquarters. On January 6th, he effected a reorganisation which relieved himself of the direct command of the Armies of the Northeast and handed it to Georges, now entitled Commander-in-Chief Northeast Front. It was a measure that would provide Gamelin with numerous outs when writing his memoirs, but somehow it did not improve the efficacity of the French Command. While he reserved the right to intervene in an emergency (a right he never exercised in battle until it was much too late), the reorganisation meant in fact that Gamelin—in sharpest contrast to his old master, Joffre—removed himself from control of what was almost certain to become the key battle area of the war. Yet Georges, on the other hand, was never vested with full powers or responsibility. The reorganisation also resulted, immediately, in the creation of yet a third headquarters:

---

* In January 1940, command of the RAF Component was transferred to Barratt, although it remained under Gort's operational control.

† It was never quite clear whether the ultimate responsibility for the BEF rested with Gamelin or Georges, and in any case Gort's instructions permitted him to appeal to the British Government before executing any order if it "appears to you to imperil the British Field Force"—which was to prove an important escape clause.

GHQ Land Forces, under General Doumenc, situated in a Roth-
schild mansion beside the Marne at Montry, midway between
Vincennes and Georges's Northeast Front HQ at La Ferté-sous-
Jouarre, which lay 40 miles to the east of Paris.

The new HQ, whose function was to prepare and elaborate
orders, was created by fission chiefly from elements of General
Georges's staff, and this breaking up of offices that had been
working well together for several months had particularly lamentable effects. The Deuxième Bureau (Intelligence) was split in
two, with its chief, Colonel Gauché,* under Gamelin's wing at
Vincennes and officers compelled to make the trip there from
La Ferté every day to obtain his signature for documents. The
Troisième Bureau (Operations) was also divided, but even more
inopportune was its separation from the Quatrième (Transport
and Supply), which was removed completely to Montry—an arti-
ficial divorce that had to be rapidly rescinded when the Germans
attacked on May 10th. General Doumenc too had to "cut himself
in two," directing affairs at Montry in the morning and at La
Ferté in the afternoon. Visiting officers from the line, such as
General Prioux commanding the elite Cavalry Corps, were not
impressed by what they saw of the new organisation; obeying
Parkinson's Law the various staff adjuncts proliferated like
amoebae, creating among themselves bureaux that specialised
in agricultural affairs, physical training and sports. Meanwhile,
the inconveniences caused to communications by this splitting up
of GQG encouraged the habit of short-circuiting Gamelin in his
Thébaïde altogether.

General Georges

Not least among Gamelin's motives in establishing this third,
buffer-state HQ at Montry was the animosity between himself
and Georges, and it seemed to be his deliberate policy to weaken
his subordinate's position by removing the more valuable members of his staff. As Gamelin's star waned in government circles
and Georges emerged as his logical successor, relations between
the two worsened to the point where they could hardly exchange
civilities. "They are so busy making war on each other," a British
general quipped in the hearing of Maurois one day, "that they

---

* Later General.

have no time to make war on the Germans." General Georges himself came of very modest origins—he was said to be the son of gendarme—and he owed a fine career entirely to professional merit, in no way to intrigue or political pull. In the Great War, he had served on the staff in Salonika, then had been picked up by Foch, and it was in the Marshal's retinue that he had ridden behind him, as a colonel, in the Victory Parade of 1919. After the war he had commanded a regiment in the Rhineland, later becoming Pétain's Chief of Staff in Morocco. On October 9, 1934, fate struck a cruel blow at Georges; while accompanying King Alexander of Yugoslavia at Marseilles he was badly wounded in the chest by the assassin who killed the king and Barthou, the French Foreign Minister. By 1940, he was still visibly suffering from the effect of his wounds; Spears noted that "he now invariably wore a woollen glove on one hand, and had been told he must not fly." Instead he drove about at high speed in a "beautiful and enormous Cadillac car, of which he was justly proud." Because of Georges's supposed associations with the more extremist right-wing factions, Daladier viewed him with mistrust and (so Gamelin claimed) for this reason would never tolerate him as C-in-C of the Army.* In 1939, Georges's pessimism about the war was widely known in the French Army; but many of the British officers acquainted with him considered Georges to be France's finest soldier. According to Spears, who should have known, he "had more influence on Churchill than any other Frenchman." There were also many senior officers in the French Army who felt that Georges—not Gamelin—should have succeeded Weygand as C-in-C in 1935.

Before the war, La Ferté, with its bourgeois houses topped by pretentious turrets that lent them an air of bogus castles, had been a popular summer retreat for rich Parisians. Here General Georges had established Northeast Front HQ at "Les Bondons," described by a staff officer as "a spacious cottage in an Anglo-Norman style, sited in the middle of a park on a wooded hill which dominated the Marne," but "as little as possible suited to be a *poste de commandement* in time of crisis." In a leisurely manner, Georges's staff officers dined at the Hôtel de l'Épée,

---

* To some extent, the bad relations between Georges and Gamelin were an extension of the rivalry between their respective political champions, Reynaud and Daladier.

boasting a renowned chef, M. Truchet, who in 1917 had presided over Pétain's cuisine. Perhaps on account of the mentally sapping consequence of Georges's wounds, the atmosphere at "Les Bondons" struck visitors as being much the same as at Vincennes; here too an order was "an excellent basis for discussion."

Reading General Spears's accounts of the French High Command in 1940,* one emerges with a feeling of a world grown old and tired. In the military corridors one runs into the same old faces one has encountered a generation earlier. Brigadiers are now army commanders or C-in-Cs; battalion commanders have divisions or corps; the captains of 1918 are now in command of brigades or divisions. But they have aged. Symbolically, here is Marshal Franchet d'Esperey, the virile hero of 1918, now aged eighty-three, in his wheelchair, and declaring to Spears and Harold Nicolson, "Well, gentlemen, you see a ghost revisiting the scenes of his past"; Gamelin, the heir to Joffre, is sixty-eight; Weygand, the shadow of Foch, seventy-three. A French historian, Marc Bloch, writing at the time describes a perhaps typical senior officer who had gone through the First War as "weighed down . . . by years spent in office work and conditioned by a purely academic training." Where then—and who—are the young men, with the young ideas?

Gamelin's strategy

In the entente of 1939, while conduct of the war by sea rested upon Britain's shoulders, the planning of land operations, on account of France's vast military preponderance, devolved in effect upon the French Generalissimo; which seemed a reasonably fair division of labour. Gamelin's long-range strategy was to wait until, in terms of men and equipment, Britain and France had caught up with the Wehrmacht, before launching any serious offensive. This could not be before 1941 at the earliest; by then, perhaps neutral America might be persuaded once again to come to the rescue. The two overriding considerations behind French strategy remained the same as they had been ever since 1919: to husband French manpower so as not to permit a repetition of the slaughter of 1914–18, and to keep the war away from the sacred soil of France. But what if, while France was building up

---

* *Assignment to Catastrophe.*

her potential, Hitler should attack first? This seemed more than likely. The two avenues open to him would be to attack across the common frontier, taking the shortest route to Paris, or to repeat 1914 and sweep through neutral Belgium. In the path of the first route lay the imposing barrier of the Maginot Line; of the second, Belgian neutrality. Given the ruthlessness of Hitler, there could be little doubt as to which barrier was the least daunting, and various Deuxième Bureau reports from October 1939 onwards suggested that it was towards the Flemish plains that Hitler was already turning his gaze.

With the Maginot Line "extension" between Longwy and the sea still far from reality, Pétain's prescription of "going into Belgium" to meet a German invasion clearly continued to hold good.* But now, of course, King Leopold's rigid neutrality eradicated any prospect of the French, at Belgian invitation, moving comfortably into their fortifications up on the German frontier as soon as war broke out. There had been no exchange consultations between the two general staffs. The Belgians based their plans on the hope that they could hold their modern defence system along the Albert Canal, of which the powerful fortress of Eben Emael was the linchpin, at least long enough for the Allies to come to their assistance. But they adamantly declined to provide the Allies with any detailed information about these plans, and requests that French officers be permitted to visit defences, in civilian clothes, were invariably turned down. The same strict neutrality applied also to Holland. Gamelin and the French military would have liked to go into Belgium without having to wait for the Germans to move first. But the politicians rightly were horrified at the impact any French violation of Belgian neutrality might have upon world (and, predominantly, American) opinion. Besides, the possibility of jeopardising eventual collaboration with the Belgian Army simply could not be entertained; for one of Gamelin's principal motives for "going into Belgium" at all was the indispensability to manpower-short France of the Belgian Army's 700,000 men and 22 divisions (plus another 10 from Holland in case of her involvement).

On October 24th, Gamelin issued orders to the Armies of the

---

* As always, it was also Britain's policy not to allow the Belgian coast to fall into enemy hands.

Northeast Front, telling them to be ready to advance to a defensive position along the Escaut (or Scheldt) River, running from Antwerp to Ghent. In terms of distance of approach march, the "Escaut Plan" represented the most prudent of the Low Countries operations open to the Allies. But it was an awkwardly long line to hold, and at the same time it covered so small a portion of Belgian territory that Brussels would be abandoned and the bulk of the Belgian Army simply left, unsupported, to its fate. General Georges, however, immediately registered the strongest misgivings about any "deeper progression into Belgium." The Army was not yet ready to risk being caught by a German offensive in unprepared positions, far from its bases. Despite Georges's doubts, on November 15th Gamelin gave out his amended Instruction No. 8, in which the Allied forces were to move up to the Dyle Line, stretching from Antwerp due south to above Dinant on the Meuse. The Dyle itself was little more than a wide stream, and the Instruction required the French Army to go out still further on the Belgian limb. Once again, General Georges expressed his reservations. On the credit side of the original "Dyle Plan," it constituted a shorter line; it protected Brussels and gave a better chance of linking up with the Belgian defenders in their Albert Canal positions; and it committed no more than 10 French divisions. Gamelin, himself, however, was not satisfied; it made no provision for lending a hand to the Dutch in case of attack.

Towards the end of November, Gamelin requested General Billotte, commander of No. 1 Army Group, to study an extension of the Dyle Plan northwards from Antwerp in the direction of Breda—which lay twice as far from the French frontier as from Germany. On hearing of this new inflationary development of Gamelin's Belgian strategy, Georges objected vigorously. In the margin of Billotte's report, he wrote: "This is of the order of an adventure. . . . Don't let's engage our effectives in this affair"; and on December 5th he sent it on to Gamelin with an accompanying memorandum which contained this highly pertinent and prescient warning:

The problem is dominated by the question of available forces. . . . There is no doubt that our offensive manoeuvre in Belgium and Holland should be conducted with the caution of not allowing ourselves to commit the major part of our reserves in this part of the theatre, in face of a German action which could be nothing more than a diversion. *For example, in the event of an attack in force breaking out in the centre, on our front between the Meuse and Moselle, we could be deprived of the necessary means for a counter-attack.**

Momentarily, Gamelin seems to have been swayed by Georges's arguments. But in addition to the essential military considerations, there was an element of personal honour and pride pushing Gamelin along; humiliatingly, as France's top soldier, he had been forced to stand by while Germany crushed first Czechoslovakia and then Poland. His enemies had never ceased taunting him for the French Army's lethargy during Hitler's conquest of Poland, and he was determined not to give them cause to say he had cast Belgium and Holland to their fates too. Then, on January 10th, there occurred one of those freak accidents of war which change the destinies of mankind.

The Mechelen incident

On January 9th, a German major of the paratroops employed on an airborne planning staff, by name Hellmuth Reinberger, received a summons to attend a highly secret conference at Second Air Fleet HQ in Cologne the following morning. Reinberger was in Münster at the time, some 80 miles distant as the crow flies. That night he was invited to the local air base. After a number of drinks and some conviviality, the station commander, a reservist major named Hoenmanns, genially proposed to Reinberger that he save him a dreary train journey by flying him down to Cologne. A First War Flyer, Hoenmanns had a civil pilot's license and wanted to get in a few more flying hours; also he would welcome an excuse to visit his wife and take home some laundry. Reinberger accepted—on condition that weather conditions were perfect.

The next day dawned cloudless, with visibility over the Ruhr up to 2.5 miles. The two majors set forth in a tiny Me–108, Reinberger hugging on his knees an imposing yellow pigskin briefcase, which bulged with top-secret documents relating to the air plan of a German operation to invade Holland and Belgium. Suddenly the weather closed in. Hoenmanns realised that he had

---

* Author's italics.

probably strayed too far west from his course, and accordingly changed direction towards the east. At that moment, the engine inexplicably cut out. Narrowly missing a high-tension line and with both wing tips ripped off by a row of poplars, Hoenmanns made a skilful forced landing in a snow-covered thicket. A quick investigation of the map revealed that they had landed just inside Belgian territory, near Mechelen, a few miles north of Maastricht. In horror, Reinberger leapt behind a bush hedge and tried to destroy the vital documents. But his lighter failed. Then an obliging Belgian peasant provided a match, and Reinberger built a small fire into which he fed the papers (always notoriously hard to burn), leaf by leaf. Soon some Belgian troops, under a captain, arrived and arrested Hoenmanns, who pretended that he had flown alone. The column of smoke from behind the thicket betrayed Reinberger, however, and the two majors were marched to a Belgian *gendarmerie* post. There, through what seems like extraordinary negligence, Reinberger was enabled to have another shot at destroying the documents by thrusting them into a stove. But he was interrupted by the Belgian captain, who rescued what remained. By nightfall, the papers were in the hands of the Belgian GHQ; though badly charred, they contained enough to indicate that the Germans intended thrusting into northern France via Belgium (and Holland), in what appeared to be a replay of the Schlieffen Plan of 1914.

The "Dyle–Breda Plan"

Belgium promptly passed this information on to the Dutch and the French. The French Army was placed in a state of alert. In terrible weather conditions, Billotte's forces closed up to the Belgian frontier. Momentarily, the Belgian High Command raised the frontier barriers and it seemed as if the Allies would be "invited" to enter. But swiftly King Leopold reversed the order, sacking his Chief of Staff. Exasperated and despondent, the French Army drew back again. After January 15th, this apparently most menacing of the various false alarms receded into the ranks of the others. But the glimpse it gave of German operational plans proved enough to fix Gamelin in his resolve.* On

---

* Since, as it later turned out, the French Army reacted in precisely the way Hitler wanted it to, for some years even after 1945 suspicions lingered that the Mechelen Incident was a cunning Nazi plant. It definitely was not.

March 20th, he issued a new directive, supplementing the former
Dyle manoeuvre with the "Breda Variant." Approved by both
French and British Governments, this would in fact be the master
plan with which the Allies met the German onslaught when it
came on May 10th. Instead of the 10 French divisions (plus the
BEF) previously earmarked for Belgian operations, now 30
would be involved; among them the very cream of the French
and British Armies—two out of France's three new armoured
divisions, five out of seven motorised divisions and all three of
the light mechanised divisions (DLMs). On the extreme left flank
of the manoeuvre, edging the sea, was placed General Giraud's
Seventh Army of seven first-rate divisions (including one DLM)
with the task of being ready to move at top speed through Belgium to link up with the Dutch Army. Hitherto the Seventh
Army had constituted a significant part of General Georges's
mobile strategic reserves; Gamelin's decision to allocate it to the
Breda Variant was to have the most far-reaching consequences
of any part of the Allied plan. Next in line came Lord Gort's
BEF,* which would advance up to the river Dyle roughly between Louvain and Wavre; south of it came General Blanchard's
crack First Army, with the role of holding the Gembloux gap down
to the fortress of Namur on the Meuse. General Corap's Ninth
Army was to wheel forward to occupy the line of the Meuse where
it runs through the Belgian Ardennes, south of Namur. The pivot
of the whole manoeuvre would be just north of Sedan, where
the Meuse leaves France, at the boundary between the Ninth
and Second Armies. To the right of Corap, General Huntziger's
Second Army stretching from Sedan to the Maginot Line anchor
at Longwy would remain static—as indeed would the rest of the
French Army encamped behind *le trou*. In essence, the final
plan meant that the main striking power of the Franco-British
Army was to be committed to whatever might transpire in Belgium and Holland, north of the line Liège–Namur.

Up to the moment of the German onslaught, misgivings lin-

---

* Explaining his reasons for placing the French Seventh Army on the left of the
BEF, Gamelin writes in his memoirs that they were "not only strategic, but psychological and moral." Similar doubts at the back of French minds about having
the British too close to the Channel and home had also existed in '14–'18, when
the French had always managed to keep Haig's army "sandwiched" between
French forces.

gered in high French circles about the Dyle–Breda Plan. Following the January 10th alarm, the Belgian General Staff had been
persuaded to prepare positions along the Dyle, in case the Allies
should be called upon to occupy them; but General Prioux, commanding the Cavalry Corps, which with some of France's best
armoured and mechanised units formed the steel tip of
Blanchard's First Army, had strong doubts of the efficacy of the
unreconnoitred defences the Belgians were supposedly erecting
in the Gembloux Gap. General Giraud, whose Seventh Army
would now have the most ambitious role to perform, complained
of the difficulties in a letter to Billotte on March 28th. Billotte,
whose No. 1 Army Group held direct responsibility for the whole
manoeuvre, had been its most enthusiastic supporter among
Gamelin's subordinates, but he too now backed up Giraud's reservations. General Vuillemin, always gloomy about German air superiority, had shared General Georges's pessimism throughout;
and Georges himself remained unconvinced. But—perhaps because of the lack of communication between him and Gamelin,
perhaps because will power had been diminished by his ailing
health—Georges was impotent to influence the Generalissimo.* In
Britain, too, there were dissenting voices; but, with only a handful of divisions in the field (by May 1940, Lord Gort still had no
more than nine under his command), it was felt that she should
keep quiet and leave the planning to the leaders of France's invincible army.†

Gamelin, buried away in his *Thébaïde,* alone remained sublimely confident. On April 15th, he dispatched a last letter to
dispel Georges's doubts, once again reiterating that "it seemed
impossible systematically to abandon Holland to Germany." In
defiance of the lessons of Poland, he somehow maintained a
simple faith in the ability of the Dutch and Belgians to defend

---

* Georges, too, seems to have suffered from his share of the sense of unreality
afflicting the French High Command. In a revealing marginal comment he appended, in August 1940, to a report on the defeat: "In the spring of 1940, did we
really have the impression of being poorly prepared?"

† Criticising this silence retrospectively, Churchill remarks (in *The Second
World War,* II, 34) that the British War Cabinet "ought not to have been deterred
from thrashing the matter out with the French in the autumn and winter of 1939.
It would have been an unpleasant and difficult argument, for the French at every
stage could say: 'Why do you not send more troops of your own? . . . Pray show
a proper confidence in the French Army and in our historic mastery of the art of
war on land.' Nevertheless we ought to have done it."

their countries. Far from fearing a German onslaught through the Low Countries, there were occasions when he gave the impression of actually longing for it; for, as he once informed the government, "the enemy would be offering himself to us in open territory."

It is difficult to conceive, however, with what forces Gamelin saw himself counterattacking the German thrust which would thus be "offering" itself. In expanding the Dyle Plan to embrace the Breda Variant and by committing General Giraud's Seventh Army to it, Gamelin was being totally loyal to the principles of the "continuous front." But behind this front he retained only the scantiest of reserves. It was all right provided the front *remained* continuous, as it had done from 1914 to 1918. In Gamelin's final alignment which was to bear the brunt of the German attack of May 1940, roughly 30 divisions were committed to the Dyle–Breda manoeuvre; 10 garrison divisions were permanently installed in the Maginot Line, while yet another 30 backed them up as "interval troops," leaving only 22 divisions in reserve. Out of these 22, seven (including two out of France's three new armoured divisions) were earmarked for Belgium, another five allocated to meet a possible German thrust through Switzerland; so that the overall strategic reserve left to General Georges amounted to between 10 and 13 divisions, or practically nothing. That an additional 30 good divisions should have to be employed "guarding" the Maginot Line seemed to point up a grave fallacy in France's whole strategic plan; as things were to turn out, the crucial phase of the battle would already be lost beyond repair before any of these 30 wasted divisions could be thrown into it.* Thus the overall picture of General Georges's northeastern front showed a powerful right flank on the Maginot Line (absorbing nearly half of all his effectives), and a powerful left flank facing northern Belgium. But the centre, along a front of little less than 100 miles behind the so-called "impenetrable" Belgian Ardennes, was held by only some four light cavalry divisions (still partly equipped with horses) and ten mediocre infantry divisions of the

---

* In his memoirs (I, 308), Gamelin tries to justify this concentration of forces on the Maginot Line by claiming: "Its existence alone guaranteed us, in the spring of 1940, that, at the moment when the Germans attacked via Luxembourg, Belgium and Holland, they could not at the same time make a decisive effort between Longuyon and Switzerland." But this was not an intention that ever for a moment entered Hitler's mind.

Ninth and Second Armies—about which more will be said later.
And behind them, emptiness.

What a standing temptation the spectacle of this French line,
then, so weak in the centre, might present to an opposing captain
of audacity and genius!

Polish lesson unlearned

Of all the attitudes struck by the French High Command during the Phoney War, none today seems more incomprehensible
than its apparent refusal to take cognizance of the lessons of the
Polish campaign. Nothing that had happened to the unhappy
Poles made France in any way alter her basic doctrine of war, review the training techniques of combat echelons, or consider possible German offensive plans against her in the light of the strategy
that had succeeded so admirably against Poland. It was not that
the French High Command was uninformed. On returning to
France in the autumn of 1939, General Armengaud, an Air Force
general sent to lead a mission to Poland, who had closely observed
events there, delivered a detailed oral report to Gamelin, which he
then followed up with a written memorandum. In this memorandum, he warned that the Wehrmacht in Poland had proven its
ability "to break through a defensive front inadequately manned."

It would be mad [continued Armengaud] not to draw an exact lesson
from this pattern and not to pay heed to this warning. The German system consists essentially of making a breach in the front with armour
and aircraft, then to throw mechanized and motorized columns into
the breach, to beat them down to right and left in order to keep on
enlarging it, at the same time as armoured detachments, guided, protected, and reinforced by aircraft, advance in front of the supporting
divisions . . . in such a way that the defence's manoeuvrability . . .
is reduced to impotence.

Armengaud considered that, of the German armour and aircraft,
it was the latter that had been the "most decisive," by impeding
the defenders' manoeuvrability and by breaching the chain of
command "in such a way that the command is made blind and
cannot get its orders through." To Gamelin, Armengaud expressed the view that the Germans would attempt a break-through
in the west, probably near the *centre* of the French front, and they
would then try to fan out to the rear, using a mass of material

and aircraft. He thought they would be able to make such a breach very quickly, possibly within forty-eight hours.

For his pains, Armengaud was relegated to an administrative post, as commander of the Paris Air Region, where, he says, he found himself powerless to stem the feckless optimism in high places—which increased as the Polish defeat receded from memory. But Armengaud was evidently also backed up by reports submitted to Gamelin by the Deuxième Bureau Chief, Colonel Gauché, one of which described how the effects of the German aerial bombardment had "resulted in almost complete paralysis of the Polish High Command, which was rendered incapable either of completing mobilisation or concentration, or of carrying out reinforcements or supplies, or of executing any kind of coordinated manoeuvre." The Deuxième Bureau also pointed out the highly relevant strategic fact that the Germans had *not* aimed at capturing Warsaw, but had sought first and foremost to destroy the Polish Army. Here, certainly, was one lesson that would prove worth considering in May 1940. On more specific but equally important matters, the Deuxième Bureau warned the High Command of the effect of German tank guns on the Polish bunkers; these had "resisted perfectly the fire of 150 mm guns; but their machine guns were often destroyed by shots in the embrasure fired by the tanks. It thus appears that every fortified work must be provided with antitank weapons." It will be seen how much notice was taken of this warning.

The French High Command attitude to all this was roughly: "We are not Poles, it could not happen here." General Keller, Inspector General of Tanks, wrote in answer to a memorandum written by Colonel de Gaulle: "Even supposing that the present fortified line were breached or out-flanked, it does not appear that our opponents will find a combination of circumstances as favourable for a *Blitzkrieg* as in Poland. One can see, then, that in future operations the primary role of the tank will be the same as in the past; to assist the infantry in reaching successive objectives." Thus inflexible remained the military doctrinaires of France. General Huntziger, commanding the ill-fated Second Army, did go to some length to circulate among his command details of the Wehrmacht technique in Poland, but few practical consequences by way of combat training ever seem to have followed.

Finland and other distractions

No less extraordinary than the French High Command's studied and arrogant disregard of the lessons of Poland was the astonishing unreality of all the Allied schemes and projects during the Phoney War, of which Gamelin's delusive optimism is but one facet or syndrome. In both French and British councils of war new mad ideas of launching diversionary operations were constantly being thought up. Of course (certainly in France) the genesis of these schemes lay understandably in the eternal anxiety about keeping war away from French soil, but all were predicated upon strength which, in early 1940, the Allies simply did not possess, and worse still, several of them would have brought Russia actively into the war on Hitler's side—the folly of which hardly bears thinking about.

On November 30th, her demands for concessions to help secure the approaches to Leningrad having been refused, Russia attacked Finland. Hitting back, the gallant Finns captured western imagination by inflicting defeat after defeat upon the ponderous Red Army. In England, Transport House condemned with angriest indignation "the Criminal Conspiracy of Stalin and Hitler" while (according to the *Daily Sketch*) at Buckingham Palace a large-scale map of Finland soon displaced one of the western front in the King's office. But in France emotions reached fever pitch; prayers were offered in the Madeleine for Marshal Mannerheim; ladies knitted vests for Finnish soldiers; gala charity performances in aid of the Finns were held at the Opera and in the Carlton at Cannes. Here was a *real* war, a man's war that one could get excited about! "The fortified front of Karelia," wrote Fabre-Luce, "evoked simultaneously the Maginot Line and a season of winter sports. It was like a highly seductive glossy magazine for skiing amateurs, obliged this year to remain at their hearth-sides." From the squalor of the concentration camp at Vernet, French attitudes struck Arthur Koestler rather less favourably; the treatment of each Finnish success as "victories of France" reminded him of "a *voyeur* who gets his thrills and satisfaction out of watching other people's virile exploits, which he is unable to imitate."

Ideologically, French emotions were compounded of several ingredients. At their highest, Russia's attack was regarded as just one more repellent act of aggression by the totalitarian powers; and had not France, that same September, entered the lists as champion of the spirit of the League of Nations? But, more powerfully, among the bourgeoisie and the right wing there were those animosities left lingering by the Front Populaire, and exacerbated by the Ribbentrop–Molotov deal. Here the "Winter War" presented prospects of a holy crusade against Bolshevism infinitely more appealing than the *drôle de guerre* against the dormant and untroublesome Hitler. The Assembly, from which the Communist deputies had just been purged, became strongly interventionist. Senator Bardoux, an independent Radical charged with "sounding out the British," represented a fair section of French bourgeois opinion when he wrote in his diary for December 23rd:

The Russian disaster in Finland is a capital event. Henceforth, far from trying to split Germany and Russia, we must—on the contrary—weld them together more tightly, for a weak ally is a ball-and-chain and opens a breach in the common front. We must enter into it resolutely. By intervening to aid Finland we shall create, together with the neutrals and Italy [he added hopefully], the definitive bloc. It is possible to offer the Crimea to Hitler, to utilise the Ukrainians, the Transcaucasians and the Persians. We can roll up everything, all the way to the Caucasus.

As the Finns continued to defeat the apparently decrepit Soviet war machine, serious thoughts of intervention spread to the military planners. An expeditionary force landed at the Norwegian port of Narvik could lend a hand to the Finns by marching across northern Sweden; at the same time a mortal blow would be struck at Hitler by depriving him of the Swedish iron ore supplies essential to his war economy. Here would be a fine side show to distract Hitler's gaze from France!

On January 15th, Gamelin wrote to Daladier proposing the opening of a front in Scandinavia. Throughout the winter, discussions volleyed back and forth between London and Paris, while the slopes at Chamonix became carpeted with British officers and men learning to ski. Briefly, Chamberlain with his declared anti-Communist bias favoured this happy means to "kill two birds with one stone," but as the full gravity of the undertaking sank in, the British Government began to try to exercise prudence upon its more impetuous ally.* Meanwhile—fortunately for all concerned—the Norwegian and Swedish Governments stalwartly rejected every overture for the expedition to pass through their territories. By March, however, parliamentary pressure upon Daladier was such that—without consulting Britain—he informed the Finns that France would be prepared to brush aside Norwegian and Swedish objections. On the 11th, he told Halifax he would resign unless Britain toed the line. The French, wrote Ironside (the British CIGS) in disgust, "are absolutely unscrupulous in everything," while the following day he recorded that the Chamberlain Cabinet—"a bewildered flock of sheep"—had reluctantly acceded to the Narvik expedition. Then, on March 13th, Finland signed peace with Russia. By a matter of days, if not hours, Britain and France had been saved from a war with Russia as well as Germany. As Colonel Josiah Wedgwood remarked in the House of Commons, "it would have been the maddest military adventure upon which this country had ever embarked." But in France, bitterest disappointment; in his diary, Major Barlone recorded: "it is a heavy moral defeat for the Allies. I realise this when I talk to the men, who are bewildered by the inactivity of the Allies. . . . We are disheartened." And this "moral defeat" was enough to cause the fall of the Daladier Government.

At the other extremity of the European war theatre, the sprightly General Maxime Weygand, commanding the French Army of the Levant, had been toying with schemes hardly less realistic than the Scandinavian adventure. Somehow Turkey and Greece would be brought into the war; the dismal Salonika front of World War I would be reactivated; and a hundred Balkan divisions would loyally march with the Allies against Hitler's "soft underbelly." Here again was a bright prospect (encouraged by Gamelin) of saving French manpower and diverting the course

---

* Gamelin, who claims that he had reservations about the Scandinavian venture but "did not feel I had the right to stand up, in this domain, against a government decision," with extraordinary lightheartedness dismisses the possibility of war with Russia by writing in his memoirs: "Of course, we could not send forces to fight side by side with the Finns without colliding with the Russians. If we wished to do anything in this direction, one had to accept this consequence." (Gamelin, II, 199.)

of war from French soil. Much talk ensued. But neither Greece nor Turkey, nor any other Balkan power, was much moved by Allied wooing; General Weygand received only two divisions of reinforcements throughout the Phoney War, and would be the only member of his army to take part in the war of 1940.*

Following the invasion of Finland, Weygand, Catholic and politically very much to the right, is to be found urging Gamelin by letter: "I regard it essential to break the back of the Soviet Union in Finland . . . and elsewhere." From here sprang notions of striking (by bombers flying out of Weygand's Syrian base) at the Caucasian oil fields which were fuelling both the Wehrmacht and the Red Army in Finland. Gamelin claims that he did his best "to deflect our thoughts from such an action," though Weygand in his memoirs declares that he received, on March 13th, a memorandum from Gamelin which "advocated an attack on the oil wells of the Caucasus." As late as April 17th, Weygand was still corresponding with Gamelin about the operation, the planes for which (fortunately) were never available. (Meanwhile, Walter Lippmann passing through Paris was helpfully offering the French Government his advice on how to breach Black Sea traffic between Russia and Germany.) How, with the absurdly small bomber potential then available to both Britain and France, it was imagined that any raid on the Baku oil wells could have caused more than a pinprick is hard to imagine. The whole lunatic venture was well summed up in a poem by A. P. Herbert published at the time:

BAKU, OR, THE MAP GAME

It's jolly to look at the map
And finish the foe in a day.
It's not easy to get at the chap;
These neutrals are so in the way.
But if you say "What would you do
To fill the aggressor with gloom?"
Well, we might drop a bomb on Baku,
Or what about bombs on Batum?

Refrain: *I'm all for some bombs on Baku,*
And, of course, a few bombs on Batum.

---

* His army in Syria was later rounded up by the British.

Meanwhile, as fervid brains in various Allied councils played "The Map Game," in apparently blissful indifference to realities on the other side of the Rhine, fighting soldiers up at the front sometimes also wondered precisely what form Hitler's plans for the spring might be taking.

7

The Sickle and the Reaper

"Quiet, friend Sancho!" replied Don Quixote. "Even more than other subjects, affairs of war are subject to continual change."

—CERVANTES, *Don Quixote*

His Majesty, Chance.

—FREDERICK THE GREAT

LONG BEFORE the war Hitler, the corporal who had endured the miseries of four years of static warfare on the western front, nurtured dreams of smashing France in what *Mein Kampf* predicted would be "one last decisive battle." To Rauschning he declared that "with an unprecedented application of all means at his command, with the most ruthless dispatch to the front of all reserves, he would nail victory to his mast in one gigantic knockout blow." Veiled in mystical imprecision, Hitler's inchoate ideas as to how this was to be achieved repeatedly sent his military advisers scurrying for shelter. The overcoming of their objections and the evolution of one of the most brilliant war plans of all time is in itself an extraordinary story, in which Chance plays a part of high importance.

When war had come in 1914, Germany possessed her long-prepared Schlieffen Plan ready to roll into instant action against France while Russia was still mobilising her unwieldy forces. But in 1939, never expecting that, on their past performance, Daladier and Chamberlain would honour their guarantee to Poland, Hitler had not instructed his General Staff to give thought to any comparable strategy. In the first place, he had no Russian foe to worry about. His generals, however, had by no means recovered from the shock of finding themselves once again at war with France and Britain when, on September 12th, Hitler told Colonel Schmundt, his chief military adjutant, that he intended attacking in the west immediately the Polish campaign was ended. On September 27th, Poland capitulated after Gamelin had shown that no threat would confront Germany from the west. At five o'clock that afternoon, Hitler held a meeting of the Commanders-in-Chief of the three Wehrmacht services in the map room of the new Chancellery.* Without any preamble and without seeking any opinion from the military experts, Hitler gave his views for an offensive against France; this year, and as soon as possible. Casting to the winds his recent promises to respect their neutrality, Hitler pronounced that the offensive would pass through Belgium and the Dutch appendix of Maastricht. By way of justification, he pleaded the vulnerability of Germany's Ruhr and alleged evidence of French collusion with the Belgian General Staff. After the minimum of discussion, tossing into the fire the scrap of paper on which he had scribbled his notes for the meeting, Hitler dismissed those present and instructed the Army leaders to draft an operational plan.

Directive Yellow

News of Hitler's decision was promptly greeted with wide protest in the Army. General Ritter von Leeb, commanding Army Group "C" along the Rhine and rated as the leading defensive theoretician of the old school, was outraged at the "lunacy" of breaching Dutch and Belgium neutrality, and (to Brauchitsch) condemned Hitler's simultaneous "peace offer" to the Allies as "simply deceiving the German people with lies." Moved more by pragmatic than moral considerations, his fellow Army Group commanders, Rundstedt and Bock, declared that any early offensive would have little likelihood of success. Halder was convinced that the motorised and armoured divisions which had fought in Poland could not possibly be reorganised before mid-November;†

---

* The Army High Command (OKH) was represented that day by its C-in-C, Colonel General von Brauchitsch and his Chief of Staff, Halder; the Luftwaffe (OKL) by Goering and Jeschonnek; the Navy (OKM) by Admirals Raeder and Schniewind; the Wehrmacht (OKW) by its Chief of Staff, Keitel and Colonel Warlimont, deputising for Jodl, the OKW Chief of Operations.

† Half their fighting vehicles were temporarily in repair shops.

the troops which had stood defensively on the Rhine were not up to scratch; and there were serious shortages of ammunition and equipment. Even the impetuous Goering had his doubts, based on the probability of bad flying weather.

The studied view of the Army High Command was that there could be no prospect of a successful offensive against France until spring of 1942.

But nothing would deflect Hitler. On October 9th, Warlimont relayed to the OKH that Hitler had fixed November 25th as the date of the offensive. The next day Hitler delivered to Halder a 58-page memorandum. Riding roughshod over all technical objections, he declared that "General Time" was on the side of the Allies, not Germany. Giving specific details for the first time, he proposed that the main weight of the panzer forces should advance on both sides of Liège; the objective of the offensive was to occupy territory on the Channel for the further prosecution of the war against England. In view of the modest limits of this goal, it seemed that Hitler was still voicing more a wild personal desire than any calculated plan when he spoke once again of the "final military annihilation" of the enemy. Working, for all their lack of enthusiasm, with the speed characteristic of the German General Staff, Halder and the OKH produced their first plan, with the code name of "Deployment Directive *Yellow*" (*Aufmarschanweisung Gelb*) by October 19th. Fundamentally it consisted simply of an enveloping movement on Ghent, designed to separate the BEF from the French, if possible, while securing air and sea bases for employment against the British Isles. The question of how the campaign would be continued in order to obtain a decision against the Allies, once the Channel had been reached, was left entirely open.

Erroneously, historians have described the first OKH "*Gelb*" draft as a variation on the Schlieffen theme, but in fact it was nothing of the sort. Schlieffen had prescribed a great Cannae battle of annihilation in which, after crashing through Belgium and striking to the west of Paris, the German Army would swing southwards to roll up the French forces from the rear and crush them against Switzerland and the Jura; on the other hand Halder's axis of advance lay *west-northwest,* and eschewed any such bold and far-reaching strategic conception as Schlieffen's.

It was manifestly a bad plan, so conservative and uninspiring that it might well have been thought up by a British or French General Staff of the interwar years, and through its many imperfections glimmered the halfheartedness of the OKH and the Army commanders. Arguments leaped back and forth as to where the panzer divisions were to be deployed. Hitler was far from satisfied. To an unreceptive Halder he began proposing visionary schemes of "special operations" in which airborne troops would capture the Meuse crossings north of Liège and cut off the Belgian Army retreating from Ghent. On October 22nd, he shocked Halder by announcing his intention of advancing the date of the western offensive to November 12th. Then, at another conference three days later, Hitler suddenly asked Brauchitsch whether a main attack *on the southern Meuse only* might be able to "cut off and annihilate" the enemy. Almost casually he injected the name of Amiens into the discussion, and then with a red pencil sketched on the map a line running from the Meuse south of Namur to the Channel coast of France. According to Bock, Brauchitsch and Halder appeared "utterly astonished." They were then packed off to reconsider the OKH plan. Meanwhile, that same day a most portentous event occurred within the Army itself; Colonel General Gerd von Rundstedt, a sixty-four-year-old officer called back from retirement to command Army Group South during the Polish campaign, arrived in Koblenz on the Rhine to take over the newly created Army Group "A," facing Luxembourg and the Ardennes country of southern Belgium. With him came his Chief of Staff, a brilliant and impulsive lieutenant general who, born Erich Lewinski, had later adopted the name of Manstein. From this day on, two channels of thought began to flow, coincidentally and quite independently of each other, which would eventually funnel together—at Sedan.

On October 29th, the OKH produced its revised plan. As before, the center of gravity (*Schwerpunkt*) of the attack remained with Bock's Army Group "B" in the north but—to meet the point Hitler had raised on the 25th—it had shifted somewhat to the south, so that the Fourth Army with four panzer divisions would now cross the Meuse both north and south of Namur. The plan still, however, envisaged a frontal attack with the same limited objectives. Hitler remained only partially satisfied, and the next day he revealed to Jodl, OKW Chief of Operations, a "new idea" which would make use of the east-west Arlon Gap in the

Ardennes to reach Sedan, on the Meuse just over 50 miles *south* of Namur, striking at it with one panzer and one motorised division. It was the first time that the fateful name of Sedan was mentioned in German councils of war. But Jodl did not bother to pass on this latest brain wave of the Führer's to the OKH.

Hitler and Brauchitsch

Meanwhile, as October ended, Hitler was becoming thoroughly aware of the OKH opposition towards his designs. On the 5th, the deadline for ordering the attack to begin on the 12th, Brauchitsch was summoned to the Chancellery for a sulphurous meeting. The Army C-in-C was a fifty-eight-year-old artilleryman, much decorated during the Great War (when he too had served his time at Verdun) and with a distinguished subsequent record. Of outstanding intelligence, he was also a quiet and withdrawn man, painfully correct in his external relations. Although emotional and high-strung, his *Junker* upbringing led him to abhor violent scenes. He had a conscience and a will, but could hardly be described as combative. Both as a soldier and a man, in every way he excelled the third-rate Keitel, the OKW's Württemberger Chief of Staff; but none of his attributes were of any assistance in standing up to Hitler. Furthermore, though not a party man, he was under some obligation to the Nazi hierarchy for having eased his divorce in 1938, the same year that he succeeded Werner von Fritsch* as C-in-C. His new wife was a rabid Nazi, who exerted a dominant influence on him. Brauchitsch's stormy sessions with the Führer in the past left him exhausted, and he tended more and more to retreat behind a passive line of "military obedience." But on November 5th he confronted Hitler fortified by a tour of the front two days previously during which all his senior commanders had unanimously and vigorously declared that the Army was not ready to launch a major offensive. To Hitler he now read out a memorandum presenting the Army's views. When Brauchitsch warned him against underestimating the French, Hitler held up his hand:

"Herr Generaloberst, I would like to interrupt immediately here, because I hold quite different views. Firstly, I place a low value on the French Army's will to fight. Every army is a mirror

---

* Disgraced on trumped-up charges of homosexuality.

of its people. The French people think only of peace and good-living, and they are torn apart in parliamentary strife. Accordingly, the Army, however brave and well-trained its officer corps may be, does not show the combat determination expected of it. After the first setbacks, it will swiftly crack up."

Though shaken, Brauchitsch rashly continued. In Poland, he said, the German assault troops had not matched up to the infantry of 1914; there were incidents where discipline had failed, which led one to question whether the troops would be up to the stresses of a campaign in the west. At this, Hitler lost all self-control. Brauchitsch was heaping "monstrous reproaches" upon *his* Army. Where had there been acts of indiscipline? Hitler demanded "concrete examples." He then vented his rage upon Brauchitsch and the army commanders; they had never been loyal to him, and the "spirit of Zossen"* had become synonymous with defeatism. Rudely, Hitler dismissed Brauchitsch and dictated a note sacking him—which he later destroyed. Brauchitsch tottered to his car, arriving back at Zossen in a state of total incoherence. He never substantiated his charges of "indiscipline," and Hitler never forgave him for the slurs he had cast upon his new young Army; the waning influence of the OKH in Nazi war councils had receded another notch. Quite unaffected by the memorandum Brauchitsch had delivered, Hitler ordered Keitel to proceed with troop movements for an attack on the 12th, as planned. But two days later, bad weather forced Hitler to delay the attack. It was the first of twenty-nine such postponements. On November 9th, an enraged Hitler once again had to call off operations, this time until November 19th.

Brauchitsch's interview of November 5th represents a high point in the OKH opposition to Hitler. Well before the war began, Hitler had already shorn his General Staff of much of its power. Although adorned with the title of Supreme War Lord, the Kaiser before him had never possessed so much influence over military affairs as did Hitler; in fact, soon after 1914 he had become the virtual prisoner of the Great German General Staff. Hitler, on the other hand, had swiftly reduced it to little more than a drafting office entirely subservient to himself as Supreme

---

* A town 20 miles south of Berlin, where—in reinforced concrete buildings, complete with bombproof and gasproof cellars—the OKH was housed.

Commander of the Wehrmacht. In military circles, OKW was liberally translated as *Oben Kein Widerstand* ("no resistance at the top"). Of the Württemberger Keitel, scornfully nicknamed "Lakeitel" (a diminutive of "lackey"), it was said that he received the appointment after the OKW C-in-C, Blomberg,* had remarked disparagingly to Hitler, "He's nothing but the man who runs my office." Hitler immediately replied, "That's exactly the man I'm looking for." And so, for the remainder of the war, Keitel ran Hitler's "office" as a kind of pliable chief clerk; while below the OKW, the C-in-Cs and their staffs of the three services possessed a mere shadow of the independence they had enjoyed in Imperial days.

Once, during the Second World War, Churchill is reputed to have grumbled in aggravation against the Chiefs-of-Staff system:

It leads to weak and faltering decisions—or rather indecisions. Why, you may take the most gallant sailor, the most intrepid airman or the most audacious soldier, put them at a table together—what do you get? *The sum of their fears.*

This was indisputably Hitler's view about *his* military advisers, and, as the success of each new gamble proved their "fears" to be groundless, he listened to them less and less. In the long run, the diminished influence of the General Staff was to prove one of the great weaknesses of Germany's superb military machine in the Second World War. Certainly the influence of the OKH was never to stand as high again after the Brauchitsch–Hitler interview of November 5, 1939.

Halder and the Resistance

Behind the OKH opposition to Hitler's plans for a western offensive in the autumn of 1939, there lay a complexity of motives which, because of its bearing on the evolution of *Gelb,* needs to be examined. It borders on the whole question of the German "resistance" to Hitler. At the time of the Czech crisis of 1938, the resistance movement, such as it was, resided principally among the conservative elements of the Army who had always regarded Hitler as an upstart and a guttersnipe, and who now were thor-

---

* Subsequently disgraced on charges of marrying a tart.

oughly alarmed as to where his policies would lead the nation. At their head stood the Army Chief of Staff,* the honourable Colonel General Beck, who was forced to commit suicide after the bomb plot of July 20, 1944. Had France and Britain stood firm over Czechoslovakia, the resistance, we are told, would have taken action against Hitler. But Hitler triumphed and the resistance lost much of its impetus as well as many of its adherents in high places, while another devastating blow was struck at its prestige by Hitler's coup in pulling off the Nonaggression Pact with Russia.

Beck had resigned before Munich, depriving the resistance of its mainspring. He was succeeded in office, reluctantly, by General Franz Halder, an artilleryman three years younger than the new Army C-in-C, Brauchitsch. Coming from an old military family which had provided Bavaria with soldiers for many generations, Halder set a precedent as the first Bavarian Catholic to break the traditional Prussian, Protestant hegemony and to become Chief of Staff. A shrewd, quick-witted and precise-minded intellectual with a passion for mathematics and botany—with his mild features and pince-nez he looked like a teacher—Halder had a brilliant career as a staff officer, in which capacity he had passed more of the First War on the static western front than in the east. In the autumn of 1939, he could definitely be counted a man of the resistance; but he possessed neither the determination nor the Army following to assume Beck's mantle. He was not one to take risks, either military or political, nor was he entirely devoid of professional ambition. Whenever he contemplated practical means for ridding Germany of the evil of Hitler, Halder was confronted with the choice of having to resort either to a political *Putsch*—against which his traditionalist sense of honour and obedience as a German officer revolted; or to assassination—which his Christian conscience overruled. Here, in the dilemma of Halder, lay the essential tragedy of what was both best and most ineffective in the German resistance as a whole. So, instead of

---

* Traditionally in Germany the Chiefs of Staff at various levels occupy positions of relatively greater responsibility vis-à-vis their commanders (especially where planning is concerned) than their British or American counterparts. At the same time, the German Army was then obviously the one body physically capable of deposing Hitler.

sharper weapons, Halder—as far as *Gelb* was concerned—settled for procrastination and obstructionism.*

After war began, Halder and his like-thinking generals had been associated with various peace feelers extended to Britain, predicated upon the removal of Hitler and the restoration of the "other Germany." But the "other Germany" they contemplated was hardly the easygoing liberal Republic of Weimar; it was much more like Kaiser Wilhelm II's pre-1914 Reich. In their "peace terms," the conspirators were not even prepared to discuss Germany's disrobing herself of Austria and the Czech Sudetenland, while from Poland they required a return to the 1914 frontiers—which was asking even more than Hitler's prewar demands. So, while prepared to renounce Hitler, they were not prepared to renounce his works. As far as British acceptance was concerned, these terms were utterly unrealistic; though perhaps not domestically so unrealistic, when it came to carrying along in a *coup d'état* a German populace elated by Hitler's cheap triumphs. As it was, in the Army alone, support for the resistance was very mixed. Of the Army Group commanders, Leeb (already, unbeknown to himself, under Gestapo observation) would have gone far, but Bock and Rundstedt—though sympathetic—took the conventional line of nonpolitical involvement. At the end of October 1939, Halder had sent out his deputy, Stulpnagel,† to sound out feelings at the front, but on his return Stulpnagel warned him that the troops and junior officers would not follow any call to overthrow Hitler.

Towards the end of November, Halder, referring to the future offensive in the west, declared (according to Ulrich von Hassell): "We ought to give Hitler this last chance to deliver the German people from the slavery of English capitalism." This was a revealing remark, as symptomatic of the deep conflict in Halder's mind as it was of that existing in the German military resistance as a whole. For the more Hitler looked like winning—both before and during the war—the less ready the resistance was to resist; and inversely. Halder had no particular desire to save the Allies from humiliation; what motivated him and his fellows,

---

* One is entitled to wonder whether British or American generals placed in similar conditions would have done better.

† Later Military Governor of France, and executed for his role in the 1944 conspiracy.

both as patriotic Germans and as military men, was that Germany should not suffer the horrors of another long war, ending in defeat. For all the radical brilliance that had gone into the shaping of the new Wehrmacht, with its panzers and its Stukas, the German military "Establishment"—of which Halder and Brauchitsch were thoroughly representative—remained fundamentally conservative, its thoughts deeply conditioned by '14–'18. In spite of the Army's staggering success in Poland, its leaders could not shake off their pessimism at the prospects of war with Britain and France; as Brauchitsch had revealed in his November 5th interview with Hitler, they could never quite suppress their awe of the once-victorious French Army. Left to themselves, Brauchitsch and Halder would have played their game with the same caution as Gamelin and Georges; they were, after all, educated in the same school. This excessive professional prudence was another factor that conditioned their planning for *Gelb* in the autumn of 1939.

If Hitler had been allowed to attack, as he wished and upon the plan then offered by Halder and the OKH, in the autumn of 1939, the chances are exceedingly slim that he would have inflicted a decisive defeat on the French. A stalemate would probably have resulted, and the war might well have limped on until, as the generals feared, it brought eventual defeat to Germany. Thus, although motivated by a desire to topple Hitler, in stalling off an abortive offensive in 1939 the OKH resistance was in fact to pave the way for Hitler's greatest triumph, prolong his survival until Germany lay in ashes, and assure their own emasculation. History knows few starker ironies.

The "Manstein Plan"

Among the professional soldiers in opposition to the *Gelb* projects of 1939, however, another skein now emerges with a quite different point of departure. The details of the first OKH plan had reached Rundstedt's newly created Army Group "A" when his Chief of Staff, Manstein, passed through Zossen on October 21st. Immediately the two generals took exception to it—on purely professional and technical grounds.

Together, Rundstedt and Manstein represented the most imposing combination in the German Army; under their leadership Army Group South had formed the right, and stronger, arm of the pincer which had smashed the Polish forces in little more

than a week. In his background at least, Rundstedt was a typical
Prussian officer of the old school. There were few wars involving
Prussia in which a Rundstedt had not taken part; as early as
1745, there is record of one serving with the Hessians in Scot-
land. In 1914, Gerd von Rundstedt had been a captain on the
staff of the 22nd Reserve Division which, during the enactment of
the Schlieffen Plan, came the closest to Paris that September.
The memory of the bitter disappointment which followed after his
division had actually glimpsed the Eiffel Tower in the distance,
only to be thrown back by the French counteroffensive on the
Marne, was to wield considerable influence upon Rundstedt all
through the campaign of 1940. From 1915 onwards Rundstedt
spent the rest of the war fighting in the mobile campaigns of the
Russian front. Between 1919 and 1933, he held almost every
staff post in Seeckt's Reichswehr. On the advent of Hitler, he was
commanding the key First Army Group in Berlin, which high
post he held for six years. At the end of 1938 (having already
applied to retire several times) he left the Army as a colonel
general to live in a rented apartment in Cassel. In 1939—like
Hindenburg and Pétain before him—he was recalled to service,
then rising sixty-four.

As a special tribute, Rundstedt on his retirement had been
made honorary Colonel of the 18th Infantry Regiment, which he
had once commanded, and during the war he always preferred to
wear the simple jacket of a regimental commander rather than a
field marshal's regalia. Frequently young officers mistook him for
a colonel. With his hair parted down the centre and a heavy jowl
even as a young man, Rundstedt's face reveals no outstanding
intelligence. But in the Army he had a deserved reputation for
being the most gifted of all the senior commanders. Despite his
age, he was resourceful and flexible. He knew how to profit
from the advice of talented subordinates; he confined his genius
to tactical problems, while his Chief of Staff, Manstein, possessed
a much wider vision on the overall conduct of war. Rundstedt
also enjoyed deep respect throughout the officer corps, and would
have made an ideal leader of the resistance; his moral principles
on the waging of war were of the highest, and he was one of the
few senior Wehrmacht commanders against whom there was
never to be any taint of war crimes. But, like a true Prussian
officer, however much he may have despised Hitler he eschewed

political involvement, just as he regarded higher strategy to be no concern of his.

Erich von Manstein, promoted lieutenant general shortly before the war, was just twelve years younger than Rundstedt. His father was an army officer of Polish-German origin, named Lewinski, but Erich had been adopted as a child by a family friend and brother officer, whose name of Manstein he subsequently assumed. Commissioned into a Prussian regiment of Foot Guards in 1906, Manstein had served as a staff captain on General von Gallwitz's group attacking on the left bank of the Meuse throughout much of the worst fighting at Verdun. The conclusions Manstein had formed from this appallingly futile struggle were directly opposed to those of his French contemporaries defending Verdun: attrition resulting from the old-style, direct, frontal attack was no way to win a war. In 1935, then a colonel, Manstein became Army Chief of Operations, under General Beck. But, extremely outspoken and with one of those minds which any army finds uncomfortably brilliant, during the military purge of 1938 Manstein—although he was not one of those hostile to Hitler*—was dispatched to command a division. It was only with considerable difficulty that Rundstedt could bring him back onto the General Staff. The beaky nose which dominated his features, the heavily arched eyebrows and penetrating eyes, gave Manstein something of the look of an eagle or a hawk. A harsh disciplinarian,† icy and unbending, he was a leader who commanded respect rather than love. Like Guderian's, Manstein's interests were purely professional, and this formed the basis of his loyalty to Hitler. Guderian, seldom lavish with praise for others, regarded Manstein as "our finest operational brain"; and as the war was to bring him one higher post after another, Manstein indeed proved himself Germany's ablest commander of large bodies of troops, besides being her outstanding strategic thinker. In fact, History

---

* Typical of Manstein's attitude to Hitler was his response in 1942, as a field marshal commanding an army in southern Russia, to an overture from the resistance; he would join in a coup against Hitler, he said, *provided* he were first allowed to capture Sebastopol.

† After the war, Manstein was tried on various war crimes charges. He was acquitted on the most serious, but sentenced to eighteen years' imprisonment (reduced to twelve), partly because he rigidly refused to enter any plea of "mitigating circumstances."

is almost certain to rate him one of the great generals of the twentieth century.

On examining the OKH "Deployment Directive *Yellow*" of October 19th, Manstein's reaction was that, at best, it could only lead to a partial success. Unlike General von Leeb, he was not deeply concerned by the fate of Belgium, but he did believe that if Germany were to breach her neutrality for a second time in a generation, it was worth doing only if it aimed at a totally *decisive* victory. Accordingly, he sat down to draft the first of six memoranda to the OKH. In it he expressed the view that success of the whole operation would lie in "defeating and *annihilating* the *whole* of the enemy forces fighting in Belgium, or north of the Somme, and not only throwing them back frontally." With this aim, the *Schwerpunkt* of the offensive must be shifted farther to the south, with its axis running from Namur through a line from Arras to Boulogne, so that the Allied wing in Belgium would not simply be rolled back to the Somme, "but cut off on the Somme." At the same time, the left flank of the German thrust must be strong enough to ward off any powerful French counterthrust coming up at it from the southwest.* Manstein concluded that he did not expect the Allies to "make the mistake of throwing too strong forces into Belgium on their northern flank" (which in fact, as has already been seen, was precisely the direction in which Gamelin's plans were heading); but if they did, the prospects for Germany of a "great success" would be just that much better.

In its initial shape, the Manstein Plan still allocated the *Schwerpunkt* to Bock's rival Army Group "B" in the north. It gave no specific details as to the employment of the panzers; it offered no comment on the timing of the offensive; nor did it mention the magic names of Sedan and the Ardennes, as did Hitler's "new idea" of October 31st. On the other hand, Manstein was putting forward a much more precise formula. And, in his proposition to "cut off" the northern wing of the Allied armies on the Somme, there was a scheme far more ambitious than anything that had yet emerged from the mind of Hitler himself.

Rundstedt entirely supported the thinking of his Chief of Staff,

---

* This was a fear which, in May 1940, was to haunt the German planners incessantly until success was finally achieved.

and on October 31st (by sheer coincidence, only a day after Hitler had voiced his "new idea" to Jodl) the memorandum was dispatched to the OKH bearing his signature. Four days later, a visit to Rundstedt's HQ by Brauchitsch gave Manstein the opportunity to discuss his plan in person. Brauchitsch refused to countenance any alteration to the existing directive; finally, however, he let himself be coaxed into promising to Army Group "A" in the south the 2nd Panzer Division and two motorised regiments. Here began the progressive escalation of Army Group "A" at the expense of "B"* (Bock). But Brauchitsch was not to be impressed by Manstein's fears of a French threat to his left flank. "Every Army Group," commented Halder trenchantly, "expects the maximum of enemy counter-measures on its own front" and doubtless Manstein's proposals struck the OKH at first as simply a subordinate formation advancing its own parochial interest. In any case, they were sat upon at Zossen and not passed on to the OKW or Hitler, nor were the new orientations in Hitler's thoughts relayed to Army Group "A."

Meanwhile, the Führer was still pursuing his "new idea" of October 30th. On November 11th, after the second postponement of the offensive, the OKH notified Army Groups "A" and "B" that Hitler had ordered a third group of fast-moving troops to be formed on "A's" southern flank, heading for Sedan. This would be composed of Guderian's XIX Corps, consisting of two panzer and one motorised divisions. Bock at once expressed dissatisfaction at this further erosion of Army Group "B"; but still the function of the Sedan thrust was regarded as purely secondary, designed to "ease" the task of Army Group "A" (which in itself remained subordinate to that of "B"). Guderian, the panzer expert, who now enters the act for the first time, was asked for his opinion and declared that the forces for an advance on Sedan via Arlon were inadequate. On the 13th, and again on the 16th, bad weather combined with the continued reluctance of the OKH (which was undoubtedly having its effect even on Hitler) once more postponed the offensive, on the latter occasion to November 26th. On November 21st, another visit to Koblenz

---

* Under OKH directive of October 29th, Army Group "A" was allocated only 22 infantry divisions; "B" 43 divisions, including 9 panzer and 4 motorised infantry divisions. By May 10th the respective proportions had shifted to "A," 45⅓ divisions (including 7 panzer); "B" 29⅓ (including 3 panzer).

by Brauchitsch, accompanied by Halder, permitted Manstein to deliver a second memorandum. Again the OKH leaders granted it no serious discussion. At this time they had still cherished hopes that Hitler would abandon all ideas of an offensive in the west, and the injection of Manstein's views into the existing plan could only lend grist to Hitler's mill. But at the same time, there was also undoubtedly an element of professional jealousy involved in Brauchitsch's and Halder's refusal to allow their subordinate generals direct access to the Führer. Relations between Brauchitsch and Rundstedt were never noticeably good, and the cautious Halder clearly evinced resentment towards the daring genius of Manstein.

Hitler berates his generals

Two days later, an extraordinary gathering took place in the Chancellery. By now thoroughly exasperated at the OKH opposition to his designs, Hitler summoned together all his top Wehrmacht leaders down to Corps commanders and their equivalent ranks in the Luftwaffe and Navy—totalling over 180—and, treating them like so many small boys, delivered a scarifying lecture. He began with the reminder that, without the Nazi Party, the rebuilding of the Wehrmacht—through which, he did not need to point out, those present enjoyed their present distinction—could never have taken place. Although he had always been surrounded by more "doubters" than "believers," his policy of annexations had paid off; now, for the first time in sixty-seven years, while the successors of Bismarck may have missed their cues, he, Hitler, had ensured that Germany would not have to fight on more than one front. He was determined to launch a crushing offensive on this one front, and "anyone who thinks otherwise is irresponsible." Now, the moment was favourable; in six months it might not be. Waving aside the question of Belgian and Dutch neutrality, he declared that "nobody would question this if Germany were victorious." As for Britain, she would be brought to her knees by U-boat and mine warfare (details unspecified).

Turning the heat on the Army leaders, Hitler all but accused them of cowardice; *he* had not created the Wehrmacht in order not to fight. He condemned obsolete notions of chivalry, and warned that anyone who opposed his will would be "annihilated."

With a reference to Brauchitsch's luckless intervention of November 5th, he declared that he was "infuriated" by any suggestion that *his* troops had been "inadequate" in Poland. "Everything depends on the military leaders. With the German soldier, I can do anything; provided he is well led." Hitler ended his homily with a call for total determination: "If we emerge from this struggle as victors—and we shall be victors!—then our epoch will enter into the history of our people. As for me," he added prophetically, "I shall stand or fall in this struggle. I shall not survive the defeat of my people. No surrender abroad! No revolution at home!"

The generals filed away, shattered by this tirade. Brauchitsch tendered his resignation. Hitler rejected it, saying that Brauchitsch had his duty to fulfil, like every simple soldier. Later Guderian, detailed off by Reichenau—one of the most steadfast of the pro-Hitler generals—went to see Hitler and voiced the "indignation" the army commanders felt at their leader's distrust. Hitler replied that he was principally getting at the C-in-C of the Army. In that case, said Guderian with some audacity, Brauchitsch should be replaced, and he went on to name some possible successors. But Hitler approved of none of these, and the interview ended inconclusively. The net effect of Hitler's taunting insults upon the generals, however, was largely to galvanise them into much more enthusiastic support of the Führer. "The reproach of cowardice turned the brave into cowards," scathingly remarked Colonel Hans Oster, a dedicated member of the military resistance. From now on the OKH opposition to *Gelb* waned steadily; at the same time, its past hesitancy had made its mark on Hitler, who now seemed rather less determined upon a winter offensive than he had been in October—despite his exhortations of November 23rd. The only one of the three main participants in the *Gelb* Plan who remained obdurate was Manstein.

In the latter half of November, Manstein invited Guderian to visit him at Koblenz, where he questioned the panzer expert as to whether it would be technically feasible to push heavy armoured forces across the Ardennes, towards Sedan. Guderian, who knew the area from the First War, reassured Manstein, with one proviso: the panzer divisions deployed there must be made as strong as possible. This was an important conversation, insofar as Manstein was first and foremost an infantryman and had hitherto given little precise thought as to use of the panzers;* nevertheless, as late as December 18th, he shows himself still thinking in terms of allocating seven panzer divisions to Army Group "B" and only three† to "A," crossing the Meuse south of Dinant. On November 30th, a third memorandum from Manstein forced Halder, for the first time, to pass some written judgement. It was noncommittal and evasive, saying that the OKH did not want to decide upon where the critical *Schwerpunkt* should lie until the first encounter with the enemy. Manstein promptly followed up with two more memoranda during December. His fourth, dated December 6th, for the first time came down categorically in favour of the *Schwerpunkt* being located on the southern flank of the attack; i.e., with Army Group "A," heading for the mouth of the Somme. By this time, Halder had had enough and decided to transfer Manstein (already earmarked to command a corps) to Stettin in the east, about as far away from Army Group "A" and the western front as possible!

Gelb *postponed*

During December, the vile conditions of snow, ice and fog which were demoralising the French Army caused four more postponements of *Gelb*. No new strategic alterations to the plan were proposed by either the OKH or Hitler, still kept unaware of Manstein's ideas. On the 28th, Hitler told Jodl that if the weather continued bad by mid-January, he would call off the offensive, perhaps until the spring. Nevertheless, on January 10th, after a period of bright, clear skies had been predicted, D Day was finally fixed for Wednesday, the 17th, at dawn. The troops began to roll, over 60 divisions strong, towards the Dutch and Belgian frontiers, the weight of both armour and infantry still preponderantly with Bock's Army Group "B" in the north. Then, that same day, the two Luftwaffe majors made their forced landing at Mechelen. At 11:45 on the 11th, Jodl braced himself to inform Hitler. Hitler flew into a terrible rage. Threats of death sentences for the flyers were uttered; the Gestapo was dispatched to interrogate their wives; General Felmy, commanding the Second Air Fleet to which Reinberger and Hoenmanns both belonged, was sacked, and re-

---

* Guderian later went so far as to claim he had provided the original inspiration for the Manstein Plan.

† Of which one was still rated only as a "light" division.

placed by Kesselring.* The German Military Attaché in The
Hague, Lieutenant General Wenniger, rushed down to interview
the interned majors and find out just how much information the
Belgians might have gleaned. Jodl wrote nervously in his diary:
"If the enemy is in possession of all the files the situation is cata-
strophic." On the afternoon of the 12th, Wenniger wired Berlin:

REINBERGER DECLARES POST BURNED.† REMAINS OF LITTLE IM-
PORTANCE.

The half-burnt papers from Reinberger's briefcase did, in fact,
betray scarcely more than the bare outlines of the operation, but
the Germans could never be quite sure. For one more day, Hitler
refused to abandon the attack. Then, yet again, the weather broke,
causing another three postponements. By the 16th, alarming reports were coming in about the extent of Dutch and Belgian mobilisation. At last, Hitler took a major decision. That afternoon
he ordered an indefinite postponement of *Gelb*. The whole operation must be replanned "on a new basis, particularly to be founded
on secrecy and surprise." This new act of chance finally saved Hitler from what might have been the grave blunder of a premature
offensive, and led him conclusively towards his finest hour.‡

For the Germans, the Mechelen Incident proved to be pure
gain. First of all, the High Command could now re-examine its
strategy at leisure and try out variations on the ground by means
of "war games." Hitler's new priorities of "secrecy and surprise"
lent added importance to the speed with which the all-out blow
should be struck. At a meeting in the Chancellery on January
20th, it was agreed to abandon the previous build-up of several
days; instead, all units would have to be ready to attack with
twenty-four hours' warning, or less. The enemy reaction to the
mid-January alarm now also gave the OKH Intelligence, "Foreign

---

* His Chief of Staff, Colonel Kammhuber, was similarly disgraced. After the war
he rejoined the new Federal German Luftwaffe and subsequently became its Inspector General.

† Reinberger was repatriated from Canada as a POW in 1944; Germany capitulated before a case against him could be heard.

‡ There is a certain historic irony about the role bad weather played in Hitler's
plans for 1940. In February 1916, the delay of a week which it imposed on the
Crown Prince's initial attack on Verdun probably saved the French from disaster;
in 1940, it was Hitler who was saved.

Armies West,* an excellent idea of the Allied order of battle and their intentions, which it did not possess before. As the French and British units rushed forward to take up their positions on the Belgian frontier in the middle of January, it was clear to the Germans that, under Gamelin's Dyle Plan, the cream of both armies was designated to be pushed into northern Belgium; and lower down, the weakness of General Corap's Ninth Army on the Meuse became increasingly apparent. As knowledge of the Franco-British dispositions made the prospects of a frontal collision less and less attractive, Manstein's alternative, which would in effect close a trap behind the elite of the enemy forces, obviously gained in appeal. Finally, it was the Mechelen Incident's revelation of apparent German intentions towards Holland that committed Gamelin, irrevocably and disastrously, to his project of strengthening his northern wing still further by the Breda Variant, thus adding his best reserves to the "bag" that Manstein was proposing to cut off on the Somme.

But Halder still held out against the persistent Manstein. On January 12th, the day after the news of the Mechelen Incident reached Hitler, Rundstedt signed Manstein's sixth and last memorandum, summing up all that had gone before, and forwarded it to Zossen with the express request that it be submitted to Hitler. Once again, Army Group "A" was told—rather tartly—to mind its own business, and Rundstedt's request was turned down. On the 25th, Brauchitsch visited Koblenz and in what must have been by now a chilly atmosphere Manstein accused the Army C-in-C point-blank of not aiming for a "full decision" in the west, and referred to the "well-known negative attitude of the OKH" to the offensive in general. He sharply criticised the OKH opportunist intention of leaving the *Schwerpunkt* question open until it had been seen which way the Allied cat would jump, citing Moltke's maxim that "mistakes in the initial deployment cannot be repaired." Two days later, Manstein was shattered to receive his posting to Stettin. It seemed that he had lost the battle.

---

* According to its chief, General Liss, this branch of OKH Intelligence had been divided on the following arbitrary basis: "countries who wear their shirts inside their trousers belong to the West, and those who wear their shirts outside, to the East."

Hitler backs Manstein

Then, on February 7th, just two days before Manstein was due to depart for his new command, Army Group "A" held its first "war game." Halder was clearly impressed by what he saw, and for the first time he showed himself veering towards Manstein's thinking. On leaving Koblenz, he at last agreed to one of the points demanded by Manstein; namely, that the Meuse crossing at Sedan by Guderian's XIX Panzer Corps be simultaneously supported by the XIV Motorised Corps. Here was yet a further step in the escalation of Army Group "A." Manstein left for Stettin with at least some satisfaction. Bock uttered another growl of displeasure. On the 14th, the war games were continued—this time in Manstein's absence—at Mayen near Koblenz. Now an important and lively disagreement took place between Guderian and Halder. Guderian wanted to push his panzers across the Meuse on the fifth day of the attack. True to the doctrines of *Achtung —Panzer!*, he conceived the armoured blow as being "concentrated and applied with surprise on the decisive point, to form the arrowhead so deep that we need have no worry about the flank." With some asperity, Halder condemned this as "senseless"; it would be impossible to mount a "stage by stage" attack across the Meuse until the infantry divisions arrived, and this could not be before the *ninth* day.* Rundstedt, no longer supported by Manstein, now took Halder's side. The games ended with this point unsettled. But, if nothing else, they had proved one other aspect; this was the extreme sensitivity of the area around Sedan for the "Red" or defending side.

Now there occurred the last of the elements of chance which were to shape the course of *Gelb*.

Shortly before Manstein's departure, Hitler's chief adjutant, Colonel Schmundt, happened to be on a tour of the front and called in at Rundstedt's HQ. Here he had a prolonged conversation with Manstein, who revealed his plan at length. This was the first Schmundt had heard of it, and he was amazed how closely it paralleled Hitler's own thoughts, though in a "significantly

---

* Just how akin Halder's First War thinking was to his French opposite numbers is revealed by the fact that Gamelin in his appreciation of German capabilities was also to reckon that the Germans could not cross the Meuse before the ninth day.

more precise form." Back in Berlin on February 2nd, he immediately told Hitler of the conversation. Though not hiding his personal aversion to Manstein,* Hitler expressed the keenest interest; Manstein must be brought before him, but how could this be done without arousing the suspicions of the OKH? Talking to Schmundt later, Lieutenant Colonel Heusinger† of the OKH operations branch, who was a warm supporter of the Manstein Plan, suggested that he should be summoned along with the four other newly appointed Corps commanders to "kiss hands" with the Supreme Commander. So, on February 17th, a fateful working breakfast took place at the Chancellery. Manstein remained until 2 P.M. pouring forth every detail of the plan he had so long been ruminating. Hitler listened raptly. The next day Brauchitsch and Halder were ordered to the Chancellery. Hitler put the Manstein Plan to them, producing it as his own homework, with no attribution to its author. The OKH leaders showed that they had in the meantime swung round towards it still further—perhaps, seeing which way the wind was now blowing, they were also anxious to avoid a repetition of the painful tirades of November. With a new spring in their step, they returned to Zossen to draft an entirely revised directive. A mood of fresh confidence replaced earlier doubts. Hitler having been navigated safely past the shoals of a winter campaign, and the Army reorganised from the war in Poland, the new design now presented to Halder's keenly professional mind a prospect of great military success. Thoughts of deposing Hitler receded. Henceforth, until the plan actually went into action, the OKH, Hitler, Rundstedt and the other front commanders are to be found all pulling together with the superbly smooth efficiency of the German military machine at its best.

Sichelschnitt

By February 24th, the new directive was ready. As it emerged from the cautious pen of Halder, it represented an even more drastic revision of *Gelb* than anything proposed by Manstein. The disputed question of the *Schwerpunkt* had been resolved; it would lie, from the very start, on the front of Army Group "A." The

---

* Based on some suspicion that Manstein (ex-Lewinski) had Jewish blood?

† In 1956 he became the first Inspector General of Federal Germany's postwar Bundeswehr.

role of Bock's Army Group "B" was now relegated, in the admirable simile of Liddell Hart, to that of "a matador's cloak," which would draw Gamelin into Holland and northern Belgium, while Rundstedt was striking the lethal sword blow elsewhere. The operation of the original Schlieffen Plan in 1914 has been compared (again by Liddell Hart) to that of a revolving door; the harder the French armies pressed in Lorraine, the more forcefully the door was intended to rotate against their back with the German push swinging round through Belgium in the north. *Sichelschnitt* ("the cut of the sickle," as the OKH's new plan was admirably christened) also functioned like a revolving door; but this time the rotation was clockwise, with the French "pushing" in the north, the Germans in the south. Bock's forces had been whittled down from his original 43 divisions to 29⅓; from disposing over all the panzer divisions, he was left with only three, and two of these would be earmarked for eventual transfer to Rundstedt. Nonetheless, Bock's role remained of utmost importance. Though substantially weaker than the numerical sum of the forces likely to be met in Holland and northern Belgium, Bock had to engage the Allied "bull" so vigorously that it would be unable to break away in order to gore the flank of Rundstedt's thrust.

Reading from north to south, the German line-up would be as follows: Army Group "B," consisting of Küchler's Eighteenth Army (opposite Holland), and Reichenau's Sixth Army; Army Group "A," with its northern boundary running south of Liège, consisting of Kluge's Fourth Army (which, transferred from Bock to Rundstedt, now brought Army Group "A" strength up 45⅓ divisions), List's Twelfth Army and Busch's Sixteenth Army; Army Group "C" (Leeb), running from Luxembourg to the Swiss frontier and consisting of the First and Seventh Armies. The seven panzer divisions handed to Rundstedt were all to be concentrated from the start (per *Achtung—Panzer!*) to break through the rugged Ardennes country of Luxembourg and southern Belgium —which the French High Command had so long considered "impenetrable." In a solid steel phalanx, 45 miles wide, they would breach the Meuse between Dinant and Sedan.

The main effort—no longer just a subsidiary thrust—would be made at Sedan, by Guderian's XIX Panzer Corps consisting of the 1st, 2nd* and 10th Panzer Divisions, aided by Hitler's elite SS Grossdeutschland Regiment of motorised infantry, and backed up by Wietersheim's XIV Motorised Corps. Further north, the 6th and 8th Panzers of Reinhardt's Corps were to head for Monthermé, while the 5th and 7th Panzers of Hoth's Corps were to provide flank cover by crossing the Meuse at Dinant. The five panzer divisions of Guderian and Reinhardt comprising the main effort were welded together under command of an integrated Armoured Group. There was some argument as to who should command this; both Guderian and Manstein were passed over (fortunately for Britain, because if either had received the key command there would most probably have been no evacuation from Dunkirk), and finally the choice fell upon General Ewald von Kleist. A conservative-minded cavalry general, Kleist had been retired at the time of the Fritsch-Blomberg purge but brought back to command a corps in the Polish campaign. Though his corps had included one panzer division, according to Guderian (who certainly did not welcome the thought of Kleist sitting on top of him) Kleist had never "shown himself particularly well disposed to the armoured force." His appointment, however, was an important success for Halder, who, always suffering some nervousness about the audacity of the new plan, reckoned that in the conservative Kleist he had a man whom he could keep on a tight rein.

At Hitler's particular instance, a major reshuffle which would make an essential contribution to the success of *Sichelschnitt* was ordained within the panzers themselves. Most of the heavier, cannon-bearing Mark III and IV tanks were to be withdrawn from Küchler's Eighteenth Army facing Holland, where they would hardly be needed, and given to Kleist and Rundstedt, who would find their guns indispensable for silencing bunkers that defended the Meuse crossing areas. Also incorporated in the new plan were various "special operations" that had been hobbyhorses of Hitler from the earliest days of *Gelb;*† these included parachute and glider operations to capture key bridges and forts

---

* Commanded by Guderian himself in the early prewar days.

† In the course of its evolution Hitler had frequently cried out at the lack of imagination his generals showed whenever the issue of "special ops" arose. "These generals are too correct. . . . No tricks ever occur to them!" This was at least one common factor which Hitler as a military mind shared with Winston Churchill.

on the Dutch and Belgian canal defence systems, as well as communications centres lying on the route of Kleist's approach march through the Ardennes. Hitler occupied himself down to the last detail with the planning of these "special operations"; as will be seen, the use of "Brandenburger" commandos wearing Dutch uniforms particularly appealed to him.

Meanwhile, *Sichelschnitt* was to be accompanied by elaborate "deception" schemes designed to keep the French constantly in fear that the *real*—or, at least, a serious secondary—attack would come from Leeb's Army Group "C" which faced the Maginot Line. In fact, Army Group "C," containing only 19 infantry divisions of moderate value, was to play no aggressive role in the coming battle. The mighty Maginot Line upon which France had spent so much of her substance would be accorded no opportunity to cover itself with battle honours. On the other hand, if it fell for Hitler's deception plan, the French High Command—it was hoped—would be hesitant to risk withdrawing from the Maginot Line the "interval troops," which constituted such a large portion of disposable reserves, for use against the Sedan breakthrough. Thus were both Leeb and Bock to act as foils for Rundstedt.

There remained some doubts and misgivings about the new plan. As late as April, Bock—possibly still smarting from the dilution of his command—was grumbling to Halder: "You will be creeping by 10 miles from the Maginot Line with the flank of your breakthrough and hope that the French will watch inertly! You are cramming the mass of the tank units together into the sparse roads of the Ardennes mountain country, as if there were no such thing as airpower! And," added Bock, "you then hope to be able to lead an operation as far as the coast with an open southern flank 200 miles long, where stands the mass of the French Army!" It was, he declared, "transcending the frontiers of reason." Rundstedt too, deprived of the reassuring presence of Manstein, continued to worry about that "open southern flank," deducing that it must be along the axis Paris–Châlons-sur-Marne–Verdun that Gamelin would logically mass his strongest reserves. His new Chief of Staff, Sodenstern, had his own doubts about the hideous traffic tangle that might ensue from the vehicles of seven panzer divisions all converging on the Ardennes. Even Guderian was seen to be having some second thoughts about whether his corps alone

GERMAN ORDER OF BATTLE — May 10, 1940

With names of commanders principally concerned

OKW
Commander-in-Chief
HITLER
(Chief of Staff: Keitel)

OKL
(Luftwaffe)

OKH
Commander-in-Chief
BRAUCHITSCH
(Chief of Staff: Halder)

ARMY GROUP "B"
(Bock)
(29 Divs. inc. 3 Panzers)

ARMY GROUP "A"
(Rundstedt)
(45 Divs. inc. 7 Panzers)

EIGHTEENTH ARMY
(Küchler)

SIXTH ARMY
(Reichenau)

FOURTH ARMY
(Kluge)
(14 Divisions)

TWELFTH ARMY
(List)
(19 Divisions)

RESERVES
42 Infantry Divisions

XV PANZER CORPS
(Hoth)

XLI PANZER CORPS
(Reinhardt)

5th PANZER
(Hartlieb)
(324 tanks)

7th PANZER
(Rommel)
(218 tanks)

6th PANZER
(Kempf)
(218 tanks)

8th PANZER
(Kuntzen)
(218 tanks)

Units reading from north (left) to south (right)

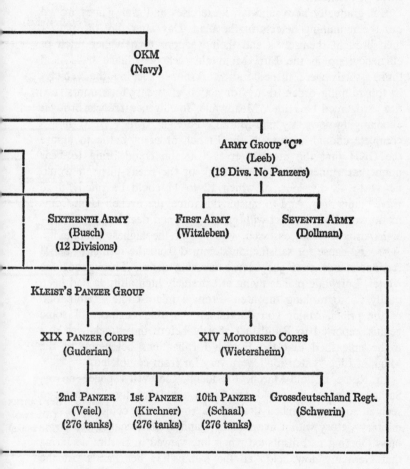

OKM
(Navy)

ARMY GROUP "C"
(Leeb)
(19 Divs. No Panzers)

SIXTEENTH ARMY
(Busch)
(12 Divisions)

FIRST ARMY
(Witzleben)

SEVENTH ARMY
(Dollman)

KLEIST'S PANZER GROUP

XIX PANZER CORPS
(Guderian)

XIV MOTORISED CORPS
(Wietersheim)

2nd PANZER
(Veiel)
(276 tanks)

1st PANZER
(Kirchner)
(276 tanks)

10th PANZER
(Schaal)
(276 tanks)

Grossdeutschland Regt.
(Schwerin)

could force the Meuse at Sedan. Halder, right to the end, harboured doubts as to whether the troops would be capable of executing this plan which called for the utmost skill and endurance; the deficiencies shown in the Polish campaign still worried him, and even by the spring of 1940 only a portion of the Army seemed to him to be up to standard, in spirit, training or equipment, and all these elite units would be committed into the first wave of the attack.

But gradually new sand-table exercises and war games ironed out the remaining defects in the plan. Day after day the panzer men brought themselves and their weapons to a higher pitch of efficiency; up in the Eifel Mountains schools, dance halls, and timber sheds were turned into workshops, keeping the vehicles in top running order, ready for action at twenty-four hours' notice as decreed by Hitler. Meanwhile, Intelligence reports brought encouraging news. By mid-March, "Foreign Armies West" had a complete enough picture of the French order of battle to assure the OKH that the most reserves Gamelin could bring to bear upon that vulnerable southern flank of the break-through would be 41 to 48 divisions, of which 12 to 17 could be rated "third wave" units only. And to muster this force, the French High Command would have to act with great speed and decision; this, "Foreign Armies West" assessed, was not of the highest probability. A second cause for satisfaction stemmed from the results of aerial reconnaissance over the Meuse crossing zones. Throughout the winter, Luftwaffe planes flying at extremely high altitude had been busily photographing the area. From a microscopic examination of the prints, Major von Stiotta, an Austrian engineer of some genius, reported to Rundstedt shortly before the attack was due to be unleashed that the French fortifications belonging to the Maginot Line "extension" were very far from completed.

In Rome in mid-March, President Roosevelt's peace envoy, Sumner Welles, was told by Ciano that recently "Ribbentrop seemed to be convinced that the German army could achieve a military victory within five months," and Welles recalled the cockiness Goering had displayed when interviewed in Berlin, declaring that Germany now held "all the trumps" in her hands. At the beginning of April, Halder's diary reveals a new note of confident enthusiasm, while later in the month General Fromm, commanding the Reserve Army, was heard to prophesy: "We shall push through Holland and Belgium at one stroke, and finish off France in fourteen days." It was not least a growing awareness of the real beauty of *Sichelschnitt* as a strategy of war that lay at the root of this self-assurance. As subsequent events were to prove, *Sichelschnitt* was one of the most inspired blueprints for victory that the military mind has ever conceived.* In its final state, it could no longer be rated as the brain child of any one person; without the drive and instinctive ideas of Hitler, and without Manstein's brilliant strategic conception, the OKH would never have contemplated a knockout blow against France. Yet, without Halder and the OKH, Hitler would probably have launched a half-cocked offensive in 1939, and it was finally Halder's organisational excellence, his ability to digest and apply technical advice, and his meticulous care that brought *Sichelschnitt* to its ultimate perfection.

But, in fact, *Sichelschnitt* was not quite perfect. If it had been, it would have won not just the Battle of France, but the whole war. Tactically perfect, strategically almost perfect; yet as an instrument of higher policy it possessed one fatal flaw. In mid-March Hitler was questioning Guderian on his plans for establishing a bridgehead across the Meuse at Sedan on the fifth day of the attack:

"And then what are you going to do?" He was the first person who had thought to ask me this vital question [Guderian recalls]. I replied: "Unless I receive orders to the contrary, I intend on the next day to continue my advance westwards. The supreme leadership must decide whether my objective is to be Amiens or Paris. In my opinion the correct course is to drive past Amiens to the English Channel." Hitler nodded and said nothing more. Only General Busch, who commanded the Sixteenth Army on my left, cried out: "Well, I don't think you'll cross the river in the first place!"

---

* Even its framers seem to have been partially unconscious of the inherent beauty of *Sichelschnitt,* as it developed; for instance, to the French High Command, when Rundstedt broke through at Sedan his ultimate objective might well have been one of three almost equally attractive ones: to swing left and roll up the Maginot Line from behind, to continue straight on and seize Paris, or to swing right and head for the Channel—as in fact the plan intended. Faced with this choice, any High Command would be like a greyhound having to make a decision on three equidistant rabbits.

The western front from Holland to Switzerland

Guderian adds revealingly: "I never received any further orders as to what to do once the bridgehead over the Meuse was captured." This reluctance of the German High Command actually to name the Channel as its ultimate objective was typical of the nagging fears provoked by the audacity of *Sichelschnitt,* which, with memories of the brilliance of the French Army of the Marne still persisting, could never quite be suppressed. Most of the energy that the OKH had lavished upon *Sichelschnitt* had been absorbed in planning the actual break-through, and but little on its immediate aftermath. Furthermore, the contingency that *Sichelschnitt* would lead to a *total* victory over France seemed so remote that, beyond the operation itself, no thought whatsoever had been given to how a knockout blow might then be administered to Britain. The vanquishing of France in one swift offensive remained altogether too startling a prospect for the First War minds of Halder and Co.; and even Hitler's inspirational vision for once failed him. Just three days before the great attack began, Hitler had an interview with Admiral Raeder, his naval chief; but neither *Sichelschnitt* nor any possible follow-up invasion of Britain was ever mentioned. All Hitler could think of was the mighty engagement by land that lay ahead.

Herein lay the Achilles heel of *Sichelschnitt,* and the seeds of Hitler's defeat.

By mid-March, 1940, *Sichelschnitt* and its dependent forces had already reached the necessary state of readiness. Everyone expected Hitler to press the button in a matter of days. But his attention was temporarily distracted elsewhere. Despite the capitulation of Finland and the collapse of their crazy schemes of intervention, the Allies were still showing a disquieting interest in Narvik and the Swedish iron ore fields. To forestall them, Hitler decided that—while the Allies dithered—he would strike in Norway first.

8

Towards the Brink

Easy training, hard combat; hard training, easy combat.
—SUVOROV

All conditions are more calculable, all obstacles more surmountable, than those of human resistance.
—B. H. LIDDELL HART, *The Strategy of Indirect Approach*

Disaster in Norway

ON DECEMBER 14th, concern about the course of the Russo-Finnish War had caused Hitler to instruct the High Command to prepare preliminary studies for an invasion of Norway. His preoccupation with *Gelb* kept thoughts of any such project well in the background until, on February 16th, the Royal Navy boarded within Norwegian territorial waters a German ship called the *Altmark,* liberating a large number of British seamen taken off ships which the *Graf Spee* had sunk. Three days later, Hitler —enraged by this *coup de main* and alarmed by Allied interest in Norway—ordered the speeding up of plans for *Weserübung* ("Exercise Weser"), the code name for the occupation of Denmark and Norway. On March 1st, he signed the directive for *Weserübung* but for two days could not make up his mind whether it should come before or after *Sichelschnitt.* Then, upon the advice of Jodl* that the two operations should be kept entirely independent of each other, Hitler decided that the Norwegian operation should be implemented first, and he began to cast around for

---

* Brauchitsch and Halder were not even consulted on *Weserübung* until the last moment, Hitler possibly anticipating the objections which the OKH would raise to this new adventure, which was even more risky than *Sichelschnitt.*

a suitable pretext for violating the neutrality of two more countries. All this resulted in further delay to *Sichelschnitt*.

Meanwhile, after months of argument, Churchill at a meeting of the Allied Supreme War Council on March 28th finally persuaded Chamberlain to permit the Royal Navy to mine the Leads, the Norwegian coastal waters along which flowed the Swedish iron ore destined for Hitler's war plants. Warning of this breach of neutrality was to be transmitted to Norway and Sweden on April 5th. By now the advent of spring had brought a new (and quite misplaced) cockiness to the men and mouthpieces of British public life. On April 4th, Chamberlain made his famous speech informing the Conservative Party that Hitler had "missed the bus"; and on the same day it reported his speech, the *Daily Express* published an interview with the CIGS, under the headline "COME ON HITLER! DARES IRONSIDE!", in which Ironside was quoted as having said, "We would welcome a go at him. Frankly we would welcome an attack. We are sure of ourselves." But while Chamberlain and Ironside were speaking, the first of some 10,000 German troops were already "embussed" for Norway, concealed aboard merchant ships and colliers, in what was to be one of the most daring strokes of the war.

On April 9th, Denmark was seized almost without a shot being fired. In five separate groups, the Germans landed in Norway at Oslo, Kristiansand, Bergen, Trondheim, and Narvik. Airborne forces seized the key airfields at Oslo and Stavanger. The Norwegians fought back courageously, though ill-prepared and surprised. The Allies, in spite of having had months in which to think about the problem, were equally taken by surprise. In Paris, the secretary of the newly created War Cabinet, Paul Baudouin, recalled that "for five minutes the Prime Minister and I vainly sought on the coasts of Norway for another Narvik, for we were sure that the Narvik where the German troops had been reported could not be the iron-ore port in the north"—1,000 miles removed from any German base. British submarines watched the German troopships creeping across the Skagerrak, but it was not until the afternoon of the 9th that they received orders to torpedo them, by which time it was too late. The fact was that the Allies, with arrogant confidence in the supremacy of the Royal Navy, had never believed that Hitler with his tiny naval forces could conceivably launch an amphibious operation of this scope. Leisurely and confusedly, they reacted. Between April 10th and 13th, the British scored a heartening naval victory by sinking all ten German destroyers covering the Narvik landings; but they carried with them no ground troops with which to follow up. It was the story of Gallipoli and Suvla Bay all over again. Further south, off Bergen, a three-hour air attack by Luftwaffe bombers on the 10th sank a destroyer and hit the battleship *Rodney* with a dud bomb. Modest as these results were, they had the critical effect of persuading the C-in-C Home Fleet, Admiral Sir Charles Forbes, to turn back out to sea. It was the first time in war that ground-based aircraft had proved their ascendancy over capital surface ships.

At Rosyth, four British battalions already earmarked for a Norwegian adventure were embarked, disembarked, then re-embarked, losing in the process much of their stores and departing almost without artillery or tanks. The first British contingent arrived at Narvik on April 15th; then between the 16th and 18th other feeble forces landed at Namsos and Andalsnes, on either side of Trondheim in central Norway, in hopes of cutting off the German bridgehead there. On the 19th, ten days after the Germans had landed, the first French troops arrived; but, according to Paul Reynaud, "they were completely incapable of moving off or offering any action whatsoever. Their artillery, tanks, antiaircraft guns, their mules and even their skis and snowshoes had remained in the auxiliary cruiser *Ville d'Alger*, which had not been able to enter the harbour because of her length—a detail which had been forgotten." By now, using 350 Ju–52 transport planes, the Luftwaffe had thoroughly established itself in central and southern Norway, and here the Stukas rendered the Allied expeditionary forces quite helpless. This extreme mobility of German airpower was a depressing foretaste of what was to come, in France, a month later.

By May 3rd, the British had been forced to evacuate all their troops from central Norway. Narvik remained the Allies' only toehold, and indeed here things went badly against the Germans; only the exigencies of the war in France were to save General Dietl and his 2,000 mountain troops from being wiped out.

In his Norwegian gamble, Hitler lost ten out of his twenty destroyers, three out of eight cruisers. Thus on a side show with no decisive bearing upon the war, he had squandered his navy without which (even had he prepared any such strategy) an invasion of the British Isles in 1940 would be utterly out of the question. This, for the Allies, was the one net gain from an operation that was otherwise an unrelieved saga of British professional incompetence and halfheartedness; "frivolous dilettantism" was Hitler's scornful verdict. Here, as at Gallipoli in 1915 (not to mention Suez in 1956), Britain failed at just the kind of operation for which both her history and her geography should have best prepared her.* Worst of all, Norway was a flagrant defeat of British seapower. Its repercussions upon the forthcoming campaign in France also deserve serious consideration; first, there was the impact that defeat in Norway had upon the already impaired morale of France; and, secondly, there were its stimulating effects upon German leadership.

In Berlin the news of Hitler's Scandinavian move was electrifying. Reactions in France were even more powerful. They were admirably summed up by a lieutenant accompanying André Maurois on a visit to General Corap's fated Ninth Army: "It's a bad business that our first enterprise in this war met with failure. A young horse must never be defeated in his trial runs. If he is, he gets the habit, loses his self-respect and comes to consider it perfectly natural that he should stay behind." Frivolously, Paris society affected satisfaction at Britain's discomfiture. Everything the caustic Ferdonnet broadcast from Stuttgart about *les sales anglais* seemed to be true. But in the Army there was the deepest apprehension; if Hitler could worst Britain in her own element, where the Royal Navy was supposedly supreme, how could the French Army stop him on land, where the odds were by no means so favourable? Was there, in fact, no stopping this apparently invincible demon? Morale descended yet another few pegs.

Unknown to the Allies, however, for all the feebleness of their counterefforts, Norway was in fact a much closer run thing than it had seemed. Hitler had been significantly shaken by the few reverses suffered there. There were two periods of what Jodl in his diary describes as "leadership chaos": from April 14th to 18th,

---

* An intriguing field of speculation opens up if one considers what *might* have happened if—in both World Wars—Britain had remained true to her amphibious traditions and maintained the bulk of her army as a truly mobile expeditionary force instead of committing it inextricably to the line in France. Certainly, in World War II, the presence or absence of the few BEF divisions in France was to have little influence in events there; whereas, properly organised, they undoubtedly could have inflicted a signal defeat on Hitler in Norway.

concerning Narvik, and until the 23rd over Trondheim. Narvik threw Hitler into a complete panic, and he actually ordered Dietl to surrender; the signal was, however, suppressed by a courageous staff officer on the OKW. Trouble with the airborne landings in Norway had made Goering and his staff extremely nervous about the operations projected for Holland; while so large a portion of Luftwaffe strength (especially in the indispensable Ju–52 transports) had been committed to Norway that even a moderate increase in the British air effort there might well have made a considerable inroad in the air support for *Sichelschnitt:* But the most important factor was psychological. Whatever the results in Norway, they would have been unlikely to halt *Sichelschnitt;* on the other hand, the panic Hitler showed over Narvik entitles one to conclude that one or two harder knocks would most probably have persuaded both him and his generals to greater caution when it came to France. And nothing would have been more likely to spell ruin to *Sichelschnitt* than excessive caution or bad nerves.

As it was, by April 24th the situation had improved so much that Hitler could now once again turn his eyes back to the west. On May 1st, more good news prompted him to order that steps be taken so that *Sichelschnitt* could be launched at twenty-four hours' notice at any time from May 4th.

Crises in France and Britain

If Norway gave the German generals renewed confidence in their Führer, in both France and Britain it resulted in a major crisis of leadership. For Gamelin, the days of April 12th and 13th were "among the most painful of my existence"; on being summoned to a Cabinet meeting, he found "an atmosphere of ice. It was as though they had just pronounced 'bring in the accused!' " Following on the Finnish debacle, public dissatisfaction had already brought about the fall of Gamelin's protector, Daladier, who was replaced (on March 21st) by a new Cabinet under Paul Reynaud, no friend of the French Generalissimo.

When France went to war in 1914, her political parties had declared a truce, forming under the Union Sacrée a coalition remarkable in the history of France. Poincaré had no love for Clemenceau, but out of patriotism was prepared to collaborate loyally with him; in 1939, although Léon Blum had declared that he would ally himself with anyone dedicated solely to winning the war, it was typical that at a dinner party where Clare Boothe was present, half the guests refused to shake hands with poor Blum. In war, the power plays of the Third Republic went on as dizzily as before. Shortly after its outbreak, Daladier had managed to purge the appeaser Bonnet* from the Quai d'Orsay, though he could not get rid of him altogether, and Bonnet had lingered on as Minister of Justice. Daladier then made an attempt at re-creating the Union Sacrée by bringing his old foe, Édouard Herriot, into the government in Bonnet's place. "Come, it is your duty," he is reputed to have said to Herriot. "At the Quai d'Orsay we need a faith, a doctrine, a capable head, endurance; in short, a man." Herriot retorted, ungraciously, "What for?", but accepted with the proviso that he should be "covered" by Pétain's also entering the Cabinet. The old Marshal's response to Daladier, however, was: "I am at your orders. But veto Herriot." Thereafter Daladier was left with no alternative but to turn himself into a one-man band—Premier, Foreign Secretary, Minister of National Defence, and Minister of War.

The Cabinet swiftly divided itself into the "hards," as represented by Paul Reynaud and Clemenceau's former hatchet man, Georges Mandel, and the "softs": Bonnet, de Monzie, Pomaret and Chautemps.† These "softs" within the Cabinet represented but a small fraction of the various dissident groups, opposed to the war in varying degree, with whom Daladier had to deal; Communists, antimilitarists of the non-Communist left, conservatives fearful of revolution, the rich trembling for their riches, defeatists and pro-Fascists such as Pierre Laval, who, though still in outer darkness, wielded a potent influence upon the "softs" within Daladier's Cabinet. Meanwhile, above it all the Head of State, who could perhaps have lent more teeth to France's wartime government, was manifestly senile; on visiting President Lebrun in the spring of 1940, Sumner Welles found his memory "failing rapidly. It was difficult for him to remember with any accuracy names, or dates, or even facts." He attempted "with a good deal of assistance" to tell Welles about the various paintings in the

---

* Typical of the mistrust festering within Daladier's War Cabinet was Gamelin's refusal to discuss France's military deficiencies in front of Bonnet; to which Daladier commented, "You did right. If you had exposed them, the Germans would have known about them next day."

† In a more modern context, they would have been rated "hawks" or "doves."

Élysée, but "was quite unable to remember the names of any of them."

Daladier

Daladier himself was neither strong nor prepossessing. A fifty-five-year-old widower and son of a baker from Vaucluse in the Midi, he had taught history before going into politics. He succeeded Herriot as leader of the Radical-Socialist Party in 1935, had been Minister of War almost uninterruptedly since 1932, and Premier at the time of the Stavisky riots in 1934 and Munich in 1938, on both of which occasions he had capitulated. Daladier was a stockily built, energetic man with a dull-brown complexion and a greasy lock of hair that imparted a slight (and deceptive) look of Bonaparte. Under the strain of the Front Populaire, he had come to depend increasingly on the more fiery French liquors. Writing in all the bitterness of 1940, Vincent Sheean describes him as "a dirty man with a cigarette stuck to his lower lip, stinking of absinthe, talking with a rough Marseillaise accent. . . . He had a certain southern eloquence, particularly over the air when he could not be seen." While Daladier was still in power, Harold Nicolson wrote in his diary that he looked "like a drunken peasant. His face must once have had sharp outlines but now it is blurred by the puffiness of drink. He looks extremely exhausted and has the eyes of a man who has had a bad night. He has a weak, sly smile." In the south, his supporters nicknamed Daladier "the bull of Vaucluse," but as Spears remarked acidly, "his horns bore more resemblance to the soft feelers of the snail than to the harder bovine variety." Others said that his was a case of a "velvet hand in a glove of iron," and certainly his rough appearance and violent fits of rage had given him a reputation for strength to which, as both Munich and the Stavisky riots had shown, he was hardly entitled. His strength, such as it was, lay in politics rather than in statecraft, and he excelled in the steamy jungles comprising the political lobbies of the Third Republic. Daladier—honest but infirm and immensely jealous of his position—seemed to epitomise the average Frenchman of his time, but for a nation as reluctantly at war as France, he was certainly not a leader to impart inspiration. In his New Year's Eve broadcast at the end of 1939, he expressed a desire to spread "a ray of joy" in each home, but all he managed to do was to propagate his own gloom. Yet, as a political juggler capable of keeping the parties of the Third Republic in some sort of equilibrium, he was indispensable.

At the beginning of January, 1940, Daladier took a weekend off to escape from the political pressures bearing down on him. Out riding, his horse slipped on frost-hardened ground and Daladier fell, with his foot caught in the stirrup. For months he suffered constant pain and insomnia, which appears to have had its effect upon his control of the government; Senator Bardoux notes that when he saw Daladier on March 6th he was still limping and seemed "even wearier, sadder and less dynamic than a fortnight previously," while grumbling, "Nothing is going right." Flandin, whose government had once fallen as a result of a car accident in which he broke his arm, commented caustically that "a politician has no right to have accidents," and on March 20th Daladier fell again—this time politically. Pierre Laval launched the attack, and the killing blow was struck by a deputy who cried tellingly: "The men who were able neither to prevent nor to prepare for war are not now qualified either to stop it or win it." After some talk about Daladier being succeeded by such "softs" as Chautemps, Laval, or Pétain, President Lebrun called for Paul Reynaud to form the one hundred and ninth government of the Third Republic.

Reynaud

Paul Reynaud was sixty-two when he came to power, for the first time. His family were farmers in the Basses Alpes, but he had established himself as a successful barrister. He had acquired a connoisseur's taste for Chinese art, and indeed there was something of the mandarin in his appearance: dapper, sharp-featured, with eyebrows that seemed to be permanently raised in a quizzical expression. He was very fond of sport—walking, cycling and swimming—and liked to advertise the fact. But the important physical feature of Reynaud was his modest stature. He had most of the attributes of the small man: agility, combativeness, vulnerability to flatterers, the self-confidence that masks a sense of inferiority —and courage. His enemies (and they were many) called him "Mickey Mouse." But to others he was a little fighting cock who, when a subject fired his imagination, would "get to his feet, put his hands in his pockets, throw back his head to raise his short figure to its full height, and hold forth in picturesque and biting phrases like quick hammer blows." In debate he showed a brilliant, quick intellect and a devastating logic; but he sought to master rather than charm, and this with his natural assertiveness and love of battle did not endear him to other politicians of the Third Republic—especially to Daladier, who loathed him. Hard-working and intensely patriotic, Reynaud had never been afraid to swim against the current. From the earliest days he had warned France about Hitler's designs, in opposition to the Flandins, Lavals and Bonnets; and it was he who had gone against official French military doctrine by taking up the views of de Gaulle. As Minister of Finance in 1938, he had achieved remarkable success in reordering France's economy after the ravages of the Front Populaire; but his tough measures had gained him many more enemies. From September 1939, he had pledged himself to total war against Hitler—though, by the time he came to power, it was a bit late, insofar as Hitler was himself on the brink of unleashing total war against France.

As the small voice in the French wilderness, Reynaud repre-sented the equivalent of Churchill (whom he hugely admired); but unfortunately he possessed neither the essential grandeur nor the support. He also was too much a product of the Third Re-public; had played the game of politics to its limit, manoeuvring and countermanoeuvring. More than this, because of the loneliness of the positions he adopted as well as his combative manner, in the Assembly he was a maverick; sitting in the centre, he pos-sessed no party of his own, and few real friends. (And his judge-ment in choosing his political "friends" was to prove far from impeccable.) Thus, in contrast to the great carte blanche given to Churchill on his accession to power, Reynaud from the start was forced to compromise and tightrope-walk in his formation of a government.

But by far the heaviest burden Paul Reynaud had to bear was his mistress, the Comtesse Hélène de Portes. As of tradition, am-bitious, busy women have exercised a powerful influence behind the scenes of French politics. At the end of the thirties there were three who had dominated the stage of the Third Republic. There was Madame Bonnet, nicknamed "Madame Soutien-Georges"; the Marquise de Crussol, a handsome and youthful-looking blonde who was Daladier's Egeria and whom the punsters chris-tened *"la sardine qui s'est Crue Sole,"* on account of the family's sardine-canning business; and there was Reynaud's Comtesse Hélène de Portes, the most powerful of them all and regarded as almost too sinister to be granted a sobriquet, although the wits occasionally referred to her, aptly, as *"La Porte à Côté."* The extraordinary thing about Madame de Portes is that, of the countless people who knew her, none can satisfactorily explain her allure. The practised eye of General Spears describes her as having "very good feet and ankles, but her complexion was sallow. Of medium height, she was dark, her curly hair, brushed upwards, looked untidy. . . . Her mouth was big and the voice that issued from it was unharmonious." Spears thought she dressed fashionably, but lacked "the attractiveness so often found in *Parisiennes,* that of being *bien soignée."*

Élie Bois, less vitriolic than most, observed in her a physical attribute which perhaps compensated for her lack of traditional beauty: "Her way of walking, quick of step, disclosed that the suppleness of her limbs and the agility of her whole body were maintained by physical exercise." But he thought her "ardent and ruthless in every way . . . a match for others at the game of secret slander." However, Bois added, "she preferred direct attack, haughty, and even violent, for thereby her will to dominate could be more surely exercised." Clare Boothe saw her as "a dark, homely, talkative little woman, in her late forties. She looked as much like a *Hausfrau* as a French *maîtresse* can. She was patriotic, energetic; she had many friends and a lot of notions about everything." But to regard her as "the Du Barry of France" was, she thought, as wide of the mark as calling "Mrs. Eleanor Roosevelt the Cleopatra of the New Deal!"

What, then, was the secret of her hold over Reynaud? Most probably it resided in his small stature. As one Frenchman remarked, "She made him feel tall and grand and powerful. Had Reynaud been three inches taller, the history of the world might have been changed." He needed and depended upon his Hélène, and thrived upon her flattery; she in her turn, dedicated to seeing her hero reach the top of the political ladder, sustained him and goaded him in his strong ambitions.

In the aftermath of France's defeat, Hélène de Portes came to be regarded by many as an out-and-out fifth columnist. Certainly before the war her famous salon had been frequently visited by Otto Abetz and members of the Comité France-Allemagne; she

was never a "hard" like Reynaud, and she was strongly anti-British
—a tendency which increased as the war went progressively worse
for France from May 10th onwards. But in retrospect it seems
fair to judge that she was no more of a fifth columnist than most
of the patriotic but self-interested *haute bourgeoisie* whose shibboleth under the Front Populaire had been "Rather Hitler than
Blum!" Perhaps the most baneful feature of her relationship with
Paul Reynaud was that she held him totally her prisoner, and
chivvied him relentlessly until he was simply worn out. Together
they lived in Reynaud's bachelor flat near the Assembly, where
much business of state was transacted. She was constantly intervening and interfering, and even in his office Reynaud was never
immune from her endless telephone calls. On at least one occasion, Madame de Portes was found actually seated at his desk,
presiding over a gathering of generals, deputies and government
officials. Once when André Maurois criticised a political appointment made by his friend, Reynaud admitted, "It was not my
choice, it was hers." Maurois replied, "That is no excuse." "Ah,"
sighed Reynaud, "you don't know what a man who has been hard
at work all day will put up with to make sure of an evening's
peace."

Another aspect of Madame de Portes's unfortunate influence
behind the scenes was the fact that she was at daggers drawn with
the Marquise de Crussol—Daladier's champion. The rivalry of
these women injected poison into the already bad relations between the two most powerful leaders of wartime France. From
about January, Hélène de Portes had begun to campaign for
Reynaud to oust Daladier, in the clumsiest fashion, filling the
salons of Paris with stories of Daladier's lethargy. This gossip the
faithful Marquise promptly passed back to Daladier, duly magnified, until the rift between him and Reynaud became almost
intolerable. To Maurois, Reynaud confided grimly: "I believe he
desires the victory of France, but he desires my defeat even more."
Of this feud, Churchill was to comment to Spears in despair,
"What will centuries to come say if we lost this war through lack
of understanding?"

Reynaud saddled with Gamelin

The tragedy for France was that Reynaud, the lone operator
with no political machine behind him, could not survive without

the backing of Daladier in his Cabinet. On the very first day of the new government, Reynaud was confronted with a vote of confidence. He scraped by with only one vote, so precarious was the balance of the government due shortly to face Hitler's onslaught. Reynaud wanted to take over the Ministry of National Defence from Daladier, but he had to renounce it because of his need for his enemy's support; he wanted to sack Gamelin but could not, because Gamelin was Daladier's man; he wanted to bring in Colonel de Gaulle as secretary to the War Cabinet, but de Gaulle would not serve with Daladier and preferred to return to his tanks.* Paul Baudouin, a director of the Bank of Indo-China, youngish, good-looking but a "soft" and a favoured protégé of Hélène de Portes, got the job instead. Bonnet was sacked at last, but later, as part of his complex balancing act, Reynaud was constrained to bring in two extreme right-wingers, Marin and Ybarnegaray. The appointment of the latter, a member of Colonel de la Rocque's Croix de Feu, was roughly the same as if Churchill had taken Oswald Mosley into his Cabinet. Daladier grumbled, "I ought not to have entered this Government. I was tired, worn out . . . I must get out of it at the first opportunity."

It was typical of how self-interest continued to prevail in a France perched on the brink of disaster. And the nation at large was all too discouragingly aware of the "swamp of personal jealousies and ministerial appetites" in Paris. At the front, Major Barlone spoke for many soldiers when he wrote in his diary of the new government: "People see a schemer and a thief in every politician. . . . Our enemies do not waste their time over parliamentary manoeuvres. . . . Spring is now here, the time of trial is probably at hand, and look what a government we have!"

Yet, for all the political ligaments binding him, restricting his movements, Reynaud came to power just as dedicated to waging war with a fresh bellicosity as Clemenceau had been. One of his

---

* De Gaulle was then commanding a tank brigade dispersed behind the Maginot Line. At the end of January he had re-entered the limelight by circulating to political and military leaders a courageous memorandum in which he warned of the danger that the Germans would smash through the French defences with an overwhelming mechanical force. The official, complacent response was that France "was not Poland." There is a curious historical parallel between Colonel de Gaulle's memorandum and one which gained disbelief and disfavour for another Colonel, Émile Driant, when he warned Joffre of the impending attack on Verdun in 1916.

first acts was to go to London to sign, on March 28th, a joint declaration with the British, pledging that neither country would
conclude a separate peace without the agreement of the other—
an undertaking to which Daladier had long been reluctant to commit himself.* Then, on April 12th, Reynaud, who had been
infuriated by Gamelin's showing over Norway, determined to precipitate a crisis here. To Baudouin he remarked: "It would be
criminal to leave this nerveless philosopher at the head of the
French Army." He was, he said, "hesitating between General
Georges and General Weygand." But in the Cabinet, Daladier immediately ranged himself behind Gamelin and threatened to resign if there were any change. Reynaud was stymied. Baudouin
claims he came out of the meeting "thunderstruck by the pitiful
spectacle of the Prime Minister's impotence to break the political
chains which bound him." At a Cabinet meeting on April 23rd,
Reynaud once again remained silent. On the 27th, Reynaud told
Baudouin that the time for procrastination was over; he would
take action within the next two or three days. But President
Lebrun, whose wholehearted support would be indispensable to
Reynaud, merely passed him a message telling him to "be patient.
Time will settle many things." Indeed it would. Then, on April
28th, Reynaud collapsed with influenza. He was confined to his
bed for a week and Gamelin was saved a second time. On returning to his office, still shaky, Reynaud prepared for a final offensive against his Commander-in-Chief.

Notices went out on the evening of May 8th for a Cabinet
meeting the next morning. Reynaud arrived with a bulky file, from
which he read for two hours. His colleagues—many of whom had
not seen him for a fortnight—"found him much altered, thinner,
feverish of eye, unsteady of voice." He closed with a warning that
France, if she persisted in the errors which had encompassed the
Norwegian operation, would almost certainly lose the war.
Gamelin could not be left in charge. There followed a painful
two-minute silence before Lamoureux, the Minister of Finance,
rallied to Reynaud. Daladier counterattacked vigorously. Reynaud wound up the session by stating that, in view of the opposition, he considered the government as having resigned and
would inform the President accordingly. All that afternoon of the

---

* This declaration was later to be a source of enduring bitterness between Britain and France.

9th, discussions went on at the Élysée. The next day the Germans attacked. A third respite was granted Gamelin.

Meanwhile in London, in the midst of questions about such grave matters as Kentish sheep being frightened by aircraft, Scottish hotels overcharging for coffee, and the advertising of patent medicines in stamp books, the Commons was concluding its debate on Norway. Chamberlain was finished. On May 10th, just as Hitler's panzers were plunging into Holland and Belgium, Churchill became Prime Minister. In those lapidary words he remarked: "I was conscious of a profound sense of relief. At last I had the authority to give directions over the whole scene. I felt as if I were walking with destiny." Britain had, at last, found her war leader and he embarked upon his task with the undivided support of parliamentarians; but there were many government matters concerning the conduct of war which were strange to him and would necessarily, and perilously, remain outside his grasp for some time. How different, though, was the scene in France on May 10th. Indubitably, time had "settled" matters, but not in the way Lebrun might have hoped. Here was a government in the throes of dissolution, a Commander-in-Chief under suspended sentence.

The opposing forces: Tanks

As one approaches the eve of the great clash, having examined the opposing plans, one now needs to have one last close look at the actual forces available to each side by May 10th. For employment in *Sichelschnitt,* by May Hitler could count upon 136 of the army's 157 divisions, of which no more than a third qualified as first-rate offensive material. Against this, France's northeast front was held by 94 French divisions of mixed value,* plus 10 British, augmented by a further 22 Belgian divisions and 10 Dutch (though, despite Gamelin's hopes, these last were able to exert only a minimal influence in the battle); a total also of 136, so that in numbers alone the Germans did not possess the overwhelming superiority which the Allies required to crush the Wehrmacht later in the war.

---

* Owing to the bloodletting of '14–'18 and the attendant fall in the birth rate, France had been able to mobilise far fewer men in 1940 than in 1914; the difference was most noticeable in the fact that whereas France in 1914 had 1,250,000 men between the ages of 20 and 25, in 1940 she had only 600,000 in this vital age group.

In the crucial matter of armour, figures have varied wildly; on May 10th, the French Deuxième Bureau estimated the Germans had 7,000 to 7,500 tanks, a vastly inflated figure which came to be extensively used in France by way of excuse for what was to follow. According to Guderian, Germany's 10 panzer divisions should have had 2,800 tanks, but they had only 2,200; as a reliable figure based on German archives, one could accept a total of just over 2,400 and well under 3,000.* For the number of Franco-British tanks available to the northeast front, Gamelin himself gives a total of 3,432 modern vehicles; Colonel Goutard, a generally trustworthy source, puts the Allied total "in the region of 3,000"; and the most recent estimate (by General de Cossé Brissac, former head of the French Army's Service Historique) calculates the French total alone at "3,100 of which 2,285 were modern." Thus, in overall tank numbers, the French and British jointly were actually superior.

Furthermore, the gulf in quality of tanks between the Wehrmacht and the Allies was not quite so wide as it had been two years previously. The mainstay of the German panzer divisions was the light Mark II tank, which carried only a 20 mm cannon; more than 1,400, or over half the total panzers, were Mark I or II; there were only 349 of the medium Mark III tanks, which carried a 37 mm gun, and only 278 of the new 24-ton Mark IV, carrying a low-velocity 75 mm gun. Against this, the French possessed their new heavy (33-ton) "B" tank—possibly the best of any nation in 1940—and the fast medium (20-ton) Somua. The "B" tank mounted a 47 mm gun in a revolving turret and a 75 mm mounted in the hull,† and had armour thicker than any German tank; the Somua also mounted the high-velocity 47 mm gun, with better penetrative power than any other gun of the period, and the numbers of these two tanks—despite all the delays in French production—totalled 800, or more than the Marks III and IV possessed by the Germans. (In addition, the 100 British infantry tanks in France were also more heavily armoured than their German counterparts, and their 2 pdr gun was more potent than the Germans' 37 mm.) The defects of the Somua and "B" tanks were that their turrets were operated by one overworked

---

* This wide discrepancy arises from the exact numbers of the obsolescent Mark I and Mark II tanks which the German Army "retired" during the winter of 1939–40.

† In this design, it was a kind of stepfather to the American "Grant" tank.

commander-loader-gunner, compared with the two- or three-man turrets of the British and Germans; the 75 mm of the "B" tank (fired and aimed by the driver) could only be pointed laterally by moving the tank itself; and French gun sights were inferior. The other modern models of tanks principally employed by the French were the R–35 (Renault, model 1935) and the H–35 (Hotchkiss, model 1935), still mounting an old-fashioned, stubby 37 mm gun that was useless against armour.

But the gravest defects of the French tanks still lay, as has been mentioned earlier, in their poor operating range and the fact that four-fifths of them carried no radio. Thus their mobility was badly impaired. Weightier than any technical advantage, however, was the superiority of the German panzer crews in training and doctrine. During the *Anschluss* of 1938, many German tanks* had broken down on the way to Austria and there was chaos on the roads. In the meantime, however, Hitler had had two years and two campaigns—Czechoslovakia and Poland—in which to put this right. He had not wasted his opportunities. Worst of all was the way in which the French tanks were scattered: 700 to 800 in the cavalry divisions or DLMs, 1,500 to 1,700 dispersed in independent battalions under the infantry. The remainder belonged to the three new armoured divisions, formed only in 1940,† and each contained just half as many tanks as the 10 powerful panzer divisions in which all the German armour was concentrated.

In antitank weapons, the German 37 mm gunners would be hard pressed to make an impression on the heavier French tanks. But the much superior French 47 mm was in such short supply that only 16 divisions possessed any; the few that existed were drawn by fifteen-year-old converted tractors, but the ammunition was carried in trucks—the guns could move crosscountry but not their ammunition. The older 25 mm lacked punch, weighed half a ton and depended largely on horse transport. It too was in short supply, with Corap's Ninth Army (which would need them most desperately) possessing only half of the established amount of 25 mm guns. The situation in antitank mines was even worse; by some extraordinary omission, not one had been ordered in France before the war, and by May 1940 they were just beginning to

---

* Jodl claimed 70 percent, though Guderian denies the number of breakdowns was "as high as 30 percent."

† The 4th Armoured, whose command was later given to de Gaulle, was actually in process of formation when the Germans struck.

reach the front-line forces. In artillery, France was numerically superior, with 11,200 guns to 7,710. But as reliant upon the horse —so pathetically vulnerable from the air—as it had been in 1918, the French artillery was equipped with none of the self-propelled guns to be found in every German panzer division.

Aircraft

In antiaircraft weapons, France's position was particularly deplorable. According to General Roton, "On May 10th we possessed 17 guns of 90 mm calibre." As to light antiaircraft, so vital in defence against dive bombers, only 22 French divisions were equipped with the 20 mm Oerlikon, and their allocation was a mere 12 pieces each; 13 other divisions had the new French 25 mm antiaircraft gun (6 each), but these had only begun to arrive at the end of April—hardly time enough to give the crews adequate training. There were 39 batteries kept in reserve at Army level; otherwise the remainder of France's antiaircraft defence was made up of 75 mm guns left over from 1918. In contrast, against a total of just over 1,500 weapons, the Germans could mount 2,600 of the powerful 88 mm and 6,700 light flak, with which each panzer and motorised division was plentifully endowed.

It was of course in the air that the inferiority of the Allies was most blatant. By the spring of 1940, the Luftwaffe stood nearly at its peak. Despite the efforts of Raoul Dautry, in April the French aircraft industry was still only producing 60 planes a month,* the same quantity it had produced during September 1939. The relative merits of the opposing aircraft have already been discussed; in numbers the balance was as follows:

	Germany[a]	France[a]	Britain[b]
Bombers	1,400	150–175	220
Dive bombers	342	54	0
Fighters	1,000	700	130
Reconnaissance and scout planes	500	350–400	50

[a] These are to some extent approximate figures, as there remain considerable discrepancies over the number of German and French machines actually in line on May 10th.

[b] Excluding planes based in Britain but used in France.

---

* Although this was the month that, for the first time, British aircraft production actually surpassed Germany's.

The French total was thus approximately 1,200; the British deployed something over 600 in France, if one also took into account the aircraft of Bomber Command which could intervene in the battle. But, according to General d'Astier de la Vigerie who commanded the Zone d'Opérations Aériennes Nord (ZOAN), because of the French system of dispersal his vital Zone supporting Billotte's No. 1 Army Group could only count on a total of 746 aircraft. Against this, Goering would be able to deploy 3,000 to 3,500 planes out of a grand total of 5,000, the remainder (including the Ju–52 transports) being kept in Norway or in reserve in Germany. What the Wehrmacht lacked in guns on the ground was more than made up for by its "flying artillery." In mobility and training, the Luftwaffe, with its experience in Spain and Poland, also had an incalculable advantage.

The French on the Meuse

The French forces which specifically would bear the weight of the German offensive, of Rundstedt's 45 divisions spearheaded by those seven panzers, were the Ninth Army of General Corap and the Second Army of General Huntziger.

As already noted, the function of the Ninth Army under Gamelin's Dyle–Breda Plan was to wheel forward upon its pivot north of Sedan to hold the Belgian section of the Meuse running from Namur southwards, which would involve an advance of up to 45 miles. The front Corap was expected to hold spanned approximately 50 air miles; but in fact, taking into account the twists and turns of the Meuse, it amounted to considerably more than this. For this task, he had only 9½ divisions. There were two Light Cavalry Divisions (1st and 4th) plus the 3rd Spahi Brigade —a mixture of horses and light armour that could in no way stand up to a German panzer division; these, acting as a reconnaissance screen, were to push into the Ardennes across the Meuse and absorb the first shock of a German attack while the infantry were taking up position along the Meuse.

Of Corap's seven infantry divisions holding this key sector of the front, only two—the 5th Motorised and 4th North African— were regulars; two (the 18th and 22nd) were "A" series, which meant that only 23 percent of their officers, 17 percent of the NCOs and 2 percent of the men were regulars, the remainder reservists; two others (the 61st and 53rd) were "B" series, which were composed almost exclusively of reservists (and the oldest

ALLIED ORDER OF BATTLE — May 10, 1940

With names of commanders principally concerned

RAF Bomber Command
(London)

VUILLEMIN
(C-in-C Air Forces)
(Coulommiers)

Other Fronts

TÊTU
(O/C Air Cooperation Forces)

British Air Forces in France ————— d'ASTIER DE LA VIGERIE
(BARRATT) (Chauny)   (Zone of Air Operations North)

RAF Advanced
Air Striking Force
(Playfair)

FRENCH SEVENTH ARMY
(Giraud)
(7 Divisions)
(inc. 1st DLM)
(174 tanks)

BEF
(Lord Gort)
(9 Divisions)
(1 Army Tank Bde

RAF COMPONENT
(Blount)

DUTCH ARMY
10 Divisions

BELGIAN ARMY
20 Divisions

CAVALRY
(4th & 1st DLC
(3rd Spahi Bde

RESERVES
(18 Divisions)
(inc. 3 Armoured Divisions)

1st DCR
(Bruneau)
(150 tanks)

2nd DCR
(Bruché)
(150 tanks)

3rd DCR
(Brocard)
(150 tanks)

[4th DCR*
(de Gaulle)]

*Not yet formed

4th N. African
Div. (R) (Sancelm

Units reading from north (left) to south (right)

GAMELIN
(Supreme Commander French
Land Forces) (Vincennes)

DOUMENC
(Major-Général)
(Montry)

GEORGES
(C-in-C Northeast Front)
(La Ferté)

BILLOTTE
(No. 1 Army Group)

No. 2 Army Group
(35 Divs.) (Prételat)

No. 3 Army Group
(14 Divs.) (Besson)

FRENCH FIRST ARMY
(Blanchard)
(10 Divisions)

FRENCH NINTH ARMY
(Corap, later Giraud)

FRENCH SECOND ARMY
(Huntziger)

CAVALRY CORPS
(Prioux)
(2nd and 3rd DLMs)
(174 tanks each)

CAVALRY
(2nd and 5th DLCs)
(1st Cavalry Bde.)

XVIII CORPS
(Rochard)

X CORPS

55th Div. (B)
(Lafontaine)

71st Div. (B)
(Baudet)

3rd North African
Div. (R)

II CORPS
(Bouffet)

XI CORPS
(Martin)

XLI CORPS
(Libaud)

5th Motorised
(R) (Boucher)

18th Div. (A)
(Duffet)

22nd Div. (A)
(Hassler)

61st Div. (B)
(Vauthier)

102nd Fortress Div. (R)
(Portzert)

Reserve

53rd Div. (B)
Etchberrigaray)

A = "A" Division

B = "B" Division

R = Regular Division

reservists at that: men of forty—unkindly nicknamed "crocodiles" by the rest of the Army) commanded by generals called back from retirement; and finally, one fortress division (the 102nd) of the kind to be found embedded in the Maginot Line, severely limited in its mobility.

Corap's mixed bag of an army was comprised largely of Normans and Bretons (good fighters, but very conscious of the past tendency of French commanders to commit them where other softer, more meridional troops might fail), men from the Loire and colonials from North Africa, Indo-China, and Madagascar. Altogether, they had certainly not made a good impression on Lieutenant General Alan Brooke when he had attended an Armistice Day parade with Corap in November 1939. Beneath a monument on which was inscribed *Ici triompha par sa ténacité le Poilu!,* Brooke watched Corap's guard of honour march past:

I can still see those troops now. Seldom have I seen anything more slovenly and badly turned out. Men unshaven, horses ungroomed, clothes and saddlery that did not fit, vehicles dirty, and complete lack of pride in themselves or their units. What shook me most, however, was the look in the men's faces, disgruntled and insubordinate looks, and, although ordered to give "Eyes left," hardly a man bothered to do so. After the ceremony was over Corap invited me to visit some of his defences in the Forêt de St. Michel. There we found a half-constructed and very poor anti-tank ditch with no defences to cover it. By way of conversation I said that I supposed he would cover this ditch with the fire from anti-tank pill-boxes. This question received the reply: *"Ah bah! on va les faire plus tard—allons, on va déjeuner!"*

The bitter, idle winter had certainly brought little improvement; and of the whole French front, there was probably no other sector less densely held than Corap's. On a visit to the Ninth Army, André Maurois was "struck by their lack of numbers. Returning to Vervins, I had the feeling of traversing an abandoned country."

At Dom-le-Mesnil, on the confluence of the Meuse and the Ardennes Canal about 5 miles downstream from Sedan, lay the boundary of the Ninth and Second Armies. General Huntziger's Second Army, whose role under the Dyle Plan did not entail any advance into Belgium, consisted of only two army corps (plus a cavalry screen similar to Corap's).

It is, however, X Corps (General Grandsard) which principally concerns this story, as his was the one to be attacked by Guderian's panzer spearhead at Sedan. To guard against an out-flanking attack on the Maginot Line, Huntziger had deployed his best divisions on the right, his poorest on the left immediately behind Sedan where they linked hands with Corap's indifferent forces. Grandsard's right wing was held by the regular 3rd North African Division, which would be almost left out of the crucial phase of the battle, while his left was held by the 55th Infantry Division—another "B" series unit, and a poor one at that. Behind, in reserve, stood the 71st—also a "B" division.

Quite early in the war, Huntziger—talking in confidence to an American volunteer ambulance driver, Florence Conrad—admitted that the poor morale of his troops was worrying him. Of the 55th and 71st Divisions, General Grandsard himself says:

Cases of ill-will were rare, but the ardour for work, for training and the desire to fight, were even rarer. Nonchalance was general; it was accompanied by the feeling that France could not be beaten, that Germany would be beaten without battle . . . the men are flabby and heavy. . . . In the artillery the men are older, the training is mediocre.

The 55th Division (General Lafontaine), recruited in the region of Bourges, has been described as a "poor relation" in terms of equipment*; it was particularly short in modern antiaircraft weapons. Of its 450 officers, only 20 were regulars; which included the colonel of each infantry regiment, and 3 out of 50 gunner officers. The 71st, recruited in Paris (including some of the more red-tainted suburbs), was probably even more mediocre than the 55th. On May 10th, owing to leave, sickness and other causes, it could muster no more than 10,000 men out of its normal establishment of 17,000, while (according to General Ruby) its commander, General Baudet, "brilliant once-upon-a-time, but now physically enfeebled, did not inspire confidence either among his troops or their leaders. His replacement was a matter of days."

Thus three third-rate "B" divisions—the 55th, 71st and Corap's 53rd—were left guarding the fateful sector of Sedan. It was, as

---

* The best equipment having been siphoned off for the Seventh and First Armies in the north.

Gamelin mildly admits in his memoirs, a "dangerous" thing to do —and a heaven-sent gift for Guderian.

Football and roses

During the bitter winter of the Phoney War, as Churchill* has commented, "visitors to the French front were often struck by the prevailing atmosphere of calm aloofness, by the seemingly poor quality of the work in hand, by the lack of visible activity of any kind. The emptiness of the roads behind the line was in great contrast to the continual coming and going which extended for miles behind the British sector."† This was an impression also shared by many Frenchmen, soldiers and civilians. Instead of ardently studying and exercising upon the sober lessons of Poland, too many French troops were employed in blancoing the curbs and steps of their barracks, playing organised football, growing roses to embellish the glacis of the Maginot forts, and—as spring came—tilling the fields, by way of dispelling boredom. Writing to Simone de Beauvoir from the front, Jean-Paul Sartre described his daily contribution to the war effort in terms that represented the futility shared by countless other French soldiers:

My work here consists of sending up balloons and then watching them through a pair of field glasses; this is called "making a meteorological observation." Afterwards I phone the battery artillery officers and tell them the wind direction; what they do with this information is their affair. The young ones make some use of the intelligence reports; the old school just shove them straight in the wastepaper basket. . . . Since there isn't any shooting either course is equally effective.

At Arras, André Maurois, on observing territorials engaged in planting kitchen gardens and raising rabbits and pigs, enquired why they could not have been set to work fortifying the river Scarpe.‡ He was told, "The enemy will never advance that far. You are a defeatist!" Hans Habe, an Austrian refugee who had joined up in a regiment that would later be thrown into the Battle of Sedan, recalled the futility of training with hopelessly rusted

---

* *The Second World War*, I, p. 442.

† It should not be forgotten, however, that the British Secretary of State for War, Hore-Belisha, was sacked (in January) for criticising the poverty of the BEF defence works.

‡ Which the panzers were to reach by the eleventh day of the offensive.

rifles on a beach near Perpignan: "Hardly an ideal drill ground. At every step you sank up to your ankles in sand; it was impossible to set up a single machine-gun or dig a single trench." The rare tank exercises had a habit of grinding to a halt—because the *Intendance* had not provided sufficient fuel in advance. Gamelin's GQG would issue instructions 19 pages long on the conduct of patrol actions—while officers at the front wondered why on earth it was not holding exercises to simulate dive-bomber attacks, so that the troops could be made to realise that safety lay, not in running about in a panic, but in staying put in foxholes and weapon slits. And during all these months of Phoney War wasted by the French, on the German side second-, third-, and fourth-line divisions were being transformed from what was described as "an armed rabble" into fully operational units.

With Corap's and Huntziger's mediocre divisions protecting the Meuse, the picture was particularly depressing. The trouble was that the urgent need for training of the reservists stood in direct conflict with the equally urgent need for work on the deficient fortifications. Four out of every five divisions were required in defending and working on the line all the time, so that on average only half a day per week could be devoted to firing practice and training; furthermore, after each of the numerous false alarms training and work had been interrupted for five to six days. The arctic weather conditions had also had effect; Grandsard noted that it was not possible until the beginning of March to send two of his infantry regiments to the rear for three weeks' training. Instructors tended to be inexperienced, and—commenting on the "general apathy" of the Second Army's "B" divisions—General Ruby remarks that "every exercise was considered as a vexation, all work as a fatigue. After several months of stagnation, nobody believed any more in the war."

In France it has always been held against Pétain that, in March 1934, he was the one to declare the Ardennes "impenetrable" (though why the French General Staff should have persisted in unquestioningly accepting this thesis is another matter!); but Pétain's rider—"provided special dispositions are effected there"—tends to be forgotten. By May 10th, just what "special dispositions" had the men of the Second and Ninth Armies, "soldiers become navvies," achieved? Some French staff officer had indeed suggested that the forest roads leading through the Ardennes towards the French frontier be blocked by the simple expedient of felling thousands of trees. But this had been rejected; why? Because these roads had to be kept clear for the advance of the French cavalry screen! At Sedan itself, General Grandsard tells us, the Meuse at the beginning of the war had been guarded by only some 40 bunkers of "type Barbeyrac." Carrying either two machine guns or a small antitank weapon and one machine gun, these could stand up to nothing heavier than a 105 mm shell. There were no concrete installations for command posts or for artillery positions. Not until November 25th was a first programme launched to double the number of bunkers. Work began only on December 5th, and by January 10th no more than a fifth of the 45,000 tons of material required had actually arrived. Moreover, the terrible cold rendered the pouring of concrete almost impossible, so that virtually two months of the winter programme had to be written off; to add to its residual disgruntlement, the 71st Division was forced to remake over 10 miles of slit trenches which winter had wrecked.

But why the delay in starting this urgent programme? Grandsard criticises the idleness and softness of his men, and lack of authority of the junior officers—but the most injurious factor seems to have been the protracted inability of Billotte and his army commanders to agree upon a standard type of fortification.

Meanwhile, in early March Gamelin had received a prophetic letter from a deputy, Pierre Taittinger, who had just completed a parliamentary inspection of the line. The defences at Sedan so shocked Taittinger and his colleagues that they foresaw it as a sector "of misfortune for our forces." Gamelin responded by reinforcing Givet, 50 miles down the Meuse, with a solitary battalion* and ordained the construction of a line of *maisons fortes* protecting Sedan midway between the Belgian frontier and the right bank of the Meuse. A *maison forte* was a small semidisguised block of masonry with a thick layer of concrete in the ceiling; above was a superstructure providing living accommodation for its garrison of four to five men. They were supposed to resist any bombardment, but in fact one Stuka bomb or even a direct hit from a big German self-propelled gun would be sufficient

---

* Compared by General Beaufre to Marshal Bazaine's "laying one cannon at St. Privat" in 1870.

to blow them apart. The garrisons of the *maisons fortes* tended to be selected from the "undesirables"—grumblers and men under suspended sentence. It was a formula that hardly spoke for success; moreover, by May 10th the right bank line covering the Sedan "bridgehead" was far from completed—as Rundstedt's keen-eyed photographic expert, Major von Stiotta, had spotted.

On April 11th, Huntziger—more anxious than ever about the state of the Sedan defences—begged Gamelin to send him four reserve divisions to speed the work. His request was refused. Thus, by May 10th, only 54 out of 100 bunkers had been completed, representing an increase in density of from 3 to 6 kilometre.* Worst of all, most of those completed had still not received their steel doors or the armoured shields protecting the weapons embrasures. The latter were left protected inadequately by sandbags, vulnerable places for Guderian's high-velocity tank cannon to seek out—and the same deficiency applied to bunkers built on Corap's front.† On the vital heights behind Sedan, only one casemate mounting two 75 mm guns—that at Bellevue—was ready when battle began. The standard of construction of many of the Meuse works also seems to have been deplorable. Sarraz-Bournet, a major on Gamelin's Deuxième Bureau, was appalled to discover that some new bunkers built by civilian contractors did not even have embrasures that overlooked the Meuse. "Was this sabotage, or was it simple forgetfulness?" Near Givet, he found barbed-wire entanglements of which the stakes were so poorly planted in the ground that they hardly held; "nobody had ever taught the officer concerned to lay out wire; no senior officer of his unit had come to supervise his work." Major Barlone recorded inspecting on the Belgian frontier an antitank ditch so unimpressive that "a quarter of an hour's bombardment and the earth would crumble away and would leave free passage, I fear, to any armoured vehicle." To back up these inadequate antitank ditches, there were of course mines. General Ruby reckons, however, that Huntziger's Second Army would have required 100,000; it was allocated only 16,000. To make matters worse, by March it was discovered that those already laid were suffering from hu-

---

* By comparison, Hitler's despised Siegfried Line could boast a density of between 20 and 30.

† Despite the fact that, as previously noted, GQG had been fully informed of what had happened to the Polish bunkers when attacked by the panzers.

midity; so they were lifted and stored in a dry place, and Ruby cannot swear that they had been replaced by May 10th.

Little effort seems to have been made to camouflage or conceal the new construction work. By the beginning of May, Grandsard admits, the building zones on his corps front "had not been cleared up and remained clearly visible to aviation, and sometimes even the mass of material hindered fields of fire." Marcel Lerecouvreux, serving with Huntziger's Cavalry, recalls being shocked by the lack of security surrounding the defence works at Sedan; on Sundays the soldiers were frequently visited by young women whom they "did not appear to have known for long." How easy it would have been, he reflected, for the Germans to infiltrate among these ladies agents crossing over the open Belgian frontier only a few miles distant!

The "impenetrable" Ardennes

Obviously the success of any French defence along the Meuse would depend to an important extent upon Belgian intentions for holding the Ardennes. The Belgians in fact had entrusted this large sector to no more than seven battalions of Chasseurs Ardennais, almost without reserves, which made the prospects of manning any "continuous front"—let alone any defence in depth —impossible. Their orders were, on being attacked in force, to destroy communications and then withdraw northwards (i.e., uncovering the French positions on the Meuse), so as to link up with the main body of the Belgian Army. Of the fortifications on the Liège–Arlon line, Paul Reynaud quotes a Belgian general as having remarked: "I piss on it, and I pass by!" The Belgians' strategy was perfectly clear and intelligible: they did not have sufficient forces to protect their whole country, so they would concentrate on defending the centres of population and industry in the north rather than the underpopulated wilderness of the Ardennes southwards of Liège. They hoped that the French Cavalry would arrive in time with strength enough to secure the Ardennes. Citing the Belgian refusal, post-1936, to discuss their defence plans with the French High Command, French writers have blamed the "surprise" at Sedan partially upon the Belgians for not revealing that it was their intention to "vanish" in the Ardennes. But the French Deuxième Bureau must have had a good idea of what the Belgian plan was, and one Belgian general,

Wanty, goes so far as to claim that the whole French High Command from Gamelin down was fully aware of it.

What of the actual terrain across which Rundstedt's mighty mechanised phalanx was to advance, described by Petrarch six centuries previously as "the savage and inhospitable forests from which warriors and arms emerge at great risk?" In August 1914, General Lanrezac of the French Fifth Army had warned the Army Commander on his right, de Langle de Cary, of the dangers which would confront his impending attack in the Ardennes: "All this country is eminently suitable for the defensive and for ambushes . . . you will not enter into this region, and if you do you will not return from it." De Langle plunged in, was ambushed, and reeled back with heavy losses. Although between the sixteenth and eighteenth centuries no fewer than ten successful military operations had been carried out in the "inhospitable" Ardennes, it was de Langle's unfortunate experience that made the most indelible impression upon the postwar French High Command, adorning the Ardennes with its reputation of being impenetrable.

There are indeed parts of the Ardennes which, extremely rugged, could constrict the passage of a large and cumbersome army. On stretches of the Meuse, as between Charleville and Givet, the approaches are protected from the east by sheer and rocky cliffs. At Dinant the river can be reached only through wooded, twisting gorges difficult for tanks to negotiate and easily blocked by resolute demolition teams. Sedan itself is protected by dense woods and a vulnerable road that winds for three to four miles up the gorge of the Semois from picturesque Bouillon, and all its eastern approaches are superbly overlooked from La Marfée heights west of the river, providing both a view and an observation point on which it would be hard to improve. But much of the landscape on the high plateau of the Ardennes provides ideal tank country. The forests are interspersed with large clearings of rolling pasturage; the triangle Arlon–Bastogne–Neufchâteau, through which would run Guderian's main approach route beyond the Luxembourg frontier, is generally flat, wide-open country. Even the minor roads are good and well-surfaced; nor was it generally true to say, as Gamelin claims in his memoirs, that the terrain "did not permit infantry and tanks to deploy from the roads." Even in the magnificent forests of oak and beech and fir where, in May, the wild raspberries are pushing up bright green shoots and the broom is bursting into saffron explosions, there are numerous tracks cutting through them, readily viable to armoured vehicles. In fact, far from being a hindrance, here the thick boskage provides superb natural camouflage from the air, so that whole panzer divisions could easily lose themselves to the enemy's sight—effecting a modern variant of Birnam Wood come to Dunsinane. To be sure, there are ravines and natural barriers such as the meandering river Semois, but none of any value unless backed by a powerful, organised defence. And, as Liddell Hart has remarked, all natural obstacles are more readily surmountable than those of human resistance.

Even allowing for the distortions of hindsight, after one has actually explored the terrain, it is hard to comprehend how anyone (except perhaps a Deuxième Bureau officer who had never set foot outside the Crillon Bar) could possibly have deemed the Ardennes "impenetrable" to a modern army. It becomes still more extraordinary when one learns that, in 1938, manoeuvres were actually conducted under General Prétélat (then commander designate of the Second Army) which *exactly paralleled* the German attack of May 1940. Hit by an imaginary seven German divisions, four of them motorised, plus two tank brigades, debouching from the Ardennes, the French "defence" in these manoeuvres was battered beyond possibility of re-establishing itself. The results were so decisive that at least one senior commander begged that they never be published—lest they "upset the troops." Studying the manoeuvres from the Citadel of Verdun, amid the opiate memories of those past miracles wrought by the French Army on the defensive, Gamelin had observed that adequate reinforcements would have been available in time for the enemy blow to be parried. Even General Ironside, the British CIGS, who was hardly an outstanding military thinker, had predicted as early as October 1939 that the Ardennes might be selected by the Germans as the sector for their main attack. It remains to be explained why, despite the lessons of the Polish campaign, despite admonitions by de Gaulle and by Taittinger, and despite the repeated warnings leaking out about Hitler's intentions during the spring of 1940, Gamelin appeared to remain blind to the danger lurking in the dark woods of the Ardennes.

Was Gamelin blind?

In 1940, one of the principal arms of military intelligence was aerial reconnaissance, and we have seen what use the Germans made of it to reveal the state of readiness of the Meuse defences. Why were the Allied air forces, then, apparently unable to observe the massive concentrations of German armour pointing towards the Ardennes? Each appeal made by Air Marshal Barratt for permission to carry out high-altitude reconnaissance flights across Belgium was turned down on political grounds. Needless to say, the Germans were not similarly impeded and are reported (by the Belgians) to have carried out some 500 flights in the eight months preceding May 1940. But the French Air Force, flying north from Alsace-Lorraine, could easily have reconnoitred the Eifel and the vital communications across the Rhine. Their failure to do so has been variously attributed (by the French) to the inferiority of their aircraft and the bad weather conditions of the winter of '39–'40.* After losses of several planes, at the end of September 1939 the Bloch 131s were withdrawn from daylight operations and put on night work only; the Bréguet and Potez reconnaissance planes were instructed to operate only "behind battery positions"; the Mureaux were permitted to "approach between one and two kilometres from the lines, on condition that they operated in patrols of two." General Ruby writes that the French reconnaissance planes "could not pass over our lines except under fear of death." Less charitably, Air Marshal Barratt, who from the very first had been appalled at the apathy and defeatism that he found in the French Air Force, declared that their reconnaissance teams simply "would not leave the floor, often they gave the *excuse* that the weather was too bad." The fact is that, during the crucial month of April, only four French airplanes were lost through enemy action; hardly an excessively high price to have paid when one considers the mortal danger then confronting France.

Despite the shortcomings, however, of French aerial reconnaissance, GQG's Deuxième Bureau had managed to acquire a remarkably accurate picture of the German order of battle; more complete perhaps even than the breakdown of the French forces

---

* Note, though, that the weather did not appear to halt Luftwaffe operations.

prepared by the OKH "Foreign Armies West." Already in March it had become aware of the German concentrations building up near Trier and in the area between the Rhine and Moselle; towards the end of March it reported that German Intelligence had suddenly begun enquiring about road conditions along the Sedan–Abbeville axis; a month later it knew the location of all the German panzers as well as of the three motorised divisions. From this massive accumulation facing the Ardennes—which, to shift elsewhere, would have required a major military operation—the French High Command should certainly have been entitled to suppose (and *know* beyond a shadow of a doubt, if it had studied Guderian's *Achtung–Panzer!*) in which direction the *Schwerpunkt* of an attack might be aimed. A Swiss military historian, Eddy Bauer, tells us that Swiss Intelligence had observed the construction of eight military bridges across the Rhine between Bonn and Bingen, and had deduced from this that the main thrust could not be coming in the north, or south through the Maginot Line; he claims that these facts were also known to the French. Probably on the basis of this Swiss intelligence work, the French Military Attaché in Berne informed GQG on April 30th that the Germans were going to attack between May 8th and 10th, with Sedan as "principal axis of the movement."

All this various information was duly passed to Gamelin, but he remained sceptical; among other things, to the bitter end he insisted that the Germans were holding twice as many troops in Army Group "C," opposite the Maginot Line, as his intelligence experts stated, and that the OKH was keeping 45—instead of 20—divisions in reserve.

The blindness of Gamelin—and, for that matter, of Georges, Billotte and the weight of French generaldom—lay partly in the genuine belief that the defences at Sedan were adequate, predicated upon that ineradicable, mystical self-assurance of the invincibility, *in extremis,* of the French Army. But also one must take cognisance of the effectiveness of German deception measures, which were all part of the final *Sichelschnitt* Plan. From February onwards, Admiral Canaris's* Abwehr was deliberately spreading reports in neutral countries telling of war-weariness in Germany, and of how the Army would be incapable of sustaining

---

* Possibly his most helpful single contribution to Hitler during the war.

a major offensive against the Allies; less than a month before *Sichelschnitt* began, the German Military Attaché in Brussels was heard to discount any attack "in depth," on grounds that "we would have an initial success, but that would lead to nothing." German "travellers," beautiful women in nightclubs, indiscreetly talked about a German offensive coming along the old Schlieffen route. But the most highly organised deception plan was that carried out by Leeb's Army Group "C." Few officers in that group were even aware that it was a "deception"; up to the last it was widely believed that they would be involved in an offensive at the southern end of the line, and there was much talk about Italy coming into the war and lending 20 divisions for such an attack. Around April 20th, the Deuxième Bureau picked up a speech by Goering in which he declared that the Maginot Line was going to be attacked at two points between May 5th and 15th and that the Germans were prepared to lose 500,000 men and 80 percent of the Luftwaffe in pursuit of success. This mass of conflicting evidence relayed by the Deuxième Bureau was undoubtedly confusing to Gamelin, who could never shake from his mind the possibility of a serious enemy effort being made against the Maginot Line; or even one outflanking it via Switzerland. But the fact is that it was the latest reports, particularly that emanating from the French Military Attaché in Berne, which should have been believed.

As May brought the unleashing of *Sichelschnitt* ever closer, some remarkable warnings came out of Germany itself, the most accurate of which were received by the Dutch.

Colonel Hans Oster, a senior officer in the Abwehr itself and one of the most active and courageous members of the German resistance,* was an intimate friend of Colonel Sas, the Dutch Military Attaché in Berlin. Four times between November and May 10th he provided Sas with precise warnings of Hitler's offensive plans; but by May the Dutch were mistrustful—partly because of the past false alarms, partly because they ardently *wanted* to believe that they would not be attacked. On April 3rd, Oster had warned Sas (correctly) of the Norwegian operation; now, on May 3rd, he told Oster that Holland was imminently to be attacked. The Dutch informed the Belgians and took some measures to

---

* Oster was executed in the aftermath of the July 1944 bomb plot.

alert their army. Sas would meet Oster once again, on the evening of May 9th.

On the brink

Seldom had there been a more marvellous spring. Parisians lingered in the *trottoir* cafés, listening to the strains of "J'Attendrai" and dreaming nostalgically of last year's holidays. Clare Boothe went into raptures at how "chestnuts burst into leaf on the lovely avenues of Paris, sunlight danced off the opalescent grey buildings, and the gold and grey sunsets, glimpsed through the soaring Arc de Triomphe at the end of the long splendid vista of the Champs Élysées, brought a catch of pain and pleasure in your throat. Paris was Paris in April!" There were art shows in the Grand Palais, racing at Auteuil, and soccer matches between Tommies and poilus in the suburbs. "The shop windows of van Cleef and Arpels and Mauboussin and Cartier sparkled with great jewels in the sunlight," she recalled. "And lots of people bought them." The Ritz, as usual, was "crowded with lovely ladies wearing simple dresses or the smart uniforms of the Union des Femmes de France service." There was also a wealthy Mrs. Corrigan who wore a uniform of her own design, embroidered with her motto, *Bien Venu!* There were meatless days, sugarless days, liquorless days, no more luxury chocolates, and the patisseries closed three days a week, but none of this made too much difference to Parisian gastronomy. On May 2nd, says Fabre-Luce, "Parisian society gave its last party. It was a charity gala at the Marigny theatre." The front seats were occupied by such dethroned monarchs as the Duke of Windsor and King Zog of Albania. About the same time, André Maurois found the Academy peaceably working away on its eternal dictionary:

The definition of the word *aile* led to a passage of arms between Abel Bonnard and Georges Duhamel. The previous edition had called a wing "a muscle." "It's perfectly ridiculous," said Bonnard. "A wing is a limb." "On the contrary," said Dr. Duhamel, "a wing is a muscle. What you eat in the wing of a chicken is the muscle, no more and no less."

And so the argument continued. Could anything, one might have wondered, could anything alter the basic facts of French life?

But underneath this veneer of "business as usual," reality was still all too evident to the discerning. Pierre Mendès-France returning on leave from Syria at the beginning of May was shocked at what he found: "Everyone, civilian and military, thought only of organising his personal life as well as possible in order to get through this seemingly indefinite period without too much risk, loss or discomfort. . . . One heard only of recreation for the army, sport for the army, art and music for the army, theatrical shows for the army, and so on." (Meanwhile, in England, Lady Astor had caused a stir in the Commons by enquiring about the number of licensed French brothels at the front.) Since January the amount of leave given the French Army had been vastly augmented; in fact, on May 7th, Gamelin had actually restored normal leave throughout the Army. Major Sarraz-Bournet of the Deuxième Bureau recounts: "Despite the warnings of Colonel Gauché, leave at the beginning of May had not been suspended, even at the Grand Quartier Général. I had myself gone off on the eve of Whitsun to go and spend a few days of a brief leave in the Dauphine." But better leave conditions had certainly done little to boost morale. Sarraz-Bournet (whose job was to control postal censorship) detected a belief widespread in the Army by the spring of 1940 that the war would end "without battle, by a diplomatic arrangement between the interested governments . . . nothing could have been worse for morale"; and Major Barlone from Blanchard's elite First Army wrote in his diary on April 30th: "The General advises us to look after the morale of our men; we must give them some distraction. The postal censorship shows that the men are fed up." Nevertheless, despite all the manifestly disturbing symptoms within the Army, at the beginning of May General Billotte could still tell some of his Corps commanders who had complained to him about arms deficiencies: "Why bother yourselves? Nothing will happen before 1941!"

In Germany, rationing had cut food consumption to some 75 percent of the prewar average; but nobody was hungry. Over the winter, Joseph Harsch of the *Christian Science Monitor* remarked, Berliners had been kept "in good humour" by a variety of "Japanese tumblers, Italian aerial artistes, Hungarian folk orchestras and clever Viennese skits, often at the expense of the Party great." After eight months during which they had not been attacked by the Allies, and particularly after the successes of the Norwegian campaign, German nerves were much restored. But still it was hard to find actual enthusiasm for the war. On Easter Sunday (March 24th) William Shirer thought the faces of the Berliners "looked blank. Obviously they do not like the war, but they will do what they're told. Die, for instance." On April 19th, the eve of Hitler's fifty-first birthday, Shirer found only some seventy-five people outside the Chancellery waiting for a glimpse of their Führer, whereas in other years "there were ten thousand." On May 1st, Shirer again visited the Rhine front; all was quiet: "Not a single airplane could be seen in the skies." His diary continues:

May 7th. For three or four days now the German newspapers have been carrying on a terrific campaign to convince somebody that the Allies, having failed in Norway, are about to become "aggressors" in some other part of Europe. . . . Where is Germany going in next? I'm suspicious of Holland, partly because it's the one place not specifically mentioned in this propaganda campaign.

May 8th. Could not help noticing a feeling of tension in the Wilhelmstrasse today. Something is up, but we don't know what.

May 9th. Headlines in the German leading papers "Britain plots to spread the war" they roar . . . it may well be, as many people over here think, that the war will be fought and decided before the summer is over. People somehow seem to feel that the Whitsuntide holidays this weekend will be the last holidays Europe will observe for some time.

At last, Hitler's panzers were ready to roll. On May 7th, he had allowed Goering to extract one last postponement—on account of the weather—from him; "but not a day longer." Then, on the evening of May 9th, the Luftwaffe announced that "weather on May 10th will be good." Like the bearer of good tidings to some oriental despot of bygone years, the head of the Meteorological Service earned a gold watch for his favourable report. Inside the Chancellery and at both OKW and OKH Headquarters, however, extreme nervousness prevailed. On the 9th, Halder recorded anxiety aroused by "alarming reports" from Yugoslavia, purporting that French and British tanks had landed there. Nevertheless, that evening Hitler and his entourage embarked on the "Führer Special" from a small railway station near Berlin, heading north. Only after dark would it turn westwards, to bring Hitler to his specially prepared battle HQ at Münstereifel, midway between

Bonn and the Belgian Ardennes. That night, at 2100 hours,* the OKW transmitted to all the formations waiting expectantly behind the western frontiers of the Reich the code word *Danzig,* signifying that the great offensive was to begin at 0535 hours the next morning. In Berlin, Colonel Sas met his friend Hans Oster again—for the last time. Oster remarked that, as there had been so many postponements, it could just happen again; but if, by 2130 no counterorder had been given, "then this is finally it." At 2130 the two colonels went to OKW headquarters. Sas waited outside in the darkness. When Oster rejoined him, he told Sas that there had been no counterorder: "The swine has gone off to the West Front. . . . Let's hope that we'll meet again after the war." Using a prearranged code, Sas then telephoned The Hague. An hour and a half later, he was rung back by the Dutch Chief of Intelligence, who said doubtingly, "I have just received the very bad news about the operation of your wife. Have you now spoken to all the doctors?" Sas, much vexed, replied, "I don't understand why you bother me now under these circumstances. You know now. Nothing can be done any more about this operation. I have spoken to all the doctors." He ended (though it seems extraordinary that German security should have allowed such a conversation to pass in clear down the telephone line), "Tomorrow morning, at dawn, it takes place." At three o'clock on the morning of the 10th, belatedly, the Dutch blew up the first of their frontier bridges.

In London as May 9th, the 250th day of the war, came to a close, Neville Chamberlain had resigned; in Paris, Paul Reynaud had offered his resignation to President Lebrun, because Daladier would not let him sack Gamelin. Near Nîmes, Janet Teissier du Cros, a Scotswoman waiting for her French husband to come home on leave, read joyfully in a newspaper she picked up late on the night of the 9th: *"Détente en Hollande."* "The cock-eyed war was going to last long enough to allow François to enjoy his leave," she thought, and nothing else mattered. Nearer the front, the staff officers of General Huntziger's Second Army HQ had spent an agreeable evening watching a play performed by the Théâtre aux Armées at Vouziers. Gontaut-Biron, a mechanised

---

* German time, i.e., one hour ahead of French time.

dragoon from the 3rd Light Cavalry Division* which was to push
into Luxembourg if the Germans attacked, recalled that his evening had been very gay. "We played bridge very late into the night.
We had no fears about anything, we had been so often told that
we would be warned at least 24 hours in advance by our Intelligence Service. Towards 11 o'clock in the evening, we separated,
and went back to our respective quarters." That same day, her
acute journalistic instinct had persuaded Clare Boothe to fly to
Amsterdam. "Motoring from Amsterdam to The Hague," she recalled, "you couldn't have told there was a crisis, except in the
wonderful tulip fields, which had reached their maximum and
were about to wither." She reached Brussels that night, where she
stayed with the American ambassador, Cudahy. "I've been on
the telephone night and day," he told her. "But now," he said,
as though he himself did not quite believe it, "it's over, thank
God. The King has reinstated all his appointments for the weekend." Near Metz, on that last day of the Phoney War, the Inspector General of Artillery, General Boris, had comforted
artillery commanders of the Third Army by telling them of the
modern guns that would be ready "next spring."

The following morning, May 10, on a tour of inspection of the
sector, General Boris heard explosions. "Is that a manoeuvre?"
he enquired. *"Mon Général,* it's the German offensive," came the
reply. In Brussels, Clare Boothe was wakened by a maid shaking
her: "Wake up! The Germans are coming again!"

So the scene opens on the confrontation of the century, of
which the Great War—the Marne, Verdun, the Somme, Pass-
chendaele and Amiens—was but a thunderous overture. On one
side, France; a nation divided and with little heart for war, led
by a Premier weakened by influenza and his mistress, who had
offered his resignation, and by a Generalissimo under suspended
sentence; guarded by an army whose morale was—to say the least
—patchy, weak in numbers and equipment, guided by outdated
doctrine and commanded by mediocre leaders, and by an air force
outclassed in every respect; and supported by a solitary ally who
could still only contribute a handful of divisions to the coming
battle. On the other side, a revolutionary Germany led by a
daemonic prophet possessed of total self-assurance, but supported

* Third Army.

by professional soldiers, many of them nervous, hostile and not sharing their Führer's certainty of success; equipped with a superlative war machine, but relatively with far fewer elite divisions than the Kaiser's army which had lumbered into Belgium a generation earlier; and marching to one of the most brilliant war plans of all time—but one so risky that any serious setback to it, any breaking of the steel cutting edge of Guderian's panzers, could but end in another calamitous defeat for Germany.

Part II

9

The Crocus Blossoms

"When the crocus blossoms," hiss the women in Berlin,
"He will press the button, and the battle will begin.
When the crocus blossoms, up the German knights will
    go,
And flame and fume and filthiness will terminate the foe.
". . . When the crocus blossoms, not a neutral will re-
    main . . ."

               —A. P. HERBERT, "Spring Song"

The Germans move

FROM THE Eifel Mountains on the night of May 9th, a forty-eight-year-old major general, Erwin Rommel, commanding the 7th Panzer Division which he had taken over less than three months before, dashed off a brief note to his wife:

Dearest Lu,

We're packing up at last. Let's hope not in vain. You'll get all the news for the next few days from the papers. Don't worry yourself. Everything will go all right.

All over western Germany, and far behind the Rhine, there were similar scenes of rapid "packing up" and the writing of last letters. The SS Grossdeutschland Regiment which was to play a key role in the coming battle received a terse order from its commander, Lieutenant Colonel Count von Schwerin: "Forward against the enemy! *Mit Gott! Es lebe der Führer!*" On returning from manoeuvres, Werner Flack, wireless sergeant in a horse-drawn unit that had fought in Poland, who was hoping to get a day's pass to enjoy the gorgeous spring weather at Bingen-am-

Rhein, was told by his *Feldwebel* (sergeant major) that afternoon that the company was to move again in four hours' time. More manoeuvres? On reaching the wireless office, he found a typewritten slip bearing the unit's action frequencies. Now knowing that it was the real thing, he later recalled: "The warmth and brilliance of the day was stunningly oppressive. But I saw neither the mountains nor the flowers, neither the meadows nor the sunshine. I simply pushed the sheet with the action frequencies on it into the Command folder."

The conditions of secrecy and speed which Hitler had imposed after the Mechelen Incident were superbly fulfilled. Even commanders of units in the van of the attack were kept ignorant of its timing until the last possible minute. On the afternoon of May 7th, for instance, Oskar Reile, an Abwehr officer stationed in Trier and charged with the important task of controlling undercover agents in Luxembourg, had asked for and been granted a few days' leave. His superior had requested him to stay in the neighbourhood, but added, "As far as I can see, nothing special will happen in the next few days." It was only on the afternoon of May 9th that Reile was recalled from his leave. Captain Count von Kielmansegg,* the second staff officer at HQ of the 1st Panzer Division which was to spearhead the attack on Sedan, noted that when they received their orders at lunchtime on the 9th, "the division's officers were completely unprepared for the news." Some had already left on Whitsun leave. Without them, the 1st Panzer departed from its quarters that night, driving with lights extinguished up the winding roads of the Eifel. "With every hour that goes by," wrote one of the tankmen, "it becomes more lively on the approach roads, more and more troops quartered here in the Eifel are getting under way. We overtake marching, riding and driving columns. The noise of the motors gets on one's nerves in this night of uncertainty. The drivers must exert the utmost powers of vision, so as not to end up in the roadside ditches. It's pitch dark. . . . Now we realise why we so often came here to carry out peacetime operations."

At 4:30† the 1st Panzer, bearing General Guderian with it,

---

* Now General von Kielmansegg, Commander of Central Forces, NATO.

† French time, which, together with British time, was one hour behind German time. French times are given throughout the rest of the narrative.

The opposing forces on the eve of the German attack: May 10th

crossed the Luxembourg frontier near Vianden where that famous propagandist of an earlier Franco-German war, Victor Hugo, had spent his declining years. But Guderian's men were not the first Germans to enter the Grand Duchy; on previous days an unprecedented number of "tourists" on bicycles and motorcycles had been checked through the unsuspecting frontier guards. Dispatched by the Abwehr, their role was to dislocate telephone communications and prevent the Luxembourgers from destroying vital road junctions. Further to the north, Rommel and his 7th Panzer were swarming across the Belgian frontier, heading for Dinant on the Meuse 65 miles away. Still further north, along the Dutch frontier facing Maastricht, German storm troops had nestled right up to the Dutch customs posts. As the first light of dawn came up, they could hear the rumble of approaching tanks; the tension grew unbearable, but still the Dutch frontier guards continued to stroll quietly up and down, apparently noticing nothing. Then the rumbling grew louder and louder as squadron after squadron of Ju–52s, containing the whole of the German 22nd Airborne Division, plus some 4,000 paratroopers, passed overhead. Meanwhile, over the German radio that dawn came the usual martial music and the first news of the day's sporting events.

Luftwaffe attacks

The Luftwaffe bomber crews too had not been warned of the imminent offensive. Roused out of their beds during the early hours of May 10th while it was still dark, they were ordered to attend briefings at fifteen minutes' notice. There was no time even to shave. Shortly before sunrise, every available aircraft left its field. Ranging far out, they laid mines off the Dutch and British coasts, struck at airfields in Holland, Belgium and France, and bombed road and railway centres deep in France. At Abbeville, a sugar warehouse was set on fire; burning for several days it produced rivers of treacle, which the inhabitants did not allow to go to waste. At the RAF airfield of Conde-Vraux south of Reims, Dornier "Flying Pencils" destroyed six of 114 Squadron's eighteen Blenheim bombers, all neatly lined up in a row, and rendered the remaining twelve unserviceable; though otherwise the RAF were fortunate enough to sustain little serious damage on the ground that day. Altogether nearly fifty French airfields, in General d'Astier's ZOAN and behind Paris, were attacked that

Popular Front memorial to the Commune: Léon Blum (with glasses and moustache), André Marty, Vincent Auriol, Maurice Thorez, Jules Moch

A disarmament parade in Paris

Munich: the formal portrait after the signing. Left to right:
Chamberlain, Daladier, Hitler, Mussolini, Ciano. *Below:* Enthusiastic
crowd at Le Bourget airport greets Daladier on his return

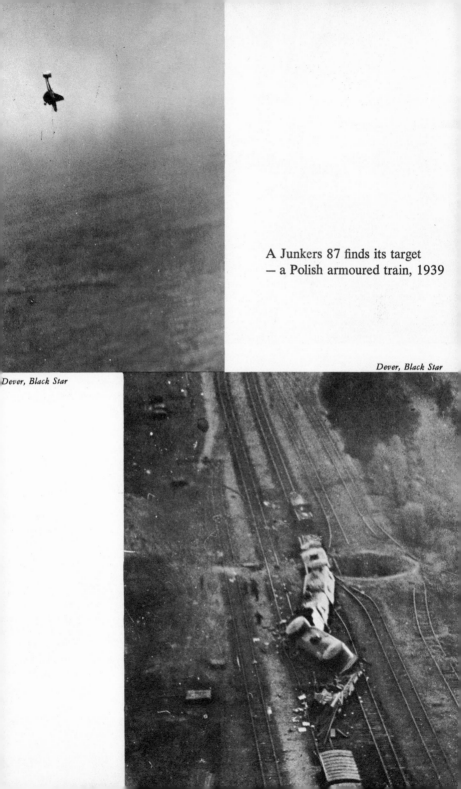

A Junkers 87 finds its target
— a Polish armoured train, 1939

French artillerymen decorate their weapons as poilu *(below)* sits
guard on the western front during the "Phoney War"

Generals Gamelin and Georges, after French Cabinet meeting

Imperial War Museum, London

Giraud

British Combin

Corap

Ironside, Churchill, Gamelin, Gort, Georges

Bibliothèque de Documentation Internationale Contemporai

Rommel

Keitel

Kleist

Manstein

Halder and Brauchitsch

Rundstedt

Balck

Reichenau

day. General d'Astier himself claims that all the fields were quickly restored, and that only four planes were destroyed and another thirty damaged. Three Heinkel 111s setting out to bomb Dijon strayed, and bombed the German city of Freiburg-im-Breisgau by mistake, killing 57 civilians, including 22 children.* It was against little Holland, however, that the main weight of Goering's fury was turned on the 10th. Flying over the Dutch pastures that morning, Theo Osterkamp, a fighter ace who had won the Pour le Mérite† in the First War, thought to himself how peaceful it all seemed: "Children playing by the stream, a white dog jumps around them barking, and they wave and laugh and are happy. How crazy! Why is this lovely peaceful land suddenly 'enemy territory'? . . . Why will those girls with rakes in their hands be threatening and screaming tomorrow, instead of waving with their coloured handkerchiefs and laughing?" The answer was not hard to arrive at, as at the same moment less idyllically-minded young Germans were already machine-gunning the streets of The Hague. Curving out into the North Sea so as to take the Dutch by surprise (not unlike the Israeli fighter-bombers of June 1967), the Heinkel 111s hammered the airfields at Amsterdam-Schiphol, Bergen-op-Zoom, and Rotterdam-Waalhaven. At Waalhaven, bombs killed a large number of Dutch soldiers who—despite Colonel Sas's warning and the ensuing alert—had been allowed to "sleep on" in vulnerable hangars. Most of the few planes of the Dutch Air Force were wiped out. After the bombing and strafing came the paratroops and German airborne force in what was to be the first major attempt in history to occupy and conquer a nation from the air.

With the main visible effort of the Luftwaffe concentrated over Holland, there was nothing here that might betray to Allied intelligence the true direction of *Sichelschnitt*. Meanwhile, over the panzers creeping slowly along the densely packed roads of the Eifel and into the Ardennes, an immense fighter umbrella flew

---

* Hitler immediately claimed that the bombers had been Allies; thereby providing himself with an admirable *quid pro quo* to excuse the launching of terror raids against Allied—as well as Belgian and Dutch—civilian centres. Goebbels's propaganda machine kept up the story of the Allied atrocity against Freiburg throughout the war, and it was not until several years afterwards that the whole truth was revealed.

† Germany's highest decoration.

cover against any Allied "spy" planes that might attempt to intrude. But few did.

To the vigilant Luftwaffe patrolling above, the roads leading towards Sedan and the Meuse presented the spectacle of a lifetime that day. Nose to bumper was the greatest concentration of tanks—between 1,200 and 1,500—yet seen in war. Kleist's massive Armoured Group was moving forward in three blocks, one densely closed up behind the other. "Like a giant phalanx," remarked General von Blumentritt, Rundstedt's Chief of Operations, "they stretched back for a hundred miles, the rear rank lying fifty miles to the *east* of the Rhine. Had this mass formation of panzers been placed in single file, the tail-end would have been in Königsberg, in East Prussia, and the head of the column in Trier." First came the tanks and the motorised infantry shock troops; then the heavy supply echelons; and finally, far beyond the Rhine, singing lustily and marching against each other as if in competition, the infantry regiments whose job would be to hold and consolidate the ground conquered by the panzers. It would be another two days before they would even reach the frontier. Occasionally, the columns would be halted by a single vehicle breaking down. But such halts were rare; the moment a tank or a car showed signs of stalling, it was ruthlessly pushed off the road. Uneasily the panzer commanders, aware of what a superb target the dense, crawling columns presented, gazed up to the skies; but there they saw only the reassuring black crosses of the Luftwaffe.

Guderian

The passage of Guderian's column through Luxembourg took place smoothly—and peacefully. Feldwebel Schwappacher of the Grossdeutschland Regiment, which was leading the panzers across the Ardennes, recorded how the outlines of the last houses in the frontier town of Echternach "appear and fade in the early morning mists. . . . An old grandmother greets us happily and gives us her blessings for the forthcoming battle . . . the Luxembourgers try to blow up the bridge over the Sauer; it only half succeeded, so that our engineers were immediately able to put it back in order by using a few boards." Other German soldiers were astonished to see farmers in the fields, continuing to plough and barely raising their heads as the panzers rumbled past. The "tourists" sent in by Admiral Canaris had performed their tasks well; there were few hold-ups caused by demolitions, and on the main Trier–Luxembourg road the advancing columns found several stretches that had been mined but not detonated. With them the German engineers carried wooden ramps, specially designed to fit over the paltry Luxembourg tank obstacles, so that the panzers could roll across them with the minimum delay. Backing up the Abwehr "tourists" was the first of Hitler's "special operations" brain children. A detachment of 125 volunteers, commanded by Lieutenant Hedderich, had been landed before dawn by 25 Fieseler Storchs near Esch on the Franco-Luxembourg frontier with the task of holding this vital communication centre until Guderian's main force arrived. After halting and turning back a number of Luxembourg workers bicycling to collect their Friday pay packets, Hedderich's group were accosted by a bewildered but amicable gendarme who informed them that they were "on neutral territory," and ordered them to leave it. He was quietly arrested. Narrowly missing the present Grand Duke Jean, who happened to be passing in a car, the Germans then settled down to wait for Guderian. By 1000 hours that morning the forward elements of the 1st Panzer had already reached the Belgian frontier after traversing all Luxembourg. Hardly a shot had been fired; total Luxembourg casualties amounted to six gendarmes and one soldier wounded, seventy-five captured, none killed.

Rommel

Out beyond the right flank of Kleist's Armoured Group, the 5th Panzer reported that its first tank to cross the Belgian frontier had bravely managed to shoot up a group of unprepared Belgian infantrymen, lolling about on a frontier bridge. Later that morning the division was attacked by two enemy bombers, which dropped their bombs aimlessly in the woods. One was shot down by the German light flak, and a parachute opened. Just south of the 5th Panzer, Rommel was encountering elaborate obstructions prepared by the Belgians:

All roads and forest tracks had been permanently barricaded and deep craters blown in the main roads. But most of the road blocks were undefended by the Belgians, and it was thus in only a few places that my division was held up for any length of time. Many of the blocks could be by-passed by moving across country or over side roads. Elsewhere, all troops quickly set to work to deal with the obstructions and soon had the road clear.

Nevertheless, the Belgian frontier works—undefended as they were—proved sufficient to slow Rommel's advance down to 6 kilometres in three hours, a first setback which made the impatient Rommel distinctly nervous. Much of the Belgian demolition work had certainly been effected with consummate skill: bridges so well dynamited that their remains provided little use for emergency bridges; roads blown up with charges dug so deep into their foundations as to make them completely impassable. At Martelange, just inside the Belgian frontier from Luxembourg, mine fields and a destroyed river bridge presented the 1st Panzer with its first check of the day, forcing it to postpone its attack on the Belgian main line of resistance until the following day. But, obeying their orders to the letter, the Belgian Chasseurs Ardennais, having completed their demolitions, withdrew from the scene. How much more the delicately balanced German timetable might have been thrown out of gear, even on the first day, if those frontier obstructions could have been supported by resolute covering fire! Here was perhaps the first of the painful consequences of Belgium's return to the neutrality of 1936.

Operation "Niwi"

So far the most demonstrative sequences in the land fighting on May 10th followed from Hitler's airborne "special operations," the first time that these had ever been employed in warfare on so large a scale. Lieutenant Hedderich's airborne commando dropped outside Esch in Luxembourg has already been mentioned, but further north in the Belgian Ardennes a more ambitious endeavour, Operation "Niwi," was also under way. "Niwi," so named because of the two villages concerned, involved a landing of some 400 men of the Grossdeutschland at Nives and Witry in the Belgian Ardennes, roughly midway between Neufchâteau and the frontier towns of Bastogne and Martelange. Neufchâteau, sitting on a very commanding height with roads radiating out of it in all directions, was potentially a most important defensive position, and its rapid capture was also essential to Guderian's advance upon Sedan. Dispatched in two groups aboard 98 of the light Fieseler Storchs, instructions were to keep open the roads running eastwards from Neufchâteau, impede the passage of enemy reinforcements through Neufchâteau, and aid the progress of Guderian's XIX Corps by attacking the Belgian frontier position from the rear. The Witry group, under the "Niwi" commander, Lieutenant Colonel Garski, landed according to schedule, but Captain Krüger's group heading for Nives was beset with the errors that so often plague airborne operations.

A sergeant with Krüger describes how "soon after take off we lost sight of the other Storchs flying with us . . . on the roads there is the endless worm of the army stretching out. People wave at us . . . we land in Belgium on a meadow. It's the wrong place, and with loud curses from us the three machines take off again." The pilots then spotted a Storch burning on the ground and landed near it; "there is a terrible muddle. The ammunition is taken into a nearby wood, the road barricaded." Stunned Belgian passers-by told the lost detachment that they had landed near the village of Leglise, about 9 miles off Nives and on the wrong side of Garski's group. "Our defence measures are strengthened, machine guns put in position . . . we requisition civilian cars . . . then suddenly our runner, Preusch, arrives with a bicycle; he has landed with the captain some 2 kilometres away." They joined up with Krüger's group, but not with Garski and the rest of the battalion until the afternoon. There was some sharp fighting against the Chasseurs Ardennais for possession of Witry, which finally fell at 1300 hours—at a cost of 19 German casualties. A short time later contact was made with the advanced elements of the 1st Panzer. The approaches to Neufchâteau were open.

The "Brandenburgers"

Although "Hedderich" and "Niwi" were more fundamental, tactically, to the success of Sichelschnitt, events up in the north were certainly more colourful and eye-catching. Holland, with her small, weak army,* predicated her defence upon the flooding of large areas and the destruction of bridges over the numerous canals. It was to forestall this that Hitler decided to strike swiftly, from behind. By the end of May 10th General Student's airborne troops had succeeded in capturing the three key airfields of

---

* In 1940 Holland, with a larger population, had an army of only 250,000 men, compared to Belgium's 700,000.

Ockenburg, Ijpenburg, and Valkenburg which ring The Hague, though they had suffered setbacks and severe losses. They had also seized the important bridges over the Maas* estuary at Dordrecht and Moerdijk, and destroyed 62 of the Dutch Air Force's 125 planes. Meanwhile, to open up Holland to Bock's panzers and infantry moving in from the east, some ruses had been resorted to that were particularly dear to Hitler's heart. As early as November 1939, he had first mooted the idea of seizing the vital Maas bridges by commandos dressed in Dutch uniforms. Canaris, although allegedly disapproving of the operation as being unethical, had provided the necessary uniforms. Their theft did not go unnoticed in Holland, where a newspaper even caricatured the uniform-loving Goering disguised as a Dutch tram conductor, but otherwise the phlegmatic Dutch were not disposed to let their suspicions be aroused. The troops for this cloak-and-dagger role originated from a body with the cover-name of *Bau- und Lehrkompanie Brandenburg*†—or "Brandenburgers" as they were more commonly christened, which was to grow from a company to a battalion, and later to a division, during the course of the war. The "Brandenburgers" had first been thought up at the time of the Czech crisis by Captain Theodor von Hippel, who had fought in Lettow-Vorbeck's brilliant guerrilla campaign behind the British lines in East Africa. They would infiltrate behind the Czech lines to link up with Sudeten "patriots." Thanks to Chamberlain, their services were never required. In October 1939, however, Canaris had instructed Hippel to set up the *Bau- und Lehrkompanie,* and their first service had been the capture intact of Danish bridges over the Belts.

The attempt on the Dutch bridges at Maastricht ended in dismal failure. There was a confused shoot-up, in which the leader of the bogus Dutchmen, Lieutenant Hocke, was killed; it was impossible to remove the explosive charges, and all three bridges blew up in the face of the waiting panzers. When Canaris's Abwehr delegate arrived outside Maastricht, he found a depressing sight of mile upon mile of panzers and vehicles jamming the roads,

---

* The Dutch extension of the Meuse.

† "Construction and Training Company." Quite by coincidence, the Germans who had pulled off without loss the greatest *coup de main* of the First War, the capture of Verdun's Fort Douaumont, the world's most powerful fortification, were also "Brandenburgers," in that they came from the III Brandenburg Corps.

and it was not until mid-morning that an assault bridge could be thrown across the Maas. A similar fiasco took place at Arnhem where the "Brandenburgers," to make up for their shortage of Dutch uniforms, utilised outlandish cardboard helmets and were immediately spotted. But at Gennep they were triumphant; under Lieutenant Walther three Dutch fifth columnists dressed as policemen marched up to the bridge with a posse of "captured" German POWs, fully equipped with machine pistols and grenades under their army overcoats, and they succeeded in securing the bridge from the surprised defenders. Walther's seizure of the bridge at Gennep had important consequences; across it the 9th Panzer Division rushed to interpose itself between the Dutch Army and General Giraud's Seventh Army, to forestall Gamelin's Breda Variant; and at the same time, General von Reichenau was able to divert northwards to Gennep some of the units of his Sixth Army bogged down before Maastricht. The *Blitzkrieg* rolled into Holland.

Meanwhile, it was also the "Brandenburgers" who were charged with securing some twenty-four objectives in Belgium, including bridges and viaducts and the tracing-out of mine fields which had previously been reported by German agents. At St. Vith, on Rommel's route to Dinant, Captain Rudloff, who had been studying the habits of the Belgian frontier guards minutely over the previous weeks, was particularly successful. There had been some wild shooting in the railway station, during which a locomotive managed to take off to give the warning; but otherwise three out of four of St. Vith's bridges fell intact into German hands. For their achievements, 3 Company of the "Brandenburgers" received no less than ninety-two Iron Crosses.

Eben Emael

But the single most striking episode of May 10th was undoubtedly the capture of the Belgian Fort Eben Emael. The nearest equivalent in 1940 to Verdun's Fort Douaumont of 1916, Eben Emael was the northernmost fortification guarding Liège and was the linchpin of the Albert Canal position, along which Gamelin anticipated the Belgians could hold the Germans at bay for five days, until the French and BEF could be established—a calculation that formed the basis of the Allied Dyle-Breda Plan. It was also a vital factor of Hitler's *Sichelschnitt* that such a delay in the north should not occur; for until the powerful mechanised forces belonging to the French First Army were engaged by frontal attack there, grave danger would always exist that they could be diverted to strike the vulnerable northern flank of the main German break-through at Sedan. Therefore, for both sides, a great deal depended on Eben Emael. Completed as recently as 1935, the fort measured some 900 yards by 700, and was protected by an enormous cutting which fell 120 feet, sheer and unassailably, into the Albert Canal. In various single and double turrets, it mounted nearly a dozen pieces of artillery from 75 mm to 120 mm as well as numerous light cannon and machine guns, and safely underground it contained a full battalion of troops. No single fort of the Maginot Line was as powerful. But, like all fixed, unmanoeuvrable and supposedly invincible strongholds, it had its Achilles' heel; it possessed virtually no antiaircraft defences and the surface of the fort itself was unmined.

The mission of capturing Eben Emael was entrusted to the Koch Storm Detachment, consisting of volunteer sappers, which, under Captain Koch, had been trained at Hildesheim in the most rigid secrecy since November 1939. Its members had been allowed no leave, were forbidden to mix with men of other units, and had been sworn to secrecy under pain of death. Initially they had practised their attack on models, and later on bunkers of the Czechs' Sudeten fortress system, so that by May they knew every detail of Eben Emael in their sleep—except its name. At 0330 on May 10th, while it was still dark, they took off from Cologne, in eleven large gliders, each carrying seven to eight men and towed by a Ju–52. The gliders were piloted by some of the star German pilots of peacetime gliding competitions—a sport at which Germany, on account of the Versailles limitations, had long excelled —including the former world champion, Sergeant Bräutigam. The reason for employing gliders was simple; in the dusk, they could cover the roughly 13 miles across the frontier unheard and unseen, and they could land on top of the fort itself within 20 yards of a given spot. The superbly precise timing allowed them to land on Eben Emael just five minutes before the bulk of the Wehrmacht crossed the frontier. After circling to gain height, the Ju–52s followed a line of beacons to Aachen where they cast off the gliders from a height of 8,000 feet. They flew on, dropping quantities of parachute "dummies" stuffed with firecrackers, to confuse the Belgian defenders. At Eben Emael, the Belgian sentries heard Dutch antiaircraft fire over the Maastricht appendix, but heard or saw nothing else until suddenly, like great black birds that seemed to hang almost motionless in the air, the gliders were on top of them.

For all its minute planning, the operation nearly failed when the towropes of two of the gliders snapped, including the one which contained the expedition commander, Lieutenant Rudolf Witzig. One landed near Düren and its disgruntled members were forced to join up on foot with the advancing ground forces. Witzig landed in a field not far from Cologne; with commendable energy, he prepared a field by chopping down willow hedges and called up another Ju–52 to tow him off. He arrived safely at Eben Emael to find that—no doubt as a by-product of the superb training the unit had undergone—his Feldwebel (sergeant major) Wenzel already had the situation well in hand, having landed unopposed plumb on top of the fort. Swiftly the German engineers blasted the thick steel carapaces which protected the subterranean gun turrets, using (for the first time) powerful hollow charges. One by one Eben Emael's turrets and gun casemates were knocked out in this fashion; the heavy twin 120 mm turret, whose armour proved too thick for the hollow charges, was dispatched by the simple device of poking explosive charges down the barrels. Some time was wasted on two turrets which proved to be dummies, but by the time Lieutenant Witzig reached Eben Emael the mighty fort had been blinded and its teeth drawn. Nearby Belgian artillery opened heavy fire on the Germans on the fort glacis, but no really dangerous counterattack had been mounted by the battalion-strong infantry garrison, nor had any mines or other obstacles been encountered. Witzig now entered the fort to clean up inside. Meanwhile, other detachments of Koch's glider-borne engineers had seized two nearby bridges over the Albert Canal. All through the night of May 10th–11th the garrison of Eben Emael held out, while Belgian infantry from outside the fort attempted to dislodge the Germans. The situation for Witzig's 85 men was becoming precarious when, at 0600 hours on the 11th, they were relieved by the advance troops of Reichenau's Sixth Army. Six hours later Eben Emael surrendered, and 1,100 men were taken prisoners. In the fighting the Belgians lost 23 killed and 59 wounded; Witzig, 6 dead and 15 wounded. Hitler promptly

awarded Koch and Witzig* (then only twenty-four) the Ritterkreuz, one of Germany's highest decorations.

Of all the successes of May 10th, none pleased Hitler more than
the capture of Eben Emael. His pleasure was indeed justified. It
was undoubtedly one of the boldest coups of war, more brilliant
even than the seizure of Fort Douaumont in 1916, which fell virtually by accident. Its capture meant that within thirty hours the
Germans had already breached the Albert Canal line and thrown
into jeopardy the whole of Gamelin's strategy. But, as already
noted, this tactical success only concerned the secondary part of
the German plan. Of still greater importance was the psychological
impact of the sudden collapse of Eben Emael. Cunningly, Goebbels's propaganda machine, suppressing all mention of Witzig's
hollow charges, made mysterious capital by referring to a "new
method of attack." The refrain was promptly taken up in the
Allied camp and dark rumours circulated about secret weapons,
such as nerve gases. Even a year later an American magazine was
claiming that Eben Emael had been blown up by Germans who
in peacetime had grown chicory in nearby caves, which they
treacherously filled with explosives. Coming so soon after Hitler's
extraordinary successes in Norway, talk about "secret weapons"
at Eben Emael's left a nasty feeling in the pit of French stomachs;
if the Germans could deal thus with the world's strongest single
fort, what would be the fate of the impregnable Maginot Line?
Eyes became nervously diverted there; eyes that should have been
fixed in gaze upon the danger hourly mounting in the Ardennes.
Meanwhile, the employment of the handful of "Brandenburgers"
disguised in Dutch uniforms was to achieve a major success of
psychological warfare for Hitler. Like wildfire the rumours of
ubiquitous fifth columnists—the nuns in hobnailed boots, priests
with machine pistols under their soutanes—spread through Holland, and then into Belgium and France, carrying paralysis and
demoralisation in their wake like the germs of a deadly plague.

The Allies move

In London, at 6 A.M. on the morning of the German attack, Sir
Samuel Hoare visited Churchill—still waiting to be summoned by

---

* After the war Witzig rejoined the army and is today a colonel, in charge of
the Engineer School of the Bundeswehr.

the King to form a government—at the Admiralty. He was smoking a cigar and eating fried eggs and bacon as if nothing serious had occurred. Two hours later the War Cabinet met to discuss events on the continent, and Churchill with supreme calmness insisted that the Cabinet listen to a report he wanted to make on a "homing AA fuse." The Cabinet listened. ("We are impossible!" exclaimed General Ironside.)

On hearing the news in Paris, Paul Reynaud swiftly agreed with President Lebrun that it was no time for the government to fall, and withdrew his letter of resignation. Equally he agreed that it was now inopportune to switch commanders-in-chief, and to Gamelin he addressed a brief conciliatory note: *"Mon général, the battle is engaged. Only one thing matters; to win it. We shall all work for this end together, with a single heart."* Speaking to the nation over the radio, he declared bravely, "The French Army has drawn its sword; France is gathering herself," and then pleaded for national unity in the coming crisis. Privately he expressed concern about the projected Allied advance into Belgium; to Baudouin he admitted, "I am disturbed. We shall see what Gamelin is worth."

At Vincennes, from 1 A.M. onwards GQG had been kept in a state of alert by reports from Luxembourg of suspicious German troop movements. Then at 0505 hours, the sirens had begun to wail. Warned of the German attack by his *chef de cabinet,* Colonel Petitbon, Gamelin came down to his office. According to one of his staff, "his face revealed no apparent emotion, no interior disquiet." Towards seven o'clock Gamelin gave the order for the Dyle-Breda Plan to get under way. Captain André Beaufre, visiting Vincennes from General Doumenc's GHQ staff, saw Gamelin "pacing up and down the corridor of the barracks, humming audibly with a martial air. . . . It has been said since that he had foreseen defeat, but I can scarcely believe that this was his state of mind at that moment." The Secretary General of the Department of War was later heard to remark: "If you had seen, as I have done this morning, the broad smile of General Gamelin when he told me the direction of the enemy attack, you would feel no uneasiness. The Germans have provided him with just the opportunity which he was awaiting." To the men under his command he drafted an order of the day, ending symbolically with a reiteration of Pétain's immortal words at Verdun: *Nous les aurons!* But somehow the message seemed banal and lacked the C-in-C's customary fluent ease. After a hasty breakfast, Gamelin drove to General Georges's HQ at La Ferté. There he heard a report sent from a French colonel attached to the King of the Belgians that "a rather serious incident has occurred at Fort Eben Emael." Otherwise the impression given by the news for the remainder of that day, as it reached GQG, seemed "favourable."

Up at the front, Lieutenant Jamet's comment in his diary on hearing of the German attack was simply "So it's war, at last?" and it was a reaction widely shared among the soldiers of No. 1 Army Group as they prepared to move into Belgium. As the eight months of the Phoney War ended, apprehension was not entirely unmixed with relief. On receiving his orders to march up to the Dyle Line, Lieutenant General Alan Brooke of the BEF's II Corps recorded that "it was hard to believe on a glorious spring day, with all nature looking its best, that we were taking the first step towards . . . one of the greatest battles of history." General Prioux of the French Cavalry Corps noted with pride the admirable route discipline of his units, and their encouraging lack of mechanical breakdowns. The air-liaison colonel accompanying him also expressed admiration, but added apologetically how sad it made him to see such fine men and equipment granted such miserable air cover. That night, after a smooth advance of 75 to 95 miles, Prioux's corps reached the Dyle Line according to schedule. But he was horrified to find there a complete absence of any defensive work, such as—he had been led to believe—the Belgians had promised.

Ninth Army

On General Corap's Ninth Army front, the infantry divisions marched forward as planned to line up along the Belgian sector of the Meuse, while the cavalry screen fanned out ahead of them into the Ardennes. Lieutenant Georges Kosak with the 4th Light Cavalry Division* recalled their rapidly altering reception as they entered into Belgium on the morning of the 10th:

At first we pass through several small villages where the people did not seem to be informed about events; then important centres where

---

* DLC.

the population mass on the sidewalks and at the windows greeting us frenziedly. French flags and garlands were hung from all windows. Women have their arms full of flowers, and their aprons full of packets of cigarettes, sweets and chocolates. . . . It is very moving. Our hearts beat; an immense pride overcomes us.

On crossing the Meuse, like Lieutenant General Alan Brooke, Kosak found it hard to believe that the battle had really begun, "everything is so gay and sunny." But on reaching the small town of Ciney, just 45 air miles from the German frontier and towards which Rommel's panzers were already advancing, "a strange feeling comes over us; the streets are quiet and silent, the shutters are closed, and a few curious onlookers watch us pass without showing any emotion . . . the atmosphere is indifferent, if not hostile; our men have become watchful and serious. After Ciney, no longer any songs, no longer any laughter."

The advance of Corap's infantry progressed somewhat less smoothly. General Martin's XI Corps seems, inexcusably, to have been taken by surprise. The 22nd Division had a number of battalions absent on exercises; in order to regroup themselves, some had to march 12 miles on foot, thus losing nearly twenty-four hours. The 18th Division, which had to cover over 55 miles in order to reach its positions around Dinant (compared with the 75 miles facing Rommel), could only rush up two battalions by truck on the first day. The rest of the 18th would not be in position until May 14th; but then it was reckoned that the enemy could not reach the Meuse until the morning of the 16th at the earliest. Meanwhile, on leaving its frontier positions XI Corps was ordered to lock up all the bunkers there and hand the keys to the staff of the 53rd Division. But this division, held in reserve by Corap, was subsequently moved southwards. The bunkers were to remain locked, inaccessible.

Second Army

Although the cavalry divisions of the Ninth and Second Armies were supposed to work closely together, in fact liaison between them was extremely poor from the beginning. On Huntziger's Second Army front, the cavalry screen at once advanced far ahead of Corap's, and it was on this sector that the first direct confrontation of the Battle of France between French and German troops took place. Covering the Arlon Gap, the advance guard of the 2nd DLC came up against reconnaissance troops of Guderian's left-hand panzer division near Habay-la-Neuve (about 8 miles northwest of Arlon) at 0900 hours on the 10th. There was confused fighting in the area, during which a German regimental commander, Lieutenant Colonel Ehermann, was killed. At Étalles, a French detachment had its 25 mm antitank gun destroyed the moment it was put into action; it was encircled and crushed after a brief street fight with the Grossdeutschland Regiment. "To our right, a group of French marching into position in a field of clover," a German rifleman of the Grossdeutschland wrote of this first encounter.

They look at us in astonishment: we ourselves don't exactly look at them cheerfully—are we to shoot? . . . Major Föst gives the order to fire! . . . One of the French somersaults in the clover, the first dead man, who looks completely white. Dead! . . . something cold grips us around the heart. We will have to get used to that yet.

There was more shooting around Étalles, during which Major Föst, a veteran of '14–'18, was killed and several men wounded. Because of their immobility, the 2nd DLC was unable to bring up its 105 mm guns in time to give support, and by midafternoon it was forced to abandon Arlon. By nightfall, scattered over far too wide an area and badly shaken by its first engagements, the 2nd DLC had fallen back on the river Semois, the last serious barrier in the southern Ardennes beyond the French frontier.

Meanwhile, at about the same time, on the right of the 2nd DLC, the 3rd DLC (belonging to General Condé's Third Army), passing the Luxembourg grand-ducal family on its flight westward, had fought a sharp engagement at Esch against Lieutenant Hedderich's group—which it erroneously reported, at first, as fifth columnists. By 0900 hours, after a French machine-gun carrier and a tank had been blown up on land mines, the 3rd DLC decided it could not force Hedderich's hastily constructed barriers and sent its H–35 tanks to try to block the roads entering Esch from the north and east. A French dragoon, Captain Gontaut-Biron, describes how the tanks were brought under fire by "very numerous antitank guns . . . while the enemy artillery pinned us down on the positions we had acquired . . . the enemy was there before us with very superior forces, and greatly helped by numerous formations of the Fifth Column in Esch-sur-Alzette which continued to fire on all isolated men." In fact, Hedderich's 90 men plus the light forward ground elements that came to reinforce them were heavily outnumbered throughout the day. Nevertheless, that evening the French withdrew from Esch; their withdrawal acutely complicated by some 25,000 desperate civilians attempting to escape down the only route towards the French frontier. It was the first of such experiences with panicking refugees that were to bedevil the French Army for the rest of the campaign.

On Huntziger's left, the 5th DLC had the task of covering the open country in the area Neufchâteau–Libramont–Bastogne. It was through here that the route of Guderian's main force lay, but because of the hold-ups inflicted by the Belgian demolitions at Martelange the 5th DLC was able to fulfil its objective for the 10th without any serious fighting. Meanwhile that day General Huntziger himself had driven up to Bouillon, the ravishing Crusader fortress on the Semois, to inform himself of the situation in the Ardennes. He was somewhat surprised by the Belgian mayor who, when requested that one of Bouillon's hotels be turned into a field hospital, replied in astonishment, "But, *mon général,* Bouillon is a summer resort, our hotels are reserved for tourists." Nevertheless, General Ruby tells us that Huntziger returned to his HQ at Senuc "in general satisfied with the course of the day." That night, however, aerial reconnaissance reports reaching Senuc identified two large mechanised masses of the enemy crossing into the Ardennes, apparently menacing both Sedan and Carignan to the southeast.

By the evening of May 10th, General Kayaerts's Belgian Chasseurs Ardennais in front of Huntziger—obedient to their instructions—had withdrawn northwards, leaving a vacuum between the French cavalry and Guderian's panzers. Only on Corap's front did they stay to fight a bitter action, thereby inflicting upon Rommel his first setback of the campaign. That night he had intended to reach the river Ourthe, but just as dark was falling he was held up by a spirited defence at Chabrehez, some 12 miles inside the Belgian frontier and about the same distance from the Ourthe. Here part of the 3rd Regiment of Chasseurs Ardennais were dug in in well-sited fieldworks, amid heavily contoured country ideally suited for the defence. Though they had no antitank weapons, the Belgians courageously kept up a disturbingly accurate fire on Rommel's 7th Motorcycle Battalion. Frustrated, Rommel was forced to abandon his aim of reaching the Ourthe that night, and Corap's cavalry were granted a respite that allowed them to move up behind the river without meeting the Germans that day.

Allied air effort

The Luftwaffe's early morning attacks on air bases in France on May 10th had been followed by a dismal tardiness on the part of the Allies to mount any riposte in the air, and damage done to airfields was by no means the chief cause. We are told, for instance, that the powerful Groupe d'Assaut I/54 equipped with Bréguet attack bombers and located in a well-placed base midway between Paris and Châlons-sur-Marne, received no instructions until midday on the 10th. Then a written order arrived, earmarking it for operations over northern Belgium and shifting it to Montdidier. But no movement order arrived until the following day, with the result that Groupe I/54 was not in action until the 12th. Almost the whole of the fighter strength of General d'Astier's ZOAN, plus strong support from RAF Hurricanes based in England, had been ordered by General Gamelin—still obsessed with the importance of his left-flank movement—to cover General Giraud's Seventh Army racing up to Breda; while only two French fighter Groupes totalling 37 planes were dispatched for the support of the Ninth and Second Armies.

In their joint air HQ at Chauny, General d'Astier and Air Marshal Barratt had spent the morning beset with frustration. At 8 A.M. they had received the following order from GQG: "Air limited to fighters and reconnaissance." This meant that the massed German columns crowding the Ardennes roads were immune from air attack during the very hours when they would be most vulnerable to it. It was not until 11 A.M. that the Allied air commanders received authority to bomb enemy columns (first priority) and airfields (second priority); and even this authorisation contained a rider added by General Georges: "At all costs avoid bombing built-up areas." Motivated by the deep French dread of Luftwaffe reprisals, and predicated on Gamelin's utterly unrealistic hopes that a "bombing war" could somehow be avoided, the order meant that Allied pilots were hamstrung by their inability to bomb the panzers when they were passing through or had halted in the innumerable hamlets on their route.

Overcome by impatience at the lethargy of the French Air Force, Air Marshal Barratt finally took matters into his own hands and ordered a first flight of Fairey Battle bombers to attack Guderian's columns advancing through Luxembourg. Barratt's Battles were the only bombers to strike there that day. Attacking without fighter support at very low altitudes, the Battles were met by a hurricane of fire from the German light flak on the ground, and pounced upon by hovering Me–109s. Immediately the Battle revealed its extreme vulnerability to attack from below, which was to prove tragically costly later at Sedan. Of the first eight Battles to attack, three were immediately shot down. More returned to make low-altitude runs that afternoon, and of 32 Battles dispatched that day 13 were destroyed and all the remaining 19 damaged.

That night a massive Franco-British operation, in which Bomber Command was to participate from Britain, was also torpedoed by General Georges's veto. Eventually, attacks were limited to bombing three airfields in Holland (by the RAF) and to scattering bombs on German airfields and roads west of the Rhine (by a few French Amiots). By the end of the 10th, Air Marshal Barratt's temper was barely under control, his view of his apparently torpid ally all but unprintable.

Hitler weeps for joy

As May 10th drew to a close, behind the scenes on the German side Hitler was well-satisfied with the day's events. As his train was arriving at his *"Felsennest"** in the Eifel that morning, the Luftwaffe was roaring overhead, going and returning on its sorties to destroy Allied air bases. When later the OKW Intelligence informed him that Gamelin had already reacted to the "matador's cloak" in the hoped-for fashion by rushing into Belgium, Hitler after a sleepless night was enraptured: "I could have wept for joy; they'd fallen into the trap! It had been a clever piece of work to attack Liège. How lovely *Felsennest* was! The birds in the morning, the view over the road up which the col-

---

* Literally "Crag's Nest." Hitler had a passion for giving his Headquarters gothically romantic names.

umns were advancing, the squadrons of planes overhead. There, I knew just what I was doing!" In his diary that night, General Halder commented succinctly on the advance of Kleist's Armoured Group: "Very good marching achievements."

Closer to the front, however, opinions were not so sanguine. In the Ardennes, despite the feebleness of the enemy reaction, there had been worrying bottlenecks and traffic snarls, and only the superb organisation and route discipline had prevented real chaos on the overloaded roads. What might have happened if Kleist's panzers had not had behind them the indispensable experience of the Austrian and Czech approach marches, and the Polish campaign, and if the Allies had attacked relentlessly from the air, surpasses the imagination. As it was, Rommel's hold-up at Chabrehez meant that Hoth's panzer corps on the northern flank of the thrust had failed to attain the day's objective, and in the south the Belgian frontier demolitions had caused the impetuous Guderian to fall behind schedule—when every minute counted! In fact at Kleist's HQ that night serious fears were expressed that the delays might have sufficed to give the French a good chance of regaining their balance. There had also been a first tactical disagreement between Kleist and Guderian. Taking an exaggerated view of the threat presented to his southern flank by the efforts of the French 2nd DLC, Kleist ordered the 10th Panzer to swing off course and move on Longwy instead of Sedan. Infuriated, Guderian demanded that the order be withdrawn, expostulating that "the detachment of one-third of my force to meet the hypothetical threat of enemy cavalry would endanger the success of the Meuse crossing and therefore of the whole operation." Guderian won, but Kleist remained anxious.

Thus, at the end of the first day, one finds a curious inversion of moods: in Gamelin's GQG, complacent optimism; in Kleist's battle HQ, nervous pessimism.

10

Through the Ardennes
MAY 11th

> Soldiers of the West Front! The hours of the most
> decisive battle of the future of the German nation has
> come.
> For three hundred years it was the aim of British and
> French governments to hinder every workable consolida-
> tion of Europe, and above all to keep Germany in weak-
> ness and impotence. . . .
> Soldiers of the West Front!
> With this, the hour has come for you.
> The battle which is beginning today will decide the
> fate of the German nation for the next thousand years.
> Do your duty.
> —ADOLF HITLER, Order of the Day, May 10, 1940

Rommel

As SOON as day broke on Saturday, May 11th, the panzers were
once again on the move everywhere. Rommel, having concentrated and reorganised his forces during the night, swiftly
smashed the courageous resistance of the Chasseurs Ardennais
at Chabrehez. By the end of the morning, leading elements of his
7th Panzer had already reached the river Ourthe, the objective
that had been denied him the previous night. On the other side of
the river, parts of the French 4th DLC had arrived. At Hotton,
Lieutenant Georges Kosak's sapper company had been detailed
to demolish a bridge which had been inefficiently blown by the
Belgians—a job greatly complicated by the masses of Belgian
refugees streaming across the bridge. At 1345 hours he finally
succeeded in clearing the bridge, and detonated charges under it
—at the very moment that the first of Rommel's armoured cars

appeared on the opposite bank. Kosak then withdrew to Marche, some 5 miles behind the river. The French cavalry made no attempt to cover the destroyed bridges on the Ourthe, and within hours the German engineers had thrown pontoons across the undefended river.

Appearing with unexpected suddenness on the other side of the Ourthe, Rommel's panzers struck their first blow savagely at the dispersed French cavalry. At Marche, Lieutenant Kosak and his troop were surprised by machine-gun fire from a German armoured car. He leaped into a small French car and tried to make off;

All of a sudden, a grey-green mass bars the road; with all my concerted strength, I brake, my hands clutching the wheel; the tyres make a noise like a large electric saw cutting wood; I swerve to the left. A quite brutal shock stops the car . . . the enemy armoured car manoeuvres; it is lying sideways on across the road, trying to turn about.

Kosak then managed to reverse and swing behind some buildings, a second before the Germans opened fire. Outside Marche, he regathered his troop and, reckoning that escape seemed impossible, decided to take up a defensive position. The sappers buried a few mines and took cover. A group of German armoured cars approached. The first one blew up with a devastating explosion on one of Kosak's mines, which also knocked out a second vehicle. Benefiting from the ensuing disarray of the enemy, Kosak miraculously managed to escape to Ciney—where only the previous day he had experienced that "strange feeling" on moving up through the first shuttered and frightened Belgian town. Here, less than 10 miles from Dinant and the Meuse, the divisional commander, General Barbe, interviewed Kosak and declared, "I am pleased with you."

Throughout the day on Rommel's axis there was confused fighting similar to that reported by Kosak. At times the tanks of the 4th DLC attacked strongly, but their Renaults and Hotchkisses were both outnumbered and outclassed. Rommel's own account of the day's action describes how "prompt opening fire on our part led to a hasty French retreat." On this first day of battle with the French he discovered "again and again that in encounter actions, the day goes to the side that is the first to plaster its opponent with fire. The man who lies low and awaits developments usually comes off second best." His panzers thus advanced, spraying the woods on either side of the roads promiscuously with machine-gun and cannon fire. Into these woods the French cavalry, horses and tanks mixed up with one another, scattered in disorder. By the evening of the 11th, Rommel was in fine fettle, having more than made up for the setbacks of the previous day. To his wife, he dashed off a second quick note:

Dearest Lu,

I've come up for breath for the first time today and have a moment to write. Everything wonderful so far. Am way ahead of my neighbours. I'm completely hoarse from orders and shouting. Had a bare three hours' sleep and an occasional meal. Otherwise I'm absolutely fine. Make do with this, please, I'm too tired for more.

The outstripped "neighbours" to whom Rommel refers consisted chiefly of the 5th Panzer Division on his right. Not led with the élan Rommel possessed, the 5th had become tangled up on the Ardennes roads and lagged badly behind the 7th. From May 11th onwards, it would never quite catch up and Rommel would seize all the limelight on the right flank of the break-through thrust.

Reinhardt

On Rommel's left, Reinhardt's corps consisting of the 8th and 6th Panzers who were to advance through Bastogne to Montherme on the Meuse, also had their problems. Reinhardt had actually set off after Guderian, so as to make room for XIX Panzer Corps on the saturated and tortuous roads of the Ardennes. But in the afternoon of the 11th, the 6th Panzer found its route bunged up by elements of Guderian's 2nd Panzer which had strayed too far to the north. At 1520 orders were given for it to hold fast until the muddle was sorted out. Finally the 2nd Panzer had to cede this route to the 6th; later Guderian also deprived it of another on the right of its axis, a factor that was to delay the division's appearance at Sedan on the critical day. In its approach march, the 1st Panzer too had also suffered inconvenience by being "squeezed" by the 10th Panzer on its left. Here Guderian appears to have been at least partly to blame; overreact-

ing against Kleist's rescinded order for the 10th to swing southwards, at 1 A.M. on the morning of the 11th he had instructed it
to aim for the river Semois at Cugnon, several miles further to
north than Florenville where it was originally directed. Back at
OKH Headquarters, Halder noted in his diary that Brauchitsch,
the Army C-in-C, wanted "to put pressure on Army Group 'A'
(they report that route difficulties have been very great on account of numerous road destructions!)." Had it not been for the
apparently almost miraculous efforts of the mechanised engineers, who seemed to have been everywhere at the right moment, destroying Belgian antitank obstacles, replacing bridges,
constructing road detours, the hold-ups would undoubtedly have
been far graver that day. As it was, the tank commanders cursed
at the tangles and delays as their engines overheated, growled
at the military police trying frantically to unsnarl the vast columns, and continuously threw nervous glances upwards into the
dazzling clear blue sky. What fantastic targets these mile-long
traffic jams offered the enemy air forces! How could they miss
such an opportunity!

Guderian

On Guderian's front, the principal action on the 11th was
fought by the 1st Panzer. Having moved his tanks up in strength
to the positions just east of Neufchâteau that had been seized
the previous day by Operation "Niwi," the divisional commander,
General Kirchner, now swept aside the few remnants of the
Chasseurs Ardennais to strike forcefully at the French 5th
DLC. Near Suxy south of Neufchâteau, some 30 tanks bearing
the white oak-leaf emblem of the 1st Panzer broke through the
French positions and swiftly surrounded a battery of 105 mm
field guns. These were modern weapons, but they were completely
unsuited for combatting armour. The whole battery was swiftly
destroyed—a first unpleasant foretaste of what was to await the
defenders on the other side of the Meuse. Shaken, General
Chanoine, the commander of the 5th DLC, ordered the Groupement forming his right wing to fall back on the Semois. Meanwhile, north of Neufchâteau, his left wing was also being hard
pressed, and during the course of the day Chanoine received
Huntziger's permission to withdraw his whole division across the
Semois. But, insisted Huntziger, the Semois must be held at all

costs. To bolster the line there, Huntziger expedited a battalion of the 295th Infantry Regiment, borrowed from one of General Grandsard's "B" divisions—the 55th—holding the key sector at Sedan.

To the right of the 5th, the 2nd DLC—licking its wounds from the previous day—was left relatively alone. The explanation for the failure of the 10th Panzer to resume its attack seems to lie in the confusion caused over its change of axis and the resulting bottlenecks; but this apparent switching of enemy emphasis from the 2nd DLC front to the 5th added to Huntziger's bafflement. Was Guderian's main effort aimed at Carignan and the northern anchor of the Maginot Line, as it might have seemed on the 10th, or now at Sedan? On its right the 2nd DLC was left somewhat out on a limb by the withdrawal, on the evening of the 10th, of the Third Army's cavalry screen (3rd DLC), which—abandoning Esch—fell back across the Franco-Luxembourg frontier. Much more serious, however, was the threat presenting itself to the other flank of Huntziger's cavalry detachments. To the left of the hard-hit 5th DLC lay the 3rd Spahi Brigade, an elite North African unit under command of General Corap's Ninth Army. Its role was to ensure liaison between the cavalry screens of the two armies. Because of the lagging of the 6th Panzer, in whose approximate path the Spahis stood, they were attacked on neither the 10th nor the 11th. Nevertheless, on learning of the 5th DLC's withdrawal, the Spahi commander, Colonel Marc, pulled his brigade back across the Semois even more precipitately—the consequences of which were to be particularly unfortunate the following day.

Thus as May 11th ended, the situation of Huntziger's cavalry was as follows: the 2nd DLC was still capable of resistance, but the 5th was badly battered, and was left holding a 20-mile front on which two of the most powerful German panzer divisions (1st and 2nd) were advancing. Both flanks of Huntziger's cavalry screen were in the air, and the whole of it had withdrawn across the Semois. Here was the last natural barrier between the French frontier and—Sedan. And it was not much of a barrier. On staff officers' maps, the Semois may look imposing; along its upper reaches it is in fact little more than a very pretty trout stream, meandering in countless loops through water meadows and wooded banks. In many places it is shallow enough to wade across; in others, narrow enough for a not particularly expert thrower to land a hand grenade on the far side. Its numerous convolutions would make it hard for an extended defence force to prevent a determined and numerous enemy infiltrating across it. The principal route over the Semois, and the one heading directly for Sedan, lay through Bouillon. Here the physical features for a resolute defence—dominating heights and clearly observable approach roads from which panzers could not easily deploy—were more promising. It was clear that Bouillon would be the scene of Guderian's major effort for the 12th. Nevertheless, an extraordinary atmosphere of business-as-usual still prevailed there.

Like Rommel's 7th Panzer, Kirchner's 1st was now leading both its neighbours. Heading west from Neufchâteau until it had reached the important road junction of Fays-les-Veneurs, it had then swung southwards to face for the first time towards Bouillon and, beyond it, Sedan. By nightfall on the 11th, the leading tanks of the 1st Panzer Regiment had reached the Semois at Bouillon. Immediately they came under heavy antitank fire from the far bank, which knocked out a tank. An undestroyed stone bridge was then discovered, but just as the panzers were about to cross it the French blew it up. Captain von Kress managed to cross by a ford discovered by regimental reconnaissance, but shortly afterwards he was bombed in error by 25 Stukas. The 1st Panzer Regiment was withdrawn, and it was decided to resume the attack the next morning, using the division's motorised infantry.

During the 11th, most of the men marching with and behind Kleist's armoured phalanx had still not caught a glimpse of the enemy, a factor which lent to the campaign in the Ardennes a phantom quality. From time to time, Guderian had spotted French reconnaissance vehicles flitting silently through the trees of the Ardennes Forest, in retreat, but apparently neither side opened fire. A young sapper lieutenant, Karl Heinz Mende, wrote home in amazement at advancing through country "as fruitful and beautiful as the German landscape," but empty and abandoned; "we are not fighting for this land, we are simply swamping it," and the whole campaign so far had reminded him of a well-conducted sand-table exercise. Indeed, as General Blumentritt told Liddell Hart after the war, it "was not really an operation, in the tactical sense, but an approach march. In making the plan we had reckoned it unlikely that we should meet any serious resistance before reaching the Meuse." In the first two days of the Ardennes campaign, the German appreciation so far had certainly held good; resistance had been only "weak opposition, and easily brushed aside. . . . The main problem was not tactical but administrative." That night Guderian with his highly mobile corps HQ took up quarters at Neufchâteau–in a much happier frame of mind. The approach march still presented "administrative problems" but, with the exception of the 2nd Panzer which continued to lag behind, the whole Panzer Corps had more than recovered the time lost on the 10th. Back at OKH, Halder recorded a visit from the Führer, lasting from 1640 until 1900 hours, during which there had been "rejoicing over the success"; on the French side of the lines, there was still "no sign of any major railway movements anywhere. Enemy air force astonishingly restrained." But in a qualifying and significantly cautious note, Halder added that there was "expectation of [enemy] attack from the south."

Air war

In the air, the Luftwaffe continued its strategic bombing of Allied airfields and communication centres, though with no greater intensity than on the previous day. According to General d'Astier, only three French planes were destroyed and one landing strip put out of action. Tactically, the main German air effort was concentrated upon the annihilation of the Dutch forces in the north. Over the Ardennes, the protective fighter cover remained dense and the panzers appear to have had as much air support as they required. Lieutenant Colonel Soldan, a Wehrmacht chronicler, states that Luftwaffe cooperation was "most admirable" during critical moments of that day: "Planes, watching the situation from above, promptly recognised any position where help was needed. Dive-bombers flung themselves on the enemy and opened the way for the countless vehicles whose motors were making a terrible noise as they laboured through this forest region of hills and mountains." But otherwise the Luftwaffe adroitly avoided any intensification of activity over the Dinant–Sedan area that might have given away the *Sichelschnitt* objectives. Meanwhile, on the 11th the Allied air forces undertook a single operation against those miles of irresistible targets worming through the Ardennes. The RAF official history relates:

"Eight Battles of Nos. 88 and 218 Squadrons were ordered to deliver a low-level attack on a column in German territory moving
up towards the Luxembourg border. Whether they managed to
reach their target area is doubtful. The only pilot to return saw
three of his companions succumb to ground fire in the Ardennes."
Again, the French Air Force took no part.

At the other end of the battle front, with similar ineffectiveness
and high losses, a squadron of Belgian Battle bombers attacked
the captured Maastricht and Albert Canal bridges, carrying 50
kg bombs which were ludicrously small for the task. Ten out of
fifteen planes were shot down. The attacks were followed up by
RAF Blenheims; on one mission, five out of six were destroyed
by flak. It was not until the end of the morning of the 11th that
General Georges's restrictions on the bombing of built-up areas by
the French Air Force was lifted. At 1630 Gamelin himself telephoned d'Astier, ordering him to "put everything to work to slow
up the German columns in the direction of Maastricht, Tongres,
Gembloux, and not to hesitate to bomb towns and villages in
order to obtain the required result." But much irreplaceable
time had been lost; and, in any case, Gamelin was concentrating
his limited air resources in the wrong place—as indeed the *Sichelschnitt* planners had intended that he should.

The Allies in Belgium

On May 11th, General d'Astier noted that Giraud's Seventh
Army in its dash towards Breda "is not being troubled" by the
Luftwaffe. In view of the merciless pounding that was being inflicted upon the poor Dutch, was there not something curious
in the apparently blind eye the Luftwaffe was turning upon
Giraud? The BEF had experienced a similarly quiet time in its
advance to the Dyle Line position. With it went a certain "Kim"
Philby, representing *The Times,* who—showing an astuteness
which would later bring untold advantage to another employer—
remarked to an American colleague, Drew Middleton: "It went
too damn well. With all that air power why didn't he bother us?
What is he up to?"*

The BEF advance—apart from one incident on the 10th when

---

* Philby's remark was recorded long before he came to fame, by Middleton in
Our Share of Night, published in 1946.

an officious Belgian frontier guard had tried to halt the passage of Major General Bernard Montgomery's 3rd Division because it did not possess the necessary permits—had indeed proceeded with exemplary smoothness. To many of its older members who had fought in Belgium once before, there was an uncanny quality about that advance. "It was almost," wrote Drew Middleton, "as if they were retracing steps taken in a dream. They saw again faces of friends long dead and heard the half remembered names of towns and villages." But the Tommies were in excellent spirits; passing them on the road back to Paris from Brussels, Clare Boothe "remembered how everybody had remarked that it was funny the soldiers didn't sing in this war. Well, these soldiers were singing . . . they stuck up their thumbs in the new gesture they had, which meant, 'OK, everything's fine,' and winked and blew cheerful kisses." By the evening of May 11th, the BEF was well dug-in on its appointed sector along the Dyle, from Louvain to Wavre; and although the river here was little more than a wide stream, the British position was relatively strong.

Not so with the French First Army of General Blanchard, earmarked to fill the Gembloux Gap, between the BEF and Corap's Ninth Army. Moving up from Valenciennes, Major Barlone sombrely noted meeting Belgian refugees racing towards France from the Liège area: "The news these people bring is pessimistic. . . . Treachery and the Fifth Column are the sole topics of conversation." On reaching Gembloux, General Prioux of the crack Cavalry Corps was "dumbfounded" to discover how little the Belgians had done to fortify this vital area; it seemed a completely open plain offering itself to the German panzers. Meanwhile, a staff captain had brought him grave news from Liège; mighty Eben Emael had fallen and the Germans were already flooding across the Albert Canal line. By the afternoon, the Germans were in Tongres and reaching out to Waremme some 6 miles west of Liège, thus threatening it from the river. At this rate, Prioux reckoned that his corps would never have time to establish itself before the enemy was on top of it. Early that afternoon he reported to Blanchard that "in view of the feeble Belgian resistance and superiority of the enemy aviation, the Dyle Manoeuvre appears to be difficult to execute and it would seem to be preferable to resort to the Escaut Manoeuvre." Blanchard passed this on to Billotte, attaching his own recommendation. Billotte, always

the staunchest supporter of the Dyle–Breda Plan among the
French hierarchy, was shocked. Visiting Prioux that night in person, Billotte told him that the Dyle Plan could not possibly be
put into reverse; he would speed up the advance of the bulk of
the First Army, but meanwhile Prioux would have to hold fast
until "D + 5"—May 14.

Holland

In Holland, the defences were crumbling at a terrifying speed.
Rumours of fifth-column treachery were multiplying; hand grenades were reported to have been filled with sand instead of
explosive, bunkers crumbled because the concrete had been cut,
children were poisoned by chocolates dropped from the air. Panic
was everywhere. The Dutch Army was still valiantly attacking
the pockets held by General Student's airborne troops, but the
Dutch Air Force had been all but wiped out and the 9th Panzer
Division had now got its tanks across the Maas (via the bridge at
Gennep captured by the "Brandenburgers") and was rapidly
striking westwards, towards Rotterdam. The advance guard of
Giraud's mechanised divisions reached its destination at Breda
only to find that the Dutch Army, to whom it had come to "extend
an arm," had been forced to withdraw northwards covering
Rotterdam. By lunchtime on the 11th Giraud had run into the
9th Panzer, in the vicinity of Tilburg. Shaken by this unexpected
encounter, his armour turned about, falling back in the direction
of Antwerp—now savagely strafed and bombed by low-flying German planes. Thus, within thirty-six hours of the opening of battle, Gamelin's Breda Variant, upon which was wagered his
irreplaceable mobile reserve, had already been rendered null
and void.

French High Command

Back at Vincennes, Gamelin's eyes were still kept rivetted upon
the north by the crescendo of events there. In London, General
Spears was told by the French Military Attaché (on the 11th
and again on the 12th) that GQG was convinced that the Germans were making their main effort between Maastricht and
Liège; while, on the 11th, *The Times* Military Correspondent
(obviously also fed by a similar *tuyau* from Vincennes) declared confidently that "this time at least there has been no stra-

tegic surprise." General Ironside recorded sanguinely in his diary: "We shall have saved the Belgian Army. On the whole the advantage is with us. A really hard fight all this summer." To outer commands such as General Weygand's in Syria, GQG concluded its summary that day: "The Allied manoeuvre is developing favourably." If there was any diminution of Gamelin's optimism that day, it lay in disappointment at the rapid disintegration of Dutch resistance and at the unexpectedly poor quality of the Belgian defence preparations. As Gamelin admits in his memoirs, during the first three days of the battle, he "was above all preoccupied with Holland." Yet the indications were mounting steadily that something serious was also afoot in the Ardennes. Already by the morning of the 11th, both French and RAF reconnaissance reports had contained such items as "numerous columns on the road from Euskirchen to Prum and on the Belgian road network to the west of Luxembourg," the unloading of tanks north of Neufchâteau and considerable motorised forces deploying towards Arlon, while in his midday bulletin General d'Astier stated: "The enemy seems to be preparing an energetic action in the general direction of Givet."* It was the actual numbers of the panzer divisions operating in the Ardennes that continued to elude GQG's Deuxième Bureau in composing its enemy order of battle. The effectiveness of the German fighter umbrella against reconnaissance intruders and the leafy natural camouflage of those "impenetrable" forests into which whole divisions could melt without trace from one hour to another all conspired to this end; and the forcefulness with which Bock was brandishing the "matador's cloak" north of Liège certainly suggested that more than just a quarter of the German panzer strength might be deployed there.

Nevertheless, it would not be true to say that—even as early as May 11th—the French High Command had received no warnings of the danger in the Ardennes, or that they were not reacting to these warnings. On that afternoon, General Georges issued Instruction No. 12 in which he "foresaw" the need to "push up onto the second position behind Sedan the 2nd and 3rd Armoured Divisions, the 3rd Motorised and the 14th, 36th and 87th Infantry Divisions," all belonging to the general reserve. The orders for

---

* About 10 air miles up the Meuse from Dinant.

the transportation of these units would be passed on between the 11th and 13th; but as events were soon to prove, they would come too late.

During the afternoon of the 11th, Gamelin visited General Georges at his headquarters, "Les Bondons." The previous day he had, on his own initiative, delegated to Georges powers to deal directly with King Leopold as Commander-in-Chief of the Belgian Army. Now he was astonished to discover that Georges in his turn had sub-delegated these powers to Billotte, to whom he also wanted to pass his "powers of coordination" over Lord Gort's BEF. It was, said Gamelin crossly, "an abdication"; yet he made no attempt to alter his subordinate's decision. When he returned to Vincennes that evening the tangle of the Allied command network had in no way been simplified; nor were relations between Gamelin and Georges any friendlier.

11

On the Meuse
MAY 12th

The Germans announce that one of the forts of Liège is
in their hands. Even if this claim is true, its significance is
diminished by the announcement that a captain and a
lieutenant have been decorated for it. That would indicate that . . . the fort was only a bunker or a small
pill-box.
                              —New York *Herald Tribune*, May 12th

DESPAIR IN BERLIN
                                       —*Sunday Chronicle*, May 12th

The attack of the German Wehrmacht in the west made
good progress on May 12th.
                              —Wehrmacht Communiqué, May 13th

The Low Countries

ALLIED NEWSPAPERS on the morning of Whitsunday, May 12th,
generally gave the impression that the German offensive had been
stemmed by the Dutch and Belgians; as indeed, according to
Gamelin's plans, it should have been. But in fact by that morning
the situation in Holland was already desperate and in the course
of the next twenty-four hours it became hopeless. In the extreme
north, the German ground troops reached the eastern shore of
the Zuyder Zee; in the centre, advancing beyond Arnhem which
the airborne troops had captured on the first day, they broke
through the Grebbe line at Rhenen after some hard fighting,
whence the very heart of the country could be threatened; in the
south, the 9th Panzer was pushing towards the great bridge over
the Maas estuary at Moerdijk, to link up with the German para-

troopers still holding it. By evening on the 12th, Moerdijk had
been captured and with it vanished all hope of assistance from
Giraud's Seventh Army. Holland was cut in two and the Dutch
Army, though it continued to fight on with bitter desperation,
was left with no option but to retreat into *Vesting Holland,* the
area containing the main cities—Rotterdam, Utrecht, Amsterdam
—with their backs to the sea. Only one airworthy bomber, a Fok-
ker, was left to the Dutch Air Force, and this was shot down over
Moerdijk the following day. General Giraud's fine mechanised
units found themselves in a menacing predicament; heavily hit
both by Stukas and German armour, their right flank was increasingly threatened by the 9th Panzer; ammunition was running
short, and many of their tanks were still moving up through Belgium on flatcars. Losses had been heavy. Giraud decided to withdraw from all but a tiny corner of Dutch soil, and try to hold a
line from Bergen-op-Zoom to the Turnhout Canal, covering
Antwerp.

After General Prioux's alarming account of the state of the
Dyle Line on the 11th, Billotte had ordered Blanchard's First
Army to speed up its advance so that it would be established in
position twenty-four hours earlier than previously stipulated—on
the 14th instead of the 15th. Moving by day instead of during
the short May nights, the French mechanised columns now came
under systematic Luftwaffe attack for the first time. In the forced
marches necessitated by this acceleration of the timetable, much
of the artillery was left behind. Meanwhile, during the morning of
the 12th the Belgian Army was in full retreat from the Albert Canal line and attempting to take up position on the line Antwerp–
Malines–Louvain, linking up with the BEF on its right. The Belgian withdrawal in turn exposed the forward elements of General
Prioux's Cavalry Corps to attack from the armour of General
Hoeppner's XVI Panzer Corps. In the general area of Hannut,
roughly midway between Liège and the Dyle, preliminary blows
were now exchanged in the first major tank battle between the
French and Germans. On that opening day, Prioux's tanks gave
a good account of themselves. The armoured forces of both sides
were overextended, and the German infantry were moving up so
slowly behind that the harassed Belgian command was given a
badly needed breather in which to effect its withdrawal without
precipitating a crisis. By the evening of the 12th, Prioux's ar-

moured screen was still clinging to its forward positions—though precariously. The day's fighting had been indecisive, but it seemed to show that—on anything like equal terms—French armour could hold its own against the German panzers. From Army, Army Group, and back to Gamelin at GQG, Prioux was showered with flattering praise for these first—alas, premature—results. But by the end of the 12th, no more than two-thirds of the First Army had reached the Dyle, and it looked as if the main weight of Hoeppner's two panzer divisions might hit Prioux on the morrow.

The BEF, entrenched along the Dyle from Louvain to Wavre, enjoyed another quiet day. That afternoon, Gort's Chief of Staff, General Sir Henry Pownall, attended what the British official historian describes as "a momentous meeting" at the Château de Casteau, near Mons of 1914 fame. Present were King Leopold and his chief military adviser, General van Overstraeten; Daladier (still Minister of National Defence), Georges, and Billotte. Under pressure of this first crisis confronting the three embattled allies, all now agreed to General Georges's earlier proposal that Billotte act as his "delegate" to "coordinate the actions of the Allied forces in Belgian territory." One of the first practical results of the Casteau conference was to resolve the defence of Louvain which, since May 10th—as one further consequence of the poor liaison with the Belgians before the offensive began—had been duplicated by both a British and a Belgian division; the sector was now handed to the BEF. In effect, however, the terms of reference within the Allied command remained vague, and with Billotte increasingly overwhelmed by the responsibilities heaped upon him by his large command, he was to have little time for "coordinating" the Belgians and the BEF with the French forces. Henceforth, Gort for one would have to carry on virtually without directives from above—a neglect that was to have its repercussions at a critical stage in the battle ten days later.

The skies on that brilliantly sunny Whitsunday once again saw the main Allied air effort concentrated in the north. It was the Maastricht bridges and the stretch of road leading from them through Tongres that attracted particular attention. Here Hoeppner's panzers were pouring towards the Dyle Line, presenting (apparently) far more threatening and obvious targets than the many times larger force "lost" in the Ardennes. At 6 A.M. on the 12th, Billotte called upon French Fighter Command to lend all its support that day to flying cover for the bombers attacking the Maastricht bridgehead. According to General d'Astier, the French bomber squadrons were still not yet ready for action. The crack ground-level attack unit, Groupe I/54, for instance, which had been ordered to shift bases on May 10th had been lacking some vital bomb-release accessories right up to the night of the 11th–12th, when these had actually been fetched by truck from the factory itself. Therefore, on the morning of the 12th, d'Astier was forced to call again on the RAF to shoulder the main burden against Maastricht. Out of nine Blenheims bombing columns between Tongres and the Maastricht bridges, seven were shot down by Messerschmitts.

By midday on the 12th, Groupe I/54 was at last ready for its first action. Flying with its leading flight of six Bréguets, Sergeant Gunner Conill gives a graphic account of a low-level attack on an enemy column at Tongres that typified the experience of many Allied bomber crews during these May days. On approaching Liège, Conill's formation was ordered to dive to zero altitude.

In front of us the Major flew his Bréguet with incredible daring, skimming the roof-tops, brushing the trees, jumping obstacles. A grand game! . . . The roofs of Tongres rose up in front of us. . . . A main road was there, the one we were looking for, flanked by trees and ditches. And what a sight! Hundreds and hundreds of vehicles rolling towards France, following each other at short intervals, mobile, and travelling fast. A lovely target! . . . at 350 kilometres an hour, right down the axis of the road, flying at tree-top level, the Major attacked. . . . Suddenly white and blue flashes sprang up underneath us and there was a hell-like outburst of fire and steel and flames, which grew bigger. I saw clearly the bursts of small-calibre shells climbing towards us by the thousands. Each one of us felt they were aimed at him personally.

Ahead, Sergeant Conill could see the German flak ripping into the major's plane; suddenly it "tipped on one wing," tore through some poplar branches, "and crashed in the midst of the German troops, right on the road." Conill then turned to see his wing man plunging earthwards in flames. Undismayed, the pilot of Conill's plane, Lieutenant Blondy, managed to drop his bombs squarely among a group of lorry-borne infantry, before his Bréguet too was riddled with flak. On one engine the Bréguet limped back to make a belly landing in a French field. The plane was a write-off, but none of the other five planes of the flight returned.

The effectiveness of the 20 mm and 37 mm flak, and the speed with which the Germans had managed both to bring up and mass these weapons around important passages, provided a singularly disagreeable shock to the French Air Force that day. The severe losses (eight out of eighteen planes in all) suffered by Groupe I/54, was also to bring a virtual end to the ground-level attack technique. That evening a dozen Léo bombers from Groupement 6 again attacked the Tongres road network, this time prudently from an altitude of 2,500 feet, but the flak still forced them to take such evasive action that accuracy suffered badly. All the Léos returned, though none was undamaged. Meanwhile, during the afternoon, Air Marshal Barratt, under constant pressure from Billotte and fully realising how suicidal future attacks on the well-guarded Maastricht bridgehead would be, took the exceptional step of calling for a volunteer effort from No. 12 Battle Squadron. The whole squadron, well nicknamed the "Dirty Dozen," volunteered. Under a strong cover of Hurricanes, five Battles went out; only one crippled plane was brought back, after the pilot had ordered his crew to bail out; the other four were never seen again. Flying Officer Garland and Sergeant Gray in the leading aircraft were posthumously awarded the VC—the first to be awarded in the campaign. One truss of the Veldwezelt bridge was knocked down. Pulled out of the burning wreck of his plane, one of the survivors was told by his German captors: "You British are mad. We capture the bridge early Friday morning. You give us all Friday and Saturday to get our *flak* guns up in circles all round the bridge, and then on Sunday, when all is ready, you come along with three aircraft and try to blow the thing up." It was not an unreasonable judgement.

According to General d'Astier, altogether that day RAF bombers made 140 sorties and lost 24 planes, while French bombers flew only 30 sorties, losing 9 planes. French fighters flew about 200 sorties, losing 6 planes and claiming 26 of the enemy; while with its 124 Me–109s that had pounced upon the Maastricht Blenheims, the German Fighter Group 27 alone chalked up as many as 340 sorties that day, losing 4 planes for a claimed 28. As regards the results achieved by the sacrificial Allied efforts against Maastricht, the war diary of Hoeppner's XVI Panzer

Corps admits that it caused "considerable delays." But at what a cost! And why were the Allied air forces continuing to waste their precious substance upon this purely secondary threat?

In his reconnaissance report for the 12th, d'Astier once again emphasised the German effort in the Ardennes: "Considerable motorised and armoured forces are on the march towards the Meuse round Dinant, Givet, and Bouillon, coming respectively from Marche and Neufchâteau." Ominously he noted the substantial amount of bridging equipment being carried by the German columns, and concluded: "One can assume a very serious enemy effort in the direction of the Meuse." But, to his amazement, by midday on the 12th Billotte was still allocating top priority for air operations to the Maastricht area, though he now switched second priority from the battered Seventh Army and the untroubled BEF to support of Huntziger. At 1600 hours, says d'Astier, General Georges intervened to grant first priority to Huntziger. Billotte, having moved into a battle HQ behind the French First Army, had his eyes fixed upon this sector of the front and was astounded. Resuming his former tack he declared: "Two-thirds of the air effort in support of the First Army, one-third in support of Second Army." To some extent, Billotte can be exculpated by the surprising fact that Huntziger himself, although informed of the bomber support earmarked for his Second Army, apparently made no appeal for it to General d'Astier that day. It was purely on his own initiative, based on the reconnaissance reports, that d'Astier requested 50 British aircraft to bomb the Neufchâteau and Bouillon areas on the evening of the 12th—from which another 18 bombers failed to return.

Guderian: Across the Semois

During the night of the 11th–12th, Guderian had swiftly exploited the precipitate withdrawal made by Corap's 3rd Spahi Brigade across the Semois the previous day. The motorcycle battalion of the 1st Panzer, deployed on the right of the division, got over the river at Mouzaive under cover of darkness, establishing itself in force on the other side before the defenders could react. Less than 5 air miles from Bouillon, the mainstay of the French defence along the Semois, the Mouzaive bridgehead gave the attackers an immediate and powerful advantage as dawn broke on the 12th. By 0600 hours Guderian had tanks across at

Mouzaive, and the left flank of Huntziger's 5th DLC, not fore-warned of the Spahis' withdrawal, was now already threatened. At Bouillon itself, men of Lieutenant Colonel Balck's 1st Rifle Regiment, who were later to cover themselves with glory on the far side of the Meuse, infiltrated down through steep and densely wooded banks until they reached a ford across the Semois which the reconnaissance unit had located the previous night. Within a short time they had carried their objectives, and the first tanks were rolling across the ford, their passage aided by the fact that the dry spring had considerably reduced the level of the Semois.

As usual, Guderian was up in the cockpit that morning, watching Balck's river crossing. After he had satisfied himself with the immediate building of a new bridge by the divisional engineers, he followed the tanks across the Semois, up the steep gorge towards Sedan. "But mined roads compelled me to return to Bouillon. Here, in the southern part of the town," Guderian admitted, "I experienced an enemy air attack for the first time; they were after 1st Panzer Division's bridge. Luckily the bridge remained undamaged, but a few houses were set on fire." In his command vehicle, Guderian then drove to the Cugnon–Herbeumont sector, where his 10th Panzer Division was engaged in crossing the Semois. This he found "an impressive sight," and he returned "without anxiety" to Bouillon, where his staff had set up corps HQ in the Hotel Panorama, well named on account of its splendid view over the Semois. In an alcove heavily decorated with trophies of *la chasse,* Guderian went to work, planning the next stage of the advance.

Suddenly there was a series of explosions in rapid succession; another air attack. As though that were not enough, an engineer supply column, carrying fuses, explosives, mines and hand grenades, caught fire and there was one detonation after another. A boar's head, attached to the wall immediately above my desk, broke loose and missed me by a hair's breadth; the other trophies came tumbling down and the fine window in front of which I was seated was smashed to smithereens and splinters of glass whistled about my ears.

After this narrow escape which might so easily have altered the course of the coming battle, Guderian moved his HQ back out of Bouillon. Once again he was bombed, and once again forced

Meuse crossings of German troops at Dinant and Sedan:
May 12th–14th

Detail of crossings at Dinant

Detail of crossings at Sedan

to move, this time to the delightful small village of Noirefontaine, on the Ardennes plateau 3 miles north of Bouillon.

Throughout the day Allied bombardment of the Bouillon bridgehead continued. From Torcy, 10 miles away on the Meuse near Sedan, French "long 155's" lobbed in shells with sufficient accuracy to make the German engineers' bridge-building a highly dangerous occupation. Rather less accurately, RAF Battle bombers, such as those that had nearly hit Guderian in the Hotel Panorama, made repeated runs on the bridges down the narrow, twisting valley. Their losses were heavy; 18 out of 50 did not return. But things did not all go the Luftwaffe's way; five American-made Curtiss fighters belonging to Groupe I/5—the Cigognes squadron to whom had passed the mantle of the legendary Guynemer of '14–'18 fame—pounced upon twelve Stukas returning from a bombing mission between Bouillon and Sedan. All were shot down, at no cost to the Cigognes, who then attacked a second wave of Stukas coming in to bomb. Several more were shot down, and the rest put to flight. The two encounters demonstrated clearly the vulnerability of the dreaded Stuka; but, alas, it was a lesson from which little benefit would be drawn.

Despite this Allied effort, by midmorning the 1st Panzer had established a sizeable bridgehead over the Semois and was thrusting down the road to Sedan—by the signposts, now just 18 kilometres distant. While Britons were reading their morning newspapers at breakfast, the first of Guderian's tanks was leaving Belgium behind it and crossing into France. As they burst out of the "inhospitable" Ardennes which had concealed and sheltered them the past two and one-half days, the panzers could make out in the distant haze the Frenois heights beyond the Meuse where, seventy summers ago, the King of Prussia and Bismarck had stood as German soldiers closed in to win that first Battle of Sedan.

Second Army

When Huntziger had realised, early that morning, that the threat to the rear of the 5th DLC by the panzer crossing at Mouzaive rendered any defence at Bouillon impossible, he ordered the cavalry to fall back on the line of the *maisons fortes,* which had been constructed that winter between Sedan and the frontier. But the withdrawal of the infantry battalion of the 295th Regiment, sent up from the 55th Division to bolster the Bouillon defences only the previous day, did not go smoothly. Its motor transport appears to have vanished and—according to General Ruby—this battalion of "B" series reservists "scattered in the woods, and, cut off from its route, lost its C.O., Major Clausener, as well as the major part of its effectives; only three hundred demoralised men were seen again, crying 'treachery' against the cavalry, and devoid of any value for the actions of the following days." It was an ominous indication of what might happen when a "B" division was really hit hard by the German panzers or Stukas.

Meanwhile, further to the right on the sector of the 2nd DLC, Marcel Lerecouvreux paints a similarly depressing picture. With the 10th Panzer now thrusting across its front on the general axis Herbeumont–Sedan, the 2nd DLC had enjoyed a relatively calm morning, but that afternoon Lerecouvreux, back at divisional HQ well behind the Semois, was astonished to hear the sound of small-arms fire close at hand. He learned that the neighbouring divisions were already pulling back across the river Chiers in retreat. Divisional HQ was hastily packed up, with the French artillery firing over its head. Lerecouvreux noted that some of the division "wept at having to leave entrenchments which they had built with their own hands, where they had hoped to halt the enemy and which now served no purpose"; nevertheless the cavalry, though fatigued after three days of combat, withdrew in good order. But it was not so with all units; at Margut, a crossing point on the Chiers, "during the two days that had passed since the departure of the civil population, there had been many depredations and pillages committed by the non-combatant troops, and the wine ran down into the gutter from barrels which had been smashed open." There was much drunkenness, leading to a particularly disgraceful incident that night:

A soldier, manifestly drunk, approached a platoon of the 18th Chasseurs who were halting at Margut after the battle, before regaining their regrouping area, and without any motive he killed an unfortunate Chasseur with a bullet square in the chest. Taking advantage of the general surprise, the murderer disappeared before he could be arrested.

Lerecouvreux also mentions the rout of a battalion of colonial infantry that day.

Guderian at Sedan

For the retreating French, the halt on the line of the *maisons fortes* was far shorter than anticipated. By 1400 hours, tanks of the 1st Panzer curling round behind the back of the 5th DLC via Fleigneux and St. Menges forced it to abandon hope of standing here, and to fall back on the Sedan bridgehead. Relentlessly the panzers pursued them. Although Gamelin's orders were to hold the city of Sedan (the greater part of which lies on the Ardennes side of the Meuse) "at all costs," within another four hours the cavalry had yielded it and retreated across the Meuse, leaving the Germans to occupy Sedan virtually unopposed. Well before dusk the forward tanks of the 1st Panzer were in the city. Sedan! The name that the visionary mind of Hitler had first spewed out, quite casually, the previous October; a small provincial French centre of some thirteen thousand inhabitants (a population little less than that of Verdun in 1916), but what magical connotations it held for German minds. The birthplace of Turenne, a castigator of Teutons in a past era, in 1870 it had witnessed France's greatest humiliation and the ascendant Prussia's greatest triumph: the unconditional surrender of Emperor Napoleon III and 100,000 men to Moltke the Elder, a surrender that had forever altered the course of European history.

Now Guderian's advance guard entered into a dead city. The streets were unnaturally empty and deserted. A few French stragglers, detached from the retreating cavalry, opened up desultory fire from rifle and machine-gun nests but were rapidly silenced. As the German infantry and engineers groped their way towards the Meuse, heavy artillery fire descended on them from the other side of the river, and suddenly there was a tremendous roar as a bridge blew up. One after another the Sedan bridges erupted until not one was standing—although, in the heat of the moment, Paul Reynaud was later to claim that some had been left intact by "treachery."

As night fell, the 1st Panzer had reached the glittering Meuse in force. General Kirchner, the divisional commander, set up his HQ just a mile or two north of Illy, the scene of French General Gallifet's last desperate cavalry charge in 1870, which had so excited the admiration and compassion of the watching King of Prussia. On the left, the 10th Panzer had also reached the Meuse in the area of Bazeilles, where another savage battle had been

fought during the war of 1870. Only the 2nd Panzer, whose delays
on the previous day had been compounded with a difficult crossing
of the Semois, bad roads and more interference with its itinerary
from other units, was still hanging badly behind—much to Guderian's annoyance and concern.

Reinhardt

On Reinhardt's XLI Corps sector, where the principal objective was Monthermé on the confluence of the Meuse and Semois,
the 6th and 8th Panzers were still making only slow progress.
The reason for this was the continued confusion on their routes
of advance; the traffic tangles had occurred not only with Guderian's 2nd Panzer, but also with elements of some of Rundstedt's
leading infantry divisions that were now beginning to press in from
behind onto the already cluttered Ardennes road network. By later
afternoon of the 12th, the War Diary of the 6th Panzer admits that
even radio communication could provide "no longer any clear picture" of just where its various units had got to. Fortunately for
Reinhardt his straggling columns were again not attacked from
the air; nor did they encounter any ground resistance that day. It
was as if they were advancing into open air. The Corps aerial
reconnaissance that afternoon could find no enemy formations
east of the Meuse, and the War Diary of the 6th tersely records
the capture of "only one drunken French soldier." By nightfall the
advance formations of the 6th Panzer—accompanied by its commander, General Kempf—had crossed the French frontier northeast of Monthermé and stood almost on the edge of the Ardennes
escarpment where it falls with dramatic suddenness down to the
Meuse. But the continued, mystifying absence of the enemy was
distinctly unnerving: "Either the French have left their senses,"
observed a Sergeant Sievert with a storm detachment of the 6th
Panzer, "and really don't know that we are just about to reach
the Meuse—or they are preparing something particularly devilish
for us."

Ninth Army cavalry withdrawal

On the French side, however, the reason for this apparent
vacuum was depressingly simple. Surprised to discover that, by
the night of the 11th, the 3rd Spahi Brigade constituting the right
wing of his cavalry screen had pulled back as far as Mézières on

the wrong side of the Meuse, Corap had promptly ordered it to turn about and reoccupy its positions along the Semois. But, as already seen, events had moved far too quickly. Guderian's panzers had got across the Semois before the main body of the Spahis had even left Mézières on their return trip. Corap now realised that this flank of his cavalry was completely exposed; at the same time he had received an aerial reconnaissance report that morning which described an enemy motorised column 15 miles long moving towards Marche, on the way to Dinant. A column this length could denote only one thing—a panzer division.* Concerned at the poor state of the defences covering Dinant, owing to the tardy approach march of his infantry, Corap had decided to order his entire cavalry screen to fall back and take up positions along the west side of the Meuse. By 1600 hours on the 12th, the order had been carried out, and all Meuse bridges on the Ninth Army front, from Dinant to the river Bar, were destroyed.

The French cavalry action was now over, having lasted just two and one-half days—instead of the five upon which the French High Command had counted when it had calculated that the Germans could not possibly mount any crossing of the Meuse before the ninth day of the campaign. Despite the disarray into which the French cavalry units had been thrown, losses on both sides had been light.

In the sector facing Reinhardt, Corap's cavalry had disengaged themselves without hindrance. It was a different story opposite Rommel's fast-thrusting 7th Panzer, and it was here that the most significant and decisive event of May 12th occurred. Lieutenant Georges Kosak describes the withdrawal across the Meuse north of Dinant of his badly battered division, the 4th DLC:

Towards midday, groups of unsaddled horses returned, followed on foot by several wounded cavalrymen who had been bandaged as well as possible; others held themselves in the saddle by a miracle for the honour of being cavalrymen. The saddles and the harnesses were all covered with blood. Most of the animals limped; others, badly wounded, just got as far as us in order to die, at the end of their strength; others had to be shot to bring an end to their sufferings.

Pursuing hotly came Rommel. By 1130 hours his 25th Panzer

---

* It was, of course, Rommel.

Regiment under Colonel Rothenburg* had captured Ciney and Leignon, just 10 miles from Dinant. Although the narrow gorges from Ciney down to Dinant should have been easy to block and difficult to clear, by early afternoon the first German reconnaissance armoured cars were rolling down to the banks of the Meuse itself. Sitting in a pillbox that guarded the western end of the railway bridge at Houx† (destroyed earlier that afternoon), Private Darche of the Chasseurs Ardennais heard the noise of their motors. It was about half past four. A few minutes later an enemy armoured car reached the other end of the bridge, little more than 100 yards from Darche. He fired his antitank rifle at it, missing with his first shot, but stopping it dead with the second. Machinegun fire from the pillbox also scattered some lorry-borne infantry imprudently debussing on the Meuse. Then Darche was killed by another armoured car firing shells straight into the gun embrasure. The survivors were forced to evacuate the pillbox, but—for the time being—they had imposed greater wariness upon the approaching Germans.

Rommel

Rommel's 7th Panzer, converted from a light division, contained only one tank regiment instead of the two allotted to the standard panzer divisions. Then, at midday on the 12th, he received a valuable reinforcement. This was Colonel Werner's 31st Panzer Regiment, which belonged to the lagging 5th Panzer Division but which Hoth, the Corps commander, now temporarily transferred to Rommel to back up the latter's already encouraging success. Werner's regiment was already well ahead of the rest of the division, and under Rommel's guidance—after some sharp encounters with the rear guard of the French 4th DLC near Ciney— it surged down to the Meuse at Yvoir late that afternoon. The last French vehicles were just crossing the bridge and Werner's armoured cars immediately tried to rush the bridge before it was destroyed. In a bunker on the other side of the river, a gallant Belgian sapper, Lieutenant de Wispelaere, pressed the demolition plunger. Nothing happened. One of the German armoured cars

---

* Later killed in Russia.

† Midway between Dinant and Yvoir, and about two and one-half miles from each.

was already moving up the incline towards the bridge. Under heavy fire, an antitank gun under de Wispelaere's command brought it to a halt, belching smoke, actually on the bridge itself. But its commander, clad in a black leather jacket, climbed out of the stricken vehicle and started running towards the spot where the explosive charges were located, a large pair of pliers in his hand. He was felled by de Wispelaere's group, and another shot from the antitank gun knocked out a second armoured car attempting to follow its precursor onto the bridge. With extreme courage, de Wispelaere now darted out into the open to ignite the demolition charges by hand, under heavy enemy fire. Miraculously he managed to light the fuse; but as he stood up to run for the shelter of the bunker, he was struck by a shell and killed outright. Almost simultaneously the bridge erupted; according to a German account "a huge plume of flame leaped into the air. There was a crash like thunder. Bits of steel, stone blocks fly high into the air, and with them the two armoured cars." Now the last of the Meuse bridges was down. Or was it the last?

By nightfall on the 12th, Rommel's motorised infantry brigade had moved up and were firmly in control of the east bank of the Meuse between Dinant and Houx. Because of the sharpness of the reaction they had encountered earlier from pillboxes like Darche's on the west bank, the leading reconnaissance detachments had carried out no more than a cursory examination of the river itself. But at Houx that afternoon they had spotted what looked like an ancient weir, connecting with a narrow island in midstream, which—unaccountably—it seemed the defenders had neglected to destroy. Under cover of darkness, and further aided by a low mist clinging to the river bed, Rommel's foot patrols now explored the weir and reported it viable. Immediately the infantry commander, Colonel Furst, ordered the divisional motorcycle battalion to infiltrate across it on foot. A divisional chronicle gives an impressionistic account of the crossing:

They grope their way out of the woods, and in one single rush are fifty yards beyond the trees. Panting, they lie down in the shell holes. . . . Onwards! They don't shoot, they don't want to bring the enemy fire down on themselves. . . . Star rockets are fired above. Their light seems to last forever, like the rays of a huge searchlight, covering the countryside far and wide with a deadly brightness. . . . At last, after what seems an eternity, their groping fingers reach the leaves and branches on the bank. In front of them runs the river. The first phase has been achieved.

The Germans reach the

thin spine with many gaps in it which comprises the old unprotected and weather-worn stone weir. . . . Right and left machine guns take up position. They give covering fire. . . . The first assault troops do gymnastics, one behind the other, with a distance in between them, on the fragile framework of the weir. Like tight-rope walkers they balance their way forwards.

The enemy did not react, and the long thin island turned out to be untenanted. Rommel's motorcyclists made their way stealthily through its scrub and bushes, until they discovered on its far side a lock gate—equally intact. They crossed this, and taking advantage of the hubbub and confusion of the night firing, they swiftly dug themselves in. Pinned under a cross fire from German and French machine guns, with friendly bullets ricochetting disagreeably off the railway line that ran along the west side of the river, the motorcyclists clung to a precarious foothold. Packet by packet they were reinforced until several companies were across; and still—strangely enough—no serious attempt was made to dislodge them. Shortly after midnight on May 12th, less than three days after the campaign had begun, German soldiers were established on the west side of the Meuse. And it had cost Rommel that day the lives of no more than three officers, six NCOs and fifteen enlisted men.

Rommel's easy initial crossing resulted from an unusual combination of circumstances. By sheer luck, at Houx he had struck a particularly sensitive point in the Meuse defences. The lock and the weir had expressly not been destroyed because it was feared (not unreasonably) that, with the exceptionally dry season, their destruction would so lower the level of the Meuse that it might actually be fordable in certain places. Yet the banks of the island were fringed with high trees so that the Germans could cross concealed from the defenders on the west bank; while on that side the road and railway both running along the river further impeded the defenders' field of fire. Westwards from Houx, the terrain climbs gently towards Anthée and Philippeville on the open plateau beyond, offering a very enticing axis of penetration for armour. Houx was therefore, from all points of view, a danger area not lightly to be ignored, and it might have been assumed that its defence would have assumed particular priority. This was not so, however.

The French at Houx

To compound the misfortunes of the sector, the German crossing point happened to fall right on the boundary between General Bouffet's II Corps and General Martin's XI Corps. Bouffet's solitary division, the 5th Motorised, which formed the left flank of Corap's army, on account of its mobility had already arrived and was more or less in position by the 12th; but its neighbour to the right in Martin's sector, the 18th Infantry Division (an "A" series unit) had only managed to get six of its battalions and a portion of its artillery into line. In fact, according to Corap's original plans, the 18th was not scheduled to be entirely in position until "D + 5," or May 14th. As a result, its companies were so thinly spread out along the Meuse that they could not hope to keep their whole front covered—and, after the more than 50 miles they had had to cover by forced marches from the French frontier, the "A" series reservists were thoroughly exhausted. Already on the 11th, General Martin had expressed disquiet about the Houx area and had obtained permission to plug the gaps in his defence with the retreating remnants of the 1st DLC. But by now the value of the chastened cavalry was not great, and what little it possessed was thrown away by dispersing it among the infantry. There was added confusion caused by a conflict in seniority between the colonels commanding the cavalry regiments and the lieutenant colonels of the infantry.

To give further teeth to the defences opposite Houx, Martin had also asked the 5th Motorised Division to transfer one of its battalions to the 18th, until such time as all that division's effectives could be in line. Although the unit concerned—the 2nd Battalion of the 39th Infantry Regiment—received its orders on the 11th, it did not reach its new position until 1600 hours on the following day; thus, at the time of Rommel's arrival on the other side of the Meuse, it was just in the process of taking over from the 66th Regiment. Observing that the riverbank was already exposed to fire from Rommel's advance guard on the east side, the newly arrived battalion had shown no predilection to send outposts down there. Instead, the 39th had sat on the high ground west of the river, whence it was impossible to cover the Isle of Houx or its approaches, and remained there even after darkness had removed the excuse of enemy fire. This error was a radical contravention of Corap's orders (No. 12 of April 22nd), which stated explicitly that the main defence must be carried forward down to the water's edge. Here was perhaps one first practical consequence of the poor discipline of the French Ninth Army on which Lieutenant General Brooke had commented the previous autumn.

It was 1 A.M.* on the morning of May 13th when General Boucher, commanding the 5th Motorised Division, learned that a German detachment had crossed the Meuse. But General Martin, the senior commander most concerned, did not receive the news until 4 A.M. As a further example of the lethal sluggishness of French communications, Martin found it quite impossible to get through on the telephone to Corap. Thus Martin was forced to coordinate plans for a localised counterattack laterally with Boucher. A wider consequence was that nobody from the Army Commander, Corap, upwards was aware of the extent of the threat at Houx until late on the 13th, by which time a much greater danger was already revealing itself at Sedan.

French High Command

At the top echelons of the French High Command—despite the repeated warnings of aerial reconnaissance and the fragmentary items of bad news from the cavalry—the day passed once again in a general atmosphere of optimism, and without any specific alarm at the turn of events in the Ardennes. Attention was concentrated on the tank battle in the Gembloux Gap which (as General Georges later admitted) the French High Command continued to regard as a greater danger to the Allied front than Sedan —because this was the way the Germans had come in 1914. In government circles the talk was all about fifth columnists and parachutists; Alexander Werth, a British correspondent, recalls one of Reynaud's chief spokesmen at the Quai d'Orsay, Duroc, telling him reassuringly, that Sunday, "After all, if the Germans

---

* Roughly two hours after the crossing.

have to resort to tricks like dressing up their soldiers in foreign uniforms—well, then they can't feel so very strong. It makes me confident they'll still lose the war." On the 12th, Gamelin is to be found suggesting to General Georges that the cavalry screen withdrawing from the Ardennes now be sent to the rear in readiness to round up German parachutists; then he changed his mind and suggested it should be sent northwards to back up Blanchard's First Army—proposals that illustrate how badly out of touch the Generalissimo was, at his radio-less GQG. Gamelin admits that he was "above all devoted to dealing with matters of overall organisation." These appear to have included all sorts of minor details concerning tactical defence against tanks in northern Belgium, and warnings to the Maginot Line of the technique employed by the Germans to capture Eben Emael. He complains at the poverty of the intelligence reaching him from the Ardennes sector, but went to bed that night contented by the evening's situation report from General Georges, which stated: "The defense now seems well assured on the whole front of the river [Meuse]."

At General Georges's headquarters in La Ferté, his Chief of Staff, General Roton, records the receipt at 1500 hours on the 12th of "a very alarming report" from Huntziger's Second Army. The cavalry had suffered "very severe losses" (something of an exaggeration), and Huntziger was calling for a fresh division to replace the 71st which Grandsard (commanding X Corps) was having to insert into the line south of Sedan. Georges was away in the north, and in his absence Roton took the initiative to order the movement "immediately" of three of the five divisions from the general reserve which Georges had earmarked for the Sedan sector the previous day: the 3rd Armoured,* the 3rd Motorised and the 14th Infantry Divisions. These were also among the best in the French Army. But at 1700 hours, surprisingly a "more reassuring" message came through from Huntziger's Chief of Staff. "Calm had returned to the front," says Roton; "he estimated that there was no urgency to push the 3rd Motorised as far as Stonne. But I held to my point of view; this division was to arrive punctually on May 14th, on the battlefield of Sedan." This would be,

---

* Note that the 2nd Armoured dropped temporarily out of sight—next day it was dispatched to the First Army.

however, at least one critical day too late. Meanwhile nothing further was done for the more immediately threatened Corap.*

Huntziger: Orders to the Second Army

With nightfall, it was abundantly clear to the French Second Army that they were going to be attacked in earnest the following day. All night long the troops opposite Sedan could hear the growl of German tanks moving up on the other side of the Meuse, and any pretence of secrecy or camouflage now appeared to be abandoned. Night reconnaissance flights reported vast motorised columns, moving with headlamps full on in flagrant contempt of the Allied air forces, along all the roads leading to the Meuse south of Namur; and heaviest of all was the traffic heading towards Sedan. That day the 1st Panzer Division had been positively identified, and, while even from the garbled reports of the French cavalry screen it was obvious that this was not the only one converging on Sedan, the fact that the 1st Panzer was known to be the pride of Hitler's armoured formations must have clearly suggested to Huntziger the scale of the pending attack. Huntziger, half Alsatian and half Breton, was rated to be perhaps the most brilliant intellect among the senior commanders of the French Army. On leaving St. Cyr in 1901 his first choice was to join the Marines. After taking part in pre-1914 colonial wars in Madagascar and Indo-China, he commanded a battalion during the First War, ending it with the rank of lieutenant-colonel as Marshal Franchet d'Esperey's Chief of Operations in Salonika. By 1938 he was appointed to the *Conseil Supérieur de la Guerre,* having already commanded the French forces in Syria as one of the youngest army commanders on record. On taking over the Second Army, he was still well under sixty—which was youthful by the standards of 1940 —a trimly elegant, alert and vigorous figure. His cold blue eyes gave away a certain tendency to be remote in his dealings with subordinates, but most of them agreed upon his "dazzling intelligence" as a theoretician, and he was generally regarded in the French Army as the likeliest successor to Gamelin.

Perhaps the most fundamental truth about Huntziger—and also

---

* It should also be noted that, by May 12th, Georges had already oriented several more of his reserve divisions—including both the 1st and 2nd Armoured—towards northern Belgium; thus away from the main threat.

many of his contemporaries of 1940—is to be found in the concluding words of his order of the day issued the night of May 12th, warning the Second Army of the coming battle on the Sedan "position of resistance":

Every portion of terrain upon which the enemy may have set foot must be retaken from him.

The honour of leaders at all levels is at stake in preserving the integrity of the position, without regard to casualties.

No *défaillance* will be tolerated.

On the Maginot Line, we shall defend the sacred soil of the nation.

I am sure of the Second Army.

Resounding, courageous and inspiring words; but they were those of a past war, redolent of the resolute but rigid linear defence at Verdun. They revealed that Huntziger's thinking, for all his intellectual power, remained rooted in the victory of 1918. The French General Staff, basing its judgements on its own capabilities, knew that it could not execute a full-scale crossing of the Meuse before "J.9"; therefore, Q.E.D., the Germans could not either. And Huntziger, by the evening of May 12th, equally still seems to have only half believed—despite all the signs—in the imminence of the danger confronting him.

Symptomatic of that fatal leisureliness with which his Second Army (and, for that matter, Corap's Ninth) carried out its final preparations was the manner in which the 71st Division was being brought up into the line. Up till March, this Parisian-recruited "B" division—probably the poorest of all Huntziger's units—had been holding a sector on the Meuse at Mouzon, but since then it had been undergoing badly needed training in the Vouziers area. On May 10th, Huntziger had ordered it to resume its position on the Meuse, between the 55th and 3rd North African Divisions, but he appears to have failed to impart to his subordinates any particular sense of urgency for this transfer. General Grandsard, to whose X Corps the 71st belonged, claims in his apologia[*] that by the night of the 12th he still had no idea of the strength of the German force approaching Sedan, details of air and cavalry reconnaissance intelligence not having filtered down to him, and his appreciation that night was that the enemy could not attack with any likelihood of

---

[*] *Le 10e Corps d'Armée dans la Bataille 1939/1940*, published in 1949.

success on the 13th. (He adds that of course he knew all about the German Stukas but had complete faith in the French Air Force to keep them at bay.) Grandsard blames Huntziger for having stationed the 71st so far away from the line on May 10th. "To demand an infantry division to march on foot," says Grandsard, "some 60 kilometres in two short May nights (6 hours approximately, each night), plus a relief, is to demand the impossible."* On the afternoon of the 12th, the commander of the 71st Division, the elderly and ailing General Baudet, requested Grandsard for a time extension. Grandsard refused. On moving into line, General Baudet found that his command post had not been set up, while the divisional telephone exchange was linked with only light temporary cables, many of which were not even buried. Meanwhile, to make way for the entry into line of the 71st, General Lafontaine's 55th Division was also in the process of extensively reorganising itself. Altogether, Grandsard reckoned that the earliest the whole of his corps could possibly be in a position was the 13th; but in fact, General Ruby tells us, General Lafontaine was not planning to complete *his* dispositions before the *night* of May 13th–14th.

In terms of artillery, Grandsard's position by the night of May 12th was somewhat rosier on paper. Early in the morning of the 12th, Huntziger had ordered up two additional regiments to support Grandsard; and the 55th Division, though short on machine guns and anti-tank weapons, had twice the normal establishment of artillery—with some 140 guns supporting its front. Without apparently informing Grandsard, the commander of the long-range 155 mm regiment had pulled back the battery at Torcy, which had been shelling the Bouillon crossing points so effectively, after it had run out of ammunition. To his annoyance, Grandsard discovered that evening that he could no longer maintain interdiction on the German approach routes.

Thus as May 12th drew to a close, the overall picture on Grandsard's X Corps front was not encouraging. Some of the artillery was still digging itself in, while other reinforcement batteries would not arrive before dawn. Of the infantry, the elderly reservists of the 71st were thoroughly fatigued from their two nights of forced

---

* Again this was thinking in '14–'18 terms; it need hardly be remarked that the German infantry divisions of 1940 would not have found such a march beyond their powers, even on foot.

marching and had little time to acclimatise themselves to their new positions; the 55th was also still moving house while this already weak unit had virtually lost one of the battalions of its 295th Regiment. Chewed up on the river Semois, the remnants straggling back across the Meuse hardly aspired to *"encourager les autres"* with their dismal narratives. Altogether, Grandsard's X Corps was hardly an imposing force to put up against the elite of the German panzers. Would the reinforcements ordered by General Georges reach the field in time? This was the big question to be answered on May 13th. Or would Guderian be able to beat them to it by bringing up enough of his corps to effect a river crossing in strength? Behind this, still more was at issue: the training and the philosophy of a whole generation; and beyond that, a whole trend of history dating back to the first Sedan in 1870.

German High Command

Would Guderian be able to cross the Meuse on the 13th? During the 12th, Hitler had sent his chief adjutant, Colonel Schmundt, to the battle HQ of Kleist's Panzergruppe to ask Kleist whether he intended to attempt an immediate crossing or to wait until the main body of the infantry arrived. The question reflected the German High Command's nervousness—still lurking just below the surface—about the audacity of the Manstein-*Sichelschnitt* Plan. Kleist, encouraged by the results of the previous three days and by intelligence reports indicating that the French had not yet begun shifting any major reserves behind the Sedan sector, replied that he preferred to "attack at once, without wasting time," so as to hit the French before they could regain their breath. A Fieseler-Storch was dispatched to fly Guderian from Bouillon to Kleist's HQ. There he received orders for his corps to attack across the river at 1500 hours the next day. For the first time, the ever-eager Guderian demurred; the 1st and 10th Panzers would be in position on time, but not the 2nd, which was still hung up along the Semois; the *Sturmpionieren*, upon whom the vital task of throwing bridges across the river would depend, were weary from their labours in the Ardennes; and Guderian himself—though he does not mention it in his memoirs—may well have been somewhat shaken from his own two close escapes that day from Allied bombers. He questioned the wisdom of moving with only two-thirds of his corps available. But Kleist was adamant, and Guderian says,

"I felt obliged to admit that there were probably advantages in thrusting forward immediately." He was much more discountenanced by Kleist's alteration in the air plan for the 13th. Guderian had previously agreed with General Loerzer of the Luftwaffe that the crossing at Sedan should be given "continuous support" throughout the operation, in order to keep the heads of the enemy gunners permanently down. Now Kleist ordered "a mass bombing attack, to be coordinated with the beginning of the artillery preparation." Guderian claimed that his "whole attack plan was thus placed in jeopardy," but again Kleist insisted. In evident ill-humour, Guderian flew back to his HQ.

On the way there was very nearly a repeat of the Mechelen Incident, which might have had much graver consequences for the Germans; the inexperienced young pilot of the Fieseler-Storch could not find the XIX Corps landing strip in the fading light, "and the next thing I knew," says Guderian, "we were on the other side of the Meuse, flying in a slow and unarmed plane over the French positions. An unpleasant moment. I gave my pilot emphatic orders to turn north . . . we just made it."

Safely back at Corps HQ, Guderian got to work on drawing up his orders for the next day. In an interesting revelation of just how thorough German training for this momentous operation had been since the redrafting of *Fall Gelb* three months previously, Guderian states:

In view of the very short time at our disposal, we were forced to take the orders used in the war games at Koblenz from our files and, after changing the dates and times, issue these as the orders for the attack. They were perfectly fitted to the reality of the situation. The only change that had to be made was that at Koblenz we had imagined the attack going in at 0900 instead of 1500 hrs.

Yet, while all eyes of the German High Command were focussed upon the Meuse crossing being prepared by Guderian, no one was aware that to the north Major General Rommel, allotted only the secondary role of providing flanking cover to the main thrust, already had a toehold on the far side of the river and was indeed about to develop a major offensive of his own.

12

The Crossing
MAY 13th

It seems that the Germans are not interested in France
this time.

—New York *Journal-American*, May 13th

*La description d'une bataille devrait être une leçon de
Moral.*

—JOSEPH JOUBERT

Rommel emerges

ON THE eve of an adventure which would launch a reputation
ultimately more familiar to the world at large than that of any
other German general of World War II, Erwin Rommel was unknown outside the army at home, and little enough known inside
it. He came from a middle-class family of moderate means, with
no military tradition; both his father and his grandfather had been
schoolteachers. Like Keitel (whom he despised), Rommel was a
Württemberger, a race more renowned for its solidity and shrewd
thriftiness than for any martial attributes. In 1940 he was forty-
eight years old. He had been commissioned in 1912—with not
particularly brilliant marks into a not particularly brilliant line
regiment. He appears to have made an early mark as a meticulous
regimental officer, intolerant of anything slipshod, but—as his
British biographer, Desmond Young, remarks—he was one of those
soldiers who only "find in war the one occupation to which they
are perfectly adapted." It was on the southern fringe of those fateful Ardennes, near Longwy, that Lieutenant Rommel had his
first opportunity three weeks after war broke out in 1914. With

only three men and suffering painfully from food poisoning, he ran into some fifteen to twenty French troops; instead of calling up the rest of his platoon, Rommel immediately opened fire and, taken by surprise, the enemy scattered. Five months later, after recovering from a thigh wound, Rommel won the Iron Cross by crawling with his platoon through barbed wire into the middle of the main French position, knocking out four blockhouses and then withdrawing with light losses before the defence could make an effective riposte. Although this was only a small-scale action, it was as characteristic of Rommel's expertise in the tactics of infiltration—which, as a senior commander, he was to bring to a supreme art—as it was of his nerveless audacity. Later in 1915 Rommel's skill at this kind of operation gained him transfer to a newly created mountain battalion, designed to perform special tasks in "Battle Groups," the commanders of which were granted a freedom of action far in excess of their rank. In the brief Rumanian campaign of 1916–17, Rommel carried out some almost incredible exploits, often with up to a whole battalion under his control, although he was still no more than a first lieutenant.

But the summit of his First War career came during the Battle of Caporetto in October 1917, against the nation that would fight under his command in the Western Desert twenty-five years later. Penetrating the Italian lines at dawn, Rommel first surprised an enemy gun battery without a shot being fired. Then, diving still deeper behind the enemy positions, he surprised from the rear a counterattacking Italian battalion. That too surrendered. After this success, Rommel was reinforced to a total of six companies and now took up position astride an important supply road well behind the enemy lines. Here he succeeded in capturing the best part of a brigade of Bersaglieri moving up towards the front. After fifty hours constantly on the move, he returned with the astonishing bag of 150 Italian officers, 9,000 men and 81 guns. For his feat, he was promoted captain and awarded the Pour le Mérite, the equivalent of the Victoria Cross when given to a junior officer.

After the First War, Rommel became a natural candidate for the elite cadres of Seeckt's tiny Reichswehr. He was promoted major in 1933 and chose to remain with his mountain troops as a regimental officer until two years later, when he was appointed instructor at the Potsdam War Academy, with the rank of lieutenant colonel. During that time he was also assigned on special attachment to the Hitler Youth, but this ended after a short time, when Rommel fell foul of their leader, the arrogant Schirach. After three years at Potsdam, he was sent to command the War Academy at Wiener Neustadt. He was by this time a full colonel —which, considering the huge expansion of the Wehrmacht, did not denote a meteoric career. But he had connections with none of the great military clans and no affiliations with the Nazi Party. His relationship with the Nazi machine in prewar days, was, in fact, not dissimilar to Guderian's; never remotely a party man, he admired Hitler as a technician, and was responsive both to his kindred dynamism and receptiveness to unorthodox ideas. It was in 1938 that Rommel first caught Hitler's eye, after publication of a simple but admirably clear textbook on infantry tactics, based on his own personal experiences from the First War and called *Infanterie Greift An.** At the time of the occupation of the Sudetenland, he was selected to command the battalion entrusted with Hitler's personal safety. On the outbreak of war the following year, Rommel was promoted major general and, as Headquarters Commandant, again made responsible for guarding Hitler during the Polish campaign. He chafed at having no operational command, found himself antipathetic to the party potentates like Martin Bormann, but was fascinated by the front-row view his job gave him of the campaign and its techniques. When it was over he asked Hitler for command of a panzer division, by way of reward for past services. This was granted. On February 15th, Rommel arrived at Bad Godesberg to take over the 7th, one of the four light divisions† to be converted into panzers that winter. Weaker than the original panzer divisions, the 7th had three instead of four tank battalions, 218 instead of 276 tanks; and over half of these were Czech-made light–medium T. 38s.

It was one of Rommel's most astonishing achievements that, in middle age, after a lifetime spent with the infantry and without any experience of armour or mechanised forces, he should within three short months have been able not only to master the technique but also to so mould a new unit that it would become perhaps the most consistently successful of all the panzer divisions employed

---

* "The Infantry Attacks."

† Mixed divisions, roughly comparable to the French DLMs, consisting of two rifle regiments and only one tank detachment. The Polish campaign proved them to be unsatisfactory.

in France—and this despite the relative lightness of its armoured contingent. Indeed, some of his critics consider that he never really understood the principles of armoured warfare. Again and again, he handled his large bodies of tanks much as he had led those few raiding companies on their deep penetrations behind the Italian lines, with a bold unorthodoxy that sometimes shocked the purists. Often he had miraculous luck. Even more than Guderian, he was a commander whose constant closeness to the front provided him with an instant grasp of events.

Rommel's opponent

The unhappy French commander against whose army Rommel would strike the first hard blow on May 13th, General Corap, was perhaps as representative of the median of the old-style French officer as Rommel was of the elite of the new, revolutionary Wehrmacht. Corap was sixty-two in 1940, a Norman who had passed out top of his class at St. Cyr in 1898. He joined the Algerian Tirailleurs, and spent most of his career on colonial operations in North Africa. He became captain in 1914, was appointed to Foch's staff the following year, and in 1918 switched to Pétain's, ending the war as a lieutenant colonel. Afterwards he returned to Morocco where, in 1926, he achieved the summit of his career by capturing the famous rebel, Abd-el-Krim. He was what in the French Army was called a typical *baroudeur,* an old sweat from North Africa, and this largely conditioned his thinking. André Maurois remarks of him: "His conversation was very interesting, but one felt his attention was directed entirely toward the past. He told me how, at the time of Fashoda, he had been mobilised against England as a young second lieutenant." Maurois describes Corap as being "a timid man, held in high esteem by his superiors, unmilitary in appearance, and running to fat around the middle. He had trouble getting into a car." In contrast to the elegant, slim and aloof Huntziger, Corap had a certain vulgar, fat-man's geniality that made him well-liked by the troops—although politically he was known to have a particularly violent antipathy towards the Front Populaire. But even more than was true of Huntziger, his military education had also ceased with 1918, and he was totally ignorant of mechanised warfare; above all, he had not the faintest idea of how quickly an opponent like Rommel could move in 1940.

Rommel crosses the Meuse

At 3 A.M. on the 13th, Rommel with his ADC, Captain Schraepler, drove down to Dinant to find out what was going on. There he saw shells falling from the French artillery on the other side of the Meuse, and a number of knocked-out tanks lying about in the streets leading down to the river. Enemy fire made it impossible for him to go any further in his conspicuous command vehicle, so he and Schraepler clambered on foot down to the river. Here his 6th Rifle Regiment was about to cross to the other bank in rubber assault boats, to reinforce the foothold made during the night by the motorcycle battalion. From here on, Rommel's own account remains probably the best and clearest of the day's events. The riflemen, says Rommel,

were being badly held up by heavy artillery fire and by the extremely troublesome small arms fire of French troops installed among the rocks on the west bank. The situation when I arrived was none too pleasant. Our boats were being destroyed one after the other by the French flanking fire, and the crossing eventually came to a standstill. The enemy infantry were so well concealed that they were impossible to locate even after a long search through glasses. Again and again they directed their fire into the area in which I and my companions—the commanders of the Rifle Brigade and the Engineer Battalion—were lying.

The early morning mist, which had provided such invaluable cover for the motorcyclists in their crossing at Houx, was meanwhile dissipating. A smoke screen was desperately needed with which to render innocuous the searching fire of the enemy infantry.

But we had no smoke unit. So I now gave orders for a number of houses in the valley to be set alight in order to supply the smoke we lacked.

Minute by minute the enemy fire grew more unpleasant. From up the river a damaged rubber boat came drifting down to us with a badly wounded man clinging to it, shouting and screaming for help—the poor fellow was near to drowning. But there was no help for him here, the enemy fire was too heavy.

At this point Rommel turned his attention northwards to Houx, where the motorcyclists were clinging precariously to their gains of the previous night. Most of the battalion had now reached the west bank, but the French resistance was mounting. Shortly after crossing, the commander of No. 1 Company, Captain Heilbronn, was wounded; then the battalion adjutant, Senior Lieutenant Pflug, and another subaltern were killed. Leading two companies himself, the battalion commander, Major Steinkeller, pushed up inland onto high ground after a brief struggle, taking the small hamlet of La Grange. But by midmorning all contact with the east bank of the river had been effectively severed, there were still enemy pockets of resistance behind, and heavy gunfire was coming down on the crossing area; the motorcyclists had not yet been able to bring over any antitank guns and, in the event of any early French counterattack accompanied by tanks, their position would be perilous.

Not particularly happy, Rommel now drove south in a Mark IV tank to the 7th Rifle Regiment which, under Colonel von Bismarck,* was trying to cross the Meuse opposite Bouvignes, about two miles south of Houx. On the way, he came under fire again several times from the west bank, and shell splinters wounded Schraepler in the arm. Bismarck had already managed to get a company across the river; but, says Rommel,

the enemy fire had then become so heavy that their crossing equipment had been shot to pieces and the crossing had had to be halted. Large numbers of wounded were receiving treatment in a house close beside the demolished bridge. As at the northern crossing point, there was nothing to be seen of the enemy who were preventing the crossing. . . .

Rommel decided that there was no hope of getting any more men over the Meuse without bringing right down to the river bank "powerful artillery and tank support to deal with the enemy nests." To effect this, he drove back to divisional HQ, where he found both his Corps commander, Hoth, and the commander of the 4th Army, Kluge, following his progress with interest. Then he returned to the Meuse, to Leffé on the northern outskirts of

---

* Later killed at the Battle of Alam Halfa in the desert, while again serving under Rommel.

Dinant, so as "to get the crossing moving there." At Leffé, Rommel continues,

> we found a number of rubber boats, all more or less badly damaged by enemy fire, lying in the street where our men had left them. Eventually, after being bombed on the way by our own aircraft, we arrived at the river. . . . The crossing had now come to a complete standstill, with the officers badly shaken by the casualties which their men had suffered. On the opposite bank we could see several men of the company which was already across, among them many wounded. . . . The officers reported that nobody dared show himself outside cover, as the enemy opened fire immediately on anyone they spotted.

The Mark IV tanks* called for by Rommel began to arrive, and Captain König of the 25th Panzer Regiment takes up the story:

> Only half the tanks reach the edge of the Meuse, the rest remain with tracks that have been thrown off and other damages, somewhere on the slope. On the Meuse all Hell is let loose—the enemy defends himself from a mass of bunkers and provisional battle positions—every house on the other side of the bank is equipped to assist the defence. Concentrated fire is coming down on the positions of our engineers, and the Meuse water is whipped up by constant artillery and mortar shell explosions.

The tanks now cruised slowly along the river road, with their turrets traversed at 90 degrees, firing at little more than 100 yards range directly into the French bunkers and machine-gun nests on the opposite bank.

> The fire of the Panzer guns [continues König], the 75mm shells as well as the well-scattered 20mm quick-firing cannon, soon show an effect . . . the companies shoot almost as if they were in training, and no recognised target, no suspicious movement of the enemy remains unnoticed. The enemy fire begins to slacken noticeably, but nevertheless the crossing of the first storm boats, the Pioneers, remains a hard task; a task from which many don't come back. In impotent rage, the tank crews watch boats torn to pieces by direct hits.

---

* The whole 7th Panzer in fact possessed only some two dozen of the new Mark IV tank with its heavy 75 mm gun.

One particularly troublesome pillbox* was engaged by Lieutenant Hanke,† who, after firing several rounds, knocked it out.

Under cover of the tanks' gunfire, the crossing slowly got under way again and a cable ferry using several large pontoons was started up. During these operations, according to Captain König: "General Rommel is everywhere. He is with the engineers, he leaps onto a Mark IV tank in order to give it the target himself. He is no easy chief for his staff." To whip up the flagging zeal of his obviously much shaken riflemen, Rommel seems to have returned to a previous incarnation that morning, and to have acted more like the junior officer leading his raiding parties behind the Italian lines at Caporetto than a divisional commander. He states:

I now took over personal command of the 2nd Battalion of the 7th Rifle Regiment and for some time directed operations myself.

With Lieutenant Most‡ I crossed the Meuse in one of the first boats and at once joined the company which had been across since early morning. From the company command post we could see Companies Enkefort and Lichter were making rapid progress.

I then moved up north along a deep gully to Company Enkefort. As we arrived an alarm came in: "Enemy tanks in front." The company had no anti-tank weapons, and I therefore gave orders for small arms fire to be opened on the tanks as quickly as possible.

From this there arose the *belle légende,* long attributed to Rommel, that he told his hard-pressed infantry to fire their Very pistols at the French tanks, to simulate the tracer effect of antigun shells. Whether true or not, the result was indisputable and the tanks withdrew, while Rommel reported that "large numbers of French stragglers came through the bushes and slowly laid down their arms."

It was now about midday, and things were beginning to look a bit better for Rommel. With Lieutenant Most he returned once more to the east bank, driving north with a tank and a signals

---

* Many of which, it will be remembered, had never received the vital armour plates protecting their embrasures.

† Hanke, according to Rommel's son, Manfred, was an out-and-out Nazi highly unpopular with the other officers. He ended the war as Gauleiter of Silesia, and conducted the last-ditch defence of Breslau. When the devastated city finally capitulated to the Russians, Hanke disappeared in a plane and has never been heard of since.

‡ Successor to the wounded Schraepler.

vehicle to where the 6th Rifle Regiment were supporting the beleaguered motorcycle battalion. Here the crossing was "in full swing," and Rommel was told that already twenty badly needed antitank guns had been forded across the river.

A company of the engineer battalion was busily engaged in building 8-ton pontoons, but I stopped them and told them to build the 16-ton type. I aimed to get part of the *Panzer* Regiment across as quickly as possible. As soon as the first pontoon was ready I took my 8-wheeled signals vehicle across.

The waiting panzer crews, their vehicles under cover just off the river, watched impatiently as the sweating engineers struggled away under a broiling midday sun. Several times the pontoons were hit, at least one of them actually sinking to the bottom of the river with a tank on it, and the commander of the engineer battalion was killed together with a number of his men.

At this point in the consolidation of the bridgehead, Rommel seems to have been struck with an excess of optimism. According to 7th Panzer's official history, in the late afternoon he summoned three subalterns commanding his light tank detachments and told them: *"Meine Herren!* The enemy is in full retreat. We shall follow up immediately, and even today we shall reach X-locality 18 kilometres west of Dinant!" But work on the ferries was further delayed by French interdiction fire, and it was not until twilight that the first of these tank detachments was able to cross, so that Rommel had to drop any intention of breaking out of the bridgehead in favour of consolidation.

Meanwhile, according to Rommel, "the enemy had launched a heavy attack, and the fire of their tanks could be heard approaching the ridge of the Meuse bank." Rommel crossed the Meuse again, heading towards the firing. Arriving at the Infantry Brigade HQ now established there:

I found the situation looking decidedly unhealthy. The Commander of the 7th Motor-Cycle Battalion had been wounded,* his adjutant killed, and a powerful French counter-attack had severely mauled our

---

* Rommel's total losses that day were 5 officers, 7 NCOs and 49 enlisted men killed, plus a considerable number of wounded.

men in Grange. There was a danger that enemy tanks might penetrate into the Meuse valley itself.

Leaving my signals lorry on the west bank, I crossed the river again and gave orders for first the panzer company, and then the panzer regiment to be ferried across during the night. However, ferrying tanks across the 120-yards-wide river by night was a slow job, and by morning there were still only 15 tanks on the west bank, an alarmingly small number.

This "powerful French counter-attack"* was in fact an exaggeration, and it remains to be seen just what the French reaction amounted to on this critical day.

Corap reacts

The sparsity and incompleteness of French accounts of the fighting exemplify the confusion enveloping this and the succeeding days, not only opposite Rommel but everywhere else where the Germans managed to cross the Meuse. Yet it is clear from Rommel's version alone that the Belgian Chasseurs Ardennais manning the pillboxes and bunkers down on the Meuse, as well as the men of the French 66th Regiment plugging the intervals, fought hard and well throughout the 13th. By the end of the day, there were still pockets holding out behind the German bridgehead, but their resources in supporting arms were very inadequate; the 66th was far too thinly spread out along the river and was already much fatigued by its approach march before the attack began. A relieving force was urgently needed.

During the 13th, the situation immediately behind the threatened area seems to have been worse even than down on the river itself—a phenomenon to be repeated, with interest, later at Sedan. As every available plane was being committed to support Guderian that day, the tactical air strikes on Rommel's front had been strictly limited—and they could at most have been only partly responsible for the chaos which was to exert so disastrous an influence in the mounting of the French counterattacks. General Boucher commanding the 5th Motorised Division had first learned of the Houx crossing, as already noted, at one o'clock

---

* The fact that Rommel considered it "powerful" is indicative of how precarious his position on the west bank was, and what might have been achieved by any resolute French riposte.

that morning. Five hours later, although his battle HQ was less than 10 miles removed from the scene of the action, he discovered that all liaison with the battalion of the 39th Regiment which he had loaned to his neighbour had somehow been broken. To restore contact, he pushed forward a squadron of motorcyclists and two troops of machine-gun carriers from divisional reconnaissance—probably the same that were repulsed by the small-arms fire and "Very pistols" brought to bear by Rommel himself that morning. At 1000 hours, Boucher decided to throw in an infantry attack on Haut-le-Wastia executed by one battalion of the 129th Regiment. H Hour was to be 1300 hours, but the battalion did not begin to move until 1400 hours and then it was almost immediately dispersed by enemy aircraft. A crack regiment of motorised dragoons under command of II Corps was then ordered to take over the task; but when this regiment said it could not arrive at the start line until 2000 hours the operation was postponed until the following morning. This was the extent of the effort mounted on the 13th from the II Corps sector north of the Houx bridgehead—by some of the best units to be found in the whole of Corap's Ninth Army.*

Between 18th Division HQ and its various regiments (the 66th, 77th and 125th) communications became extremely poor in the course of the morning. General Doumenc notes: "Lines are cut. They had ceased with the 77th, and could not be re-established with the 125th. The radio did not function. There were no more motor-cycles." General Martin, having received no news of the crossing at XI Corps HQ, less than 15 miles from Houx, visited the 18th Division early that afternoon, where he called up the colonel of the 39th Regiment, which did not seem so far to have distinguished itself. The colonel, in some agitation, told him that he had only just managed to escape from a group of German scouts whom he had met, in his staff car, on a railway bridge at Sosoye—8 miles west of the Meuse. Martin then ordered the 39th to prepare a counterattack aimed at recapturing Surinvaux Wood

---

* The sluggishness and lack of punch with which these first ripostes were executed characterised almost all the French counterattacks subsequently carried out at various levels; in contrast, right through to the last days of the war, the art of the counterattack was something in which the German Army was particularly skilled. As many American and British veterans can testify, the German capacity to hit back with an instant and weighted blow with whatever forces that happened to be at hand was often little short of miraculous.

and at throwing all the enemy troops on the west bank back into
the Meuse. The operation would be supported by three artillery
groups and a squadron of tanks; H Hour was to be 7:30 P.M.
Meanwhile, the battered 66th Regiment had "begun to show
signs of exhaustion," says General Doumenc; and "little was
known of the rest of the division. The 77th* appeared to have
fled. Of the 125th* nothing was known." All this had been
achieved by Rommel's dozen or so infantry companies, unsupported by any heavy weapons on the west side of the Meuse.

Then, at 1830 hours, just one hour before Martin's counterattack was due to go in, according to General Doumenc:

the Colonel of the 39th Infantry Regiment communicated by telephone
that he would not be ready at the appointed hour. H-Hour was fixed
for 2000 hrs. At 1945 he reported once again that the attack could
not take place at 2000 hrs. Thus it happened that, alone, the squadron
of tanks moved forward to the Bois de la Grange; the tanks swept all
that they found in front of them, and brought back 8 prisoners as
night was falling.

Realising that there was no infantry following them to consolidate
on the captured ground, the tanks then withdrew.

Thus ended the sum effort of Corap's Ninth Army on May 13th
against the malignant, mortal tumour swelling in its side; just
one "hit-and-run" raid by a squadron of unsupported tanks. A
golden opportunity to wipe out Rommel's bridgehead and inflict
a severe reverse upon him had been lost. All that day, events had
been balanced upon a knife's edge; much more finely balanced,
indeed, than was apparent to the French defenders at the time.
Without Rommel's personal leadership on the one side, with just
a little more determination on the other, the story might have
been different. Presumably Rommel would have made a fresh
river-crossing attempt on the 14th or the 15th; but, as his subsequent career after the tide of war had begun to flow against Germany showed, he was a commander exhilarated by success but
easily dejected by adversity. If his motorcyclists and riflemen had
been pushed back into the Meuse on the 13th, the reverse might
well have seriously blunted the cutting edge of the 7th Panzer;
but indisputably it would have gained for Corap at least some

---

* Like the 66th Regiment, both were "A" series reservist units.

of the commodity which the French Army was to need most desperately throughout the campaign—TIME. Even through the night
of the 13th and the early morning of the 14th, Rommel's position
remained extremely critical. His bridgehead was only a couple of
miles deep and perhaps three wide; pockets of resistance were
still holding out in its rear, and it was by no means certain that
he could get his tanks across in sufficient strength before a concerted attack by French armour might overrun it completely. As
the night dragged on, the waiting panzer crews listened impatiently to the sappers hammering away at their bridge, which had
been slightly damaged in an enemy bombing raid the previous
evening.

At lunchtime on the 13th, the first news of Rommel's crossing
was transmitted to Gamelin by General Georges's headquarters,
in a brief signal which added simply: "A battalion had been
knocked about." Colonel Minart at GQG tells us that the news
created "a lively emotion." A short time later, GQG was informed
that a counterattack with tanks was in process. Now, at last, all
attention was concentrated on what was happening on the Meuse,
says Minart:

But two long hours went by without being able to know if the announced counter-attack had succeeded and if the Germans had been
thrown back onto the right bank of the river. Various rumours, unchecked, began to reach as far as Vincennes. The Germans were supposed to be at Mézières. Anxious about being incorrectly informed,
General Gamelin, at two various attempts (1400 and 1415 hrs) telephoned—the only time—direct to 9th Army. General Thierry D'Argenlieu,* Chief of Staff to Corap's Army replied with his usual calm—
"Nothing to report at Mézières; we are surveying the region of Monthermé. The incident at Houx is in hand; General Martin is on the spot
with General Duffet."†

After this report, some hours elapsed without any further news
from the Ninth Army. Then, suddenly at 1615 hours a first smattering of ill-tidings came through about Huntziger's Second
Army. At 2125 hours that night, General Georges rang through
to tell Gamelin tersely that there had been *"un pépin assez*

---

* D'Argenlieu was killed a few days later.
† Duffet was commander of the 18th Division.

*sérieux"** just south of Sedan. It was the understatement of the century.

Guderian's panzers

That morning at 0715 hours Guderian had issued his final orders for the crossing operation that afternoon. It would have the support, he promised in only a modest exaggeration, of "almost the whole German Air Force." The French defences would be smashed "by means of uninterrupted attacks lasting for eight hours." At 1500 hours his XIX Panzer Corps would effect crossings on either side of Sedan, between the mouth of the river Bar† and Bazeilles. If it arrived in time, the 2nd Panzer would form the right flank of the assault, crossing the Meuse at Donchery. In the centre, the 1st Panzer would strike at Glaire, on the root of the Iges peninsula formed by a sharp loop in the Meuse, and Torcy on the northern outskirts of Sedan. The 10th Panzer was to cross south of Sedan, securing the left flank with the capture of the high ground running along the west bank of the Meuse above Pont Maugis.

But the main effort of the day was to be made by General Kirchner's 1st Panzer. The task Guderian prescribed for it was to mop up inside the Iges peninsula and push forward to the Bellevue–Torcy road; then to attack the dominating Bois de la Marfée heights, the anchor of the whole French position at Sedan, and finally to establish itself on a line from Chéhéry‡ to Chaumont. For this task the division would be reinforced by the SS Grossdeutschland Regiment, transferred from the strength of 10th Panzer; an entire battalion of *Sturmpionieren* (Assault Engineers); and the heavy artillery battalions belonging to each of its sister divisions. A tremendous concentration of firepower could thus be brought to bear on 1st Panzer's front of less than 2 miles in width; but the success or failure of the day would in the final analysis depend upon the three rifle battalions of Lieutenant Colonel Hermann Balck's 1st Rifle Regiment, the four of Lieutenant Colonel Graf von Schwerin's Grossdeutschland, and the

---

* "A rather serious pinprick."

† It is to be recalled that this also marked the hinge between the French Ninth and Second Armies.

‡ Note the two different, closely situated place-names over which confusion was later to arise: *Chéhéry* and *Chémery*.

various *Sturmpionieren* companies. As with Rommel at Dinant, there would be no question of tank support on the west bank until the infantry had secured the bridgehead.

To provide his panzer corps with further encouragement, Guderian added the information that the other two panzers in Kleist's group, Reinhardt's 6th and 8th, would also be crossing the Meuse that day, in the Monthermé and Nouzonville areas. Meanwhile, behind Guderian, Wietersheim's XIV Motorised Corps would be assembling, ready to support and exploit their success.

Battle for Sedan

An intense, nervous hubbub surrounds that morning—mingled with a new wariness. From contemporary German newsfilms one has glimpses of the assault troops covering on foot the last few kilometres of the approach march down to the Meuse: tough, bronzed, enormously fit young men striding in shirtsleeve order through meadows knee-high with lush grass and spring flowers, brimming over with arrogant self-confidence. The sun beats down on them. On the way, they pass innumerable heavy weapons destined to help get them across the river. Everywhere the crews are breaking off branches of trees to camouflage their vehicles. Overhead there is a steady, comforting drone of friendly airplanes. Inevitably there are moments of confusion; there is still the residue of the traffic tangles in the Ardennes to be sorted out, separated units to be reunited. Sergeant Prümers, with a signals unit of the 1st Panzer, recalls being ordered the previous day to prepare an assault pack, because "for two days we would no longer see the transport." At midnight his unit began to move. In the pitch darkness,

we observed radio silence, so as not to betray ourselves. When we come upon a long transport column, there were hold-ups in the darkness, and suddenly we lose contact. We overtake, and find ourselves on the edge of a huge bomb crater; we attempt to take the road to the right, this was also filled with vehicles, and nobody knows where the Regimental Staff has gone. So we wander about until morning, before we finally come upon Rifle Brigade HQ.

Then the enemy artillery began to open up: "The French are shooting at every single vehicle, even motorcyclist signalers. Shot upon shot." Voicing the thoughts of hundreds of young Germans that day, Prümers wondered nervously: "What on earth will it be like on the other side?"

As the morning went on, General Kirchner several times informed Guderian that the enemy gunfire was rendering his own movements practically impossible, warning him that the crossing could only succeed if the Luftwaffe knocked out the French artillery. Yet on the whole the French interdiction fire that morning was sporadic and not outstandingly accurate; although, to some of the panzer crews, it seemed almost impossible that any single enemy shell could fail to hit a target. Tanks and soft vehicles were cramming into every gulley and hollow leading to the river; the Fond de Givonne, a long open valley of fertile farms and orchards that runs down to Bazeilles on the Meuse partially concealed from the west bank, held the main body of Guderian's armour in one of the most formidable concentrations of mechanised might ever assembled. With tracks almost touching, the deafening roar of their motors was audible well beyond the French first-line positions on the other side of the Meuse. Using the houses along the river as cover, gunners of the light artillery and flak worked their weapons forward into their firing positions. Engineers, panting under the weight of the heavy rubber assault boats, struggled with them to the dead ground nearest the river, which they aimed to reach in one bound as soon as the signal to attack was given. With the brilliant sunlight shining in their eyes, in many places the assault teams could not make out the individual French strong points just 60, 80 or 100 yards across the sleek, silver ribbon of water. But from almost all angles, apprehensively they could gaze up at the imposing heights of La Marfée which seemed to dominate the battlefield in every direction. How could anything approach this imposing redoubt unseen or undestroyed?

From La Marfée, the French observers' view of Guderian's line-up was indeed superb. Over the whole of his corps frontage, from first light onwards, says General Grandsard, they could see "the enemy emerging from the forest . . . the deployment is general; everywhere observation points report an almost uninterrupted descent of infantrymen, of vehicles either armoured or motorised." To the gunners there poured in signals pinpointing "at least 200 tanks in the St. Menges area . . . another 200 in the outskirts and centre of Sedan." What targets! "What an opportunity," wrote a French military critic, General Menu, "for the artillery to rain down those 'hammer blows,' to practise those 'sweeping concentrations' which constitute, in the manipulation of fire-power, the high point of the five hundred very scientific pages of the *General Instruction on Artillery Fire!*" But the French guns "hammering" Guderian's tank concentrations on the morning of the 13th limited their fire to thirty to eighty rounds apiece. Why? Grandsard explains that he was anxious "to spare ammunition" (though at Sedan within the next few days large dumps of shells were to fall, unexpended, into German hands). Despite all the evidence of this rapid build-up of enemy might on the opposite bank, Grandsard for one still seems to have been clinging—even on the morning of the 13th—to the archaic belief that Guderian could not attempt a river crossing that day. To General Lafontaine of the 55th Division he declared reassuringly: "The enemy would be unable to do anything for four to six days, as it would take them this long to bring up heavy artillery and ammunition, and to position them."

Strictly speaking, and by all the canons of conventional 1918 warfare, Grandsard's appreciation was correct. On the 13th, Guderian would only be able to bring up a fraction of the heavy artillery available to the defenders, and—according to Kleist—his guns were rationed to "only fifty rounds *per battery*," as a result of the ammunition columns being delayed by the road congestions in the Ardennes. This was indeed a problem which Guderian had foreseen when he wrote *Achtung–Panzer!* four years previously; but in the meantime the artillery had been substituted by a powerful air weapon, and it is typical of the unreal world in which the French commanders existed that, by May 13th, 1940, Grandsard should not have been capable of envisaging the part that the Luftwaffe would play in a Meuse crossing.

The Luftwaffe attacks

For the massive air support promised that day, the Luftwaffe had allocated the whole of Lieutenant General Bruno Loerzer's Fliegerkorps II, one of the principal components of the Third Air Fleet, commanded by General Hugo Sperrle; plus Major General Wolfram von Richthofen's Fliegerkorps VIII, borrowed from Kesselring's Second Air Fleet operating in the north. Kesselring and

Sperrle (later promoted field marshals for their work during the French campaign) were both regular army officers who had transferred to the Luftwaffe in the 1930s, while Kesselring—an artilleryman—had only learned to fly when he was forty-eight; Sperrle, a vast brooding figure, had gained invaluable experience as first commander of the "Condor Legion" in Spain. Loerzer was what was known as "an old eagle," who, claiming forty-four victories, had tied for seventh place in the German list of First War aces. Freiherr von Richthofen, cousin of the famous "Red Knight" who had also been a junior member of his "Flying Circus" in the First War, had succeeded Sperrle in the "Condor Legion," establishing a reputation as the Luftwaffe's outstanding expert on close-support tactics. It was his Stukas particularly that were to make their mark at Sedan. Between them, Loerzer and Richthofen disposed over nearly 1,500 aircraft*—roughly equivalent to the combined British and French total available air strength in France. Certainly by 1940 standards, it was a staggering concentration of airpower to be brought to bear on just a few miles of front.†

At 0700 hours Loerzer's level bombers, mostly Dornier 17 "Flying Pencils," started bombing the French positions. But these were "harassing attacks," hardly heavier than the raids of the previous days. The bombing continued for four hours, gradually mounting in intensity. It was particularly the communication links of the defenders that were hit by this preliminary "softening-up." Grandsard stated that his artillery fire plan was greatly hindered by repeated breaks in telephone lines, and as the morning progressed the fire began to slacken. Visiting the HQ of General Baudet's newly arrived 71st Division, Grandsard found that the makeshift divisional telephone exchange had been destroyed, and that Baudet, still disgruntled at the accelerated movement into line of his division, had already "been affected by this bombard-

---

* In the Luftwaffe of 1940, the basic unit was the *Staffel*, comparable to an RAF squadron and containing 10–12 planes; 3 Staffeln comprised a *Gruppe*, equivalent to an RAF wing; 3 Gruppe made up a *Geschwader*, which consisted of approximately 120 planes. Then came the *Fliegerkorps*, constituted of Geschwader of different types of aircraft. The two Air Fleets deployed in the west between them contained five Fliegerkorps.

† Though, in terms of weight of explosive delivered, it was still probably eclipsed by the German artillery bombardment on the opening day of the Battle of Verdun, in February 1916.

ment." Grandsard says he tried to "comfort" Baudet, telling him too that "it did not seem the enemy would be able to attack on the 13th with important forces." Meanwhile, General Lafontaine of the 55th Division was complaining to Grandsard that he was being bombed without any intervention from Allied aircraft, and this was of course shaking the morale of his soldiers. Grandsard promptly passed on these views to Huntziger, coupled with a plea for immediate air cover; but, according to Grandsard, Huntziger gave a most "unsatisfactory" response: "They must receive a baptism of fire."

The total failure of both Allied air forces at Sedan on May 13th is one of the more extraordinary, in some ways inexplicable, features of the whole battle. If any simple, general explanation is to be found, it must lie in the dreadful quagmire of liaison links between the various French ground armies and combat units of the air forces. As far as bombing missions to break up the German concentrations east of the Meuse were concerned, General d'Astier tells us that at 0940 hours on the 13th, he was at last asked by Billotte to allot top priority to air support for the Second Army. But he claims that he was given no inkling of the imminence of a German river-crossing attempt, Billotte speaking only in vague terms of "the next two or three days." It was not until midday that the Second Army reported tank concentrations near Givonne, and it added that for the moment it did not require intervention by bombers, as its artillery "was engaging these targets." Thus, in the stereotyped mind of the French artilleryman, simultaneous aerial bombing could only upset his observation. (Meanwhile Billotte, reporting Rommel's crossing at Houx, also refused air support, on the grounds that armour had already been sent for—the sequel to which has been recounted.)

What about the British? In the absence of any desperate plea for assistance from General Georges, Barratt's AASF spent the 13th licking its wounds. They were painful. For the previous three days, the rate of loss had amounted to 40 percent of all sorties on the 10th, 100 percent on the 11th, and 62 percent on the 12th. By the evening of May 12th, the AASF's total of 135 serviceable bombers had dwindled to 72, and perhaps not surprisingly Barratt had received a signal from the Chief of the Air Staff in London, expressing concern at his heavy losses, and warning: "We cannot continue indefinitely at this rate of intensity.

. . . If we expend all our efforts in the early stages of the battle we shall not be able to operate effectively when the really critical phase comes." It would be hard to conceive of a more "critical" day than May 13th; nevertheless, with this caveat of the previous night, Barratt made no call on his Blenheims, and the Battles restricted themselves to blocking a crossroads near Breda in the north.

As for Allied fighter cover over Sedan, General Ruby—who was then at Huntziger's HQ—claims that all Grandsard's requests were immediately passed on to the air command, but the latter's "appalling organisation" somehow swallowed them up. General d'Astier states that his fighters in fact made 250 sorties that day between the Ninth and Second Army fronts, shooting down 21 enemy planes for the loss of 12; but this was a mere drop in the bucket compared with the number of planes put in the air by the Luftwaffe. Typical of what the French fighters were up against was this entry in a squadron diary: "Between 10 and 11 o'clock, a three-plane patrol flying over the area Carignan–Sedan runs into 50 enemy bombers protected by 80 Messerschmitts. Free-for-all in which Lieutenant Wrana is shot down." Against this kind of competition, the French Curtisses—60 mph slower than the Me–109s—were at a grave if not hopeless disadvantage. Considering the seriousness of the threat on the 13th, one does get the impression that the French fighter squadrons—their pilots already short on sleep—did not press home their attacks with every ounce of vigour.

At midday the intensity of the bombing rose sharply, with the Luftwaffe sending over hundreds of planes in dense formations. Sergeant Prümers of the 1st Panzer, still being heavily shelled by the enemy artillery, was among those to watch with awful fascination the first appearance of Richthofen's Stukas:

Three, six, nine, oh, behind still more, and further to the right aircraft, and still more aircraft, a quick look in the binoculars—*Stukas!* And what we are about to see during the next 20 mins. is one of the most powerful impressions of this war. Squadron upon squadron rise to a great height, break into line ahead (*"Reihenformation"*) and there, there the first machines hurtle perpendicularly down, followed by the second, third—ten, twelve, aeroplanes are there. Simultaneously like some bird of prey, they fall upon their victim and then release their load of bombs on the target. We can see the bombs very clearly. It becomes a regular rain of bombs, that whistle down on Sedan and the bunker positions. Each time the explosion is overwhelming, the noise deafening. Everything becomes blended together, along with the howling sirens of the *Stukas* in their dives, the bombs whistle and crack and burst. A huge blow of annihilation strikes the enemy, and still more squadrons arrive, rise to a great height, and then come down on the same target. We stand and watch what is happening as if hypnotised, down below all hell is let loose! At the same time we are full of confidence . . . and suddenly we notice that the enemy artillery no longer shoots . . . while the last squadron of *Stukas* is still attacking, we receive our marching orders.

The Stukas operated in three groups, each of about 40 planes; the first, coming in at about 5,000 feet would attack with two or three planes at a time, while the second group hovered watchfully at 12,000 feet, looking for the targets missed by the first group and then—after that had expended its bombs—moving in in turn; the third group operated in isolation, picking out single or moving targets. After the Stuka waves, the Dorniers would resume their work; then more Stukas. Around them buzzed the Me–109s and the heavier Me–110 "destroyers" pouncing on any slower French fighter that attempted to get at the vulnerable Stukas.

Watching the steady procession of the bomber formations, Guderian suddenly realised that the Luftwaffe was carrying out the tactics he and Loerzer had agreed upon—and not the massive, once-for-all bombardment dictated by Kleist. Though puzzled, Guderian "sighed with relief." When the day was over he questioned Loerzer; shrugging his shoulders, the First War ace explained that Kleist's change of orders had arrived "—well, let's say, too late. They would have muddled the *Geschwader*. So I didn't pass them on!"

The Stukas kept on coming in. Down they screamed, sirens howling, loosing their two 500-pound bombs upon the thin-skinned French pillboxes, on the infantry crouching exposed in their trenches, and on the gun crews. It was against the French artillery in their poorly concealed and shallow gunpits that the rage of the Stukas was particularly concentrated; and among them, the new reinforcements arrived the previous night, who, with insufficient time to dig themselves in, suffered most. The explosive force of the heavy bombs literally turned batteries up-

side down, wrecked guns and filled the working parts of antiaircraft machine guns with earth and grit. Observers in concrete
bunkers were blinded by the dust and smoke, and everywhere
telephone lines were ruptured. The noise was terrifying.* Grandsard's reservists had the impression that each plane was about
"to land right on top of him," that it simply could not miss. In
some uncanny way, the German pilots seemed to know just exactly where every gun and bunker lay. Nowhere was one out of
sight, nowhere out of range of this dreadful weapon.

Yet, owing to the inaccuracy of the Stukas, casualties were
not great. But as an instrument of terror it was far more effective
than the Kaiser's "secret weapon" of 1914, the "Big Bertha"
shells that had plunged down on the Belgian forts; more effective than the gas attack at Ypres; more than the first appearance
of flame throwers, or even the tank. This was a new dimension of
war for which not even tough regulars had been prepared; and
Grandsard's men were flabby civilians whose morale was not conspicuously high, and who had received absolutely no training in
how to cope with dive bombing. For what ensued they could not
entirely be blamed. Says General Ruby:

The gunners stopped firing and went to ground, the infantry cowered
in their trenches, dazed by the crash of bombs and the shriek of the
dive-bombers; they had not developed the instinctive reaction of running to their anti-aircraft guns and firing back. Their only concern
was to keep their heads well down. Five hours of this nightmare was
enough to shatter their nerves, and they became incapable of reacting
against the enemy infantry.

To add to their demoralisation, over their heads they could see
no sign of any Allied planes coming to their assistance. Plea after
plea from the 55th Division went apparently unanswered.

Seen from the German side of the river, the whole of the west
bank had disappeared in a blanket of smoke. Even at a distance
the waiting Germans suffered disagreeably from the tremendously

---

* It was perhaps the noise that was the most unnerving feature of the Stuka attack. In Florence Conrad's field ambulance, the French wounded kept repeating:
"The noise, the horrible noise! . . . You feel the bomb coming, even if it falls
50 or 100 yards away. You throw yourself to the ground, certain of being blown
into thirty pieces. And when you realize it was only a miss, the noise of this shrieking *vous casse les pattes.*"

high pressure caused by the bomb blasts. In awe, they wondered how anything could possibly survive such an inferno. Then, half an hour before H Hour, Guderian's artillery joined in the hideous fugue with a short but ferocious barrage. Meanwhile, taking advantage of the stunning effect of the Stukas, the flak gunners moved their weapons out of cover, manhandling them right down almost to the very river's edge to engage with flat trajectory fire the French bunkers just across the river. At this close range, the twin-barrelled 20 mm and 37 mm automatic cannon swiftly sought out the bunker slits and gun embrasures. Against those bunkers where the protective armour had not arrived, the consequences were deadly; though much less so with those that were properly equipped. But the most lethal work was effected by a piece that was later to achieve renown as the most feared antitank gun on any side, possibly—with the Russian T-34 tank—as the most successful single weapon of the whole war. This was the German 88. Designed by Krupp as the Wehrmacht's standard heavy antiaircraft gun, it was a direct descendant* of the weapon hastily produced (also by Krupp) in 1870 to shoot down the French balloons escaping from besieged Paris. The 88 mm imparted a very high muzzle velocity; therefore, at close ranges, tremendous hitting and penetrating power. The 88 had been tried out experimentally in the early part of 1939, firing at close range into the embrasures of the French-designed bunkers among the Czechs' "Little Maginot Line"—supposedly at Hitler's own instance. The results were devastating—and it is worth noting that (according to General Menu) they were reported upon in detail by the then French Military Attaché in Prague. The first combat employment of the 88 in a horizontal role occurred purely by accident; during the Polish campaign, an isolated flak unit had been attacked by surprise by Polish cavalry, and, in the emergency, brought their 88s to bear—firing them over open sights. The success achieved surprised even the Germans. Suddenly new possibilities presented themselves. Now at Sedan, the French bunkers designed to stand up to the oblique fire of all calibre guns up to 210 mm proved desperately vulnerable to the direct fire of the 88s—limited in number though they were. One by one the guns in the bunkers were smashed, their crews blinded by splinters or

---

* It was also the antecedent in design of most present-day tank guns.

horribly mutilated by shells exploding within the confined space of the bunkers; or else simply forced by the torrent of light flak fire to abandon guard at the embrasures.

Sedan: The fatal moment

Abruptly at 1500 hours, the Stuka bombardment lifted, shifting to targets further behind the Meuse. Though few of the soldiers confronting each other across this narrow strip of water can have had time to reflect upon it, the moment of crisis in the whole battle had arrived. Here was the culminating point of all the elaborate plans of *Sichelschnitt*—indeed, of Hitler's aspirations to become the founder of a "Thousand Year Reich." If the crossings at Sedan were to fail, if Guderian's spearhead were to be smashed, who could foretell Germany's future? It was the crisis for France, for western civilisation; and it would come to be regarded as one of the crisis moments of the twentieth century. At such a moment suddenly the great, complex stratagems of both sides, in which armies are moved about like chess pieces, become reduced to the isolated actions of one or two men. As in the adage of the nail, the horse and the rider, the success or failure of such lone combats leads to the success or failure of a platoon; from a platoon to a company; a company to a regiment; and so on, until the whole battlefield is in flux and the day is decided.

At Sedan, events now move with such brutal speed that the historian is left floundering—as blinded by the all-obscuring smoke of the Stuka bombs as the French defenders. Unlike the leisurely four months of siege warfare around Paris in 1870, or the ten months of static warfare at Verdun in 1916, minutely and superbly recorded at every level, the decisive acts at Sedan pass in confused, unchronicled minutes—or even seconds. On the French side, there would be little time to enter up the regimental diaries; whole pages of the story of that day have disappeared forever with the participants; others are, alas, so shaming to French *amour-propre* that—like the details of the Mutinies of 1917—they will probably lie forever hidden from sight in the archives contained in the gloomy dungeons at Vincennes. Even on the German side, where headquarter units were not destroyed or dispersed, the pressure of events results in an unfortunate lack of cohesive reports on the course of the battle. Thus one is forced to build up a picture of the day upon snatches and fragments of small, isolated actions; and to rely to a large extent upon the German accounts, with their occasional distortions imposed by National Socialist bombast.

Scene One—the 10th Panzer

Even before the smoke from the last Stuka bombs had cleared, the attackers were appearing everywhere on the river in their inflated rubber dinghies.* There were many casualties among the first wave. To the survivors, the 60-yard crossing seemed to last interminably. On the left of Guderian's corps, the 10th Panzer—crossing "according to the last war-game at Bernkastel"†—made a bad start. The boats for the right-hand group, composed of the 86th Rifle Regiment, reached the water's edge too late for it to take full advantage of the Stuka bombardment. On its left the 69th reported (at 1600 hours) to Lieutenant General Schaal, the divisional commander, that it could not move on account of heavy flanking shellfire from guns‡ apparently left untouched by the Luftwaffe, which rained down upon it in the flat, exposed meadows bordering the Meuse near Bazeilles. Out of some fifty small rubber dinghies, all but two had been shot up. A vivid account is provided by Sergeant Schulze of the 69th. His platoon had come under heavy artillery fire at Givonne that morning, and—after being ordered to "dig in" for the first time during the campaign —it had been particularly gratified to see the first Stukas come shrieking down on the enemy guns. At H Hour, Schulze's team began to work its way through the village of Balan:

A large meadow lies in front of us. On a hill about 800 yds. away, the enemy is dug in.§ To begin with we move forward well, the meadow is wet, finally we are wading up to our calves through the water, here and there shots fly over our heads. Barbed wire is cut through, and we move on ahead. In the next second everything breaks loose. Machine-gun bursts whistle over us, there are strikes before, near and behind us. The enemy is shooting well. Under this fire it is impossible for anybody to get forward. The least movement . . . brings the fire down anew. We are lying in the water, we hug the

---

* At the Riom Trials, French Army witnesses claimed—surprisingly—that the use of these boats "came to us as a great surprise."
† On the river Mosel.
‡ Belonging to Grandsard's 71st Division.
§ On the far side of the Meuse.

ground very close, and are delighted when a particularly high grass hummock keeps us out of the sight of the enemy. To the left of us some of our own troops are going back, but for us any movement is impossible. About 300 to 400 metres further to the right is *Oberfeldwebel* S.P. with his platoon. The men have already reached to within 80 yds. of the river. . . .

The enemy artillery, whose shots hitherto have fallen far behind Balan, have adjusted their fire forwards, and now it is very close behind the attackers. Enemy infantry in front of one, behind a separating river, artillery bombardment behind us, here it is impossible to move either forwards or backwards. Unexpectedly, over to the right appear engineers, men hard as iron, who bring up assault boats. There *Oberfeldwebel* S.P. decides to risk it with the engineers. He and three of his men spring forward and leap into one of the boats. In a second the boats are in the water . . . they are on their way to the safe shore. The second boat follows with reinforcements and the Battalion Adjutant, Lt. M. By the time a third boat is about to enter the water, the artillery has adjusted its fire so far towards the Meuse, that the assault boat is destroyed. The engineers fall. But a small group of 10 to 12 men has made it. The first on the other side of the Meuse. They lie close up against enemy bunker. What are they to do? If there is any French counter-thrust they are lost.

From the Balan side of the river, Schulze then observed that the enemy bunker appeared to be knocked out, having received a direct hit from a German gun a short time previously. A German officer was seen to disappear behind the bunker;

soon he comes back with five prisoners, the bunker was still occupied—then they lay out white sheets, because from the other side, our own troops are often still firing; they have no idea, that our own people are already over there. Meanwhile hours pass by, while *Oberfeldwebel* S.P. has crossed the Meuse, the Company is stuck in the water, pinned down by the enemy fire.

Schulze's platoon falls back on Balan that evening, and is told to stand by as reinforcements. "The enemy artillery shoots on Balan. We are sitting in our wet uniforms in safe cellars. There was no thought of sleep, for the evenings are bitterly cold. Teeth chatter and limbs tremble."

By nightfall on the 13th the prospects on Schulze's immediate front did not look brilliant. That the 10th Panzer obtained a foothold on the opposite bank at all that day seems to have depended largely on the initiative of individual detachment leaders of the assault engineers such as *Feldwebel* Rubarth. Specially equipped with explosive charges for knocking out bunkers which had survived the Stukas and flak, Rubarth and his section of eleven men assembled their gear in the private park of a mansion near Balan. Across the wide stretch of open meadow where Schulze had been pinned down, Rubarth could clearly recognise the enemy strong points on the river at Wadelincourt; but he noted that "the terrain is extremely unfavourable for an attack." Moving down to the Meuse over this dangerously exposed ground as H Hour arrived, Rubarth records: "Immediately we were met by strong machine gun fire. There are casualties. With my detachment I reach the bank of the Meuse under cover of a row of trees and a sportsground." He appears to have had available only two small rubber dinghies designed to carry no more than three men. Cramming four into each, however, Rubarth paddled out under a hail of fire, into the 60-yard-wide river. Because of the extra weight, plus their heavy equipment of wire cutters, grenades and hollow charges, the water came perilously close to the gunwales of Rubarth's dinghy. He ordered his men to throw out all unnecessary ballast, entrenching tools included, remarking grimly: "No digging in for us—either we get through, or that's the end." To upset the defenders' aim during their crossing, the *Feldwebel* ordered his driver, Corporal Podszus, to blaze away with a machine gun into the weapon slits of a particularly menacing-looking bunker immediately to their front, using another man's shoulder to steady his aim in the wildly unstable dinghy. On landing (near Wadelincourt), Rubarth speedily finished off this bunker.

The enemy artillery is now laying down heavy artillery fire on our crossing [continues Rubarth's own story]. Crawling past the next bunker in dead ground out of reach of its guns, the section attacked it from the rear. I made use of an explosive charge. In the next second part of the rear bunker wall is ripped out by the power of the explosion. We utilise the opportunity to reduce the occupants of the bunker with hand grenades. After a brief fight they appear with white flags, and a few seconds later our Swastika flag flies over the bunker. From the other bank the sound of loud cheers of our comrades comes over to us. Thus encouraged we fling ourselves at two further field works we had spotted some 100 metres half left of us. To get to them we have to go through a patch of swamp where part of the time we stand up to our thighs in water. With reckless audacity Corporal Bräutigam alone attacks the left bunker and through a clever action captures the occupants. Together with Sergeant Theophel and Corporals Podszus and Monk, I take the second bunker. Thus the first line of bunkers immediately behind the Meuse is broken through over a stretch of some 300 metres.

The facility with which Rubarth and his few men succeeded in knocking out this row of bunkers, one after the other, suggests the state to which the French defenders had been reduced. What were the "interval troops" entrusted with guarding the vulnerable flanks of these important bastions doing? There is virtually no mention of them in Rubarth's account; where were they? Clearly, not all was well with the river defences at Wadelincourt.

Rubarth's own account continues with his detachment pushing forward to the railway embankment 100 yards or so from the riverbank. Here, for the first time, he came under such strong fire that "temporarily we have to seek cover." Taking stock of the situation, Rubarth ascertained that the other dinghy bringing his section across the river had been hit in midstream, its occupants presumably killed. Thus:

With one sergeant, four men and the group of infantry which were covering our right flank, I am alone on the far side of the river. Moreover our ammunition is exhausted so that we cannot continue our attack. In order to bring up reinforcements and ammunition, I go back to the crossing place and discover that the crossing operation has been interrupted by very heavy enemy fire. The dinghies are partly deflated or shot to pieces. Four men of my detachment have been killed there. My Company Commander, who is still on the other side of the river and has watched the course of the battle, immediately orders the bringing up of new dinghies and appoints new crews.

While waiting for these reinforcements under the blazing sun, Rubarth's Corporal Bräutigam, a French-speaker, ordered one of the prisoners to go back into his bunker and get something to drink. He returned with a bottle of wine. During the interval the Wadelincourt defenders suddenly rallied and launched a surprise attack on Rubarth. They were beaten off, but Bräutigam was killed and Corporals Monk and Podszus wounded. Shortly after this critical moment, an infantry group arrives and Rubarth joins up with it. With fresh reinforcements of assault engineers reaching him at last from the east bank, he goes on to blast a gap in the second line of bunkers. By nightfall, exhausted and having lost six dead and three wounded out of his original eleven men, Rubarth, together with riflemen of the 86th Regiment, had reached his objective on the heights above Wadelincourt. For his achievements, Rubarth was immediately awarded the Ritterkreuz and a lieutenant's commission.

Thus, by dusk, the 10th Panzer had a firm but small toehold on the west bank, between Wadelincourt and Pont Maugis.

Scene Two—the 1st Panzer

With the tremendous concentration of firepower supporting it, the 1st Panzer was having a somewhat easier time. On its left flank, the job of clearing the west-lying suburbs of Sedan and then rushing La Marfée heights, fell to the SS Regiment Grossdeutschland. One of the elite fighting units of Nazi Germany, the Grossdeutschland could trace its origins in the 1870s as the Berlin "Guard Regiment." In the turbulent twenties it was employed to put down any attempted *Putsch* in the capital, while in more peaceful times its principal function was to march three times a week with bands thundering out "Deutschland über Alles," to change the guard at the Brandenburger Tor, and to provide guards of honour for such visiting dignitaries as Ciano of Italy and Horthy of Hungary. Just three months before war began, Hitler had issued a proclamation changing the regiment's name to Grossdeutschland as a martial symbol of the unity of all Germans within the new Reich. Officers of the Grossdeutschland Regiment (which later in the war was expanded to a division, and eventually to an army corps) were specially selected from the rest of the Army. As with the British Brigade of Guards, the men had to be over a certain height, and the regiment always fought as a separate unit, its name proudly emblazoned on the sleeves of its members. Regarded as a crack force set aside for especially tough operations, the Grossdeutschland had been earmarked by Guderian ever since February for the role of smashing a hole in the French lines through which the panzers could then pour. At that time Guderian had evidently made some disparaging remarks about infantry who "slept instead of advancing at night"; to which the regimental commander, Lieutenant Colonel Graf von Schwerin, rose testily, betting Guderian a case of champagne that this would not be true of the Grossdeutschland. All through April it had undergone rugged toughening-up exercises: marching on short rations, river crossings on the Mosel, and night attacks.

At midday on the 13th the shock troops of the Grossdeutschland had been issued their iron rations, their field flasks had been filled with coffee, and weapons inspected. Then Colonel von Schwerin arrived, jauntily carrying a stick, and the regiment set off through Floing less than a mile from the appointed crossing area. Senior Lieutenant von Courbiere, commanding No. 6 Company which was to be second over the river, was struck by the unnatural stillness at Floing: "Not a shot falls, the inhabitants have fled, dogs and cats roam through the streets whose destroyed houses bear witness to the fearful force of this war." Apprehensively, he wondered whether the silence of the French guns meant that they "had already been hit so hard, or are they just waiting for the moment in which we get moving to cross the river?" Then, as his company reached the cloth factory with blue-tinted blackout windows on the river, where it was to embark:

At last the French recognise the danger threatening them, and begin to fight back, without worrying about the bombs exploding around them. The engineers bring up their assault boats, but they cannot reach the river. Despite our covering fire the enemy can watch all movements out of his bunkers and hits back at us—assault guns roll up, but even their shells can do nothing against the concrete and iron—valuable time is lost, until finally a heavy 88 mm Flak silences the enemy. Once again the assault boats are brought up, but this attempt also brings down enemy fire. The young lieutenant of the 7th Company, Lt. Graf Medem, and two engineers are killed. The wounded are brought back—once again a heavy Flak is brought into action. Under its protection the first sections of the leading (No. 7) Company cross the Meuse. The Crossing has succeeded! Swiftly, as we already practiced in the winter, 6th Company follows.

A little over two miles ahead, Courbiere could clearly make out the forward slopes of La Marfée. The Stukas were still hurling their bombs into the fortifications on top of it, often apparently only a "hair's-breadth" from the leading attackers. Approaching the main Sedan–Donchery highway, Courbiere saw the first French appear, with their hands up. At the same time, No. 7 Company on his right was coming under heavy fire from several bunkers along the road.

A quick reconnaissance shows that a large bunker with 6 weapon-slits some 200 yards south of the road on the edge of a vegetable garden, offers good prospects of approach; . . . after a short fight the bunker is reached by a sergeant and two men. The enemy are smoked out by hand grenades; they are completely vanquished, they come out. Their faces reveal the psychological strain of this fighting. Close to each other they stand with their backs to their bunker and raise their hands: "*Tirez!*" they cry.

Courbiere's company cleaned out a second bunker and then an antitank position concealed in a barn; here to their delight they discovered a cache of bottles of soda water with which they slaked their thirst in the sultry heat of the late afternoon. After a short rest, they were even more delighted to make contact with elements of Lieutenant Colonel Balck's 1st Rifle Regiment, which had also successfully crossed the Meuse. It was now about 5 P.M. After some savage hand-to-hand fighting, just as daylight was fading Courbiere's company reached their objective atop Height 247, not far from where Moltke had directed the first Battle of Sedan seventy years previously.

Together with the Grossdeutschland, it was the 1st Rifle Regiment* that was to play the most important role in the early phases of the break-through at Sedan. Its commander, Lieutenant Colonel Hermann Balck, was a tough front-line soldier who had gone through Verdun and been wounded five times during the First War. A most forceful personality (Chester Wilmot† rates him, perhaps too harshly, as "a notorious optimist with a reputation for ruthless aggression," and the American official history, *The Lorraine Campaign,* portrays him as a swashbuckling martinet), there were certainly not many Second World War commanders who could exact more from their troops. After Sedan, Balck's hitherto slow rise was vastly accelerated, and there were few campaigns from which he was absent; a divisional, then

---

* The motorised infantry belonging to the 1st Panzer Division.
† *The Struggle for Europe,* pp. 538, 565–66.

a corps commander in Russia; an army commander in Poland and Hungary; finally, as a full general, an Army Group commander in the later stages of the retreat from France. On the 13th and the next two days his qualities as a leader undoubtedly contributed most significantly to Guderian's success.

Balck's orders for May 13th were to cross in the Glaire–Gaulier area, in the tracks of the Grossdeutschland, push up onto the northern slopes of La Marfée, then swing round it to thrust along the main road running southwards from Sedan to Vouziers. The Grossdeutschland having borne the brunt of the fighting, Balck's riflemen had perhaps the easiest time of any of the German assault units that day. According to Guderian, watching at Floing and chafing with impatience to get over the Meuse himself, their crossing developed

as though it were being carried out on manoeuvres. The French artillery was almost paralysed by the unceasing threat of attack by Stukas and bombers. The concrete works along the Meuse had been put out of action by our anti-tank and anti-aircraft artillery, and the enemy machine-gunners were forced to keep down by the fire of our heavy weapons and artillery. Despite the completely open nature of ground, our casualties remained light.

Balck himself, who had the impression that the French gunners had already begun to desert their batteries, noted that the cessation in French artillery fire had a remarkable effect on the morale of his riflemen: "A few minutes before everyone was seeking refuge in slit trenches, but now nobody thought of taking cover. It was impossible to hold the men." An hour and a half after H Hour, Balck with the leading elements of his regiment had reached the railway line running from Sedan to Donchery; another hour (1730 hours), and he had beaten his way through to the main road lying parallel to it—thus breaking into the main French line of defences. Meanwhile, the division's motorcycle battalion which had crossed over the Meuse loop at Iges had cleaned up the whole Iges peninsula, rejoining Balck on the banks of the canal that traverses the root of the peninsula. By 1930 hours, the 1st Panzer had elements of six battalions established in a substantial bridgehead. A large part of the all-important La Marfée heights—crowned by pine woods, First War cemeteries, and a monument to a French infantry regiment which, in August 1914, "threw back the Germans on the Meuse by a *contre-attaque à la baïonnette*"–had already fallen into their hands.

On the west bank of the Meuse, however, Guderian still had no tanks, antitank guns or artillery. Like Rommel to the north, he now faced an anxious night during which the French might prepare an armoured riposte to crush his unprotected infantry before the first panzers could be pushed across the river. Every priority was now devoted to rushing construction of ferries and bridges. While the east bank was still under machine-gun fire from the bunkers opposite, Senior Lieutenant Grubnau, commanding a special bridging company of the engineers, had already reconnoitred "a completely level field with firm dry ground and good approaches to the river bank. . . . But there is no cover." It was close to the cloth factory at Gaulier, under cover of which the engineers assembled their heavy equipment. The Meuse is here approximately 70 yards wide. Although some of Grubnau's transport had been held up in the Ardennes, by 1630 hours–while Balck's riflemen were still struggling across in their assault boats –work was already beginning on the first pontoon bridge. "The engineers leap from their vehicles and unload the pontoon trucks," recorded Grubnau, adding in surprise at the lack of antitank obstacles:

It is astonishing how easily heavy bridge-building could be carried out today. An enemy bombing attack causes everyone to take refuge in the little cover that is at hand. Our nine light machine-guns fire . . . the bombs fall far from us. With undiminished strength the construction continues. Now enemy artillery fire begins. The enemy artillery plane is however driven off by our fighter cover. . . . It seems that the French are expecting our bridge to be built at another place . . . shells fall 50 yards from us . . . fortunately, the village of Glaire hinders any observed fire.

Throughout the afternoon, the young sappers, half-naked and their steel helmets cast aside in the torrid heat, worked away at the bridge in almost casual detachment, despite the intermittent rain of shot and shell. In the record time of thirty-eight minutes, Grubnau's men had the first light ferry operating; shortly before midnight a 16-ton bridge was ready, with a tremendous concentration of armour queuing up behind it on the east bank.

Scene Three—the 2nd Panzer

On its right hand, the performance of the 2nd Panzer stood out in even sharper contrast to the successes registered by the 1st than did the limited progress of the 10th on the left flank. Guderian's old division, the 2nd Panzer had taken part in the march into Austria in 1938 and, remaining as part of the garrison troops of Vienna, had become known in the Wehrmacht as the "Vienna Division." Its formations contained a large number of Austrians and Bavarians. Led by Lieutenant General Rudolf Veiel, its commander since the *Anschluss,* the "Vienna Division" had spearheaded the occupation of the Sudetenland and during the Polish campaign had thrust into Poland on the southern flank, via Czechoslovakia. Its limited contribution to the crossings on the 13th was expected; the night before, Guderian had warned Kleist that the 2nd, still bogged down on the Semois, would not be in position on the Meuse at H Hour, and in any case it had forfeited its heavy artillery support to the 1st. When it did get over the Meuse (at Donchery), its orders from Guderian were fairly ambitious: after seizing the high ground behind Donchery it "will then swing immediately westward, will cross the Ardennes Canal to the Bar bed inclusive, and will roll up the enemy defences along the Meuse." On the higher strategic plane, the role of the 2nd Panzer would assume great significance—for it would be the formation to force the hinge between the two French armies of Huntziger and Corap.

Against expectations, on the morning of the 13th the 2nd made surprisingly rapid progress and by midafternoon some of its elements were already reaching Donchery, a gloomy small Meuse village straddling the river, roughly two miles downstream from Sedan, where at a humble weaver's house in 1870 Bismarck had first met Louis Napoleon to discuss the terms of the French capitulation. As soon as the first German tanks deployed down into the river valley, they were met by a storm of artillery fire. The French observation from the overlooking hills was excellent; while with the sinking sun now glistening brilliantly behind the Meuse the panzers found it extremely difficult to pinpoint the well-camouflaged French positions. The tanks fanned out, slowly groping their way into the abandoned portions of Donchery lying on the east bank. Pinned down under the heavy fire the *Sturm-*

pionieren persuaded the tank crews to carry them and their rubber dinghies down to the river on the backs of the tanks. Corporal Frömmel with a squadron of tanks describes how, under fire from a French antitank gun sited in a superbly covered position:

The engineers leap off and attempt under this hail of fire to get their boat to the Meuse. There are only a few metres separating them from the bank, and yet each step means hell. The tank shoots with all its guns, it attempts to give fire cover to the determinedly working engineers. The boat is already in the water, and paddles cutting deep into it. Like a shower a machine-gun bursts from the bunker and falls on this single boat. All around it the water springs up high, and several brave engineers are killed. It is impossible! Back! They come back to the bank, and attempt to find cover in the deep grass. The same fate occurs several minutes later to men whose inflatable dinghy has been brought down by three further tanks to this death dealing river.

A company commander of the engineers, Lieutenant Zimmermann, is seriously wounded in midstream and barely manages to struggle back to the bank. Here several more German wounded lie in agony in the grass, still under French machine-gun fire. Tanks carry them back to safety behind a railway embankment. In the growing twilight a murderous duel goes on between the tanks and the French bunkers across the Meuse. Tracer shells whizz back and forth like fireworks. Says Sergeant Major Keddig:

We fired off shell after shell, always at the recognized bunkers, to try and silence them. It became unbearably hot inside the tank's turret, which was filled with powder smoke. A beautiful summer evening lay across the countryside. But the firing of the French artillery continued with undiminished violence. We couldn't dream of opening any of the tank's hatches.

Despite the French artillery and antitank fire, few of the panzers appear to have been knocked out. Finally, one of the bunkers is silenced and a white flag is spotted. The first *Sturmpionieren* dinghy makes a safe crossing, and shortly afterwards triumphant white Very lights arced up from enemy bank.

Their ammunition exhausted, the tanks withdraw after nightfall. Greatly aided by the hole driven in the centre of the French lines by Balck and the Grossdeutschland, the 2nd Panzer too had gained a foothold over the Meuse. Hurrying back and forth across the river that night with reinforcements, one of its infantry officers noted in the moonlight—among the destroyed enemy bunkers and the huge Stuka craters—the extraordinary number of incomplete fortifications: "The wooden scaffolding still stands there, the foundations have not yet been dug. Astonishing these Frenchmen! They have had now nearly twenty years to build their lines of defence."

Sedan: The French view

As noted earlier, the French view of what happened down on the Meuse on the 13th is perforce scanty and confused. It was General Lafontaine's 55th Division which, almost exclusively, had borne the brunt of Guderian's attack. Undoubtedly, most of the odds were against it from the start. Its elderly, poorly trained reservists were in no way a match for the best troops in the German Army; backed by pulverising airpower, they were caught partly moving house, and one battalion had already been mauled almost to death on the Semois. On the other hand, the 55th had very strong artillery support and a fabulous natural position in La Marfée. Here and there the men of the 55th fought back with gallant, unsung heroism, and Captain von Kielmansegg on the staff of the 1st Panzer himself pays tribute to the "numerous bunkers which defended themselves desperately." But out in the open the French infantry seem to have melted away under the aerial onslaught, and by and large most French military historians concur with the summing-up of Colonel Goutard—one of the more outspokenly objective among them—that "in general, resistance was very feeble."

The news reaching divisional and corps headquarters was fragmentary. At 1710 hours, one of the first reports received by Grandsard from the 55th Division stated tersely: "The Meuse has been crossed by some 40 men* at reference 1572 south of Wadelincourt. A barrage has been opened up. Donchery occupied by a battalion and a half of infantry. Divisional artilleries firing." It added ominously: "No longer any contact with the infantry regiment on the left." At that moment General Huntziger had himself arrived at Grandsard's PC (Command Post), com-

---

* Presumably Rubarth and his mates.

menting calmly on the numbers of enemy reported crossing at Wadelincourt: "There will be just that number of prisoners." Huntziger did not intervene in the battle, says Grandsard, leaving him to cope with the situation. Grandsard explains that his first appreciation was that "nothing was lost, provided that the P.R. (position of resistance) defended itself, and provided that orders given to reserves were executed." However, he continues: "The hours that followed were to give a cruel disappointment to the hopes of the Commander of X Corps. From 18–19 hours approximately, the situation evolved with a disconcerting rapidity towards catastrophe." At 1830 hours there came a most disquieting report from the commander of a battery of guns at Chaumont that enemy *tanks* had been spotted in the area of La Marfée. This was followed up a quarter of an hour later by an item that was even more disturbing. According to Grandsard:

The colonel [Dourzal] commanding Group B of the Corps Heavy Artillery at Bulson reported to the colonel [Poncelet] commanding the Corps Heavy Artillery that violent fighting had broken out 400–500 metres from his PC and was requesting orders to withdraw; on a request for details from his Chief, he confirmed that there were definitely German machine-guns and that he would be encircled within five minutes; he received from his Chief the authority to withdraw. . . .

At more or less the same time, Colonel Poncelet also evacuated his PC back at Flaba, well behind Bulson and over five miles from the nearest Germans, while giving the order for the heavy batteries under his command to withdraw. (It should be noted here that not one German tank reached the west side of the Meuse until the following morning; and that no German infantrymen reached anywhere near Bulson that night.) Yet (according to General Ruby) Poncelet was heard to declare that "the German tanks were arriving as he left his PC at Flaba." Both these gunner colonels, General Ruby comments scathingly, "bear a particularly grave responsibility" for the panic which was to follow. Incredibly, no one seems to have made any attempt to verify these alarmist reports, including Grandsard himself, although later that night he ordered the panicky colonels back to their PCs. Colonel Poncelet, apparently shattered by what had happened at Sedan, fell into a deep depression and committed suicide twelve days later.

Meanwhile about three hours after the first crossings had taken place, General Lafontaine of the 55th Division was taking stock of the situation at his PC at Fond-Dagot, just behind Bulson, with a certain calmness. The bombing had ceased; he had established liaison with the 53rd Division belonging to Corap on his right; and he had dispatched a battalion to reinforce La Marfée (which would in fact succeed in checking the German advance there until dawn the next day). Then, suddenly, says General Ruby:

A wave of terrified fugitives, gunners and infantry, in transport, on foot, many without arms but dragging their kitbags, swept down the Bulson road. "The tanks are at Bulson!" they cried. Some were firing their rifles like madmen. General Lafontaine and his officers ran in front of them, tried to reason with them, made them put their lorries across the road. . . . Officers were among the deserters. Gunners, especially from the corps' heavy artillery, and infantry soldiers from the 55th Division, were mixed together, terror-stricken and in the grip of mass hysteria. All these men claimed actually to have seen tanks at Bulson and Chaumont! Much worse, commanders at all levels pretended having received orders to withdraw, but were quite unable to show them or even to say exactly where the orders had come from. Panic brooked no delay; P.C.s emptied like magic.*

There is no doubt that the real collapse at Sedan began with the gunners. Ever since Napoleon, in the French Army the artillery has always occupied a far more exalted position than in other armies. During the First War it became almost axiomatic that, so long as the artillery "held," the infantry would hold. But when the guns fell silent, the infantry would give up. By a strange coincidence, the Germans' first success on the opening day of the Battle of Verdun had also come when they broke a second-line territorial unit of elderly *"pépères"* comparable to the "B" divisions of 1940. But in contrast the French artillery at Verdun had stood its ground, and the hole had been plugged by counterattacking infantry—though at terrible cost. Why had the French

---

* The "panzers at Bulson" were almost certainly their own tanks, belonging to Grandsard's reserve tank battalions. One more ingenious variation of the story, recounted to Madame Conrad at her Field Service Unit by fugitives several days later, was that the wicked Boche had confused the defenders by utilising Renault tanks captured in Poland!

gunners at Sedan not been able to "endure" as their fathers had? Undoubtedly the mass onslaught of the Stukas that afternoon had been a horrifying experience, difficult to recapture at this range in time; but was not the terrible hammering of the German 210s and 150s at Verdun, over an infinitely longer period, just as injurious—if not more so—to human nerves? And had not the Polish artillerymen in 1939, though fighting at even greater material disadvantages, stood by their guns under Stuka attack until they were literally pulverised? But the Poles were fighting for their very existence; and, in May 1940, what were the Frenchmen of the Third Republic fighting for? In attempting to isolate the reasons for the breaking of the Sedan gunners, one comes face to face once again with the twenty-four corrosive years separating the poilus of Verdun from the men of Sedan; here is the terrible harvest of those years of mutual mistrust, disunity, despair at the losses of '14–'18, *je-m'en-foutisme* and defeatism in France.

Paradoxically, there were still determined and courageous pockets of French infantry continuing to hold out *in front of* the artillery, while the commanders of the latter were pulling out. But when the word got round that the gunners had deserted their guns, panic and all its repercussions spread like a vast, ugly oil slick. There seemed to be no stopping the fugitives of the 55th Division, or the escalation of the rumours they carried. As far back as Vouziers, the Second Army provost marshal, Colonel Serin, called in two companies of Gardes Mobiles in an attempt to "canalise" the flood. Still, according to General Ruby, the fugitives managed to reach Reims before they could be rounded up —having "pillaged from top to bottom Ste. Ménéhould and Vouziers." Even Huntziger's HQ at Senuc was not immune to this tide of panic. "Towards 21 hours," says General Ruby, "two sapper officers presented themselves to the General; much affected, they testified to having seen German tanks at Vendresse. Coldly, General Huntziger called them liars. They had taken our 7th Tank Battalion for a panzer unit!" Still further afield, Jean Muray at a village where his division was in reserve behind Corap's front, 35 miles from Sedan, met men from Sedan the very next morning, bearing terrible tales: "They had seen it; the scattering of French divisions. The pulverising of a whole army . . . the courage of some, the cowardice of others." Roland Dorgelès, the famous novelist, tells of ten gunners and a medical officer fleeing from Sedan in a truck who were stopped at Auxerre—in the middle of France—six days after the debacle; interrogated about his departure from the front, the officer replied, "*Mais, mon capitaine,* bombs were falling!" In the ensuing days, wretched tales like this could be multiplied a thousandfold.

Closer to the front at Sedan, however, the consequences of this wave of panic were much more immediately disastrous. Never pausing to check the rumour "the panzers are at Bulson!", General Lafontaine requested Grandsard to be allowed to move his PC back to Chémery. Grandsard said Lafontaine must decide what was best. Lafontaine did. Half in transport, half on foot, his headquarters staff hastily retired. This in itself, according to Grandsard, had a baneful effect; officers presenting themselves for orders at Lafontaine's former PC during the night found it abandoned, and "deduced a definitive withdrawal on the part of the 55th Division. They saw therein an argument for their own pride."* At Chémery, General Ruby tells us, Lafontaine

fell into the middle of unimaginable chaos; the flood of fugitives traverses the village without pause; all the echelons of the division, accumulated in this region—fighting units, regimental HQs, supply columns, vehicle parks . . . —all are heading for the south, swelled by stragglers; as if by magic, their officers have naturally received a mysterious order to withdraw. Barriers established by the military police are swept aside.

Amidst this scene of anarchy, with *ad hoc* lines of communication even worse than those at Bulson, so badly disrupted by the German bombing, Lafontaine was attempting to organise a counterattack. But the commander of his principal reserve formation, Lieutenant Colonel Labarthe of the 213th Infantry Regiment, depressed by the effect the prevailing atmosphere was

---

* In the wake of Sedan, the quest for "an argument for their own pride" seems to have been carried out at all levels. General Lafontaine himself, in a report to Gamelin dated May 18th, attempts to utilise the old, untenable bogey (about which more will be said) of the German fifth column. "One must note the almost certain presence," he declares, "of doubtful characters, certainly of parachutists charged with a definite mission to fulfil, who transmitted the orders for withdrawal." As with so many major French debacles throughout history, there has to be somewhere a "traitor" or an enemy agent—*nous sommes trahis!* Needless to say, no hard evidence has ever been produced for this "fifth column" activity at Sedan.

having upon his men, kept mumbling to him: *"Surtout, pas de contre-attaque!"*

Next, the impact of the panic on the 55th's front swiftly made itself felt upon its sister "B" division, the 71st, which—although still slowly moving up into line—had suffered little during the day's fighting. Almost immediately after receiving the first news of the purported enemy tanks at Chaumont and Bulson, Grandsard had relayed it to General Baudet, requesting him to make the necessary dispositions. Baudet at once decided to pull *his* freshly established PC at Raucourt back three or four miles, taking with him the commander of the divisional artillery. This withdrawal of the division's chief gunner had its attendant repercussions on the various batteries; in the absence of authority, the personnel of some dispersed in the woods, where they wandered all night, only returning ("naturally, incomplete," says Ruby) to their guns in the morning; others, on notional orders, destroyed their weapons and headed for the rear. All too few were the battery commanders who, like Major Benedetti of the 363rd Regiment, actually manhandled their guns forward during the night, against the demoralising flood tide of fugitives. On the 71st Division's front, says General Ruby, already "three groups of 75s out of four had been abandoned by their crews . . . four out of six groups of the heavy artillery." These were the guns which had halted the German crossings at Wadelincourt by their flanking fire. The prospects for the 71st, if attacked the following day, were hardly auspicious.

Sedan: The French counterattack

We have seen the results of the first French counterattacks mounted against Rommel's bridgehead at Dinant; what was being prepared to repulse Guderian's at Sedan? Under his command Grandsard had in reserve two tank battalions, the 4th and the 7th, and two infantry regiments, the 205th and the 213th, the latter led by the reluctant Lieutenant Colonel Labarthe. Behind them, the powerful units ordered up by General Georges —the 3rd Armoured and 3rd Motorised Divisions—were now arriving to be placed under Huntziger's control. Grandsard had put all four of his reserve units at Lafontaine's disposal, and at 0130 hours on the morning of the 14th the harassed Lafontaine ordered them to carry out a two-pronged dawn counterattack. If the

Barricaded Dutch road is no barrier to Germans

German engineers swarm over Belgian roadblock

Rotterdam after the Nazi air raids

German paratroopers
landing in the Netherlands

German troops storm Belgian fortified bunker

Germans penetrate the "impenetrable" Ardennes

Crossing the Meuse near Dinant: 37 mm antitank guns cover the troops

A German motorcycle reconnaissance unit in France

German tanks pass demolished French column

The end for a French B tank

The end for a German motorcyclist

operation had been executed as planned, before Guderian's armour had begun to reach the west side of the river and before the Luftwaffe returned, it would have had a good chance of success; and even if it had not overrun Guderian's soft-skinned riflemen, it would at least have gained valuable time for Huntziger to swing his main punch.* But not one unit was ready to attack on time. Lieutenant Colonel Labarthe managed to persuade Lafontaine that, in view of the uncertain morale of the 213th Regiment, it would be too risky to undertake a night march through all that calamity-crying debris reeling back from the front; the 7th Tanks, detailed to accompany it, claimed it did not get the order in time. The 205th Regiment (belonging to the 71st Division) was held up in the approach march by lorry-borne fugitives crying, "Infantrymen, don't go forward! The Boches are there!", and finally received orders from a dispatch rider to halt ("From whom came this counter-order?" queries General Ruby); while its supporting tank battalion, the 4th, having been met by one of Grandsard's own staff captains at about 9 P.M. and told that there were panzers at Chaumont, decided to camp down for the night—never meeting up with the infantry from the 205th until morning. There was, says Grandsard with admirable restraint, "too great a facility to interpret an order than to execute it as received; too great a facility to modify under the pretext of initiative, when confronted by unchecked information." As a result, instead of getting off the ground at 0400 hours, Grandsard's counterattack would not start until three hours later. By then, the whole picture in the German bridgehead would have changed. In essence, the story was much the same as at Dinant. The French Army had forfeited its second big opportunity of the campaign.

As night fell, Lieutenant Colonel Balck, sitting comfortably on his objective just beyond Frenois, became aware of the fading away of French gunfire. An inkling of what was going on among the enemy gunners seems to have occurred to him. His riflemen were dog-tired from the day's exertions but, infusing his own energy into them in a notable feat of personal leadership, he rallied

---

* "If the ill-starred French had not been still dogged by misfortune," commented Captain von Kielmansegg, giving a German view of this missed opportunity, "they would have made a spirited counter-attack to remove while it was still small the bulge which had developed in their lines and destroyed all the German units on their side of the Meuse before they could be reinforced."

them and got them on their feet again. Bullying and driving, Balck led the weary regiment in a five-mile night march towards the south, so that by dawn—without opposition—they had reached Chéhéry, thereby at one bound doubling the depth of the bridge-head. On the left flank, nightfall and the diminution of the flank-ing fire from the 71st Division enabled the stalled rifle battalions of the 10th Panzer to get across the Meuse. Creeping from one bomb crater to another, "ideal positions" thrown up by the Stukas, Sergeant Schulze noted how many bunkers seemed to have been abandoned by their occupants. Swiftly the divisional engineers began construction of a bridge for the 10th Panzer, just south of Sedan. On the 1st Panzer front, Guderian—who had al-ready crossed the river closely on the heels of Balck's riflemen—stood by, watching anxiously as Lieutenant Grubnau's men put the finishing touches to their bridge at Gaulier. The regimental historian of the Grossdeutschland notes: "The noise of fighting had almost stopped; only occasionally there was one shot, other-wise silence—the enemy is beaten!" Shortly before midnight, the pontoon bridge was ready, and "we roll slowly over onto the other bank, turn sharply to the right and follow the road running along the Meuse some thousand yards to the small village of Villette. A crater-like Stuka bomb hole forces us out onto the fields . . . around us are burning houses, shimmering with heat." As the first panzers rumbled into the Sedan bridgehead, it measured some three miles wide by four to six miles deep at the point where Balck had completed his night march. "Pleased and proud with what I had seen," Guderian returned to his HQ at La Chapelle to prepare operational orders for the 14th. It was clear, he felt, that this day would "bring a decision." At the same time, he could not resist sending off a telegram to General Busch, the commander of the Sixteenth Army who, at that meeting with Hitler, had told Guderian he would never get across the Meuse.

Reinhardt's difficulties

If on both wings of the *Sichelschnitt* thrust—at Dinant and Sedan—the results on the 13th left little to be desired (from the German point of view), the same could hardly be said of the cen-tre. Here, at Monthermé, Reinhardt's XLI Corps was badly stuck, and would remain so for the next two days. The story of Reinhardt's difficulties makes an interesting comparison to the easy successes of Rommel and Guderian, though they were not really his fault. The terrain around Monthermé is some of the ruggedest in the Ardennes; the approach roads—on which Reinhardt's supply columns had become so badly entangled with those of Guderian's 2nd Panzer on the previous days—are few and poor. The defenders, unlike the troops on Corap's northern wing at Dinant who had had to take up unfamiliar positions after a 60-mile march into Belgium, were on French territory and had been dug in there since the beginning of the war; also, in contrast to Huntziger's troops at Sedan, they were not "B" reservists but regulars of the 102nd Fortress Division. With its main weight concentrated on Sedan, the Luftwaffe could only lend relatively small support to Reinhardt; and against the well-prepared French positions in this heavily wooded country, its bombs had but limited effect. (In fact, the Germans seem to have suffered almost as much as the French, when Stukas mistakenly attacked a detachment of the 6th Panzer, knocking out several guns and vehicles and killing eleven personnel.) On the other hand, Corap, judging the Charleville–Mézières gap to be the most vulnerable portion of this sector, had located most of the available artillery there, leaving the defence of Monthermé largely to the 42nd half-brigade of colonial machine-gunners—a number of them Indo-Chinese.

During the morning of the 13th, the advanced elements of General Kempf's 6th Panzer cleared the parts of Monthermé lying on the right bank of the Meuse. Kempf himself arrived at the Roche à Sept Heures, a famous tourist halt overlooking the town a mile to the north, to plan his attack. Around him stretched one of the most memorable panoramas of the whole Ardennes. Below, the heights dived almost perpendicularly through great slabs of slippery rock and treacherous shale, broken with belts of thick forest, down to the Meuse several hundred feet beneath. Beyond the river, he could see the whole Monthermé isthmus protruding from its narrow base like a swollen thumb (the Germans promptly nicknamed it the "bread-roll") into the folds of the Meuse and rising to heights quite as dominating as the Roche à Sept Heures—a superb natural defensive position. In the Meuse at his feet, faster flowing and wider than at Sedan, lay the half-submerged trusses of the destroyed road bridge. It was by no means an ideal place for a major river crossing, though Kempf was agreeably surprised at the astonishing resemblance to the Lahn in Germany where the division had been posted to carry out its preparatory training for *Sichelschnitt*. He ordered his 4th Rifle Regiment to prepare for an immediate attempt, deploying, like Rommel at Dinant, all his available Mark III and Mark IV tanks to provide close covering fire.

Painfully the riflemen scrabbled, stumbled and slid down the steep slope with their weighty machine guns, mortars and ammunition boxes. Small avalanches of loose stones started up from beneath their boots, and there were many painful falls. The valley, however, was filled with a welcome pall of smoke, and gratefully they noted how sparse was the French artillery fire. On reaching the level of the river, there was an uneasy silence during which the riflemen could distinctly hear the asthmatic sounds of the foot pumps inflating the rubber assault dinghies under the cover of dead ground. Just across the river they could read the signs *Café* or *Boucherie* on the riverside buildings, but there was no sign of life from the enemy. The moment the first team reached the water with their dinghy, however, devastating machine-gun fire opened up. Several men were wounded, the remainder dropped the boat and ran for shelter. The next team was also shot up, and it was difficult in the smoke and confusion to pinpoint just where the fire was coming from. At last a bunker was located carefully camouflaged underneath a terrace café, where in happier times tourists had sat and gazed out over the Meuse. Tanks were brought to bear on the café, and under cover of smoke from a burning coal barge more assault teams were launched. They noted that the tanks had reduced the bunker beneath the café to a gaping hole; meanwhile it was also discovered that dinghies launched upstream and carried away by the current were jamming into the spans of the demolished bridge, where they appeared to be covered from fire by the remaining French bunkers. Swiftly the engineers capitalised on this discovery and brought up planks and more dinghies, creating a rickety footbridge lashed to the remnants of the bridge. In the twilight, the remainder of one of the rifle battalions made its way across the bridge, establishing by midnight a small bridgehead on the Monthermé peninsula. But there was no indication here of French resistance being broken, and Kempf's riflemen—tired and having suffered distressing casualties—were forced to dig in defensively, under heavy fire from the French-held heights, and with little prospect of getting their tanks across the Meuse the next morning.

Holland: A matter of hours

For all the new, menacing fury of the fighting on the Meuse, developments in northern Belgium and Holland were not without gravity on the 13th. The Dutch had reached a point where clearly it was a matter of hours before the end would come. The 9th Panzer was hammering its way towards the outskirts of Rotterdam. Still the Dutch fought back, and by the evening an exasperated General von Küchler (commander of the Eighteenth Army) was issuing orders for his forces "to break the resistance in Rotterdam with all means." Meanwhile, Giraud's Seventh Army had retired more or less out of harm's way towards the estuary of the Scheldt. Further south, the main body of the Belgian Army had made its way back behind the Dyle Line, and on the BEF front Lord Gort could once again state: "No event of major importance occurred during the day."

It was General Prioux's Cavalry Corps which, still standing ahead of Blanchard's First Army, bore the main burden of the fighting in northern Belgium. What had been armoured skirmishes on the 12th had turned into the first full-scale tank-versus-tank battle of the campaign. Adroitly supported by Stukas, powerful concentrations of tanks from the 3rd and 4th Panzer Divisions hammered at Prioux's two Light Mechanised Divisions. All day the battle had seethed like a cauldron around Merdorp, a village just west of Hannut and a few miles from Marlborough's battlefield of Ramillies. Although contemporary German accounts admit to few losses on their side, it is clear that they were much disconcerted at first by the "unbelievable" armour of the medium Somuas, which could stand more than one hit by all but the heaviest German tank cannon. Then the German panzer commanders began to detect that the French tanks consistently seemed to fire short and at a slower rate than their own. So the Germans closed the range whenever possible. But, according to a German panzer officer who was there, they learned a far more basic lesson about French armoured techniques that day at Merdorp: "their lack of manoeuvrability and the fact that they fight single and in loose formation, not altogether under one com-

mand. They cannot take advantage of strength and number."
Never again in the campaign would French tanks fight on such
closely equal terms with the enemy; at Merdorp they fought with
tenacity and courage, but too often in penny packets that were repeatedly outmanoeuvred, and it was the panzers which, at the
end of the day, held the field. That night Prioux drew his tanks
back behind the Belgian antitank obstacle at Perwez. Both sides
had suffered heavy losses,* but the French losses were to have
much more far-reaching consequences on the overall strategic
position.

The Allies: Tears and ignorance

As this eventful Whitmonday came to a close, at the upper
echelons of the French High Command General Georges for one
seems at last to have been awakened as to what was at stake on
the upper Meuse. Captain Beaufre recalls drawing in on General
Doumenc's situation map early that morning a large arrow, de-
noting that the main German effort was being made, "not in Belgium, but on the axis Luxembourg–Mézières." He claims that
Georges's Deuxième Bureau had arrived simultaneously at the
same conclusion, but had dismissed it on the grounds of the "defensive value of our position" at Sedan. During the day, dispatch
riders rushed back and forth between Doumenc's GHQ at Montry
and Georges's at La Ferté, bearing a flood of reports. Late that
evening, Beaufre informs us, he was awoken by a telephone call
from General Georges, asking him to "tell General Doumenc to
come at once!" Accompanied by Beaufre, Doumenc arrived at
La Ferté at about 3 A.M. Georges's staff officers were clustered
together in the *grand salon* of "Les Bondons," which had been
transformed into a map room. The lights were low, and had been
extinguished in the rest of the villa.

At the telephone, Major Navereau repeats in a soft voice the information he is receiving. The others are silent. General Roton, the Chief-
of-Staff, is slumped in an armchair. The atmosphere is that of a family
keeping vigil over a dead member. Georges rises briskly and comes
up to Doumenc. He is terribly pale. "Our front has been pushed in
at Sedan! There have been some failures (*défaillances*). . . ." He
falls into an armchair and a sob silences him.

---

* The Germans claim to have knocked out 30 Somuas and 70 Hotchkiss H–35s.

It was the first man that I had seen weep in this battle. I was to see many others, alas. It made a dreadful impression on me.

Doumenc, says Beaufre, did his best to comfort the C-in-C. There were collapses like this in all wars, he said reassuringly. "Come, let's look at the map. We'll see what can be done."

Gamelin, meanwhile—and beyond him the French and British Governments—remained blissfully unaware of Georges's state of mind, cushioned from the full gravity of the situation by sheer lack of Intelligence. After General Georges's first lustrous communication, warning of the *"pépin assez sérieux"* at Sedan, Gamelin's last news that night from Sedan, via Georges, announced that the Second Army was "holding" and concluded, superbly: "Here we are calm." Baudoin, the secretary to Reynaud's new War Cabinet, declares that after three vain attempts on May 12th to gain accurate information from GQG, Colonel Villelume, the Cabinet's military liaison officer, succeeded in bringing in the news at about 6 P.M. on the 13th that "our advance guards had been violently thrown back in the Ardennes." Finally, from the depths of his isolated *Thébaïde,* Gamelin issued the following somewhat meaningless order of the day to the French forces at large:

The onslaught of the mechanical and motorised forces of the enemy must now be faced. The hour has come to fight in depth* on the positions appointed by the High Command. One is no longer entitled to retire. If the enemy makes a local breach, it must not only be sealed off but counterattacked and retaken.

In London, the British CIGS, Ironside, summed up this momentous day in his diary:

There is yet no sign of the Germans having done anything except move forward their mechanised columns under cover of intense air activity.

---

* The last thing for which the "continuous front" philosophy was in fact designed!

13
Consolidating the Bridgeheads
MAY 14th

In the area south of the line Liège-Namur our troops
have left the Ardennes behind them and reached the
Meuse between Namur and Givet with their advance
guard. . . . Under the protection of German fighter,
Stuka and "destroyer" units, which attacked non-stop,
and with a shattering effect, it was also possible to cross
the Meuse on French territory.
—Wehrmacht Communiqué, May 14th

In general it may be said that the Germans have not yet
made contact with the bulk of the French and British
forces, except possibly in the Longwy area, where they
are said to be challenging the underground hill fortresses
of the Maginot Line.
—*The Times*, May 15th (dispatch dated May 14th)

Onhaye: Rommel attacks

FOR THE Germans, May 14th was a day devoted to consolidating
their bridgeheads over the Meuse, in preparation for the great
armoured break-through across northern France; for the French,
a day of building up major counterstrokes against the two German
bulges.

For Rommel, positioned at Dinant, it did not seem to begin under the most brilliant of auspices. The dawn attack (postponed
from the previous night) by a battalion of French motorised
dragoons (the 14th) from General Boucher's 5th Division succeeded in capturing the village of Haut-le-Wastia and some forty
of Rommel's motorcyclists. Not pressing their advantage, however, the French had then withdrawn to a "line of containment"
fixed by General Corap. On the other side of the bridgehead,

Colonel von Bismarck signalled that under cover of darkness his 7th Rifle Regiment had pushed up to Onhaye, three miles down the main road west of Dinant. It had overrun enemy positions there, but was being engaged by powerful French forces. Rommel rushed back and forth, positioning his antitank guns and urging on the tanks which were beginning to cross the barely completed pontoons, but with what seemed like agonising slowness. Suddenly he received a wireless message from Bismarck stating that his regiment was "encircled." Thereupon Rommel decided "to go to his assistance immediately with every available tank." By 0800 hours his 25th Panzer Regiment, under command of Colonel Rothenburg, had succeeded in assembling just 30 tanks on the west bank. All of these now moved up behind Bismarck, but encountered no opposition. Says Rommel, "It transpired that von Bismarck had actually radioed 'arrived' instead of 'encircled'!"*

With five tanks providing mobile support fire, Bismarck's riflemen now carried out a flanking attack to seize Onhaye from the rear. From Dinant the main road climbs steeply through woods to Onhaye; but once Onhaye is passed, one stands on the height of land, with flat open country ideal for armoured deployment leading westwards to Philippeville, and beyond it the featureless plains of northern France. Thus the securing of Onhaye (which had been the object of a special exercise conducted by Rommel at Bad Godesberg) was of paramount importance to the breakout phase of the 7th Panzer's advance. To keep a tight control over the action, Rommel mounted himself in a Mark III tank and followed closely behind Colonel Rothenburg. This typical audacity nearly brought an end to his career. Approaching the corner of Onhaye Wood,

suddenly we came under heavy artillery and anti-tank gunfire from the west. Shells landed all round us and my tank received two hits one after the other, the first on the upper edge of the turret and the second in the periscope. The driver promptly opened the throttle wide and drove straight into the nearest bushes. He had only gone a few yards, however, when the tank slid down a steep slope on the western edge of the wood and finally stopped, canted over on its side, in such a position that the enemy, whose guns were in position about 500 yards away on the edge of the next wood, could not fail to see it. I had been

---

* *Eingetroffen* instead of *eingeschlossen*.

wounded in the right cheek by a small splinter from the shell which had landed in the periscope. It was not serious though it bled a great deal. I tried to swing the turret round so as to bring our 37 mm. gun to bear on the enemy in the opposite wood, but with the heavy slant of the tank it was immovable. The French battery now opened rapid fire on our wood and at any moment we could expect their fire to be aimed at our tank, which was in full view. I therefore decided to abandon it as fast as I could, taking the crew with me. At that moment the sub-altern in command of the tanks escorting the infantry reported himself seriously wounded, with the words: *"Herr General,* my left arm has been shot off." We clambered up through the sandy pit, shells crashing and splintering all round.

Just ahead of him, Rommel was shocked to see Rothenburg's tank "with flames pouring out of the rear."

The adjutant of the Panzer Regiment had also left his tank. I thought at first that the command tank had been set alight by a hit in the petrol tank and was extremely worried for Colonel Rothenburg's safety. However, it turned out to be only the smoke candles that had caught light, the smoke from which now served us very well. . . . It was only the involuntary smokescreen laid by this tank that prevented the enemy from shooting up any more of our vehicles.

Meanwhile, Rommel's own armoured signals vehicle pushed into the wood where it too was immobilised with a shot in the engine. Rommel got away from the fracas, though his biographer, Desmond Young, claims that he narrowly escaped being captured by French native troops.* He then ordered Stuka strikes to liquidate the troublesome French gun positions. Later his riflemen winkled out a courageous French gunner captain from the cellar of a half-destroyed house, where—"smoking cigarettes and drinking red wine on a sofa"—he had remained to telephone observations to his battery as the German columns marched past his refuge. His capture did not immediately silence the French guns, but thenceforth their fire fell wildly all over the place. However, on account of the morning's setback, it was not until evening that Rommel could lay hands on his vital assembly area at Onhaye.

---

* From the newly arrived 4th North African Division.

Onhaye: The French counterattack

On the French side, there was more fatal procrastination in the dispatch of reserves to counterattack Rommel's bridgehead. The most powerful piece that General Georges could bring into play —in fact one of the most powerful pieces on the whole French chessboard—was the 1st Armoured Division. Originally earmarked by Gamelin to back up the Dyle manoeuvre, on May 11th the 1st Armoured had been sent to Charleroi to be at the disposal of Blanchard's First Army, with the specific object of covering the Gembloux Gap. Commanded by General Bruneau, the 1st Armoured contained only 150 tanks, compared with Rommel's 228, but half of these were the excellent heavy "B" model. On the other hand, it possessed no armoured liaison cars; it lacked signals units, and among the tanks which were equipped with radios it was found that the accumulators were inadequate to maintain transmissions over any length of time. Fear of the Luftwaffe forced the division to make its approach march to Charleroi by night; which, in the short May nights, would have required four stages to cover 130 kilometres.* Then, following the rapidity of the German progress, it was decided to reduce the stages to two, the second being carried out by daylight; finally, a third decision prescribed that Bruneau reach Charleroi in one hop. Much confusion resulted. In fact, German bombing of the railways delayed the division's arrival by eighteen hours, and as soon as Bruneau had established his PC at Lambusart (near Charleroi) on the night of May 12th he received a request from the local Corps commander to help him round up parachutists reported in his region. Wisely Bruneau refused.

All through the 13th the 1st Armoured remained inactive there, less than 25 miles from where Rommel's bridgehead was developing. That day General Georges had promised it to Corap, but Billotte—alarmed by the course of the fierce tank battle in which Prioux's Cavalry Corps had become engaged in front of the sensitive Gembloux Gap, and still disinclined to accept that the main German thrust was materialising in the south—continued to hesitate. Only at midnight on the 13th did Bruneau receive preliminary instructions preparing the 1st Armoured to strike south in

---

* Not much faster than the rate of advance of the panzers through France.

order to aid General Martin's XI Corps. Then another twelve hours were frittered away by muddled staff work until, at 1300 hours on the 14th, it was ordered to move to the Florennes area just over 20 miles to the south. "It took them a long time to reach their positions," wrote Colonel Bardies, "for the roads were cluttered with fleeing troops and civilians. . . . It took the armoured division seven hours to cover those twenty miles. It was short of petrol. It would be unable to fight that day." One battalion lost its way, and it was not until after midnight that Bruneau had three battalions of tanks in the Florennes assembly area; meanwhile, mistakenly, he had relegated his petrol trucks to the rear of the divisional column, and thus it seemed doubtful whether the 1st Armoured would even be in a fit state to attack early on the morning of the 15th.

By this time, the whole picture would have altered radically. How different things might have been if it could have hit Rommel on the 13th, when only his infantry were across the Meuse; or even on the morning of the 14th when Rommel was still being vigorously resisted around Onhaye!

The other major force at Corap's immediate disposal for a counterattack against Rommel was General Sancelme's 4th North African Division, which had been standing by in reserve. A tough regular unit comprised of Zouaves and Algerian Tirailleurs— many of whose kinsmen would be fighting against France less than two decades later—and constituting the finest division* in the Ninth Army, it should ideally have been employed in a forceful attack coordinated with the 1st Armoured. Corap, however, true to the 1918 doctrine of "containment," immediately cast it in a defensive role, to hold the line at Onhaye. Fighting splendidly, it had been the Tirailleurs forming its advanced elements which had checked Rommel here during the morning of the 14th, but the defensive tone of Corap's order did not have an encouraging effect on the hard-pressed remnants of his 18th Division. The news from its left flank, opposite Rommel's original crossing place at Houx, was particularly bad. Here the battalion of the 39th Regiment

---

* As will be seen on subsequent occasions, it was frequently the French North African and colonial units which put up the best resistance in 1940. On the other side, German troops inoculated with Nazi racial doctrines are repeatedly to be found protesting at the "shame" of the *Herrenvolk* having to fight against inferior "nigger-people" in France.

detailed off to attack Surinvaux Wood at dawn had stumbled into it too early during the night. At daybreak it was swiftly rounded up by the Germans, supported with tanks. Then, fighting gallantly, the remains of the 66th Regiment were submerged. After which, says General Doumenc, "the whole line ebbed back and attempted, without much success, to anchor itself to the Anthée–Sosoye defence line. The Luftwaffe raged relentlessly around the sector; communications were cut, orders could not be passed; it became impossible to control the battle."

Corap in trouble

Control was not aided by Corap's own movements that day. Having found that his HQ at Vervins was too far from the battlefield to keep abreast of events, in the morning he had moved up to General Martin's PC at Florennes and had then spent the rest of the day visiting the various divisional PCs. Liaison officers urgently requiring instructions for orientating the 1st Armoured and 4th North African Divisions found it difficult to locate him. What Corap saw and learned that day depressed him in the extreme. In addition to Rommel's bridgehead, a German infantry division was getting across the Meuse at Yvoir, to the north of Dinant. Worse still, another infantry division had partly overrun the southerly division—the 22nd—of General Martin's XI Corps which was holding the line near Givet. As bad luck would have it, the divisional commander, General Hassler, had been injured in a car accident the previous month and did not return to his division until May 15th, and Hassler's Chief of Staff, losing his head, ordered the 22nd Division to abandon the strong point guarding Givet and fall back some six miles behind the river. Furious, Corap threatened him with a court-martial and formally ordered him to counterattack. But it was too late; as Colonel Goutard acidly comments: "Here was another division which disintegrated at the first blow."

Everywhere Corap found indications that morale was flagging, and especially among the "A" reservists of the 18th Division which had so far absorbed the hardest blows from Rommel. Officers seemed to be giving up all too readily. To the Ninth Army at large he addressed an exhortatory signal with the following words:

Some *défaillances* have occurred at certain points. . . . At this mo-

ment when the destiny of France is in the balance, no weakness will
be tolerated. At all levels, leaders have the duty to set the example, and
if necessary force obedience! Pitiless sanctions will fall upon any leaders who fail.

By evening Rommel had succeeded in wresting Onhaye from
the North Africans. Although they were still fighting back hard,
at seven o'clock General Martin, concerned at the shaky position
of his 18th and 22nd Divisions and their poor state of morale, gave
the order for the whole corps to fall back behind a "barrier" line
running through Florennes. Moving up to the front that evening,
the 13th Zouaves, the reserve regiment of the 4th North African
Division, was astonished to pass Martin and his HQ staff heading in the opposite direction. The Zouaves had begun to move up
from their positions on the Belgian frontier on May 10th, repeatedly attacked by German bombers and Stukas, and during the
night of the 13th they had circuited the burning town of Philippeville. Now, still not having seen the enemy, they were "thrown
into the ditches alongside the road, and remained there immobilised
for more than three hours, watching without comprehension," as
the HQ of XI Corps—accompanied by a flotsam of fighting troops
—withdrew through them. Hard upon its heels came Colonel
Rothenburg's panzers, who by nightfall on the 14th had pushed
down the Philippeville road as far as Anthée. Rommel's bridgehead was now over seven miles deep—at a total cost of 3 officers,
7 NCO's and 41 men killed that day. The tanks of both Rommel's
division and those of Colonel Werner's from the 5th Panzer,
which were still at his disposal, were flowing into the bridgehead
with ever-increasing speed, despite Allied air attacks on the pontoons, and all was now set for the breakout phase. In this, Rommel
was still one jump ahead of Guderian at Sedan.

About the only comfort Corap, the portly old colonial soldier,
could find on his front that day was the continued resistance that
the colonial machine gunners of the 102nd Fortress Division were
putting up at Monthermé. Here General Kempf's 6th Panzer was
not having an easy time. During the early hours of the morning,
accurate French artillery fire had destroyed the footbridge of
rubber dinghies. The riflemen clinging to the west bank of the
Monthermé isthmus had been repeatedly counterattacked, and
were much hampered by the nonarrival of the divisional heavy

artillery—still held up in the Ardennes traffic blocks. With heavy losses, Colonel von Ravenstein's riflemen managed to push up onto Height 325 during the morning, but by midday Kempf was forced to tell his Corps commander, Reinhardt, that he saw little prospect of any further progress that day. There was certainly no question of building a heavy pontoon bridge to get the tanks across. All through the day and the following night the French gunfire kept up. But the few heavy weapons available to the defenders were slow-firing, First War models of the "long" 155 which with their flat trajectory had difficulty in hitting the Germans on the steep reverse slopes of the Monthermé isthmus. To help them, Corap sent up a group of sixty-year-old 220 mm howitzers. At midnight these were found by the commander of the French 42nd Half-Brigade, abandoned on the road by their personnel, presumably after being attacked by the Luftwaffe. That same evening a solitary 47 mm antitank gun was also sent up to Monthermé; according to General Menu, it too was discovered by the enemy the following day, abandoned by its crew without having fired a single shot.

German infantry reach the Meuse

Despite the continued agglomeration of traffic in the Ardennes, the first of Rundstedt's infantry divisions which were to play a vital role in "lining" the corridor of the panzer break-through had now reached the Meuse. On the 14th, three established crossings on either side of Rommel's bridgehead, and two divisions of General Haase's III Corps,* the 3rd and 23rd, fought their way down to the Meuse at Nouzonville, roughly midway between Monthermé and Charleville–Mézières. One of the first officers of the 23rd across the Meuse was Axel von dem Bussche, a twenty-one-year-old regular who was later to become distinguished for his participation in various bomb plots against Hitler. Up till now, the march through the Ardennes had seemed like a jolly picnic, and—until the commanding officer had berated them for unmartial practices—his footsore men had taken to wheeling their weapons along in commandeered baby carriages. Then, fighting his way up the western bank of the Meuse, von dem Bussche, with his arm raised

---

* Its immediate forebear, the III Brandenburg Corps of '14–'18, had pulled off the remarkable coup of capturing Verdun's Fort Douaumont.

in the act of lobbing a grenade into a French position, saw a frightened Annamite face taking aim at close range. The bullet removed
his right thumb, and for von dem Bussche the campaign was over.

Lieutenant Karl Heinz Mende of the engineers had shared
similar experiences of the campaign so far. Still not having seen a
shot fired, he recalled how, when passing a customs-house on the
French frontier that morning, his men had acquired a rubber
stamp marked "*Douane Française, 9 Mai 1940*," which they
adjusted to the right date, and frivolously stamped their letters
home with it. One even tattooed his breast with it. There was an
occasional sound of gunfire in the distance, but that was all. Then
suddenly Mende's unit was plunged into the inferno. In spite of
repeated Stuka attacks on Nouzonville, the French 102nd Fortress
Division fought back tenaciously from well-hidden positions, and
it was only on the third attempt that his division got across the
river. Later Mende wrote home describing this first confrontation
with war in more pensive terms, which perhaps typified the emotions of many a young German during these days:

We have it behind us . . . after everything that I have experienced
I do not know whether I have become richer or poorer and whether
the experience of such things is the true new value of this campaign.
I only know one thing—and I have also found this conviction among
brave comrades; the worst thing in battle is not the danger, which
stands burning before one's eyes; the worst feeling is nervousness
about success.

After the crossing had succeeded:

I cannot say that we were worried or uncertain, we simply had no feeling left in us. That was the mood of the battle. And only, when in
front of us, an infantryman who was hit collapsed and a dead comrade
lay nearby, did there awake a piece of the old feeling and we thought
for one second how dangerous it all was and that we were after all human beings of flesh and blood.

By the end of the 14th, however, it was not the crossings at
Monthermé and Nouzonville that were most endangering Corap's
right flank but the change in direction of Guderian's thrust, which
now threatened Sedan.

The French: "A mission of sacrifice"

As an indication of just how well according to plan *Sichelschnitt* was going, the main directive in Guderian's brief orders for the 14th read: "The divisions will capture their objectives according to the map exercise." By dawn a substantial number of the 1st Panzer's tanks had already trundled across Lieutenant Grubnau's bridge. The concentration of vehicles queuing up on the east bank was so enormous that it was impossible for anything to move in the opposite direction. Thus, noted Grubnau, the cloth factory from which the first crossings had been launched on the 13th had been transformed into a field hospital in which all the German wounded—plus some two hundred French—were being tended. The 1st Panzer tanks immediately headed towards Chéhéry (where Colonel Balck was sitting somewhat precariously) and Bulson. These happened to be the same routes along which General Lafontaine's two counterattacking groups, each comprised of an infantry regiment and a battalion of support tanks, were advancing. The first head-on collision between Guderian's panzers and the French armour was now imminent. But, on top of all the delays of the previous night, Lafontaine's two groups still proved incapable of coordinating with one another. The right-hand group (comprised of the 4th Tank Battalion and the 205th Infantry Regiment of the 71st Division) were still not ready for action. So only the 7th Tanks and Lieutenant Colonel Labarthe's 213th Infantry Regiment went, piecemeal, into battle. Still complaining about the state of his regiment, Labarthe begged to be allowed to adopt a defensive position in the villages of Chéméry and Maisoncelle. But he was overruled by Lafontaine (backed by Grandsard), and finally set forth at 0700 hours, muttering *"C'est une mission de sacrifice!"* The 213th carried with it not one antitank weapon, artillery support was doubtful, and the 7th Tanks was equipped only with the light FCM infantry model mounting an obsolete 37 mm gun with little penetrating power. Nevertheless, the battle started well enough for the French armour. Near Chéhéry they came upon vehicles of the 1st Panzer that were refuelling and a savage encounter at short range ensued, in which the first two leading German tanks were knocked out and the commander of the 1st Panzer Brigade, Colonel Keltsch, was severely wounded. Even the German accounts admit that this was an ugly moment for them, and it leads one to speculate what havoc the 4th and 7th Tanks might have inflicted on Balck's soft-skinned infantry had they only been able to attack a few hours earlier. With that mixture of optimism and misinformation still prevalent in the French High Command, half an hour later General Georges was reporting to Gamelin "that the breach at Sedan has been contained and that a counter-attack with strong formations was carried out at 4:30 A.M." Shortly afterwards, the tide of battle was already turning against the 7th Tanks. With extreme courage, a nearby German *Sturmpionier* battalion flung itself on the French tanks, hurling hollow charges between the tracks and under the motors; during which the commander, Lieutenant Colonel Mahler, lost his life. The French tanks seemed hesitant to press their advantage. As in the armoured battle in northern Belgium at Merdorp, they were seen to be manoeuvred slowly and clumsily by their commanders. While the few German antitank guns that had reached the battle line (plus two 88s) held the 7th Tanks at bay, with customary speed the 1st Panzer prepared a smashing counterblow. Towards 0830 hours, a mass of panzers struck in the area of Connage (midway between Chéhéry and Chémery), accounting for 11 out of the 15 FCMs there. A similar fate overtook the French tank companies deployed on the dominating high ground at Bulson. Now it could be said with truth, "The *Panzers* are at Bulson." The 7th Tanks reeled back, having lost more than half of their machines on much the same ground where the French cuirassiers had sacrificed themselves at the 1870 Battle of Sedan. German armour hooking left from Chémery then tore into the flank of the unprotected 213th Infantry Regiment. Its commander, the reluctant Labarthe, was wounded and taken prisoner, and the broken remnants of his regiment streamed back to the 55th Division's second line of defence at Mont-Dieu.

It was about 9:30 when General Lafontaine heard of the failure of his counterattack. Under the circumstances, he considered it pointless to throw in the right-hand combat group. Instead he ordered it to fall back behind Raucourt, the 4th Tank Battalion dispersing without ever having been engaged that day. This, says General Ruby, "marked the end of the 55th Division." Some three hours later, an exhausted and saddened Lafontaine, alone with his HQ staff, reported to Grandsard's Corps HQ. Two days later he was officially removed from command of a division that no longer existed.

The 71st, though still not attacked, was not long to survive its sister "B" division. Poor General Baudet, ill and overdue for retirement, who had been told by Grandsard only the previous morning, "The enemy cannot possibly attack today with forces of any size," had wandered about all night in a state of bemusement, from his own PC to that of his right-hand neighbour, the 3rd North African Division, and to Grandsard's HQ. During the night he moved his PC from Raucourt back to La Bagnolle, and once again in the morning to Sommauthe, seven miles further south. Thus, at a moment when the 10th Panzer was beginning to press in from Pont Maugis and Thélonne and grim reports were percolating through about the fate of the 55th, General Baudet had lost all contact with his troops. There were cries of "Tanks to the rear and to the left!" and, says General Menu:

This cry re-echoed from group to group, from section to section. Riflemen and machine-gunners got up and fled, taking with them in their flight those of the artillerymen who had not already beaten them to it, mingled with elements flooding backwards from the neighbouring sector . . . by 1400 hours there was no one any longer in position.

Except for the 205th Regiment earmarked for Lafontaine's counterattack *manquée,* which continued to hold out bravely around Raucourt, the 71st Division—with no one visibly in command—just disintegrated. By the evening of the 14th, it had—in the acid words of General Ruby—"literally faded away at the mere threat of the enemy." Baudet's head too fell into the basket, along with Lafontaine's.

The contagion of fears seems to have spread to Grandsard's X Corps HQ also during the morning of the 14th. Its chief Signals officer, who (according to Grandsard) "since the previous day had shown a regrettable agitation and nervousness," had evacuated the HQ telephone exchange without any orders. "When, towards midday, I wanted to call up Army once again, the exchange no longer replied. Going down to it, I discovered that it had been completely taken apart!" By nightfall, Grandsard himself possessed only the empty husk of a command. All that remained of his corps artillery was one 105 mm and one 155 mm gun which had been in the repair shop. His one intact division, the 3rd North African, was transferred by Huntziger to XVIII Corps. The remaining fragments of X Corps were then placed at the disposal of General Flavigny, commander of the newly constituted XXI Corps which, with the 3rd Armoured and 3rd Motorised Divisions, was hastening up towards the Sedan bulge. With this, Grandsard's X Corps and its hapless "B" divisions disappear from the story, to be replaced by the first of a steady flow of new names and new units.

Guderian swings west

On the morning of the 14th, Sergeant Schulze with the riflemen of the 10th Panzer, who had had such a hard time crossing the Meuse the previous day, reached the heights above Thélonne once tenanted by the 55th Division. "We found their artillery positions left as if they had fled. Some of the guns were still loaded; the enemy had not had time to render the weapons unserviceable." The size of the hole rent in the French defences was also immediately apparent to the German field commanders. During the morning Guderian had driven across the Meuse again to the front of the bridgehead, passing thousands of French prisoners on the way, and had been present while General Kirchner gave the 1st Panzer his orders for warding off the French tank attacks. Shortly after leaving Kirchner, the 1st Panzer concentrations at Chéméry had been attacked with heavy losses by Stukas, unaware that their own troops had advanced so far. Meanwhile, since early morning there had been reports from Luftwaffe Intelligence of hectic transport movements from Verdun, Metz and Soissons towards Sedan —despite heavy bombing of road and rail networks. It deduced that "movement up by railroad of the French Army reserve is apparently beginning."* Going back to the Meuse bridge, Guderian ordered the tank brigade of the 2nd Panzer to hasten across the river immediately behind the 1st, to be in a position to meet the main French counterthrust. The principal task of the 1st Panzer and the Grossdeutschland Regiment must be, with all urgency, to secure the vital high ground at Stonne which commanded the whole Sedan bridgehead. Then, by early afternoon, the breaking

---

* These reserves would have been principally the 3rd Armoured and 3rd Motorised Divisions.

up of Lafontaine's counterattack and the lack of any other immediate French threat made the weakness of the whole enemy
position apparent to Guderian. He returned once more to the 1st
Panzer—which was now facing south on the line Chémery-
Maisoncelle—to put a most important question to General Kirchner: "I asked him whether his entire division could be turned
westwards or whether a flank guard should be left facing south on
the east bank of the Ardennes Canal." By way of reply, Kirchner's
senior staff officer, Major Wenck, promptly interjected Guderian's
own favourite slogan: *"Klotzen, nicht Kleckern."** "That," says
Guderian, "really answered my question." He immediately issued
orders for the 1st and 2nd Panzers "to change direction with all
their forces, to cross the Ardennes Canal and to head west with
the objective of breaking clear through the French defences." To
Kirchner, Guderian supplemented his orders with the dramatic
words: "For the right wheel, road map Rethel!" Driving back to
Corps HQ on the east bank of the Meuse to prepare his detailed
orders for the 15th, Guderian paused on the heights above
Donchery, and, "as I looked at the ground we had come over,
the success of our attack struck me as almost a miracle."

Guderian's order was perhaps the most significant event of the
campaign to date, and with it was introduced a third, decisive
phase. The first phase had been the tricky approach march through
the Ardennes, with its accompanying deception of the "matador's
cloak" operating to the north; the second, the crossing at Sedan
and the constitution of a bridgehead. Now, by facing westwards,
Guderian was poised in readiness for the dash to the Channel
which would cut in two the Allied armies. The Battle of Sedan was
over, and the Battle of France about to begin, bringing with it a
complete change in the character of the campaign. By swinging to
the right, across the Ardennes Canal—the hinge between the
French Second and Ninth Armies—Guderian was also altering the
immediate tactical situation, gravely to the detriment of his opponents. His back turned upon the battered Huntziger, he would
now be striking at the southern flank of Corap's Ninth Army—
already in disarray where it faced Rommel in the north. But Guderian was undoubtedly taking a colossal risk by offering his south-

---

* Literally, "Wallop them, don't tap them"—i.e., Strike as a whole and don't
disperse the effort.

ern flank to the major counterthrust by those reinforcements that
Intelligence had warned were on their way. This flank, of which
Stonne was the keystone, was to be guarded by only the Grossdeutschland and the 10th Panzer. But the Grossdeutschland had
already suffered considerable losses, and it would still be some
time before the tanks of the 10th could intervene effectively.
Would they be able to hold until the consolidating infantry reinforcements, still marching up through the Ardennes, could arrive?
Meanwhile, there was a second contingent source of worry confronting Guderian; would the Allied air forces be able to destroy
the pontoon bridges across the Meuse, those tenuous life lines on
which everything depended?

Allies bomb Sedan

Towards midday on the 14th, Rundstedt, the Army Group commander, had arrived at Sedan to examine the situation. Guderian
reported to him "in the very middle of the bridge, while an air raid
was actually in progress. He asked drily: 'Is it always like this
here?' I could reply with a clear conscience that it was." Throughout the 14th, French and British bombers attacked the Sedan
bridges with a reckless courage that impressed even the German
flak gunners. The news of Rommel's and Guderian's crossing of
the Meuse had reached Air Marshal Barratt on the night of the
13th. Accordingly Barratt, although the AASF had already lost a
quarter of its bombers, had warned Playfair to be ready to throw
in his full strength the next day, but also to prepare plans for retirement. Shortly after daybreak, 10 Battles from Nos. 103 and 150
Squadrons took off for Sedan on two separate missions. Catching
the German flak by surprise in the early morning mist and encountering no Messerschmitts, they returned without loss; but—
with their lightweight bombs—they caused only small damage to
the pontoons which was speedily repaired. It was then Barratt's
intention to switch to Rommel's bridges at Dinant, but—following
the failure of Lafontaine's counterattacks—General Billotte made
an urgent "victory or defeat" appeal to him for all available Allied bombers to be thrown in at Sedan. At midmorning it became
the turn of the French Air Force, which could only scrape together
the pitifully small total of 28 bombers. First of all, 8 Bréguets
from Groupement d' Assaut 18, escorted by fighters, attacked
troop concentrations on the west bank. Heeding the disastrous

losses from the ground-level attacks earlier in the campaign, they flew in at over 2,500 feet; this confused the German flak gunners but it did not make for accuracy. Five of the Bréguets were hit, but only one came down—behind French lines. Next, shortly after noon, 13 lumbering and elderly Amiots and 6 Léos attacked the outskirts of Sedan. Five of the French bombers were shot down, and by evening on the 14th, Groupe 1/12 had only one serviceable machine; consequently, the French air command called off its remaining operations for the day.

In the afternoon, Barratt's AASF returned, throwing in every available Blenheim and Battle. Like the French, the British made the mistake of attacking in small packets; and, in any case, as had already been proved in the north, the slow and under-armed Battles were horribly vulnerable both to enemy ground fire and Messerschmitts.* By now the German defences were thoroughly prepared. Against an impressive escort of 250 Allied fighters, Loerzer and Richthofen fielded 814 machines; the German flyers called it "fighter's day." But in truth the day belonged at least as much to Guderian's light flak teams. With that extraordinary organisational brilliance which characterised the whole Sedan operation, Guderian had somehow disentangled his flak batteries from the columns still stretching across the Ardennes and rushed them forward so that they now ringed the pontoon bridges with an imposing concentration of firepower. Captain von Kielmansegg stood watching near the 1st Panzer bridge at Gaulier:

The summer landscape with the quietly flowing river, the light green of the meadows bordered by the darker summits of the more distant heights, spanned by a brilliantly blue sky, is filled with the racket of war. For hours at a time, the dull explosions of the bombs, the quick tack-tack of the machine-guns, the different notes, and the various effects of the separate flak calibres, mingles with the droning of the aircraft motors and the roar of the divisions passing over the bridges unimpeded. The flak soldiers serve their guns with rolled up shirt sleeves, covered in sweat, and carry out their defensive role with almost sporting ambition, encouraged by the spectators occasionally coming up from the ranks of the troops waiting at the crossing. Again and again an enemy aircraft crashes out of the sky, dragging a long black plume

---

* Against fighter attack from the rear the Battles (designed in 1933) had only one flexibly mounted Lewis gun; roughly the same armament as that carried by the aircraft of 1914–18.

of smoke behind it, which after the crash of the succeeding explosion remains for some time perpendicular in the warm air. Occasionally from the falling machines one or two white parachutes release themselves and float slowly to earth. . . .

In the short time that I am at the bridge, barely an hour, eleven planes alone were brought down.

For the RAF the Meuse that day was an unimaginable hell, a real Valley of Death from which few returned. In it, the targets they had to hit were mere threads 60 yards long by a few feet wide, and more than one German writer testifies to the "unbelievable bravery" with which the hopelessly outclassed Battles pressed home their attacks. No. 12 Squadron—the "Dirty Dozen" which had already suffered so heavily at Maastricht—lost four out of its remaining five planes; No. 150 Squadron, four out of four. Altogether, out of 71 bombers engaged, 40 did not return. As the RAF official history soberly remarks: "No higher rate of loss in an operation of comparable size has ever been experienced by the Royal Air Force."

That evening 28 Blenheims from Bomber Command continued the attacks; they lost a quarter of their numbers. The Germans later claimed to have shot down 200 Allied planes, bombers and fighters; Guderian's flak—the commander of which, Colonel von Hippel, was decorated with the Ritterkreuz for his work that day— was said to have accounted alone for 112 aircraft. These claims were certainly exaggerated,* but the losses were high enough to break the back of the Allied tactical bombing potential. The Luftwaffe too had suffered fairly heavy casualties, including the death of two of its most senior combat leaders: Major General von Stutterheim and Colonel Schwartzkopf, the Stuka ace. The constant bombing attacks had undoubtedly shaken German nerves, and an entry in the XIX Panzer Corps War Diary for that evening notes: "The completion of the military bridge at Donchery had not yet been carried out owing to heavy flanking artillery fire and long bombing attacks on the bridging points. . . . Our fighter cover is inadequate." But the bridges had not been destroyed; the procession of Guderian's armour and supplies across the Meuse had been briefly delayed, but not halted. Thus it was a grotesque

---

* Total French and British losses from the Sedan action on May 14th were probably nearer 90.

piece of wishful thinking on the part of General Georges to inform Barratt in the evening that the air attacks had enabled Huntziger to "contain" the bridgehead, and to add a prediction that the "centre of interest" would shift next day to Dinant. As it was, that black day marked the supreme effort of the Allied bomber forces; an effort that could never again be repeated in this campaign—and it had failed in its objective.

The heroic sacrifice of Barratt's Battle squadrons had certainly not halted the impetus of the crucial right wheel by the 1st and 2nd Panzers. During the morning, even before Guderian's momentous decision, the forceful Colonel Balck had already seized a crossing point over the river Bar and the closely parallel Ardennes Canal near Omicourt against light resistance. All the way down to its confluence with the Meuse, the Bar valley is very wide and open and there are no natural defensive positions comparable to La Marfée heights to the east, now lost to the French. The Bar itself is no more than what is sometimes described in France as a *pipi du chat,* 30 feet wide in most places, and the bridges over it appear not to have been destroyed. Westwards from the Bar, the country transforms itself rapidly into the great monotonous plain of northern France, stretching all the way to the Channel, with no serious defensive feature until the river Oise just short of St. Quentin. Swiftly the tanks of the 1st and 2nd Panzer began pushing over the Bar crossing places secured for them by Balck's riflemen. Shortly after midday, there was a third French tank attack, coming up from the southwest, against the 1st Panzer, which had to refurnish its tanks with ammunition right up in the firing line. But by 3 P.M. there was a noticeable slackening in the French resistance southwest of the Bar. At least in this direction, the audacity of Guderian's right wheel seemed justified so far.

French reinforcements to Sedan

On the French side, the forces sent by Huntziger (on the night of the 13th) to hold the Bar consisted of the 5th DLC and the 1st Cavalry Brigade—both badly knocked about during the early skirmishes in the Ardennes—under command of General Chanoine. To link up with them, on the Second and Ninth Army hinge, General Corap had dispatched Colonel Marc's 3rd Spahi Brigade—which had retired with such disastrous precipitancy from the Semois—and the 53rd Division. But, owing to a series of typical counterorders which had sent the 53rd chasing around in circles all night, only the Spahis and Chanoine's group were in position that morning and it was upon them that the weight of Guderian's right wheel had fallen.

Commanded by General Etchberrigaray, the 53rd was the third of those French "B" divisions so disastrously located around Sedan at the time of the German attack. It had spent the winter building the fortifications in the north, and the early spring working on farms outside Paris. Constituting Corap's reserve for his right-hand sector, on May 12th, the 53rd had been ordered to back up General Libaud's XLI Corps, between Mézières and the Bar. At 2100 hours on the 13th, Corap warned Libaud that contact had been lost with the Second Army at Sedan, and therefore the 53rd Division should be sent to hold the Bar, facing east. Then, three-quarters of an hour later when the 53rd was already under way, Libaud received another message from Corap, announcing (for no very clear reason) that the situation had become less critical and that the 53rd was to resume its position facing *north*—i.e., in support of the Ninth Army, anticipating a threat coming via Mézières. At 2230 hours, Libaud retransmitted this latest order to General Etchberrigaray; but on his way the liaison officer carrying it received another counterorder direct from Corap, instructing the 53rd once again to deploy along the Bar. Meanwhile, to add to its sense of insecurity the division in its peregrinations was soon running into those demoralising fugitives encountered by other reinforcements on that night of May 13th. Says General Doumenc: "Elements of our own artillery passed with their trucks but without any guns. Their officers declared that there was no longer any infantry in front of them; that the Germans had crossed the Meuse near Donchery, that they were already on the Ardennes Canal." In this nocturnal confusion, General Etchberrigaray had the greatest difficulty catching up with his troops to marshal them. By morning, the 53rd Division was so dispersed that it would be unable to reach the Bar in time to be of any use during the 14th. Thus neither in its quality nor in its location was it exactly the ideal formation with which to bar the vital gateway between Huntziger and Corap against the all-out onslaught Guderian was about to mount.

After some hard fighting in which the French cavalry put up a splendid resistance, by nightfall on the 14th of May Colonel

Balck's German riflemen—still at the apex of Guderian's thrust—had reached their objective at Singly. Their losses had by no means been light; Balck had lost a large number of his officers and riflemen, and only three-quarters of the 1st Panzer's tanks were still fit for action. But the division had already captured 3,000 prisoners and 28 guns, and had knocked out some 50 French tanks. During the night, the 1st and 2nd Panzer brought all their tanks across the Bar in readiness for the big push westwards on the 15th.

Grossdeutschland at Stonne

On the other side of Guderian's bridgehead, Sergeant Major Rubarth and his exhausted engineers had been overjoyed to see the first of the 10th Panzer's tanks coming through the morning mist, after an anxious night. But during the day, a combination of flanking French artillery fire, RAF bomb damage to the pontoons and various technical difficulties had delayed crossings still more than in the 1st and 2nd Panzer sectors. Consequently, the 10th would not be able to lend its full weight to the vital, defensive role allotted it in Guderian's right wheel until the 15th. Meanwhile it was up to the Grossdeutschland—now detached from the 1st Panzer and returned once more to the 10th—to secure the key heights around Stonne, some 12 miles south of Sedan, against the enemy's anticipated major counterattack. Moving up towards Stonne, the Grossdeutschland was strafed by French Moranes. The war diarist of the 15th Company watched with detached curiosity as the Moranes released two bombs on it:

Helplessly we shoot back with our weapons! We look at each other. Where is the explosion? Somebody cries "It's a dud." Corporal Waldemar Kiedrowski from Essen . . . leaps out of the ditch onto one of the duds . . . Kiedrowski throws it onto the street—the bomb blows up! There is nothing left of Corporal Kiedrowski! Corporal Schieg loses a leg—further behind us the Morane crashes, a victim to our machine-guns—Kiedrowski is our first dead. Nobody can find him, nobody can bury him!

And what of the counterattack by the Second Army, to be launched with the powerful units that General Georges had dispatched to it? In the carefully measured words of General Ruby, such a thrust against the flank of Guderian's bridgehead at a moment when the main weight of the panzers was performing its

90-degree turn, leaving the flank to be guarded by the infantry of the Grossdeutschland, would probably have gained—on the evening of May 14th—"a fine local success, the repercussions of which . . . would have been felt beyond the boundaries of the (Second) Army."

The 3rd Armoured at Stonne

General Brocard's 3rd Armoured Division—together with its sisters, the 1st and 2nd—constituted one of the rooks of the French chessboard; they were the most powerful pieces that General Georges had to play. It had two battalions of new Hotchkiss H–39s, and—although fewer in overall numbers—these should have been a match for the extended 10th Panzer, half of whose tanks were light Mark I and II, which were not designed for tank-versus-tank engagements. Its morale was excellent; on the other hand, it was such a newly constituted division that its battalions had only started divisional training on May 1st, and some of its tank engines were not yet properly run in. The 3rd Motorised Infantry Division (General Bertin-Boussu) was also a first-rate unit, at the peak of its training. When the 3rd Armoured received its movement orders on the afternoon of May 12th it had been in training north of Reims, some 40 miles away, and it was then generally believed that the division was being transferred to another training area; not that it was going to be pitched into battle. Though not actually bombed on its approach march by the Luftwaffe, the 3rd Armoured encountered many delays resulting from bomb damage, and it lacked engineers or sappers to put the roads in order. The heavy "B" tanks had had difficulty crossing the Aisne, and at one place the encumberment caused by refugees and military fugitives was such that they were compelled to force a passage by crushing cars that obstructed their way.

What the reinforcements moving up to Sedan ran into on the roads is graphically described by Marcel Lerecouvreux.* Well behind the front, bridges and telephone exchanges were discovered to have been destroyed with precipitate haste, on "superior orders"—the origins of which were never traced, but were later

---

* His unit, the 2nd DLC, having regrouped after its withdrawal from the Ardennes, was due to attack on the right of Flavigny's group, comprising the 3rd Armoured and the 3rd DIM.

wildly attributed to the fifth column. Meanwhile, fresh bands of fugitives were arriving the whole time.

One squadron of the 5th Cuirassiers discovered a sergeant major who had torn off his badges of rank, so as to take flight more easily, both from the enemy and from his own responsibilities; later a lieutenant of the divisional anti-tank battery reported fugitives among whom were found two lieutenants who had similarly degraded themselves; he made this troop turn about under threat of his sub-machine gun. All these cowards were causing terrifying rumours to run around, notably about the aerial bombardments to which they had been subjected, and about the avalanche of tanks which was closely pursuing them. . . . One had to seek proper justification for the rout. . . . The fugitives said that they had been pursued by formidable masses of tanks (some spoke of 400, others of 500, or even of 5,000!).

Such panic-spreading tales, Lerecouvreux goes on to explain, "were probably one of the causes that had made excessively nervous commanders carry out the hasty demolitions which had taken place behind us." Closer to the front, the rumours had caused the wholesale disappearance of a battalion of sappers charged with organising the defences of the village of Vaux. In the confusion, some French units "reacting to mutual suspicions had machine-gunned and fired at each other with rifles; near Raucourt in particular two battalions had thus inflicted upon each other some fairly serious losses." At Sommauthe on the way towards Stonne there were scenes of chaos and pillage where "vehicles lay about on the side of the road, smashed during the precipitate retreat without this even being the work of the enemy, and left by their drivers who had completely lost their heads." Here were also some abandoned horse-drawn artillery, one gun of which was still harnessed to its dejected horses, standing in the middle of a small stream. Despite the haste of their flight, the fugitives had nevertheless found time to pillage everything, even the medical stores. "The spectacle of all this debris, which inscribed our defeat upon the ground," says Lerecouvreux, "was lamentable and it gripped my heart."

For all the delays and degrading panic it had experienced on the approach march, the 3rd Armoured reached its assembly area behind Stonne at 6 A.M. on the 14th, full of spirit and eager to have a go at the enemy. General Brocard promptly reported to Second Army HQ at Senuc, where he met the commander of the newly constituted XXI Corps,* General Flavigny, who handed him these orders: XXI Corps was to

(A) take up positions along the second line to the east of the Bar . . . and contain the bottom of the pocket created by the enemy. . . .
(B) having contained the enemy, counter-attack at the earliest in the direction of Maisoncelle–Bulson–Sedan. . . .

Specifically, the 3rd Armoured was to hasten its refuelling and attack in coordination with the 3rd Motorised, "as soon as possible," towards Bulson with the object of "throwing the enemy back across the Meuse." But, as Colonel Goutard points out, the two terms of "containment" (that old stand-by from 1918) and "counter-attack" in Flavigny's orders were contradictory: "Containment is defensive and demands linear dispersion along a front; counter-attack is offensive and requires concentration in depth at one point. . . . How could one group fulfil these contradictory missions simultaneously, or even one after the other? And when containment has been effected, the opportunity for counter-attack would be over; it would be too late. It was obvious that, with our mania for an unbroken front, the containing mission would have priority."

Flavigny's orders ended ominously: "The time of the counter-attack will be fixed later." Brocard then brought to Flavigny's attention the state of his division after its night march of a full 30 miles. He did not think it would be ready to attack for some ten hours. (How closely this resembled the story of the 1st Armoured Division at Dinant!) Rejecting Brocard's suggestion that H Hour be fixed for 4 P.M., Flavigny told him by word of mouth to attack at 11 A.M. But Brocard seems to have been tardy in issuing his orders, while refuelling proceeded with painful slowness, so that the 3rd Armoured was not ready to set off for its start line before 1 P.M. Even its progress was impeded by the results of bombing and more waves of fugitives to such an extent that the division was not in fact deployed for attack until 4 P.M. Meanwhile, the 3rd Motorised Division had experienced still worse hold-ups on its approach march, and instead of reaching the bat-

---

* Comprising the 3rd Armoured, 3rd Motorised, 5th Cavalry Divisions and the 1st Cavalry Brigade.

tle area on the morning of the 14th, by 4 P.M. it was only able
to support the 3rd Armoured with three reconnaissance groups.
But there yet remained four hours of daylight for the counterattack, and—says General Ruby—"the tank crews were champing at
the bit in their eagerness."

By this time, however, the speed with which the battle front
was changing had made its impression on General Flavigny. He
was now alone at Senuc; Huntziger, fearing Second Army HQ
to be threatened by the enemy, had moved it back to Verdun.
Himself an old tank man, Flavigny (according to General Ruby)
also seems to have begun to entertain doubts as to the technical
qualities of Brocard's division, with its limited training. Whatever the combination of his motives, at 3:30 P.M., Flavigny
made a fateful decision. He would abandon the attack part of
his orders in favour of that 1918 principle of "containment first."
"The most important thing," he said, "was to ensure the safety
of the second line."

In consequence, the 3rd Armoured was ordered to disperse
itself defensively over a front of some 12 miles, from Omont west
of the Bar to Stonne. On all tracks and potential corridors of
penetration it was to form "corks," each comprised of one "B"
and two H–39 tanks. During the night this powerful, modern unit
was thus broken up into a series of penny packets. "From then
on," says Colonel Goutard, "there was a line, a few tanks but no
3rd Armoured Division. The steel lance was buried for ever,
and so was the counter-attack." The best—and last—opportunity
of administering a severe check to Guderian before he burst out
of his bridgehead had been thrown away. It was a tragic error of
judgement.

The generals: Georges and Huntziger

On May 13th General Georges, in order to relieve the over-
burdened Billotte from responsibility for the fighting at Sedan as
well, had transferred the Second Army from No. 1 Army Group
to his direct control. Thus it was to Georges that Huntziger had
to report back on the 14th. Although his headquarters attempted
to fob British correspondents off with the bland statement that
"we are withdrawing our advance posts, as has always been our
intention," Huntziger warned Georges that morning that some
of his troops were not holding; "that men had been seen emerg-

ing from block-houses with uplifted arms and that he had given orders to open fire on them."

Huntziger's references to Flavigny's counterattack seem, however, to have been so discreet as to be almost evasive. At 7 P.M. his Chief of Staff told Georges that it had been unable to begin "for technical reasons." Half an hour later Huntziger was on the telephone himself, claiming with ill-founded optimism that "the enemy advance has been contained by Flavigny's *groupement* between the Ardennes Canal and the Meuse."* Georges, obviously much vexed by Huntziger's procrastination but at the same time still only partially aware of the full gravity of the situation at Sedan, replied sharply:

The 3rd Armoured Division was put at your disposal in order to counterattack at Sedan. Tomorrow, therefore, you must vigorously pursue the operation so well started (sic!) today by pushing on as far as you can towards the Meuse, and consolidating with the infantry the terrain conquered by the tanks. This is the only way to gain a supremacy over the enemy and to paralyse his whole advance to the west and south.

By the end of the 14th, Huntziger was in fact far from feeling the optimism which he attempted to impart in his messages to Georges. To one of his officers, he remarked sadly, "I shall always be *le vaincu de Sedan.*" In his depression at the buffeting his army had received he now made a miscalculation on an even graver scale than Flavigny's halting of the counterattack and dispersal of the 3rd Armoured. Reacting in a manner typical of the epoch in which the Maginot Line had come to be regarded as the be-all and end-all of French military policy, Huntziger concluded that Guderian's thrust was aimed principally at outflanking the Maginot Line and then rolling it up from the north. Thus he decided to meet this notional threat by pivoting on his right heel, which was planted where the Line ended near Longwy, and swinging back the centre of his army from its position astride the Meuse at Mouzon to one further back at Inor. In effect, this would mean the relinquishment, without fighting, of over 130 bunkers along the Meuse, and the expansion of the 4-mile-wide

---

* This was duly passed on to Gamelin, with the addition of a little extra saccharine at "Les Bondons."

Donchery–Wadelincourt pocket into a large breach more than 15 miles across. It also meant that the 10th Panzer crossing point could no longer be brought under interdiction fire by Huntziger's flank artillery, a circumstance which in turn critically reduced the prospects of any counterattack that might be launched on the 15th. But worst of all, Huntziger's decision meant that the Second Army would in fact be *pulling away* from the Ninth, thereby increasing the gap through which Guderian was planning to burst.

The generals: Guderian and Kleist

At his HQ near La Chapelle that night Guderian was drafting his orders for the breakout by the 1st and 2nd Panzers the next day. In one hop of over 20 miles they were to "reach as primary objective the line Wasigny–Rethel," while the Corps reconnaissance was to probe as far ahead as Montcornet. These orders immediately provoked another heated disagreement between Guderian and his superior, Kleist. Having studied the Intelligence reports on the movement of Flavigny's reinforcements towards Stonne, Kleist—further removed from battlefield realities than Guderian—had become extremely nervous for the safety of that southern flank. It was an anxiety that would plague the German senior commanders repeatedly from this day on, as indeed it had during the planning stages of *Sichelschnitt*. Kleist and other German officers of his generation could not help being haunted by memories of how, in 1914, victory had been snatched from them on the Marne after Kluck had wheeled inwards prematurely, thereby exposing his flank to Gallieni's counterattack out of Paris.* Instead of pushing on to Rethel, Kleist now told Guderian that he would prefer to halt and consolidate on the line Montigny–Bouvellemont, just a mile or two beyond where the panzers had come to rest that same night. Guderian was furious. According to the XIX Corps War Diary, he "bitterly criticised this plan which throws away the victory." After some forceful argument, Guderian won and his orders for the 15th were issued as intended. If any additional justification was required for Flavigny's launch-

---

* Another factor was the serious shortage of fuel threatening the panzers at this stage in the campaign. To an important extent the planning of *Sichelschnitt* had been predicated on the German ability to supplement its own reserves from captured enemy supplies.

ing his counterattack on the 14th—Kleist's hesitancy certainly seems to provide it.

Terror at Rotterdam

Holland was at her last gasp. During the morning of the 14th, negotiations for a cease-fire had begun between Dutch and German representatives outside Rotterdam. Meanwhile the Luftwaffe was preparing a "terror" blow against the city in case the Dutch there continued to resist. At 1400 hours, 60 He–111s bombed the old centre of the city for twenty minutes, utterly unopposed, as the Dutch Air Force had been annihilated. The Germans have since claimed that efforts were made to call off the raid, but the planes—already airborne—never received the signals. Whatever the explanation, it was a brutal act which shocked world opinion at the time. Just under 900 people were killed, but in the terror of the moment the Dutch Foreign Minister put the figure at 30,000 —an exaggeration which only added to the paralysing alarm felt in France at the apparently invincible ferocity of the German war machine. Shortly before 10 o'clock that night Parisians listening to their radios heard Holland announce the news of her capitulation.

Tank battle in the Gembloux Gap

On the front in northern Belgium, the BEF had faced its first serious challenge on the 14th. Bock's forces attempted to take Louvain, but were repulsed by a fierce barrage from the 60-pounders of Montgomery's 3rd Division. But it was further south, on the French First Army's front, that the heaviest fighting again took place. The previous night Prioux's Cavalry Corps had withdrawn, after the savage tank battles of that day, behind the Belgian antitank obstacle running south of Perwez. Shortly after dawn on the 13th, Hoeppner's panzers began to smash through it, supported by powerful concentrations of artillery. They succeeded in forcing a 200-foot breach, but by throwing in every gun, tank and soldier Prioux managed to push them back. By late afternoon Blanchard's First Army had at last established itself in position in the Gembloux Gap. The role of the Cavalry Corps was now fulfilled, and in the late afternoon it was pulled back for reorganisation in the rear of Blanchard's main line. The first great tank battle of the campaign was over. In Paris the papers claimed victory, and indeed Prioux's tank crews had fought with fiercest determination—something very different from the performance already evinced on the French Second and Ninth Army fronts. But Prioux's losses had been appallingly heavy; one-third of the new medium Somuas and two-thirds of the Hotchkisses had been knocked out, with some units losing up to 60 percent of their effectives. The strategic impact of this on the course of the battle as a whole was not to be underestimated. That night Gamelin was contemplating the concentration of all armoured and motorised forces on the right of the First Army so as to attack the northern flank of the Ardennes break-through. The crippling of the elite Cavalry Corps now rendered this proposition hardly feasible.

Gamelin ill-informed

Back at GQG, Gamelin's light had been observed burning well after midnight on the 13th–14th. The next morning he visited Georges's HQ at La Ferté, and again in the afternoon. In his memoirs he says that his "presence there was necessary from a point of view of morale." Georges had evidently not recovered from the breakdown which Beaufre had witnessed the previous night—no doubt exacerbated by the debilitating effects of his old wound. However shocked he was by what he saw at "Les Bondons," Gamelin nevertheless admits elsewhere that—at the time—the situation at Sedan seemed to him less grave than it really was. For this Huntziger's overoptimistic reports, to which General Georges had added his own rose-tinted glaze, are to be blamed. At 0730 hours Georges had fed the following misleading fragments of information to the Generalissimo: "Ninth Army—the counter-attack at Houx did not succeed, the infantry not having followed the tanks. . . . Second Army—the breach at Sedan has been plugged on the halt line. . . . Counter-attack with serious forces was unleashed this morning at 0430 hours." At 1030 hours, fuller reports gave GQG the impression that the Second Army was "in hand and that the troops are holding." A couple of hours later, Captain Beaufre telephoned news that was rather more disquieting: "Panic, with the 5th Light Cavalry Division. The Germans are at Omicourt, on the Bar Canal." At 1625, Gamelin heard the first news that Rommel had got his tanks across the Meuse. Late that evening he received a disagreeable canard (part

of the Germans' skilful deception plan) about an imminent
enemy attack through Switzerland; Goebbels was reported as having declared that "within twice 24 hours there will no longer be
any neutral states in Europe." Could it indeed be that the attack
at Sedan, for all its apparent force, was *not* the main German effort. The Wehrmacht communiqué of the 14th still continued to
make no great capital out of the Meuse crossings. Were the Germans perhaps keeping up their sleeve a flanking attack on the
Maginot Line from the Swiss end as well? Obviously, one had to
remain cautious about moving reinforcements from behind the
Line. The day ended for Gamelin with a last unrealistic report
about Sedan from "Les Bondons":

Not much has changed since the last report. Still some small infiltra-
tions in the area of Mézières–Charleville. There has not been any
counter-attack at Sedan, but violent aerial bombardment and blocking
action. The German advance appears to be blocked. . . . All the
prisoners indicate the fatigue of the German troops.

Says Colonel Bardies acidly of Georges's optimism:

It aimed at nothing but minimising the setbacks, at reassuring General Gamelin, and above him the Government, and above the Government, public opinion . . . one has the impression that GQG did not
yet believe in a disaster, and as a result did not envisage any means of
major scope to counteract it.

For all the reassuring noises emanating from La Ferté and Vincennes, there were those in Paris who on the 14th already sensed
that not all was well at the front. Alexander Werth of the *Manchester Guardian* noted in his diary: "Gloom at the office. . . .
The parachutist who descended on Paris yesterday was only a
deflated sausage balloon." Paul Baudouin, the secretary to Reynaud's War Cabinet, relates how he had just been to

a lunch in honour of the Prime Minister and the Foreign Minister of
Luxembourg, and of the Belgian Foreign and Finance Ministers, and
I was just coming out when Colonel Villelume said that he wanted
to speak to me urgently. At that moment I was walking on the big lawn
of the Quai d'Orsay in glorious sunshine, but a chill came over me.
. . . The news was very bad; Huntziger's Army had been violently

attacked and some fortifications in the Sedan district had been lost. We felt that the situation had suddenly become tragic.

A meeting of the War Cabinet was convened at the Élysée that afternoon at which Gamelin confirmed that the news was bad. (But just how bad he did not say, for the simple reason that he did not know.) He admitted he was "surprised," but externally continued to show every sign of Joffrian sang-froid.

In London the British Government also remained oblivious of the full gravity of events.

14

The Breakout
MAY 15th

If our tanks are distinctly superior to those of the enemy,
our fighters dominate perhaps even more the enemy
airforce.
—*Le Temps,* May 15th

Responsible circles lay stress on the fact that north of
Sedan, inclusive, a war of movement is in progress, and
the conflict must therefore inevitably sway to and fro
until the main bodies get to grips and a continuous front
is established. . . . Under a seemingly endless torrent of
bombs, backed up by artillery barrage from the
French forces, the Germans wavered and then began
to fall back. They found the roads to their rear choked
and blocked in many places by wrecked and overturned
lorries, tanks, armoured cars, and supply transport.
—*The Times,* May 16th

Upon the crossing of the Meuse in the area of Sedan,
with the closest cooperation of the Luftwaffe, the protective wall of France—the Maginot Line—has been
broken in its extension to the northwest.
—Wehrmacht Communiqué, May 15th

Corap: Another terrible day

MAY 14TH had been a terrible day for General Corap. What the
incessant bombing by the Luftwaffe, which had concentrated its
attention on the Ninth Army that day, had done to the morale of
his battered divisions made a deep impression upon him. But
most of all he was concerned at the growth of Rommel's pocket
west of Dinant; and now Guderian was slicing deep into his other
flank. Late that night he took a fatal decision, and at 2 A.M. on
the 15th he was telephoning Billotte to report that he had intended

to abandon the whole line of the Meuse. He proposed withdrawing the Ninth Army behind the French frontier positions which they had left just five days earlier in fulfilment of the Dyle Plan. Billotte raised no objection in principle, but instructed Corap to "establish an intermediate stop line on the line of Walcourt–Mariembourg–Rocroi–Signy-l'Abbaye,"—roughly along the main road running north to south from Charleroi to Rethel. But Billotte's "intermediate line" existed solely on paper, and in the chaos of communications inside the Ninth Army this order marked the beginning of its disintegration. Some of Corap's units only received orders to halt on the barrier position which General Martin had been trying to establish behind Florennes the previous evening; others duly pulled back to the "intermediate line." Some were unable to move at all; others, receiving no orders, simply disbanded and straggled westwards of their own accord. In a state of high emotion, Corap telephoned General d'Astier begging for air support at dawn to cover his withdrawal. Although his orders were to devote all forces to Huntziger's front, d'Astier said he would see what he could do; but Corap was even unable to tell him precisely where his own front lay.

Such was the situation at Army level as dawn broke on the 15th. In effect, Huntziger the previous evening had opened one sluice gate; Corap was now opening the other. Through the pair of them the flood was about to burst into France.

Rommel strikes again

Opposite Rommel's bridgehead, the "stop line" decreed by Corap ran close by Philippeville, some 12 miles from where Rommel had come to a halt on the 14th. But his orders to the 7th Panzer for the 15th were to "thrust straight through in one stride" to the Cerfontaine area—8 miles to the *west* of Philippeville. Rommel himself intended to ride with Rothenburg's tanks so as to direct operations from up forward, leaving divisional HQ in the hands of his senior staff officer, the able Major Heidkämper who was to end the war as a lieutenant-general. Guarding his right flank, but slightly behind, came Colonel Werner's tanks from the 5th Panzer. At about 0800 hours a Luftwaffe liaison officer informed Rommel that Stuka support would be available for the 7th Panzer that day. Rommel called for them to go into action immediately just ahead of his tanks, which were already beginning

The panzer advance: May 15th–17th

to move forward. Within the next hour they came up against General Bruneau's 1st Armoured Division, positioned near Flavion, in what Rommel describes as a "brief engagement."

On reaching its concentration area late on the night of the 14th, Bruneau's tank battalions had adopted a defensive stance of *"rassemblement gardé"* while waiting for the arrival of the fuel tankers which Bruneau had mistakenly placed at the rear of his column. Agonisingly the hours ticked by and still the tankers, held up by the appalling chaos on the roads, did not arrive. Finally Bruneau had told General Martin that he could not possibly attack at dawn, as prescribed by XI Corps. Refuelling, he now reckoned, would be complete only by the end of the morning. Accordingly, he sent back his artillery, deploying one lone battery out of six in support of his immobilised armour.* Soon after dawn, Bruneau learned that his units were being heavily dive-bombed. Then at 0830 hours his two battalions of heavy "B" tanks were caught by a dense concentration of Rommel's panzers just as they were refuelling. A confused action ensued at close range. One French squadron managed to counterattack, inflicting noteworthy losses. Once again the Germans discovered that their 37 mm guns could not penetrate the massive "B" tanks, that their best bet lay in shooting off the tracks. But many of these superb instruments, tragically immobilised like hobbled elephants by the lack of fuel, simply had to be set on fire in haste by their own crews.

With that magical feeling for the situation which characterised all his movements, Rommel then swung round Bruneau's flank to continue his thrust towards the west. Having struck one first hard blow at the 1st Armoured, he left the *coup de grâce* to be administered by the approaching 5th Panzer. Bruneau, making an accurate appreciation of Rommel's intent from the consequent lull in the fighting, at 2 P.M. ordered his division to regroup north of Florennes, facing southeast. But by the time the order reached his tanks they were inextricably engaged in heavy fighting—this time with Colonel Werner's "Red Devils"† from the 5th Panzer.

---

* This decision exemplified the French commanders' unawareness of the speed with which the panzers were about to move; that same morning General Sancelme of the 4th North African Division, the other component in Corap's counterattack against Rommel, had also sent his guns to the rear.

† So called from the insignia of the 31st Panzer Regiment.

The afternoon's armoured battle—from the French point of view —is described by a subaltern fighting in a "B" tank of the 37th Battalion:

"En avant!" orders the *Adour,* the Captain's tank. . . . The *Gard* is on my right, the Captain is to the right of the *Gard.* . . . At that moment, a shell strikes the armour on the left side! Towards the road, red lights flare up on the level of a low hedge; another shell in the armour plate! I hesitate to shoot back, because I thought it was a mistake by one of ours; then I traversed my turret towards the flames, and shoot off 5 high explosive shells at the hedge, after which nothing moves any longer. I continue my advance and arrive at the woods which mark the edge of the plateau, and it is there that the battle begins. The driver shouts: "A tank on the edge of the wood in front of us!" It was certainly an enemy! A Mark IV on which I directed the fire of the 75. . . . Near a burning German tank, men are climbing and crawling towards the undergrowth. The whole of our left flank is crowded with big German tanks; I can make them out more or less indistinctly, because they are camouflaged, broad-side on and immobile.

At this moment, the co-driver of the Captain informs me that the Captain, wounded in the stomach and in the legs, is handing over the command to me. The new Mark IVs burst into flames under our fire, but my radiators are themselves smashed in; my 75 is hit on the side of the muzzle, and remains in a position of maximum recoil; I continue with the 47. Feeling myself harassed, I try to change position and to move myself in a thicket further to the south. The wood is being hammered by a 105 mm., and shell holes open up not far from us. From a distance, I can make out the *Gard,* the door of whose turret is open. . . . On my right a knocked out tank of the 28th; the line of German tanks forms a semi-circle of vehicles which I estimate in number at between 50 to 60.

I give the order to the tanks of my Company to retire . . . *Ourcq* and *Yser* withdraw slowly, while I observe *Hérault* burning.

By the late afternoon the 37th Battalion was reduced to four "B" tanks; its sister, the 28th, had only two left in fit state to comply with Bruneau's order to withdraw; and the 26th could muster less than a score of its light tanks. Only the 25th (light) Tank Battalion remained more or less intact, having lost its way the previous night and arriving too late to take part in the action. Thus was the first of General Georges's "rooks" destroyed as an effective force. The tank crews of the French 1st Armoured had fought bravely and well, and claimed to have knocked out some 100 German tanks.* But they had been squandered, not in a bold armoured counterstroke, but piecemeal in a battle of encounter. The division had been engaged, remarks Colonel Bardies, "as in times gone past squadrons of cuirassiers were engaged, to cover a rout in giving them the order to die." Under cover of night the 1st Armoured crept back to Beaumont, and then to Solre-le-Château behind the French frontier positions. When Bruneau saw it the next day, it had only 17 tanks left, the remainder having lost their way or run out of fuel during the night's withdrawal.†

Meanwhile, sweeping around the 1st Armoured, Rommel's panzers were now out in the open, inflicting havoc upon the Ninth Army's "soft" rear areas. On the way to Philippeville, Rommel himself noted passing

numerous guns and vehicles‡ belonging to a French unit, whose men had tumbled headlong into the woods at the approach of our tanks, having probably already suffered heavily under our dive-bombers. Enormous craters compelled us to make several detours through the wood. About 3 miles north-west of Philippeville there was a brief exchange of fire with French troops occupying the hills and woods south of Philippeville. Our tanks fought the action on the move, with turrets traversed left, and the enemy was soon silenced. From time to time enemy anti-tank guns, tanks and armoured cars were shot up. Fire was also scattered into the woods on our flanks as we drove past.

Already by midday Rommel had occupied Philippeville, and was pushing on to Cerfontaine 6 miles beyond, thereby breaching in one swift bound Billotte's and Corap's "intermediate line" even before it could be occupied. Men and machines were exhausted. One of his panzer commanders records:

A number of vehicles broken down, even my command vehicle could no longer keep up and I had to have it towed by a truck. . . . I'm dead tired . . . two days and three nights, not a moment of rest, food

---

* The total may have been exaggerated.

† But the fact that the 1st Armoured had virtually ceased to exist was not learned by Ninth Army HQ, No. 1 Army Group, nor GQG until much later.

‡ Very probably the artillery and supply echelons that Bruneau had sent to the rear.

consists of two slices of bread, a hellish thirst. Next day we are to have a rest.* The vehicle badly needs service, wire has wound itself around the drive wheel, and the batteries are run down. . . . We look like pigs, muddy, sticky and without a shave for several days. I am tottering with fatigue, and have to help myself with Pervitin tablets. The radio operators can only be kept awake with difficulty.

But Rommel was a hard taskmaster. Furious to discover that Bismarck's weary riflemen were lagging nearly 10 miles behind the tanks, creating a gap into which enemy elements were infiltrating, he turned about and headed eastward to chase them up. Along the route Rommel had covered that morning, he found two tanks which had broken down.

Their crews were in process of collecting prisoners, and a few who had already come in were standing around. Now hundreds of French motorcyclists came out of the bushes and, together with their officers, slowly laid down their arms. Others tried to make a quick getaway down the road to the south.

I now occupied myself for a short time with the prisoners. Among them were several officers, from whom I received a number of requests, including, among other things, permission to keep their batmen and to have their kit picked up from Philippeville, where it had been left.

His mission accomplished, Rommel headed westwards once again at high speed and just short of Cerfontaine he met "a body of fully armed French motorcyclists coming in the opposite direction, and picked them up as they passed. Most of them were so shaken at suddenly finding themselves in a German column that they drove their machines into the ditch and were in no position to put up a fight." From his panzer camp at Cerfontaine, "looking back east from the summit of the hill, as night fell, endless pillars of dust could be seen rising as far as the eye could reach—comforting signs that the 7th Panzer Division's move into the conquered territory had begun." Rommel's losses for that day had totalled just 15 killed; he had advanced over 17 miles, taken 450 prisoners, knocked out or captured 75 tanks, and struck a decisive blow against the Ninth Army and its hopes for a counterattack.

---

* This was optimism!

The Ninth Army breaks

At 4 A.M. on the 15th, Billotte had informed Georges on the telephone that "the Ninth Army is in a critical position." By nightfall on the same day its condition was one of rout, all along its 50-mile front. Describing the effect of the German bombing, a staff officer of the 18th Division recounts:

We passed through clouds of smoke from a petrol convoy which had just been bombarded by a plane and was burning along the road close to the route. Elsewhere an artillery group had been attacked whilst on the march. On the road and elsewhere there was a series of enormous bomb craters and very numerous corpses of horses, which indicated that the attack had been devastating. . . . On the road to Fraire, there arrives upon us at full gallop a group of disbanded artillerymen. Halted, they declared that the enemy was behind them.

Hammered since the day Rommel had first set foot across the Meuse, the 18th Division now dissolved. Having lost most of his staff, its commander, General Duffet, spent the day roving the battlefield, in an attempt to regroup his scattered units. With a handful of men he ended the day trying to set up a defence at Beaumont, just inside the Belgian frontier, through which the remnants of the 1st Armoured were retreating. On his right, General Hassler's 22nd Division, which had given no particularly commendable account of itself the previous day against the German infantry forcing the Meuse at Givet, shared a similar fate. "Aircraft do not cease to follow us, to bombard us and machine-gun us," recorded one of its battalion commanders.

We passed through Couvin where all kinds of columns were mixed up together . . . the disorder worsened, and our men in whom fatigue had exceeded anything that one could imagine, mounted on any vehicles they encountered, despite their officers who attempted to stop them. But, understanding that this was the only way of pulling out a force completely exhausted, I gave them the order to allow them to do this. . . . [But] at the exit to Couvin, we were once again attacked by enemy machine-guns. There were scenes of horror which occurred with women, children, lying alongside the road, dead or wounded, stretched out in the ditches. Grown men also fell . . . the planes came in quantity, machine-gunning and bombarding in turn, increasing the confusion.

By nightfall this division consisted of nothing but fragments, straggling back over the frontier. Thus General Martin's XI Corps had all but vanished. Nevertheless he was ordered by Corap to "do everything possible to halt the enemy on the frontier line." It was an impossible demand. As General Martin notes, "the first task was to get the engineers to open the doors of the bunkers!" But the keys to the bunkers, locked up when the Ninth Army moved forward on the 10th, had disappeared—either with units that had been dispatched elsewhere, or on the persons of local mayors who had taken off among the growing stream of refugees.

To the north the 5th Motorised Division covering Yvoir, though not heavily engaged that day, was also forced to withdraw in mounting disorder after its flank had been exposed by the breaking-up of XI Corps. In Corap's northern sector there thus remained only General Sancelme's 4th North African Division, and the fate of this fine unit on the 15th was particularly poignant. After its admirable defence against Rommel at Anthée on the 14th, the division had been pulled back to hold the Hemptinne–Philippeville line. But deprived of artillery support—since Sancelme, like Bruneau, had sent his guns to the rear—it had been unable to assume a proper defensive position before being sliced up by Rommel in his drive around the flank of the 1st Armoured. The experience of Lieutenant Édouard Leng, a reservist officer of the 13th Zouaves, pushed off the roads by the retreat of General Martin's HQ the previous day, was perhaps typical:

From the early hours of the morning, I fought on the Vodecée crossroads and at Villers-le-Gambon, enduring fire from German tanks and Stukas, and finding myself almost without contact with the other elements of the division. Towards 1830 hours, we received the order to withdraw in the direction of Philippeville. . . . Closely pursued by the enemy in the course of this movement, sustaining losses in both men and weapons (which were almost out of ammunition), with two other officers and a group of our men I ran into a score of German tanks at Vachefontaine, about one kilometre south-east of Philippeville. . . . We were encircled, and any resistance became useless.

Other tanks of the 7th Panzer overran the HQ of the 25th Algerian Tirailleurs at Philippeville itself, and an hour later reached the divisional PC at Neuville, from which General Sancelme only narrowly escaped behind a barricade of antitank guns. Cut off

from his regiments, that afternoon he dispatched three separate
liaison teams to Martin's HQ—but none returned. By the end of
the 15th, the 4th North African, like the 1st Armoured, was no
longer an effective fighting force.

Havoc at Monthermé

Further south on XLI Corps front the break-up of Corap's
army proceeded with even more dramatic swiftness. Here the
repercussions of Corap's order to withdraw behind the Rocroi–
Signy-l'Abbaye proved particularly disastrous; for the 102nd Division—whose colonial machine gunners from Indo-China and
Madagascar had so valiantly been holding Reinhardt at bay in
the Monthermé peninsula during the past two days—was a fortress
unit devoid of transport, while the 61st Division to the north had
insufficient vehicles, and these were not close enough for a quick
getaway. During the small hours of the 15th at Monthermé, German engineers equipped with flame throwers and riflemen of the
6th Panzer crept up to within a few yards of the bunkers held by
a gallant colonial rear guard. At 0330 hours they attacked under
a powerful artillery barrage. While it was still dark the Germans
were through the first defences, and by 0830 hours they had captured the French reserve positions. Immediately, the hitherto
stymied tanks of the 6th Panzer began to swarm across the Meuse
at Monthermé. At this moment a French truck loaded with a
thousand desperately needed antitank mines arrived at the front,
tragically late. With considerable courage the driver persisted in
trying to push through to his destination, but was caught by tanks
"which opened fire and the truck blew up with a formidable explosion." Upstream from Monthermé, the German 3rd and 23rd
Infantry Divisions completed their river crossings and began erecting bridges to get Reinhardt's other panzer division, the 8th,
across the Meuse.

Now Reinhardt more than made up for the time he had lost on
the previous four days of crawling through the Ardennes and bat-
tling his way into the Monthermé peninsula. The transportless
French 102nd Fortress Division, forced to abandon all its guns
and even its machine guns, was overtaken and rounded up with
incredible speed. Rushing out from the Monthermé bridgehead,
the motorcyclists of the 6th Panzer roared past

a French munitions dump, and past numerous guns which stand abandoned on the road. The enemy has had no time in which to take them with him in his flight. Also in the wood to the right a battery all ready to fire has been abandoned. It must have been completely surprised. . . . Near the leading group, a few carbine shots ring out. Then the enemy soon comes out with raised hands from the bushes. Some 30 men were there, and four negroes. They are muddy and unshaven, and their eyes are full of fear.

On reaching Arreux, some 6 miles from Monthermé, "Frenchmen come out from cellars and surrender of their own accord. . . . In Renwez it is the same story. The French give themselves up without having fired a single shot." On the left of the 6th Panzer, motorised infantry occupied the sprawling twin cities of Charleville–Mézières. Karl von Stackelberg, a war diarist travelling with them, noted that "the shops were closed and barred, the houses locked up. All the inhabitants had flown, and we moved through lonely and dead quiet streets." Later he was astonished to meet a French column marching in the opposite direction, in perfect order, headed by a captain:

They had however no weapons and did not keep their heads up. . . . They were marching willingly without any guard into imprisonment. Behind this first company which I saw followed new groups, ever new groups. . . . There were finally 20,000 men, who here in the sector of our Corps, in this one sector and on this one day, were heading backwards as prisoners. Unwillingly one had to think of Poland—and the scenes there. It was inexplicable. How was it possible, that after this first major battle on French territory, after this victory on the Meuse, this gigantic consequence should follow? How was it possible, these French soldiers with their officers, so completely downcast, so completely demoralised, would allow themselves to go more or less voluntarily into imprisonment?

Everywhere on the far side of the Meuse where Reinhardt's panzers had passed, Stackelberg encountered the same indescribable havoc:

All along the side of the road lay dead horses, abandoned baggage waggons, from which the cases had tumbled down, their contents strewn about the ground, rifles thrown away, steel helmets, saddles and all kinds of other pieces of equipment. I saw dead Frenchmen lying in the ditches, I saw abandoned guns, riderless horses roaming about, and often this scene escalated to regular barricades compounded of vehicles, guns and dead horses that had all been shot up together.

Reaching the small village of Brunehamel, close to where the PC of the French XLI Corps commander, General Libaud, had been that morning, Stackelberg found more barricades manned by dead Frenchmen and a deathly silence broken only by the crackling of flames. In the middle of a street a horse with crazy eyes stood unmoving; as Stackelberg approached, it suddenly collapsed and died. In another village he came upon two German soldiers playing that old hit of the Phoney War, "We'll Hang Out Our Washing on the Siegfried Line" on a "liberated" gramophone. As the tinny music blared out, a tearful French colonel watched the forlorn columns of prisoners file past. Interrogated by Stackelberg, they expressed hopeless amazement at the speed with which the panzers had overrun them.

By the end of the morning, the commander of the 42nd Half-Brigade which had defended Monthermé was captured; of its right-hand neighbour, the 52nd Half-Brigade, only 10 officers and 500 men remained from its established strength of 70 and 2,600 respectively. The following day, the divisional commander, General Portzer himself was rounded up and the total strength of the division then numbered no more than 1,200. This marked the end of the 102nd as a fighting force.

The fate of the 61st Division, which had not been subjected to any serious frontal assault, was even less distinguished. Outflanked, its "soft" transport was overhauled by Reinhardt's racing panzers in the kind of action tankmen dream about. On one road near Brunehamel alone, four tanks ran up and down a column of 40 French vehicles, shooting them up. A hundred men surrendered. Just as the Germans were beginning to run short of ammunition, another column of 75 vehicles was sighted and duly destroyed. When joined by the main force the following day, the four tanks and their crews numbering 13 had, between them, accounted for 500 prisoners and several hundred vehicles. Under this kind of treatment, the 61st—another "B" division—broke up like its sisters at Sedan. Its commander, General Vauthier, reported sadly to Ninth Army HQ the following day that there was only himself left, though in fact during the course of the 16th some 700 to 800 men straggled back, with three light machine guns between them—while other survivors of the 61st were picked up as far away as Compiègne over the succeeding days. By the end of the 15th, it could be said that Corap's XLI Corps had also ceased to exist.

In the heady spring sunshine, the extraordinary scenes on every side of a disintegrating enemy began to induce an entirely new mood in the German troops. Rapidly vanishing was the nervous apprehension of the legendary *furia francese,* of the insuperable victors of 1918; its place was taken by a kind of intoxication, the lightheartedness of the excursion that swept the panzers on at an increasingly reckless speed. "A perfect road stretches before us," wrote a member of the 6th Panzer, "and no enemy fliers over us. The air is completely dominated by our own fliers. A wonderful feeling of unconditional superiority. We rush on at 50 mph at Montcornet on the Serre. In front of the town there is a short collision with a French company, who give themselves up almost without fighting." Against somewhat stronger opposition, Montcornet itself was captured by nightfall. Since the morning, Reinhardt's panzers had covered 37 miles from the Meuse, bringing them to within a bare half-hour's drive of the HQ of the Ninth Army itself, at Vervins to the northwest. It was by far the most outstanding advance made by the Germans, and even Reinhardt seems to have been taken by surprise. At midnight he ordered the 6th to halt at Liart—which was 17 miles *east* of the point they had already reached that evening. Corap's "intermediate line" had been smashed wide open, from top to bottom.

Back to Sedan: The battle for Stonne

But Reinhardt would not have had his lucky break had it not been for the earlier successes, on either side, of Rommel and particularly Guderian. One now returns to Sedan, still the key sector. On the morning of the 15th, two separate battles confronted Guderian: an offensive, breakout battle to be fought by the 1st and 2nd Panzers westwards from Singly–Bouvellemont, and a dynamic defensive battle by the Grossdeutschland Regiment (principally) facing southwards at Stonne.

All through the night of the 14th–15th, General Georges had chafed at the way Huntziger was employing the 3rd Armoured

Division which had been rushed up to help him. At 6 A.M. he telephoned Second Army to confirm his order of the previous night, calling for a vigorous counterattack, and added: "Its execution is rendered even more indispensable by the situation of the Army on your left" (Corap). Passing these instructions on to General Flavigny, Huntziger—though by now he would have been much happier to remain on the defensive—called for a "tank-supported" attack on the Bulson–Sedan axis. At 1130 hours (note the further loss of time), Flavigny ordered the 3rd Armoured and 3rd Motorised divisions to attack at 1500 hours. They would move in three systematic bounds: the first taking them to the line Chémery–Maisoncelle–Raucourt; the second to the heights south of Bulson; and the third back onto the Marfée–Pont-Maugis position commanding the Meuse. It was to be carried out along the methodical, classical lines of an infantry-backed-by-tanks operation such as had been taught at the École Militaire ever since 1918. No initiative was allowed to the executants, and typically the whole operation was placed under the command of an infantryman—Bertin-Boussu of the 3rd Motorised rather than Brocard of the 3rd Armoured.* Meanwhile, the 3rd Armoured—deployed to form "corks" the previous evening—had become dispersed over a wide area on both sides of the Ardennes Canal. It was additionally suffering from an unusual number of technical breakdowns, which perhaps reflected both the newness of its equipment and the inexperience of its crews. By 1430 hours Brocard was telling Flavigny that he could not get his "B" tanks into position in time. The attack was consequently postponed until 1730 hours. It was the same old story that had bedevilled all the French counterstrokes to date.

True to its training, the Grossdeutschland did not just sit still and wait to be attacked by the French. Early in the morning it was pushing forward up onto the high ground on both sides of Stonne, with orders to establish its defence line around this key village. This unexpected movement further helped throw Flavigny off balance, and he was forced to commit piecemeal in the defence of Stonne some of the tanks and infantry that were being husbanded for the afternoon's set-piece attack.

---

* As one French military historian, Colonel Le Goyet, remarks, by now Brocard "no longer commanded anything. He had simply become a provider of tanks."

Stonne sits on a steep hill, surrounded by undulating country on which thick woods and scrub alternate with small patches of open moorland. Seen from a distance, in May 1940 its clustered houses gave the impression of an impregnably fortified hill town from the Middle Ages. Possession of it would provide an attacker with an indispensable point of departure, while for a defender it constituted a secure position from which he would be hard to dislodge. All through the 15th the battle swayed back and forth at Stonne in some of the most violent fighting yet seen on the Sedan front, with the village itself changing hands several times in the burning May heat.

Moving up with the 10th Panzer, one company commander related to his tank crews how his grandfather had died at Sedan with Moltke in 1871, while his father had been killed fighting in the same area in the First War. He added: "And if I die, that is the end of a military clan." Near Raucourt his tank ran into French antitank guns. Commanding from an open turret, he brought his gun to bear, but was evidently beaten to it by a French weapon. His tank halted, and one of his men found him being supported by his crew, his head smashed by the French shell. The tragic saga had been completed. But, with the 10th Panzer's tanks still only partly deployed across the Meuse, for the Germans it was essentially an infantryman's day at Stonne, and the Grossdeutschland was by no means having an easy time of it. Towards midday, General Schaal of the 10th Panzer received from it "alarming reports" of French tank attacks.

It was very largely thanks to the impressive celerity with which the Grossdeutschland was able to deploy its antitank guns (once more an attribute of the excellence of Wehrmacht training, at its best, in 1940) that the regiment was not overrun at Stonne on the 15th. Lieutenant Beck-Broichsitter commanding the 14th Antitank Company gives a vivid description of the fighting that day. Moving into the village after a Stuka attack,

we find abandoned houses, overgrown gardens, romantic old springs . . . a high water-tower standing apart from the rows of houses dominates every place in the village. We go along the village streets. Grenadiers of all Companies are running about independently. They have no orders. A shot-up German tank lies in a ditch. An officer and a sergeant standing with pistols nearby. One of the tank crew lies in a dusty black uniform nearby on the grass, dead. His face is yellow. From the water-tower there comes rifle fire! A cloud of dust rises from the road. A French tank comes towards us. We spring behind a house; it thunders past very close. . . . The edge of the village comes under machine-gun fire from the water-tower. Hidden guns are firing often unsuspected from the wooded hill behind us—it's a completely confused situation!

After the company had brought up three of its light 37 mm antitank guns, six French tanks appeared and a bitter duel ensued. Several of the tanks were knocked out, but one of their shells lodged in a wall close to where Beck-Broichsitter was standing:

The shots come gradually closer; single French tanks are bringing fresh infantry. In the gardens their strength is difficult to estimate. The situation is becoming critical, the fighting will of the soldiers is slackening in the heavy fire. All are at the end of their strength, because of the fighting since May 10th.

The German fire begins to slacken off. After a fresh French attack from the water tower, more tanks appear from a different direction.

The situation is very serious [continues Beck-Broichsitter]. The other anti-tank section have their hands fully occupied with the enemy on their front. How are we going to stop these new attacking tanks? The fire gets even heavier, everything seems to be burning! On the street lie our dead, and more and more wounded disappear to the rear! . . .

Some ten French tanks roll in on a wide front. At some 25 miles an hour, the drivers swing their vehicles about, and then fire. They are firing from the water-tower, the three guns are hit in the middle of the road; immediately there are wounded, but the section holds! The duel begins! In an hour long running battle, Hindelang's section holds the attacking infantry with their fire as well as the flank fire from the water-tower and also from the wooded hill. The fight for the village slackens. Against the tough French attacks some of our Rifle Companies gradually crumple away. Self-propelled guns help again and again; . . . four heavy infantry guns are brought into open positions, and fire with 15 cm. shells on the water-tower. But it does not budge. The losses are getting greater. Some of the anti-tank guns are shot full of holes. They carry on shooting.

Beck-Broichsitter's guns now came under fire from three of the 3rd Armoured Division's 32-ton "B" tanks:

At 100 metres, one of them shoots up the gun; then it machine-guns the wreckage. The Commander is wounded—it is Sergeant Kramer, his gun layer is badly wounded, the other dead. Kramer himself wounded crawls under machine-gun fire to the gun layer and drags him with unspeakable difficulty into a house.

The fire of the three heavy tanks threatens to wipe out the anti-tank section. But it remains in position. One moment, one of the colossuses crosses the front. The left gun commander, Senior Corporal Giesemann, discovers in the middle of its right side a small-ribbed surface; apparently it is the radiator! It is not much bigger than an ammunition box. He aims at it. A tongue of flame shoots out from the Panzer. . . . Both gun commanders now fire only at this small square in the side of the 32-tonners. The left gun is shortly afterwards wiped out by a direct hit—now Hindelang retreats with the one remaining gun into the village. The three 32-tonners are knocked out!

According to the Grossdeutschland regimental history, Oberfeldwebel Hindelang's action saved the front at Stonne that day; for which, both he and Beck-Broichsitter were later awarded the Ritterkreuz. The 14th Antitank Company's losses during this 10-hour battle numbered 1 officer and 12 men dead and 16 men wounded. Twelve of their vehicles and 6 out of 12 guns were destroyed, while they claimed to have knocked out 33 French tanks. Seen from the German point of view, the situation at Stonne undoubtedly at one time seemed critical. Visiting the Grossdeutschland while a French attack was actually in progress, Guderian himself remarks that "a certain nervous tension was noticeable." Shortly after 5 P.M. Graf von Schwerin, the regimental commander, was reporting to General Schaal that his men had been forced out of Stonne again and that they were "in a state of complete physical exhaustion and hardly fit for combat." All available rifle companies from the 10th Panzer were rushed up to support the flagging Grossdeutschland, while armour was dispatched to meet a new French attack by an estimated 50 tanks in the direction of Raucourt. Then, at 1800 hours, the 10th Panzer War Diary reported a fresh "strong enemy armour thrust on Chémery," adding the comment that this move was "considered to be extremely dangerous, because in the event of success it would strike the westward swing of XIX corps in the flank."

Precisely what, in fact, had constituted the French effort which caused the Germans such concern? During the morning, just one battalion (the 45th) of H–39 light tanks and a company of "B" tanks from the 3rd Armoured, plus one battalion of infantry, had been thrown into the reflexive counterattacks attempting to check the Grossdeutschland's movements upon Stonne. Then, at 1730 hours Flavigny's long-awaited set-piece attack went in. But, in the words of General Ruby, it was reduced to "a fist blow." Of the armour, only the 49th Battalion of "B" tanks and a handful of H–39s moved; and no sooner had they entered into action than General Brocard gave the order calling off the attack. Brocard's other two tank battalions, deployed to the west of the Ardennes Canal, never joined in the counterstroke that day. As the German accounts testify, the French tank crews that did see action fought well; Captain Aulois, a First War veteran commanding one of the "B" tank companies, having lost four of his tanks near Stonne, was dragged badly wounded out of his wrecked machine and "congratulated" by his captors on the admirable action he had fought. But what Flavigny's force *might* have achieved had it struck with all its available strength, even as late as the afternoon of the 15th, can also be deduced from the gravity with which 10th Panzer HQ viewed the thrust on Chéméry by this mere handful of tanks. Writing after the war, General Hoth (Rommel's Corps commander) reckoned that in the postponement of Flavigny's operation, "the French missed a favourable occasion; this counterattack, conducted in a resolute manner, would have transformed defeat into victory."

It was certainly the last "favourable occasion" to be granted on the Sedan battlefield. That evening Brocard was sent by Huntziger to swell the ranks of sacked generals. Both the French and the exhausted Grossdeutschland recoiled from Stonne. But early the next morning the Germans re-entered it against only "slight resistance." Later that day relief for the Grossdeutschland arrived in the form of the 29th Motorised Division,* the first of Wietersheim's XIV Motorised Infantry Corps that had been hastening up behind Guderian. It was, says Kielmansegg, "a very welcome

---

* One of the crack German divisions, later lost at Stalingrad.

relief and certainly a necessary one for the worn-out defenders of the southern front." The Grossdeutschland had lost 9 officers and 94 other ranks killed; 30 officers and 429 other ranks wounded and missing—probably the heaviest casualties of any German unit in the campaign so far.* But the crucial battle for Stonne had been won. Colonel von Schwerin had more than deserved the case of champagne wagered with Guderian. All that remained on the 16th was the mopping-up of the scattered tanks belonging to the 3rd Armoured, which had been so dismally cast away by the French command.

The 1st and 2nd Panzers: Bitter resistance

In comparison with the flamboyant performance of Reinhardt's XLI Panzer Corps in their breakout from Monthermé, the physical achievement of the 1st and 2nd Panzers during the 15th looks almost unimpressive on the map. Their energies were chiefly absorbed in completing the complicated change of direction imposed by Guderian and in smashing the last elements of resistance which stood between them and the soft interior of France. Of what did these elements consist?

The previous day General Georges had summoned General Touchon—a much wounded hero of the First War, when he had commanded a regiment of the Chasseurs Alpins—and dispatched him to the front to take over an "Army Detachment." His ambitious orders were to "reestablish liaison and weld the flanks of the Second and Ninth Armies, by coordinating the activities of the units in the area." Touchon appears to have frittered away the 14th, calling on various subordinate commanders in his new zone of operations, and only reaching Huntziger's PC by 4 P.M. and Rethel at 7 P.M. The next day, having set up his own PC at Château Porcien, at 2 P.M. he promulgated his first order—which was "to hold at all costs the second line at Liart, Signy-l'Abbaye, Poix Terron and Bouvellemont." He then set off to find General Libaud of XLI Corps. But Libaud's headquarters camp was deserted. Returning to Château Porcien, Touchon was shot at by enemy armour near Rozoy-sur-Serre, and made a narrow escape.

---

* Though they were light compared with any equivalent action at Verdun in 1916.

He decided to withdraw his PC to Hermonville, some 10 miles northeast of Reims.

The forces placed initially at the disposal of "Army Detachment Touchon" (later to become the Sixth Army) were XLI Corps, the southernmost unit of Corap's army; General Etchberrigaray's 53rd Division; Chanoine's cavalry groupement; the 14th Division, and later the 2nd Armoured Division; plus the valueless shell of Grandsard's X Corps. We have already examined the fate of XLI Corps at the hands of Reinhardt's panzers during the 15th, and seen how the confusion of repeated counterorders on the 14th had diminished the effectiveness of the 53rd Division, which, as a "B" unit, was modest enough even before the tide of battle caught up with it. The tragic, futile saga of the 2nd Armoured Division—the last of General Georges's "rooks"—will be followed later. The 14th Division, commanded by General de Lattre de Tassigny who had led a company at Verdun and was to become a Maréchal de France and one of the great heroes of the liberation, was one of the finest infantry units in the French Army. But, sent from Lorraine, it had just arrived at Château Porcien, on the Aisne west of Rethel, with the result that only one of its regiments, the 152nd, could reach the front in time to take part in the day's fighting. Thus it was that the main resistance against Guderian's swinging lunge on the 15th was put up by this one regiment around the village of Bouvellemont and, just to its north, by Colonel Marc's 3rd Spahi Brigade at La Horgne.

On the other side, the hardest fighting once again fell to the redoubtable Colonel Balck and his riflemen of the 1st Panzer. All day he hammered away against a magnificent defence put up by the Spahis and de Lattre's men. At one point, Balck's troops—already much fatigued by their unremitting efforts of the past days—seem to have become extremely dispirited by their losses. More than half their officers were either dead or wounded, and many companies were little above half strength. They had received hardly anything to eat or drink during a day of burning heat. Some of the officers complained at the new demands being made on the regiment; Balck alone was fully aware that what now confronted them was the very last of the French defensive lines. "Suddenly," wrote one of his NCOs, with perhaps just a touch of hero worship, "there appeared our Regimental Commander. Like a tower in the battle he stood between us, equipped with only a field cap, a walking cane, gas-mask and a pistol. Quickly he put himself in the picture, and immediately produced the order expected by us all." Visiting Balck in the burning ruins of Bouvellemont the following day, Guderian tells us:

Ammunition was running low. The men in the front line were falling asleep in their slit trenches. Balck himself, in wind jacket and with a knotty stick in his hand, told me that the capture of the village had only succeeded because, when his officers complained against the continuation of the attack, he had replied: "In that case I'll take the place on my own!" and had moved off. His men had thereupon followed him. His dirty face and his red-rimmed eyes showed that he had spent a hard day and a sleepless night.

By nightfall on the 15th, de Lattre's regiment, abandoning Bouvellemont, was forced to fall back towards Rethel. Though it had claimed some 20 German tanks, all its antitank guns and a third of its men were lost. At La Horgne, the 3rd Spahis had fought back with perhaps even grimmer determination—fully atoning for their disastrous withdrawal from the Semois three days previously. Attacked by both tanks and infantry, the brigade resisted until 6 P.M., when it was literally wiped out. Colonel Marc had been captured at his post; his two regimental commanders, Colonels Burnol and Geoffroy, were both killed. Out of 37 officers, 12 were killed and 7 wounded; casualties among the other ranks were roughly proportionate. For his leadership that day, Balck was awarded the Ritterkreuz and singled out for the rare privilege of a special mention in the Wehrmacht Communiqué.

Although the resistance at La Horgne and Bouvellemont succeeded in checking the impetus of the 1st Panzer, to the north the main weight of the 2nd Panzer smashed through the disordered elements of the 53rd Division without much difficulty, and by the close of the day its reconnaissance detachments were already making contact with Reinhardt's panzers at Montcornet. The Signy-l'Abbaye–Poix Terron line which Touchon had only that afternoon ordered to be held "at all costs" was no longer anything more than an entry in a staff officer's logbook. Guderian's route westward lay open, virtually without obstacles ahead of it. Of even more fundamental significance was the fact that, whereas twenty-four hours previously the German bridgeheads across the Meuse had consisted of three isolated bulges, they now formed one continuous pocket 62 miles wide—with no bottom. Thus it is hardly an exaggeration to say, as has more than one French historian, that May 15th was the day France lost the war.

The French 2nd Armoured cut in two

On paper, there remained General Bruché's 2nd Armoured Division. But of all the units sent to stem the German breakthrough none was subjected to a sadder or more wasteful Calvary. Formed in January 1940, the 2nd Armoured—like its sisters—had been located in the Champagne area on May 10th. The next day Georges had earmarked it to reinforce the Second Army, along with the 3rd Armoured, but then appears to have forgotten about it for the next forty-eight hours. On the afternoon of the 13th, Georges finally dispatched it towards Charleroi—in the tracks of the 1st Armoured and *away* from the main danger area at Sedan where Guderian had already crossed the Meuse. Because of the shortage of tank transporters, the tanks and other tracked vehicles were sent by train on flatcars while the wheeled transport constituting the supply echelons went by road under their own steam; furthermore, as the movement of the 1st Armoured had taken up most of the available railway flatcars, the loading of Bruché's tanks at Châlons station was protracted from the afternoon of the 14th to the morning of the 15th—little aided by the repeated German bombing attacks. Consequently, the 2nd Armoured became thoroughly scattered over a wide area at the worst possible moment. Reporting early on the morning of the 14th at First Army HQ in Valenciennes, Bruché was forced to admit to General Blanchard that he did not know where his various units were, or in what order they would arrive. The poor man was then told that his division had now been put at Corap's disposal. The next day, when Bruché's liaison officer reported to Ninth Army HQ, pointing out that the change in plan made it impossible to attack before midday on the 17th, he was told: "The 2nd Armoured no longer belongs to us. It has been given to the 'Army Detachment Touchon,' to whom we are transmitting your report." Meanwhile, on General Georges's instructions the road column which had just reached Guise was redirected eastwards to Signy-l'Abbaye, the southern anchor of Corap's "stop line"; the tanks were to be unloaded at Hirson, as soon as they reached it, and then to go under their own power to Signy.

But just at the time when this manoeuvre—so complex that it would have required all the skill of a Guderian—was being executed, Reinhardt's panzers were already tearing through Signy on the way to Montcornet. Caught on the road at Blanchefosse (near Brunehamel) at about 1700 hours on the 15th, one artillery battery of Bruché's division had 10 out of its 12 guns overrun by tanks; another tractor-drawn battery, sent by road since there were no flatcars for its guns, simply disappeared into thin air. In effect, Reinhardt—without realising it—had driven a wedge slap through the centre of the 2nd Armoured. The road column, having progressed farther than the armour, was forced southwards and took refuge beyond the Aisne at Rethel. Moving in a southeasterly direction from the rail terminal at Hirson, the tanks made a totally unexpected first contact with the panzers along the Liart–Rozoy road, and had promptly headed away—towards the north. Thus, by dawn on the 16th, almost all of General Bruché's armour lay scattered over a vast area between St. Quentin and Hirson on one side of Reinhardt's panzer thrust, without any means of supply and having lost half its supporting artillery. On the other side, south of the Aisne was General Bruché himself, with all the wheeled transport of the division, one gun battery, a company of H–39 light tanks, four solitary strayed "B" tanks, and two companies of chasseurs. So the third and last of Georges's powerful "rooks" had simply broken up before it could even be committed to the battle. To make matters worse, for a considerable period both Generals Georges and Touchon were to remain disastrously unaware of the true state of affairs with the 2nd Armoured.

Giraud replaces Corap

At dawn on the 15th, Billotte had telephoned Georges: "The Ninth Army is in a critical position. . . . It is absolutely essential to put some life into this wavering army. General Giraud, whose vigour is well known, appears to me to be best fitted to take on this difficult task." In a telephone call with the unhappy Corap later in the morning, Georges realised that he had "lost his sangfroid" and that evening what broken fragments there remained of his army were removed from the old colonial soldier. "I left at

0400 hours on the 16th," wrote Corap, "heartbroken."* Giraud, his successor, is described by Beaufre as having been "our most ardent commander"; less flatteringly by Lieutenant General Alan Brooke as a Don Quixote who "would have ridden gallantly at any windmill regardless of consequences" and who "inspired one with little confidence when operating on one's left flank." But more than Quixotic ardour was required to restore the situation on the Ninth Army front; and would the elements of Giraud's own Seventh Army, which had survived the Breda fiasco and were now following him to the Ninth Army, prove sufficient to plug the gaping holes that had been rent there? That night Giraud sent a first disquieting message to Billotte, summing up the situation as he found it:

I have no news of the XIth Army Corps. Sancelme's Division (the 4th North African) appears to have elements in the region to the west of Philippeville. No news of the 18th and 22nd Divisions, which seem to be disorganised. Vauthier's Division (the 61st) has abandoned Rocroi and is withdrawing to the second position . . . the 1st Armoured Division has this morning struck a blow in the Mettet region. It is to strike another blow in the region of Philippeville, but I have received no information. *Mon impression est grave,* especially on my right because of the rapid advance of the panzers.

Then, in the middle of the night, Giraud received the devastating news of the arrival of the panzers at Montcornet, just 12 miles south of Army HQ at Vervins.

Meanwhile . . . in Belgium

In northern Belgium, the BEF was again attacked by the German Sixth Army with orders to "prevent consolidation of the Allied forces" on the Dyle Line. Once again the Germans were driven off. At the end of the day Lord Gort had cause to be satisfied with the BEF's performance, and the troops—seeing only their immediate front—were confidently aware of no reason why they should not continue to sit on the Dyle indefinitely. To their right a small breach was made during the afternoon on the French

---

* Huntziger retained his command throughout. In retrospect it is difficult to see that he handled the battle any more brilliantly than Corap, who had faced the far greater test.

First Army front, but by and large the line from Antwerp to Namur held well. It was the sudden exposure of Blanchard's right wing caused by the disintegration of the Ninth Army which abruptly became the dominant factor. At 6 P.M. on the evening of the 15th, General Billotte, recognising for the first time the full gravity of the German break-through on the Meuse, decided to retire the whole Allied line in the north back to the Escaut—the position which the Allies were to have held originally before Gamelin imposed the more ambitious Dyle Plan. The withdrawal would take place in stages of three nights and was to be completed by May 19th. Blanchard was promptly informed of Billotte's intention. Gort, on the other hand, only learned of it at 5 A.M. the next morning when, disquieted at the news trickling in from the south, he sent a senior officer to No. 1 Army Group HQ, who there happened to see the order before its dispatch. Gort then sent Major General Needham, head of the British Military Mission at Belgian Army HQ, to inform the Belgians what was afoot. But Needham was seriously injured in a car accident and the unfortunate Belgians did not hear of Billotte's intention until 10 A.M. on the 16th. Gort's confidence in the French High Command was further shaken, and the Belgians were greatly embittered; their Deputy Chief of Staff, General Derousseaux, claims it was "my worst memory of the campaign. The General Staff was stunned by it." When the troops of the BEF heard of Billotte's order to retire, after their successful holding operation of the past two days, they too were "stunned"—and greatly disappointed. No one could comprehend just what had taken place to the south.

RAF bombs Ruhr; Reynaud pleads for more Hurricanes

In the air war on May 15th, a number of extremely important events occurred. At 6:30 A.M. General Têtu had rung through from General Georges's HQ to order d'Astier to switch air priority from the Second to the Ninth Army. It was symptomatic of the self-delusion still prevailing in the higher echelons of the French Command that he added: "I am told that the situation of the Ninth Army is less serious than one might believe; its withdrawal is a controlled operation." But the forces the Allies were able to put into the air that day in support of this new priority now reflected all too faithfully the grim losses of the previous five days. To cover the whole of the northeast front and Paris, General d'Astier could mount no more than 237 serviceable single-seater fighters, 38 night fighters and 38 bombers. By midday, he was forced to admit that half of his fighter capacity had been knocked out by enemy bombing. In all, his *aviation de chasse* could make only 200-odd sorties that day, compared with 340 on the 14th, claiming 21 enemy planes for a loss of 7. This was hardly enough to shelter Corap's army from the Stukas plaguing it as relentlessly as flies upon carrion.

Of France's remaining bombers, just six Léo 45's were thrown in to support Flavigny's counterattack in the Sedan sector, while nine Bréguets from Groupement 18 bombed Reinhardt's armour debouching from Monthermé. With all notions of ground-level attack now abandoned, the Bréguets released their bombs from a height of over 1,500 feet; all returned safely to base, a fact which raised the morale of the Groupement—though apparently without its examining too closely just how effective the results had been. Typical of the feebleness of French air effort on the 15th was the nocturnal bombing of one Heinkel base by a solitary French aircraft, which dumped its missiles in woods more than a quarter of a mile from the barracks and then headed for home.

Meanwhile the relentless bombing of French reinforcements and supply columns continued. All over northern France the roads told the same story of troops caught on the move, the wounded soldiers crying for help amid piles of abandoned equipment. Day by day the sinister Arado observer planes—which seemed immune to small-arms fire and were never chased off by Allied fighters—stalked French reinforcements moving up to the line, until the Heinkels and Dorniers were ready to pounce.

The British record for the 15th was hardly more outstanding than the French. After their appalling losses of the 14th,* the vulnerable Battles were in process of being withdrawn from daylight operations, so that the day's main effort consisted of some dozen Blenheims striking at Rommel's columns near Dinant —an attack reported neither by Rommel nor the divisional war diary. But that night an operation was mounted which, although it did nothing to influence the course of the battle, was certainly to

---

* According to Churchill (Vol. II, p. 38) by the night of the 14th, there were only 206, out of 474, serviceable RAF aircraft left in France.

change the character of the war. Outraged by the Luftwaffe's raz-
ing of Rotterdam, the British War Cabinet banished the scruples
that had hitherto restrained it from launching a strategic bombardment of the German Ruhr. It persuaded itself that such a
heavy bomber attack by night would, in the first place, force the
Luftwaffe to divert fighters from France to protect the Ruhr;
and secondly, that the German outcry for retaliation would result
in some of the bombers, which were breaking up the French Army
to such deadly effect, being redirected against the British Isles.
With somewhat less altruistic motives, the Air Staff also had at the
back of its mind the hope that—daylight bombing having been
proved so ruinously expensive—cheaper returns could be gained
by night. Accordingly, that night 96 Wellington, Whitley and
Hampden bombers were dispatched to northwest Germany. Of
these, 78 were directed against oil plants; but, in the words of the
RAF official history, "Only twenty-four of the crews even claimed
to have found them." Like so much of the subsequent history of
strategic bombing, this first attempt had only the most negligible
results. Not a single plane or antiaircraft gun was deflected from
France. Goebbels's propaganda machine indeed howled for
vengeance, but this would not be exacted until after the Fall of
France, until the Blitz on London.

That same day a second decision of strategic, indeed of historic importance was taken in London. At the time of the German
onslaught, ten of Britain's all too few fighter squadrons were committed in France, and on May 13th the equivalent of two more
Hurricane squadrons had been dispatched. Accounts by German
bomber crews testify to the impact made by the Hurricane pilots,
who tended to press home their attacks with much greater energy
than the French pilots in their outclassed Moranes; yet this was
all a drop in the bucket. On the evening of the 14th, Reynaud
telephoned Churchill with a new note of urgency in his voice,
to beg that another ten fighter squadrons be sent to help reestablish the line at Sedan. The next day this request became the
subject of bitter controversy within the Cabinet. Air Chief Marshal
Dowding, of Flight Command, vigorously objected to the dispatch of any more of his squadrons to France. His face white with
strain, Dowding rose from his seat and walked round the long
conference table until he came up behind Churchill's chair. Years

later Dowding remarked, "I think some of the others thought I was going to shoot him"; but all he did was to place in front of the Prime Minister a single sheet of paper with a graph on it. It predicted what would be the probable rate of loss over the next ten days if further Hurricanes were sent to France. On the tenth day, the graph line touched the zero point. If the current rate of wastage were to continue over another fortnight there would no longer be "a single Hurricane left in France or in this country," Dowding solemnly told Churchill. The graph, he says, "did the trick." In an atmosphere highly charged with emotion, the Cabinet was reluctantly swung over to Dowding's side.

Meanwhile, in France the close of May 15th brought with it a new threat to the AASF. A score of fighters were lost just protecting the forward bases from the incessant Luftwaffe attacks, and now some of these airfields were seriously endangered by the advancing panzers. Shortly before midnight Air Marshal Barratt decided to shift southwards a number of the menaced combat units—an awkward move to make in mid-battle with the limited transport facilities available to him. At the same time he closed down his own Advanced Headquarters at Chauny and retired back to Main HQ in Coulommiers.

Kleist and Guderian at odds

Behind the scenes of the German Command, where one might have presumed to find jubilation after such a promising day, contrary to every expectation the prevailing tone was one of uncertainty and discord. Its overt expression took the form of a third fundamental disagreement between Kleist, the commander of the Panzergruppe, and Guderian. The more cautious Kleist wanted to confine Guderian to a small bridgehead west of Sedan and to build up forces within it before continuing the next stage of the advance. That night Kleist's HQ, says Guderian,

ordered a halt to all further advance and to any extension of the bridgehead. I neither would nor could agree to these orders, which involved the sacrifice of the element of surprise we had gained and of the whole initial success that we had achieved. I therefore got in touch, personally, first with the Chief of Staff of the Panzer Group, Colonel Zeitzler, and since this was not enough with General von Kleist himself, and requested that the order to stop be cancelled. The conversation became very heated and we repeated our various arguments several times.

Thoroughly enraged, Guderian shouted down the telephone a pointed comparison to the Marne in 1914 when (at least according to the view widely accepted in German military circles) an untimely interference from the High Command had caused the German armies to halt and turn about on the very brink of victory. It was a reminder, notes Guderian, "that was no doubt not very well received" by his superiors. However, Kleist—with some reluctance—gave way once again, restoring to Guderian the "freedom of movement" he demanded.

15

"We Have Lost the Battle!"
MAY 16th

The enemy has not succeeded in breaking through our
battle front and emerging from the Sedan–Mézières
region. He has thrown wave upon wave, division on
division, into the furnace. Our plains, our fields, our
roads are filled with his corpses. . . . We must say this
and say it again and cry it out to the four winds of
France's skies: "He wanted to break through, as he
wanted to at Verdun, and he did not get through!"

—L'Époque, May 16th

Southwest of Namur our divisions extended their successes on the west bank of the Meuse and once again
struck at French armoured forces. South of Sedan,
French counter-attacks, which included the employment
of the heaviest tanks, were warded off. . . .

—Wehrmacht Communiqué, May 16th

A certain number of German fighting vehicles were
able to push right forward, but they were not strong
enough and operated like "lost children." . . . The
German tanks will soon have no more petrol or ammunition.

—HAVAS, May 17th

Round Sedan the French were still holding the positions
they took up yesterday after containing the enemy attack there. On the left bank of the Meuse the situation
is less clear, though such progress as the Germans may
have made there has been relatively slight.

—The Times, May 17th

ON THIS seventh day of the campaign, abruptly the scene of predominant interest shifts from Corap's and Huntziger's broken
fronts to the higher councils of war on both sides, where from

now on the leaders would find themselves striving desperately to keep up with the incredible tempo of events. For the Germans, the rapidity of the advance was accompanied by fresh doubts and fears of setbacks to come. For the Allied High Commands, it was the night of May 15th and the early morning of the 16th which at last brought home the extent of the disaster on the Meuse. But before coming to this tardy moment of awakening, it may be well to retrace the activities which had ensued at Vincennes and La Ferté on the preceding days.

May 10th–15th: Was Gamelin to blame?

Having made his plans and troop dispositions, Gamelin as C-in-C had then in effect left it to General Georges, commander on the northeast front, to do the best he could with them. The relationship was not unlike that of Generals Alexander and Montgomery later at Alamein (except that one must not forget the deep-seated dislike Gamelin and Georges held for each other); and doubtless if Sedan had gone as well as Alamein, historians would now regard Gamelin as a war lord of distinction. On May 10th, Gamelin revealed himself as well pleased with the apparent form the German offensive was taking, and during the first three days he had busied himself with "matters of overall organisation" with a particular emphasis on Holland, to which, through his Breda Variant brain child, he felt personally committed. Although we have seen how badly informed he was kept on the course of the battle, he refrained from making more than one trip (on May 11th) to see Georges at La Ferté. Then he had learned with "some astonishment" of Georges's subdelegation to Billotte of his "powers to coordinate" the movements of the BEF and the Belgian Army. Although criticising Georges's order as an "abdication," he went along with it on the grounds that "it is often better to accept a *fait accompli* than to risk hampering a commander's actions." On the 12th he deliberately kept away from La Ferté, explaining that it would have been "improper" for him to go there while Georges was away visiting the front in Belgium. The next morning, when Guderian was about to cross the Meuse at Sedan and Rommel already had a toehold at Houx, Gamelin revisited Georges and claims (in his memoirs) to have been "shaken by the realisation that no major reserves appeared to have been sent to the front." But nothing is on record to indicate that Gamelin intervened or made any alternative suggestion at this point. On the 14th, he was at La Ferté both morning and afternoon and records that he was astonished to discover there had been no reserves immediately behind Sedan when the Germans attacked, and also that—"for reasons that I have been unable to elucidate" —Huntziger had failed to launch his counterattack. Again, although he claims that his presence there was necessary from a point of view of morale," Gamelin still appears to have made no personal intervention at La Ferté that day. On returning to Vincennes, he could do nothing (according to Colonel Minart) to enlighten his own GQG, beyond stating the fact that the Meuse crossings "seemed incomprehensive, inexplicable," and that there had been "grave errors of execution." On the morning of the 15th, during another visit to La Ferté Gamelin was surprised* to hear that Georges had given the Ninth Army the order for a general withdrawal from the Meuse.

So great were the confusion and the duplication of duties in the French command network that it is still not entirely clear who was ultimately responsible—Gamelin or Georges—for the various orders sent out during the crucial days of May 10th to 15th. If, as Generalissimo, Gamelin was not aware of the specific measures Georges was taking to counter the German threat on the Meuse, the responsibility rests upon him; just as, in the final analysis, he cannot escape blame for *allowing* Georges to keep him so incompletely informed as to the real state of affairs at the front. But Gamelin must have been aware at least of the movements of Army reserves ordered by Georges; and assuming this, one has to conclude either that he should have intervened if he disapproved of these movements, or that they had his tacit support. Gamelin never did intervene; for which, in his memoirs he advances the rather feeble reason that "a commander-in-chief executes badly what he does not understand."† On the other hand, nothing in his copious apologia indicates that he would have handled his reserves other than Georges did. Thus—although *ex post facto* he may criticise the tardiness with which Georges dispatched his reserves—it seems fair to accept that Gamelin did endorse the di-

---

* The words "surprised," "shocked," "astonished," appear with revealing frequency in these sections of the Gamelin memoirs, *Servir*.

† A retort originally attributed to one of Napoleon's generals upon whom he had wanted to impose his own plan of campaign.

rection in which they were sent. Having established this, it may be useful briefly to summarise the troop movements between May 10th and 15th for which Gamelin and Georges were jointly responsible.

Altogether 17 divisions and 2 brigades, representing more than 300,000 men, received orders committing them to battle. On May 10th, the 1st Armoured was sent to the First Army; May 11th, two more divisions to First Army, and another two dispatched to protect the northern flank of the Maginot Line; May 12th, yet another two divisions to First Army, two (the 3rd Armoured and 3rd Motorised) to Second Army,* while one (the 53rd) was removed from direct control of the Ninth Army and sent to back up the front behind Mézières. On May 13th, one division (2nd Armoured) was sent to First Army, and one (the 36th) was sent to Ninth Army, but only to replace the 53rd removed from it the previous day; and in fact events overtook the 36th before it could ever reach its destination, so that it remained stuck on the Aisne. On the 14th, out of nineteen different movement orders, sixteen involved a change of direction; and among the divisions affected, no less than seven had their missions altered within twenty-four hours—the consequences of which were to prove particularly disastrous to such units as the 53rd Division and the 2nd Armoured. That same day the 14th Division (de Lattre) was sent to bolster the Ninth Army; but, like the 36th, it too never arrived and was left holding the Aisne under Touchon's command. By the end of the 14th, orders had been issued dispatching to Huntziger's Second Army eight fresh divisions, with the object to prevent any rolling-up of the Maginot Line from the north; of these, half were to remain unemployed during the decisive battle. Finally, on May 15th, one division (1st North African) was detached from First Army and sent down to reinforce the Ninth. Thus the total reinforcements ordered up by the French High Command read as follows:

---

* Although they were sent with the primary purpose of protecting the northern end of the Maginot Line, the dispatch of these two units to Sedan was perhaps Georges's happiest stroke; as already seen, it was the fault of the local commanders —not Georges—that they were so misused. A less happy stroke was Georges's change of mind about the 2nd Armoured—also earmarked on May 11th for Sedan —which, two days later, was ordered northwards to First Army.

To First Army: five divisions, of which three were subsequently redirected.

To Second Army: eight divisions, four of which played no part in the decisive battle. By contrast, the army most sorely in need of reinforcement—Corap's Ninth—did not receive a single division until May 15th, when it was far too late. Nothing could illustrate with greater clarity how completely Georges and Gamelin had been deceived by the "matador's cloak," how completely they had misread German intentions. And the end of the deception was not yet in sight.

At Vincennes, May 15th had begun with renewed fears of a German left hook on the Maginot Line via Switzerland, with Intelligence from Berne reporting the situation along the German frontier now to be "critical." It was, says Colonel Minart, "a gloomy day, interminable, smelling of death." The communiqués arriving from La Ferté continued to be noncommittal, but their very laconicism was becoming increasingly suspect—while liaison officers dispatched from Vincennes were treated with a marked brusqueness. On liaison duty between Vincennes, La Ferté, and Doumenc's headquarters staff at Montry himself that day, Minart sensed "that our command organisation was steadily breaking down, and that a paralysis was creeping up, hour by hour." Within the grim fortress it was more than ever like being in "a submarine without a periscope." Nevertheless, ugly rumours direct from the front were beginning to filter through to Vincennes in increasing quantity. Although at meals "everything was done to avoid painful subjects," what Minart describes as "the obsessing perspective of defeat" made its way, unspoken, through the dark corridors of GQG. The nervous tension that day was further played upon by mysterious comings and goings, private telephone conversations between Gamelin and Georges, and a call from Reynaud's office purporting to relate to an urgent intervention made to the British Government. Gamelin himself, though still externally serene, gave the appearance of a man "stricken by a dull and pervasive fear," and increasingly sought the insulation afforded by his *chef de cabinet,* Colonel Petitbon, and his ADCs. Still he declined to intervene directly in the battle.

At La Ferté, General Georges's attention during the 15th appears to have been principally concentrated on the fighting around Stonne and Flavigny's belated counterattack. That evening, at

1700 hours, he personally telephoned the commander of XVIII Corps holding Huntziger's *right* wing, with the emphatic order: "You must hold at all costs the anchor position Inor–Malandry. Upon this can depend the whole outcome of the war." Inor–Malandry was the line upon which Huntziger (disastrously) had fallen back during the night of the 14th; its significance was that it protected the northern flank of the Maginot Line, for which purpose Georges had sent those eight divisions. Herein lay the key to Georges's thoughts that day. First it had been the threat to the Gembloux Gap; now it was the outflanking threat to the Maginot Line which stood paramount in Georges's mind. Meanwhile, as Guderian preparatory to his swing westward was on the defensive at Stonne, the reports reaching Georges from Huntziger sounded as if the French were more than holding their own in this sector. Gradually towards evening of the 15th a new note of quite ill-founded hope seems to have begun to replace the terrible debility that Georges had displayed the previous day. On the basis of Georges's renewed optimism, Gamelin was inspired to conclude that day's signal to the C-in-Cs of the North African and Levant theatres with the following absurdly unrealistic summary: "To sum up, the 15th seems to show a lessening in intensity of enemy action which was particularly violent on the 14th. Our front, which was shaken between Namur and the area west of Montmédy, is gradually pulling itself together."

Gamelin: "Suddenly his eyes were opened"

That evening, Gamelin delivered a similarly encouraging report to the War Cabinet. But, at about 8:30 P.M., shortly after Daladier, the Minister of National Defence, had returned from the meeting to his office in the Rue Saint-Dominique, Gamelin was on the telephone with an entirely different note in his voice. For the first time the Joffrian *sang-froid,* the sugary tone of reassurance which he customarily reserved for his political masters had vanished. What combination of events and intelligence led to this sudden change of heart is not quite clear; in all probability it was caused by a report from a GQG staff officer, Lieutenant Colonel Guillaut. Gamelin had dispatched Guillaut that day as his personal liaison officer to the Ninth Army—the only occasion so far when he had adopted such a measure—and reporting back Guillaut stated: "The disorder of this Army is beyond description. Its troops are falling back on all sides. The Army General Staff has lost its head. It no longer knows even where its divisions are. The situation is worse than anything we could have imagined. . . . The roads are choked with routed troops." According to Pertinax, up to this moment Gamelin "seems to have cherished the illusion that everything could be 'patched up.' Suddenly his eyes were opened." Now he knew that the Germans had consummated their break-through, while the major part of the French reserves were irrevocably committed, or had already been partly destroyed. William Bullitt, the American ambassador, was with Daladier when Gamelin telephoned from Vincennes. Obviously caught off balance by the change in the Generalissimo's demeanour and the tale of disaster that he had to tell, Daladier was heard by Bullitt to exclaim:

"No, what you tell me is not possible! You are mistaken! It's not possible!"

When the extent of the catastrophe revealed by Gamelin had sunk in, Daladier shouted again down the telephone: "We must attack soon!"

"Attack! With what? I have no more reserves."

The conversation ended with the following exchange:

"Then it means the destruction of the French Army?"

"Yes, it means the destruction of the French Army!"

Daladier then demanded an explanation, after which Gamelin stated: "Between Laon and Paris I do not have a single corps of soldiers at my disposal."

Within an hour of this dramatic conversation, General Georges at La Ferté was receiving the first, "stupefying" news that Reinhardt's panzers had reached Montcornet. For the French High Command, the whole picture was suddenly transformed. No longer was the main threat pointing at the Maginot Line, but— of course—at Paris herself! Late that night a meeting was convened by Paul Reynaud in the Ministry of the Interior, at which Daladier, General Hering, the elderly Military Governor of Paris, and Lieutenant Colonel Guillaut—representing Gamelin—were present. In a thoroughly panicky atmosphere the first measures for defending the capital, and for the possible evacuation of the government, were discussed. To begin with, the decision was taken to withdraw forty squads of Gardes Mobiles from the armies and place them at the disposal of General Hering—to maintain order in Paris.*

Reynaud takes a hand

Meanwhile, the head of the civil government, Paul Reynaud, had arrived independently at his own sombre conclusions on the Battle of the Meuse—and much earlier than his discredited generalissimo. At 5:45 P.M. on May 14th, Reynaud had wired an urgent message to Churchill in London. The chronological context of this message needs to be noted carefully; it was sent *before* anyone in Paris could possibly have known that Rommel had smashed the counterattack by the 1st Armoured; *before* Reinhardt had broken out from Monthermé; *before* Flavigny had launched his action towards Sedan; only hours after Guderian himself had made up his mind to swing westwards, and while General Georges was still very much preoccupied with the notional threat developing against the Maginot Line. Said Reynaud to Churchill:

Having just left the War Cabinet, I am sending you, in the name of the French Government, the following statement:

"The situation is indeed very serious. Germany is trying to deal us a fatal blow *in the direction of Paris*.† The German Army has broken through our fortified lines south of Sedan. . . .

"Between Sedan and Paris, there are no defences comparable with those in the line which we must restore at almost any cost."

The Germans could only be stopped, Reynaud concludes, by isolating the panzers "from their supporting Stukas." And for this more fighters were desperately needed. "It is essential," Reynaud urged Churchill, "that you send immediately ten additional squadrons. Without such a contribution, we cannot be certain that we shall be able to stem the German advance."

On having Reynaud's wire relayed to him, General Ironside, the British CIGS, ordered that a liaison officer be sent direct to Georges's HQ "to find out what the real situation is"; but

---

* It was revealing that the first measure taken to defend Paris should have concerned the preservation of order; presumably against a popular revolt by the left, such as had been a perpetual bugaboo since the Commune of 1871.

† Author's italics.

later that day he noted, "We could get nothing out of" either Gamelin's or Georges's HQ. Reynaud, he thought, was being "a little hysterical." There is no doubt that the French leader was not in a good state, physically or mentally. He had not shaken off the depressing aftermath of his influenza; the strain of the previous weeks of political juggling had told on him; his condition was not improved by Madame de Portes constantly importuning him with suggestions for running the war, and France, or with requests for advancement for friends or sons of friends. Because of the estrangement existing between Reynaud and the Generalissimo, whom he had been on the brink of sacking, his communications with Vincennes were just as unsatisfactory as Gamelin's with Georges. Paul Baudouin tells of an absurd situation when, having heard from his Military Secretary, Colonel Villelume, of Corap's collapse on the morning of the 15th, Reynaud had been "unwilling to telephone direct to General Gamelin in order to avoid a breach with M. Daladier, who is hypersensitive in matters of this sort. . . . He therefore rang up Daladier to ask him what were Gamelin's counter-measures, to which Daladier replied, 'He has none.'" After Colonel Villelume had in fact rung up Vincennes for information, Gamelin's *chef de cabinet,* Colonel Petitbon, snapped back: "If this goes on, I will not give any information at all."* From the start, however, Reynaud in his profound distrust of Gamelin had relied upon his own "spies." The information they brought him, compounded with his small man's hyper-developed intuition, led him to conclusions closer to reality—even though they may have been tinged with "hysteria"—than either Gamelin's or Georges's. When he told Churchill on the 14th that the defences between Sedan and Paris had been "broken," he also spoke with the technical knowledge of a Cassandra who had long preached and studied the possibilities of armoured warfare. He knew that "if our front were broken . . . *everything was lost.*† There was no question of a repetition of the battle of the Marne. We had cast our lot in favour of a continuous front. We had to abide by such a decision."

---

* This incredible episode appears at least to have steeled Reynaud to one resolve, though rather late in the day. "It is time to put an end to this comedy," he told Baudouin. "I must be Minister of National Defence. Daladier will have to go to the Ministry of Foreign Affairs or resign."

† Reynaud's italics.

At 7:30 A.M. on the 15th, the morning after he had received
the French Prime Minister's first wire, Churchill records:

I was woken up with the news that M. Reynaud was on the telephone
at my bedside. He spoke in English, and evidently under stress. "We
have been defeated." As I did not immediately respond he said again:
"We are beaten; we have lost the battle." I said: "Surely it can't have
happened so soon?" But he replied: "The front is broken near
Sedan; they are pouring through in great numbers with tanks and
armoured cars"—or words to that effect.

Still evidently half-asleep, Churchill replied reassuringly:

"All experience shows that the offensive will come to an end after a
while. I remember the 21st of March, 1918. After five or six days
they have to halt for supplies, and the opportunity for counter-attack
is presented. I learned all this at the time from the lips of Marshal Foch
himself." Certainly this was what we had always seen in the past and
what we ought to have seen now. However, the French Premier came
back to the sentence with which he had begun, which proved indeed
only too true: "We are defeated; we have lost the battle." I said I was
willing to come over and have a talk.

After this more alarming communication, Churchill promptly
rang up Ironside (who was then in the process of talking to Gort)
to relay Reynaud's message, commenting that the French Premier
had seemed "thoroughly demoralised" and that he (Churchill)
had told him "to keep calm." Ironside informed Churchill that
"we have no extra demands from Gamelin or Georges, both of
whom were calm, though they both considered the situation serious." Churchill tells us that he now personally "rang up General
Georges, who seemed quite cool, and reported that the breach
at Sedan was being plugged. A telegram from General Gamelin
also stated that although the position between Namur and Sedan
was serious he viewed the situation with calm." With a candor
that would have looked well if encountered in the memoirs of
General Gamelin, Churchill admits: "Not having had access to
official information for so many years, I did not comprehend
the violence of the revolution effected since the last war by the
incursion of a mass of fast-moving heavy armour." Thus on May
15th the judgement of Gamelin and Georges prevailed over that

of Reynaud in Churchill's appreciations. At the Cabinet meeting convened to consider the French plea for more fighters, Churchill did not overrule Dowding's arguments that the home defences should on no account be further weakened. Britain's decision to hold back her fighter squadrons will ever remain a source of extreme bitterness in France; but the influence exerted upon this decision by the misleading "calmness" of the French C-in-Cs in these early days cannot be overlooked.

By the morning of the 16th—the day of general awakening—Churchill too had begun to appreciate the full grimness of the situation in France. A new SOS sent late on the 15th by Reynaud announced tersely: "Last evening we lost the battle. The way to Paris lies open. Send all the troops and planes you can." Churchill remarks that, although "no clear view can be formed of what was happening, the gravity of the crisis was obvious. I felt it imperative to go to Paris that afternoon." Accordingly, at about 3 P.M. he flew off in an unarmed Flamingo at a steady 160 mph, accompanied by General Ismay and the Vice CIGS, General Dill.

Vincennes—May 16th: The news is all bad

At Vincennes, May 16th began with a seemingly endless succession of dismal tidings. "Just as the day of the 15th had been a day of waiting on the fringe of events, so that of the 16th with one blow plunged the PC of the Commander-in-Chief into the atmosphere of the battle itself," says Colonel Minart. After news had come through in the small hours that the panzers were now nearing Laon, just 82 miles from Paris, "it was as if the old fort, witness of so many historic scenes, were pounded by the first breakers heralding the tidal wave which was about to engulf France. Never had the situation seemed so grave." At 0630 hours, Gamelin issued a desperate order instructing all troops "to hold out even when encircled, to constitute centres of resistance." Still the information being passed on via Georges remained at a minimum, and at 1015 hours Vincennes learned that telephonic communication with Blanchard's First Army had been cut off. But there now followed a series of direct communications from the front abruptly bringing Gamelin into immediate contact with the battle. First, Lieutenant Colonel Ruby of Huntziger's staff telephoned on his own initiative to report on developments around Stonne, the failure of the 3rd Armoured counterattack and the sacking of General Brocard. It was the first time since May 10th that any such detailed report had reached Gamelin without being filtered through La Ferté. Almost immediately afterwards a call came in from Amiens, from the Chief of Staff of the Second Region, explaining that he had, "in view of the extreme gravity of the situation, decided to get directly in touch with Vincennes." Giving an itemised account of the German forces which had passed through Montcornet, he then described the "withdrawal in disorder of units of all arms" from Corap's army into the eastern areas lying under the Second Region's jurisdiction. Already some 20,000 men, among them fugitives from the 61st Division, had reached Compiègne; another call from the Second Region two hours later elevated the figure to 30,000. Again, this was the first precise news about the Ninth Army to reach Gamelin. Finally, towards the end of the morning, General Touchon's Chief of Staff telephoned to reveal the full extent of the breach the panzers had made.

Evacuate Paris?

Everything seemed to confirm that the Germans were now moving on Paris at a horrifying speed. Early that morning Reynaud was with Daladier when Gamelin telephoned to warn him that "the Germans may be in Paris tonight." According to Baudouin, Gamelin then disclaimed any responsibility for the safety of the capital, as of midnight. "Which," Reynaud observed to Baudouin, "is a polite way of washing his hands!" Gamelin telephoned the same warning to Georges Mandel at the Ministry for the Colonies, supposedly adding, by the way of explanation, that the Army, "permeated with Communism," had not held. At ten o'clock the senile Military Governor of Paris, General Hering, evidently in a state of collapse, sent a letter to Reynaud:

Mr. President,

In the present circumstances, I deem it wise, for the purpose of preventing any disorder, to suggest that you order the evacuation of the Government. . . . I should be obliged if you would inform me of your decision as soon as possible.*

---

* The next day, when the panic had temporarily abated, Hering wrote anew to Reynaud saying: "It was my duty, yesterday, to suggest to you the departure of the

Once again, it is curious to note that, by singling out the danger of civil "disorder," the Military Governor of Paris obviously sensed at his back the spectre of the Front Populaire and of a resurrected Commune as a threat no less great than that of the approaching enemy.

At midday, Reynaud summoned a meeting attended by General Hering, M. Langeron (the Prefect of Police), the leaders of the Senate and Chamber of Deputies—Jeanneney and Herriot respectively—and those ministers that happened to be available, including Daladier, de Monzie (one of the most committed "softs" in the Cabinet), Dautry, the Minister of Arms Production, and Clemenceau's old lieutenant, the cold and unshakeable Georges Mandel. The French leaders met amid an atmosphere of undisguised panic. Thick columns of smoke arising from Ministries that were already beginning to burn their secret files brought home all too brutally the fact that, for the third time in living memory, Paris was directly menaced by the vile Boche and his diabolical war machine. Could anything now stop it? Everyone spoke at once. Some wild suggestions were put forward, including one that shallow-draught warships should sail up the Seine to defend Paris. Governor Hering explained the measures he had taken to defend the city; but he had no explosives. There was discussion about destroying industrial plants, but this was rejected on the grounds of the working-class riots which such measures might provoke. Reynaud, showing signs of being thoroughly alarmed, had come to the meeting prepared to order that the government leave Paris for Tours at four o'clock that afternoon, and was drafting a proclamation calling upon the populace also to evacuate the city. But Daladier felt that the cure would be worse than the disease, and was resolutely opposed, on psychological grounds, to any departure of the government; Dautry declared dramatically: "We will fight in the streets and everywhere"; Mandel, who appears throughout to have shown the most self-control,* was also silently obdurate; finally, de Monzie clinched matters by announcing that there was simply not sufficient transport to carry out a large-scale evacuation. Another call from Reynaud to Gamelin

---

Government and the Chambers from Paris. You have decided to remain. My heartiest congratulations. Yours respectfully, Hering."

* "What a man!" one of Mandel's colleagues remarked to Élie Bois that day. "What a pity he's not Prime Minister!"

(who was meanwhile allocating four divisions, plus another three light infantry divisions earmarked for Norway, for the defence of Paris) ascertained that the government could still have until midnight before deciding about its departure. Reynaud's resolve now hardened. He declared that the government "ought to remain in Paris, no matter how intense the bombing might be"; though he then added, somewhat Delphically, that "it should, however, take care not to fall into the enemy's hands."

The civilian front

Meanwhile, sparked by the panic within the French Government and the High Command, for the first time since May 10th alarm had begun to spread among the civil population.

Barring an occasional twinge of uneasy disquiet, life in Paris—and in the provinces for that matter—had run on since May 10th with remarkable normalcy and calm. Going to see the first night of Bernstein's *Elvire* on the evening of May 10th, Vincent Sheean recalled that there had been only a score of people in the theatre, and those few "wept a good deal." But thereafter such displays of emotionalism vanished rapidly. The theatres remained open (until May 20th) and flourished. The restaurants were filled, often with functionaries evacuated at the beginning of the war who, bored to death with exile in the provinces, had drifted back to Paris. Shops in the Rue de Rivoli kept up a busy trade in china Aberdeen terriers lifting a leg on a copy of *Mein Kampf*. But there was nothing which had distracted Parisian minds from the approaching peril more than this particularly wonderful springtime itself. Wrote Clare Boothe on returning from Brussels:

Paris in the spring was still Paris in Maytime. The air was sweet and in the gardens of the Luxembourg and the Bois, the unstartled birds sang. . . . In the gilded corridors of the Ritz, although now nearly all of them had gone, one or two bosomy old women with bleached hair and painted faces and less imagination than their sisters still minced along cuddling their pedigree dogs. Taxis tooted on the boulevards, glasses clinked on the marble tops of the bistro tables.

News and censorship

As a preserver of civilian illusions, hand in hand with the insidious beguilements of spring 1940 stalked the shadowy, mute

and all-powerful intermediary figure of the French Censor. The
organs of censorship resided under the Ministry of Information,
in the Hotel Continental. There one of the most powerful figures
was the "official spokesman," a Colonel Thomas whose closely
cropped hair, moustache and pince-nez reminded one British war
correspondent of the unhappy Dreyfus, and he was supported by
numbers of hard-faced ladies who had taken to sporting small imi-
tation scissors in their hats. Right from the opening of hostilities,
Gamelin had made it clear he did not care to have journalists at
the front and every effort had been made to limit their contacts
with the fighting troops to a minimum. The experiences of a group
of British war correspondents attached to the Second Army on
May 10th seem fairly representative. Because of the bureaucracy
of censorship, their "eve of battle" stories did not reach London
before Huntziger's men were in full retreat; over the next critical
days they were permitted no nearer the front than Vouziers and
received their news through a captain in charge of Huntziger's press
section, who addressed them "as if giving a conference on military
strategy," and who seems to have been no better informed on
events at the front than they themselves. The little extra they were
able to glean of what was really happening came from the in-
coherent mouths of refugees. Then, when Army HQ withdrew
from Senuc, they were dispatched back to Paris—bombed and
strafed in a nightmarish train journey lasting eighteen hours.

Thus the Allied press was largely dependent upon the information percolating through Colonel Thomas and his minions, and
upon unilluminating official communiqués; moreover, dispatches
based on these handouts had to be reprocessed, scissored and
blue-pencilled in the Hotel Continental. Often British correspondents found that the copy ultimately reaching their papers at home
added up to little more than gibberish. One of the journalists attached to the Second Army, Gordon Waterfield of Reuters, claims
that they were forbidden even to mention the existence of refugees, and that when he referred to the Maginot Line as being "almost impregnable," the word "almost" was swiftly excised.

Over the long term, the severity and mendacious editing of
French censorship meant that, for historians, the documentation
of those world-shaking days of May 1940 was even slimmer than
it might have been. But immediately it resulted in the complete
deception of the French public, so that when the truth finally

seeped through, the impact was all the greater. On the 11th and
12th, there had been nothing disturbing to read in the newspapers.
On the 13th a few fragments of bad news began to find their way
past Colonel Thomas, but not enough to cause anxiety. On May
14th, Arthur Koestler picked up *L'Époque* in a train and read
Kerillis's declaration: "The spirit of the heroic days of 1916 has
returned; yesterday, in reconquering an outer fort of Sedan, our
troops have shown a bravery worthy of the glorious days of
Douaumont." Chilled by the words, he went off to tell his friend,
Joliot-Curie, "They are at Sedan." "Sedan? You are dreaming.
. . . I did not know you were such a *paniquard*." But as Koestler
left Joliot-Curie's laboratory, *Paris-Midi* had just come out, with
the words "We have evacuated Sedan" blazoned across the front
page. "That," declares Koestler, "was the moment when the chair
under us broke down." That same day, Alexander Werth of *The
Manchester Guardian* recorded "Gloom at the office"; while on
the 15th he went to hear Colonel Thomas announce that the situation "is not unlike that of March 1918. The situation is serious;
but it is neither critical nor desperate." To his diary, Werth confided: "God, fancy saying that on the second day of the attack
on France!"

In the provinces

Intellectuals like Koestler and journalists like Werth in sensing
the imminence of catastrophe belonged to a slim minority, and it
was not until the 16th that alarm began to assume any proportion
among the public of Paris. That the picture was similar in provincial centres of the north is testified by an excellent and detailed
account of life in Amiens during these days, provided by Pierre
Vasselle.* According to Vasselle, that beautiful Sunday of May
12th had passed in utmost tranquility. During the next day, Whitmonday, some Belgian cars began to appear in the city; but this
was regarded as part of the plan for evacuating the fortified areas
of Belgium and provoked no anxiety. Some people, however,
thought they could hear gunfire when the wind blew from the
east. On the 14th, the delay with which the official communiqués
appeared to be reporting events caused some uncertainty, and
there was talk about evacuating women and children. The num-

---

* Pierre Vasselle, *La Tragédie d'Amiens*, Amiens, 1952.

ber of itinerant Belgians increased. But life continued unchanged; the shops were full, and children made ready to return to school after the Whitsun holidays. The 15th also passed without incident. There were reports that Arras had been badly bombed during the night; some cars with AF (Aisne) and NA (Pas-de-Calais) number plates now joined in the Belgian traffic, but it still flowed smoothly through the city and there was no move towards any organised evacuation. The sun continued to shine down, brilliant and hot as in July. The earliest moment of serious disquiet came that evening with the first official admission that the Germans had crossed the Meuse between Namur and Mézières. Then, on the morning of the 16th, word got around that it was no longer possible to get St. Quentin on the telephone. The cars bearing AF and NA plates multiplied, and occupants who paused at cafés were subjected to intense questioning. By midday, cars were beginning to pour out of Amiens towards the west—greatly favoured by the superb weather.

May 16th: Panic hits Paris

Amiens, however, remained a good deal calmer than Paris that day. From the earliest hours ugly rumours had begun to ripple through the city: "Rethel has been overrun" . . . "The Boches are at Laon" . . . "They'll be in Paris this evening." For confirmation of the worst, one only had to drive through the Place de la Concorde where the Ministry of the Marine was frantically heaping its files onto navy lorries. There was suddenly a tremendous run on walking shoes and suitcases at the Galeries Lafayette. Senator Bardoux, on his way to the Chamber of Deputies, noted that at half past ten "I did not have a bad impression; Paris seemed normal. But at a quarter past twelve, my impression was quite different. The requisitioning of buses, the increase in the traffic and the arrival of refugees had made Paris frantic." From every direction the first heavily laden motorcars began to appear on the roads, and throughout the day the traffic built up as more and more Parisians sought to escape from the city while there was still time.

Probably the worst centre of rumours and panic was the National Assembly itself. Outside, one of Reynaud's ministers was greeted that morning by a group of "spivs," who "looked towards

the Madeleine, 'waiting,' they said, 'for the arrival of the enemy.'"
Inside, Senator Bardoux on his arrival found

the corridors were invaded by a disgusting crowd, dirty and badly
dressed, malodorous and enveloped in smoke. The gravest rumours
were circulating—and hawked about moreover by two *quaestors*,
Barthe and Perfetti. "The Germans have entered Laon and Rheims.
They are advancing in a motorised column, flanked to right and left
by two armoured divisions. They will be in Paris this evening."

Other prominent politicians assured him that the broken line
on the Meuse had been held by two Parisian divisions which had
been "got at by the Communists."* These had "disbanded" after
being attacked by tanks and flame throwers, and the fugitives
from them were now marching on Paris "to proclaim revolution."
The Paris taxis (shades of the Marne!) were being mobilised for
an unspecified purpose that night. Pierre Mendès-France, back on
leave from Syria, recalls how one minister he knew "spent literally
the whole morning telephoning his friends to advise them to
leave the capital immediately. He was particularly concerned
about the Jews, painting a lurid picture of the risks they were
likely to run."

Reynaud addresses the Assembly

At three o'clock that afternoon Reynaud was informed by telephone that the *couloirs* of the Chamber were seething with excited deputies now spreading "the wildest rumours" to the effect
that the government's departure from Paris was imminent. He
decided to go and address the Chamber himself. To Élie Bois,
who saw him just before he spoke, Reynaud "looked like a man
taxed to the uttermost by fatigue, distress and responsibilities,"
but he managed to summon up the courage that had apparently
deserted him in the morning. With some prevarication, he hotly
denied that there was any truth in the rumours that the government had been contemplating flight, declaring: "We shall fight
before Paris; we shall fight in Paris, if need be!" When he got up
to speak, his manner struck listeners as "very noble, very firm."
Hitler, he said,

---

* The 71st was specifically mentioned. This was the thesis to which even Reynaud, in his memoirs written after the war, continued to subscribe.

means to win the war in two months. If he fails he is doomed, and he knows it. . . . The period we are about to pass through may have nothing in common with the one through which we have just passed. We shall be called upon to take steps that only yesterday would have seemed revolutionary. Perhaps we shall have to change both methods and men. For every weakness there will be the penalty of death.

On this Draconian line, the deputies rose to their feet and applauded long and loudly. Herriot, the President of the Chamber, ended this dramatic meeting amid renewed applause with the words: "France is alive to the grandeur and tragedy of this ordeal. She will live up to her past and her destiny!"

Churchill in Paris

Such was the atmosphere as Churchill landed in Paris. "From the moment we got out of the *Flamingo*," says Churchill, "it was obvious that the situation was incomparably worse than we had imagined. The officers who met us told General Ismay that the Germans were expected in Paris in a few days at most." Ismay was "flabbergasted." Driving through the streets of Paris, he noticed "the people seemed listless and resigned, and they gave no sign of the passionate defiance that had inspired the cry, *Ils ne passeront pas!* in the previous struggle. . . . There were no cheers for Churchill." At half past five Churchill's party arrived at the Quai d'Orsay for a meeting attended by Reynaud, Daladier, Gamelin, and various others. "Everybody was standing," recalls Churchill. "At no time did we sit down around a table. Utter dejection was written on every face. In front of Gamelin on a student's easel was a map, about two yards square, with a black line purporting to show the Allied front. In this line there was drawn a small but sinister bulge at Sedan." According to French accounts of the meeting, Churchill expressed surprise at the gravity of the situation, confessing that "he did not quite understand what stage had been reached when he heard that the Government was thinking of leaving Paris." Reynaud, says Paul Baudouin, then

beckoned to General Gamelin, who, like a good lecturer, took his stand by the map, and gave an admirable discourse, clear and calm, on the military situation. . . . His ladylike hand marked here and there on the map the positions of our broken units and of our reserves on the move. He explained, but he made no suggestions. He had no views on the future. . . . While this was going on M. Daladier remained apart, red in the face, drawn. He sat in a corner like a schoolboy in disgrace.

Daladier interrupted to admit in an aside to Baudouin: "The mistake, the unpardonable mistake, was to send so many men into Belgium."

Noting that, after Gamelin had spoken for about five minutes, "there was a considerable silence," Churchill continues his recollection of the meeting with an immortal passage:

I then asked: "Where is the strategic reserve?" and, breaking into French, which I used indifferently (in every sense): *"Où est la masse de manoeuvre?"* General Gamelin turned to me and, with a shake of the head and a shrug, said: *"Aucune."*

There was another long pause. Outside in the garden of the Quai d'Orsay clouds of smoke arose from large bonfires, and I saw from the window venerable officials pushing wheelbarrows of archives onto them.

The air outside was filled with whirling scraps of charred paper —projected pacts, state secrets of the highest order, all intermingled with meaningless interdepartmental memos. Every once in a while another heavy packet of documents thrown from the upper storeys of the Quai d'Orsay would strike the ground with a dull thud in front of the Allied statesmen's eyes.

"No STRATEGIC RESERVE," repeated Churchill.

*"Aucune."** I was dumbfounded. What were we to think of the great French Army and its highest chiefs? It had never occurred to me that any commanders having to defend five hundred miles of engaged front would have left themselves unprovided with a mass of manoeuvre. . . . What was the Maginot Line for? It should have economised troops upon a large sector of the frontier, not only offering many sally-ports for local counterstrokes, but also enabling large forces to be held in reserve; and this is the only way these things can be done. But

---

* French accounts of this exchange broadly agree with Churchill's, with the exception that Gamelin claims that, when speaking of the strategic reserves, he did not say, "There are none," but "There are no longer any."

now there was no reserve. I admit this was one of the greatest surprises I have had in my life. Why had I not known more about it?

Why indeed! The question certainly pointed up an appalling gap in liaison between the two Allies. Several times in his bewilderment Churchill returned to the window to gaze distracted at the curling wreaths of smoke rising from the bonfires of French state documents. "Still the old gentlemen were bringing up their wheelbarrows, and industriously casting their contents into the flames." Then he would return to fire questions at the French leaders: Why were the Allied Armies retreating from northern Belgium, thereby abandoning Brussels and Louvain? Should they not, on the contrary, be counterattacking the northern flank of the German break-through? "This is the moment to advance and not retreat," he reiterated. He hesitated to take the threat of the German tanks so seriously; so long as they were not backed up by strong infantry units they were just "so many little flags stuck in the map," unable either to support themselves or to refuel.

According to Baudouin, Reynaud, "seeing that the English Prime Minister did not appear wholly to grasp the seriousness of the situation," took over Gamelin's place at the easel, explaining:

"The hard point of the German lance has gone through our troops as through a sand-hill." He pointed out the importance of the battle in progress in the bulge marked in red on the map. He twice said, "I assure you that in this bulge there is at stake not only the fate of France but also that of the British Empire."

Turning back to Gamelin, Churchill asked point-blank: "When and where are you going to counterattack the flanks of the Bulge?* From the north or from the south?"

His reply was: "Inferiority of numbers, inferiority of equipment, inferiority of method"—and then a hopeless shrug of the shoulders.

There was no argument. Here was the admission of the bankruptcy of a whole generation of French military thought and preparations.

The French now turned the heat on Churchill to help stop the

---

* Ismay observed that "boolge" was the nearest Churchill could approach in French.

gap which the panzers had ripped. He must send still more fighter squadrons. Churchill replied at length, pointing out how disastrously the very outcome of the war might be affected if the defences of the British Isles were denuded. He referred to the grievous losses the RAF had suffered during the daylight bombing of the Sedan bridges, contrasting them with the felicitous results and small losses of the recent night raids on the Ruhr. He revealed that four more fighter squadrons were in fact already on their way to France,* but ended by declaring firmly (and pointedly): "It is the business of the artillery to stop the tanks. The business of the fighters is to cleanse the skies (*nettoyer le ciel*) over the battle." Having lasted two hours, the meeting ended. "This was the last I saw of General Gamelin," wrote Churchill, dismissing him with the withering epitaph: "No doubt he has his tale to tell."

On repairing to the British Embassy for dinner, Churchill instructed Ismay to telephone to London that the Cabinet should assemble at once to consider an urgent telegram which he was about to dictate. With a touch of John Buchan, Ismay carried out this order in Hindustani, having previously arranged for an Indian Army officer to be standing by in London. At 9 P.M. Churchill's telegram was dispatched. Stressing "the mortal gravity of the hour," he estimated: "At least four days required to bring twenty divisions to cover Paris† and strike at the flanks of the Bulge." Describing the burning of files which had made so strong an impression on him, Churchill went on:

I consider the next two, three, or four days decisive for Paris and probably for the French Army. Therefore the question we must face is whether we can give further aid in fighters . . . I personally feel that we should send squadrons of fighters demanded (i.e., six more) tomorrow, and, concentrating all available French and British aviation, dominate the air above the Bulge for the next two or three days, not for any local purpose, but to give the last chance to the French Army to rally its bravery and strength. It would not be good historically if their requests were denied and their ruin resulted.

---

* This had been sanctioned by the Cabinet just prior to Churchill's departing from London that day.

† It should be expressly noted that, by the night of the 16th, there was no considered thought by either Churchill or the French leaders that the German thrust might be aiming at the Channel and not at Paris.

Prophetic words!

At about 11:30 P.M. the reply came back—in a single word of Hindustani, *Han* ("Yes") via Ismay. The British Cabinet had agreed to the call for the six extra squadrons. Churchill immediately "took Ismay off with me in a car to M. Reynaud's flat. We found it more or less in darkness. After an interval M. Reynaud emerged from his bedroom in his dressing gown." A scene now ensued with Churchill putting on his most powerful histrionic performance in a deliberate attempt to inspirit his French colleague. It reminded Ismay of parents watching their children open presents; Churchill "was about to give Reynaud a pearl beyond price, and he wanted to watch his face when he received it." He insisted on reading out with great emphasis the telegram he had sent to London. Reynaud thought it was "admirable." Following this, says Churchill, "I told him the favourable news. Ten fighter squadrons! I then persuaded him to send for M. Daladier." This proposal, Ismay observed, did not greatly please Reynaud. But Daladier arrived; Churchill read through his telegram once again, and repeated the Cabinet's response. "Daladier," Churchill continues, "never spoke a word. He rose slowly from his chair and wrung my hand." Churchill now launched into what Reynaud described as "a forthright harangue on carrying the war to the enemy." One of the French eyewitnesses records Daladier as being "crushed, bowed down with grief; Reynaud silent and with his head erect, like some small broken piece of machinery," while Churchill paced back and forth, exhorting them: "You must not lose heart! Did you ever suppose we should achieve victory except after dire setbacks?" Warming to his subject with true Churchillian vehemence, he began to exert a potent charm over his important audience.

"Crowned like a volcano by the smoke of his cigars," wrote Baudouin in his diary, Churchill declared

that even if France was invaded and vanquished England would go on fighting. . . . Until one in the morning he conjured up an apocalyptic vision of the war. He saw himself in the heart of Canada directing, over an England razed to the ground by high explosive bombs and over a France whose ruins were already cold, the air war of the New World against the Old dominated by Germany. . . . Mr. Churchill made a great impression on Paul Reynaud, and give him confidence. He is the hero of the war to the end.

Meanwhile that same evening the French radio was broadcasting a confident and assertive address by Reynaud, which revealed an almost excessive swing from his mood of the early morning. "The absurdest rumours have been put about," he assured the French public:

It has been said that the Government intends to leave Paris: that is false. The Government is, and will remain, in Paris. . . .

It has been said that the enemy was in Reims. It has even been said that he was in Meaux, whereas he has merely managed to form a broad pocket, south of the Meuse, that our gallant troops are striving to fill in.

We filled in plenty in 1918, as those of you who fought in the last war will not have forgotten!

In this new frame of mind, before the day was over Reynaud was also warning his colleagues that the government might have to be prepared to go, at a moment's notice, to North Africa, to continue the war from there.

The Ten RAF squadrons

Next morning Churchill flew back to England, feeling that perhaps he had managed "to revive the spirits of our French friends, as much as our limited means allowed." But in fact what he, Dill and Ismay had seen and heard that day in Paris gave birth to an irremediable lack of confidence in the French High Command. From now on British policy assumed an increasingly sober view of the Battle of France. "Encouragement" towards the French would go hand in hand with retrenchment at home; operations at Narvik (which were beginning to look most hopeful) would be suspended to enable a build-up of the home forces; the Local Defence Volunteers would be formed to deal with German parachutists, and a sharp line would be drawn on the dispatch of any more fighter squadrons to France. As it was, after the atmosphere of jubilation which Churchill had deliberately fostered by the manner of his announcement, the facts about the six extra squadrons promised to France were to come as a grave disappointment.

During Churchill's absence on the 16th, Air Chief Marshal Sir Hugh Dowding had followed up his stand of the previous day with an important and strongly worded official letter to the Air

Ministry reminding them "that the last estimate which they made as to the force necessary to defend this country was 52 squadrons, and my strength has now been reduced to the equivalent of 36 squadrons." At the emergency Cabinet meeting summoned by Churchill from Paris that night, although Ironside had "recommended that we should send all we could—up to ten squadrons," saying that "it was a battle that might lay France low and we must not stand out," the Chief of the Air Staff, Sir Cyril Newall, had strongly backed Dowding. He finally produced a rabbit out of the hat, in the form of a conversation with Barratt's HQ in France which had pointed out that their bases could, in any event, accommodate only three more squadrons. In view of the fact that the AASF was being forced by the panzers' advance to abandon some of its fields that day, this was an argument difficult to refute. It was thus agreed that, as a compromise, the six additional Hurricane squadrons should be concentrated in the south of England and should fly to France daily (three in the morning, and three relieving them in the afternoon) for operations over the battlefield. The British Official War History explains: "Thus the equivalent of ten extra squadrons for which the French had asked was operating from French or English bases by the 17th." But, considering the short maximum range of the fighters of 1940 (300 miles for a Hurricane), this was by no means the same as what the French thought they had been promised on the night of May 16th; based on England, the Hurricanes certainly could not, as Churchill had envisaged, "dominate the air above the Bulge for the next two or three days." In any case, such was the superiority now achieved by the Luftwaffe that 100-odd fighters could not possibly tip the balance. Moreover, as Churchill had pointedly remarked to the French, it was only on the ground that the panzers could be stopped.

Vincennes: "A wind of panic"

How, after all the comings and goings of this eventful day, did Gamelin and Georges now propose to eliminate the "Bulge"?

In the course of the important political happenings on the afternoon and evening of the 16th, more fragments of bad news had kept on arriving at Vincennes. Liaison officers brought with them depressingly uniform accounts of the "bad appearance" of troops. Even in the suburbs of Paris the bars and bistros, says Colonel

Minart, were "filled with topers in uniform of all arms. Disorder, indiscipline reigns everywhere." In GQG itself, Minart records, something like "a wind of panic" was blowing by the end of the day: "Colonel Petitbon* had sited in the court of the fort itself, pointed in the direction of the great south portal, a 75 mm gun arrived from no one knows where, which would have been better used elsewhere. Secretaries were rapidly initiated in the service of this cannon." This order Minart considered as indicative of just how completely everybody had lost his head. One staff officer had even "had his kit brought down to his office so that he could carry it away with greater ease in case of flight." Meanwhile Gamelin himself, "sad and unoccupied, inspiring a profound pity, came and went between his chief staff officers and his ADCs, endeavouring to grasp at some intangible fetish. Nobody dares tackle him."

Nor, for that matter, was Gamelin yet prepared to tackle General Georges and take control of operations out of his hands; despite his *ex post facto* grumblings at Georges's handling of operations and the fact that one Army commander (Corap), one Corps commander (Martin), and three divisional commanders had already been (or, in Martin's case, were about to be) sacked for their responsibility in the disaster on the Meuse. Meanwhile, by the end of the 16th, both Gamelin and Georges continued deluded as to the Germans' strategic goal. Paris was now their overriding fixation. Yet at the same time fresh alarums from Switzerland combined with renewed hard fighting at Stonne still kept alive in the backs of their minds nagging fears for the safety of the Maginot Line, with the result that they could not quite bring themselves to deploy elsewhere all those idle reserves and "interval troops" guarding the line. No serious thought was given to the possibility that Rundstedt might be heading for the Channel coast with the aim of encircling and annihilating the Allied armies now in northern Belgium. From General Georges's Northeast Command, two important orders went out during the 16th. The first, General Order No. 14, specifically referring to the enemy thrust "in the general direction Givet–Paris," decreed that Billotte's armies were to "make every effort to re-establish themselves" along the line running from Antwerp through Charleroi, Anor,† Liart,

---

* Gamelin's *chef de cabinet*.

† On the fortified line behind the French frontier, Ninth Army sector.

Signy-l'Abbaye, Omont to the anchor position at Inor. But this meant that the armies in northern Belgium were to continue to hold the Germans frontally, regardless of any possible threat to flank—or rear; while the line from Liart to Omont had already been broken through the previous evening. The order then prescribed that, in the event of its proving impossible to reestablish the "continuity" of this front, the French forces were to "oppose any lateral extension of the enemy by holding all the passages over the Aisne and the Oise, as far as their confluence." Georges's Special Order 93, however, called for "a counter-attack by tanks" on the morning of the 17th aimed at "cleaning up" the whole area between Hirson-Liart and Château Porcien on the Aisne. The attack was to be conducted by Giraud, using the 1st and 2nd Armoured Divisions with reinforcements from the 1st Light Mechanised and 9th Motorised Divisions which had belonged to his old Seventh Army. From the south, General Touchon was to attack with the "de Gaulle group," about which much more will be said later. Was this, then, to be the concerted action against both flanks of the Bulge which Churchill had urged? Alas, no. Georges was totally misinformed as to the true state of the units designated to take part: the 1st Armoured had lost most of its tanks, the 2nd was split in two and dispersed, and de Gaulle's group was literally being assembled that very night under the fanciful title of the "4th Armoured Division." Furthermore, as far as the 2nd Armoured was concerned, Georges's instructions were mutually contradictory in exactly the same sense as Flavigny's handling of the 3rd Armoured on its arrival south of Sedan: on the one hand, it was expected to launch a counterattack; on the other hand, its scattered tanks were being called upon to "cork up" the various river crossings along the Oise. Once again, as events would swiftly prove, France's waning armoured strength was about to be thrown away in penny packets.

At the front: Stonne again

On Guderian's front, the fighting at Stonne continued to seesaw back and forth fiercely throughout the 16th. During the night of the 15th–16th, a fresh local attack mounted by General Flavigny succeeded in pushing two companies of "B" tanks into the village, where they destroyed some dozen German tanks. But—as so often before—infantry and tanks were poorly coordinated, so that by midday the occupying French infantry were once again pushed out of Stonne by German counterattacks. That day the battered Grossdeutschland Regiment was pulled out of the line for its well-earned rest,* replaced by the first of the infantry divisions hastening up by forced marches in Guderian's wake. On the way, they encountered scenes of destruction caused by accurate French artillery fire such as were seldom to be seen elsewhere behind the German lines during the whole campaign: "shell hole upon shell hole, shot-up tanks, motorcycles; in one vehicle . . . the driver is still sitting at the wheel, half his skull torn away, a terrible sight." Huntziger's men swiftly noticed the difference between the second-line German relief troops and the magnificent elite that had stormed Sedan. "The prisoners," says Ruby, "are sorry specimens." One letter found on a young officer revealed: "Our losses are very heavy . . . the French artillery decimates entire companies. We are fed up with this." But still the French could make no perceptible headway. "The fighting," Colonel Ruby tells us, "took the form of a war of position." From the French point of view, at Stonne this was quite the wrong form; yet now, in what was still the most sensitive part of the German front, Huntziger no longer had the armoured striking power for a serious counterstroke. At this point, Huntziger and his Second Army are left behind by the rapid-flowing tide of battle and assume but a minor role in this story; Huntziger, now ensconced with his HQ in one of the sinister forts at Verdun, reappears only to place his name on the document of capitulation which had its beginnings at Sedan.

Guderian breaks through

To the northwest of the static battlefield around Stonne, the right wheel of the 1st and 2nd Panzers moved into top gear on the 16th. Guderian, now restored his "freedom of movement" by Kleist, was himself riding up with the leading tank company in a signals half-track, repeatedly intervening in the conduct of the advance. Although Luftwaffe reconnaissance could provide no clear-cut picture of the situation to the west, it was rapidly becoming clear to the men with the armoured spearhead that there

---

* The Grossdeutschland's next battle would be against the British at St. Omer, on May 23rd.

was no longer any defending force worthy of the name ahead of them. "One had the impression," wrote Captain Kielmansegg with the staff of the 1st Panzer, "as if he (the enemy) were staring half-paralysed, half-hypnotised at the original break-through area at Sedan." Driving up from Sedan, Kielmansegg noted that, as far as Bouvellemont where Balck had fought so hard an engagement against de Lattre's men the previous day,

there was not a place that was not either shot to pieces or burnt, in which only a few houses could offer a possibility of accommodation. The smell of burning lay everywhere in the air, and in many places the flames had still not been extinguished. Then suddenly all this ceases. There is neither any sign of the enemy nor of our own troops anywhere. A wonderful spring morning . . . that is not characterised by fliers in the sky but by singing birds. . . . In this peaceful landscape, human beings were absent. Everything is dead and empty, not even the old people have remained . . . the second thing that I remember, is the bellowing cattle in the fields and in the cowsheds.

The troops were ordered whenever possible to milk the swollen udders of the cows, but "by now the speed of the campaign made this seldom possible."

"We were in the open now," wrote Guderian, and the realisation acted like the most potent of stimulants on his jaded troops. Driving through to Montcornet that day,

I passed an advancing column of the 1st Panzer Division. The men were wide awake now and aware that we had achieved a complete victory, a break-through. They cheered and shouted remarks which often could only be heard by the staff officers in the second car: "Well done, old boy," and "There's our old man," and "Did you see him? That was hurrying Heinz," and so on. All this was indicative.

In the market place of Montcornet, Guderian found General Kempf of the 6th Panzer which had captured it the previous night. With three panzer divisions now pouring through this one centre and no boundaries laid down by Kleist, it was imperative to allot new routes to the various divisions. Guderian and Kempf settled on these between themselves and then "ordered the advance to go on until the last drop of petrol was used up." By the end of the day, the leading elements of Guderian's corps had reached Marle

and Dercy on the river Serre—over 40 miles from that morning's
starting point and 55 miles from Sedan. Corps HQ was established
at Soize, just east of Montcornet. To the north, Kempf, after capturing Vervins—the former site of Corap's Army HQ—had pushed
his reconnaissance units as far forward as Guise on the Oise.
(Meanwhile, back on the Meuse, the German 3rd Infantry Division after a hard fight had just completed its bridge at Nouzonville,
thereby enabling Reinhardt's other panzer division, the 8th, to
get its tanks across the river, which it hitherto had been unable
to do. Fresh, and having suffered negligible losses, it now
speeded to catch up with its sister division.) Behind Guderian's
and Reinhardt's leading panzer divisions, however (so the Official History of the 1st Panzer tells us), there was

hardly a single German soldier to be found, except for a few supply
services, up to 25 to 30 miles behind the 1st and 2nd Panzer Divisions. Munitions and petrol were brought up over a single very thin,
almost unprotected supply road. They were also, however, tanked up
from petrol dumps and public petrol stations captured from the French.

By the night of the 16th, the foremost infantry divisions were only
just reaching the Sedan area. Here was a situation to alarm sober
minds back at Panzergruppe HQ and beyond, though not the impetuous Guderian.

During the 16th, offensive actions against Kleist's advancing
Panzergruppe by French formations, disorganised as they now
were, amounted to almost nil. After several days of rest behind
the Maginot Line at Longwy, the French 3rd Light Cavalry Division had returned to the front via Reims and was under orders to
join in de Gaulle's thrust into the southern flank of the Bulge
which Georges had ordered for the 17th. On the 16th the divisional
commander, General Petiet, decided to send a reconnaissance in
force towards Montcornet. On reaching the Dizy-le-Gros, some
five to ten miles short of Montcornet, it ran into the 2nd Panzer
and was badly battered late that afternoon. The cavalry force was
dispersed and did not rejoin the division until two weeks later,
while only two and one-half platoons of motorcyclists and armoured cars were able to disengage themselves. Guderian, in
Montcornet at the time, speaks of an entire tank company taken
prisoners, which he mistakenly states "belonged to General de

German troops on the move — panzer column above, infantrymen below

Refugees on the western front

Gort and Barratt

War comes to England:
Children watch battle in
the skies, 1940

A couple of happy, drunken French soldiers surrender

German victors jeering at column of French prisoners

German infantry on the march in France, singing

Germans in Berlin follow progress of war against Poland

Lebrun and de Gaulle, 1940

Weygand, Baudouin, Reynaud, and Pétain

Truck pulling armistice railroad car to Compiègne

Ribbentrop, Keitel, Goering, Hess, Hitler and Brauchitsch at armistice ceremony in Compiégne, June 21, 1940

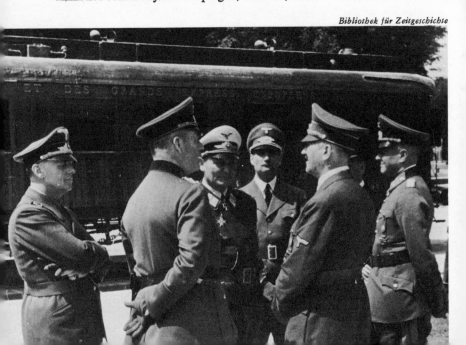

Gaulle's division."* Meanwhile, a battalion of dragoons in Hotchkiss medium tanks, dispatched by Petiet to take up a defensive
position near Sisonne, encountered no panzers, but was almost
overwhelmed by an unstoppable flood of fugitives from broken
French units. Another battalion of dragoons was ordered to occupy
the village of Liesse and make contact with de Gaulle's force,
supposedly concentrating in the Forest of Samoussy, just east of
Laon. It arrived in Liesse just as the curé, "a big old man with an
energetic expression and a moustache cut sharply above his upper
lip, locked up his church and pulled out." At about 7 P.M. the
dragoons met a solitary tank belonging to de Gaulle. Three hours
later machine-gun fire was heard, indicating that the panzers were
already close.

And what of General Bruché's bisected 2nd Armoured Division, supposedly preparing for its attack against the northern flank
of Kleist's Bulge the next day? Because of the chaos on the railways, some of the trains were halted near Bohain *west* of the
Oise. When the order came to disembark, the troops were on the
wrong side of the river and were ordered by Giraud (in accordance
with the defensive part of Georges's Order No. 14) to disperse
and "cork up" the crossing points. (Meanwhile, the fine brigade
of Somua tanks from the 1st Light Mechanised Division which
was on its way southwards through Belgium was stuck at Soignies,
northeast of Mons, by a breakdown in the Belgian railways.†)
The rest of the 2nd Armoured's tanks, left on the north side of the
Bulge, found themselves disembarking at scattered points between
Etreux (on the Oise), Le Nouvion, and Hirson, completely out
of touch with Bruché at divisional HQ now safely south of the
Aisne, and receiving conflicting instructions from half a dozen
different commands. Two companies of "B" tanks disembarking
at Le Nouvion received orders on the 16th (before receipt of
Georges's No. 14) from General Giraud directly to strike southwards at once towards Montcornet. There followed a saga which
revealed sadly the mechanical deficiencies of France's best tank.
At Le Nouvion, Second Lieutenant Perré, son of the division's
second-in-command, found that his "B" tank, *Tempête,* would not

---

* De Gaulle's attack was not due to begin until the following day. Guderian
would err again later in attributing an action to de Gaulle.

† Caused, apparently, by posters instructing engine drivers to take off to their
homes.

shift into fourth gear. On reaching Voulpaix, it had only third gear left and was abandoned by the remainder of the company. Perré spent the morning trying to repair his tank, and towards 3 P.M.—hearing that the enemy had already captured Vervins—he decided to limp on regardless, in third gear. But, coming to a hill, the motor rebelled. To his agreeable surprise he then met another tank, *Martinique,* which was having fan trouble. Like the blind leading the blind, the two tanks took turns to tow each other. Then, just as *Martinique* was giving up the ghost for good, they came upon *Aquitaine* and *Toulon,* also broken down, which were being nursed along by *Bourrasque.*

It was now midnight. *Martinique* and *Aquitaine* were set on fire, but *Bourrasque* managed to tow the two surviving tanks. They advanced for three hours, passing 10 German tanks which failed to recognise them. At 5 A.M. on the 17th, *Bourrasque*'s petrol pipe broke under the strain. Just at that moment the tanks were attacked by lorried infantrymen. These were driven off by the tanks' machine guns; then a few minutes later two men—French prisoners—came up with a white handkerchief, calling upon the tanks to surrender. They were sent back with a burst of fire, and the Germans moved away. Its petrol pipe repaired, *Bourrasque* alone remained roadworthy and moved off—destroying two German vehicles that came too close. The commanders of the two immobilised "B" tanks, Perré and Rollier, then ordered their crews to escape and make for the French lines, taking with them the tank machine guns. All through the 17th, the two commanders stayed with their tanks, manning the 47 mm turret. That evening Perré blew up a German ammunition truck and then knocked out a light tank with an armour-piercing shot. Meanwhile Rollier chalked up two tanks and a car. That night, running out of ammunition, they blew up *Tempête* and *Toulon* and—after watching from a ditch as a column of 60 panzers trundled past—finally made their way back to the French lines at La Fère.

The few fighting elements of the 2nd Armoured south of the Aisne had meanwhile been absorbed by General de Lattre, and he put them to use defending Rethel. On the evening of the 15th, a chasseur came to de Lattre reporting that three "B" tanks from the 2nd Armoured were in mechanical difficulties just north of the river. During the night de Lattre had them brought in and positioned guarding bridges over the Aisne. The next day, *Téméraire* spotted an enemy staff car approaching at almost point-blank range. A well-placed round from the 47 mm gun destroyed it, and in the wreckage was found a German colonel who had had his foot shot away. On him was a briefcase containing the whole of Guderian's order of attack for the following day, together with detailed itineraries for the panzer columns. The documents were at once dispatched—supposedly to GQG. Hearing the roar of enemy motors to the northeast of Rethel, the crew of *Villers-Brettonneux* were horrified to discover simultaneously that the 47 mm gun was jammed, while a swollen cartridge could not be rammed home in the breech of the hull 75 mm. The co-driver finally bashed it into place with a tremendous blow from a hammer, in time to halt an enemy column with a couple of shots. Thirteen German trucks were then shot up. Without being knocked out themselves, the three "B" tanks kept up their action for four days and nights, thereby forming the backbone of de Lattre's spirited stonewalling defence at Rethel. But this was not what these offensive weapons were there for; and de Lattre's fight, admirable as it was, in fact did no more than hold one of the gateposts through which the stampede had already passed.

Rommel: The Avesnes raid

On Rommel's front the 16th began modestly enough; so much so that around the middle of it the new Ninth Army Commander, Giraud, was beginning to derive false hopes that the front had been "stabilised." But it was to end with the most spectacular German exploit of the day—possibly of the whole campaign—and one which, more than any other, was to establish Rommel's reputation. His principal task that day was to smash through what he always subsequently referred to as the "Maginot Line." The Line proper, of course, terminated at Longwy, but Rommel too, like the Allied press, seems to have fallen for French propaganda that the Line had been extended to stretch from Switzerland to the sea. In fact, what faced him was a shallow belt of antitank obstacles and pillboxes which had been run up behind the French frontier during the winter; they had now been manned hastily in part by remnants from Martin's broken XI Corps, who, for reasons already noted, had even encountered difficulties in occupying many of the pillboxes. Rommel, however, seems to have regarded this line as a serious barrier and to have concentrated his forces for a heavy and deliberate blow to smash through it. By midmorning he was still preparing his plans when, quite unexpectedly, in walked the Army Commander, Kluge. On his way forward Kluge had been reassured by the scenes he had witnessed:

Troop detachments are closing up, the rear services are moving forwards, prisoners marching back. Once again there is evidence of defeat, for numerous French tanks lie shot-up in the terrain on both sides of the road. One sees the effect of the German Stuka attacks along the road with their bomb craters particularly thick at the crossroads. The hits are mostly in the immediate neighbourhood of the road. Vehicles and horses that have been hit have been pushed to one side, and craters on the edge of the road have been rapidly filled in. The artillery fire of the early morning has meanwhile died away . . . men of the Army Staff . . . take prisoner two Frenchmen, who, according to their story, have been wandering around in the woods south of Anthée for three days. In their troop they have received no regular food for the last days. They seem to be strongly impressed by the effect of the German attack.

Coming across an abandoned French camp, his staff noted the horses left still tethered to trees, or else wandering about serenely grazing. Everywhere there were signs of utter panic. Arriving at Rommel's HQ, Kluge—perhaps rather censoriously—"was surprised that the division had not already moved off." Rommel then elaborated on his plan for a set-piece attack on the "Maginot Line"; Kluge gave complete approval.

One of the first units to come in the way of Rommel's advance upon the French frontier was the remains of General Duffet's hard-tried 18th Division—the same that had first felt the bite of Rommel at Houx. After a brief stand they were rounded up at noon. Duffet himself lost contact with his troops and, like a lost soul, wandered from PC to PC in search of them all through the following day. Finally, with a handful of men he escaped through the German lines, arriving back in Paris to place himself at Gamelin's disposal again. Early on the 16th, General Sancelme of the 14th North African was also a commander without a division. While withdrawing from Neuville the previous night, deprived of any information about its formations, divisional HQ heard the dread cry of "Here come the panzers!" There was a shot from an antitank gun, and a tank was discovered knocked out. It turned out to be a French Hotchkiss, the crew of which had been killed—the leading vehicle of a company (presumably belonging to the 1st Armoured) which had not been engaged in that day's battle and was now also retreating across the frontier. Taking the tank company along with him, Sancelme arrived at General Martin's PC on the morning of the 16th, where he was greeted with some amazement, because it had already been assumed that the whole division had been taken prisoners. Still he could gain no news about it; nevertheless Martin ordered him to install what remained of his division in a defensive posture at Anor, and then (with total inaccuracy) informed Giraud* that "the 4th North African has just arrived with all its infantry and a portion of its artillery." By this time, after the appalling strain of the past week, Martin seems to have been making little sense. Having issued these and other orders to hold fast, in the afternoon he received unconfirmed (and inaccurate) reports that the Germans were already threatening the bridges behind him on the Sambre and upper Oise. Without reference to Giraud, he now ordered an unconditional withdrawal back across the Oise—the line which Georges's Order No. 14 was just decreeing was to be held at all cost.

Of the 4th North African, about all that reached Anor (on the 17th) was a colonel and a thousand of his Tirailleurs who had escaped through the German net at Philippeville, though losing the whole of Regimental HQ. After a 70-mile march, without rations, they were forced to turn and face the Germans in a state of complete exhaustion. This was the tragic end of a division which had acquitted itself bravely. That same night, General Sancelme was taken prisoner with his staff at La Capelle.

Rommel was across the French frontier, travelling, as on the previous day, in Rothenburg's command tank. Moving towards the village of Clairfayts, the tank column was warned that the road through it had been mined, so they

bore off to the south and moved in open order across fields and hedges in a semi-circle round the village. There was not a sound from the enemy, although our artillery was dropping shells at intervals deep into their territory. . . . Suddenly we saw the angular outlines of a French fortification about 100 yards ahead. Close beside it were a

---

* Who, Vervins having been overrun by the enemy, was in the process of moving Army HQ back to Wassigny behind the Sambre–Oise Canal.

number of fully-armed French troops, who, at the first sight of the tanks, at once made as if to surrender. We were just beginning to think we would be able to take it without fighting, when one of our tanks opened fire on the enemy elsewhere, with the result that the enemy garrison promptly vanished into their concrete pill-box. In a few moments the leading tanks came under heavy anti-tank gunfire from the left and French machine-gun fire opened over the whole area.

Taking up the story, one of Rommel's tank commanders describes coming up against one of the French bunker positions towards evening:

It spits fire. Two vehicles knocked out; and also from the right an anti-tank gun fires and hits the Command tank of the heavy company. The radio operator has a leg shot off, commander unhurt. I am close by with my tank, but take cover. Enemy artillery fires heavily on us with medium calibre guns. How are we going to get through the bunker line? Big question. In front of us is a thick wire entanglement, behind it a broad and deep panzer ditch, and in the middle of the road anti-tank obstacles have been built. Are there still further obstacles? The only possibility, to blow up the anti-tank obstacles, and then rush through, hoping for luck. Meanwhile it is night. The Divisional Commander as ever accompanies us in our attack in a tank.* Explosion, silence full of apprehension, then two Very lights, the road is passable. Now with a rush, shooting wildly between the bunkers. There are one or two casualties, but the mass get through.

Heavy artillery fire now plastered the French fortified zone. Under cover of smoke, engineers crept up to demolish the anti-tank "hedgehogs." Rommel watched as another assault troop dealt with the pillbox ahead of him:

The men crawled up to the embrasure and threw a 6-pound demolition charge in through the firing slit. When, after repeated summonses to surrender, the strong enemy garrison still did not emerge, a further charge was thrown in. One officer and 35 men were then taken prisoner, although they shortly afterwards overcame the weak assault troop and escaped, after French machine-guns had opened fire from another pill-box. Slowly the sky darkened and it became night. Farms were burning at several points in Clairfayts and farther west. I

---

* Rommel.

now gave orders for an immediate penetration into the fortified zone, and a thrust as far as possible towards Avesnes.

With jubilation, Rommel wrote in his diary:

The way to the west was now open. . . . We were through the Maginot Line! It was hardly conceivable. Twenty-two years before we had stood for four and a half long years before this self-same enemy and had won victory after victory and yet finally lost the war. And now we had broken through the renowned Maginot Line and were driving deep into enemy territory. It was not just a beautiful dream. It was reality.

Now the fighting took on an entirely different character, that of a mad nocturnal pursuit. There was a bright moon, and Rommel ordered his tanks to advance at top speed, firing on the move to discourage any enemy antitank gunners or mine-laying parties. "We'll do it like the Navy," he said. "Fire salvoes to port and starboard."

In the moonlight we could see the men of the 7th Motorcycle Battalion moving forward on foot beside us. Occasionally an enemy machine-gun or anti-tank gun fired, but none of their shots came anywhere near us.

The French were clearly taken by surprise: first, that Rommel should have broken through the frontier fortifications with such speed; and secondly, that—against all the rules—he should be continuing the advance by night.

The people in the houses were rudely awoken by the din of our tanks, the clatter and roar of tracks and engines. Troops lay bivouacked beside the road, military vehicles stood parked in farmyards and in some places on the road itself. Civilians and French troops, their faces distorted with terror, lay huddled in the ditches, alongside hedges and in every hollow beside the road. We passed refugee columns, the carts abandoned by their owners, who had fled in panic into the fields. On we went, at a steady speed, towards our objective.

As always, Rommel was leading the raiding party in much the same way that, as a young captain, he had led his infiltrators behind the Italian lines at Caporetto; occasionally he transmitted a brief radio message to his divisional staff, well to the rear. Towards Avesnes, progress became slower:

Military vehicles, tanks, artillery and refugee carts packed high with belongings blocked part of the road and had to be pushed unceremoniously to the side. All around were French troops lying flat on the ground, and farms everywhere were jammed tight with guns, tanks and other military vehicles. . . . Always the same picture, troops and civilians in wild flight down both sides of the road.

On reaching Avesnes, the small town from which Ludendorff had directed the Germans' last-gasp offensive of March 1918, Rommel appreciated that it might be occupied by strong French forces. Nevertheless, he ordered the panzer column to thrust forward at full speed. In Avesnes, Rommel's advance guard caught by surprise the remnants of Bruneau's 1st Armoured, on its way to La Capelle. There was a disagreeable moment for Rommel when some of the surviving "B" tanks managed to push into a gap in the panzer column, "shooting wildly around them." Several German tanks were knocked out; then, as dawn was coming up, Lieutenant Hanke—the diehard Nazi who had proved himself on the Meuse—moved in with his Mark IV and polished off the remaining "B" tanks. Of the whole French 1st Armoured Division, only three tanks crept off the battlefield. Later that day its artillery was also mopped up; with the exception of one battery, it had not fired a solitary shell. Having lost his division, General Bruneau "gave his staff officers their freedom," and himself disappeared into the night. The following night he too was captured east of St. Quentin by two engineers of the 6th Panzer.

After cleaning up in Avesnes, Rommel signalled Corps HQ for further orders. No reply. He decided to continue the headlong rush and try to seize Landrecies and its crossing over the Sambre, 11 miles west of Avesnes. Ammunition was running out, so his column now "drove westwards through the brightening day with guns silent." But Rommel was convinced that the rest of his division, infantry and supplies was following up closely behind him. Once again, he passed more columns of wretched refugees mingled with utterly astonished French troops on the march:

A chaos of guns, tanks and military vehicles of all kinds, inextricably entangled with horse-drawn refugee carts, covered the road and verges.

By keeping our guns silent and occasionally driving our cross-country vehicles alongside the road, we managed to get past the column without great difficulty.

One of Rommel's panzer commanders recalled simply shouting, loudly and impudently, at the French troop columns to throw away their weapons. "Many willingly follow this command, others are surprised, but nowhere is there any sign of resistance." Several times his tank men were questioned, hopefully: *"Anglais?"* There was evidently one rare, recalcitrant exception, who brought out the ruthless streak in Rommel: a French lieutenant colonel overtaken by Rommel as his staff car was trapped in the road jam. On being asked by him for his rank and appointment "his eyes glowed hate and impotent fury and he gave the impression of being a thoroughly fanatical type." Rothenburg signalled to him to get in his tank. "But he curtly refused to come with us, so, after summoning him three times to get in, there was nothing for it but to shoot him."

Through Landrecies and across the Sambre via an undamaged bridge, the panzer spearhead drove into a barrack full of troops. After a tank there had been swiftly destroyed, Lieutenant Hanke ordered the officers to have all their troops paraded and marched off eastwards. Almost out of ammunition and petrol, Rommel finally halted his column on a hill just east of Le Cateau, and 19 miles on from Avesnes. It was now 0515 hours on the 17th. Though his tank crews were utterly exhausted, Rommel himself immediately hastened back to bring up the rest of the division.

End of the Ninth Army

Since the previous morning, Rommel had advanced nearly 50 miles. By all the existing canons of warfare the way he had driven this thin finger, perhaps less than a mile wide, deep into the French lines by night seemed almost an act of recklessness. But its effect on an already demoralised enemy was devastating. Over the two days of the 16th and 17th, Rommel's own casualties amounted to one officer and less than forty men and NCOs; while some *ten thousand* enemy prisoners were counted and a hundred tanks knocked out or captured. The wider consequences of the Avesnes Raid were even more significant; by seizing their starting-off points, it shattered what little prospects there were for the counterstrokes on the northern flank of the Bulge scheduled to take place on the 17th; and, by capturing the bridge at Landrecies, it breached the Sambre–Oise line which Georges in his Order No. 14 had been determined to hold, come what may. Finally, it virtually administered the *coup de grâce* to the Ninth Army. The fate of II Corps and its solitary division, the 5th Motorised, was a case in point. On the left wing of the Ninth Army, this formation had played only a marginal part in the battle so far. During the afternoon of the 16th, General Bouffet (the Corps commander) ordered Boucher (commanding the 5th) to withdraw on Avesnes that night. Almost immediately afterwards a violent air attack wiped out II Corps HQ, killing Bouffet and nearly all his staff. Shaken, the 5th Motorised began to withdraw in some confusion. Then, on reaching Avesnes, it was stopped dead by Rommel. Panic sown by fear-ridden fugitives spread like fire in the dark. In the vivid words of General Doumenc, out of the ensuing chaos the division emerged "volatilised." Gone was the last of the divisions originally under Corap's command. As Victor Hugo wrote of Waterloo: "There faded away this noise which was a great army."

16

The Panzers Halt
MAY 17th

We can always recover ground, but never lost time.
—FIELD MARSHAL GRAF VON GNEISENAU

The spokesman of the French Ministry of Information, referring to reports of a penetration of the French lines by German armoured columns, said that "a very marked improvement" had taken place in the situation.

He described the penetration of the German armoured columns as being "in a long straight line," and said that some short lapse of time had been necessary before measures were taken to deal with this armoured column . . .
—*The Times,* May 17th

There is no ground for a suggestion that the French Army showed itself "overwhelmed" by the striking force of the German armoured divisions and bombers [at Sedan]. It is true that they lost ground in several places and had their line of advance ruptured; but that is only the inevitable outcome of the advantage the attacker has in choosing his point of attack. The French General Staff were prepared for such a temporary reverse; and more are bound to occur before the Allies succeed in stabilising the front.
—*Manchester Guardian,* May 17th

All quiet on the Kurfürstendamm

INSIDE GERMANY, the tremendous developments of the first week of the campaign had aroused astonishingly little excitement. True, as part of the German deception campaign, the full scope and direction of the break-through had been extensively played down. Not until May 15th did the Wehrmacht communiqué even mention that the Meuse had been crossed at Sedan, and then it was subordinated to news about the capitulation of Holland. That same evening German radio commentators also dwelt at length on the glories of the Dutch surrender, adding almost *en passant* that "the crossing of the Meuse south of Namur . . . offers the best prospects of threatening the fortress of Namur from the flank and of taking the northern sector of the Dyle Line from the rear." Nevertheless, announcements of such triumphs as the conquest of Holland, the capture of Liège and the seizure of Fort Eben Emael were given tremendous emphasis—interpellated with loud fanfares and occasional bursts from the "Deutschlandlied," or "We Sail Against England"—and it was quite clear from the occasional hints dropped by Berlin officialdom that other startling successes were being scored at the front.

Yet, by comparison with the electric days of August 1914, the lack of enthusiasm among the German public amounted almost to apathy. On May 10th, housewives gave the appearance of being principally concerned with laying in provisions for the Whitsun holiday. William Shirer noted how few even "bothered to buy the noon papers which carried the news" that day. Two days later he recorded: "A typical Sunday in Berlin today, with no evidence that the Berliners, at least, are greatly exercised at the battle for their thousand-year existence." As a modest air-raid precaution, cafés were closed at 11 P.M., instead of 1 A.M., and dancing was *verboten* for the time being. The next day, Shirer's diary begins to reveal a sense of astonishment at the speed of events:

May 13th. Astounding news. . . . No wonder a German officer told me today that even the *"Oberkommando"* was a little taken aback by the pace. . . .

May 14th. We're all a little dazed tonight by the news. The Dutch army has capitulated—after only five days of fighting. What happened to its great water lines? . . .

May 15th. Very long, stunned faces among the foreign correspondents and diplomats today. The High Command claims to have broken through the Maginot Line near Sedan. . . . It seems almost incredible. . . .

May 17th. What a day! What news! . . . I would not have believed it except that the German land army has seldom misled us. . . . At the *Rundfunk* tonight I noticed the military people for the first time spoke of a "French rout."

But still the window shoppers on the Kurfürstendamm, the strollers peacefully enjoying spring in the Tiergarten, continued to betray no visible excitement.

Hitler nervous; Halder confident

It was quite otherwise within the various headquarters of the German High Command. The hard-pressed Allied leaders would have been amazed, and encouraged, could they but have seen the nervousness, apprehension and confusion which by May 17th prevailed at the summit of the enemy camp—in sharp contrast to its very tangible successes. When one recalls the positions taken during the drafting of *Sichelschnitt,* a marked change in attitudes becomes apparent among the German principals. Hitler for one—the gambler whose audacity had previously terrified his professional advisers—was showing signs of losing his nerve; whereas the cautious, professional Halder was now bursting with confidence.

On May 10th the Führer had taken up his battle HQ in an austere nest of concrete works belonging to the Siegfried Line amid the bleak uplands of Münstereifel. Even the mess was located in a bunker, while the focal point was a small wooden hut, no more than 12 feet square, serving as a map and briefing room where all the most important OKW conferences took place. According to Jodl's testimony at Nuremberg, life at the *Felsennest* resembled "a cross between a cloister and a concentration camp . . . a martyrdom for us soldiers; for it was not a military headquarters at all, it was a civilian one and we soldiers were guests there." Although Brauchitsch and Halder had their OKH headquarters close at hand, so deep-rooted had Hitler's contempt for his Army General Staff become that contact between the two headquarters was minimal and strained. The Luftwaffe continued to roar overhead and army units heading for the front poured down the roads past the *Felsennest,* but Hitler remained curiously remote from the battle, informed largely through the eyes of the sycophantic Keitel, who tells us that he "was on the road literally every other day, mostly in the area of von Rundstedt's Army Group," which now had for its Chief of Staff* General von Sodernstern, an old friend of Keitel's.

---

* Succeeding Manstein.

On May 16th Hitler was already showing visible concern for
the safety of the lengthening left flank of the panzer break-
through. The infantry divisions marching up to protect it seemed
to be arriving much too slowly. Jodl noted that Hitler that day
"was pressing hard for the transfer of all armoured and motorised
formations from Army Group B to Army Group A," while he was
heard bellowing down a field telephone at Reichenau, the commander of the Sixth Army, for procrastinating over the release
of Hoeppner's XVI Panzer Corps.* This and other interferences
in the Army's conduct of the campaign added to the tension already existing between Hitler and the OKH. Meanwhile Halder,
its Chief of Staff, who had long since abandoned his cautious
pessimism about *Sichelschnitt* (once he had been persuaded as to
its intrinsic military virtues), in no way shared Hitler's alarm for
the left flank. Here lay the essential difference between the ra-
tional intellect of the professional and the irrational, instinctive
functioning of the unschooled genius. In his diary for May 16th,
Halder wrote with manifest satisfaction that "the breakthrough
is developing along completely classical lines." Following with
scrupulous care the intelligence reports from "Foreign Armies
West," which on the whole proved to be highly accurate, Halder
noted that there was still no sign that the French were throwing
their main reserves into battle, while by seven o'clock that evening
incoming reports stated that all attacks† against the left flank
had been warded off. The next day, fresh intelligence from "Foreign Armies West" made it quite obvious to Halder that there
was also little danger now of a serious Allied counterattack on
the northern flank of the Bulge. In the opening entry for the 17th,
Halder wrote in his diary that the "picture shows clearly that the
enemy has still not taken any major measures to close the break-
through gap." He noted that the French had brought up "at least
6 divisions" along the Germans' critical southern flank; but "here
we do not intend to attack, and his forces do not suffice for
an attack."

In his new mood of complete confidence, Halder then went on
to voice an opinion which signified a radical departure from the
original *Sichelschnitt* blueprint as well as a remarkable swing of

* Which had been striking at Prioux's Cavalry Corps and the French First Army.
† Referring presumably to Flavigny's action.

the pendulum from his own earlier mood of conservative caution. So well did the overall situation seem to be developing, thought Halder, "one may conclude that we can now consider continuing the operation towards a *southwesterly direction.** In his view, France could at this point be smashed in a single battle —instead of the two separate operational phases called for in Manstein's thinking. To Bock's Army Group "B" alone would fall the task of "encircling and annihilating the enemy north of the Sambre," while Rundstedt's Army Group "A" should now swing away eccentrically to roll up the French to the southwest— with a possible right hook enveloping Paris. He could see no conceivable threat to the southern flank, "because for the time being the enemy is too weak." Accordingly, at 1030 hours he telephoned Rundstedt's Chief of Staff, Sodernstern, instructing him not to halt on the Oise, and not to let his forces become pinned down along the southern flank. At midday in OKH C-in-C Brauchitsch was summoned to Hitler and evidently experienced another of those disagreeable sessions that so discomfited him. Says Halder laconically: "Apparently little agreement of ideas. The Führer emphasises that he sees the main danger coming from the south. (At present I don't see any danger at all!) Therefore infantry divisions must be brought up as quickly as possible to protect the southern flank."

Rundstedt supports Hitler

Distrustful as ever of his OKH advisers, Hitler then set off himself that afternoon to see Rundstedt at his HQ in Bastogne. Arriving in a state of extreme nervousness, Hitler found Rundstedt's views closely approximating his own. (Indeed, in retrospect one may well wonder to what extent Rundstedt in his recurrent anxiety was the principal breeding ground for Hitler's loss of nerve; not only during the period of May 17th to 19th, but also later at the time of the historically far more consequential "Halt Order" before Dunkirk.) The utterances of all three Army Group commanders show them to have been completely taken aback by the initial successes of *Sichelschnitt;* after the Meuse crossings, Bock exclaimed, "The French seem to have taken leave of their senses," while by May 18th Leeb, obviously overwhelmed by the speed

---

* Author's italics.

of the German advance, was writing in his diary, "It's fantastic!" But Rundstedt seems to have been the most surprised of the three; his loyal Chief of Operations and biographer, General von Blumentritt, refers to the Meuse crossings as a "miracle which Rundstedt could not understand." At various crucial moments, Rundstedt shows himself to have been almost as strongly conditioned by his personal experiences of '14–'18 as any of his French opposite numbers. His own unit having come within sight of Paris in 1914, he could not forget how Kluck's misguided change of direction had forfeited the victory apparently within Germany's grasp, and upon no other German senior officer had the French Army's capacity to recuperate from shattering reverses and fling itself into a devastating riposte left so ineradicable an impression. Any talk about a deviation to the southwest* immediately aroused in him the worst memories of Gallieni's lethal attack on Kluck's flank which preluded the Marne. His esteem for the French General Staff remained unshakeably high, and—so Blumentritt tells us—from the earliest moments of the breakthrough he and Sodernstern had lived in expectation of the wily enemy launching "a great, surprise counteroffensive by strong French forces from the Verdun and Châlons-sur-Marne area, northwards towards Sedan and Mézières."

Already by May 15th, the Army Group "A" War Diary is expressing Rundstedt's concern about his southern flank:

The question has arisen for the first time as to whether it may not become necessary temporarily to halt the motorised forces on the Oise . . . the enemy is in no circumstances to be allowed to achieve any kind of success, even if it be only a local success, on the Aisne or later in the Laon region. This would have a more detrimental effect on operations as a whole than would a temporary slowing-down of our motorised forces.

The War Diary continues:

---

* Although events proved Halder to have judged the threat to the southern flank more accurately than either Rundstedt or Hitler, his proposed "two-in-one" operation might well have dangerously dispersed the panzers and their indispensable air support. This opportunism of Halder's was typical of what traditionally provided German staff planning with both its greatest tactical strength and its strategic weakness; which, at its worst, had led to the disaster on the Marne and Ludendorff's final catastrophe in 1918.

The extended flank between La Fère and Rethel is too sensitive, especially in the Laon area . . . an open invitation for an enemy attack. . . . If the spearheads of the attack are temporarily halted it will be possible to effect a certain stiffening of the threatened flank within twenty-four hours.

In consequence, Rundstedt had issued orders to Kleist on May 16th instructing the Panzergruppe to mark time and *not* cross the Oise before the 18th. Now Hitler in his visit to Army Group HQ on the following day accorded Rundstedt his complete support, declaring:

The decision at the moment depends not so much on a rapid thrust to the Channel, as on the ability to secure as quickly as possible an absolutely sound *defence* on the Aisne in the Laon area, and, later on the Somme. . . . All measures taken must be based on this, even if it involves temporary delay of the advance to the west.

Fortified by his talks with Rundstedt, Hitler drove back to the *Felsennest* with renewed rage against his OKH advisers. That night Halder summed up in his diary: "A very disagreeable day. The Führer is enormously nervous. He is anxious about our own success, doesn't want to risk anything and would therefore be happiest to have us halt." His visit to Army Group "A," added Halder, "has only caused unclearness and doubt." From the OKW, Hitler's devotee Jodl concurred: "A day of great tension," he wrote. "The C-in-C of the Army [Brauchitsch] has not carried out the decision of building up as quickly as possible a new flanking position to the south. . . . Brauchitsch and Halder are called immediately and ordered peremptorily to adopt the necessary measures at once." Halder was forced to abandon the southwest operation—though, bravely, he still clung to his original viewpoint.

Kleist orders Guderian to halt

Meanwhile, what was the net effect of all this discord at the top on the actual executants and their conduct of operations? As previously noted, Kleist, the Panzergruppe commander—activated by Rundstedt—had already attempted twice, unsuccessfully, to put a brake on Guderian. There was little love lost between the two generals with their totally different personalities and doctrines of warfare, and during the last argument (on the night of the 15th) tempers had risen. Then, very early on the morning of the 17th, Guderian received a message from Panzergruppe HQ:

The advance was to be halted at once and I was personally to report to General von Kleist, who would come to see me at my airstrip at 0600 hrs. He was there punctually and, without even wishing me a good morning, began in very violent terms to berate me for having disobeyed orders.* He did not see fit to waste a word of praise on the performance of the troops. When the first storm was passed, and he had stopped to draw breath, I asked that I might be relieved of my command.

The angry Kleist, says Guderian, was "momentarily taken aback," but then he nodded and ordered Guderian to hand over to his most senior divisional commander—General Veiel of the 2nd Panzer.

Guderian was shaken to learn that Hitler himself, the former fairy godmother of the panzer arm, "who had approved the boldest aspects of the Manstein plan and had not uttered a word against my proposals concerning the exploitation of the breakthrough, would now be the one to be frightened by his own temerity." Guderian signalled to Rundstedt, announcing his intention to fly to Army Group HQ that afternoon to report on what had happened. Back came the answer: Guderian was to remain at his headquarters and await the arrival of General List, commander of the Twelfth Army, "who had been instructed to clear this matter up." Meanwhile, until List arrived, Guderian's panzers were also to stay put. On his arrival early that afternoon, List "asked me at once what on earth was going on here. Acting on instructions from Colonel-General von Rundstedt he informed me that I would not resign my command and explained that the order to halt the advance came from the OKH and therefore must be obeyed." Guderian's vehement exposition of the true state of the French collapse on his front (backed up by similar views expressed by the other Panzer Corps commander, Reinhardt) seems to have persuaded List and, through him, to have at least partially reassured Rundstedt. But not Hitler. Finally List,

---

* Presumably those initiated by Rundstedt on the 16th, instructing the panzers to mark time while allowing the infantry flank protection to catch up.

with Rundstedt's approval, produced an admirable compromise. He ordered Guderian: "Reconnaissance in force to be carried out. Corps headquarters must in all circumstances remain where it is, so that it may be easily reached." Thus, while giving Guderian enough latitude to stifle his petulance, Rundstedt must have thought that, by immobilising Guderian—as he would never lead his panzers "from the rear"—he would effectively have halted the advance. But he did not know Guderian; meanwhile, through what appears to have been connivance at junior levels between the OKH staff and Rundstedt's, "reconnaissance in force" was formally defined as being inclusive of all but the rear echelons!

Guderian's "Blind Eye"

A delighted Guderian was now provided with exactly the blind eye he required. Obediently, his Corps HQ remained at Soize; but "a wire was laid from there to my advanced headquarters, so that I need not communicate with my staff by wireless and my orders could not therefore be monitored by the wireless intercept units of the OKH and the OKW." The "reconnaissance in force" was set in motion. After the best part of a day's inaction, by the evening of the 17th the panzers were rolling forward again—unbeknown to Hitler and the High Command. It was a splendid piece of inspired military insubordination.

Among the panzer troops themselves, however, there was no doubt that the halt order of the 17th was regarded as an unmitigated blessing. It was, points out Kielmansegg, "the first real day of rest since the beginning of the campaign." Besides enabling the outdistanced infantry and supplies to catch up, here at last was an opportunity to get some badly needed sleep, to grease up the tanks and replace their numerous worn-out parts. But if there had been no such ruthless and self-assured commander as Guderian to keep the advance rolling, if Rundstedt had had subordinates sharing his anxieties on the 15th and 16th, could events have taken a less unhappy turn for the French? Colonel Goutard, the French historian, is one who thinks that such a two-day respite "might perhaps have given our Command time to collect itself."

De Gaulle: The chance to act

May 17th, the day the panzers halted, was also the day appointed by Georges for the first coordinated attacks on the Bulge

from north and south. But in fact it was solely de Gaulle's group
that made any concerted effort. Then aged forty-nine—exactly
a year older than Rommel—and still a full colonel, this haughty,
totally dedicated figure who had chosen to return to his tanks
rather than accept a political appointment as secretary to Reynaud's War Cabinet, had only received command of the 4th
Armoured Division on May 11th. As de Gaulle himself remarks,
the division "indeed did not exist" and its various elements were
only gradually arriving from distant points. On the 15th, de
Gaulle was summoned to Georges's HQ and informed that General Touchon was endeavouring to establish a defensive front
barring the way to Paris; operating from the Laon area, the 4th
Armoured was to "gain time" for Touchon and it was left to de
Gaulle to decide how. General Georges, "calm, cordial but visibly
overwhelmed," sent him on his way with the words: "There, de
Gaulle! For you who have so long held the ideas which the enemy
is putting into practice, here is the chance to act." De Gaulle
hastened to Laon where the next day he was joined by an embryo
staff and the scattered remnants of General Petiet's 3rd Light
Cavalry. A dismal spectacle greeted him:

Miserable processions of refugees crowded along all the roads from
the north. I saw, also, a good many soldiers who had lost their weapons. They belonged to the troops routed by the panzers during the
preceding days. Caught up, as they fled, by the enemy's mechanised
detachments, they had been ordered to throw away their arms and
make off to the south so as not to clutter up the roads. "We haven't
time," they had been told, "to take you prisoner!"

At the sight of this routed rabble and "at the tale, too, of that
contemptuous piece of insolence of the enemy's," de Gaulle declares in his *War Memoirs*:

I felt myself borne up by a limitless fury. "Ah! It's too stupid! The war
is beginning as badly as it could. Therefore it must go on. For this,
the world is wide. If I live, I will fight, wherever I must, as long as I
must, until the enemy is defeated and the national stain washed clean."
All I have managed to do since was resolved upon that day.

Having carried out a reconnaissance, de Gaulle decided he
would try to sever Guderian's communications by striking for the

important road junction at Montcornet, some 20 miles northeast of where his group was assembling; striking in the direction, in fact, which Hitler and Rundstedt most feared. De Gaulle would attack the next morning "with whatever forces might have reached me." By dawn on the 17th, he had received just three battalions of tanks. Two of these consisted of light Renault R–35s, mounting the obsolete short-range 37 mm gun; only one (the 46th) was a "B" tank battalion, and this had but recently been converted from light tanks. It had never taken part in tactical manoeuvres, and had had only one firing practice with the 75 mm gun. There was also one company of modern D–2 light (16 tons) tanks, equipped with the powerful 47 mm gun. In the course of the day a solitary infantry battalion, the 4th Chasseurs, would arrive—transported in buses that were highly vulnerable from the air. In sharp contrast to Guderian's lavish equipment, de Gaulle's 4th Armoured had no proper antiaircraft weaponry; nor could it call upon any air support worth the name.

Nevertheless, at daybreak de Gaulle set forth on his mission, through the "sad columns" of army fugitives, clad in a leather jacket and puffing incessantly at a cigarette, an exacting leader of his improvised division. Amid the harsh setting of mechanised warfare, there is a certain note of romance as its two great French and German protagonists—de Gaulle and Guderian—confront each other on the field of battle for the first time. The day began well for de Gaulle, with his tanks sweeping all before them up the road from Laon to Montcornet. Advancing through Dizy, Captain Idée, commanding the independent company of "D" tanks, observed with pride the professional way in which his fourteen tanks were deploying themselves, but was concerned to see only two of the battalion of "B" tanks which should have been on his right. At Chivres, Idée's tanks overran a German reconnaissance column amid scene of frightful carnage:

Hell breaks loose. There are their motor-cycles, their passengers inert, crumpled up in the side-cars or slumped over the handle-bars; a truck in flames; an armoured car knocked out by our 47s; infantry-men mown down while they were withdrawing behind a farm; yet another armoured car, shot up on the road to Machecourt. Chivres is cleaned up, we continue towards Bucy. A feeling of success.

Another German column of soft vehicles was overtaken, and left "a long line of fire," and at 3 P.M. de Gaulle's tanks fought their way into Montcornet, "destroying everything which had had no time to flee."

De Gaulle's attack: The German view

Here the command post of the 1st Panzer came close to being overrun that day. General Kirchner had himself become a casualty two days earlier when a vehicle had run over his knee as he lay catching up on a few minutes of badly needed sleep. Since then, he had lain immobilised, "cursing and with a menacing expression, on a stretcher near the situation map," but refusing to relinquish command and relying heavily on his two staff officers, Wenck and Kielmansegg. Leaving his command past at Lislet just outside Montcornet, Kielmansegg was driving alone to the division's advanced HQ, some 8 miles to the west:

As I came out of Montcornet and continued along the main road—the division's only route—I saw several German soldiers running back towards me. They were engineers, who insisted that French tanks were coming behind them. I was disinclined to believe it, because the direction in which they pointed lay towards our own front! My ordnance officer, however, who had meanwhile hastily driven up a hill, confirmed it. There was no longer any time to consider where the tanks were coming from. I ordered the engineers, who had already laid some mines, to set up a barricade at the entry to Montcornet.

The town was filled with all kinds of vehicles, including Kielmansegg's own ammunition columns, which were piling up on top of each other. Having established an *ad hoc* defence, Kielmansegg rushed at full speed back to Lislet, which was left completely open to the French tanks. Here he found "lying blissfully and peacefully ignorant in the warm sunshine, a field service ammunition column halted in two of the roads leading to the village, and waiting to push on ahead." Kielmansegg shouted at them to turn about. While they were reversing, the Feldwebel he had posted as a lookout ran up:

"They're coming, Herr Hauptmann, they're coming!" Soon I also heard shooting. At the same moment it occurred to me that among the other orders I had forgotten to inform my runner and clerk, who were in accommodations somewhere further off . . . then, the last one to leave, I pulled out of the still very quiet Lislet, as the first French tanks swung round into the village streets. Under these circumstances prudence was the better part of valour, for even with the best will in the world, one cannot hold up a dozen enemy tanks with a pistol.

Kielmansegg then hastened back to warn Guderian's HQ at Soize. On his way, he met a few German tanks coming out of workshops. These he immediately ordered to head for the oncoming French; meanwhile some flak guns also opened up fire from the heights behind Lislet. Several of de Gaulle's tanks were knocked out and the remainder were beaten back, but Kielmansegg notes that about 25 tanks had actually got in behind the 1st Panzer's fighting troops. Among the German casualties was Kielmansegg's fellow staff officer, Major Wenck, wounded on his way back from attending the sulphurous meeting that morning between Guderian and Kleist. On returning to Lislet, Kielmansegg found it "burning from one end to another, two shot-up French tanks stood in the village itself and several others lay before Montcornet and Lislet. My HQ was somewhat battered." Later in the afternoon there was a second tank attack, this time led by four heavy "B" tanks. But,

In spite of the fact that my light flak guns (which I had brought up in the interim) could not penetrate their thick armour, by firing at the tracks of the French machines they forced them to turn about. Here [claims Kielmansegg] the lack of fighting spirit of the enemy became abundantly clear to us—German tanks against so weak a defence would certainly not have turned round.

Captain Idée's account of the close of the day's operation strikes a depressingly familiar note:

1900 hours. Petrol is running low. The "B" tanks have just turned about. They are leaving Lislet. The infantry had not been able to follow them, and what can we do without them? There must be some infiltration at our rear. The enemy platoon commanders have a terribly enterprising air about them. . . .

His company of "D" tanks then withdrew, though he noted proudly that he had lost only one machine in the fighting. Mean-

while, another column of de Gaulle's tanks had been stopped
dead on the river Serre and forced to retreat from Montcornet
by German self-propelled guns firing across the river, which de
Gaulle with his lack of artillery was unable to engage. On its
way back to its starting point, the 4th Armoured—unprotected
by any air cover and desperately short of antiaircraft guns—was
attacked remorselessly by waves of Stukas. Captain Idée recalls
the incendiary bullets ricochetting by the thousand off his armour as he thought grimly: "We shall not get out of this. I am
blinded by sweat. I wipe myself with my sleeves—and the medal-
lion of Ste. Thérèse which I carry on my wrist smiles at me. I
kiss it." Idée survived, though he lost one more tank from the
air attacks. Now the alerted German armour began skirmishing
in the rear of de Gaulle's force.

We were lost children twenty miles in advance of the Aisne [says de
Gaulle]; we had got to put an end to a situation that was, to say the
least, risky.

What did de Gaulle achieve?

Thus ended de Gaulle's first action, within the same twenty-
four hours that it had begun. Two days later he would attack
again, this time due northwards from Laon, and with further reinforcements, but with no greater success. In view of the fame
which his armoured operations of 1940 were later to receive at
the hands of the Gaullist *mythomanes,* thereby creating the
second of the four pillars on which his historical reputation rests,*
it may be well to analyse briefly here just what was achieved
at Montcornet on May 17th. De Gaulle himself states that his
attack had left "several hundred German dead and plenty of
burned-out lorries on the field. We had taken 130 prisoners. We
had lost less than two hundred men."† But, unsupported (once

---

* The first pillar, roughly speaking, is constituted by de Gaulle's reputation as
an avant-garde military thinker of the interwar period; the second, by his performance as an armoured commander during the Battle of France; the third, by his
career as leader of the Free French from 1940 onwards; and the fourth, by his
achievements in the postwar world as President of France.

† It should be noted in passing that de Gaulle's account of the action has to be
drawn entirely from his own memoirs, insofar as he alone of the French Armoured
Division commanders of 1940 steadfastly refused to testify at any of the sessions of
the official Serre Commission investigating (in 1947) the failure of French armour
in 1940.

more) by any infantry follow-up and with no backing on either flank, it could hardly be described as anything more than an armoured raid of ephemeral consequence. It is doubtful whether it gained any breathing time for Touchon's covering force to establish itself; and it certainly did not, as some Gaullist historians would claim, bring Guderian's advance to a halt. (As has already been seen, an entirely different explanation lies behind the German halt on the 17th.) From Kielmansegg's account, it is clear that the surprise of de Gaulle's attack did create some momentary alarm within the 1st Panzer; but the German archives disclose none of the note of real concern to be found in the reports on the earlier defensive battles around Stonne, or the still greater anxiety which was to be evoked by the British counterattack at Arras on May 21st–22nd. After the war, Kleist stated revealingly to Liddell Hart: "It did not put us in any such danger as later accounts have suggested. Guderian dealt with it himself without troubling me, and I only heard of it the day after." Doubtless Guderian had his own motives for not informing Kleist, but the fact remains that the German High Command knew nothing of de Gaulle's counterthrust until the order to resume the advance had already been promulgated. Considering its state of extreme nervousness, if de Gaulle's blow on the southern flank *had* been forceful enough to make itself heard at Rundstedt's HQ, the German High Command would almost certainly have imposed an extension of the halt order. For the relative impact of de Gaulle's attack on the German break-through, one is reluctantly reminded of Samuel Johnson's dictum: "A fly, sir, may sting a stately horse and make him wince; but one is but an insect, and the other is a horse still." Under the circumstances and with the force available to him, it seems unlikely that de Gaulle could have been expected to inflict *more* than an insect bite,* and he certainly led his division at all times with the utmost personal courage. But the facts hardly justify his elliptic boast made in London on March 1st the following year: "I know of a certain armoured division, improvised in the midst of combat, which

---

* The fact that de Gaulle's counterattack, feeble as it was, should have gone down in the records as the one bright armoured effort by the French perhaps serves to emphasise how pathetic were those which the other three French armoured divisions had carried out previously.

inflicted on the Germans exactly the same treatment that their eleven *Panzer-divisionen* inflicted on us."

French attacks from north

On paper, the attacks on the northern flank of the Bulge which Georges had decreed for the 17th, to link up with de Gaulle's action, sounded impressive enough. But in fact—for reasons already outlined—they amounted to nothing. The 1st Armoured had ceased to exist—although Georges still remained ignorant of its true state—and what forces might have been available had been deprived, with one stroke, of their starting point by Rommel's night advance to Le Cateau and thrown on the defensive. Still dispersed over a wide area behind the Oise, the tank battalions of General Bruché's 2nd Armoured Division were given no chance to regroup themselves before Kleist's halt order came into effect, and were simply committed in packets guarding various crossing points. Shortly after dawn they were attacked by advanced elements of the 2nd Panzer and succeeded temporarily in beating them off from the bridges in the vicinity of Moy; although farther south the 1st Panzer managed to seize the important Oise bridge at Ribemont just as Guderian and Kleist were in the midst of their wrangle. The 2nd French Armoured remained throughout the 17th a division without a commander, with General Bruché frantically roaming in search of his lost sheep, and himself in turn being vainly sought by General Giraud. Meanwhile Giraud's 9th Motorised Division from his former command also found itself dispersed during the night of the 16th in consequence of Rommel's Avesnes Raid. Arriving on the Oise, it received no order from Giraud to hold the bridges and fell back as soon as the enemy presented itself, abandoning the bridges at Hirson and Guise. With Landrecies and Ribemont already in German hands, this meant in effect that the line of the Oise–Sambre, on the retention of which Georges had placed so much store the previous day, was already compromised. General Didelet's 9th Motorised managed to regroup during the course of the 17th and was instructed (hopefully) by Giraud to destroy "the few squadrons of German tanks" which were reaching out towards Le Cateau.* Giraud then added: "I order the bridge at Landrecies to be taken by a

---

* Rommel's.

night attack." The other division from the "old" Seventh Army, the 1st DLM, much depleted from the fighting around Breda, was also in no position to attack that day. Once again, what had been designated as a day of counterattack by the French High Command ended with the forces everywhere (with the exception of de Gaulle's) on the defensive.

Rommel consolidates

One of the legion of prisoners taken by Rommel during his Avesnes Raid was Lieutenant Georges Kosak of the 4th Light Cavalry, who had already had one lucky escape from Rommel's advance guard east of the Meuse on the 11th. Captured at Maroilles, some 6 miles west of Avesnes, Kosak managed to escape a second time by wading down the course of stream in water up to his neck. Reaching Wassigny, he was rushed to General Giraud's HQ where he was cross-examined. Giraud and his staff appeared astonished to learn from him that the panzers were already in force at Maroilles. So, for that matter, was Rommel's own Corps commander, General Hoth, who that morning —to Rommel's amusement—ordered him to "continue" his attack *towards* Avesnes. For Rommel, the 17th was spent in consolidating his gains of the previous night and early morning and rounding up prisoners; but it was not devoid of excitement. There was an anxious moment in the early morning, when, after halting outside Le Cateau, Rommel discovered that in fact "only a small part of the Panzer Regiment and part of the Motor-Cycle Battalion" had been following his lead. Displeased, he sent an officer back to the rear at once.

Then I tried myself to drive back to establish contact but soon came under anti-tank fire from Le Cateau and had to return. Meanwhile, Rothenburg with part of Panzer Battalion Sickenius had been in action with French tanks and anti-tank guns on the hill east of Le Cateau, but had soon disposed of them. I returned to the Panzer Battalion, which had meanwhile formed a hedgehog.

After further elements of the motorcycle battalion had arrived, Rommel felt the situation at Le Cateau was secure, and still in the belief that the rest of the division was somewhere close behind, he hastened off in his signals vehicle, escorted by a single Mark III tank, to bring it forward.

On the way we came across several stranded vehicles belonging to the Motor-cycle Battalion and Panzer Regiment, whose crews told us that it was wise to go carefully in Landrecies as a number of our vehicles had been fired on there by enemy tanks. I then drove on [eastwards] at high speed to Landrecies, where the Panzer III, which was in the lead, lost its way in the town. When at last we reached the road to Avesnes, we saw a German vehicle standing in the road a hundred yards ahead, where it had been shot up by enemy guns. There must have been a French tank or anti-tank gun somewhere around, but we had no time for a long palaver and so—through! As we drove past, wounded motor-cyclists shouted frantically to us to take them along. I could not help them, unfortunately—there was too much at stake.

Then, near Maroilles where Lieutenant Kosak had fallen into German hands, the escorting Mark III broke down. It could hardly have been a more awkward moment:

Alongside the road there were French officers and men bivouacked close beside their weapons. But they had apparently not yet recovered from the fright which the German tanks had spread, and so we put them on the march so far as we could by shouts and signs from the moving vehicle. There were no German troops to be seen. On we went, at top speed, through Maroilles. East of the village we suddenly discovered a Panzer IV, which had been stranded by mechanical trouble and had its 75 mm gun in working order. We sighed with relief. A Panzer IV was a strong protection at such a moment.

A short time later Rommel spotted a motorised rifle company on the horizon, travelling fast down the road from Marbaix, midway between Maroilles and Avesnes. Thinking that this meant further detachments would be following in its wake, Rommel pushed on further towards Avesnes, "but found nothing." At this moment,

A French car came out of a side-turning from the left and crossed the road close in front of my armoured car. At our shouts it halted and a French officer got out and surrendered. Behind the car there was a whole convoy of lorries approaching in a great cloud of dust. Acting quickly, I had the convoy turned off towards Avesnes. Hanke swung himself up on the first lorry while I stayed on the cross-road for a while, shouting and signalling to the French troops that they should lay down their arms—the war was over for them. Several of the lorries had machine-guns mounted and manned against air attack. It was impossible to see through the dust how long the convoy was, and so after 10 or 15 vehicles had passed, I put myself at the head of the column and drove on to Avesnes.

Here Rommel at last encountered the lagging elements of the 7th Panzer. One can imagine that they were administered a rigorous dressing-down. It was not until approximately 1500 hours that Rommel's own HQ reached Avesnes and unit after unit began to occupy the territory overrun the previous night. In the course of this move, Rommel tells us that his gunners

successfully prevented 48 French tanks* from going into action just north of Avesnes. The tanks stood formed up alongside the road, some of them with engines running. Several drivers were taken prisoner still in their tanks. This action saved the 25th Panzer Regiment an attack in the rear by these tanks.

Having arranged the deployment of the 7th Panzer to his satisfaction, Rommel says he then "took an hour and a half's rest." But he was soon restored, and—according to one of his tank officers—at Le Cateau that evening, Rommel

gathered together the Panzer Commanders and gave orders in his classic manner: "Our further line of march—Le Cateau—Arras—Amiens—Rouen—Le Havre!" We were somewhat shocked by this unreasonable demand, because we were completely exhausted by the battles of the last days and lack of sleep. It was thus almost welcome to us that the execution of this order initially failed, because our tanks had almost no more petrol.

Between the long narrow tongue formed by Rommel's foray and the hernia formed by Reinhardt's and Guderian's panzers in the Oise bend, on the 17th German infantry divisions smashed through the Anor and Trelon Gaps, thereby breaking the last of the "Maginot" extension along the Belgian frontier. Guarding the first, the remnants of General Hassler's 22nd Division were

---

* Probably belonging to the 1st DLM.

scattered into the Forêt de St. Michel; at Trelon, it was the 1st North African Division—sent down as reinforcements from the First Army on May 15th—which suffered, and by the following day two of its battalions had been reduced to some 260 men each.

On Reinhardt's front, crossing tracks with the 6th Panzer, the 8th had at last entered the battle and was pushing along the upper Oise south of La Capelle before the halt order came into effect. To the south, tanks of the 6th under Colonel von Ravenstein seized an undestroyed bridge at Origny against weak resistance. That evening its bridgeheads at Hauteville and Neuvillette were sharply attacked by "B" tanks of the 2nd Armoured. Once again, the official German accounts relate how ineffective the German antitank weapons were against the thick French armour; one "B" tank was apparently hit twenty-five times before it was immobilised by a shot in the tracks. The 6th Panzer War Diary adds scornfully that "if German crews had been sitting in these superior French tanks," the bridgeheads would have been hard to hold. Finally, by nightfall, they were secured by the bringing up of those deadly 88 mm flak guns.

Before the halt order came into effect, Guderian's 1st Panzer had taken Ribemont on the Oise and Crécy-sur-Serre.* By night-fall on the 17th, the Germans had occupied most of the prom-ontory of land within the Serre and the Sambre and Oise rivers. From Landrecies southwards to Moy on the Oise, some 6 miles north of its confluence with the Serre, the various panzer com-manders—under guise of the "reconnaissance in force" permitted by Kleist—had established a number of important bridgeheads across Georges's river barrier. Guderian for one was poised ready to resume his march towards the Channel the moment Kleist gave the signal.

German infantry man the flanks

Meanwhile, the German infantry divisions whose role in "picketing" the walls of the Bulge formed so vital a part of the German design were at last beginning to reach their positions during the day's halt. At Stonne, far back at the root of the break-through where the French were still attacking, General Forster's VI Army Corps had arrived; which meant that the motorised

---

* Not to be confused with the Black Prince's Crécy-en-Ponthieu, near Abbeville.

divisions of General von Wietersheim's XIV Army Corps could now move forward to hold the flank at Rethel where de Lattre was fighting resolutely but defensively. Also at last released from its defensive role at Stonne was Guderian's 10th Panzer, which now hastened forward to rejoin the main armoured phalanx. In the course of the 17th it was already passing Rethel to its south. Two days later Wietersheim would again be "bumped" westwards by the arrival of the Brandenburgers of III Corps, marching south-westwards from Charleville–Mézières. And so it continued, with the German flank protection divisions always coming up just be-fore the French reinforcements, bombed and strafed on their approach routes and generally disorganised, could possibly insert themselves in the vacuum between the panzer and the following echelons—as Hitler and Rundstedt had feared they might.

The manning of the flanks of the Bulge (or the "Panzer Corri-dor," as it was about to become) was undeniably an organisational triumph on the part of Halder and the OKH, and its contribution to the overall success of *Sichelschnitt* has perhaps never re-ceived sufficient acclaim by historians. But it also reflected a notable triumph of endurance by the ordinary German foot soldier. In these days, on every highway to the rear of the advanc-ing panzers the picture is the same: on one side of the road, the endless dejected columns of French captives limping eastwards; on the other, the companies and battalions of young Germans, bareheaded and with sleeves rolled up, as always singing on the march, *"Sollte ich einst liegen blieben auf blutdurchtränktem Feld"** or that old favourite from bygone times, *"Siegreich wollen wir Frankreich schlagen"*†—and marching, marching, march-ing. For them, there is little motor transport. Supplies and baggage are brought up on horse-drawn drays, the infantry move on their feet—an illustration of how, behind the thin armoured veneer of the superb elite forces in the Wehrmacht, relatively few in number—in 1940 the great mass of its divisions were probably less well equipped with the panoply of modern war than either the French or British. Up and down the marching columns dart the Feldwebels, keeping route discipline, herding on the stragglers; while at their back are the battalion commanders, Rundstedt, and

---

* "If I should ever lie dead on a blood-soaked field."
† "Victoriously we'll rout France."

ultimately Hitler—all exhorting the hard-pressed infantry to greater efforts. In the heat and dust of that relentlessly sunny May, the strain of the prolonged marches day after day is immense; wrote one German footslogger: "The first 15 kilometres a day are a country walk, the next 10 an exertion and the remainder—into the evening—sheer torture."

Slowly, but slowly, the German engineers were getting the captured railway networks running again; by the 17th, troop trains were coming up as far as Libramont in the Ardennes, three days later to Dinant. At the same time, the Luftwaffe was leapfrogging its bases forward so that its squadrons were always there to provide the advancing panzers the close support they needed. The organisation functioned with superlative smoothness; experiences in Spain and Norway paid off. Close up behind the panzer spearheads came special Luftwaffe task forces, with the function of putting back into service at top speed all captured enemy airfields. They were followed by signals units that had been training all winter so that they could lay cables from vehicles and motorcycle sidecars moving at 25 mph, thus providing immediate communications with the Luftwaffe's new forward bases. But the backbone of the whole operation was the work-horse Ju–52, in which spares, fresh crews, bombs and ammunition were flown into airfields within hours of their capture from the Allies. Even fuel came up this way; by siphoning out its own tanks and carrying an additional seven big drums, each Ju–52 could fly in nearly a thousand gallons a trip (a noteworthy feat in those days)—enough to keep a Messerschmitt squadron in the air for an hour.

Allied air forces withdraw

On the other side of the lines, the withdrawal of the Allied air forces during the 16th and 17th proceeded with considerably less smoothness. By the 16th, Barratt's AASF bases astride the Aisne were forced to evacuate. Fortunately they had somewhere to go, as—with commendable foresight—some grass landing fields had been prepared around Troyes during the months of the Phoney War. But they had virtually nothing to go in, despite Barratt's urgent representations of the past winter. "Its transport resources," says the RAF official history, "were still hopelessly insufficient for a simultaneous move of the kind now required. Six hundred vehicles short even of its official complement, the

Force would have been crippled but for two pieces of good fortune." The first of these was that the Germans did not try to cross the Aisne southwards, and the second the fact that the AASF in some mysterious way managed to "borrow" three hundred new American lorries from the French, which "in spite of protestations" they kept until the final evacuation. Airfield accommodation was also aided by the "rolling-up" of four of the worst-hit* of Barratt's ten bomber squadrons. Barratt himself moved his HQ from its dangerous position in the path of the panzers, at Chauny west of Laon, back to Coulommiers south of the Marne. On the 17th, the Air Component backing Gort in the north was also forced to withdraw, and Barratt—south of the enemy Bulge— henceforth found himself completely out of communication with it. Two days later the Air Component would be removed to England. Needless to say, in the highly charged emotions of the moment, the withdrawal of the RAF bases was widely regarded by the French as a sign that it was "running away"—a rumour that hardly improved French morale.

At the same time as Barratt, however, General d'Astier was also obliged to move his ZOAN HQ back from Chauny to Chantilly. On the 16th, some ten French units had to withdraw from the Reims–Mézières–Laon triangle, and the next day they were followed by a further four Groupes of fighters and one of bombers. It was at this point that the weakness of the French Air Force supply organisation began to show up. General d'Astier notes that, incredibly enough, it was the responsibility of each Groupe to send its own pilots to the rear to ferry up replacement aircraft; meanwhile, even at the peak of battle, the depots closed down on Sundays and after hours! In the chaos that accompanied the withdrawals of the Allied air forces, air activities were reduced to a minimum—at the worst possible moment. On the 16th, 250 sorties were flown by French fighters (compared with 340 on the 14th), of which only 153 were over the critical fronts;† on the 17th, a similar effort was made, but also dispersed across an area stretching from Antwerp to the Maginot Line. Only 22 victories were claimed. While the Luftwaffe was launch-

---

* Two Battle squadrons—Nos. 105 and 208—had only four planes left between them; the two Blenheim squadrons—Nos. 114 and 139—had nine.

† The British were largely absent from the battle that day.

ing single attacks on communications of 100 bombers at a time, all that could be scraped up to support de Gaulle's attack towards Montcornet was about 12 Léos escorted by about 30 fighters. The air supremacy of the enemy was becoming more and more marked. In the French Air Force, units such as Groupe I/54 had been reduced to one serviceable aircraft. In an encounter over Gembloux (northern Belgium) on the 17th, 11 out of 12 Blenheims from No. 82 Squadron were shot down, the sole survivor heavily damaged. The useless, lethal Battles had now been withdrawn from daylight operations for service only at night; yet, in the words of the official historians:

In fact, so many Battle crews now dropped their bombs with no more precise identifications of their target than that provided by their watches, that Barratt was compelled to forbid bombing "on estimated time of arrival." After that the phrase ceased to appear in the pilots' reports. The practice, however, continued.

"Why don't our planes protect us?"

So strained had the Allied air resources become that, among their many tasks, they were unable either to come to the aid of the Second Army, which was still being heavily bombed by the Germans to break up any fresh threat to the flank at Stonne, or to assist the withdrawal of the armies in northern Belgium. This absence of friendly planes above them was having its cumulative effect on the morale of the French ground troops. Their progressive despair is well summed up by an account kept by a French NCO, René Balbaud, moving up with reinforcements towards Maubeuge. On first being machine-gunned by enemy aircraft on the 14th, he wondered: "How the devil did these planes escape being pursued by our squadrons? Probably an accident." The next day, after his unit headquarters had been bombed, he remarked: "But they can't really know where it is. It's just luck. We don't, in fact, see much of the French planes." On the 16th, following more bombing, he is questioning: "Why don't our planes protect us? No one says it aloud any more, but everyone is thinking it." After a night spent in hastily dug trenches, and still more bombing, he admits: "This bombing has tired even the toughest. What can one do with light machine-guns against 150 bombers?" Finally he concludes: "Not to see the enemy face to face, to have no means of defence, not to see the shadow of a French or Allied plane during hours of bombing, this was one of the prime reasons for the loss of our faith in victory."

Meanwhile, on the morning of May 17th there had been some disagreement between Barratt and the French High Command on the employment of the additional RAF fighter squadrons promised by Churchill. Should they be used to escort Allied daylight bombing missions, or to shoot down the German bombers attacking the ground troops? The two tasks were obviously irreconcilable. General Georges pleaded that the troops could not stand up to the devastating combination of tanks and aircraft. Finally it was agreed to reduce still further the modest French daylight bombing effort, so as to concentrate on providing the ground forces with more air cover.

Retreat from Belgium

In northern Belgium the methodical withdrawal of the Allied armies began on the 16th and continued through the 17th. The 3rd and 4th Panzers of General Hoeppner's XVI Corps, still hammering away at the Gembloux Gap, were now transferred from Bock to Rundstedt's Army Group "A," swinging southwest for Charleroi and Maubeuge to assure the northern flank of the Bulge. Thus all but one of the ten German panzers were now concentrated in the encircling thrust towards the Channel. But the bulk of Bock's forces continued to push hard behind the retreating Allies, so as to grant them no possibility of disengaging. Although the Germans were nowhere able to breach the Allied positions, over the 16th and 17th the BEF experienced its hardest fighting of the campaign so far. On rereading his diary the next day, Lieutenant General Alan Brooke found the following entry: "I was too tired to write last night, and now can barely remember what happened yesterday. The hours are so crowded and follow so fast on each other that life becomes a blur and fails to cut a groove in one's memory." General Prioux—depressed and annoyed at seeing most of his Cavalry Corps dispersed in small packets to fill the *ad hoc* needs of the First Army—went on the 17th to Army Group HQ at Douai to see Billotte, who told him, "We are on the way to a new Sedan, and more terrible still than that of 1870." Despite the speed with which Rundstedt's drive in the south was moving, bearing with it the threat of annihilation for

Billotte's armies in the north, their withdrawal was proceeding with painful slowness. Nevertheless, on the 17th Billotte proposed that the move back to the Dendre line scheduled to take place that night be postponed twenty-four hours. In agreement with the Belgian High Command, Gort managed to dissuade Billotte, and the original plan was adhered to—amid some confusion and costly errors. By nightfall on the 17th, German troops were marching into Louvain and Brussels for the second time in a generation. Falling back with his unit on Maubeuge that day, René Balbaud wrote, baffled: "We don't understand. A liaison officer's driver brings strange news. The Germans, he says, have entered France at Sedan. We have no radio. . . . Somehow the old jokes about our coming occupation of Germany have become scarce."

French High Command: A bogus calm . . .

Back at La Ferté, General Georges came to the disagreeable conclusion during the morning of the 17th that there was now no good prospect of holding the panzers on the Oise. Accordingly, he sent out another special order stipulating: "Should No. 1 Army Group be forced to abandon the Sambre-Oise line north of La Fère, it must reestablish itself on the line of the Escaut at Valenciennes, Cambrai, Le Catelet, St. Quentin, St. Simon, the Crozat Canal, and La Fère in conjunction with Touchon's Army Detachment." To block the approaches to Paris, Georges decided to create a "new" Seventh Army and introduce it into the hole left by Giraud's vanishing Ninth Army, to link up Touchon's forces with the rest of No. 1 Army Group, along a line southeastwards from Péronne on the Somme. To command this army he chose General Frère, a Corps commander from a quiet sector, whom he had summoned urgently to La Ferté to receive his orders. At Frère's disposal would be some ten divisions, mostly drawn (at last!) from those standing as reinforcements behind the Maginot Line or the Alps; as well as the 3rd Light Division which had originally been dispatched to Brest for embarkation to Norway, then recalled and placed at the disposal of Governor Hering for the defence of Paris. But on the morning of the 17th, the "new" Seventh Army comprised only General Frère and two staff officers.

After the panic of the previous day, a kind of bogus calm

descended once more on Vincennes as the dawn of the 17th brought the realisation that the Germans were no nearer to Paris. At eight o'clock, Gamelin received a brief letter from Daladier asking him to produce a report on the conduct of operations and his personal appreciation of the situation. This was very much Gamelin's forte, and with gusto he sat down to devote his day to preparing a copious memorandum—while the battle for France raged less than 100 miles away. Once again, there would be no intervention in Georges's handling of the battle that day from Gamelin. After completing his paper work, he visited La Ferté, where "they seemed to be calm." At this time, reassuring news was reaching Georges's HQ that the panzers had been halted and were possibly even turning away from Paris. Certainly the threat did not seem as acute as it had on the 16th. Meeting General Frère, Gamelin made vague reference to a major counteroffensive he was contemplating, whereupon (says Gamelin) "I saw his face light up; he has the soul of a great leader."

That day Gamelin received a telephone call from Reynaud, insisting that he should draft a new order of the day for broadcasting to the forces. "I showed some coolness towards this," says Gamelin, "having addressed two already to the troops." However, Reynaud's wish prevailed and an order was prepared ending on a Verdun-like note that, however, somewhat lacked conviction:

Every soldier who might not be able to advance must let himself be killed on the spot rather than abandon the portion of national soil which has been entrusted him.

As always, in the grave moments of our history, the order today is: *Conquer or die. One must conquer.*

GAMELIN

Meanwhile, another telegram was sent off to Churchill suggesting that perhaps the German supply columns might be impeded if the RAF were to drop magnetic mines in the Meuse.

In Paris too

The false sense of relief was general to Paris on the 17th. Senator Bardoux noted that "this morning, the press seem to have unwound, slightly. The taxis have received a counter-order." Later

he picked up a dangerously, falsely comforting rumor to the effect
that Churchill had promised to send France every single fighter
based in England. Paul Baudouin also recorded: "The military
situation appears to be no worse, possibly because the German
armoured divisions have had to regroup and revictual. The truth
is that everybody is optimistic because Paris is not yet under fire
from the German tanks." This showed some profundity. But in
the evening: "The news brought by Colonel Villelume was not so
good. The German columns are turning away from Paris towards
the Channel Ports. The enemy advance has become very rapid
again, and it seems as if it cannot be stopped."

Recalled to duty: Weygand and Pétain

Reynaud had now firmly decided to get rid of Gamelin. But
when he broached the subject at a Cabinet meeting that day,
Daladier once again sprang to Gamelin's defence, and—as at the
stormy session of May 9th—no conclusion was reached. Reynaud,
however, had already taken other steps in utmost secrecy. The
following telegram had been dispatched to seventy-three-year-old
General Maxime Weygand, commanding the French forces in the
Levant: "The gravity of the military situation on the western front
is increasing. Please come to Paris without delay. Make suitable
arrangements to transfer your functions to the high authority
you may choose. Secrecy of your departure is desirable." Weygand received it in Syria on the 17th and immediately packed his
bags.

Meanwhile, Reynaud had also sent a special envoy by night
train to Madrid to bring back the French ambassador there, another old soldier of renown—Marshal Philippe Pétain.*

---

* In the Assembly that day Laval was reported as already calling for a government led by Pétain and Weygand.

17

The Dash to the Sea
MAY 18th—20th

They never knew. Nobody knew anything. They were
evacuating. There was no way to house them. Every
road was blocked. And still they were evacuating. Somewhere in the north of France a boot had scattered an
ant-hill, and the ants were on the march. Laboriously.
Without panic. Without hope. Without despair. On the
march as if in duty bound.
—Antoine de Saint-Exupéry, *Flight to Arras*

As for the German armoured column so often mentioned during the last few days . . . this column seems
to have gone astray, inasmuch as it moved straight forward for too long and ultimately found itself too far
away from the mass of the German army.
—*Daily Telegraph*, May 18th

It may be assumed from the reticence of the French communiqués, and from the sibylline ring of French newspaper comment, that General Gamelin has his counterthrust ready.
—*The Times*, May 18th

Every day which elapses without a catastrophe must be
regarded as a day of victory.
—*L'Époque*, May 19th

The high point of the crisis is over . . . our soldiers are
now accustoming themselves to the German methods of
attack and know how to counter them.
—*Paris-Soir*, May 20th

Panzers advance again

As soon as day broke on the 18th, the panzers resumed their
advance. Over the ensuing three days "these hideous, fatal

scythes," as Churchill so aptly called them, now encountering steadily lessening resistance in their path, moved with a new and terrible impetus. Such was the acceleration of events that entries in the war diaries on both sides are reduced to a minimum. Bursting out from its bridgeheads on the Oise, Guderian's 2nd Panzer Division rushed forward to grab the city of St. Quentin 10 miles to the west by 8 A.M. On its left, the 1st Panzer—once again in the lead—reached Péronne and the important nearby bridges over the Somme at the end of the morning after sweeping forward some 30 miles. More columns of retreating French troops were taken by surprise and rounded up, including several staffs who, according to Guderian, "had arrived at Péronne to find out what was happening." Meanwhile the 10th Panzer was drawing level to provide mobile "blocking detachments" (*Sperrverbände*) along that sensitive, ever-lengthening southern flank. Northwards from Guderian, Reinhardt's 6th Panzer pushed out from its bridgeheads to make the welcome discovery that the "B" tanks of Bruché's 2nd Armoured Division, which had given it such a hard battle the previous day, had now "disappeared" in a west-southwesterly direction. Reinhardt reported back: "The enemy does not represent a very serious danger . . . and his local attacks are nothing more than pin-pricks, deprived of any unified command. There is only one mission for the XLI Army Corps; to push on without bothering about either the right or the left."

Towards the middle of the afternoon, however, the 6th Panzer's "Combat Group Ravenstein" ran into heavy resistance around Le Catelet. Once more the superiority of the French "B" tanks made itself felt. For two and one-half hours the fighting raged. Finally the last coherent units of the French 2nd Armoured, under command of Lieutenant Colonel Golhen, were submerged by sheer weight of numbers. Ravenstein's tanks pushed into Le Catelet, where they overran the headquarters of the ill-fated Ninth Army. The entire HQ staff, including the Army Chief of Staff, were taken prisoners. Only the commander himself, General Giraud, who happened to be away at his advanced command post, *behind* the panzers, managed to escape—temporarily. By nightfall Reinhardt's corps had established itself astride the main road some 6 miles south of Cambrai. Summing up the day's events (after the war), the reluctant Kleist admitted that Ravenstein's engagement had been "the only noteworthy incident" to confront the Panzer-gruppe.

On the northern flank of the Panzer Corridor, the 5th Panzer (still lagging behind Rommel) captured the fortress of Maubeuge and encountered fierce resistance in the Forest of Mormal from the 1st North African Division and the 1st DLM, which had been sent down from Prioux's Cavalry Corps for the abortive French counterstroke of the 17th. Confused fighting continued in the forest during the next day.

Rommel too fought one brisk engagement that day. Shortly after midnight on the 17th he had received orders to push on to-wards Cambrai, 15 miles down a ruler-straight road from Le Cateau. Some six hours later the adjutant of Rothenburg's 25th Panzer Regiment, still stuck out on the tip of the tongue left by Rommel's Avesnes Raid, arrived at HQ to report that "a powerful enemy force" had established itself midway between Landrecies and Le Cateau. He had managed to get through under cover of darkness in an armoured car, but Rothenburg's line of communications was now threatened—and he urgently needed petrol and ammunition. Rommel promptly set his remaining panzer battalion in motion towards Le Cateau, "with orders to push through to the regiment and get the ammunition and petrol up to it." Needless to say, he then followed closely in its wake. He soon caught up with it, finding its tanks in action against French armour which barred the way. Says Rommel: "Violent fighting developed on the road and there was no chance of out-flanking the enemy position on either side. Our guns seemed to be completely ineffective against the heavy armour of the French tanks."* After watching the action at close range for some time, he disengaged the tank battalion and struck out with it south-westwards. Again they ran into French armour and slowly fought their way through. It was not until midday that Rommel finally reached Rothenburg, who reported that he had held his ground against heavy enemy tank attacks, but was "now in-capable of further movement." For some reason, the petrol and ammunition column had not followed Rommel; thus "I was not at that moment in a position to help him. . . . Meanwhile, French heavy artillery had begun to lay down a heavy barrage on our

---

* These were presumably Somuas from the 1st DLM.

hedgehog position. Their fire was accurate and part of the position had to be vacated."

Despite the evident precariousness of his situation, Rommel —like Reinhardt—appears to have recognised that the French attacks represented desperate "pinpricks" rather than any serious, coordinated counterattack. Accordingly, he ordered Rothenburg's Panzer Regiment to form up for the attack on Cambrai even before arrival of the supply trains was assured. Revictualling of the main body of Rothenburg's regiment did not take place until some hours later, towards the evening. In the meantime a composite battalion of motorised infantry was already streaking out towards Cambrai, led by only a few tanks and two troops of self-propelled flak guns. It was a calculated risk* typical both of Rommel and of the revolutionary dynamism of the Wehrmacht which had already carried so much before it. According to Rommel:

The battalion advanced over a broad front and in great depth straight across the fields to the northwest [of Cambrai], throwing up a great cloud of dust as they went. Tanks and AA guns scattered fire at intervals into the northern outskirts of Cambrai. The enemy in Cambrai, unable in the dust to see that most of our vehicles were soft-skinned, apparently thought that a large-scale tank attack was approaching the north of the town and offered no resistance.

By nightfall, the town was firmly in Rommel's hands. Following along his route later, a German war correspondent described a 12-mile swathe of wreckage:

Tanks, trucks, guns, command vehicles, horses and also human beings

---

* The episode later caused something of a domestic furore, in itself illustrative of the stresses which the campaign was beginning to impose upon the Germans. Rommel's extremely competent staff major, Heidkämper, complained to him in a memorandum that, as divisional commander, he should have stayed farther to the rear. Furious, Rommel confided to his wife:

"I shall have to have him posted away as soon as I can. This young General Staff Major, scared that something might happen to him and the Staff, stayed some 20 miles behind the front and, of course, lost contact with the fighting troops which I was commanding up near Cambrai. Instead of rushing everything up forward, he went to Corps HQ, upset the people there and behaved as if the command of the division were no longer secure. And he still believes to this day that he performed a heroic deed."

A few days later, however, Heidkämper was forgiven.

—in fact everything that found itself retreating on this road. Most numerous of all are the vehicles, which were surprised in the middle of the road by the advancing panzers, and which drove into the ditches and were dispatched. It was a picture of horror that no one could ever forget.

Here and there were French tanks with whole slabs of their turrets ripped away, presumably the result of near-hits from Stuka bombs detonating their ammunition; while on one airfield near Cambrai, some 42 French planes were counted—shot up on the ground by the Luftwaffe. The 7th Panzer's losses for the 18th amounted to 35 killed, including 4 officers.

Hitler comes round

Back at the German High Command, oblivious of events at the front, the argument of the previous day had continued on an even higher note. At 9 A.M. there was a meeting at Hitler's HQ, attended by Brauchitsch and Halder, at which (according to Halder) there was "an extremely unpleasant discussion." Hitler was still displaying "an incomprehensible anxiety" about that southern flank: "He rages and bellows that we are on the way to wrecking the whole operation and heading for the danger of a defeat." Then, around midday, news arrived at OKH that Antwerp, Cambrai* and St. Quentin had been captured. Apparently without further reference to Hitler, Halder issued orders for the panzers to "win the line Cambrai–St. Quentin," and push on westwards with reconnaissance forces. At a second, 5 P.M. meeting with Hitler, Halder explained the new situation "and demanded freedom of movement. This was accorded." (By this time, however, it could do little to alter operations at the front.) Thus, says Halder acidly and with a certain smugness, "the correct thing finally came to pass; but with ill temper all round and in a form that, seen from the outside, gave the appearance of being a measure concluded by the OKW"—i.e., by Hitler.

The following day the German radio announced the capture of St. Quentin and Le Cateau and claimed that since May 10th, 110,-000 prisoners had been taken—not including the Dutch Army.

---

* This was obviously somewhat premature, as Rommel did not take Cambrai till much later in the day.

Giraud captured

On the French side, there was no sign of any consolidated effort on the 18th. There was in fact little available for one. General Georges's armoured divisions had virtually ceased to exist: the 1st had been destroyed by Rommel; the 2nd, split in two, had been blotted out piecemeal; the 3rd, reduced to a fraction of its strength, was still operating feebly and fruitlessly in the Stonne area; while de Gaulle's *ad hoc* 4th Armoured Division, licking its wounds from its blooding on the 17th, was preparing for a second action on the 19th. The 6th Army, Touchon's "blocking" force formed behind the Aisne, stood guarding the unthreatened road to Paris, but as its function was purely defensive it could in no way influence the tide of the panzers flooding to the coast. The futility of its role is depicted by Hans Habe, an Austrian refugee who had volunteered for the French Army and whose division had been pushed up into the Le Chesne sector, at the root of the Panzer Corridor, just 20 miles south of Sedan. "Our officers, to be sure, spoke of a counter-offensive," he says, "but no one believed them." For three weeks they sat passively on their positions: "They said we were going to spend some time in the Forest of Noirval . . . we seriously discussed where we should be sent on furlough after forty days in the front line." It sounded like the Phoney War all over again.

Of the other hastily constituted "cork," General Frère's new Seventh Army on Touchon's left, the 23rd and the 3rd Light Division arrived on the morning of the 18th, but could only get as far as the wrong side of the Crozat Canal between Ham and La Fère before having to dig in to meet the rapidly approaching enemy. North from Ham almost as far as Douai, 40 miles distant, stretched a gaping hole in which lay the now worthless fragments of the French Ninth Army. Between this hole and the Channel, nothing—except for two British territorial divisions. These, the 12th and 23rd, had been in France a month; neither fully equipped nor trained, they had been employed on line-of-communications duties between the BEF and its rear bases. Their strength was equivalent to little more than half that of a normal division, and many of their fieldpieces could fire only over open sights because of the lack of proper instruments. Now they too, the only units available, were flung into the hole in the dyke.

The 23rd was given the task of holding 16 miles of the Canal du Nord, from Douai and behind Cambrai where Rommel was pressing forward; the remaining 14 miles southwards to Péronne was to be occupied by Frère's troops, who could never arrive in time. The British 12th Division was distributed in small packets guarding the widely separated centres of Abbeville, Amiens, Doullens and Cléry-sur-Somme. It was not much to set in the way of seven highly experienced panzer divisions. On the evening of the 18th, a light detachment of Guderian's 1st Panzer made their first contact with British troops, the Royal West Kents, just outside Péronne. Temporarily the Germans withdrew into the town, but the British were ordered to fall back on Albert as night fell. Meanwhile, a train carrying a brigade of the 12th Division was hit that afternoon during the first Luftwaffe air raid on Amiens.

The night of May 18th–19th witnessed the consummation of the tragedy of the French Ninth Army. Out of contact both with General Frère and with most of his own troops during the 18th, General Giraud had been ordered by Billotte to pull back his HQ to Le Catelet, but—as "the only way of maintaining morale"—he insisted on staying put himself in his command post at Wassigny, 15 miles to the east, with a minimum of staff. At 1600 hours he decided to withdraw to Main Army HQ at Le Catelet, little knowing that it was about to be overrun by the 6th Panzer. Accompanied by two of his officers, he got to within 6 miles of Le Catelet when he heard reports that German armour was in the neighbourhood. For the next three hours the group worked their way cross-country by compass. Arriving at the burning town of Le Catelet, Giraud and his group exchanged shots with a panzer detachment. They then took refuge in a wood, and Giraud ordered his companions to separate. Slowed down by a wound acquired in the First War, Giraud was picked up by a French column with a gun carrier in the lead—into which he climbed. More German tanks were encountered, the first being knocked out by Giraud's gun carrier. Later Giraud was forced to seek refuge in an isolated farmhouse. At 6 A.M. on the 19th it was surrounded by German troops, and Giraud was forced to surrender—according to the French, to a group of tanks; according to the War Diary of the 6th Panzer, to the men of one of its field kitchen units. That same day the division also captured General Bruneau, the commander of the annihilated French 1st Armoured Division. Giraud's command had lasted exactly three and one-half days. He had done the best he could in an already hopeless situation.

With the disappearance of Giraud the Ninth Army, which the portly General Corap had taken into battle just nine days earlier, also disappeared. One of Gamelin's liaison officers returning from the front reported:

Complete disintegration. Out of 70,000 men and numerous officers, no single unit is commanded however small . . . 10 percent at most of the men have kept their rifles. . . . Out of the thousands we sifted, it wasn't possible for me to form one company for the defence of the bridge at Compiègne. However, the losses had not seemed to be high. There were no wounded among the thousands of fugitives . . . they don't understand what has happened to them. The sight of an aeroplane induces terror in them. The service troops broke up before the infantry and it was they who spread disorder everywhere.

Covering the BEF sector for the *New York Times,* Drew Middleton encountered some of the tattered remains of the Ninth Army straggling through Amiens: "They were the clerks, the cooks, the anti-aircraft, and the heavy artillery of the Army that had been decisively beaten and routed. As they sat on their horse-drawn carts in their dirty uniforms, they did not look like soldiers but like gypsies." It was not a heroic epitaph.

Fugitives and refugees

The spectacle of broken French soldiers who had lost touch with their units, or were simply on the run, was becoming common throughout northern France as the panzers speeded their advance. One typical Odyssey was that of Jean Muray, a gunner on leave at Signy-le-Petit in the Ardennes when the Germans attacked. He and several hundred others were told to await transportation back to their division, but transportation never arrived. On May 15th, fugitives from the battle on the Meuse began to pass through Signy and the rumble of guns was audible in the distance. Finally a sergeant major distributed one rifle to every five men and ordered them to try to make for safety in small groups. Still lugging their heavy leave kits with them, Muray's group headed westwards. Soon they joined up with a retreating column commanded by a lieutenant; it was all that was left of an artillery regiment mauled on the Meuse, plus a sprinkling of infantrymen. They had already been on the road for three days, rifling what food they could from abandoned villages. During the night of the 16th, says Muray:

We marched incessantly, with a surprising continuity for two long hours, and then the column suddenly stopped. A powerful light was fixed upon us at a turn in the road . . . profiting from this unhoped for halt, men sat down on the side of the road. A quarter of an hour passed. Then an officer came to the back of the column, to announce that we were prisoners and that we must throw away our arms. In front of us was a machine-gun carrier. The Commander had already been taken away by the Germans. . . . I threw my rifle away in the ditch. How simple this had all been!

But a short time later Muray and his companions realised that the Germans had all departed, taking with them only the commander of the column, so they resumed their flight. Passing through a wood they heard a fusillade of shots, then came on some civilian refugees whom some soldiers were contemplating shooting as spies. There was also a twenty-year-old infantryman who had been beaten up and was in such a state he could not explain which unit he came from. He was taken along with the fugitives, under escort. The next day, reaching Brunehamel, strewn with dead horses with horribly distended stomachs—the remnants of a column shot up during Reinhardt's break-out from Monthermé —Muray and his group were surrounded by Germans. Trying to flee across some fields he was shot in the thigh and taken prisoner.

The luckier army fugitives made their way not only as far as Amiens, where Drew Middleton saw them, but to the very gates of Georges's GHQ at La Ferté. A "centre of regroupment" was set up but there were simply not enough military policemen to cope with the numbers. Stories circulated of fugitives, including several officers, being shot at Mont Valérien—*pour encourager les autres*. Certainly the demoralisation they caused as they straggled through the villages and towns, throwing away their arms and leaping onto any available horses or cars, was extreme.

But whatever emotions the disbanded military might exact, the condition of the civilian refugees, driven from their homes by nameless fears, was incomparably more pitiful. At one point it was estimated that as many as 2 million Dutch and Belgians and nearly 8 million French refugees were on the roads; some nine-tenths of the population of a city like Lille departed. During the first five days of the battle, the French kept the Belgian frontier closed. Then the human flood burst into northern France, resembling more one of the great migrations fleeing before the Barbarian in times of yore than any event hitherto seen in modern Europe. The number plates on the cars of the refugees, telling the truth the censors were trying to hide, in turn set more and more in motion as they realised the speed at which the Barbarian was approaching.

Pierre Mendès-France, back on leave from Syria, watched the fleeing hordes pour through his hometown of Louviers (south of Rouen) of which he was Mayor:

During the first few days, we had seen high-powered American cars driven by uniformed chauffeurs. Their occupants, elegant women with hands resting on their jewel-cases . . . then came the older, shabbier cars . . . a day or two later came the most extraordinary procession of veteran cars . . . then came the cyclists, mostly carefree young people . . . there were also the pedestrians, sometimes whole families . . . last of all came the heavy waggons of the peasants from Flanders; they advanced slowly, laden with the sick and the aged . . . strings of these waggons stretching for a mile or more would represent the combined evacuation of an entire village, with its mayor, its priest, the old schoolmaster, the policeman. It was a colossal uprooting.

At first there were no soldiers among the refugees; later whole detachments "were swept into the great river of humanity which flowed towards the west and the south." Apart from the most common sights of the countless wheezing old crocks, their roofs heaped high with mattresses, and the huge lumbering hay waggons with the family grouped under the shade of an umbrella (they reminded Simone de Beauvoir of "a tableau staged for a ceremonial procession"), almost everything that could move took part in the exodus. There were racy Paris tourist buses, with *Paris la Nuit* still written upon the side; furniture vans and fire engines; ice-cream carts and hearses, and pathetic pedestrian groups pushing battered prams laden with the precious acquisitions of a lifetime. Those without any transport besieged the railway stations. Around the station at Amiens, Maurois found "a torrent of refugees . . . seated on their bags, on sidewalks, on pavements, they made an immense human carpet worked in dull and lifeless colours. They had emptied the larders of the restaurants, the ovens of the bakeries, the shelves of the groceries, as completely as necrophagous insects clean out a corpse."

There were refugees who had made a similar pilgrimage at least once before; to a French officer caught up in the retreat, one old man remarked plaintively, "I'm eighty-two. Eighty-two, do you hear? I went out in '70. I went out again in '14. I thought all the same they'd let me die at home, in my own house." On the road, the wretched columns of refugees were alternately bombed and machine-gunned by German planes, and pushed off the road by Allied units trying to get up to the front. As the exodus gathered momentum, the condition of the refugees deteriorated, and their plight did not always bring out the best in human nature. Lieutenant Georges Kosak of the cavalry was involved in a sadly typical scene during the retreat from Charleroi. A huge man

tries to pass four abreast with an enormous chariot which is too heavily laden, drawn by six magnificent animals. He strikes with his whip at everything which is in range. The enormous vehicle, bulging with packs, pitches and jolts, and ends by getting hooked up with and upsetting a wretched cart drawn by a little donkey; then he sends two wheelbarrows and a child's pram into the ditch amidst cries of protest and despair. People leap onto him, but the man is a real colossus, at least six feet tall, with a red face, and wide shoulders. Some women and old men try to master the brute, but he grabs his whip by the small end and strikes with the heavy end against the spines of these wretched people. Why was such a Hercules not at war?

In the end, Kosak drew his pistol on the brute. He blanched, dropped his whip, and abandoning his ponderous vehicle disappeared at top speed.

Initially, the civil population treated the refugees with kindness. In Paris, Clare Boothe noted, "the stations were full of volunteers. Tireless, white-faced little French boy scouts helped them off the trains and stacked their bicycles and bundles in careful confusion. Then, as the numbers multiplied and locust-like they denuded the countryside of foodstuffs, kindness turned to hostility." By the end of May, says Fabre-Luce, the French "had expended their pity. They now greeted the new arrivals with

closed faces." Requests for bread, petrol, or even somewhere to
sleep, were increasingly met with refusal. In their turn, the refugees often showed undisguised hatred towards the French troops
they encountered on the road—which at times seemed to exceed
what they felt for the enemy. A German officer overtaking the
wretched refugees in their thousands during the rapid advance
claimed, "They don't hate us, and they don't love us. For them
everything has come upon them as an act of God; they don't concern themselves with the causes of catastrophe."

The fifth column: Myth or reality?

To the Allied forces the encumberment of the refugees on the
roads presented an impossible problem. Reinforcements desperately needed at the front were held up for hours at a time;
wounded soldiers died in ambulances trapped in endless traffic
blocks. The military police tried to force the refugees to camp in
the fields during the day, but gradually they would drift back on
to the roads. Short of actually gunning them down, the troops
were helpless. Meanwhile the plight of their kinsmen had a
markedly depressing effect on the French troops—and even on the
British, fighting though they were on foreign soil. "This continual
sight of agonising humanity drifting aimlessly like frightened cattle
becomes one of the worst of day-light nightmares," Lieutenant
General Alan Brooke confided to his diary. "One's mind, short of
sleep, is continually wracked by the devastating problems of an
almost hopeless situation, and on top of it one's eyes rest incessantly on terrified and miserable humanity cluttering the lines of
communication on which all hope of possible security rest."
Earlier the BEF had worked out an elaborate scheme for evacuating some 800,000 inhabitants from the industrial areas of
northern France, but as the panzers curled around their escape
routes westwards Brooke encountered these unhappy evacuees
crowding back towards the east.

Many women were in the last stages of exhaustion, many of them with
their feet tied up with string and brown paper where their shoes had
given out. . . . I was informed by the Prefect that these were the 800,-
000 people whom we had evacuated westward. They had run into the
German armoured forces, and into rumours of these forces where they
did not exist. Like one big wave, the whole of this humanity, short of

food and sleep and terrified to the core, was now surging back again and congesting all roads at a moment when mobility was a vital element.

The mass exodus of the refugees proved to be one of Hitler's most successful "secret weapons" of the French campaign. To what extent was it a diabolically contrived policy of the Germans? What were the motivating causes behind this mass migration? In Allied countries during and after the campaign, it was widely believed that German radio broadcasts and fifth-column activity had been responsible for getting the refugees in motion, and that the Luftwaffe had then kept them moving by deliberately strafing them. Dr. Goebbels's "terror" propaganda was undoubtedly angled at sowing panic among the civil population, but no one in Germany calculated on the migration's attaining such a scale. German troops frequently affected surprise that the neutral Belgians and Dutch they were coming to "protect," as well as the French civil population, should regard them with such fear; but they forgot how deeply engrained were memories of German "beastliness" in occupied territories during 1914–18. Superimposed on these memories was the impact made by news films of German terror bombing during the Spanish Civil War and in Poland, not to mention the more recent example of Rotterdam. Many reliable witnesses* testify to the fact that refugee columns *were* machine-gunned and bombed in open country. Possibly the strafing could on occasions be attributed to inexperienced pilots genuinely mistaking the refugee columns for troops; and on others to the viciousness of individual Germans. But there is little to suggest that it was Luftwaffe policy. The refugees, however, *expected* to be attacked from the air, and this added to the uncontrollability of their panic.

Maurois tells a pathetic story of a Belgian woman who, "having noticed that our lorries and tanks were camouflaged with branches, had picked up four leaves and spread them neatly in line along the top of her baby-carriage."

The stories, widespread at the time, of a vast malevolent network of fifth. columnists mingling with the refugees and trans-

---

* Among those already mentioned in this story, just to name a few: General Prioux, Drew Middleton of the *New York Times* and Gordon Waterfield of Reuters.

mitting bogus instructions to propagate terror also rarely stand up to examination. Louis de Jong, a Dutchman who made a sober and careful assessment of the whole fifth-column background,* goes so far as to declare of France that "in not a single concrete case have we any evidence that the flight of the population was furthered by false orders circulated by enemy agents." It is impossible to avoid the conclusion that many of the allegations in this context stemmed from an instinct on the part of the French authorities to explain away their own failings. Often it was the very people who should have attempted to curb the mass panic who led the exodus. Accounts of the scene behind the Ninth Army front frequently refer to gendarmes passing through villages and telling the inhabitants, "*Il faut partir.*" At the huge Pechiney works near Compiègne, the managing director (according to Senator Bardoux) took the entire factory into flight with him. In the north, Saint-Exupéry, watching the refugees teem past as if "a boot had scattered an ant-hill," asked them:

"Who ordered you to evacuate?"
It was always the mayor, or the schoolteacher, or the mayor's clerk.
One morning at three the order had run through the village: "Everybody out!"
They had been expecting this. For two weeks they had seen the passage through their village of refugees who no longer believed in the eternity of their homes. . . . The villages were on the move. And no one so much as knew why.

And so the chain reaction passed from hamlet to village, from town to city. In view of the appalling dislocation the refugee hordes caused the Allied war effort, it was a grave failure on the part of the French and Belgian Governments not to have taken drastic measures. They could, for instance, have stopped the sale of petrol, closed the Belgian frontier completely to civilian traffic, and used the radio to *order* the population to remain at home— instead of as a means to fill the ether with tranquilising dance music and untruthful communiqués.

No less powerful a "secret weapon" in Hitler's armoury was the much-vaunted fifth column—or the *belief* in its sinister ubiquity. "Spy mania" had gripped France during the darkest

---

* *The German Fifth Column in the Second World War.*

moments of defeat in both 1870 and 1914—but never more devastatingly than in 1940. Shortly after the collapse of the Ninth Army, a group of journalists were trying to make their way out of Cambrai. Percy Philip of the *New York Times* was dragged out of a train by some soldiers after it had been bombed, his war correspondent's uniform, blue eyes and fair hair having given rise to suspicions that he was a German parachutist. He was about to be shot out of hand when some gendarmes arrived and confirmed that his papers were in order. But they would take no responsibility for his safety, because of the "dangerous mood" of the crowd. Philip finally escaped with the aid of three French Army doctors. About the same time, Maurice Noël of *Le Figaro* was seized while bicycling through a French village. Like the *tricoteuses* of the Revolution and the harpies thrown up by the Commune, women seem to have led the mob, shrieking, "The newspapers have told us to kill all parachutists." An Arab soldier announced to Noël: "I can tell by your accent that you are not a Frenchman." Then the police intervened. On searching him they found a box of white powder which Noël carried as a remedy for indigestion. At once the crowd shouted, "There it is! There is the explosive!" To demonstrate that it was not, Noël lit a match, but before he could put it to the bicarbonate of soda three police officers and a dozen bystanders flung themselves on him, "in a desperate attempt to save the police station from total destruction." Noël was only saved by the intervention of a courageous mayor.

Episodes such as these multiplied with the panic that spread before the approaching panzers. In the early days of the fighting, a demolition squad of the Belgian Chasseurs Ardennais was arrested while retreating over the French frontier, disarmed, and placed in grave danger of being shot. In Paris, Fabre-Luce recorded: "The songstress whom one applauded under a French name is in a concentration camp at the Vel' d'Hiv; she was German. The professional anti-Nazi whose diatribes against Hitler one used to read in the newspapers has been arrested; he was a spy." There were frequent cases of Allied flyers being manhandled, but particularly dangerous was the predicament of the rounded-up "aliens" like Arthur Koestler. From cells bursting with "fifth columnists" at Abbeville, twenty-two such prisoners were arbitrarily taken out and shot near the city bandstand. Out of a group of Belgian refugees shot without trial at Abbeville, the Fascist leader Léon Dégrelle was one who evidently escaped notice. "As for the spy problem, we have solved that," one French soldier declared to an American correspondent. "We simply shoot all the officers we do not know!" That this was no idle boast is confirmed by Major Barlone, who wrote in his diary for May 22nd: "Our orders are to shoot all spies and strangers who are unable to justify their presence"; and later: "Dispenser Charbonnier, at our hospital, had five persons shot, one a beautiful young girl; by showing lights and curtains of different colours, they had guided German aircraft, signalling to them and thereby causing fires in the neighbouring chemical factory."

To what extent *was* there an organised fifth column working ahead of the panzers? Insisted Major Barlone: "The Fifth Column really does exist; every night blue, green and red lights appear everywhere. A regiment cannot remain two hours in a tiny spot without being invariably bombed with enormous bombs." At the time, the vast majority of Frenchmen agreed with him, and certainly the lists of deeds attributed to various insidious underground agencies covers an imposing range.* The stories started in Poland, where it was rumoured that the *Volksdeutsch* had ambushed Polish troops and insinuated mustard gas into the water the troops washed in; and there were reports of German spy planes dropping poisoned chocolates and cigarettes.† In Holland, the *fact* of the handful of "Brandenburgers" in purloined Dutch uniforms multiplied a thousand times with incredible rapidity. On May 16th, the distraught Foreign Minister of Holland, van Kleffens, himself assured the press in Paris that parachutists had descended on his country "by the thousand," clad in "French, Belgian and British uniforms, in the cassocks of priests and in the garb of nuns or nurses." Here began the legend of the "nuns in hobnailed boots." In Belgium, the Security Service warned that parachutists in civilian clothes had landed in various places, and

---

* Some French press reports referred categorically to 100,000 German agents as having been deployed in the Low Countries and Luxembourg alone.

† The story of the Polish "poisoned chocolates" is an interesting example of how, in an atmosphere of rampant terror, even the craziest allegations can gain wide credence and reappear in countless different contexts. After the invasion of Holland, orders went out for all "unexplained" chocolates to be instantly destroyed; as for France, Alexander Werth's diary for May 21st reveals this entry: "Another woman says they dropped poisoned sweets at the Gare d'Austerlitz the other day, and that one child died after eating one."

it requested that all placards advertising "Pasha" Chicory be removed from telegraph poles, etc., because on their reverse side "drawings have been found which can give the enemy valuable information." After the Germans had traversed the Ardennes, word went around in France that they had been able to do so at such speed only because the fifth column had prepared secret petrol dumps in advance of the panzers. The debacle at Sedan was immediately followed with rumours that the Meuse bridges had been abandoned intact to the enemy through treachery;* that officers detailed to blow them up had been mysteriously shot down by disguised German agents. Here, and on many subsequent occasions, local disasters were attributed to bogus orders telephoned by fifth columnists, and purporting to come from some staff officer—or from the mayor of a village ordering its evacuation. General Spears relates a typical story (told him by Saint-Exupéry, "who said he could vouch for its truth"), of how

a group of the best heavy guns in the French Army, the 155-millimetre Rimaillots, was halted near Laon when a pale-faced Staff Officer appeared declaring he had come post-haste from Corps H.Q. to say that a German Panzer division was converging on them and would be there in a matter of minutes, and the Corps Commander adjured them as good Frenchmen not to allow their guns to fall into enemy hands. Within a few minutes 35 of these priceless guns had been damaged beyond repair. No such order had been sent from Corps H.Q.

This dissemination of false orders was one of the commonest activities for which the fifth column was held responsible, and its consequence was often that orders transmitted by genuine but unidentified officers were simply disobeyed—all adding to the chaos of the French command network.

Another common allegation was that German agents signalled to invisible aircraft or to other agents. Looking out from Montmartre one night, Peter de Polnay† claims: "I saw signals in

---

* This assumption was perpetuated by no less a person than Paul Reynaud who, in his "la Patrie est en danger" speech of May 21st, erroneously declared that "through unbelievable faults, which will be punished, bridges over the Meuse were not destroyed." (According to General Doumenc, all the Meuse bridges were blown.)

† Peter de Polnay, "Death and Tomorrow," London, 1942.

Morse all over Paris. The fifth column was at work." Hans Habe*
writes also of a suspicious sergeant major who used to disappear
mysteriously every evening and who, he claims, was later discovered "giving signals to German planes under the pretext of
lighting his pipe. According to some he was shot on the spot by
an artillery lieutenant. . . . I never saw him again."

Only a fraction of these specific allegations of fifth column
activities have been substantiated. None of the works written
analytically in the aftermath of the war sustain the legend.
Brigadier General Telford Taylor, who served with the U.S. Army
Intelligence in Europe during the Second World War and was later
Chief Counsel at the Nuremberg Trials, states that ". . . careful
investigations . . . have abundantly proved that in Holland, as in
Norway, the reports of subversion and sabotage were uniformly
exaggerated and often utterly groundless."† De Jong puts the
total number active in Holland at one thousand, including about
one to two hundred Dutch citizens. He adds: "It is worthy of
note that in not one of the German documents bearing on the
preparations for the offensive is there so much as a single passage
referring to such a Fifth Column." As in Holland, in Belgium
there was a smattering of "Rexist" traitors who may have helped
the Germans, and de Jong mentions Abwehr agents who were
infiltrated into Belgium as "refugees"; these he also numbers at
between one and two hundred. In Luxembourg, as has already
been seen, the German "tourists" who flowed over the frontier
prior to the invasion did help the panzers by preventing demolitions and disrupting communications. But, apart from a few
Abwehr sabotage squads attempting to infiltrate with the refugees
—and about whose achievements little is known with accuracy—
no serious effort seems to have been made by the Germans to
operate a fifth column in France. De Jong categorically refutes
the myth of bogus orders: "Nowhere has it appeared that false
instructions were circulated by the fifth column.‡ At least two
French generals, Menu and Ruby (who was Huntziger's Chief of

---

* Hans Habe, *A Thousand Shall Fall,* London, 1942.

† Telford Taylor, *The March of Conquest,* New York, 1959.

‡ Walter Schellenberg, the famous SS Intelligence operator, boasted that he had
been responsible for sending out "false news items" in French over powerful German transmitters, but he makes no claim however of bogus orders having been
among his repertoire.

Staff), also scoff at the notion of fifth columnists being responsible for the chaos and confusion on the Meuse. Says General Menu: "We say emphatically that we do not believe in this argument. . . . Was he an agent of the fifth column, the officer of X Corps, who telephoned at the end of the afternoon of May 13th that the panzers were at Chaumont and then at Bulson? . . . We say, No." A Swiss historian, Eddy Bauer, goes so far as to declare: "One thing is however clear, that in France there never was a fifth column."

On the German side, out of the welter of personal memoirs and war narratives published since 1945, the sheer absence of allusion to organised fifth-column work in France is in itself instructive. The Abwehr, to be sure, had its networks of "V-men," spies and informers inside France, but these seem to have been strictly limited both in numbers and quality, and for the most part established in haste at the beginning of the war. From its own accounts, the Abwehr depended for its intelligence more upon the less romantic forms of espionage, such as aerial reconnaissance and signals interception. The fact is that Canaris's Abwehr proved itself, throughout most of the war, to be one of the least effective organs of Hitler's war machine; added to which, the German character has seldom shown a marked propensity for the subtler forms of underground warfare.

There were diverse reasons why the bogey of the fifth column became magnified out of all proportion in France. There was the impact of Goebbels's propaganda coupled with the boasts of Hitler himself.

In the midst of peace [he had declared—or so the faithful Rauschning told the world—] troops will suddenly appear, let us say, in Paris. They will wear French uniforms. They will march through the streets in broad daylight. No one will stop them. Everything has been thought out. . . . We shall send them across the border in peace-time. Gradually. No one shall see in them anything but peaceful travellers.

In this form of psychological warfare, the Nazis were aided in the west by knowledge of the precedent of subversive actions which the Sudeten Czechs created in 1938; but they were also succoured by the panic-inspiring utterances of Allied leaders—such as Kleffens on the hobnailed nuns; Reynaud declaring that the Meuse bridges had been captured undestroyed, and proclaiming (on May 13th) that all German combatants caught out of uniform would be shot on sight.* But, as with the refugee exodus, even the Nazis never quite expected to get such returns with the fifth-column bogey as they did.

There was also the cumulative effect of Hitler's string of light-ning successes, enhanced by rumours of his armoury of "secret weapons." Surely, there had to be some simple answer to explain these successes? How had Norway and Denmark succumbed so easily? Had Fort Eben Emael been taken by means of some deadly nerve gas or death ray? Had the Germans crossed the Meuse with some kind of amphibious tank kept afloat by compressed air? Were they using 60-ton tanks with such heavy armour that noth-ing could penetrate? These were all stories that made the rounds. But where else could an explanation be found to all these devas-tating successes? Could it lie in the fifth column? In treason?

"Nous sommes trahis"

Treason! Faithfully that terrible word reappears on French lips the moment there is a major disaster, revealing one of the less admirable national traits. Gallic pride can never admit that the nation has been collectively at fault; inevitably, she has been betrayed by an individual or a faction. Repeatedly during the Franco-Prussian War, and again in the most adverse moments of 1914–18, the expression *Nous sommes trahis* rings out across the ramparts. But the soil had never been more fertile for such an interpretation of France's woes than in May 1940. Clare Boothe relates a conversation with an elderly Red Cross nurse, who asked her:

"Madame, you are an American?" I said: "Yes," and she went on: "Then you must tell me the truth: *Qui nous a trahi?* Who has betrayed us?" That was the first time I heard the word *trahi* ("betrayed") in Paris. At first it was no more than a whisper, like the little winds that come in the dim days before the hurricane.

Then, as the debacle at the front escalated, it became "a sullen

---

* The Nazis retorted that for every one shot, they would execute ten French prisoners. "Nice pleasant people the Germans," commented Shirer. "That takes us back a thousand or two years."

roar." All the suspicions and mutual mistrusts of Third Republic France bred by Stavisky, the Croix de Feu and the Front Populaire now surged to the fore. On entering Paris with the victorious German Army at the end of June, William Shirer was assured that there had been "treachery in the French Army from top to bottom—the Fascists at the top, the Communists at the bottom." The left accused the *Cagoule** of having conveniently established arms and fuel dumps for the Germans beyond the Meuse; the right blamed the catastrophe there on Communist influence. The defeatists and "softs" in the government were men bought by German money; the right-wing generals were bought. And so the nightmare fantasy of the pervasive fifth column spread, in ever-widening ripples. Even intellectuals such as Simone de Beauvoir seemed prone to believe in it ("Had there been treachery?" was her immediate reaction on hearing of Corap's defeat. "No other explanation seemed possible"); and from London General de Gaulle later cloaked it with historical respectability. For those in high places, treachery and the fifth column provided an admirably convenient explanation for otherwise inexplicable disasters. Almost on the last page of his copious memoirs, Gamelin appends—and apparently endorses—a report blaming the break-up of the 55th Division at Sedan on those bogus orders put around by "parachutists"; and at the time, he made repeated allegations about the responsibility of the Communists. Whatever the Communists may have done to augment demoralisation, both inside and outside the French Army, they never constituted a fifth column in its conventional sense. It was indeed "what is false within" that principally betrayed France.

Real or imagined, however, the role played by the fifth column in the defeat of France should never be underestimated. What it meant to the simple French fighting man was eloquently summed up by René Balbaud, a senior NCO:

We felt ourselves spied on, betrayed on all sides. . . . When we learned that the Germans had entered France, our first reaction was to think once more of betrayal. We talked of generals being retired, of the commander-in-chief being replaced. And so? But, real or imagined, these betrayals all had the same result: collapse of the army's

---

* The extremist organ of the right-wing "Leagues," which, just before the war, had perpetrated one or two minor bomb outrages.

morale. We talked of King Leopold. . . . And our aircraft? vanished into dreamland. Betrayed. And our equipment, said to be tip-top, but which we never saw a sign of? Betrayed. Well, why fight? Everyone we trusted had betrayed us.

The French now know: The Germans are heading for the Channel

May 18th was the day that the French High Command at last knew for certain that the Germans were heading for the Channel —that they were swinging away from Paris, while covering their flank defensively along the Aisne. As already noted, on the 16th orders containing the complete itineraries for the panzers were taken off a badly wounded German colonel near Rethel. There is some mystery about their subsequent fate; the German documents were apparently handed to General Touchon's (Sixth Army) HQ, but for some reason—perhaps simply the chaos existing in French channels of communication—they were not immediately passed on to La Ferté or Vincennes. On the 17th, the Deuxième Bureau at Billotte's No. 1 Army Group HQ intercepted a German signal in clear which also disclosed that the thrust was aimed at the Channel and not Paris; again, this intelligence does not seem to have made its way promptly back to GQG. That same morning another German staff officer with similarly revealing orders destined for the 1st Panzer was captured by a formation of the French 2nd Armoured Division. The divisional second-in-command, Colonel Perré, set off towards Compiègne to take them to the Ninth Army commander, General Giraud. But Giraud could not be traced. Colonel Perré also seems not to have thought about transmitting this valuable booty directly to GHQ, reasoning that it would arrive too late to be of any use. Thus it was not until well into the 18th that the sum of all this intelligence reached Georges or Gamelin, confirming the rumours of the previous day. By this time, even the Germans were no longer making great efforts to conceal the true objective of *Sichelschnitt.* Shirer spotted an item in a Berlin newspaper hinting "that the German armies now converging on Paris from the north-east may not try to take Paris immediately, as they did in 1914, but strike north-west for the Channel ports in an effort to cut off England from France."

Gamelin still hesitates and Pétain arrives

The rumours that Hitler was turning away towards the Channel ports had provoked a fleeting, ill-founded elation among Parisians. Shares on the Bourse fluttered briefly upwards. "Maybe he's going to England first" were the whispers overheard by Clare Boothe. Gamelin himself may not have subscribed to this view, but there was no doubt that on the 18th he struck his staff as being "in better form than on the day before. Visibly the Commander-in-Chief had pulled himself together." In the mind of the faithful staff officer of Joffre, the man who had actually prepared the orders preluding the immortal victory of the Marne in '14, a chord was struck. By swinging away from Paris and presenting such a long, open flank, were the Germans about to commit the same error as Kluck in 1914? Thoughts parallel to those which had plagued the minds of Hitler and Rundstedt now began to preoccupy Gamelin. At Vincennes it was sensed that the Generalissimo was about to produce his master stroke. That afternoon (the 18th) aerial reconnaissance reported a "complete vacuum" in the Laon–Montcornet area immediately behind the cutting tip of the panzers. But still Gamelin hesitated. . . .

Visiting La Ferté that morning, Gamelin affects to have found none of the newly regained composure which his staff were detecting in him. The atmosphere at "Les Bondons" struck his tidy mind as "extremely detrimental to regular work." In the office of Georges's Chief of Staff, General Roton, there reigned "utter disorder" with staff officers continually coming and going through it. The situation was hardly better in the room where Georges himself presided, and he betrayed to Gamelin "incontestable signs of lassitude." The monastic Generalissimo wondered how his subordinate could possibly "dominate events" in such an atmosphere of chaos where no reflection was possible. He voiced his misgivings privately to General Doumenc. After making conventional noises of loyalty to Georges, Doumenc expressed agreement and said he thought the time was approaching when Gamelin should take direction of the battle into his own hands. Gamelin replied, "Of course, let me know the right moment"—as if this had not long since passed. After a further, inconclusive discussion with Georges about restoring the "continuity of the front," Gamelin was warned that Reynaud and Daladier were coming to visit him at three o'clock that afternoon and he sped back to Vincennes.

At the appointed hour, Daladier arrived; but no Reynaud. On telephoning his office, Gamelin learned that Reynaud—accompanied by Marshal Pétain, newly returned from Madrid—had left a good hour earlier. Consternation! Had the Premier been involved in an accident? Finally word came through ("brusquely," says Gamelin) that Reynaud and Pétain had gone to see Georges first. Gamelin and Daladier were to await their arrival. The two passed the time in "affectionate and confident conversation," with Daladier (in the words of Gamelin) displaying "the soul of a good Frenchman." It was, he admitted, "the first time for ten days that I had remained without any precise occupation"—which seems a curious admission at such a moment in Allied fortunes.

At 1820 hours, after more than three hours had passed in chat between Gamelin and Daladier, Reynaud arrived with Pétain. According to Reynaud's account, on the earlier visit to La Ferté, General Georges had

explained the situation to us on a large map, which, with his hand covered by a grey glove, he pulled up and down on its roller. We saw on the map the positions of the Armies, and, prominently marked, those of the ten panzer divisions. Two or three times he broke off his account to tell us, his brown eyes brooding sorrowfully on us: "It is a difficult situation."

At Vincennes, Gamelin treated Reynaud and Pétain to a similar rundown on the situation. When the eighty-four-year-old Marshal climbed back into his car, he clasped Gamelin's hand warmly and murmured, "I pity you with all my heart." As Reynaud had made no reference to his intentions for the Generalissimo's future, the full meaning of Pétain's expression of sympathy was not apparent until the following day. Gamelin then returned to his office to sign the wordy report which he had been preparing at Daladier's behest. He had still made no move to assume control of the battle.

For the French High Command, the 18th ended with extremely grave news reaching Georges's GHQ from General Billotte. "We had hoped to be able to contain them today, but we were twenty-four hours too late," said Billotte. Seeing little prospect now of sealing the hole which gaped between the French First Army and General Frère's *ad hoc* Seventh Army, Billotte added ominously: "One must reflect upon the conduct to adopt in the event that our forces should find themselves separated." In his final order for the day, Georges spoke hopelessly of the importance of "envisaging the prolongation of our barrage along the Somme, from Péronne to the sea"—a measure which in itself certainly envisaged no means of halting the panzers before the Channel. Finally, on the following day, de Gaulle's 4th Armoured was to make another jab into the southern flank of the panzers along the axis Laon–Crécy-sur-Serre.

On the political scene that Saturday, Reynaud invited Pétain to join his government as Deputy Premier. Pétain accepted. According to Reynaud, when he told the Senate that the "Victor of Verdun" was now at his side, there were widespread shouts of "At last!" Spears, who had not seen him since the First War, describes the aged Marshal shortly after his return to France as being "still erect but so very much older, and in plain clothes which emphasised the break with the past . . . but he seemed dead, in the sense that a figure that gives no impression of being alive can be said to be dead . . . when occasionally I looked towards him he seemed not to have heard what was being said." From now on this venerable but pessimistic old soldier, tragically recalled from the glorious past, was to play a role of increasing weight in France's fate.

Upon Pétain's acceptance Reynaud proceeded to the first stage of reshaping his Cabinet. Daladier at last was ousted from the Ministry of National Defence—which Reynaud took over himself, handing to Daladier the Quai d'Orsay as a sop. The tough Georges Mandel, Clemenceau's old hatchet man, was transferred from the Colonies to the Interior, a key post when civilian morale was gravely threatened. But, to take the lead part in his reshuffle, Reynaud was still awaiting the arrival of General Weygand.

May 19th: De Gaulle's second chance

In his orders for May 19th, Guderian stated: "The Commander-in-Chief of the Army* has explicitly approved further advances by Group von Kleist." His XIX Panzer Corps were to seize

---

* Brauchitsch.

bridgeheads over the Canal du Nord to the west; at the same time, looking ahead to the second phase of the Battle of France, it was to establish bridgeheads over the Somme between Ham and Péronne, in order to be ready "to swing south-west when the time comes." The progress registered on the 19th would, as it happened, be less spectacular than that of the previous day. Technical priorities of the divisions enforced a day essentially of badly needed consolidation and regrouping in preparation for the final lunge to the coast.

Despite all the good omens, the 19th began on an anxious note for Guderian. At 1:35 A.M. XIX Panzer Corps HQ received a radio message reporting that the fuel depot at Hirson had been "burnt out." This was extremely serious news, as it was from here that Guderian's tanks were to be refuelled that night. Consequently, they would have no more than *one day's ration of fuel.* Later in the morning the 10th Panzer reported that its attack against Ham had failed. Then Luftwaffe reconnaissance revealed the massing of around 100 tanks south of Crécy-sur-Serre. This was accompanied by a report that one of the *Sperrverbände* ("blocking detachments") had been overwhelmed by an enemy attack on the south flank.

De Gaulle had begun to move forward at dawn. The objective of his second attack was to strike across the Serre bridges near Crécy and then cut Guderian's line of advance through La Fère. He had received further reinforcements in the form of an artillery regiment of 75s, the famous cannon of the First War, and two squadrons of Somua tanks, bringing his armour to a total of about 150 tanks. Of these, however, only 30 were "B" tanks, 40 Somuas or D–2s, the remainder obsolete R–35s. The Somua crews consisted of a commander-gunner who had never fired the gun and a driver who had done no more than four hours' driving. With only a single battalion of infantry he was once again poorly supported.

At first de Gaulle seemed to be advancing into empty space. After overwhelming or dispersing light enemy forces, he reached the Serre within four hours. Here his tanks came up against heavy opposition. Guderian had reacted with his customary speed. "Crécy is a fortress of antitank guns, an enormous ambush," declared Captain Idée. "The R–35s lost their footing and withdrew in a shambles. Already several are burning." His D–2s now moved up. Just before the bridge over the Serre the first tank blew up on a mine, the second had a track blown off. In third position Idée's own tank, the *Rocroi*, came under violent fire:

A formidable shock. The turret shakes, struck at the base. The traversing gear is jammed. The turret won't move any more. I struggle furiously with it, strike the gear, and just at the moment when I am despairing, unjam it. The turret moves. I fire. Bing! A heavy shell strikes obliquely at the top of my turret, which glows red.

As on the 17th, the infantry never materialised, so—having lost two tanks—Idée decided to withdraw. In the two days' fighting, his company of 14 tanks had lost 6 destroyed and 2 "missing."

De Gaulle's misfortunes on the 19th were compounded by a piece of bad liaison that was typical of the inefficient communications between the French ground and air forces. To ward off the shattering Stuka attacks that had disrupted de Gaulle's first attack, General d'Astier had been called upon to provide the most powerful fighter cover that his reduced circumstances would allow. But the time of the attack was changed without d'Astier being informed. The Stukas once again descended on de Gaulle's column out of an empty sky. Answering a desperate plea for help, d'Astier ordered up every fighter patrol already in the air at the time. But by the time they arrived over the Serre it was too late; de Gaulle's force had been badly knocked about. Early that afternoon he received an order from Georges, instructing him "not to commit himself too deeply, as the division was needed on another front." Under repeated Stuka bombing, de Gaulle once more pulled his forces back in good order, behind the Aisne. In most bitter frustration, he says:

I could not help imagining what the mechanised army of which I had so long dreamed could have done. If it had been there that day, to debouch suddenly in the direction of Guise, the advance of the panzer divisions would have been halted instantly, serious confusion caused in their rear, and the northern group of armies enabled to join up once more with those of the centre and the east.

May 19th: The Germans consolidate

From Guderian's point of view, the various local difficulties besetting him that morning—of which de Gaulle was one—imposed three choices of action: he could halt his westerly advance and establish a defensive face towards the south; counterattack southwards with the main weight of his forces; or change nothing in his orders and continue the advance as before. Typically he chose the third possibility, leaving it to the 10th Panzer alone to block de Gaulle's attack. Once again events proved his decision right.* Meanwhile, as de Gaulle's attack was in progress, a corrective radio signal resolved Guderian's major anxiety: the report about the Hirson fuel depot should have read "ready for distribution" instead of "burnt out"!† The panzers could forge on.

During the afternoon, Guderian's 1st and 2nd Panzers crossed the Canal du Nord and reached the old Somme battlefield of the First War—an event giving rise to strong emotions among the many veterans who had sat there for months on end in 1916, under gruelling attack by the British and French. There were now warnings from both men and machines that seemed to make a brief pause imperative; when the commander of his prize 1st Panzer Brigade, Colonel Nedtwig, collapsed from sheer exhaustion,‡ even Guderian had to take note. That night the main weight of his Corps halted on the line Cambrai–Péronne–Ham.

To Guderian's immediate north, Reinhardt's panzers mopped up French resistance around Le Catelet by the middle of the day, after more brisk fighting. With nightfall, they too stood shoulder to shoulder with Guderian in a consolidated position west of the

---

* Guderian's coolheadedness is all the more remarkable in that, through an error, he seems at the time to have exaggerated de Gaulle's threat. Although in his memoirs (*Panzer Leader*) he describes it as "slight," he goes on to say: "During the next few days de Gaulle stayed with us and on the 19th a few of his tanks succeeded in penetrating to within a mile of my advanced H.Q. in Holnon wood. The headquarters had only some 20 mm antiaircraft guns for protection, and I passed a few uncomfortable hours until at last the threatening visitors moved off in another direction." The fact was that after the 19th, de Gaulle disengaged to the south and did not attack again until the 27th. Furthermore, Holnon where Guderian came in jeopardy lies nearly 25 miles northwest (beyond St. Quentin) from the farthest point reached by de Gaulle on the 19th. It seems more likely that the infiltrating tanks belonged to units of the dispersed French Second Armoured.

† *Ausgabebereit* instead of *ausgebrannt*.

‡ He was replaced by the indestructible Balck.

Canal du Nord defence line. For Rommel the fast going of the previous days came to an end with the capture of Cambrai. He too was forced on the 19th to pause in order to regroup and give his exhausted crews some sleep. By nightfall he had pushed forward a bare 6 miles to Marquion, where the Canal du Nord crosses the Arras road. Visited by his Corps commander, General Hoth, during the afternoon, the impatient Rommel asked to be allowed to mount another night attack so as to seize the vital high ground southeast of Arras, some 20 miles on, by daybreak on the 20th. Hoth demurred, on the grounds that the men could not take it. "The troops have been twenty hours in the same place," countered Rommel, "and a night attack during moonlight will result in fewer losses." Hoth yielded and Rommel was allowed to prepare to move towards Arras shortly after midnight. On Rommel's right flank, the 5th Panzer was sharply engaged again in the Forest of Mormal with elements of the 1st DLM and the 1st North African Division. But, pushing on towards Solesmes, its advanced units also began to draw level with Rommel. Meanwhile, still further north the 3rd and 4th Panzers of Hoeppner's XVI Corps now transferred to Rundstedt were battering back the southern anchor of Blanchard's First Army in the direction of Valenciennes. Thus by the end of the 19th, after their various itineraries, all but one of Hitler's ten panzers* were now lined up as a dense phalanx of armour in what has been called the "rendezvous of May 19th." Here they stood poised for the final act of *Sichelschnitt*, just 50 miles from the sea.

The Maginot Line: The forgotten army

Down in the Maginot Line, life during the previous eight days of the battle had continued very much as in the months of the Phoney War. The desperate struggle to the north left it untouched. Inside its steel and concrete turrets, observers peered out—waiting for an enemy who never came. There was an occasional long-range artillery duel, but that was about all. Then, on the 18th, General von Witzleben's First Army suddenly attacked a small fort, curiously enough called La Ferté. It lay in an awkward defensive position, and after a savage struggle La Ferté fell on the 19th. This first capture of a Maginot Line fortress was

---

* The 9th was still deployed against Antwerp.

greeted with maximum acclaim by the German radio, though its strategic significance was negligible. The action, however was not just braggadocio. It was carefully and deliberately timed; for the French High Command had at long last given the order to withdraw the hitherto immobilised "interval troops" as reinforcements for the battle in the north. Here, then, was a warning not to go too far in denuding the Maginot Line—one which, as the Germans expected, the French High Command would be bound to heed; by the end of May it was actually *sending back* precious tanks to help guard the forts.

The Luftwaffe ascendant

In the air, the 18th and 19th witnessed a further marked deterioration of Allied strength.* By the 19th, General d'Astier's ZOAN could count on no more than 170 serviceable fighters, and —because of damage to the telephone lines—it was becoming increasingly difficult for his group commanders to bring their planes into action. There were still six *groupements* of bombers left; but two consisted of Amiots and Blochs which could only be used by night; of the three equipped with Léos and Bréguets, two were on the move, while the third was caught (on the 19th) by the Luftwaffe just as it was about to take off on a mission and lost two-thirds of its machines; the sixth, comprised of newly arrived American Glenn Martins, was waiting to have the bomb release mechanisms fixed. As far as the British were concerned, on the 18th Barratt's Advanced Air Striking Force was still virtually out of action on account of its move. The following day telephone contact between Barratt and the Air Component with the BEF had been severed by the German advance, and Lord Gort agreed with the Air Ministry that it should not be withdrawn to operate from southern England. Within two days nothing but a few Lysander liaison planes remained in France. The evacuation of the Air Component was, alas, carried out in such haste that most of its ground equipment and stores had to be abandoned to the enemy. A total of 261 Hurricanes had flown with the Component; 75 had been destroyed, but only 66 of the remainder returned to England. The balance of 120 consisted of damaged machines

---

* Although, on the 18th, *L'Époque* felt inspired to claim: "The German air force loses some of its advantage every day. Nowhere does it now have mastery of the air."

that also had to be abandoned in France. Thus in ten days' operations over northern France alone, Britain had lost 195 Hurricanes —roughly a quarter of her entire strength of modern fighters. Henceforth based on Kent and under control of the Air Ministry, the Component was too far removed from the battle to provide effective collaboration with the BEF, and its activities were largely limited to night operations of doubtful value.

The RAF continued to pound the Ruhr by night with its heavy and medium bombers, and continued to deceive both itself, the government and the public as to the results. *L'Oeuvre* on May 19th spoke of "catastrophic effects" reported by eyewitnesses; the disorganisation following the raids was claimed to have "almost crippled the movement of reinforcements to the front over the past 24 hours." In his diary, General Ironside quoted a pilot who "said that over Hamburg he could read a book at 10,000 feet. They also touched up the Ruhr again, finding very little A.A. defence guns"—a statement that perhaps reveals just how lightly the Germans were regarding these raids. Passing Cologne aerodrome on the 19th, William Shirer noted:

It was packed with planes, but the hangars had not been touched. Beautifully camouflaged with netting they were. Obviously these night attacks of the British have failed not only to put the Ruhr out of commission, but even to damage the German flying fields. A phoney sort of war the Allies still seem to be fighting.

Meanwhile, Churchill was grumbling to his Chief of the Air Staff at the Allied impotence to strike at the panzers which were doing all the damage: "Is there no possibility of finding out where a column of enemy armoured vehicles harbours during the dark hours, and then bombing?" On the evening of the 19th, 20 Chance-Vought dive bombers belonging to the French Navy and based on Boulogne and Berck were thrown in for the first time to help the forces desperately engaged in the Forest of Mormal; but 10 were shot down, the remainder badly holed, and the effect on the panzers apparently was minimal. With the steady extension of the Panzer Corridor and the decreasing number of Allied planes available, it was becoming more and more difficult to pinpoint the spread-out enemy columns. Early on May 19th, reconnaissance spotted a large armoured force (presumably Rommel's) moving in the direction of Arras; but no bombers were on hand at the time, and the panzers were allowed to move on unmolested. The next morning two RAF bomber squadrons were dispatched from England to attack panzer columns spotted at 8:30. The first reached the target area at 11:30 and bombed a column moving westwards; shortly afterwards the second could find nothing at the same point. Both had in fact arrived too late to attack the initially designated target—an advanced unit of the 6th Panzer —which was by then well dispersed.

On the German side, the Luftwaffe was now well established in Belgian airfields close behind the front, so that its Stukas were able to fly as many as six or seven missions a day—thereby multiplying its already imposing numerical superiority. Apart from this never-failing tactical close support work, the medium bombers of the Luftwaffe were concentrating effectively on smashing up the French railway system by which Georges was trying to bring up reinforcements to the Aisne and Somme. At midday on the 19th, a powerful force of German bombers struck savagely at Amiens, "softening up" for the next day's panzer attack. The city appears to have been all but undefended, whether by fighters or antiaircraft. Four-fifths of the population had already left the threatened city, but casualties were heavy; fortunately twenty ambulances manned by volunteers of the American Field Service happened to be passing through the city and were able to help with the wounded.

Retreat from northern Belgium

In northern Belgium, the Allies completed their withdrawal behind the Escaut line on the 19th, with the Belgian Army in position from Terneuzen on the coast down to Oudenarde. Below them—the BEF occupied a strong position on the river Escaut as far as Maulde on the French frontier. The 5th Division had been pulled back to Seclin, just south of Lille, as Army reserve, and on the night of the 19th Gort ordered the 50th Division— minus one brigade group—to concentrate north of Arras on the Vimy Ridge of First War fame. Here it was "to prepare for offensive action." South of the BEF, Blanchard's First Army had the task of holding a "mole" anchored on Condé, Valenciennes and Bouchain around the end of which the irresistible flood of the panzers swirled westwards. Bombed repeatedly during the

last stage of its withdrawal, the BEF was extremely tired. Lieutenant Miles Fitzalan-Howard with Montgomery's 3rd Division
recorded in his diary what was a typical experience for those days:
"In five nights I have had eight hours sleep; 18th, up all night;
19th, up till 3, sleep till 7; 20th, up till 3, sleep till 7; 21st up;
22nd up; 23rd in bed." Nevertheless, the BEF was in much better shape than Blanchard's forces which had consistently borne
the brunt of the fighting in the north since the first encounter with
the enemy, and had suffered higher casualties than either the
British or the Belgians.

Retiring across the French frontier near Condé-sur-l'Escaut,
Major Barlone was one of those who experienced a momentary
sense of relief: "There at least, behind our defences, we can
breathe. But refugees, fleeing towards the interior of France, tell
us that our pill-boxes are unoccupied. During a long halt, giving my mare a chance to rest, I gallop forward on another horse
and am astonished to find our blockhouses empty." The staff of
Barlone's divisional HQ (the 2nd North African) billeted itself in
the town of St. Amand, where fewer than fifty civilians remained.
The troops, according to Barlone, were permitted "to take from
the houses anything they need, for we know that the Germans
will be here within a few days. The officers can dip into the cellars of the Hôtel de Paris, on the Place du Beffroi, to their heart's
content; a sentry stands at the door and only officers are allowed
to enter." Despite the faulty discipline implicit in this surprising
admission of legalised looting by "officers" only, Barlone states
that the morale of his men was good; they were "bewildered
rather than discouraged."

The same was also true of Prioux's Cavalry Corps, despite the
repeated drubbing it had taken from the panzers. But the troops
were dead tired and it required all the energy of the officers to
prevent them from sleeping at their posts. The 1st DLM was still
fighting bravely far away in the Forest of Mormal, though nominally it was supposed to be under Prioux's control; many of his
other tank companies had been farmed out in supporting roles to
other divisional commanders, who—despite Billotte's strict orders
to the contrary—were now proving reluctant to return them to
their rightful master. Therefore, with his Cavalry Corps thus de-
bilitated, Prioux was surprised to receive an order from
Georges at midnight on the 18th, instructing him to "attack to-

morrow, May 19th, in the direction Cambrai–St. Quentin with a view to breaking up the armoured elements operating there"— i.e., the bulk of nine German panzer divisions. It was one more revelation of just how hopelessly out of touch the French High Command was with realities at the front. Prioux at once sought out Billotte to explain precisely why he would be unable to comply.

Are the British leaving?

Early in the afternoon of May 19th, an important telephone conversation took place between Generals Georges and Billotte, while Georges was in session with Gamelin and a British delegation headed by General Dill. In the course of it, Billotte remarked:* "I learn that the British are said to have decided to fall back on Calais in three or four stages, and to evacuate." The supposition was erroneous, based on a misunderstanding between Billotte's and Gort's staffs; nevertheless it illustrated the direction in which Gort's thoughts were beginning to run. The various factors governing the British decision to evacuate the BEF concern this story only marginally. They require mention, however, insofar as they touch upon the last Allied counterstroke that had any prospect of slicing through the Panzer Corridor and releasing the armies about to be encircled in the north.

During his visit of the 16th to Paris, Churchill had miraculously managed to boost the sagging spirits of Reynaud and Daladier. But he and his entourage had returned to London profoundly alarmed by what they had seen and learned—more so than they revealed to their ally. The very next day Churchill wrote a memo to Neville Chamberlain, asking him to examine in general terms "the problems which would arise if it were necessary to withdraw the B.E.F. from France."

At this moment, Ironside was revealing in his diary that he for one no longer had much confidence in the ability of the French to halt the Germans: "We have lived in a fool's paradise. Largely depending upon the strength of the French Army. And this Army has crashed or very nearly crashed. . . . At the moment it looks like the greatest military disaster in all history." If the German advance continued, the BEF's line of communications through

---

* According to General Roton. (See also Gamelin, III, 431–32.)

Amiens would be threatened, and in this eventuality Britain would be forced to try "to evacuate the B.E.F. from Dunkirk, Calais and Boulogne." It was, thought Ironside, "an impossible proposition." Nevertheless, that day he suggested to the Admiralty that they begin collecting all small vessels.

Then, on the night of the 18th–19th, there was a critical meeting between Lord Gort and General Billotte. At about midnight the French Army Group commander drove to Gort's command post at Wahagnies. For the past week, the BEF had received no orders from Billotte; it was the first time that he had come to confer with Gort and report on the full extent of the crisis. Hitherto the French had tended to regard both Gort and Britain's small contribution to the land war effort with a certain amount of contempt. Now suddenly in this moment of crisis it was apparent that France would have to rely upon the "amateur" but relatively intact BEF to play a key role in future strategy, and accordingly its commander assumed a new importance in French eyes. Gort's experiences over the past week had already greatly reduced his confidence in the judgement of the French High Command, and what Billotte now told him only confirmed his gloom. According to Gort, Billotte described

the measures which were being taken to restore the situation on the front of the French Ninth Army, though clearly he had little hope that they would be effective. Reports from the liaison officers with French formations were likewise not encouraging; in particular I was unable to verify that the French had enough reserves at their disposal south of the gap to enable them to stage counter-attacks sufficiently strong to warrant the expectation that the gap would be closed.

What if the gap could not be closed? Then nine German panzer divisions would be curling round the unprotected rear of Gort's nine divisions. Two alternatives presented themselves to Gort: he must withdraw either to the line of the Somme or to the Channel coast. The first had the obvious advantages that the BEF would be falling back on its lines of communication, and would keep touch with the French; on the other hand, it meant that the Belgian Army would be forced to relinquish Belgian soil, or its allies—and, should evacuation of the BEF finally become inevitable, it would obviously be that much more difficult if the Channel ports were abandoned. But if the BEF *did* fall back on the Channel, this

would involve the departure of the B.E.F. from the theatre of war at a time when the French might need all the support which Britain could give them. It involved the virtual certainty that even if the excellent port facilities at Dunkirk continued to be available, it would be necessary to abandon all the heavier guns and much of the vehicles and equipment.

Henceforth Gort would be torn between a desire to aid the French loyally in their attempts to counterattack, and concern at not letting his nine divisions—the cream of the British Army—be cut off from the sea. However, what Billotte had revealed to him of his prospects for "closing the gap" were so discouraging that, on the 19th, Gort warned the War Office that it might have to consider evacuating the BEF. "I realised that this course was in theory a last alternative," said Gort. "Nevertheless, I felt that in the circumstances there might be no other course open to me." That same day the War Office and the Admiralty began joint discussions—under the code name of *Dynamo*—on the "possible but unlikely evacuation of a very large force in hazardous circumstances."

Exit Gamelin

May 19th was a Sunday. Although the French Government placed its hope for a miracle that day in two earthly champions —de Gaulle who was attacking on the Serre, and Weygand momently expected from Syria—the soul of France turned instinctively to Notre-Dame—as it had done when the Governor of Paris had invoked the aid of patron Ste. Geneviève at the worst moment of the Siege in 1870; as it had done during countless other crises in the long course of French history. That day there was a moving service of intercession attended at Notre-Dame by the entire government and representatives from all French public life. Outside on the parvis was also gathered a large congregation "that aroused the emotions by its piety and unanimity," said Senator Bardoux. There was "a splendid evocation of the saints of France; while the relics of Ste. Geneviève, of St. Louis were paraded . . . each of the saints was invoked and the crowd responded in chorus. Bullitt,* who was in the front pew, was unable to hide his tears."

There would be no divine intervention that day on behalf of General Gamelin. It was to be "the last day of my military existence"—although he had no inkling of this as it began with a telephone call from General Doumenc, at about 5 A.M. "I thought it was pointless waking you earlier," said Doumenc, "but I have the very clear impression that the time has now come for you to intervene. I can't say any more over the telephone." Gamelin replied that he would be at "Les Bondons" at eight o'clock. "Today, the hour has come," Gamelin declared dramatically in his memoirs. "I hope that it is not too late." Arriving at "Les Bondons," Gamelin found Georges still agitated and depressed in the extreme, amid an atmosphere of chaos similar to what he had seen the previous day. Colonel Minart, on liaison to Georges that day, describes the scene vividly:

A large number of officers of all ranks, in particular several generals, some very busy, others downcast, come and go in the different rooms of this enchanting property of Les Bondons. . . . Telephones, maps (events have moved so quickly that the maps of Finland and Norway have not yet been removed from the walls), dossiers, scribbling pads, notebooks of all sorts are spread out, as if for a jumble sale.

A grand piano was heaped high with kepis, while nearby liaison officers from the various armies were ringed about by interrogators;

Some of them, having succeeded in passing through the enemy columns, have achieved remarkable deeds . . . adding to the disorder, through the thin partitions of this bungalow of grand luxe there filters a noise of typewriters, the ringing of telephones, the inadequately silenced noises of motor-cycles housed outside, the musty smells of the kitchen or blocked lavatories, the infantile waggeries of orderlies, secretaries or chauffeurs, witnesses that were generally unaware of— and too close to—this decomposition. One had the impression of attending a consultation without hope of a hundred done-for doctors, specialists of different kinds brought in *in extremis* to a dying man who had already been given up.

---

* The American ambassador.

Gamelin announced to Georges diplomatically that he felt it necessary now, "as Allied Commander-in-Chief, to formulate a general scheme of manoeuvres." Asking for a pen, he then retired to a small room to draft his famous Personal and Secret Instruction No. 12—his first and last intervention in the battle. Some of his staff, says Gamelin, wanted him to take matters entirely in his own hands. "But I did not want to inflict upon General Georges this humiliation in front of everyone. I was anxious to maintain 'form,' to preserve his *amour-propre* and his authority"—perhaps a curious consideration at this moment of French destiny.* Accordingly, Gamelin began self-effacingly:

Without wishing to interfere in the conduct of the battle now being waged, which is in the hands of the Commander-in-Chief of the northeast front . . . I consider that, at the present time:

1. There are grounds . . . for extending the front of our Eastern Armies and those covering Paris towards the west, and for maintaining the link with No. 1 Army Group.

2. That, as regards No. 1 Army Group—rather than let it be encircled—we must act with extreme audacity;† first by forcing, if necessary, the road to the Somme, and secondly, by throwing in particularly mobile forces against the rear of the panzer divisions and the motorised infantry divisions which are following them. It seems that there is, at present, a vacuum behind this first echelon.‡

3. To prepare with all available resources an offensive against the bridges at Mézières. . . .

4. The complete strength of the French and British aviation must now devote itself to joining in the battle. . . .

5. Everything depends on the next few hours.

M. GAMELIN

This was hardly the language of a supreme war lord, of a Joffre or a Foch, vigorously grasping the reins in his hands; it seemed

---

* Gamelin later chided Georges for the lack of gratitude he showed towards this concern for his "susceptibilities."

† Gamelin originally wrote "we must get away from classical notions," but altered it on the objection of his staff.

‡ Like Gamelin (and, before him, Hitler and Rundstedt), Churchill had also arrived at the same conclusion; on the 19th he wired Gamelin in colourful terms: "The tortoise has protruded its head very far from its shell. Some days must elapse before their main body can reach our lines of communications. It would appear that powerful blows struck from the north and south of this drawn-out pocket could yield surprising results.

more like a justification before the court of History. The vaguely
worded concept of striking at the rear of the panzers was obviously correct, but it had come hopelessly late in the day. A
"few hours" was more than the Allies had left at this point; and
where now were the "particularly mobile forces" called for by
Gamelin's plan?

At 9:45 A.M., Gamelin put his signature to what General Roton
termed his "military testament." Having read it out in a "calm
and measured voice" to Georges's assembled staff, he then went
for a stroll in the garden of "Les Bondons" with General Vuillemin of the Air Force, while Georges began acting upon Instruction No. 12. Afterwards he stayed for a "quick lunch" with
Georges produced by the chef who had cooked for Pétain a generation and a war earlier. "Dispirited like all of us by the defeat,
he had put all his frustrated patriotism into the confection of a
true wedding banquet," recalled one of the staff officers present;
but the lunch assumed more "the atmosphere of a funeral repast.
. . . Then came the dessert; a huge raised pudding covered with
cheveux d'ange. It was grotesque and pathetic." Only Gamelin
seemed to eat with a good appetite.

Returning to Vincennes, Gamelin's party (according to Colonel Minart) found that

all activity had practically halted as if on the eve of a move. Everybody,
thinking about his own personal affairs, was packing in all haste. The
cupboards were practically empty. The 75 cannon, installed in the
court, had been withdrawn. At the first signal, Vincennes could be
evacuated like a fireman's barracks.

In this setting, a travel-worn General Weygand arrived, at about
half past three. He informed Gamelin simply that he had been
summoned to Paris by Reynaud, and had been instructed to put
himself in the picture. Gamelin described the situation to him.
Then he asked permission to call on Georges. As he left, he remarked to Gamelin enigmatically: "You know Paul Reynaud
doesn't like you?" Weygand was followed by a visit from a broken
General Corap, to whom Gamelin expressed a few sympathetic
words and an assurance that his "honour as a soldier was beyond question." Towards nine o'clock that evening, a car arrived
bearing an emissary from Reynaud. He handed to Gamelin a

letter succinctly announcing his replacement by Weygand, and thanking him for services rendered "in the course of a long and brilliant career."

Early next morning (May 20th) Weygand arrived at Vincennes to take over. In the C-in-C's office, overlooking the moat where the Duc d'Enghien had been shot, an unusual exchange took place between the two generals—if one may accept Gamelin's version of it. Gamelin expressed his belief that "the execution of my order is the only solution to save the situation"; to which Weygand apparently replied, tapping his notebook, "But I have the secrets of Marshal Foch!" "I could have retorted," says Gamelin, "that I had those of Marshal Joffre and they had not sufficed." With hurt feelings, Gamelin noted that during the brief final interview Weygand could not bring himself to express "one word coming from the heart"; he did not even seem to recall that "it was I who had obtained for him the command in the Levant in August 1939." On this sadly petulant note Gamelin left Vincennes forever. Weygand thought he was "manifestly relieved at being spared a heavy responsibility." The dismissed Generalissimo said good-bye to no one. A few inquisitive secretaries watched his departure discreetly from the windows. The sentries saluted. Some of those watching felt that the gloomy courtyard at Vincennes had just witnessed another execution. Gamelin then returned to the ground floor flat in the Avenue Foch which he had bought for his retirement, and began mulling over his memoirs. The war went on.

Enter Weygand

The new Commander-in-Chief who now held the waning fortunes of the Allies in his hands was seventy-three at the time of his appointment. Supposedly of Belgian parentage, he was an illegitimate and to this day his parentage remains a subject of speculation. Some have it that he was the offspring of a Belgian industrialist and a Polish woman; others that Leopold II, the exploiter of the Congo, was his father; while a strong faction contend that the unhappy Emperor Maximilian and a Mexican woman were Maxime Weygand's parents.* Mexican blood would

---

* As a variation on this theme, the German radio promptly claimed on Weygand's appointment that he was the son of Maximilian by a Saarlander; thus claiming good German blood for the poor misguided general.

certainly have explained the high cheekbones and deep-set eyes
that gave him an increasingly un-French look as he grew older.
A small, dapper man with a foxy face (he reminded one Englishman of an "aged jockey") that revealed a quick intelligence,
Weygand had passed into the cavalry through St. Cyr. Right at
the beginning of the First War he had been picked by Foch, more
or less at random, as his Chief of Staff and had remained with
the Marshal—like a constant shadow—until the Armistice, and
after. He had thus never commanded troops in battle, and—as
Spears remarked of him—between this and being a Chief of Staff
was "as different as riding in the Grand National from taking
photos of its jumps." On leaving Foch's side, he went to Poland
where his admirers consider him to have been chiefly responsible
for the great Polish victory of 1920 against the Russians. In 1923
he was appointed high commissioner in Syria, and then in 1931
became Commander-in-Chief of the French Army. Retiring in
1935, he was called back in 1939 (by Gamelin) to return to Syria
as military commander.

Weygand was very much that particularly French creature, a
"political general." He was almost as deeply committed to the
right wing as he was to the Catholic Church. Clemenceau described him as being "up to his neck in priests," and he often
seemed to harbour an inquisitional notion that sinful France
would be required to suffer for her wickedness. It was also
Clemenceau who had once issued the warning, "Look out. If ever
a *coup d'état* is attempted, it will be by him." On more than one
occasion Weygand had addressed meetings of de la Rocque's
Croix de Feu, and at one time it was whispered that his passionate conservatism had carried him as far as relations with the
Cagoulard terrorists. Certainly, during the Russo-Finnish War he
had been in the van of those anxious to "have a go" at the
Bolsheviks. Spears claimed that Weygand had "only two preoc-
cupations; his haunting fear of revolution, and his dislike of Reynaud." Both were to have their effect on his conduct of the war
as Generalissimo.* Reynaud in his turn had little love for Weygand; about the best thing he could say about him in his memoirs
was that he "had the gift of explaining things clearly." Why then

---

* At the most critical moment in June, Weygand insisted that he be left those
divisions which remained fresh, "in order to maintain order"—on the assumption
that, by then, the threat of revolution was more dangerous than the Germans.

had Reynaud called forth the elderly general at this most dire moment? He was, in de Gaulle's caustic words, "a brilliant second" who had never commanded troops in action; he had not had the advantage of studying the German *Blitzkrieg* technique at first hand, as had—for instance—General Huntziger; and out in the Levant he had not kept himself in particularly close touch with events since May 10th.* The fact was that his selection was first and foremost an act of patriotism, intended by Reynaud to tap and draw strength from the "Verdun stream" flowing through the French soul. In the popular mind, if Pétain represented endurance in adversity and honour, Weygand was still Foch's right hand—and Foch signified victory and *la gloire*. Not every French soldier, however, was thus impressed; many shared the cynicism of Lieutenant Claude Jamet who, on hearing of the new appointment, wrote in his diary:

Gagamelin. Weygand, on the contrary, he's pure blood. The spirit of Foch. "When in danger, call for Weygand," etc. . . . what sluggishness of intellect, and heart! And Weygand is summoned, regardless . . . because Foch is dead. For this "modern war," one might just as well have called for Napoleon, the Great Condé—or Vercingetorix!

Certainly the emotive summoning of Pétain and Weygand to stiffen France's war effort was one measure that would backfire badly on Paul Reynaud.

Weygand had had a gruelling flight from Syria, his aircraft constantly dogged by misfortune. On the 18th he had hoped to make Tunis in one hop, and then Paris by the evening. But there were strong head winds, and over Benghazi (then in Italian hands, Italy being a dubious neutral) he was forced to turn back to refuel at Mersa Matruh in Egypt, thereby losing three precious hours. Finally, in landing at Étampes, the undercarriage of the plane collapsed, and Weygand had to creep out through the upper gun turret. Just at that moment there was an air-raid warning, and he did not reach Paris until 11 A.M. on the 19th. Despite this harrowing journey for a man of his age, Weygand surprised those who saw him; Alexander Werth thought he "looked good in uniform"

---

* On arriving from Syria and having first seen a map of the German advance Weygand is reported to have exclaimed: "If I had known the situation was so bad I would not have come" (on which Spears commented acidly, "It meant he was thinking of his reputation").

—in contrast to Pétain who was accompanying him ("Poor old boy—fancy being dragged into all this at his age"). On arriving at La Ferté, Captain Beaufre (who admittedly became a lifelong devotee of Weygand) was struck by his displaying "a swagger, a passion and a fierce will which contrasted sharply with the pale and curdled calm of his predecessor." Almost immediately the seventy-three-year-old astonished his new staff at Montry* by performing a hundred-yard sprint on the lawn.

On his first brief interview with Georges on the 19th, Weygand at once got an idea of just how serious the situation was. In ten days' fighting the French Army had lost 15 divisions and in the north another 45 were in danger of being thrown into the sea; there were no reserves; the arsenals were almost empty. Between Valenciennes and Montmédy, the gap to be filled measured nearly 100 miles; the proper moment for a coordinated counteroffensive here, assessed Weygand, should have been on the 15th or 16th— therefore it was now too late. As for the unnerved and dejected General Georges, Weygand decided that he must remain (at least nominally) at his command; it would be too complicated, as well as too demoralising for the army, for him to be replaced at this point. But—in contrast to Gamelin—from the beginning the actual conduct of the battle would be in his, Weygand's, hands. Meanwhile Gamelin's Instruction No. 12, decreed only that morning (the 19th), was cancelled. Returning from Georges's HQ, Weygand had gone to Reynaud's office in the evening and, having told the Premier he would accept the "heavy responsibility" cast upon him, added pessimistically: "You will not be surprised if I cannot answer for victory, nor even give you the hope of victory." As he left, Baudouin enquired about his immediate plans, to which Weygand replied: "I am dead tired, for I had only three hours sleep at Tunis. I shall begin by getting some sleep." All decisions would be postponed to the morrow. Thus passed another twenty-four of the "few hours" remaining to France.

On to the Channel

Monday, May 20th, was the day of Guderian's triumph. The previous evening he had once more been granted complete free-

---

* So as to be closer to the conduct of operations, but also perhaps to rid himself of the shade of Gamelin lurking in the gloom of Vincennes, Weygand decided to move his headquarters in with General Doumenc's staff at Montry.

dom of movement, and at midnight he ordered his Corps to strike out for Amiens and Abbeville—prefacing his orders with the words: "The enemy opposite the corps front has been defeated." The latest aerial reconnaissance reports certainly confirmed this view; they could find virtually no Allied formations ahead of the panzers. On the Allied side, General d'Astier's patrols spoke of a "whirlpool of armour" about to burst westwards. With the Canal du Nord behind them, there was now no natural barrier between the panzers and the coast; just mile upon mile of the flat, featureless Picardy plain, a paradise for armoured commanders.

Guderian himself was on the road at 4 A.M. with the 1st Panzer, desirous of being present at the historic moment of the capture of Amiens. The morning began with a sharp row involving Colonel Balck, now commanding the 1st Panzer Brigade, who had moved out from the Péronne bridgehead without waiting to be relieved by the 10th Panzer. His successor, Colonel Landgraf, was enraged by Balck's casualness, and particularly at his retort: "If we lost it you can always take it again." At the familiar Battle of the Somme name-place of Albert, the riflemen formerly commanded by Balck came up against British troops* for the first time. The 1st Panzer official historian describes them as having "fought toughly and bravely without however being able to prevent the fall of Albert." Swinging round the hold-up at Albert, Balck's tanks were at the gates of Amiens by midmorning, having advanced nearly 35 miles.

Never had the armour moved faster. "We had the feeling," said Kielmansegg, "such as a fine racehorse may have, of having been held back by its rider, coldly and deliberately, then getting its head free to reach out into a swinging gallop and speed to the finishing post as winner." William Shirer, who that day had at last been allowed to follow in the wake of the German advance, was fascinated by the spectacle of this army on wheels, which

simply went up the roads . . . with tanks, planes, artillery, antitank stuff, everything . . . all morning, roads massed with supplies, troops going up . . . curious, not a single Allied plane yet . . . and these endless columns of troops, guns, supplies, stretching all the way from the German border . . . what a target! . . . Refugees streaming back along the roads in the dust and heat . . . tears your heart out.

---

* The Royal West Kents.

Notwithstanding all the years he had observed the build-up of the new Wehrmacht in Germany, the speed and efficiency with which the German columns moved made a deep impression on Shirer:

It is a gigantic, impersonal war machine, run as coolly and efficiently, say, as our automobile industry in Detroit. . . . thousands of motorised vehicles thundering by on the dusty roads, officers and men alike remain cool and business-like. Absolutely no excitement, no tension. An officer directing artillery fire stops for half an hour to explain to you what he is up to.

On an airfield outside Amiens, the panzers nearly surprised an RAF unit which had lodged there for the night, and the fighters took off literally in the face of the first German tanks. The city was almost empty; the previous afternoon the last line-of-communication troops had marched out,* accompanied by nuns from the Community of the Holy Family; and about the same time, the defeated General Corap was passing through on his way to see Gamelin. Fires caused by the previous day's bombing had raged all night, and dawn brought the Luftwaffe over again, bombing relentlessly. About all that was left holding Amiens was a battalion of the Royal Sussex Regiment, belonging to the 12th (Territorial) Division, which stood and fought to a finish against Balck's tanks, and was completely destroyed. By midday the Germans had spread a large Swastika flag in front of the post office, to show the Luftwaffe that the city was in German hands. Methodically, they then pushed on southwards to seize bridgeheads over the Somme—in preparation for Phase Two of the Battle of France. Guderian was there, as intended, to inspect the great city which even Ludendorff had failed to capture in 1918, and somehow found time to visit the cathedral before rushing off to see how the 2nd Panzers were getting on.

He discovered General Veiel and the 2nd Panzer at Albert, where they had just captured a British gun battery which had exhausted its ammunition. The division was nearly out of fuel, and was proposing to halt at Albert. Guderian says "they were soon disillusioned," and he ordered them at once to push on to

---

* Surprisingly, the Gare du Nord was still sending trains off from Paris to Amiens as late as the evening of the 19th.

Abbeville. Having somehow mastered their fuel problem, the 2nd Panzers reached Abbeville by six o'clock that evening after an advance from Albert of 45 miles, taking by surprise a French unit drilling on its parade ground. Its tanks then broke in between positions held by territorials of the British 35th Brigade, only a few remnants of which managed to fall back across the Somme. Abbeville too had been bombed—indiscriminately, like Rotterdam, it seems—all through the 20th, and severe damage caused. But in fact the Luftwaffe probably granted the hard-pressed British territorials a respite by mistakenly bombing the bridgeheads which the Germans had seized—forcing them to withdraw that night until the error was resolved.

Because of a delay in the transmission of orders, Reinhardt's troops did not move until 8 A.M. on the 20th. At 1400 hours they ran into their first British at Mondicourt, who—in the words of the 6th Panzer War Diary—"in contrast to the French, cause surprise by their tough way of fighting and are only overcome after a one hour battle." Two hours later Ravenstein's force was once again fighting a hard battle against the British 36th Brigade defending Doullens, which, though hopelessly outnumbered, managed to hold out until shortly before nightfall. Nevertheless, despite this stubborn resistance, Reinhardt's armour swept around Doullens to reach its objectives at Hesdin and Le Boisle. By the end of the day the two British Territorial Divisions, the 12th and 23rd, had all but ceased to exist.* Widely dispersed, and inadequately prepared as they were to encounter German panzer divisions, each had given a good account of itself against impossible odds, as the various German accounts testified.

As agreed with Hoth the previous day, Rommel launched forth on another of his famous night attacks just after midnight on the 19th. By five A.M. he had reached the village of Beaurains, two and one-half miles south of Arras. But, as had happened at Avesnes, his motorised rifle regiments did not follow the armour as closely as intended. Rushing back in an armoured car to find them, Rommel was nearly trapped by French cavalry tanks infiltrating across his lines of communication. These knocked out Rommel's accompanying tanks, and for several hours he and his signal staff were surrounded. The situation was restored only by

---

* At one point even a mobile bath unit was thrown into the battle.

the arrival of an infantry regiment and artillery. Once again Rommel had the narrowest of escapes. For the rest of the day the 7th Panzer hammered unsuccessfully at Arras, held by British troops under Major General R. L. Petre. It was his first serious check since crossing the Meuse, his casualties the highest since the 13th. On the evening of the 20th, the 7th Panzer was placed on the defensive around Arras—an unusual posture for Rommel.

Meanwhile, as night descended over northern France on May 20th, Guderian's men pulled off the ace achievement of the campaign so far. Pushing out down the Somme from Abbeville, Austrians from Lieutenant Colonel Spitta's battalion from the 2nd Panzer reached Noyelles on the Atlantic coast, not far from the Hundred Years' War battlefield of Crécy-en-Ponthieu. They had advanced over 60 miles since the morning. The dog-tired panzer crews filled their lungs with sea air and wondered in amazement at how much more they had already achieved than the Kaiser's Army before them. In ten short days they had covered some 200 miles* and had encircled the cream of the Allied armies. What could they not aspire to! In his orders that night, Guderian told his Corps: "Today's battles have brought us complete success. Along the whole front the enemy is in retreat in a manner that at times approaches rout." Far back at the rear, both the OKH and the OKW were taken by surprise at the news. On the 19th, Jodl had been worrying that the Allies in northern Belgium might slip out to the south, and even on the morning of the 20th Halder was expressing concern lest Bock's pressure in the north might result "in driving the game away, as it were, past Kleist." But at the *Felsennest* Jodl found a Hitler "beside himself with joy. Talks in words of highest appreciation of the German Army and its leadership. Is working on the peace treaty. . . . First negotiations in the Forest of Compiègne as in 1918."

In Paris, Alexander Werth recorded:

Cheerful news reached me from the censors' office at night that all telephone (and telegraph?) communications between Paris and London had been broken off—lines cut; Fifth Column at work? or what? . . . Colonel Thomas said there was some heavy fighting "around"

---

* By comparison, it is interesting that in mid-April 1945 when Germany was all but defeated, the American 5th Armoured—in what was held to be a record—took *thirteen* days to advance the same distance.

St. Quentin and Péronne. He tried to suggest that the German progress was slowing down. I've noticed that when they mention places
"round" which there is fighting, it means these places are already in
German hands.

As usual the French Censor was forty-eight hours behind with
the news. For the Allies this was unquestionably the darkest day
of the war so far, and few in the next five years to come would be
darker.

18

Encirclement
MAY 21st — 23rd

In the West, the greatest offensive of all time has had its
first strategic result, after a series of major tactical successes; our forces have reached the sea.
    —Wehrmacht Communiqué, May 21st

The Germans have not yet stood the final test . . . we are
the old opponent of the Marne, the old opponent of
Verdun. Pétain appears to us like a symbol, a promise.
Weygand brings back to us the genius of Foch.
    —Le Journal, May 21st

A serious technical fault in the cable, it was learned,
caused the cancellation of the public telephone service
between London and Paris and beyond on Monday
night and yesterday. . . . A Post Office official said:
"We have no idea when the service will be restored."
    —Daily Telegraph, May 22nd

The recapture of Arras may prove to be a turning-point
in the present battle which will have a vital effect on
the whole war.
    —Daily Mail, May 23rd

German High Command: More vacillations

FOR THE jubilant Germans, the next three days would be potentially the most dangerous of the campaign. The vulnerable "tortoise head" of the panzers was now further extended than ever
before,* the vacuum between them and the weary, forced-

---

* General Schaal, for example, was reporting back in alarm that his 10th Panzer
covering the western end of the flank along the Somme was spread out over a
distance of 60 miles.

marching infantry divisions greater than it had been when Hitler had lost his nerve on the 17th. Would the Allies, despite their disarray, yet be able to launch a successful counterattack to break through the Panzer Corridor before this frail wedge between their armies became a thing of steel?

At no time since May 10th had the outcome of the battle become such a race for time. On the German side, Guderian up in the forefront with his panzers was supremely aware of this. After his remarkable achievements of the 20th, he fretted that night that "we did not know in what direction our advance should continue." Nor, he added, had Kleist himself received any further instructions on how to proceed. In his orders for the 21st, Guderian simply told his panzers to regroup and "mop up" on the positions gained the previous day.

So the 21st of May was wasted while we waited for orders. I spent the day visiting Abbeville and our crossings and bridgeheads over the Somme. On the way I asked my men how they had enjoyed the operations up to date. "Not bad," said an Austrian of the 2nd Panzer Division, "but we wasted two whole days."

"Unfortunately," Guderian commented bitterly, "he was right."

The reasons for this delay in the transmission of orders lay in renewed vacillations within the German High Command, again partially caught off balance by its own successes. The objective of *Sichelschnitt* had been reached, the Allied armies in the north were encircled; but the master blueprint had laid down no precise directives as to what the next step should be. Halder seemed to be still toying with notions of immediately continuing the advance southwards from the bridgeheads gained across the Somme, and leaving Bock's Army Group "B" to "mop up" the encircled Allied forces in the north. Meanwhile Hitler's jubilation was once again tempered with renewed misgivings about the weakness of that southern flank, and later that day he was again lecturing Brauchitsch on the slowness of the infantry to catch up with the panzers. It was thus not until midday on the 21st that the German High Command decided to concentrate all its forces upon reducing the Allied forces trapped in the north, so that by the time Guderian received his orders to swing northwards to seize the Channel ports the campaigning day was over. In the meantime, Rommel and the forces grouped around Arras had run into serious trouble.

Allied High Command: More delays; Ironside's Plan

In the Allied camp, where time was even more vital, the change of command—however desirable it may have been—could hardly have come at a worse moment. Before any forces could have been concentrated for the attack towards Mézières from the south and the Somme from the north, as called for by Gamelin's Instruction No. 12 of the 19th, the order was cancelled by Weygand. On Weygand's first visit to Georges's HQ that day, Georges had offered to give him a detailed briefing on the situation. Weygand, weary after his fatiguing trip from the Levant, had replied, "No, tomorrow." After his briefing then by Georges, Weygand had taken one or two important measures. He ordered the roads to be cleared (at last); civilians were to be allowed to move only between 6 P.M. and midnight. Struck by the lack of antitank weapons, he had ordered all the famous 75s of the First War to be brought out of mothballs and used in combination with the infantry, "like revolvers." The most serious problem, as he rightly saw it, now lay not south of the Panzer Corridor but in the north. But Weygand discovered that all communications with the forces there were cut off; he was only in contact tenuously with Billotte through London. Therefore, he told Georges: "I must go and see on the spot what the situation is." It was Foch who had taught him "the value of personal contact maintained at frequent intervals." Later that afternoon he announced to Reynaud that, if the railway were still working, "I will go by train to Abbeville tonight; if not, I will go by air tomorrow morning." Pétain, who was present, supported Weygand's decision, saying that nothing was equal to the presence of a commander-in-chief. Reynaud, however, managed to dissuade Weygand from entraining for Abbeville, on the grounds that "it would be a fatal blow to France if you were to be taken prisoner"; which indeed might have been the case, as Abbeville was just about to pass into enemy hands. Finally it was decided that Weygand would fly north the following morning—on condition that, Cinderella-like, he would be away no more than twenty-four hours. But this would still mean the loss of two more precious days to the Allies.

Meanwhile, as Weygand was being briefed at La Ferté and the panzers were fanning out towards the coast, on the morning of the 20th the British CIGS, General Ironside, had arrived in the north on an important mission from his government. His visit followed upon Gort's call to the War Office of the previous day warning that he might be forced to consider evacuating the BEF. Churchill viewed Gort's fears with considerable disfavour, and stated that General Ironside "could not accept this proposal, as, like most of us, he favoured the southward march." Accordingly, Ironside was dispatched to Wahagnies to tell Gort that he was to "force his way through all opposition in order to join up with the French in the south." The phrasing of this brief revealed just how misinformed the Churchill Government remained—even as late as May 19th—on the true situation prevailing in France.* Ironside arrived at Gort's HQ at 8 A.M. on the 20th, and promptly delivered to him a written order embodying the government's views, which said that the CIGS would inform General Billotte and the Belgians accordingly. General Dill, already in Paris, would also inform Georges of the British view; which, in effect, constituted the very first intervention by Britain in the French General Staff's handling of land strategy since the war had begun.

Ironside put his case for executing the southward march towards Amiens. Gort revealed obvious consternation. Then, according to Ironside, "after some thought, Lord Gort did not agree. I asked him to try, but the C-in-C said no, he could not agree." Firmly Gort pointed out that seven of his nine divisions were in close contact with the enemy on the Escaut; even if they could be disengaged, their withdrawal would open a gap on his left between the BEF and the badly shaken Belgian Army through which the enemy would be bound to penetrate. In response to Ironside's contention that the advancing German panzers were "tired," Gort said he was sure the French were even more tired. Everything he had seen of the French forces and their leaders in recent days increasingly led him to doubt whether they could stage "an organised counteroffensive on a large scale"; therefore he was inclining more and more to his "last alternative." How-

---

* However, by way of reinsurance, on the morning of the 20th Churchill did follow up with a decree that "as a precautionary measure the Admiralty should assemble a large number of small vessels in readiness to proceed to ports and inlets on the French coast."

ever, he told Ironside that he "already had plans in hand" to launch the following day a *limited* attack southwards from Arras with his two remaining "free" divisions. In the absence of any fresh orders from the French, he would carry out this attack. Ironside then asked Gort "under whose orders he was now acting."

The answer was General Billotte, who had a headquarters under the Vimy Ridge near Lens. Billotte had given the B.E.F. no orders for some eight days, nor had Gort complained to the Cabinet or to me.*

Asking if he could take Gort's Chief of Staff, Lieutenant General Pownall, along with him, Ironside then set off in an ill humour to see Billotte.

Gort

Like actors in a play, the minor characters of history have their moments when they advance from the rear of the stage to dominate briefly the whole scene in the full glare of the footlights, before receding once more into the background. Now, for the next ten days, the unassuming, bulldog figure of Lord Gort emerges to the fore as the most important in the battle—perhaps in the war at large. At the time, John Standish Surtees Prendergast Vereker, 6th Viscount Gort, was fifty-four years old. After joining the Grenadier Guards in 1905, he had earned an almost legendary reputation for bravery during the First World War. Four times wounded, nine times mentioned in dispatches, he won the Military Cross, the Distinguished Service Order and two Bars—and finally the Victoria Cross, when commanding his battalion at the crossing of the Canal du Nord in September 1918.† After the war he held various staff jobs at home and in India, and was CIGS when selected to lead the BEF. Up to that moment he had never commanded any unit larger than a brigade.

Utterly straightforward, with a limited intellect, he had always held himself completely aloof from any kind of extramural intriguing; in marked antithesis to the French "political" generals

---

* As further instance of the poor liaison existing between the French High Command and the BEF, Gort only learned indirectly on the 20th that Weygand had taken over and was now directing operations; the British Government was not consulted on the change of command.

† Close to where Guderian crossed it (in the opposite direction) on May 19th.

like Weygand, or the cerebral Gamelin—or, for that matter, to his own forerunner, Sir Douglas Haig. His reaction to the reforming but perhaps too adroit Hore-Belisha (appointed Secretary for War in 1937) was typical: "We mustn't upset the people in the clubs by going too fast." Adored among the Brigade of Guards (known there by the affectionate but hardly flattering nickname of "Fat Boy") in the eyes of Brooke, his subordinate (who could be far from uncritical of his superiors), Gort was

one of those pre-eminently straight characters who inspired confidence. He could never have done anything small or mean. . . . He had one of those cheerful dispositions full of vitality, energy and *joie de vivre*, and the most wonderful charm, and was gifted with great powers of leadership. . . . I could not help admiring him and had feelings of real and deep affection for him.

But, added Brooke, "I had no confidence in his leadership when it came to handling a large force. He seemed incapable of seeing the wood for trees." During the winter of the Phoney War—perhaps when he should have been voicing to the British Cabinet his doubts on the French Army and its strategy—Gort had busied himself tirelessly with such details as the proper use of hand grenades, the art of patrolling and night small-arms fire, and map reading in the snow. Visiting his HQ, Maurois noted in evident surprise:

Never has a generalissimo had a simpler office. A scrawled card, affixed to the door by four thumb tacks, read: "Office of the C-in-C." Inside the room, which contained no other furniture, two trestles of white wood supported a bare plank. This was Lord Gort's work table. . . . Extremely active by nature, he found, in time of war, his only sport and relaxation in walking. He was to be seen at dawn on the muddy roads around Arras, his elbows close to his body, his head thrust forward.

Gort's French colleagues, as Spears aptly remarks, tended to regard him "as a sort of friendly and jovial battalion commander" —and they treated him as such. Certainly with his hearty demeanour, the occasionally worried expression, the breeches and the Guardsman's highly polished knee boots, Gort did seem the image of the old-style British battalion commander, and to a large

The panzer advance: May 18th–21st

extent this was the key both to his character and his actions. On being sent to lead the BEF in 1939, Gort's instructions from his government were that he was to take his orders from General Georges, as C-in-C Northeast Front; but if any order received from the French should appear to Gort "to imperil the British Field Force," he would be at liberty to appeal to the British Government before executing it. Gort had interpreted these instructions with the rigid, unquestioning instinct for loyalty of a Guards battalion commander. Both during the Phoney War and after the German offensive had begun, he had observed much that had disturbed him about the French conduct of affairs, and he clearly resented the offhand way in which Georges and Billotte had never bothered to offer him anything but the minimum of consultation and information—such as the commander of a very junior formation might expect. But the French leaders were his appointed superiors, and—true to his instincts—Gort doggedly accepted his lot, without exercising his right to complain or express his misgivings to his own government. At the same time, as the situation following the German break-through became progressively graver, so Gort's concern grew that Churchill and his government should be unaware of just how bad things were in France;* but again—at least until May 20th—Gort was not inclined to challenge the fallacious views of those set above him.

Yet there was much more to Gort than just the laudable virtues of a Grenadier battalion commander. He was endowed to excess with the singlemindedness which so often accompanies great personal courage; and by the third week in May this singlemindedness had taken the form of a determination to save his BEF from destruction, come what may. A man who had won the VC as Gort had would not be deterred from pursuing what he considered to be his line of duty, regardless of the opposition, even if it should include a will as formidable as that of Winston Churchill. In 1914 it was popularly said of Jellicoe that he was the only man who could have "lost the war in an afternoon" (although, in view of the poor subsequent performance of battleships on both sides, this claim may have been somewhat exaggerated); but in 1940,

---

* For the British Government's misconceptions, Gort must himself be held partly to blame in his failure to communicate earlier his doubts about the French conduct of the battle; he seems certainly to have erred in not complaining much earlier to Ironside about his receiving no orders from Billotte.

Gort by May 20th was certainly the man who—by forfeiting Britain's only land force—could easily have lost the war at least in a week of afternoons. It was also once said of Jellicoe that he had "all Nelson's qualities except disobedience." Gort, the Guardsman, would never be disobedient; but in a tight corner his single-mindedness and courage would make him defiant—which, when clear and realistic directives from above were lacking, would amount to almost the same thing. Over the next week, the responsibility resting on Gort alone would be gigantic. Fortunately for Britain—and ultimately for France—events would prove that Gort had the strength to bear it.

Ironside visits Billotte

On his way to Lens to see Billotte, Ironside had an unpleasant journey. The road was

an indescribable mass of refugees, both Belgian and French, moving down in every kind of conveyance. Poor women pushing perambulators, horsed wagons with all the family and its goods in them. Belgian units all going along aimlessly. Poor devils. It was a horrible sight and it blocked the roads, which was the main difficulty.

At Lens, Ironside found Billotte with Blanchard, the commander of the French First Army. They were both, he said, "in a state of complete depression. No plan, no thought of a plan. Ready to be slaughtered. Defeated at the head without casualties. *Très fatigués* and nothing doing." There ensued an angry scene. The British CIGS was also—to foreign eyes—something of a caricature of an Englishman; aged fifty-nine, he had been the original prototype for Buchan's Richard Hannay and stood six foot four (inevitably, this had gained him the nickname "Tiny").* In Army circles he had openly referred to Secretary of State Hore-Belisha as "that little monkey," the Cabinet as "the old gentlemen," and had a healthy, Kiplingesque contempt for those "lesser breeds." In a rage he must have presented a daunting figure before the two distressed French generals of modest stature. Ironside admits he lost his temper and "shook Billotte by the button of his tunic. The man is completely beaten," he added contemptuously for the

---

* One of the French present at the meeting that day, Captain René de Chambrun, says that Ironside struck him as the tallest man he had ever seen.

benefit of his diary. "There is absolutely nothing in front of them. They remain quivering behind the water-line north of Cambrai while the fate of France is in the balance."*

He then bulldozed Billotte and Blanchard into accepting the British proposal to attack towards Amiens, and (according to Ironside), "Billotte drew himself up to attention to say that he would make an immediate plan to attack and I left him to do it." Next, Ironside telephoned Weygand and "told him that there was no resolution here and that there was no coordination. I told him that Billotte should be relieved." Finally it was agreed (with Billotte and Blanchard) that the British and the French First Army would each attack on the 21st with two divisions. That the French were acquiescing only under Ironside's formidable pressure was obvious; before the CIGS departed for London, Gort assured him "that they would never attack."

On his return home, the tone of his diary entries shows that, after his experience at Lens, Ironside at any rate regarded the situation in France with more sober realism. He writes: "I begin to despair of the French fighting at all. The great army defeated by a few tanks." He was increasingly despondent about the prospects facing Gort's divisions. With perhaps only another four days' food left, Ironside was doubtful whether they could even fight their way back to the Channel coast:

Situation desperate. . . . Personally, I think we cannot extricate the B.E.F. Only hope a march south-west. Have they the time? Have they got the food?

"God help the B.E.F.," Ironside added bitterly. "Brought to this state by the incompetence of the French Command." After seeing Churchill on the 21st, he found that the Prime Minister still "persists in thinking the position no worse."

Gort goes it alone at Arras

At Wahagnies, Gort pushed ahead with his plan to attack southwards from Arras on the 21st. Coordinating the operation was Major General Harold Franklyn of the 5th Division. Known

---

* The exaggeration of this remark again indicates how incompletely Ironside and the War Cabinet in England understood how disastrous the French defeat had already been.

Carl Mydans

Refugees clog the road out of Paris, five days before the city's fall

The debris of the defeated

Bibliothek für Zeitgeschichte

Dunkirk

Wide World Photos

Rommel's own situation map of May 21st; British

attack by "five divisions" at Arras

The vanquished

Keitel reads the surrender terms

Huntziger signs

Military sight-seers at Sacré Coeur

A *gendarme* gives directions to touring German officers

as "Frankforce," the troops at his disposal nominally consisted
of two infantry divisions (5th and 50th) and the 1st Army Tank
Brigade, but in the event only a much smaller force could be
committed. The infantry divisions had between them only four
brigades, instead of the usual three apiece; one from the 5th Division had been detached, partly to relieve the French cavalry on
the river Scarpe so that they could join in the attack, and General
Franklyn decided to hold its other brigade (the 17th) in reserve
until after the first phase had been completed; from the 50th Division, one of its brigades was sent to bolster the defences of the
Arras garrison and to hold the river line immediately east of the
city. Thus when the operation actually started on the 21st, instead of two British divisions only two battalions (from the 151st
Brigade, 50th Division) would in fact initiate the attack. Meanwhile, instead of the 100 tanks at its disposal, through the mechanical wear and tear of the long marches of the past days,
"Frankforce" could only mount a total of 58 Mark I and 16 Mark
II infantry tanks. Both were extremely slow machines, but heavily
armoured. The Mark I carried only a medium machine gun; the
Mark II, later christened the "Matilda," was armed with a
2-pounder gun* and—weighing 25 tons—had the thickest armour
of any tank on the battlefields of France. "Frankforce" would be
led into battle by Major General G. le Q. Martel, the commander
of the 50th Division and one of Britain's foremost experts of tank
warfare of the interwar period.

At Gort's HQ what had started life as a limited operation designed simply to disengage Arras had, in the meantime, as a consequence of the forceful pressure applied by Ironside during his
visit, imperceptibly escalated to the point where it was now regarded as the first blow in the concerted Allied attempt to close
the gap. But none of this was revealed to either Franklyn or Martel. Their orders remained unchanged: to "support the garrison
in Arras and to block the roads south of Arras, thus cutting off
the German communications (via Arras) from the east." Little
thought seems to have been given to what enemy strength Martel's rather slender force might expect to encounter "south of
Arras" by the 21st.

After Ironside's departure, Gort—still harbouring fears that,

---

* The British 2-pounder had a slightly larger calibre but considerably more hitting power than the 37 mm then carried on the German Mark III panzer.

as he had predicted to Ironside, the French "would never attack" —had instructed his liaison officers with Billotte and Blanchard to make it clear that "if our counter-attack was not successful the French and British Armies north of the gap would have their flank turned and could no longer remain in their present positions." Nevertheless, when at 6 P.M. on the 20th there was a conference at Franklyn's HQ to coordinate the next day's operation, no representative arrived from General René Altmayer's French V Corps, which Billotte and Blanchard had undertaken would attack with two divisions east of Arras, in the direction of Cambrai. Shaken by Ironside's rage, Blanchard had in fact sent a special liaison officer, Major Vautrin, to Altmayer to urge upon him the importance of attacking simultaneously with the British on the 21st.* But, Vautrin reported back, "General Altmayer, who seemed tired out and thoroughly disheartened, wept silently on his bed." He told Vautrin that one had to be realistic, and that "the troops had buggered off, that he was ready to accept all the consequences of his refusal and go and get himself killed at the head of a battalion, but he would no longer continue to sacrifice the army corps of which he had already lost nearly half." Accordingly, late that night a letter from Blanchard reached Gort telling him that Altmayer would not be able to move until the 22nd or the following night—because the roads were so badly blocked. Instead, Prioux and his Cavalry Corps would lend flanking cover to the west of "Frankforce."

Prioux—who seems to have retained the most fighting spirit of any French general in these days—had indeed wanted to use his armour to slice into the panzers' tenuous communications in a cavalry-style raid. But he had his own problems at that moment. A good part of his 1st Light Mechanised Division had been destroyed in the bitter fighting in the Forest of Mormal, and on the 19th he had been unable to reassemble those others of his tank companies, farmed out to various infantry divisions, in time to combine with de Gaulle's attack from the south. The reluctant infantry generals seem to have turned a deaf ear to the injunctions of Billotte, and finally—at 5 P.M. on the 20th—he sent out a Draconian order: "The greater part of the fighting vehicles have not

---

* Although Colonel Goutard blames Blanchard for saying in his orders to Altmayer, "The attack will start *from May 21st onwards*, nothing then was imperative about the order . . ."

been returned to the light mechanised divisions. . . . This order will be carried out immediately. I will not hesitate to bring any formation commander who disobeys this order before a court martial!" But it came too late for Prioux to offer more than a few weak detachments of his 3rd DLM to help "Frankforce" on the 21st.

At the same time, General d'Astier reveals, ZOAN had been called upon by Georges to lend "powerful support" on the morning of the 21st to an operation of "first importance" being launched against Cambrai by Blanchard's First Army. But no front, no targets, no time had been given; Georges seemed completely out of the picture, and d'Astier had been unable to make contact himself with either the First Army or the British Air Component now back in Kent. His reconnaissance planes were either shot down or turned back, and it was not until 4 P.M. on the 21st that they were able to get through—by which time they reported that nothing was happening round Cambrai. From the Air Component, just completing its move back to Kent, no RAF cover was forthcoming either.*

Despite this confirmation of his worst fears about French participation, Gort stuck doggedly to his plans for the Arras attack, his French critics suggesting that he was "perhaps anxious to be done with the thing." In any case, instinct and experience decided him not to wait for the French. Thus, by two o'clock on the afternoon of the 21st when—after various hitches in the morning—"Frankforce" finally attacked, the massive counterblow called for by Ironside had been whittled down from four French and British divisions to a jab by two British battalions (territorials at that) supported by tanks of which only the 16 "Matildas" were useful against German panzers, and with flank cover from a few squadrons of light French armour. The sad story of all the previous French counterefforts was being repeated; the only difference was that the effects would be marginally dissimilar.

Martel's attack

Leading it as Rommel would have done, from an open car, General Martel opened his attack by striking southwards around

---

* D'Astier, apparently, had not yet been informed of the withdrawal of Air Component.

the west of Arras with two mobile columns. Each consisted of a tank battalion and an infantry battalion (of the Durham Light Infantry), plus a battery of field artillery and one of antitank guns. There was no air cover. The objective was to reach the river Cojeul that night. Almost at once the right-hand column unexpectedly came up against the enemy at Duisans.* The village was cleared after a fight, and a number of prisoners taken; but two precious companies of infantry and some antitank guns had to be left behind to hold it. The remainder of the column then pushed on towards Warlus, which it had to capture against substantial opposition. Next it took Berneville and threw an advanced guard out across the Doullens–Arras road. Here the British infantry found themselves pinned down by heavy machine-gun and mortar fire, while for twenty minutes the Luftwaffe attacked the main body unopposed. Nevertheless, Martel's tanks swept around to the left and pushed on to Wailly, where they hit the newly arrived SS *Totenkopf* motorised infantry division. But the right-hand column had shot its bolt, and that evening was forced to fall back defensively on Warlus after heavy losses. Here an unfortunate incident took place when a detachment of Prioux's tanks attacked some British antitank guns, taking them for Germans. A spirited engagement followed, in which one British gun was knocked out and several men killed, and more than one French tank hit, before the French commander realised the mistake and made his apologies. Six of these tanks then played a useful role in freeing rear links with Duisans where Rommel's tanks were threatening to infiltrate. That was about the extent of French support that day.

Martel's left-hand column also had to fight all the way, but it made faster progress and (as will be seen from Rommel's own account) inflicted heavy casualties. Occupying Dainville, its tanks smashed up a motorised column, destroying its transports, while the following infantry took a considerable number of prisoners. Two miles further on, six "Matildas" found little difficulty in overrunning a German antitank battery near Achicourt. The left-hand column then pushed on to Agny and Beaurains, and a small advanced party reached Wancourt on the river Cojeul. Throughout

---

* Motorised infantry of Rommel's 7th Panzer who were just resuming their advance northwestwards. The fact that their presence was unreported reveals the incompleteness of the hasty Franco-British reconnaissance.

The Allied counterattack at Arras: May 21st–23rd

most of the afternoon a savage battle raged in the area of Agny–Beaurains between the heavy infantry tanks of the 4th Royal Tank Regiment and Rommel's 6th Rifle Brigade, backed by a powerful line of guns. There were heavy losses on both sides; but, like Martel's right-hand column, the left also had no troops to follow up its success or even to make good the ground won. Meanwhile, east of Arras, Brigadier Haydon's 150th Brigade (50th Division) had made a harassing raid across the Scarpe towards Tilloy, and the 13th Brigade had established a bridgehead further east in preparation for the second phase of "Frankforce's" operation. But, realising that he could not hold the ground occupied on the first day and that Rommel's panzers would soon be threatening his rear to the west of Arras, Franklyn decided to call off the attack. The British counterattack at Arras had come to a halt. It had advanced a maximum of 10 miles, taken more than 400 German prisoners* and destroyed a large number of tanks and transport; but it had lost all except 26 of its Mark I tanks and 2 of its valuable Mark IIs.† The remainder, with their tracks breaking from the excessive wear of the past days, had to fall back to the rear, constantly harried by German Stukas.

The German view

This, in brief, is the British view of what was effectively their first major armoured engagement of the war. The German accounts reveal, however, that the drive Martel instilled into the "Frankforce" attack, combined with the almost impenetrable thickness of the armour on the British infantry tanks, made an impression out of all proportion to the numbers involved. The SS Totenkopf division apparently abandoned its first line in haste when attacked at Wailly, and even Guderian states that it "showed signs of panic"—a comment not to be found previously in his forthright account of the campaign. Rommel's eyewitness account of the day's events is, as so often, the most instructive. At almost exactly the moment that Martel began his attack, Rommel had ordered Rothenburg's 25th Panzer Regiment to advance again around the northwest of Arras. He intended to accompany the tanks himself, together with his faithful ADC, Lieutenant

---

* Probably the biggest bag of prisoners taken in any isolated action against the Germans since May 10th.

† The commanders of both the British tank battalions had also been killed.

Most. But once again he had to retrace his footsteps to shepherd forward his lagging infantry regiments. He could not find the 7th, but just south of Wailly,

we eventually came across part of the 6th Rifle Regiment, and driving alongside their column, turned off with them towards Wailly. Half a mile east of the village we came under fire from the north. One of our howitzer batteries was already in position at the northern exit from the village, firing rapidly on enemy tanks attacking southward from Arras.*

Rommel continues:

As we were now coming under machine-gun fire and the infantry had already taken cover to the right, Most and I ran on in front of the armoured cars towards battery position. It did not look as though the battery would have much difficulty in dealing with the enemy tanks, for the gunners were calmly hurling round after round into them in complete disregard of the return fire.

But on reaching Wailly itself, Rommel found that the British tank fire had created "chaos and confusion among troops in the village and they were jamming up the roads and yards with their vehicles, instead of going into action with every available weapon to fight off the oncoming enemy. We tried to create order."

West of the village, Rommel came across a light flak troop and some antitank guns, "most of them totally under cover." Close to this position British tanks had shot up a Mark III panzer, and other tanks approaching from Bac du Nord were pressing in closely upon Wailly. "It was," says Rommel, "an extremely tight spot." He watched while "the crew of a howitzer battery, some distance away, now left their guns, swept along by the retreating infantry." The scene was almost more reminiscent of the French debacle at Sedan than anything previously recounted by Rommel. To restore this perilous situation, Rommel continues,

With Most's help, I brought every available gun into action at top speed against the tanks. Every gun, both anti-tank and anti-aircraft, was ordered to open rapid fire immediately and I personally gave

---

* This was the right-hand column of Martel's force.

each gun its target. We ran from gun to gun. . . . Soon we succeeded in putting the leading enemy tanks out of action. About 150 yards west of our small wood a British captain climbed out of a heavy tank and walked unsteadily towards us with his hands up. We had killed his driver.

Rommel then switched the fire of his guns to another group of British tanks, knocking out several and forcing the remainder to retreat: "Although we were under very heavy fire from the tanks during this action, the gun crews worked magnificently. The worst seemed to be over and the attack beaten off, when suddenly Most sank to the ground behind a 20 mm anti-aircraft gun close beside me. He was mortally wounded." Lieutenant Most was the second of Rommel's ADCs to fall at his side during the campaign,* but this episode marked the final halting of Martel's right-hand column.

Turning now to the progress of the left-hand column, Rommel speaks of "very powerful armoured forces" which had inflicted "heavy losses in men and material" on his 6th Rifle Regiment.

The anti-tank guns which we quickly deployed showed themselves to be far too light to be effective against the heavily armoured British tanks, and the majority of them were put out of action by gunfire, together with their crews, and then overrun by the enemy tanks. Many of our vehicles were burnt out.

The attack was finally brought to a halt after Rommel had established a strong gun-line between Beaurains and Agny, formed from his divisional artillery and 88 mm antiaircraft batteries. Firing over open sights, the German fieldpieces proved too much even for the thick armour of the "Matildas," and once again the 88s proved their deadliness, one battery alone claiming nine tanks. Later that evening Rommel was striking with his tanks northwest of Arras at the flank and rear of "Frankforce." There was another fierce engagement, during which seven more heavy British tanks were knocked out, but at a cost of nine of Rommel's.

The day's fighting cost Rommel considerably more tanks than

---

* The first, Lieutenant Schraepler, recovered from his wounds and returned to Rommel a few days later.

any other operation so far. His casualties amounted to 89 killed (including 7 officers), 116 wounded and 173 missing.* For one of the few times in the campaign, German eyewitnesses, as their accounts reveal, were particularly struck by the number of their own burnt-out tanks visible on the battlefield, and it is perhaps instructive that in the German propaganda film *Sieg im West*, Martel's action at Arras is the only Allied counterstroke to be singled out for special mention. There is no reference to de Gaulle. That Rommel for one was even more concerned than his diaries reveal is apparent from his magnification of Martel's four battalions in his own immediate appraisals; his communiqué on the 21st speaks of being attacked by "hundreds of enemy tanks," while situation maps marked up in his own hand display arrows purporting a counteroffensive by *"five* enemy divisions."

Rommel's anxiety echoed back all the way up the German chain of command. His Army commander, Kluge of the Fourth Army, admits in his communiqué that the 21st was "the first day on which the enemy had met with any real success," and he was inclined to halt any further advance westward from Arras until the situation there had been resolved. In Kleist's Panzergruppe, the 6th and 8th Panzers were ordered by Rundstedt to swing back from Le Boisle and Hesdin which they had reached, respectively, to assume defensive positions along the flank of the "five enemy divisions"; while Guderian's 10th Panzer, still badly needed to guard the southern flank of the Panzer Corridor, was placed in reserve, to be ready in case of emergency to move up to the Arras front. In front of the Nuremberg Tribunal, Rundstedt declared:

A critical moment in the drive came just as my forces had reached the Channel. It was caused by a British counter-stroke southward from Arras on May 21st. For a short time it was feared that our armoured divisions would be cut off before the infantry divisions could come up to support them. None of the French counter-attacks carried any serious threat as this one did.

---

* Or four times the losses suffered during the break-through into France. One of Rommel's battalion commanders, Major von Paris, had a very lucky escape. After his unit had been overrun by Martel's tanks, he evidently took refuge in a house, under a bed. Some British officers apparently came in and rested on the bed, and von Paris was only able to get out when the British withdrew the next day.

Back at OKH, Halder recorded in his diary early on the 21st: "The day begins in a quite nervous atmosphere! . . . a rather heavy pressure is being exerted on the north flank of the 4th Army." As the day ended, returning to his prevailing mood of confidence, he wrote: "The situation on the right wing of von Kluge cannot be very serious. Only local affairs," but by the following morning his first entry betrays a new note of concern: "Army Group 'A' has temporarily decreed a halt . . . of the panzer movement in the direction of Calais which we ordered yesterday and will only unleash it when the situation at Arras is cleared up . . . everything depends on getting the infantry quickly up to Arras and westwards." Finally, the shock received at Arras infected Hitler himself, resulting in a new nervousness which was to contribute directly to the Germans' greatest failure of the campaign. On the Allied side, the breakdown of the operation convinced Gort finally that the only hope for the BEF was to fall back on Dunkirk, rather than to try to hack its way through to the south as Ironside and Churchill had hoped.

Weygand flies north

As Gort was about to launch his "Frankforce" attack, the new French C-in-C had departed on his trip to the northern commanders. Once again the journey (in both directions) had been such as might have broken the spirit of a far younger man. Arriving at Le Bourget airport with a solitary aide, Weygand found that the authorities there "seemed to have heard nothing of this journey. We were sent from one end of the airfield to the other." Having wasted an hour in this manner, he took off shortly after dawn with a flight of fighters as escort. The first unmistakable sign that the enemy had broken through to the coast came when, crossing the river Canche,* his plane was sharply greeted with antiaircraft fire. A little further on, his escort had to drive off some attacking Messerschmitts. Arriving safely at the airfield of Norrent-Fontès, northwest of Béthune, Weygand found it abandoned as "unserviceable" on account of enemy bombing.

After wandering past empty hangars in which everything indicated a precipitate departure [says Weygand], at last we met a small soldier,

---

* Running inland from Montreuil through Hesdin.

very dirty but with an attractive face, who told us what had happened
and asked me what he was to do with 20,000 litres of petrol about
which he was greatly concerned, having received no orders.

There was no sign of any transport awaiting the Generalissimo;
later it transpired that cars had been sent to collect him from
Abbeville, but had arrived to find the city in flames, and returned
—narrowly escaping Guderian's panzers. At last, however, Weygand and his ADC discovered an ancient military truck, of which
the small soldier with the grubby face appeared to be the driver.
After some misdirections, Weygand found his way to a village
with a functioning civilian post office "where, after long efforts,
the postmaster secured communication, abominably bad though
it was, with the General Staff of No. 1 Army Group. In this way
I learned that General Billotte had been trying to find me, though
nobody could say in what direction he had gone." Weygand then
decided to take off again for Calais. While waiting for the necessary order to be given, tortured with hunger, he went to an inn in
a half-deserted village and ordered an omelette. He was served
by a woman whose husband was away at the front, and who told
him "she did not wish to go away, for she did not know where to
go, and what was the use?" On the wall there was a lithograph of
the signing of the Armistice in November 1918, and from it she
suddenly recognised Weygand, exclaiming: "How can I be
frightened now you are here?" With this small encouragement,
Weygand flew on to Calais, where he learned that the King of the
Belgians (as C-in-C of the Belgian Army) was waiting for himself and Billotte at the Ypres town hall. Through roads appallingly encumbered with refugees and army convoys, Weygand was
driven to Ypres, which he reached at 3 P.M. King Leopold had
already arrived, but not Billotte—nor Gort. The only British representative there was Admiral Sir Roger Keyes, who was attached
to King Leopold. Such was the unpromising confusion surrounding the advent of the new Allied Generalissimo.

In the mayor's office of Ypres town hall, there ensued what the
King of the Belgians described as "four hours of confused talking." Three separate meetings took place that day. The first was
between King Leopold, attended by his ADC, General van Over-

straeten, and General Weygand.* Outside were waiting three
Belgian ministers—Premier Pierlot, General Denis, the Minister of
National Defence, and the immortal Paul Henri Spaak, then
Foreign Minister. Later they alleged that the King, highhandedly,
had refused to allow them to join in the conference and that they
had only "learned by chance" that this meeting of Allied commanders was going to take place at all; the King in his turn accused his ministers of adopting "an aggressive and disagreeable
attitude." Consequently, in this state of strain between the Belgian King and his ministers, accounts of what took place in the
meeting with Weygand vary radically. According to Weygand, he
told King Leopold that the Belgian Army, now standing on the
river Escaut (Scheldt), "had remained too long in the east" and
should now retreat further west as soon as possible—if necessary,
as far as the Yser. Leopold said this was impossible; his army
"was too tired to do this after the forced marches it had made."
Instead, he seemed to want to "form a vast bridgehead at Ostend." This conflicted diametrically with the project already
formulating in Weygand's mind. He wanted the Belgians to fall
back and hold the line of Yser—as they had done from 1914 onwards—so that, with the left flank shortened and secured, the
BEF would be free to strike southwards with all its strength. But
this would, of course, mean abandoning all but a few square miles
of Belgian territory. General van Overstraeten claims that, on
behalf of the King, he objected that it was "absolutely necessary
to suspend withdrawal because the divisions were beginning to
disintegrate under a succession of night retreats—the bane of
discipline." Weygand says that the King refused then to come to
any decision; "he said he would think it over and let me know
later." Weygand thought he detected signs already of "profound
discouragement" in the Belgian King, while Premier Pierlot, who
saw Leopold immediately after his tête-à-tête with Weygand,
has stated: "The King considered the position of the armies in
Flanders almost if not quite hopeless." Certainly it seems true to
say that in refusing to withdraw to the Yser, King Leopold was in
effect anticipating defeat.

While this discussion was going on, through the chaos of communications Billotte had at last managed to trace Weygand's

---

* Believed by some to be the King's bar-sinister uncle.

whereabouts and had arrived at Ypres. But there was still no
sign of Gort or any of his staff, and Blanchard—who shared an
equally vital interest in the plans being discussed—had apparently
not been invited. Billotte was to be granted no opportunity to set
down his own recollection of what transpired at this second meeting in the Ypres town hall, so—once again—accounts of it vary.
Apparently Weygand outlined his projected scheme in broadest
terms; this would be to strike simultaneously southwards from
around Cambrai and northwards from the Somme, the two thrusts
meeting somewhere in the neighbourhood of Bapaume. According to General van Overstraeten, Billotte then pointed out that
the French First Army was in a very confused situation, tired and
severely tested, incapable of launching an attack, and barely capable of defending itself. In his opinion, only the BEF still constituted a powerful offensive force. Weygand comments: "I had
long been aware of the intelligence, decision, and energy of General Billotte. . . . The fatigues and anxieties of the past two
weeks had left a deep mark on him, but he realised the capital
importance of the manoeuvre to be carried out and shared my
view of its urgency." But it is questionable whether Billotte gave
Weygand the full facts concerning the "Frankforce" attack then
in progress: namely, that Blanchard had declared himself unable
to launch a two-division attack until the 22nd–23rd, and that
Gort had only been able to find one brigade group, with which
he was attacking at that very moment. If Blanchard and Gort had
been at the Ypres meeting it seems improbable that Weygand
could have returned to Paris harbouring any serious belief that
the northern armies could ever attack concertedly on anything
like the scale that he would be promising in front of Reynaud and
Churchill twenty-four hours later. Once again a French C-in-C
was to deceive his government with false hopes.

Gort misses Weygand: Billotte mortally injured

Annoyed that Gort had neither turned up nor sent any ex-
planatory message, Weygand waited in Ypres for him until 7 P.M.
"I could not go back without meeting him," thought Weygand,
and—despite his undertaking to Reynaud to return to Paris within
twenty-four hours—he wondered, "Ought I spend the night where
I was and try to succeed better next day?" At this moment, Ad-

miral Abrial, the French Commander of the Naval Forces of the North, presented himself and, warning Weygand that enemy bombing of airfields had now made it impossible for him to fly out, offered to place at his disposal a 600-ton torpedo boat, the *Flore*. Weygand accepted and left forthwith for Dunkirk. There he embarked in the midst of a violent air raid, with the *Flore* crossing the harbour bar at full speed, "amidst fountains of water thrown up by bombs falling in the sea, and alongside the quays set alight by incendiaries." After a detour via Dover, the *Flore* deposited Weygand at Cherbourg shortly after dawn on the 22nd. From there he went on, to reach Paris—still showing no trace of fatigue—at about 10 A.M.

Approximately an hour after Weygand left Ypres, Gort arrived. Previously, both King Leopold and General van Overstraeten had urged that efforts be made to bring Gort to the meeting, since nothing could be decided without his views being known. In vain, van Overstraeten had tried to reach him on the telephone and then had driven with Admiral Keyes to Hazebrouck, where Gort was thought to be. Eventually he was tracked down to his new command post, at Premesques, between Lille and Armentières, where he had just moved from Wahagnies. According to Gort, all he knew of Weygand's visit was a signal from Churchill to Keyes, copy to Gort, received the previous night (20th), which stated simply: "Weygand is coming up your way tomorrow to concert action of all forces." A message sent by the British mission at French GQG warning that Weygand would land at Norrent-Fontès at 9 A.M. apparently miscarried; there is no record of its receipt either at BEF GHQ or Gort's command post. Meanwhile, he had spent the whole day waiting for notification of Weygand's whereabouts. Until van Overstraeten's intervention, no one on the French side seems to have thought of sending messengers to scour the countryside for the British commander.

Weygand was to go into German captivity still believing that Gort "had purposely abstained from coming to the Ypres conference." To this day, Gort's absence remains a matter of acute controversy in France. Did he stay away in a state of pique because Altmayer had not materialised at the "Frankforce" conference the previous night, and because the French had failed to participate in the Arras attack? J. Bénoist-Méchin* suggests that Gort deliberately absented himself, because he had already become "a partisan of evacuation" and any involvement in Weygand's offensive schemes would have placed him "in an inextricable position." On Gort's side, there is the fact of the appalling communications and the signal which never arrived; he had just shifted his command post, on the 21st, and his preoccupation both with the Arras counterattack and the awkward predicament of two of his corps on the Escaut front would seem to offer sufficient excuse for not attempting to track down Weygand.† But principally, any such complex, devious thinking as Bénoist-Méchin attributes to Gort is simply out of character.

The failure of Gort and Weygand to meet on the 21st was in any event disastrous. At Ypres the third meeting of the day took place between Billotte and Gort, at which Billotte relayed Weygand's intentions. Gort in turn reported on the not very encouraging progress of the Arras operation, pointing out that all his available reserves were now committed. The Belgians were finally persuaded to fall back from the Escaut to the Lys, so as to relieve British divisions for Weygand's offensive. But this was a poor compromise; as the map reveals, the Lys line hardly offered any shortening of the front, and Gort reckoned that the switch-over could not be completed in time for the relieved divisions to attack before May 26 at the earliest. As the last meeting ended, King Leopold informed his waiting ministers that Gort had agreed to cooperate in Weygand's offensive, but: "The British General considers that the chances of the manoeuvre in which he is going to take part are practically nil. The situation is desperate." Thus in effect nothing specific had been decided about the proposed offensive. The Belgians had not committed themselves to withdrawing to the Yser. Gort had not heard anything that might restore his faith in the capacity of the French First Army to join effectively in an attack; and the Belgians had certainly given him no confidence in the security of his left flank. Weygand had re-

---

* Bénoist-Méchin's *Soixante Jours qui Ebranlèrent l'Occident* (Paris, 1956), partly written while he was serving a commuted death sentence for collaboration, contains a mass of inaccuracies, but it made a considerable impact in France.

† On the other hand, Weygand has been equally criticised by French historians for not waiting for Gort in Ypres; and Churchill questions the wisdom of Weygand's making the journey at all and thereby sacrificing another precious day.

turned to Paris thoroughly mistrustful of Gort, and imbued with notions which Gort could swiftly have persuaded him were impractical had the two men but met in Ypres. The meetings broke up, according to van Overstraeten, in a very depressed atmosphere.

Then followed yet another of the tragic twists of fate that had seemed to dog the Allies from the very beginning of hostilities. Shortly after the Ypres conference, some young British officers were about to appease their hunger by sharing out a bottle of milk found in a nearby farmhouse. Abruptly the door opened and in came a senior French general. Spotting the milk he exclaimed "*Ah! du lait!* Excellent!" and without any further formality grabbed the bottle, drained it, and then departed before the Britons could register their indignation. This was Billotte, and it was probably the last time he was seen alive by any member of the BEF. Carrying him on through the darkness to brief Blanchard about Weygand's intentions, a few hours later Billotte's car apparently skidded and ran into the back of a refugee lorry. The driver, who was wearing a steel helmet, survived; Billotte, not so protected, was gravely injured, and, after lying in a coma for two days, died. His removal from the scene could hardly have been more catastrophic for the Allies. He was the only French or British commander with the northern armies who knew of Weygand's plan at first hand,* and he was the one person in whom both Gort and King Leopold still had some confidence. With Billotte fighting for his life, another three days were allowed to elapse before the badly shaken Blanchard was confirmed as his successor, and General Prioux was then moved up to command the First Army. Thus in these crucial days there was to be no coordinating hand to harness the three Allied armies in the north to the "Weygand Plan." Meanwhile, demoralising rumours swiftly ran round the French camp that the unfortunate Billotte had committed suicide.†

Churchill's second meeting with Reynaud

In Paris that afternoon, Reynaud had made a courageous—indeed, a great—speech before the Senate. For the first time he

---

* General d'Astier rates him as having been the most outstanding of the French commanders, and the only one who could possibly have averted the final disaster.

† About the same time, rumours were also rife in Paris that Gamelin had done the same.

revealed to France just how grave was the situation. "The country is in danger!" he proclaimed. "It is my first duty to tell the Senate and the nation the truth." Murmurs swelled into a roar; there were demands for the names of the guilty. The Premier continued, enumerating some of the terrible facts. He spoke of the "serious failures" of the Ninth Army, condemned General Corap and disclosed that "through unbelievable faults, which will be punished, bridges over the Meuse were not destroyed." When he revealed the news that Amiens and Arras had been lost, Alexander Werth in the gallery recorded: "A gasp of bewilderment rises from the senators' benches." The air cleared only a little when Reynaud went on to offer a source of hope:

In the midst of our country's misfortunes we can take pride in the thought that two of her sons, who would have been justified in resting on their laurels, have placed themselves at the nation's service in this tragic hour: Pétain and Weygand. (Prolonged cheers.)

Pétain, the victor of Verdun, the great soldier with the human touch, the man who knows how a French victory can come out of a cataclysm.

Weygand, Foch's man, who halted the German onslaught when the front was broken in 1918 and who was afterwards able to turn the tables and lead us to victory. . . . France cannot die.

For my part, if some day I were to be told that only a miracle could save France, that day I should say: "I believe in the miracle,* because I believe in France."

After Reynaud's speech, as Senator Bardoux recorded, the atmosphere in the corridors was "terrifying." "Faces are distorted. Groups form and re-form." Now at last the veils were down.

That evening Reynaud suffered fresh gloomy forebodings as to what would happen if Weygand on his journey should fall into German hands, and to Baudouin he even began to speak of General Huntziger as a possible successor. The following morning (the 22nd) he anxiously waited for Weygand to report in at the Rue Dominique. Despite his arduous experiences of the past twenty-four hours, the seventy-three-year-old Generalissimo arrived full of bounce and launched into his analysis of the situation

---

* Werth commented sceptically: "Reynaud's belief in miracles somehow reminds me of the Russian communiqué after the Battle of Tannenberg: 'God will not desert Holy Russia.'"

on an evident note of optimism. "So many mistakes have been made," he began, "that they give me confidence. I believe that in future we shall make less." The BEF, he declared—apparently without mentioning its engagement at Arras—"is in a very good state, for up to the present it has hardly been in action. Some elements in Blanchard's army have been shaken, but . . . this army still constitutes a powerful force." He then offered to Reynaud the plan he had outlined to King Leopold and Billotte the previous day; namely, the joint thrusts from north and south meeting at Bapaume. In conception, it was roughly the same as Gamelin's short-lived plan, contained in his Instruction No. 12 of May 19th; the main differences were that the pincers were to close further to the west, three days later, and it would be a heavier blow. Weygand said that he had "thoroughly explained" his plan "to everybody I have seen;* I think they understood me, and that I have convinced them. I cannot waste my strength running after armour. It is better to try this manoeuvre of a junction." He then concluded† with a curiously revealing remark: "It will either give us victory or it will save our honour." In the coming days, the expression "save our honour" was to appear with increasing regularity on Weygand's lips, and it indicated which way his thoughts were already beginning to turn. As Colonel Goutard acidly points out, "As soon as it became a question of 'honour,' we were in a bad way!"

Reynaud declared himself entirely in agreement with Weygand's project, and informed him that Churchill was due in Paris at 11:15. After collecting the British Prime Minister, Reynaud recalls: "At midday we went together to the stronghold of Vincennes under a sky whose very beauty seemed implacable in those tragic days." On this second visit of immense importance to Paris, Churchill was once again accompanied by the inseparable General Ismay and General Sir John Dill, who was about to succeed Ironside as CIGS. Ismay noted that, despite the change in command since their last visit, "the *Beau Geste* flavour of the old fort was just the same—spahis with white cloaks and long curved swords, on guard duty, and the floors and chairs covered with oriental rugs." (In the light of all these disastrous revelations of

---

* But he had not seen Gort, and Billotte was dying.

† As the scene is recorded by the secretary of the War Cabinet, Paul Baudouin.

the past weeks, how anachronistic the power of the French Army must suddenly have seemed!) But Ismay was at once agreeably surprised by Weygand's appearance: "He gave the appearance of being a fighter—resolute, decisive and amazingly active, in spite of his wizened face and advanced years. He might have been made of indiarubber. One dared to hope that the Allied armies would now have the leadership that had hitherto seemed lacking." Churchill admits to having been equally taken by the Generalissimo: "In spite of his physical exertions and a night of travel, he was brisk, buoyant, and incisive. He made an excellent impression upon all." The absence of Daladier and his aroma of absinthe was also clearly an improvement.

Weygand's plan

The meeting, says Ismay, "was short and businesslike." Weygand described the situation as he had found it on his trip to Ypres, and then once more gave an exposé of his plan. This met with general agreement, and accordingly Weygand retired to draft his General Operation No. 1,* which read as follows:

(I) The forces grouped with No. 1 Army Group (the Belgian Army, the B.E.F., and the First Army) will make it their principal task to block the German advance to the sea in order to maintain contact between themselves and the remainder of the French forces.

(II) The German Army will only be stopped and beaten by counter-attacks.

(III) The forces necessary for these counter-attacks already exist in the group, the linear defence of which is much too densely held, and they are:

some infantry divisions of the First Army;

the cavalry corps;

the B.E.F., which must be withdrawn from the line by extending the Belgian sector, and used as a whole.

These counter-attacks will be supported by all the R.A.F. based in France.

(IV) This offensive will be covered on the east by the Belgian Army on the Yser.

The light enemy units which are trying to cause disruption and panic in our rear between the frontier and the Somme, supported by air-

---

* Which was not, however, dispatched to the now headless No. 1 Army Group until 2050 hours on the 22nd.

raids on our aerodromes and ports, are in a dangerous position and will be destroyed.

Weygand ended his order by declaring that, having been "rounded up," the panzers "must not escape again." One might as well have said the same of the Soviet spy George Blake, after he had been "sprung" from a British maximum security prison.

To write off the seven panzer divisions which had driven through the Allied armies as "light enemy units" might seem to bear little enough relationship with the facts of life,* but it was nothing as compared to the telegram Churchill now sent to Gort summarising the talks at Vincennes:

It was agreed:—
1. That the Belgian Army should withdraw to the line of the Yser and stand there, the sluices being opened.
2. That the British Army and the French First Army should attack south-west towards Bapaume and Cambrai at the earliest moment, certainly tomorrow, with about *eight divisions,*† and with the Belgian Cavalry Corps on the right of the British.
3. That as this battle is vital to both armies and the British communications depend upon freeing Amiens, the British Air Force should give the utmost possible help, both by day and by night, while it is going on.
4. That the new French Army Group which is advancing upon Amiens and forming a line along the Somme should strike northwards and join hands with the British divisions who are attacking southwards in the general direction of Bapaume."

In the first place, the Belgians had *never* agreed to withdrawing to the Yser. Secondly—as both Blanchard and Gort could have pointed out to the Allied leaders—how could eight divisions, or 100,000 men, turn their backs on the enemy pressing hard from the east and attack southwards, at a day's notice? One of the "secrets of Marshal Foch," to which Weygand had archly alluded during his valedictory interview with Gamelin, was that Foch had always known exactly the value of the forces he could throw into battle at any given moment. This was something Weygand clearly did *not* know on May 22nd, despite his journey of the previous

---

* Certainly as they stood by May 22nd.
† Author's italics.

day. Thirdly, it was gross exaggeration to speak of a "new French Army Group . . . advancing upon Amiens"—as Weygand must well have known. The truth was that behind the Somme, between the coast and the Crozat Canal nearly 90 air miles to the east, there were only the five divisions that General Frère had now managed to scratch together in his new Seventh Army; plus the badly mauled 2nd and 5th Light Cavalry, and the newly arrived and unblooded British First Armoured Division. In a separate order dispatched by General Georges on the 22nd, these units were summoned up to take their place to the left of General Frère, under command of General Robert Altmayer.*

Above all, the enticing vacuum that had existed behind the German spearhead on the 20th and 21st would exist no longer by the 23rd.

Churchill's hopes

In Reynaud's private ear, Churchill complained that four consecutive days had been allowed to pass without Gort's receiving any orders whatever. "Ever since Weygand had assumed command three days had been lost in taking decisions. The change in the Supreme Command was right. The resultant delay was evil." Nevertheless, carried along by the vigour with which Weygand had put his case, the Vincennes meeting (so Ismay records) "ended on a note of restrained optimism." Before he left, Churchill remarked flatteringly to Weygand: "There is only one fault in you; you are too young!"

Throughout his career, Churchill would always show himself susceptible to a general who gave the appearance of being a fighter, and Weygand—in sharp antithesis to the pallid intellectualism of Gamelin—clearly struck him as such. Shaken as he had been by the dreadful revelations in Paris of May 16th, as the British statesman who had once cried out, "Thank God for the French Army!" Churchill still harboured some romantic faith in that army. Indeed, could this magnificent weapon upon which all the calculations of British European policy had been founded since 1919, could it really be proved a broken reed by the events of just twelve terrible days? As both historian and participant,

---

* Not to be confused with his brother, General René Altmayer, commander of V Corps with the First Army. On May 30th, Robert Altmayer's new Groupement was to be designated the "Tenth" Army.

Churchill retained the memory of Foch and the "miracle of the Marne" and July 1918 constantly before his eyes. Surely, as on both those occasions, the French Army would spring back again at the eleventh hour? Now if a *fighting* French general—the spiritual heir to Foch—declared that such an offensive operation was possible, then it must be tried—without being too pragmatic. And here, as far as experience with practicalities is concerned, Churchill shares some of Weygand's own limitations. Like Wavell in Greece the following year, Weygand had been plunged into the middle of battle with no previous firsthand knowledge of the speed and momentum and utter destructiveness of a modern armoured *Blitzkrieg;* similarly Churchill—and this must always be borne in mind when considering his actions in May 1940—after those years in the wilderness, remote from the pragmatism of public office, had had less than a fortnight of unrelenting crisis in which to acquaint himself with the practical logistics of an army at war in 1940. Now, Weygand had rekindled Churchill's faith. In the vivid words of Spears, the Weygand Plan "hung like a limp sail from the mast," but Churchill in his turn, "like a new Aeolus, filled it momentarily with the power of his lungs." (But, added Spears, "the ship did not move.")

At 7:30 that same night Churchill was back in London and holding a Cabinet meeting. General Ironside noted dejectedly that "he was almost in buoyant spirits." The impression Weygand had made upon him remained markedly observable, and he stuck to his belief in the feasibility of his plan. Some of Churchill's military advisers were much less happy. Ironside, for one (although, about to be replaced as CIGS, his views no longer counted greatly with Churchill), now completely disillusioned by what he had seen on his visit to Billotte two days previously, thought that "when it all came down to things it was still all *projets.*" The BEF, he said gloomily, had "lost a chance of extricating itself." But even Churchill's faith in Weygand's "project" would begin to wilt in the face of events before many more hours went by.

The panzers drive for the Channel ports

After the well-deserved day of rest forced upon his panzers, Guderian was on the move again early on the morning of the 22nd. His orders now were to swing northwards and seize the

Channel ports. Originally he had wanted to throw the relatively fresh 10th Panzer towards Dunkirk at full speed; this was refused him, on account of "Frankforce's" attack at Arras on the 21st which had persuaded Kleist to keep the 10th back as Panzergruppe reserve, in case the situation worsened.* Guderian says "it was with a heavy heart" that he changed his plans. The 1st Panzer, bolstered by the Grossdeutschland Regiment which was now back in the fold after recuperating from the fighting at Stonne, was to head for Calais while the 2nd swept up the coast to Boulogne. By 7 A.M. his forces had crossed the river Authie, some 15 miles north from Abbeville, though Guderian noted, significantly, that they could not move in full strength since units of both divisions had to be left behind to secure the Somme bridgeheads until the motorised infantry of Wietersheim's XIV Corps caught up to fill its now familiar relieving role. That afternoon there was fierce fighting on the approaches to Boulogne, and for the first time Guderian recorded being vigorously attacked by Allied aircraft—"while we saw little of our own Luftwaffe." Owing to the speed of the advance, the German tactical air support was now operating at long range, at the same time that the battlefield was coming within comfortable radius of the RAF Air Component units relocated in Kent.

But on the ground resistance was patchy and ill-organised, so that by nightfall on the 22nd Guderian was at the gates of both Boulogne and Calais, having made another staggering advance of over 60 miles (to Calais). Kleist having in the meantime decided that the crisis at Arras was past, the 10th Panzer was returned to Guderian, who promptly ordered it to replace the 1st Panzer before Calais on the morning of the 23rd. The 1st was then to hasten eastwards to strike out for Gravelines and for Dunkirk just 25 miles by road along the coast from Calais. During the 23rd, however, it encountered much tougher resistance and halted that night on the Aa Canal after progressing only some 15 miles. The 2nd Panzer was also involved in heavy fighting at Boulogne, which was stoutly defended by Irish and Welsh Guards of the 20th Guards Brigade (only two days previously they had been in

---

* Here at least was one most tangible benefit gained by Martel's effort. What the consequence might have been if Guderian had been able to break through to Dunkirk on the 23rd with the ease that he did to Boulogne and Calais is not pleasant to contemplate.

training in Surrey) and improvised French garrison defence forces. For several hours the thick medieval ramparts of the old port kept even the panzers at bay; then an 88 was brought up, and it blasted a hole in the wall through which the tanks were able to make their way. But it was not until the 25th that the 2nd Panzer was able to hoist the Swastika over Boulogne, thereby providing another important setback in Guderian's timetable for grabbing the far more important booty of Dunkirk. Meanwhile, under personal orders from Churchill not to surrender, Brigadier C. N. Nicholson held out at Calais until late on the 26th in one of the finest stonewalling actions of the British Army*—thereby pinning down the 10th Panzer, which otherwise might also have been deployed against Dunkirk.

On the 21st, elements of Reinhardt's 6th and 8th Panzers had been ordered to swing inland to meet the threat developing at Arras, and on the next day they were in turn pushing menacingly at Gort's right flank west of the Béthune–Arras line. At the same time, once Martel's attack had been brought to a halt, Reinhardt's main force (now reinforced by a motorised SS division moved up from Holland) thrust northwards on a course parallel to Guderian's, so that by the end of the 23rd it too was standing on the Aa Canal, in the area of St. Omer.

As soon as Rommel had recovered his breath from the shock at Arras, on the 22nd he was attacking again, using his armour in his favoured technique of slipping round the enemy flank while his riflemen kept it pinned down frontally. At Maroeuil, Rothenburg's tanks overran some British gun batteries supporting Martel's rear. They then pushed up onto Mont-Saint-Éloi, an important height overlooking Arras from the northwest, where they were temporarily driven off in a spirited counterattack by a regiment of Prioux's motorised Dragoons. On the 23rd, General von Hartlieb's 5th Panzer drew level with Rommel, almost for the first time since the crossing of the Meuse, and Colonel Werner's tanks (31st Panzer Regiment) now joined Rothenburg's in the flanking drive to the west of Arras. By the evening of that day Werner stood on the dominating Lorette Heights, the scene of so

---

* When called upon to surrender by the 10th Panzer, Nicholson replied: "The answer is no, as it is the British Army's duty to fight as well as it is the German Army's." He later died in a German prisoner-of-war camp.

much bitter fighting in 1915, where a French war memorial bears the inscription: "Who holds the Lorette Heights holds France."* Rommel's advance guard was within sight of the outskirts of Béthune and threatening the Lens road, "Frankforce's" principal line of access to Arras. Meanwhile German motorised infantry were attacking the city itself—which was being subjected to constant dive bombing—from three sides.

All the time more and more second-line infantry divisions were pouring into the Panzer Corridor, to plug any possible breaches that the Allies might exploit. By-passing Hoth's panzers, Hoeppner's 3rd and 4th Panzer Divisions were now moving into line to take up positions between Rommel and Reinhardt; thus all the German armour† would shortly be concentrated in an arc facing eastwards, opposite (principally) the BEF. At the same time as the German armour was thrusting into the western flank of the encircled Allied armies, Bock's infantry divisions were also stepping up their pressure against the Escaut line, and by the 23rd the tired Belgians‡ had been forced to abandon the anchor points of Terneuzen and Ghent.

William Shirer was there to watch the German preparations for crossing the Escaut:

Heavy artillery—and this is amazing to see—six inch guns, pulled by caterpillar trucks, and on rubber tyres, are being hauled up a hillside at forty miles an hour. (Is this one of the German military secrets, such big guns being hauled so fast?) . . . Over the front all afternoon hover two or three reconnaissance planes, German, obviously, directing artillery fire. They cruise over the battlefield unmolested. . . . The lack of observation planes alone puts the Allies in a hole. In fact we do not see an Allied plane all day long.

Once again Shirer was struck by the calm organisation of the Wehrmacht going about its business: "Even the wounded seem to play their part in this gigantic businesslike machine. They do

---

* In his diary for the 23rd, Halder exclaimed: "Notre Dame de Lorette! The fate of France is in our hands!"

† With the exception of the 9th Panzer, arriving from Holland, which would be deployed guarding the Somme flank.

‡ Who for the four days following Billotte's accident on the 21st received no instructions from the French.

not moan." But what particularly impressed him was the morale of the German troops. It was "fantastically good":

I remember a company of engineers which was about to go down to the Scheldt River to lay a pontoon bridge under enemy fire. The men were reclining on the edge of the wood reading the day's edition of the army daily paper, the "Western Front." I've never seen men going into a battle from which some were sure never to come out alive—well, so nonchalantly.

In contrast, Shirer sadly recalls some unaddressed letters he had found near the recent graves of two dead French soldiers: "They must have been written before the push began. They tell of the boredom of army life and how you are waiting for your next leave in Paris, 'ma chérie.'"

In these days the smell of victory was unmistakably in German nostrils. Rommel, in one of his brief notes to his wife, wrote on the 23rd:

Dearest Lu,
With a few hours' sleep behind me, it's time for a line to you. I'm fine in every way. My division has had a blazing success. Dinant, Philippeville, break-through the Maginot Line and advance in one night 40 miles through France to Le Cateau, then Cambrai, Arras, always far in front of everybody else. Now the hunt is up against 60 encircled British, French and Belgian divisions. Don't worry about me. As I see it the war in France may be over in a fortnight.

Lieutenant Karl Heinz Mende, with one of the infantry divisions now pouring into the Panzer Corridor, wrote home about the same time: "Don't try to form impressions of what is happening here. What is logical and what can be estimated, that is too small a yardstick for these days; out of all that is happening there is only one thing that is certain—every day something new, every hour something new." Reflecting the admiration many young Germans felt for the astonishing successes run up by their Führer, he speaks glowingly of "an infallible victorious deed of a genius," and later declares: "This war is good."

May 22nd: The French attack

While "Frankforce" was having a hard time holding its ground west of Arras, at 9 A.M. on the 22nd General René Altmayer launched the attack originally agreed between Ironside and Billotte and which had failed to materialise the previous day. But instead of the projected two-division thrust, as had happened with "Frankforce" the French effort was whittled down to one infantry regiment (the 121st, belonging to General Molinié's 25th Motorised Division), supported by two armoured reconnaissance groups and artillery. Striking from the east of Douai towards Cambrai, the 121st executed its orders brilliantly, administering a hard blow to the German 32nd Infantry Division. French light tanks penetrated quickly to the outskirts of Cambrai. Then they were heavily bombed by formations of Henschel 123s,* and strafed by cannon-firing Messerschmitts; finally, yet again, it was German 88s—firing at a range of 150 yards—that halted the French armour. Twelve hours after the beginning of the French attack, orders came through from First Army for it to halt and withdraw behind its start line. That the attack took place at all when, in theory, the First Army and the BEF should have been conserving their strength for Weygand's "eight-division" counterstroke projected for the 23rd, in itself reveals the disastrous breakdown in coordination which followed Billotte's fatal accident; Gort, for one, had also not been warned of Molinié's operation.

The exercising of command in the encircled armies of the north was becoming increasingly difficult. General Blanchard's HQ had been driven out of Lens after a Luftwaffe incendiary raid had turned the town into a sea of fire. It moved to the village of Estaires until that was bombed to pieces; then on to Attiches, which was also soon blasted by the Luftwaffe. The headquarters' power plants were destroyed so there was no electric light or radio. Around it were constantly milling large numbers of dejected soldiers who had lost their units, their equipment and their rifles and were too tired to march any further. Under the ceaseless air attacks, there were inevitably signs of still further cracks in French morale. In Paris, Weygand told Baudouin (on May 23rd) he had received information that forty French officers from the armies in the north had taken refuge in London; they were to be

---

* The Henschel 123 was the old biplane dive bomber that was predecessor to the *Stuka*. That it had to be thrown into the battle at all at Cambrai is further indication of the strain that the Luftwaffe, having suffered heavy casualties among its relatively few Stukas, was temporarily feeling on May 21st and 22nd.

arrested and brought back to France. There had been times recently, Weygand added, when he had "not been able to recognise the morale of the French troops; both in conduct and demeanour they were so different from those I left when I gave up my command."

As for the relief counterstroke coming from south of the Somme which Weygand had depicted so favourably at Vincennes, by the end of May 23rd virtually nothing had happened. Elements of General Frère's Seventh Army "made contact" with the river, while Senegalese troops of the 7th Colonial Division—exhausted after a 20-mile approach—were halted on the perimeter of the German bridgehead south of Amiens, some 3 miles from the city. There could be no possibility of General Robert Altmayer's new Groupement doing anything effective for several days. There was some basis for Ironside's bitter statement that the deployment of the French forces on that side of the Somme was purely defensive and they appeared to have "no intention of attacking but were trying to prevent the Germans from advancing on Paris."

Gort decides: Save the BEF

Over the past three days, Gort's frustration had been steadily mounting because of his government's apparent inability to see how grave the situation was in the north. It reached a peak, bordering on despair, when he received Churchill's directive following the Vincennes meeting of the 22nd. How on earth, in their present state, were the northern armies to mount an eight-division effort by the 23rd? As Gort well knew, the French First Army now totalled no more than eight divisions—plus the much reduced elements of the Cavalry Corps—and the most they had so far been able to produce for an attack was one regiment; the BEF's two divisions formerly kept in reserve were fighting for their lives around Arras; and nothing could be expected from the Belgians. Most annoying of all, he had not even been told in advance of the French attack; with Billotte dead and still not replaced, the absence of any overall control of the three different national forces augured extremely ill for any concerted effort. By the morning of the 23rd—the day on which the Weygand Plan called for the attack to begin—Gort had still not received any specific orders; so, resorting to a rare use of his prerogative, he sent a telegram to the Secretary of State for War, Anthony Eden, pleading that "coordination on this front is essential with the armies of three different nations." He requested that the universally respected Sir John Dill fly out that day to make an on-the-spot appreciation, and warned Eden forthrightly: "My view is that any advance by us will be in the nature of a sortie and relief must come from the south as we have not, repeat not, ammunition for serious attack."* Arriving at Gort's HQ that morning, General Blanchard expressed agreement with this view.

Churchill's immediate response to Gort's plea was to protest to Reynaud in a new and sharper tone: "I demand the issue to the French commanders in north and south and Belgian G.H.Q. of the most stringent orders to carry this out and turn defeat into victory. Time is vital as supplies are short." This hardly helped Gort in his own difficulties, but (although Gort could not have been aware of it) Churchill was beginning to revise his opinion of Weygand's intentions. At a Cabinet meeting held that morning after he sent his demand to Reynaud, Churchill pointed out "that the whole success of the Weygand plan was dependent on the French taking the initiative, which they showed no signs of doing." That night—when still no Allied action either to north or south of the Panzer Corridor had materialised and no orders had been received by either Gort or the Belgians—Churchill followed up with an even tougher signal, addressed to Weygand via Reynaud, and asking:

How does this agree with your statement that Blanchard and Gort are *main dans la main?* . . . Trust you will be able to rectify this. Gort further says that any advance by him must be in the nature of sortie, and that relief must come from south, as he has not (*repeat* not) ammunition for serious attack. Nevertheless, we are instructing him to persevere in carrying out your plan.

But the most reassuring communication to reach Gort in these days was one from Eden on the 23rd, which read as follows: "Should, however, situation on your communications make this [Weygand Plan] at any time impossible you should inform us so that we can inform French and make naval and air arrangements to assist you should you have to withdraw on the northern coast." At last, it seemed to show, the government was beginning to face

---

* The BEF was placed on half rations that day.

up to realities. As far as Gort was concerned, here now was an opening for him to act according to his own judgement.

Gort's judgement was now already formulated. It was that the Weygand Plan would never materialise, that the French would never attack, and that the only hope of preserving anything of the BEF was to fall back on Dunkirk while there was still time.* The French Army, at any rate in the northern pocket, was finished. Meanwhile, at Arras, Gort was faced with an immediate, compelling danger. For two days, long after any hope of resuming its attack had vanished, "Frankforce" had held its own against the bulk of two panzer divisions. Now, creeping around its flank and rear, Rommel was threatening to encircle it completely. There were only two roads left still available for its extrication. At 7 P.M. on the 23rd, Gort ordered the withdrawal of "Frankforce" and the abandonment of Arras. During that night the British 5th and 50th Divisions pulled back some 15 miles,† behind the Haute Deule Canal northeast of Arras.

In the atmosphere of mounting recrimination between the Allies, the British withdrawal from Arras provoked considerable bitterness. It was said that—although General Franklyn had warned the French units on either side of him—Gort had not informed Blanchard of the move.‡ It was said that the speed and depth of the British withdrawal jeopardised the French forces in this part of the line. It was said (by Weygand) that it thereby abandoned the start line for the Weygand Plan's attack from the north, and that it demoralised the French forces by conveying the impression that the BEF had renounced participation in it. But, even assuming that the Weygand Plan still offered any prospect of success by the 24th, if Franklyn had not abandoned the start line of Arras, Rommel would almost certainly have enveloped it that day, plus the better part of two British divisions, as well as the

---

* Many of those close to Gort felt it was already too late; Brooke confided to his diary on the evening of May 23rd: "Nothing but a miracle can save the B.E.F. now, and the end cannot be very far off," while Ironside wrote in much the same tone: "I cannot see that we have much hope of getting any of the B.E.F. out now."

† Not, as Weygand and Reynaud claimed at the time, 25 miles.

‡ Whether this was owing to poor communications or the precipitancy with which the move had to be made, before "Frankforce" was completely cut off by Rommel, is not quite clear, but it seems that the British Government was also taken by surprise; Ironside comments: "Why Gort has done this I don't know. He has never told us that he was going to do it or even when he had done it."

remnants of the French Cavalry Corps. Whatever the truth of the matter, the British withdrawal brought from Paul Reynaud a reproachful and ominous telegram, dispatched to Churchill on the 24th:

You wired me this morning that you had instructed General Gort to continue to carry out the Weygand plan. General Weygand now informs me that, according to a telegram from General Blanchard, the British Army had carried out, on its own initiative, a retreat of twenty-five miles towards the ports at a time when our troops moving up from the south are gaining ground towards the north, where they were to meet their allies.

This action of the British Army is in direct opposition to the formal orders renewed this morning by General Weygand. This retreat has naturally obliged General Weygand to change all his arrangements, and he is compelled to give up the idea of closing the gap and restoring a continuous front. I need not lay any stress upon the gravity of the possible consequences.*

Reynaud's claims of the southern forces "gaining ground towards the north" was however a palpable exaggeration, and there is more than an element of truth in Spears's† countercharge: "I feel certain that Gort's inevitable withdrawal is being seized upon as an excuse for the fact that no French forces have advanced from the south."

Although on May 24th the Weygand Plan attack was finally fixed for the 26th, Gort's decision to withdraw across the Deule in fact marked the end both of the plan and of any sensible hope for a breakout across the Panzer Corridor. Even if there had been no prior retreat from Arras, one is forced to conclude that the 24th would have marked the end of such hopes in any event. For already by the beginning of the 23rd the steel-capped vacuum of the 21st had become what Pertinax aptly describes as a "solid-limbed army." The German infantry divisions had arrived and the panzers were now deployed to meet any threat of a break-out by the encircled Allied forces, or to thrust in with the *coup de grâce*

---

* Reynaud's telegram provoked an angry, baffled query from Churchill to Ironside: "I must know at earliest why Gort gave up Arras, and what actually he is doing with the rest of his army. Is he still persevering in Weygand's plan, or has he become largely stationary? . . . Clearly, he must not allow himself to be encircled without fighting a battle."

† Sent by Churchill to be his personal representative to Paul Reynaud, Spears arrived in Paris on the 25th.

at a moment's notice. At every point of the invested perimeter, the Allied forces were on the defensive; and there was no prospect of relief from the south. Even if the Allies could then have effected a temporary break-out from the northern pocket, the counterattack itself would have been extremely vulnerable to attack on both its flanks by much stronger German forces. From the German point of view, the tenuous Panzer Corridor was now inviolable. *Sichelschnitt* had succeeded.

Thus faded the great Allied stratagems for a concerted counterstroke that would sever the head of the German tortoise. All they had amounted to—the Gamelin Plan, the Ironside Plan, and finally the Weygand Plan with its aim of striking eight divisions strong—had been two blows, separated by twenty-four hours, by one British infantry brigade and 74 tanks, and one French infantry regiment plus a few light tanks. The British attack at Arras on the 21st was but a straw in the wind, far too light to do more than throw the Germans temporarily off balance; yet the shock it caused indicates what a strong, well-coordinated and resolutely led effort on May 21st, or preferably earlier, could have achieved. One is tempted to speculate what might have happened if Martel had disposed of even 50 instead of just 16 "Matildas"; if his attack could have been accompanied by one of the excellent French armoured divisions squandered so uselessly early in the battle; and possibly supported by the local aerial superiority which, for the first time in the battle, the Allies were capable of attaining on the 21st. This was the day of extreme danger for the Germans. The thinly lined Panzer Corridor was only 25 miles wide south of Arras; the opportunities missed at this time are implicit in a report written by the commander of the French 2nd DLM: "My impression is that if I had my division intact, especially my tanks, I could quite easily reach Cambrai. But all I have is the non-armoured element." At the same time, one is forced to conclude that, although a harder Allied punch on the 21st might have inflicted heavy losses and have stopped the Germans temporarily, they would have come on again, sooner or later; for by May 21st, in terms of men, material and morale, the French Army had already lost too much of its striking power to be able to recuperate. But without venturing onto the hazardous quicksands of speculation, there can be little doubt as to what material results the "Frankforce" attack at Arras *did* achieve. It upset the

German timetable for seizure of the Channel ports, without which the "miracle of Dunkirk" would have been born dead.

This is what, at this moment of destiny, raised Lord Gort momentarily above the level of the other Allied war leaders. It was on his own responsibility that Gort decided to attack singlehanded on the 21st; and on his own responsibility that he decided to disengage on the night of the 23rd and begin the withdrawal that he knew would culminate in evacuation. As far as the overall conduct of the war was concerned, the latter was the most far-reaching decision that could have been taken in May 1940 on the Allied side; and Gort was the only person who could take it. If Gort had been a romantic visionary, a kind of Lawrence, one could conceive that in his imagination he saw those British divisions which he was about to save from the cauldron of Flanders leading the liberation of Europe four summers later. But Gort was not a visionary. Nor was he communicative, and all that can be stated with some certainty is that, by May 23rd, he knew that the French Army was finished and that it was his simple duty to save the BEF to fight another day, on some other field. Had the BEF been wiped out in northern France, it is difficult to see how Britain could have continued to fight; and with Britain out of the battle, it is even more difficult to see what combination of circumstances could have aligned America and Stalin's Russia to challenge Hitler.

19

The End in the North
MAY 24th – JUNE 4th

Since the retaking of Arras, it has been reported that
Amiens and even Sedan and other important points had
been retaken by counter-attacks.
　　　　　　　　　　　　　　　　　—*Daily Herald,* May 25th

German military circles here tonight put it flatly. They
said the fate of the great Allied Army bottled up in
Flanders is sealed.
　　　　　　　—WILLIAM SHIRER, *Berlin Diary,* May 25th

According to an estimate by the French War Ministry,
at least 2,000 German aircraft and 1,400 tanks have
been lost in the operation in Holland, Belgium and
France.
　　　　　　　　　　　—*National Zeitung,* Basle, May 26th

We must be careful not to assign to this deliverance the
attributes of a victory. Wars are not won by evacuations.
—WINSTON CHURCHILL, speaking to the House of Commons,
　　　　　　　　　　　　　　　　　　　　　　June 4th

THE COLLAPSE of the Weygand Plan meant that the campaign
was now lost beyond recovery. The "decisive battle" against
France of which both Hitler and Manstein had separately
dreamed had been fought and won. Henceforth minor ripostes
and local actions of extreme gallantry would impose an occasional
check upon the German progress to complete victory, but what
follows during the next month of hostilities until the inevitable
finale in the railway coach at Compiègne is little more than a
grim and protracted postscript to the story already unfolded. Of
this postscript, its most dramatic episode, the evacuation from

Dunkirk, belongs more properly to the first act of the Battle of Britain than to the closing scenes of the Battle of France. Yet, to complete the narrative, the events of the remaining weeks before France finally laid down her arms require to be sketched in brief. They begin with the sequel—one of historical importance, and still a subject of active dispute—deriving from the saga of past discord within the German High Command.

Hitler orders: "Halt"

On May 24th, after a day in which hard pressure on the encircled Allied perimeter at all points had culminated in the British withdrawal from Arras, General Ironside observed with puzzlement in his diary: "The German mobile columns have definitely been halted for some reason or other. Rather similar to the halt they made before. It is quite certain that there is very little movement about." Ironside was correct in his supposition. Early on the 24th Guderian and Reinhardt had secured a number of bridgeheads across the Aa Canal. Guderian was limbering up for his final drive on Dunkirk. Then, like a bolt from the blue, Guderian says:

Hitler ordered the left wing* to stop on the Aa. It was forbidden to cross that stream. We were not informed of the reasons for this. The order contained the words: "Dunkirk is to be left to the Luftwaffe." . . . We were utterly speechless.

But, as it was a "Führer Order" and no reasons had been given for it, Guderian says that this time "it was difficult to argue against it." His panzers were even instructed to withdraw from the bridgeheads they had established across the Aa. Many explanations have been given for this famous Halt Order, which was to last for two critical days; the muddy Flanders terrain, crisscrossed with canals and drainage ditches, was unsuitable for tanks; the Germans had to husband their depleted tank force for the next phase of the battle against the French; Hitler wanted to grant the BEF a "golden bridge" back to England, so as to ease the conclusion of a peace treaty with the British; Goering, discountenanced by the Army's brilliant successes, had demanded his share of glory for

---

* Which now contained virtually all the German armour.

the Luftwaffe; and finally, the vast forces now converging on the compressed Allied pocket were administratively in a tangle. At best these are half-truths. Historians will continue to argue over motives involved, but the facts briefly seem to be as follows.

On May 23rd, Goering had telephoned Hitler at the *Felsennest,* urging him that the moment had come for the Luftwaffe to administer the *coup de grâce* in the north; after which, the Army would be required solely to "occupy the territory." He resorted to politico-philosophic arguments, declaring that the ultimate triumph should fall to the "National Socialist" Luftwaffe, rather than to the conservative Army; it came down to a question of Hitler's personal prestige as opposed to that of the OKH generals. Goering expressed total confidence that the Luftwaffe could indeed finish the job singlehanded. Doubtless the argument made its mark with Hitler, though Jodl, the OKW Chief of Operations, remarked acidly of Goering: "He's shooting his mouth off again."

At 10:30 the next morning, Hitler went to Rundstedt's Army Group "A" HQ, which—at Charleville—was now many miles behind the battle being fought out in Flanders. Rundstedt explained the situation in detail. He told Hitler that once again the security of the southern flank was still bothering him. According to Army Group "A" War Diaries, "The possibility of concerted action by Allied forces in the north and French forces south of the Somme had to be reckoned with." He stressed the extreme nervousness which had been caused to Kleist's Panzergruppe by the British attack at Arras, and pointed out that Kleist had reported up to 50 percent of his tanks *hors de combat;* although neither he nor Kleist mentioned that the large part of these would in fact be repaired during the next few days. What if, in the marshy Flanders terrain which Hitler and Rundstedt knew so well from twenty-five years ago, the British "Matildas"* should inflict even more grievous losses on the German armour? How then would they be able to muster the tanks with which to pursue Operation "Red," the battle to crush the still considerable French forces protecting the rest of France south of the Somme? The capitulation of the encircled Allied forces in the north was but a matter of time; preparatory groundwork for Operation "Red" must assume prior-

---

* They did not know that by now there was only one battleworthy "Matilda" left in the north.

ity. The previous night he had sent out a preliminary order to Kleist's and Hoth's panzers to halt where they were the next day, in order "to allow the situation to clarify itself and to keep our forces concentrated." This was the burden of what Rundstedt told Hitler.

For the second time in the campaign, Hitler found himself in complete accord with Rundstedt. He was delighted by the measures the Army Group commander had already taken, and agreed particularly with the necessity to husband the armour for the next phase of the battle. Orders were thereupon sent out calling for the indefinite halt of the panzers and bearing the stamp "By the Führer's orders"—which made total compliance mandatory.

It was, as two eminent German historians* have pointed out, a situation "probably unique in modern German military history." What Hitler was in fact doing (not for the last time) was deliberately short-circuiting his top Army advisers, the OKH. As might be expected from the stands previously taken, Brauchitsch and particularly Halder strongly disagreed with Rundstedt's and Hitler's appreciation. Already by midday on the 22nd, Halder had noted down in his diary "a decrease in tension in the overall situation: the enemy is yielding at Arras, west of Arras our panzers have come up against only a weak enemy." The next morning, he was showing himself principally concerned over administrative friction between the two Army Groups, Rundstedt's and Bock's, now jostling each other in increasingly confined quarters. Noting the considerable difficulty Army Group "A" was having to control its huge mass of 71 divisions,† Halder added—in what was obviously a slap at Rundstedt—"It seems to me questionable whether it is sufficiently flexible and energetic with its staff." Later that afternoon, doubts were exchanged concerning Kleist who "feels himself not entirely up to his task, so long as the crisis at Arras is not resolved. Losses in panzers up to 50 percent. I tell him that the crisis will be overcome within 48 hours. I know the size of the task imposed. Tenacity must be demanded." The following day (May 24th), Halder's entries continue in much the same vein: "The power of resistance of the enemy is no longer to be rated

---

* H. A. Jacobsen and J. Rohwer, *Decisive Battles of World War II: The German View*, London, 1965.

† Increased to this total as a result of various transfers and additions made during the course of the battle.

very highly, apart from local fighting. Thus matters will take their own course; we must only have patience, let them mature." Then, that night, Halder baldly records the transmission of the Halt Order, adding that it was "on express wish of the Führer! Within the area specified, the Luftwaffe is to settle the fate of the encircled armies!!" The exclamation marks themselves contain a wealth of meaning. Ulrich Liss, the Intelligence chief of "Foreign Armies West," noted that the usually punctual Halder arrived nearly an hour late for the OKH evening conference, "in a clear state of rage, such as I have never before nor afterwards seen him in. 'For the decision that has just fallen the General Staff is not to blame . . .' were his approximate words."

The 25th, Halder records, "began again with unpleasant disagreements between Brauchitsch and the Führer." Hitler, with Rundstedt ranged behind him, steadfastly held out against any repeal of the Halt Order in the face of strongest representations from Brauchitsch and Halder. In evident despair, Halder wrote in his diary:

A complete upset is thus occurring. I wanted to make Army Group "A" the hammer, and Army Group "B" the anvil; but now "B" is to be the hammer and "A" the anvil. Since "B," however, is faced with an organised front, this must necessarily be very costly and take a long time. Another thing, the Luftwaffe, on which so much hope is now being placed, is completely dependent on the weather.

The whole thing was "more wearing to the nerves than the entire organisation of the campaign itself."

Finally, at 1230 on the 26th Brauchitsch was called to the *Felsennest*. To his great satisfaction, Hitler informed him that he had given orders, though with certain reservations, for the panzers to advance on Dunkirk again—in order to end the evacuation of the British there. But it would take a further sixteen hours to get them moving again. By then, says Guderian, "it was too late to achieve a great victory." For, during the three days the Halt Order had been in force, much had happened. Four British divisions and a number of French had managed to escape from the cauldron forming at the bottom of the pocket, around Lille— which they certainly would not have done had Rommel been allowed to continue his encircling thrust. The construction of a tough perimeter defence line guarding a Dunkirk bridgehead was well under way. In Britain, the *Dynamo* evacuation fleet was assembled and—as Hitler informed Brauchitsch—the first embarkations were already being made from Dunkirk. Finally, there were the first signs of a possible break in "Goering's weather," so crucial to the Luftwaffe if it were to "finish the job from the air."

Before leaving this episode, which—as Guderian rightly remarks—was "to have a most disastrous influence on the whole future course of the war," three myths can be usefully dispatched. In the first place, the excuse that the Flanders mud was responsible for the Halt Order is supported by none of the German tank experts who fought over the area; Guderian, who should have been able to judge better than anybody else, simply dismisses it as "a poor one." Secondly, the notion of the "golden bridge" offered by Hitler to the BEF now finds few supporters, and it certainly stands directly at odds with the very definite orders given to the Luftwaffe, which were the "destruction" of all the encircled enemy forces. The myth in fact appears to have been propagated, if not originated, by Rundstedt during his interrogation by Liddell Hart immediately after the end of the war. Thirdly, the fault for the Halt Order cannot be placed solely at Hitler's door. Since the war, German generaldom has been committed for various reasons, which include both self-preservation and professional pride, to blaming every wartime error and crime upon Hitler, and in this instance even Guderian is to be found disputing the view that Rundstedt was responsible for holding up the panzers. But if anyone was primarily to blame, both on the evidence of the episode itself and of his past performance during the campaign, it was Rundstedt. In his exchange with Hitler, he was a completely free agent, not a party hack just playing back Hitler's own wishes. Rundstedt's integrity as a soldier was too great for this. He was an outstanding battle commander, but as a strategist he showed himself throughout to be almost as preconditioned by the experiences of the First World War as his French counterparts. On May 24th, it was the shock of what the British *had done,* coupled with his ineradicable fears of what the French still *could do,* which principally decided Rundstedt, and—through him—persuaded Hitler, to halt the panzers.

Here, in this disarray within the German High Command, of which the Halt Order of May 24th was the culminating episode,

lay the Achilles' heel in Hitler's superlative machine and its superlative plan. Through it the BEF was to be saved; if the Allies
could have taken advantage of this Achilles' heel by more resolute
action earlier in the battle, could still more have been saved?

The panzers move again

During the panzer halt, the German infantry formations were
still keeping up an unremitting pressure on all sectors of the encircled area. For the Allies, the principal danger points were in
the east along the line held by the rapidly flagging Belgian Army,
and at the bottom of the pocket where the French First Army,
now commanded by General Prioux, was situated. As King Leopold had finally agreed, following the Ypres conference, the Belgians had withdrawn from the Escaut to the Lys on the 25th,
but almost immediately Reichenau's infantry had broken through
the new line on either side of Courtrai. The next day the Belgians were trying to anchor their right wing between Ypres and
Roulers. Blanchard, having succeeded Billotte, was urging them
to fall back on the Yser—as Weygand had wanted originally. But
the Belgian Chief of the General Staff, Michiels, declared that a
further retreat was out of the question, and would only result in
the disintegration of his units. On the afternoon of the 26th, the
Belgian High Command warned Blanchard: "The limits of Belgian resistance are very close to being reached."

On the rescinding of the Halt Order, Rommel's first task was
to break across the La Bassée Canal east of Béthune, which was
held by the BEF. Once again, Rommel had the armour of the 5th
Panzer placed under his control. After some hard and costly fighting, by the end of the 27th* he had broken through the British
line. The 5th Panzer surged forward to capture Armentières,
while Rommel swung eastwards to meet German infantry advancing from the opposite direction. Nearly half the French First Army
was now cut off in a smaller pocket around Lille. For four more

---

* The previous day Rommel was awarded the Ritterkreuz by Hitler, principally
in recognition of his exploits at Avesnes. He noted that the 7th Panzer's total losses
in the campaign to date amounted to 27 officers killed and 33 wounded, and 1,500
men dead and wounded—"That's about 12 percent casualties. Very little compared with what's been achieved," commented Rommel. By the end of the month,
the division had only 86 tanks fit for operations—of which no more than five were
Mark IVs: on the other hand, many of the tanks on the unfit list would be ready
for action again in a few days.

days General Molinié fought an immensely courageous but hopeless action (largely with North African troops), which in fact enabled the BEF and the remainder of the First Army to fall back
safely into the Dunkirk bridgehead.* But when the jaws of the
trap closed, one of those to be taken (along with some 35,000
French troops) was the valiant General Prioux, captured at his
PC in Steenwerck by men of the 4th Panzer. During the fighting,
Rommel once again came close to losing one of his nine lives
when German heavy shells landed by mistake a few yards from
his signals vehicle, killing one of his battalion commanders. On
May 29th, the 7th Panzer was pulled out of the line for six days'
rest and reorganisation before taking part in Operation "Red."
The encirclement of Lille marked the end of Rommel's role in
the first phase of *Sichelschnitt*.

Guderian, after the lifting of the Halt Order, pushed across the
Aa Canal to capture Wormhoudt and Bourbourgville on May
28th and Gravelines, midway between Calais and Dunkirk, on
the 29th. (Meanwhile Boulogne had been captured on the 25th;
Calais on the 26th, after a last-ditch resistance by the Rifle Brigade under Brigadier Nicholson.) Then, like Rommel and the
7th Panzer, Guderian's XIX Corps was withdrawn to prepare
for Operation "Red." Bitterly he remarks of the brakes applied
to his panzers in these critical days: "What the future course of
the war would have been if we had succeeded at the time in taking
the British Expeditionary Force prisoner at Dunkirk, it is now impossible to guess."

French despair

Behind the lines in France, the appointment of Weygand and
his flight to Flanders had been accompanied by another brief
flicker of optimism. It was to be the last. On May 23rd, Alexander
Werth in Paris observed that the bookstalls along the *quais* had
reopened and that workmen were busy completing the pedestal
of one of the statues on the Pont-du-Louvre—which struck him,

---

* In recognition of its heroic defence, the Germans allowed the Lille garrison to
march out with full battle honours on June 1st. But this tragic episode provided
one more source of mounting French bitterness towards the British. Blanchard
complained to Weygand that, despite his protests, Gort had taken the BEF withdrawal to Dunkirk entirely into his own hands; thus, it was said, the British had
left the French First Army in the lurch at Lille.

under the circumstances, as being rather "queer." At a cocktail party two days later he found people expressing confidence that things were "going far better"; there was talk that "Weygand has organised his Somme front; that the Flanders and Somme armies will, within the next twenty-four or forty-eight hours, join and cut the German pincer, and that Hitler made a mistake in not attacking Paris on 16th May." On the 26th, French Army spokesmen were still deriding the "armchair strategists" who concluded that the Flanders armies had been encircled. The following day, Werth recorded a further sign of continuing normalcy in the shape of Picasso—"dark jealous mistress and all"—holding forth at the Café Flore, but now even Colonel Thomas in the Hotel Continental was half-admitting the loss of Calais, while "the juncture of the Somme and Flanders armies is no longer even mentioned."

In this last week of May, defeatism began to spread unchecked in France. The signs of despair assumed varied shapes; Vincent Sheean first sensed it on visiting the Quai d'Orsay when he spotted that one of the grand old *huissiers,* the guardian dragons defending the portals of French diplomacy, had allowed his heavy silver chain, the badge of service, to fall askew so that it was almost dropping off one shoulder. "It was an arrow pointing toward disaster; anybody who ever knew those stiff, proud lackeys of the Third Republic would have known by this that the Republic was dying." Arthur Koestler, in between arrests as a suspicious "alien," discerned the advent of despair in

The onslaught on the railway stations. The disappearance of the buses and taxis from the streets. The melting away of the town, as if infected with consumption. The tommy-guns of the "flics" at the street corners. The peculiar glance of the people in the Underground, with the dim candles of fear lit behind their eyeballs. The parachutist scare. The Fifth Column psychosis.

Then he was rearrested, along with the leading German anti-Nazis who had sought refuge in France, some of whom now began to take cyanide.

General Spears phrased his first reports to Churchill on much the same lines. Churchill, he said, had been misinformed when told Paris was getting angry. The city was fast emptying of the well-to-do, . . . the populace was merely bewildered and apathetic. There was absolutely no sign of the effervescence and excitement that had vibrated through the city in the early days of 1914.

At the same time, from deep within the Maginot Line, Lieutenant Claude Jamet was sadly reflecting:

In whom—officer or soldier—have I discovered a true sacred fire? a sincere ardour, the dedication of one's whole being towards one solitary goal? the sole and complete will to "make war"—and to win it? Oh yes, we should be vexed to be beaten. . . . But how can one get worked up about something that one simply cannot imagine?

On Sunday, May 26th, there had been a repetition in Paris of the solemn religious invocations of the previous week. The relics of Ste. Geneviève had been displayed in front of the Pantheon, the resting place of the great men of France's past; but for Senator Bardoux, who was again present, the spectacle there of the "stricken and silent crowd, which has lost its voice so that it can no longer even sing the Marseillaise and recites the litanies mechanically, is incapable of comforting me. . . . The shadow of 1870 is spreading over the country."

Belgium capitulates

As the news got around that the BEF was beginning to embark from Dunkirk, French despair was accompanied by an emotional rift, rapidly growing, between the Allies. Spears, ever sensitive to the prevailing atmosphere after a lifetime of experience in French affairs, says that on his arrival, "for the first time I sensed a break in the relationships between the two nations, no more perceptible than a crack in crystal, but going right through, irreparably. We were no longer one." The implications of the widening breach were equally horrifying to neutral observers. "I watched with fear the hatred of the French for the English growing by giant leaps and bounds," wrote Clare Boothe. "Many people now quite openly blamed the whole horrible fiasco on the British High Command."

On May 28th, France learned of another cause for rancour. In the small hours of that morning, Belgium had surrendered. The

surrender of the Belgian Army on its left indeed provided the final
blow to Prioux's First Army in the Lille pocket (it also left a gaping hole between the BEF and the sea); but, from the hints
dropped by King Leopold and General Michiels for the past several days, it should have been abundantly clear to the French
High Command that it was only a matter of hours before Belgium
succumbed. Nevertheless, in the despair of the moment, Reynaud
reacted with ferocity. Broadcasting to the nation that night, he
declared that Leopold had laid down his arms "without warning
General Blanchard, without a thought or word for the French
or British troops who went to the aid of his country in response
to his agonised appeal." He rated it "a deed without precedent
in history."* Anger towards the defaulting ally swept through
France. Listening to Reynaud's broadcast in a bistro, Gordon
Waterfield observed two women burst into tears, crying: *"Les
salauds, les salauds!"* Parisians threw Belgian refugees out of
their houses, countrymen set fire to their wretched carts; French
refugees heckled and buffeted them in stations and on the roads.

Weygand and the "Separate Peace" lobby

Within Paul Reynaud's Government, the twin viruses of defeatism and anti-British sentiment had established themselves even
before they had begun to cast their malaise in wider circles. May
24th and 25th were critical days, and they marked a kind of
watershed. Henceforth Weygand, the "political general," is to be
found exerting an influence over French councils far transcending
his military functions as Generalissimo; it was he, not Pétain, who
first assumed lead of the separate peace lobby. At 10:30 A.M. on
the 24th, Weygand arrived for a meeting in the Prime Minister's
office at which Baudouin and Pétain were also present. According to Baudouin, who reveals himself increasingly in support of
Weygand, the new C-in-C whispered to him on entering: "The
situation is very serious, for the English are falling back on the
ports instead of attacking to the south." Weygand claimed that

---

* At first, Churchill's reaction was far more restrained. He told the House of
Commons that he had no intention of passing judgement on the King; and Duff
Cooper, the British Minister of Information, declared on the BBC that the Belgians had "fought bravely . . . suffered heavily," and that it was no time for recriminations. Later, however, under strong French pressure, Churchill swung
round to condemning King Leopold in much the same terms as Reynaud.

he was not surprised by the British manoeuvre, for on the previous evening General Ironside's tone over the telephone had made an unfavourable impression upon him. "I would willingly have boxed his ears," he exclaimed to Baudouin. In the course of his conference with Reynaud, Weygand still appeared to be adhering to his original plan, despite the British withdrawal from Arras. Then, at six o'clock that evening Weygand telephoned Baudouin from Vincennes, where he was with General Georges, and asked him to come to him.

On Baudouin's arrival, Weygand confided that the situation caused by the British withdrawal now seemed much graver than it had in the morning, and as a result he saw himself forced to abandon his plan of two days previously. Weygand, says Baudouin, "seemed to me overcome by the defection of the English." He had summoned Baudouin because he wanted him to explain this to Reynaud and also to point out to him the condition in which the French Army would find itself if the forces in the north capitulated. It would then consist of only some 50 divisions, of which 18 were immobile fortress units, and it would have to hold a front from the Somme to the Maginot Line nearly 350 miles long. Weygand described this remaining force as a "wall of sand" which would soon be pierced by the enemy. He then outlined to Baudouin his plans for the future:

The French Army ought to resist desperately on the Somme and Aisne positions. Then, when the enemy has broken this resistance, what is left of the French Army should continue to fight where it stands until it is annihilated, *to save the honour of the French flag.**

Weygand repeated to Baudouin what he had told Reynaud that morning; namely, that it had been "criminal" for France, the previous September, to have declared war without any of the means for carrying it on. Baudouin then expressed his doubts as to whether the Army's morale was up to waging any new desperate struggle on the Somme and the Aisne:

Would it be possible to apply the measures envisaged by the General to save the national honour?

---

* Author's italics.

I said to him, "We have only one object—to get France out of the ordeal which she is undergoing so as to allow her, even if defeated in the field, to rise again." . . . With tears in his eyes, the General told me that he shared my fears.

After this meaningful exchange, the two men parted in wide agreement with each other. The fateful word *armistice* had never once been mentioned, but—as Reynaud points out—this was clearly what was in both their minds, behind the talk about "saving national honour."* Weygand had now been in command for just four days.

At noon on the following day, May 25th, discussions were held in Reynaud's office, lasting two and a half hours. Before they began, Churchill's emissary, General Spears, had arrived to present his credentials to Reynaud, whom he had known well in the past. Reynaud, says Spears, launched in with some acid comments on "how British generals always made for harbours." Spears begged him "to set his face against recriminations," saying that the only hope for France and Britain now was to "act together as brothers."

Reynaud nodded his head in approval. He got up once or twice, his small figure very erect, the shoulders of his black jacket thrown back, and walked up and down, his hands behind his back. Several times he stretched his neck and turned his head to one side as if putting on too high and too tight a collar. His Chinese eyes, always ready to emphasise his wit with a twinkle, did not smile. . . . He looked not in the least rattled. I said to myself as I had often done before: "This is a likeable, gallant little man."

To Spears and to members of the French Government with whom he spoke that day, Reynaud declared—as he was to declare repeatedly in the ensuing weeks—that he would fight, tooth and nail, to the end. Reynaud then invited Spears to attend the session of the War Cabinet which was about to take place.

Inside Reynaud's office, Spears found Marshal Pétain, General Weygand, Admiral Darlan and Paul Baudouin waiting. Weygand

---

* At the Commission of Inquiry in 1949, Baudouin admitted, "I was certain . . . on May 24 that the struggle was lost," and he considered Weygand was of the same opinion.

had with him a liaison officer from Blanchard's HQ, a Major Fauvelle, whom he requested should be heard. Says Spears:

The idea of defeat, or even the shadow of such an idea, never crossed my mind, but, as Commandant Fauvelle told his story in fragments, revealing an appalling state of affairs, and as I realised that his cata-strophic defeatism seemed to some extent at least to be accepted as the reflection of the real position, I felt cold fingers turning my heart to stone. . . . In my view nothing short of throwing Fauvelle out of the window would have been adequate.

Fauvelle ended his pessimistic report on Blanchard's situation by declaring: "I believe in a very early capitulation"; which pro-voked a censure for exceeding his brief simultaneously from both Reynaud and Weygand. The discussions continued with Weygand expressing utmost gloom over the prospects of the French Army "retreating in good order and defending successive positions" in the face of a new German attack. Weygand then turned on Rey-naud and (according to Spears) "with a voice like a saw," said: " 'This war is sheer madness, we have gone to war with a 1918 army against a German Army of 1939. It is sheer madness.' "

During this and other conferences of such extreme gravity, Spears was shocked to note the number of interruptions on the French Prime Minister's "harmonium-like telephone." If it was not his mistress, Hélène de Portes, the caller appeared to be some parliamentarian requesting "that his son-in-law serving in the north should be transferred to a part of the front where there were fewer Germans." Spears found this revelation that the "Re-public of Pals" still prevailed in France horrifying: "The Chair-man of a reputable board in the City of London would never allow himself to be interrupted at a meeting where he was dis-cussing the retail price of soap with his colleagues, to deal with a personal question. But here we were, when the fate of France was in the balance, interfered with in this way." At the same time, Spears admits that his admiration for Reynaud's courage grew, when—following this first meeting—"I gradually came to appreciate what he was up against, the defeatism in high places and the trance into which France had fallen."

After Spears departed, a second, still more important meeting*
of the French War Cabinet was held at the Élysée that evening,
at which President Lebrun was also present. Weygand opened
with a brief and gloomy résumé of the disastrous course of military operations since May 10th. He claimed still to be adhering
to his plan for the north–south operation towards Bapaume
(despite what he had confided to Baudouin the previous day),
now due to begin on the night of the 26th–27th, but he was hardly
optimistic any longer and he regarded it as "my duty to prepare
for the worst." At this point, Reynaud interrupted to announce
receipt of a telegram from Churchill that afternoon, which now
confirmed the retreat of the British from Arras, and recognised
that the northern forces were to all intents and purposes surrounded, their communications cut–save for Ostend and Dunkirk. Weygand continued with his report, forecasting the course
of events that would follow the loss of the northern armies.
France would find herself "called upon to fight against odds of
three to one." She must fight a last ditch stand on the Somme–
Aisne position; here "each section of the army must fight to the
last to save the honour of the country." Weygand concluded
by repeating yet again his reproaches about France's unpreparedness to declare war.† "It is probable," he prophesied (according
to Reynaud), "that she will pay dearly for this imprudence." It
was time to think of the resurrection of the country.

President Lebrun‡ now intervened to voice for the first time
the unspoken thought in the mind of Weygand and his supporters.
What if the French armies were scattered and destroyed as Weygand envisaged? "Of course," he said, "we have signed engage-
ments§ which prevent us from concluding a separate peace, but
if Germany makes any relatively advantageous offer we ought
nevertheless to examine it closely and objectively." Weygand ex-

---

* The principal source here is Baudouin, who in his role as secretary was the
only one to take notes: therefore caution has to be exercised in accepting exactly
what transpired.

† Referring to Weygand's own stewardship during the thirties as French C-in-C,
Reynaud remarks that he "took great care not to recognise the responsibility he
bore for the 'great mistake' which he denounced."

‡ Of the President of the Republic's role in these days, Mandel made this caustic
comment to Spears: "He raises his hands to heaven and weeps. . . . *Il pleure.*"

§ Referring to the Franco-British Declaration signed by Reynaud in London on
March 28th. (See page 172.)

pressed sympathy with the President's point of view, and thought
that the government ought to take up this issue with the British
right away. Pétain questioned whether there was in fact complete
reciprocity of obligations between the two countries; after all,
had not Britain put only 10 divisions into the field while 80 French
divisions were fighting? On the same theme, General Vuillemin of
the Air Force* stated that while the French were losing some 30
machines a day, RAF fighters had hardly been engaged at all. Although at times the BEF troops on the ground might have shared
the same view, it was hardly a true picture. Nevertheless, Vuillemin continued that there were only 65 British fighters on the
Continent while 600 were kept in England for the defence of the
island. "It is said," he claimed, "that during the last three days
the English have sent a hundred fighters a day over the Continent,
but I have not been able to verify the statement. I do not know
in any detail what has been done by the English fighters in
France.† M. Campinchi, the Minister of the Marine, injected the

---

* Vuillemin, who seems never to have recovered from the shock the Luftwaffe
prepared for him on his visit to Germany in 1938, seldom contributed at War
Cabinet sessions; instead, says Spears pungently, he "just looked on with the bewildered washed-out eyes of an ancient celluloid doll floating on the opaque waters of the bath it seemed bewildered to find itself in." *"Vuillemin, nul comme
d'habitude,"* was Baudouin's verdict.

† On May 21st it had in fact been agreed that the RAF should henceforth support the armies in the north, with d'Astier's ZOAN backing the Somme and Aisne
fronts. During the last week of May, virtually the whole of the RAF Bomber
Command's strength of some 500 bombers was continuously employed. The official
RAF history states that, from May 22nd onwards, "something like two hundred
fighter sorties a day were flown from England over northern France." Some of
Dowding's most treasured possessions, the Spitfire squadrons earmarked for the
defence of Britain, were even drawn into the battle by the end of May. In the
course of the whole campaign, only ten out of Britain's total of 53 fighter squadrons were not engaged in France; and of these ten, two were committed in Norway, three were night fighters and two were nonoperational. Though General
Vuillemin may not have been aware of it, the Germans certainly noticed RAF
intervention in the battle in the north from May 22 onwards. Jacobsen and
Rohwer write:

"For the first time VIII Air Corps was compelled to admit that its Stukas had
suffered heavy losses from the unexpected appearance of numerous British fighter
planes. Many RAF planes until now held back for the defence of the United
Kingdom had obviously been flown from their bases in southeast England, and
taken part in the air war on the Continent. With this, the situation in the air
suddenly grew critical."

Meanwhile, as far as the French air effort was concerned, as late as May 30th
the Minister of Air, M. Laurent-Eynac, revealed that, in all but fighters, the
French Air Force was actually *stronger* in numbers than on May 10th; 660 air-

ingenious suggestion that, if France wanted to conclude a separate peace without British consent, she might be freed of her
obligations if the present French Government, which had signed
the joint declaration, were simply to resign. The session ended
with Reynaud announcing that he would fly at once to London
and that he would explain France's military plight clearly to
Churchill. Weygand and his supporters urged that Reynaud should
specifically raise the question of the Franco-British Declaration.
There was no discussion of whether, in the event of defeat in
France, the French Government might follow the example of the
other invaded nations and go into exile in London or elsewhere.

As a result of these meetings of the 25th, Reynaud says, "If
I did not know all, at least I knew . . . that Pétain and Weygand
were in favour of asking for an armistice on the day the battle
of France was lost, and of allowing the Government to be captured in Paris." In London the next day, he relayed to Churchill
the full gravity of France's dilemma and the problem now confronting him from the "softs" within his own government. He
also expressed concern that Mussolini was about to bring Italy
into the war against France. What could Britain do to help here?
Reynaud declared his own determination to fight on to the end;
but he declined to raise the delicate issue demanded by Weygand.
At 7:30 that evening he was met at Le Bourget by Baudouin,
who at once asked him:

"What did you say of the necessity in which we may shortly find ourselves of breaking off the fight? In what conditions will the English free
us from our promise?" "I was not able to put the question," he replied.
I told him that he had done wrong; that he had not fulfilled the mission
with which the War Cabinet had entrusted him.

That so junior a minister* should have expressed himself in these
terms to the Prime Minister of France is in itself indicative of
the growing ascendancy of Paul Baudouin. Behind Baudouin one
may descry the shadowy agency of the Comtesse de Portes, his

---

craft had been lost, but 571 new machines had been delivered. According to
French sources, by the Armistice of June 22, the French Air Force was *still*
stronger and better equipped than it had been on May 10th.

* As secretary to the War Cabinet, Baudouin's official status was that of Under
Secretary.

political patroness, indefatigable, inflamedly anti-British and already dedicated to a separate peace, but (for once) apparently unable to use the weapons of the boudoir to influence her lover, Reynaud, determined as he now was on fighting to the end.

During Reynaud's absence in London, Pétain had called upon Baudouin. He revealed to Baudouin that he too did not believe in a fight to the finish. The old Marshal who had gained his reputation for husbanding the lives of his men at Verdun thought that it was "easy and stupid to talk of fighting to the last man; it is also criminal in view of our losses in the last war and of our low birthrate." He felt that a part of the Army must be saved, for without it "to maintain order a true peace is impossible." In the days to come, these last words were to correspond faithfully with Weygand's own views.

From the South: The last Allied attack

Thus in Paris the days of May 24–26th saw the crystallisation of a "separate peace" lobby, of which its hard core was formed by the Weygand–Pétain–Baudouin axis. It was a turning point in the affairs of France. From now on the lobby would be increasingly conscious of its combined strength against Reynaud. It was also the time when the fire which Churchill had thought he detected in Weygand on the 22nd finally flickered out. On the 27th, the long-awaited effort from the south began. Under the reinstated General Grandsard (formerly of X Corps), the 7th and 4th Colonial Infantry Divisions, backed by a scattering of Somuas, attacked towards Amiens. They got to within sight of the city, apparently causing the German defenders some passing anxiety; then, after suffering heavy losses, the French colonial troop (many of them Senegalese with no battle training) were thrown back to their start line by an enemy counterattack. On the 28th, de Gaulle executed his third offensive action with customary courage and dash, supported by the British 51st (Highland) Division—this time against the German bridgehead around Abbeville. De Gaulle claims: "There was an air of victory on the battlefield. Everyone held his head high. The wounded smiled. The guns barked joyously. The Germans before us had fallen back after a pitched battle." Five hundred German prisoners were claimed; but once again the attack petered out, on the second day without the German bridgehead having been erased—

Encirclement of Allied forces: May 23rd–31st

and certainly without any incursion having been made into the Panzer Corridor. The French forces along the Somme now resumed their defensive posture.

Herewith faded the last Franco-British offensive effort, and the final flicker of the Weygand Plan. Its author had lost hope well before it began. On the 29th, while de Gaulle was still attacking towards Abbeville, Weygand presented a memorandum to the War Cabinet in which he made an unfavourable comparison with the lost war of 1870. At that time, when the regular armies had been crushed, France had been able to raise *ad hoc* forces which had "prolonged the resistance for five months and saved the honour of France." Now, even if the equipment were available for fresh armies, "the enemy would not allow us the time to organise them." Pétain congratulated Weygand on his memorandum and approved its contents. Weygand then said verbally to Reynaud: "I hope to stand on the Somme–Aisne line, but it is my duty to tell you that I am not sure of being able to do so." His meaning was now abundantly clear; he would fight one more battle, "to save the honour of France," and that would be the end. Reynaud replied to Weygand's memorandum with a resolute written rejoinder in which, for the first time, he declared his intention of continuing the war—if necessary—from North Africa.

Dunkirk

During these days, Gort—with dogged determination and deflected neither by Blanchard's pleas nor Churchillian growls—was beginning the evacuation from Dunkirk of the force upon which would depend the immediate safety of Britain and the ultimate salvation of France. Although Gort had been acting (at any rate, until May 26th) in direct opposition to his will, Churchill wrote of him later in *The Second World War:*

Confident in his military virtue, and convinced of the complete breakdown of all control, either by the British and French Governments or by the French Supreme Command. . . . In all this Lord Gort had acted upon his own responsibility. But by now we at home, with a somewhat different angle of information, had already reached the same conclusions.

Accordingly, on the 26th Gort received official notice from the War Office "to operate towards the coast forthwith." Few then held hopes of saving more than a fraction of the BEF; Ironside was reckoning in private that the British would be lucky to get out 30,000 men,* and Gort himself signalled back in reply to the War Office's instruction of the 26th: "I must not conceal from you that a great part of the B.E.F. and its equipment will inevitably be lost even in best circumstances." On May 28th Churchill warned the House of Commons to "prepare itself for hard and heavy tidings." Certainly, without Gort's decision to disengage from Arras and without Hitler's Halt Order to the panzers, the probability is that few in excess of Ironside's pessimistic calculation would have been rescued.

The story of the "miracle of Dunkirk" has been told and retold. Little needs to be added here. During the three-day respite afforded by the halting of the panzers, Gort had managed to throw up a strong protective shell around the Dunkirk bridgehead. But it was in the air that the holding of the bridgehead was predominantly decided. The RAF now threw in every single plane available. Day and night its bombers blasted the attacking Germans, while fighter pilots flew sometimes as many as four sorties a day. Altogether the British fighter cover totalled 2,739 sorties while the evacuations lasted. For the first time since the campaign began, the cruelly beautiful "Goering's weather" that had so aided the Luftwaffe now deserted it; during at least half of the nine-day epic of Dunkirk, fog and bad visibility limited flying. On the good days, the Luftwaffe—considerably weakened by the losses and strain of three weeks constantly on the offensive†—found itself sorely pressed by the furious concentrations of aircraft that the RAF, flying from bases just across the Straits of Dover, was able to put in the air over Dunkirk. Only on two days, May 27th and June 1st, did the Luftwaffe enjoy outstanding success. Each day that went by proved Goering's boast that he could "finish the job" to be a little further from realisation.

By the evening of May 27th, the disappointing total of only 7,669 men had been embarked from Dunkirk. But the next day

---

* The German High Command itself erroneously estimated that the encircled Allied forces in the north totalled no more than 100,000 all told.

† Some bomber *Gruppen* could now only put 14 to 16 aircraft in the air, instead of 30.

the Royal Navy began to be reinforced by the vast armada of small boats collected from all over the south coast of England, and that day's figure reached 17,804. On the 29th, the arrival of French warships helped hoist the day's results to 47,310; and so on, until a peak of 68,014 was reached on May 31st. That day Gort himself sailed for England, having been issued strictest orders by Churchill to hand over to one of his Corps commanders as soon as the BEF left in France was down to the equivalent of three divisions.* Also that day, Churchill was in Paris again attending a meeting of the Supreme War Council and was able to tell it that the astonishing figure of 165,000 men had already been evacuated. Weygand promptly questioned—in what Spears describes as a "high, querulous and aggressive" voice—"But how many French? The French are being left behind?" When Churchill revealed that only 15,000 of these had been French, not unnaturally there were resentful comments. (In fact, it transpired that Blanchard—to Gort's amazement—had received *no orders* from Weygand to begin evacuating French troops until May 29th.) At the meeting of the 31st, Churchill promptly decreed that henceforth the evacuations should proceed on equal terms between the British and the French—*"Bras dessus bras dessous,"* as he put it in his robust French.†

By the morning of June 3rd, the last British troops were embarked. The Germans were within a mile and a quarter of the sea, but still held back by a courageous French rear guard. At the dawn the next day, the last ship left Dunkirk, taking with it a final contingent of French soldiers. The remarkable total of 337,-000 men, of whom 110,000 were French, had been got out of the *Sichelschnitt* trap—at a cost of six British and two French destroyers, as well as many lesser craft. But the knowledge that

---

* General Blanchard followed on June 1st.

† It was also at that meeting that Churchill delivered one of his greatest orations, with the intent of boosting the morale of the French Government: "The peoples of France and Britain," he declaimed, "were not born to slavery, nor can they endure it. It is impossible that a temporary Nazi victory should bring to a final conclusion the glorious histories of France and Britain." Britain, he insisted, would "carry on with the war if every building in France and Great Britain is destroyed. The British Government is prepared to wage war from the New World if through some disaster England herself is laid waste. The British people will fight on until the New World re-conquers the Old. Better far that the last of the English should fall fighting and *finis* be written to our history than to linger on as vassals and slaves."

30,000 French troops, the last of the rear guard, had to be abandoned to the Germans—in addition to the many thousands forced to surrender in the Lille pocket—was to provide another lasting source of anti-British bitterness in French hearts.

Although, as Churchill warned the House of Commons on June 4th, "Wars are not won by evacuations," Dunkirk will always be regarded by the British as one of the great triumphs of the island race. But to the French, for whom, in any case, water was a hostile rather than a friendly element, Dunkirk could only represent defeat, and desertion by an ally. But it was Hitler who—in terms of overall war strategy—suffered the most injurious defeat at Dunkirk.

20

One Last Battle
JUNE 5th – 22nd

Defeat is a thing of weariness, of incoherence, of boredom. And above all of futility.
—ANTOINE DE SAINT-EXUPÉRY, *Flight to Arras*

One can only think with a shudder of our unawareness during the past eight months, in which our noblest duty seemed to consist of making the leisure hours of the soldiers at the front pleasant.
—*L'Oeuvre*, May 30th

Soldiers of the West Front!
Dunkirk has fallen . . . with it has ended the greatest battle of world history.
Soldiers! My confidence in you knew no bounds.
You have not disappointed me.
—ADOLF HITLER, Order of the Day, June 5th

While the German army suffers unheard-of losses, the French army remains intact.
—RADIO STRASBOURG, June 12th

Operation "Red": The opposing forces

AT MIDNIGHT on the day Dunkirk fell, Hitler decreed that bells throughout the Reich should be tolled for three days in celebration of the end of this "greatest battle in World History." An hour later, on June 5th, the OKW communiqué announced: "The second great offensive is being launched today." To be in at the kill, Hitler had moved westwards from his headquarters at the *Felsennest;* before doing so, he ordered that the entire area in the Eifel should be preserved as a "national monument"—every room was to be kept unchanged, every name plate to remain upon its door.

On a rare note of concord and satisfaction, Halder wrote in his diary for the 4th: "In the evening, a glass of wine with the C-in-C at his country residence.* Wonderful eventide peace, harmonious atmosphere!"

In the six days of rest since they had been withdrawn from the northern battle, the German panzers had been completely reorganised and redeployed with superb flexibility. For the final battle, they were now divided into five armoured corps, each consisting of two panzer divisions and one of motorised infantry. Three of these corps were given to Bock, still standing on the right of the German line, and two to Rundstedt, who was now facing the French from east of Laon to the northern anchor of the Maginot Line at Montmédy. On the far right of the German line, along the lower Somme, were Rommel's 7th Panzer and the 5th, once again with Hoth as the Corps commander. Then, facing Amiens and Péronne, came Kleist's Panzergruppe, now comprised of two armoured corps;† further east, facing the Rethel area along the Aisne, came Guderian, now promoted to command his own Panzergruppe of two corps.‡ Altogether, from the sea to the Meuse, the Germans mustered some 104 fully manned divisions.

Against this, along a front 225 miles long, Weygand could dispose of only 43 infantry divisions,§ plus three much reduced and only partially reconstituted armoured divisions, and three similarly weakened DLCs. Twenty-five of Weygand's available infantry divisions had been pulled out (belatedly) from the Maginot Line area, but another 17 still remained there. In addition, there were the British 51st (Highland) and 1st Armoured Divisions; the latter was now down to about a third of its strength, and its armour consisted chiefly of lightly clad cruiser tanks. On their way were two more divisions (one of them Canadian)—the only two equipped formations now left in the British Isles. In the air,

---

* Together with Hitler, Brauchitsch and the OKH had also moved westwards onto Belgian territory, west of Givet on the Meuse.

† Containing the 9th, 10th, 3rd and 4th Panzers.

‡ The XXXIX and XLI Panzer Corps, containing Guderian's old 1st and 2nd Panzers and Reinhardt's 6th and 8th.

§ According to Weygand's figures, French losses up to the fall of Dunkirk amounted to the equivalent of: 24 infantry divisions (including 6 out of 7 motorised); 3 out of 3 DLMs; 2 out of 5 Light Cavalry Divisions (DLCs); 1 armoured division.

Southward advance of German forces into France: June 1st–22nd

French production and American consignments had helped replace a good part of the losses suffered; Glenn Martin bombers
and new Dewoitine 520 fighters, mounting a cannon and four
machine guns, were seen in the air for the first time. General
d'Astier's ZOAN could now mount 125 bombers, of which 93
were modern and suitable for daylight operations, and about 225
fighters. To General Vuillemin's pleas for another 20 RAF squadrons, the British had continued to present a firm front. But by
June 5th Barratt's AASF—after falling to 30 aircraft by May 20th
—had once more risen to a total of 100, 30 fighters and 70 bombers, a fact not generally appreciated in France at the time. Some
250 bombers from Bomber Command in England were also used
in support of operations in France. In all, d'Astier says that 980
aircraft were engaged in the second phase of the battle; but the
pilots and organisation to keep them in the air were desperately
thin on the ground.

Thus Weygand assessed his total strength at a maximum of
60 divisions; while, against what the Luftwaffe could throw in, he
regarded his air forces as "ridiculously weak." For the main
strength of the Weygand Line behind the Somme and the Aisne,
Weygand—at last abandoning the ruined "continuous front" philosophy—relied principally on a chequerboard system of "hedgehogs." Each hedgehog consisted of troops well dug in around a
natural obstacle—a village or wood—and armed with 75s which
were to be used in an antitank role. Many of them First War
weapons brought out of retirement, the 75s were to be pointed
"like revolvers" at the enemy armour. The hedgehogs were designed to hold out even when surrounded or bypassed by the
enemy. Behind them were *groupements de manoeuvre* constituted from the few remaining units of Allied armour. It was at
last an attempt at a defence in depth, but unfortunately the Weygand Line lacked the forces with which to provide anything like
the depth needed to halt panzers. True to his belief that he should
fight one last battle, "for the sake of honour," and then persuade
the government to sue for peace, Weygand had prepared no succeeding positions on which to fall back once the Weygand Line
was broken.

The French fight back

The German plan called for Bock to open the attack on June 5th and Rundstedt to follow four days later. At once Bock's forces ran into unexpectedly tough resistance. Desperate as their situation was, the French defenders fought back with a determination and a spirit of sacrifice that had not been seen on the Meuse. No longer did the screaming Stukas bring panic in their wake. The French gunners stayed and died with their 75s, knocking out considerable numbers of German tanks. Karl von Stackelberg, the military diarist who had followed the German advance all the way from Nouzonville on the Meuse, wrote: "In these ruined villages the French resisted to the last man. Some hedgehogs carried on when our infantry was 20 miles behind them." Both at Amiens and Péronne, Kleist's two panzer corps were prevented from breaking out of their bridgeheads, after managing to advance only a few miles; and even Rommel had been halted most of the day at Hangest and Le Quesnoy in the marshes of the lower Somme. By the end of the day, Weygand was impressed that his troops had held their own better than expected. There were grounds for hope. But the cost had been high, and the material odds were enormous. A sequence in the German film, *Sieg im West*, taken at this time shows a monster German self-propelled gun (probably 150 mm) reducing a solitary French sniper in a house, with shot after shot at point-blank range. Nothing could demonstrate more clearly the disparity of might between the two sides in these desperate days.

Rommel again

On the 6th, the French once again stopped Kleist south of Amiens and Péronne. In these two days of battle, one of his panzer corps had some 65 percent of its tanks disabled. But disaster overtook the French on the flank. It was precipitated by Rommel, who broke through west of Amiens after some fierce fighting and advanced 20 miles southwards from the Somme. The next day (his wife's birthday), Rommel swept forward another 30 miles to Forges-les-Eaux on the Beauvais–Dieppe road and only 25 miles from Rouen. With his customary swiftness to adapt himself to new situations, Rommel had mastered Weygand's chequerboard system by taking his division cross-country so as to avoid the French hedgehogs, leaving them to be dealt with by the following infantry. His advance that day split in two General Robert Altmayer's Tenth Army, of which one of the units left on the coastal flank was the British 51st (Highland) Division. Next, on the 8th, Rommel pushed on to take Elbeuf on the Seine, thereby sealing off the great city of Rouen. He wrote to his wife on the 9th in high spirits: "Two glorious days in pursuit, first south, then south-west. A roaring success. 45 miles yesterday"; and on the 10th: "Our successes are tremendous and it looks to me inevitable that the other side will soon collapse. We never imagined war in the west would be like this." The 5th Panzer had meanwhile captured Rouen, and on Rommel's left the lower Seine had been reached by the XXXVIII Infantry Corps, commanded by General Erich von Manstein—allowed at this late date to participate in the triumph which owed so much to his genius. Rommel was now ordered to countermarch to the northwest, swing round Rouen, and head for the sea near Fécamp in order to cut off the retreat of Altmayer's isolated left wing. After another 60-mile advance, Rommel reached the coast in a day, and began to push back up it towards Dieppe. At the small port of Saint-Valéry-en-Caux he fell upon the cut-off part of Altmayer's army, then attempting to form a bridgehead prior to evacuation. But no ships arrived, and on June 12th the Allied garrison surrendered. That day Rommel took 40,000 prisoners, including 12 generals. They included the whole of the 51st Highland Division with its commander, Major General Fortune—one of Britain's finest fighting units.

On the 14th, Rommel occupied Le Havre. Then, after two days' rest, he was ordered to advance on Cherbourg, passing through terrain which, as a field marshal and almost exactly four years later, he would be called upon to defend against American tanks enjoying almost the same numerical superiority that the Germans had had in 1940. On June 17th he established an alleged all-time record by advancing 150 miles in a single day. Two days later he accepted the capitulation of Cherbourg. This was the end of the campaign for Rommel and the 7th Panzer, nicknamed by the French the "Phantom Division." In six remarkable weeks, it had captured 97,648 prisoners, together with 277 guns, 458 armoured vehicles, and over 4,000 trucks. Its own casualties had totalled 682 killed (including the relatively large number of 52 officers),

1,646 wounded and 296 missing; while its loss in tanks was only 42 complete write-offs.*

Guderian again

On June 9th, Rundstedt's attack had duly gone in. In an order of the day to the French armies that morning, Weygand declared: "We have come to the last quarter of an hour. Stand firm." The German assault was led by Guderian's Panzergruppe, which—after a 150-mile march largely retracing the route of his victorious advance—was concentrated on either side of Rethel. Meanwhile, the main weight of the Panzergruppe belonging to his former chief and antagonist, Kleist, was also being switched eastwards to the Aisne, after being checked south of Amiens and Péronne on the direct route to Paris. In contrast to the Meuse crossings, this time the infantry were to attack first and seize bridgeheads across the Aisne before Guderian committed his panzer divisions. But, says Guderian:

At 1100 hours I received messages from the front on either side of Rethel that the Rethel attacks had failed. My observers from the other fronts reported that the infantry had only succeeded in establishing a single bridgehead, a small one a mile to a mile and a half deep, in the neighbourhood of Château-Porcien.

Once again, the French defenders were fighting back heroically; de Lattre de Tassigny's tough 14th Division alone claimed some 800 German prisoners. If only Grandsard's men could have put up the same kind of resistance at Sedan when the odds had been so much less in favour of the Germans! Guderian now decided to move tanks of the 1st Panzer into the solitary bridgehead under cover of darkness. The next day the armour pushed out of the bridge-head, but made only slow progress; in the afternoon a hard tank-versus-tank battle was fought around Juniville against the remnants of Guderian's old adversary, the French 3rd Armoured Division. Colonel Balck personally captured the colors of a French regiment, but Guderian admitted to having suffered heavy casualties. On the 11th, Guderian records that 1st Panzer pro-

---

* By the end of May, Rommel in fact had only 86 tanks (of which just five were Mark IVs) fit for operations, out of his complement of 218. But many of the remainder were back on the road within the next few days.

gressed "as though this were a manoeuvre." French resistance on the Aisne sector of the Weygand Line was clearly coming to an end. Soon Reinhardt's two panzer divisions, then Kleist's four, were across the Aisne—thrusting southward in an irresistible mass of armour. By nightfall, Reims was reached; the following morning (May 12th) Guderian captured Châlons-sur-Marne.

Paris abandoned

The capture of Rouen in the west and the crossing of the Marne in the east now meant that Paris, the sacred capital, was irretrievably compromised. On June 3rd, Paris was bombed for the first time and over 250 people were reported killed. By the 8th, the sound of distant cannon had become almost continuous. For the third time in seventy years, Paris began to resemble a city under siege. "The restaurants emptied," said Fabre-Luce. "The Ritz, abandoned by its last clients, resembled a palace in a spa on the day the baths closed down." The following day, GQG Northeast packed up at "Les Bondons" and departed for less commodious lodgings at Briare on the upper reaches of the Loire. The next night (June 10th), the French radio announced: "The Government is compelled to leave the capital for imperative military reasons. The Prime Minister is on his way to the armies."

At midnight, the car containing Reynaud and his new Under Secretary of State for National Defence, General Charles de Gaulle, left for the future seat of government at Tours. Behind them an endless stream of refugees poured out along the Boulevard Raspail. Ilya Ehrenburg, who—as a correspondent representing Hitler's Russian ally—remained, was moved to compassion while, as he watched, "An old man laboriously pushed a handcart loaded with pillows on which huddled a small girl and a little dog that howled piteously." In contrast, de Gaulle relates how in the course of his arduous journey through the night, past a long stationary line of refugees: "Suddenly a convoy of luxurious, white-tyred American cars came sweeping along the road, with militiamen on the running-boards and motorcyclists surrounding the procession; it was the Corps Diplomatique on its way to the châteaux of Touraine." It was dawn by the time Reynaud and de Gaulle reached Orléans.

Until this moment, the French Government had kept on repeating in Gambettaesque terms that it would fight in front of Paris, behind Paris, and only that weekend it had announced that the city had been placed "in a state of defence." Every fifty yards or so down the Champs Élysées buses had been placed diagonally, with the object of preventing German airborne troops from landing. Then on the night of the 11th, Weygand decided to declare Paris an "open city." That Paris should have capitulated without a struggle, while Warsaw, London, Leningrad and Stalingrad opted to accept battle and be devastated, has ever since remained a source of contention; at the time there were many loyal Frenchmen who—like André Pertinax—considered its capitulation "quite unprecedented" and pointed out that "in 1870–71 the war had continued in the provinces only as a result of the capital's heroic resistance." By June 11th, the situation was such that there would, however, have been little military advantage gained in fighting for Paris, stone by beautiful stone. But psychologically its abandonment struck a grievous blow to what remained of French morale. André Maurois recalls being warned, on June 10th, that Paris would not be defended: "At that moment I knew everything was over. France deprived of Paris, would become a body without a head. The war had been lost."

As the Germans approached Paris, a drizzle of rain fell on the capital after the long weeks of peerless weather. Early on the morning of June 14th, an officer on the staff of Küchler's Eighteenth Army, Lieutenant Colonel Dr. Hans Speidel,* received two French officers who came under flag of truce with instructions to deliver up the capital. Later that morning troops of the German 87th Infantry Division, led by an antitank gun detachment which occupied the Hôtel de Ville and the Invalides, made a bloodless and orderly entry into Paris. Following in its wake just three days later, William Shirer felt an ache in the pit of his stomach at the sight of the familiar but lonely streets: "I wished I had not come. My German companions were in high spirits." Going round the Place de l'Opéra, he noted

---

* Four years and a few weeks later, Speidel, now Lieutenant General, was defending Paris against the Americans and Free French as Chief of Staff, Army Group "B." After ending the war in a Gestapo prison camp, he returned to Paris in 1951 to negotiate the rearmament of Federal Germany. In 1957 he was in Paris again, as the first German Commander of Allied Land Forces in Europe.

for the first time in my life, no traffic tie-up here, no French cops shouting meaninglessly at cars hopelessly blocked. The façade of the Opera
House was hidden behind stacked sandbags. The Café de la Paix
seemed to be just reopening. A lone *garçon* was bringing out some
tables and chairs. German soldiers stood on the terrace grabbing them.

The following day, he observed there was already "open fraternising" between German troops and Parisians:

It seems funny, but every German soldier carries a camera. I saw them
by the thousands today, photographing Notre-Dame, the Arc de
Triomphe, the Invalides. . . . Two newspapers appeared yesterday in
Paris, *La Victoire* (as life's irony would have it) and *Le Matin*. . . .
It (*Le Matin*) has already begun to attack England, to blame England
for France's predicament!

The day after Paris fell, Halder entered in his diary: "Another
important day in military History!" Verdun, the mighty fortress
and spiritual symbol for which hundreds of thousands of German
lives had been spent in vain in 1916, had fallen after twenty-four
hours' fighting and at a cost of less than 200 dead. For the Germans
the campaign was rapidly becoming a pursuit down the highways
of France. Rommel was rushing from Le Havre to Cherbourg. On
the 14th Guderian entered St. Dizier—to find Colonel Balck relax-
ing peacefully on a chair in the market place; by the 15th the 1st
Panzer had captured the old fortified town of Langres and pushed
on to Gray-sur-Saône in the foothills of the Jura. The next day,
Guderian's columns took Besançon and on the 17th (it was his
birthday) Guderian learned that his 29th Motorised Division had
reached the Swiss frontier at Pontarlier. At the same time, Kleist's
armour pushing along the upper Seine had taken Dijon. The
Maginot Line—that exorbitant Great Wall—and the powerful
forces* guarding it were now turned and completely isolated from
the rest of France which the Line had been built to protect. Like
the triangle player in a school orchestra waiting for his solitary bar
of music, the moment had at last arrived for the Maginot Line.
Attacked on all sides, little aware in their deep, sunless caverns
of what was happening in the rest of France, the defenders of
this white elephant of French interwar policy fought on until the

---

* Four armies totalling 400,000 men.

very end. Not one of the major fortresses of the Line actually succumbed.

Mussolini declares war

As if France's cup were not full enough, scavengers, scenting that her wounds were mortal, had moved in. Mussolini had long been champing at the bit to grab a piece of French territory as well as a crumb of the glory. He told Marshal Badoglio: "I need only a few thousand dead to ensure that I have the right to sit at the peace table in the capacity of a belligerent." Several times President Roosevelt had interceded with the Duce, sending firmly worded pleas for Italy to remain neutral. But Hitler's reluctance to have Mussolini as a co-belligerent (with good reason, as it later turned out) carried more weight. Finally, Mussolini could bear the postponements no longer: "I can't just sit back and watch the fight," he exploded at the beginning of June. "When the war is over and victory comes I shall be left empty-handed!" On June 10th, the day the French Government left Paris, Italy declared war on France, bringing forth from Roosevelt the angry condemnation: "The hand that held the dagger has stuck it in the back of his neighbour." Italy's act had little military consequence. After five days of fighting before the armistice was signed, an Italian army of 32 divisions had barely dented France's Alpine front, held by General Olry and three divisions; on the Côte d'Azur the Italian invasion was held up by a French NCO and seven men.*

The soldiers: Last resistance

For the French soldiers, the retreat seemed to go on without end:

You could catch the smell of the earth, the smell of a good June rain [wrote Hans Habe], the smell of sweating horses, the smell of the starched white blouses of the peasant girls. And then your eyes turned back to the flood of limping soldiers, trying in vain to look like men in the presence of the fleeing women. You saw children screaming

---

* A squadron of RAF Wellingtons, sent to Marseilles to bomb northern Italy, found, however, that it also had to contend with the French; lorries were driven onto the airfield to prevent the bombers taking off, in anxiety at possible Italian reprisals against French targets.

desperately or still as death; officers' cars blowing their strident horns and trying to open a path; bright cavalry uniforms on nervous, weary horses; wagons with their sleeping drivers; cannon without ammunition; the whole disordered funeral procession of a disintegrated army.

In these last terrible days, the quality of resistance was mixed. But perhaps it was almost miraculous that, under the circumstances, soldiers could be persuaded to fight at all. At Vierzon, it is said, a tank officer wanting to defend the city was lynched by angry burghers. There were signs of mutiny in some units, while disbanded soldiers were reported to be robbing passers-by in the forests near Paris. There were also revelations that—whether through incompetence or lack of will—France had never reached right down into the depths of her military potential. As the Germans advanced, they came upon huge depots of weapons, ammunition, clothing, fuel and even new tanks which appear, inexplicably, never to have reached the armies. At the same time, Spears on his way to the government's final resting place at Bordeaux wondered angrily at the fact that "nearly all the towns and villages I passed through were full of gaping, idle soldiers. . . . How came it then that we were constantly told that all resources and man-power had been exhausted?" The validity of such reproaches may never be determined. Yet, amid all the adverse accounts from these days of France's expiring agony, one episode at least will always leap forth from French history books in a blaze of glory, the kind of glory belonging almost to a past age. On June 19th, the day Pétain was asking for an armistice, Bock's panzers had reached Saumur on the Loire, the site of the famous cavalry school. Though still under instruction, the young cadets decided that they would not allow the school to fall without a fight. Armed only with training weapons, they held the Saumur bridges for two whole days against panzers—until at last their ammunition ran out.

Doubtless there were other such epics of hopeless heroism, which will never now be recognised.

The politicians: Last resistance

While the German mobile columns were thrusting and tearing into the entrails of France, branching and rebranching like the tendrils of some rampant fungus or a nightmare man-eating plant, a bitter political struggle was being waged within Allied councils. Though forced to be more or less an impotent spectator at this stage of France's agony, Britain's position was a relatively simple one. Every hour that France remained in the fight delayed the German invasion of Britain by an hour—an hour in which Britain would be rearming herself to meet the attack. Should not the undefeated French armies withdraw into a Breton redoubt where —supplied by the Royal Navy—they could hold out until, in due course, new armies from Britain, the Empire and possibly America came to their aid? Or if all hope failed in metropolitan France, would not the French Government and what remained of the Army transfer itself to North Africa, there to recuperate behind the joint shield of the French and British Navies? These were the anxious hopes of Britain. But above all, Churchill and his government were concerned at the fate of the French Fleet. If this were to fall into enemy hands, it would mean the end for Britain—the end for everybody.

On June 11th, Churchill made his fourth visit to France—in response to an urgent summons from Reynaud who had just established himself at Tours. Among those present at this meeting in Briare were, as usual, Pétain and Weygand, and—for the first time—General de Gaulle, whom Reynaud had brought into his Cabinet from the front line in an attempt to strengthen his position against the "softs." With the exception of the calmly phlegmatic de Gaulle, Spears recalls: "The Frenchmen sat with set white faces, their eyes on the table. They looked for all the world like prisoners hauled up from some deep dungeon to hear an inevitable verdict." Churchill at once urged that Paris be defended: "I emphasised the enormous absorbing power of the house-to-house defence of a great city upon an invading army." Weygand countered by demanding that every available British fighter squadron be thrown into the battle. "Here," he said (according to Churchill), "is the decisive point. Now is the decisive moment." No, replied Churchill adamantly; the decisive moment would come when the Luftwaffe hurled itself against the British Isles. This can hardly have been encouraging to French ears; nor any more so Churchill's promise that, if France could hold on until the spring of 1941, Britain would send her 20 to 25 fresh divisions. Spears says, mildly, that he was aware of Reynaud's "suppressed irritation" at the inadequacy of this offer.

Reynaud remarked pointedly: "No doubt history will say the Battle of France was lost through lack of aircraft." "And through lack of tanks," retorted Churchill.

Weygand, having made it clear all along that he would fight his one last battle, was all defeatism: "I am helpless, I cannot intervene for I have no reserves. . . . *C'est la dislocation.*" He repeated what he had told the Army in his proclamation of June 9th: "We have come to the last quarter of an hour."* Weygand concluded by giving his opinion that France might soon have to ask for an armistice. According to Churchill, Reynaud snapped back: "That is a political question." Then Churchill, deeply moved by the agony of the French, erupted into a new explosion of inspired, visionary oratory, once more declaring Britain's determination to fight to the end. Prophetically, he added: "It is possible that the Nazis may dominate Europe, but it will be a Europe in revolt, and in the end it is certain that a regime whose victories are in the main due to its machines will collapse. Machines will one day beat machines." Then, without waiting for an answer to it, he threw in the question that was obviously uppermost in his mind: If France's armies were to succumb, what would the French Navy do?

After the meeting ended, Churchill took aside General Georges, the French general on whom—from prewar days—he placed the greatest reliance. He was shattered to discover that Georges was now largely in agreement with Weygand. At dinner that night Churchill, turning in a friendly manner to Pétain, said:

"Think back! We went through difficult times in 1918 but we got over them. We shall get over these in the same way!"

"In 1918," Pétain replied coldly, "I gave you forty divisions to save the British army. Where are the forty British divisions that we would need to save ourselves today?"

The question was unanswerable. Churchill and his advisers returned to London, anticipating the worst.

---

* Spears records that in this moment of extreme gravity, "fancy came to my rescue. . . . I saw Big Ben with a French General's cap on, marking time at the double, chiming the last quarter of an hour incessantly, at ever accelerating speed, while the dial of the clock became Weygand's face."

The "softs" versus the "hards"

Behind the scenes of the French Government, the struggle between the "softs" and the "hards" raged on. On one side was Reynaud, backed principally by the cold, unconquerable will of Georges Mandel, by Campinchi (Navy) and Marin (Minister of State), and now by de Gaulle; determined to be loyal to the Anglo-French Declaration, to fight to the end in France and continue from North Africa.* Against them were arrayed Weygand, Pétain, Baudouin, Chautemps and Ybarnegaray (both Ministers of State without Portfolio)—and Hélène de Portes—all the time bringing over new recruits to their side. The case of the "softs" was that it was imperative to negotiate at once a separate peace; the validity of the Anglo-French declaration was questionable, because—although (in the views of some) she had pushed France into the war—the British had not upheld their part of the bargain, by keeping back the RAF in Britain and by evacuating the BEF.

To his song about fighting one last battle to "save honour," Weygand had added a new refrain. Haunted by the precedent of the Commune (which he was almost old enough to remember), he now began expressing fears that in the wake of defeat would follow revolution. The prospect clearly seemed to afflict him more than surrender to the Germans.† On the 12th he warned the Cabinet to remember 1917 in Russia, "when Russian soldiers formed *Soviets* in the regiments and in the armies." He urged that Army divisions be kept intact, so as to "maintain order." The following day, Weygand announced that he had received a telegram via the Ministry of the Marine, stating that "serious disturbances have broken out in Paris, and that Thorez has installed himself in the Élysée." President Lebrun jumped, and the rest of the Cabinet were aghast, except for Mandel, who, as Minister of the Interior, declared with crushing certainty: "There are no riots in Paris and M. Thorez, *Monsieur le President,* will not sleep in your bed this evening." But the era of the Front Populaire had

---

* Whether or not a French continuation of the war in North Africa would have been swiftly followed up by a German invasion—and therefore disastrous to the Allies in the long run—lies beyond the scope of the present book.

† This repetition of history is interesting. One of the considerations urging General Trochu and the French leaders to hasten capitulation to the Prussians in January 1871 had been the threat of left-wing revolt in Paris—which, indeed, came to pass.

planted one last paving stone on the way to France's downfall.

For all their disagreements during the interwar years, Pétain was now completely at one with Weygand, both in his fears about "internal order" and in the need to stop the fighting. Ever since Verdun, horror at the losses suffered by "his" French soldiers had left an ineradicable mark upon the eighty-four-year-old Marshal. There is something infinitely pathetic about Pétain in these days. Except when mention of the troops and their suffering would snap him to life, there were long periods when he seemed not to be aware of what was going on. Reynaud notes in his memoirs that after Weygand had delivered his account of the fighting at the Cabinet meeting of June 9th, "Marshal Pétain said nothing. He seemed to be asleep, prostrated. I questioned him. 'Don't you want to express an opinion, Marshal? These gentlemen are anxious to hear you.' 'I've nothing to say,' he replied." Listening to "that thin voice and cough" on the radio, Arthur Koestler was reminded of "a skeleton with a chill" and somehow it was such images of the grave and "the snows of yesteryear" that most struck people on encountering Pétain in these days. Making his first call on the Marshal at his office near the Invalides, Spears was struck by the complete "sense of unreality" there; "it was as dead, as somnolent, as the chambers of a provincial lawyer on a Sunday afternoon." On a later visit in June, the impending fall of Rouen made Spears remark to Pétain that what France needed was another Joan of Arc. The name promptly roused Pétain and he asked Spears whether he had ever read his speech about Joan of Arc ("When was it, in 1937, '38?"). Bringing down a bound volume of typescript from a bookshelf, he proceeded to read out the complete speech in a dull monotone. Spears was unable to recall a single sentence; but what he did remember "was the terrible sadness I felt as I watched him, a sadness now based on pity for a very old man for whom I had, till so recently, felt the deepest affection and regard. He was infinitely pathetic in his childish satisfaction as he read." Even more saddening, Spears reflected, was the enormous influence Pétain wielded in France; what French man or woman in these days, he wondered, was not saying, "He will save us as he did at Verdun." The next day Spears warned Churchill that he was certain the Marshal would never leave France; there would be no question of his following any French Government into exile.

General Spears in his illuminating, vivid account of this page of history speaks of Reynaud staggering not only under the burden of his own responsibilities, but "the additional cross of the entourage with which he had handicapped himself. He was like those savage warriors who, not contented with the wounds inflicted by the enemy, gash themselves with knives." The source of perhaps the most crippling wounds Reynaud received from his entourage was the one which in these terrible days should have lent him the most comfort: his mistress, Hélène de Portes. The same ruthless, relentless energy she had once applied to pushing her chevalier to the top rung of the political ladder was now devoted to the cause of obtaining an early separate peace. Following the government to Tours, then to Bordeaux, the Comtesse de Portes was everywhere, plaguing the Prime Minister incessantly, without mercy, in a manner that astounded the British officials who came in contact with her. Paul Baudouin, who was completely her man and came to represent her will within the Cabinet, wrote with the utmost restrained chivalry: "If she acted as the controller of the Cabinet her one desire was to save the country by defending and fortifying the man she admired." Certainly the impression one gets from those others who were present is that Reynaud was never for a moment left alone, never allowed to make a decision or an appointment without Hélène de Portes being party to it. In the middle of deliberations of the War Cabinet she would ring him on his private telephone; if in despair he should disconnect it, she would summon ushers to take in written messages to him; and finally she would often burst into the council chamber herself. On one occasion at Tours, Spears (who admittedly was no devotee of the Countess) was astonished to see her in the courtyard of Reynaud's residence, clad "in a dressing gown over red pyjamas, directing the traffic from the steps of the main entrance." This was relatively harmless; but on another occasion Spears also found her intercepting one of Reynaud's stenographers and reading over his shoulder a most important and top-secret communication from Churchill.* Again, when a secret telegram from the French Embassy in London had been missing for some hours, Reynaud's *chef de cabinet* from the

---

* This was, in fact, his eleventh-hour proposal for an indissoluble Franco-British Union.

Quai d'Orsay, Roland de Margerie,* eventually produced it with the hushed whisper, "It was in Madame de Portes's bed." In Spears's opinion, as he left France, it was Reynaud's mistress who did him the greatest harm, because she "had imposed on him as collaborators the men who were now his bitterest opponents."

The breaking of Reynaud

Certainly she must greatly have added to the physical and nervous strain imposed on Reynaud in these last days. By June 12th, Reynaud was beginning to break. That night he was persuaded by the "softs" to telephone Churchill and ask him to fly to Tours, once again, to discuss the prospect that France would conclude a separate peace with Germany. The following afternoon Churchill arrived, accompanied by Halifax and Beaverbrook. According to Churchill, over lunch Baudouin "began at once in his soft, silky manner about the hopelessness of the French resistance." Only if the United States declared war on Germany might it now be possible for France to continue. After lunch, Churchill was received at the Prefecture by Mandel, who in marked contrast to Baudouin was "energy and defiance personified. . . . He was a ray of sunshine. He had a telephone in each hand, through which he was constantly giving orders and decisions. His ideas were simple: fight on to the end in France, in order to cover the largest possible movement into Africa." Then Reynaud arrived. The meeting began with the French declaring that the position of the Army was desperate. Now Reynaud put the fateful question to the British Prime Minister: Would Britain agree that France, having nothing further to contribute to the common cause, should be released from the joint declaration and be permitted to negotiate a separate peace? Spears, watching him closely, noted that Reynaud no longer mentioned the possibility of fighting on in Africa: "He was a very different man from the cheerful, determined little chap of a few hours ago. For a moment I saw him as a ventriloquist's dummy voicing the views—of whom? Pétain? Weygand? Could it be Madame de Portes?"

Meanwhile—according to Élie Bois—the Countess was trying

---

* It was hardly surprising that de Margerie was in the habit of characterising her, uncharitably, as "ugly, *mal soignée*, dirty, nasty and half-demented, and a sore trial to me."

to get into the conference room. Prevented from doing so, she grew impatient and sent for Baudouin: "Tell Paul that we must give up—give up. We must make an end of it. There must be an armistice! Tell Paul so, won't you?—from me. I insist on it."

In response to Reynaud's agonising question, Churchill expressed his understanding of France's predicament. In no case would Britain waste time in reproaches and recriminations. But that was a different matter from consenting to release France from her pledge. He added, however, a solemn promise that was to be fulfilled five hard years later: "If England won the war France would be restored in her dignity and her greatness." As a final suggestion, Churchill urged that Reynaud send one last new appeal to the President of the United States, with which Britain would identify herself. Reynaud agreed, but made it clear how grave matters would be in the event of an unfavourable reply. With that Churchill returned to London; it was the last time that he would set foot on French soil for four years. After the meeting, Reynaud was violently reproached for raising the separate peace issue by Mandel and the Presidents of the Senate and Chamber of Deputies, Jeanneney and Herriot, the latter in tears. In the meantime Baudouin was insidiously putting it about that Churchill had released France from her engagement. Later that evening when Spears saw Reynaud, he was struck by how "ghastly" he looked; "with a completely unnatural expression, still and white." By the end of that day, he was convinced that "the possibility of France remaining in the war had almost disappeared."

The plea to America

During the small hours of June 14th, Reynaud dispatched his appeal to President Roosevelt, making it dramatically clear that "unless you can give France firmly to understand, in the hours ahead, that the United States will enter the war in the very near future, the destiny of the world will change." In other words, France would capitulate. It was the last of a series of communications—ranging from the beseeching to the admonishing—addressed to the President by the British and French Premiers. At the beginning of June, Roosevelt and General Marshall had rushed through a deal whereby Britain purchased some six hundred freight cars of First War arms and ammunition—virtually everything the U.S. Army could spare at the time—but none of it

was to reach Europe before France fell. In harbouring any anticipation whatever that the United States would instantaneously
send him "clouds of planes" or ever declare war on Hitler, Reynaud was under a hopeless delusion.* The fact was that America
—no more prepared to play a role in Europe than she had done
during the past twenty years—had no planes to send; and with a
presidential election coming up in November, no politician alive
could have brought America into the war that June. Roosevelt's
response to Reynaud's appeal was bound to be negative.

The last quarter of an hour

On June 14th, the day the Germans entered Paris, the Government of the Third Republic departed for its final seat at Bordeaux.
Reynaud was clearly reaching the end of his tether and seemed
to have lost all his old vigour in dealing with the "softs." He kept
on repeating that everything depended on Roosevelt's answer to
his telegram. He would try one last ploy, however, within the
confines of his Cabinet. That afternoon he proposed to Weygand
that, like the Dutch, France should seek a military capitulation,
"binding only the Army but leaving the government freedom of
action." Weygand was outraged. "I refuse," he declared indig-
nantly, "to bespatter our colours with this shame!" But this was
a political decision, beyond the prerogative of a Commander-in-
Chief, and—as Churchill points out—Reynaud would have been
within his rights to have dismissed Weygand. It was a decision,
however, that he no longer had the strength or the will to take.
Next Camille Chautemps suggested a compromise solution: Why
not ask the Germans what their conditions of armistice would
be, remaining free to reject them? The proposition had a dangerously Faustian smell about it; said Churchill, "It was not of
course possible to embark on this slippery slope and stop."

When the Chautemps proposal was relayed to London, Churchill's reply was that Britain would give her consent for France to

_____

* For this, the American ambassador in Paris, William Bullitt, must be held
greatly to blame. In an age when ambassadors carried weight and were more than
merely the post-office clerks they tend to be today, Bullitt appears to have sinned
by misleading both his own country and France as to the true situation in the
other; Washington was persuaded by Bullitt that France's fighting capacity was
much greater than it was, while through him the French Government was led to
expect far greater aid than could possibly have been forthcoming from the
United States at that time.

ascertain the terms of an armistice *"provided, but only provided, that the French Fleet is sailed forthwith for British harbours pending negotiations."** Britain, in her resolve to continue the war, would in no way associate herself with such an enquiry.

That evening Reynaud received Roosevelt's answer. Spears was with him when it arrived: "As he read it he grew still paler, his face contracted. . . . 'Our appeal has failed,' he said in a small toneless voice, 'the Americans will not declare war.' "

Meanwhile, in England de Gaulle, who had flown there on the 14th to ask for shipping to transport troops to Africa to continue the fight there, had impressed upon Churchill the need for some "dramatic move" to keep his government in the war. In the words of Churchill, de Gaulle "suggested that a proclamation of the indissoluble union of the French and British peoples would serve the purpose." So, on the afternoon of Sunday, June 16th, such a "Declaration of Union," of staggering historical implications, was duly drafted. De Gaulle then dictated it over the telephone in person to Reynaud.

With him in Bordeaux, Spears records that as Reynaud put down the telephone "he was transfigured with joy, and my old friendship for him surged out in a wave of appreciation at his response, for he was happy with a great happiness in the belief that France would now remain in the war." A Cabinet meeting was immediately called. But Reynaud's colleagues did not share his elation. From the front, reports had arrived that the Germans were at the gates of Besançon and Dijon. Baudouin claims that the French ministers were stunned by the British offer: "It in no way satisfied our expectations. It did not loosen the stranglehold on the country." Chautemps declared that he "did not want France to become a Dominion." In the middle of the discussion, an usher entered with a cryptic note ("I hope that you are not going to play at being Isabella of Bavaria")† hastily scribbled by Hélène de Portes, giving Reynaud the last orders he would receive from her as Prime Minister of France. Suddenly the tough little Frenchman with the mandarin face collapsed. Physically and mentally

---

* Churchill's italics.

† Isabella was Queen of France from 1389 to 1435; she gave her daughter Catherine in marriage to King Henry V of England, whom she recognised as heir to the King of France, and is generally held responsible for the surrender of France to the English; Isabella was buried, without honours, at St. Denis.

exhausted, he could no longer stand up to the "softs." No vote was taken on the British "Declaration of Union" proposal; Churchill's telegrams concerning the safety of the French Fleet were not even presented to the Cabinet. Reynaud announced his intention to tender his resignation to the President. He would propose that Marshal Pétain be sent for.

At about eleven o'clock that night, President Lebrun relates that he told the eighty-four-year-old Marshal:

"Well, there it is. Form a government." Without hesitation the Marshal opened his brief case with a characteristic gesture, showed me a list and said to me: "Here is my Government." I must say that, despite the deep sadness of the moment all the same I felt a small ray of comfort. I recalled those difficult negotiations about forming administrations . . . and here I had one given me ready made . . . I thought that this was excellent.

Two hours later Pétain called for the Spanish ambassador, Señor de Lequérica, and requested him to approach the Germans about an armistice. Later on that morning of June 17th, Spears—his mission ended—prepared to fly back to England. By a prearranged plan, de Gaulle (only just returned from his own journey to England) came to the airstrip, affecting to see Spears off. After the engines had started up, Spears reached out a hand as if to say good-bye and yanked de Gaulle into the plane. Georges Mandel was less fortunate; attempting to get to North Africa and set up a "government in exile" there with other leading politicians among the remaining "hards," he was arrested and returned to France. Four years later he was murdered by Vichy *Milices*. De Gaulle alone "carried with him," said Churchill, "in this small aeroplane, the honour of France."

In France, the news that Pétain had requested an armistice was greeted by emotions of widespread relief; "at last, the nightmare is about to end" was the common reaction. Crowds of refugees gathered around the government buildings in Bordeaux to cheer the old Marshal. People wept publicly in grief and in gratitude.

In Germany, the immense events of the past weeks seem to have provoked—at least, on the surface—astonishingly little excitement. At the end of May, Shirer recalled three Germans betting him that the Wehrmacht would be in London within three weeks,

but a week later—as the battle round Dunkirk was about to end—
he admitted that the scene in Berlin "confounds me." Strolling
down the Kurfürstendamm in the evening, Shirer found it

jammed with people meandering along pleasantly. The great sidewalk
cafés on this broad, tree-lined avenue were filled with thousands, chat-
ting quietly over their ersatz coffee or their ice-cream. I even noticed
several smartly dressed women. Today, being the Sabbath and a warm
and sunny June day, tens of thousands of people, mostly in family
groups, betook themselves to the woods or the lakes on the outskirts
of the city. The Tiergarten, I noticed, also was thronged. Everyone
had that lazy, idle, happy-go-lucky Sunday holiday air.

Shirer was equally taken aback at the lack of elation the normally
excitable Berliners displayed on hearing the unbelievable news
that Paris had fallen. The city took it

as phlegmatically as it has taken everything else in this war. Later
I went to Halensee for a swim, it being warm and I feeling the need of
a little relaxation. It was crowded, but I overheard no one discussing
the news. Out of five hundred people, three bought extras when the
newsboys rushed in, shouting the news.

He added: "It would be very wrong though to conclude that the
taking of Paris has not stirred something very deep in the hearts of
most Germans. It was always a wish-dream of millions here."

21

Aftermath

Can it be that France has had her day like Athens, Rome, Spain or Portugal in the past? Is it Germany's turn now? No. Our virtues and our culture which only twenty years ago proved so strong and full of life, have not been killed by a mere handful of politicians.
—MAJOR D. BARLONE, *A French Officer's Diary*

There are no Allies any more. There remains only one enemy: England!
—Wehrmacht Communiqué, June 25, 1940

FRENCH SIGN PEACE TREATY: WE'RE IN THE FINALS.
—Newspaper vendor's sign in London, 1940

The clearing at Rethondes: Hitler's revenge

SHORTLY BEFORE noon on June 20th, Pétain received radio instructions from the Germans for the dispatch of the French armistice delegation. They were to present themselves "at the Loire bridge near Tours" early that evening. There would be a temporary cease-fire in the area. After some argument, the unfortunate General Huntziger, erstwhile commander of the Second Army, had been selected to lead the delegation. Reluctantly he had accepted. His orders were to break off talks instantly if the Germans called for the surrender of the French Fleet or the occupation of any colonial territory.

So great was the clutter of refugees and military traffic on the roads that Huntziger and his convoy did not reach the appointed rendezvous until late that night. A German escort then whisked them, with no time for sleep or a proper meal, to Paris where they arrived at 7:30 A.M. They still had no clue as to the site chosen by the Germans for the cease-fire negotiations. Then, after only a few hours' pause, they were driven on to Compiègne some 50 miles northeast of Paris. Finally, just after three o'clock that afternoon, the cavalcade halted at the clearing in the forest at Rethondes. There stood the historic *wagon-lit* where, in November 1918, Marshal Foch and Weygand himself had received the defeated German emissaries. With characteristic efficiency, German Army engineers had hacked down the wall of the museum housing the railway coach and brought it out to where it had stood twenty-two years earlier. A large Swastika was draped over the monument to the 1918 Armistice. The cycle of revenge could not be more complete. France had chosen as the setting for the final humbling of Germany in 1919 the Versailles Hall of Mirrors where, in the arrogant exaltation of 1871, King Wilhelm of Prussia had proclaimed himself Kaiser; so now Hitler's choice for the scene of his moment of supreme triumph was to be that of France's in 1918.

When Huntziger and his co-delegates, dazed and weary from the journey, realised they were being led to Foch's *wagon-lit,* they were deeply shocked. Together with his service chiefs, Ribbentrop and Hess, Hitler had already arrived at the clearing. In warm sunshine he strode up to the great granite block and meticulously read the inscription on it:

HERE ON THE ELEVENTH OF NOVEMBER 1918 SUC-
CUMBED THE CRIMINAL PRIDE OF THE GERMAN
PEOPLE . . .

Fifty yards away, Shirer was intently studying Hitler's expression through binoculars:

It is afire with scorn, anger, hate, revenge, triumph. He steps off the monument and contrives to make even this gesture a masterpiece of contempt. . . . Suddenly . . . he throws his whole body into harmony with his mood. He swiftly snaps his hands on his hips, arches his shoulders, plants his feet wide apart. It is a magnificent gesture of defiance, of burning contempt for this place now and all that it has stood for in the twenty-two years since it witnessed the humbling of the German Empire.

Then Hitler led the way into the railway coach.

After the French delegation had seated itself, Keitel began

proceedings by reading out a brief preamble, explaining that the site had been chosen as "an act of reparatory justice." France was now defeated; in her armistice terms, Germany's chief aims were to prevent any resumption of hostilities and to provide herself with the requisite conditions for pursuing the war against Britain. When Keitel had finished, at 3:30, Hitler got up, gave a Nazi salute and marched out to the strains of "Deutschland über Alles." Keitel now handed the French delegates copies of the German terms. No discussion was to be allowed. Huntziger and his team returned to Paris late that night, and over an infuriatingly bad telephone line relayed the armistice terms to Weygand in Bordeaux. To Pétain, Weygand described the terms as "harsh but not dishonouring." All through the night and most of the next day Pétain's Cabinet debated the terms. An extension of the deadline was granted, ill-humouredly, by Keitel. Finally, at 8:50 P.M. on Saturday, June 22nd, the armistice was signed. The shooting would officially end at 35 minutes past midnight on the 25th. In a voice seized with emotion, Huntziger—addressing Keitel—said he hoped that, "as a soldier," the German leader would understand how onerous this moment was for him. Keitel then declared, "It is honourable for the victor to do honour to the vanquished." He asked those present to stand in silence for a minute, in honour of the fallen on both sides. "Military honour," commented Weygand, "was safe."

As the delegates emerged from the *wagon-lit*, those observing outside in the clearing felt a drop of rain fall. The skies had become heavily overcast. Soon the drops grew to a violent storm. The few black flags hung out by French householders drooped limp and sodden. The wonderful days of sunshine, "Goering's weather," that extraordinary run of good fortune which had so assisted the Germans in their conquest, had at last broken with a vengeance. In the darkening sky lay auguries for the future; Britain was not yet suing for peace; and in exactly one year to the day, Hitler would be sending his victorious legions to their doom in Russia.

Immediately the armistice had been signed, German engineers prepared to move Foch's *wagon-lit* in triumph to Berlin.* With a barbarity worthy of Genghis Khan, Hitler decreed that—except-

---

* Where it was later destroyed in an RAF air raid.

ing Foch's statue—the site should be totally razed. He then set off on a tour of First World War battlefields, together with two old comrades from the company in which he had served as a corporal, taking in some of the Maginot Line forts—like any German tourist—before returning to Berlin to organise the celebrations that would suitably commemorate this astonishing victory. For Hitler, as for many of his soldiers, the war was over. France, the arch-enemy, was prostrate at last; Britain no longer counted, she would fall like a plum from a tree in due course. Russia did not exist; America did not exist. Ever since that day of humiliation at Versailles, it was France alone that had obsessed German thoughts. Karl Heinz Mende summed them up well when, writing home about the armistice, he said; "The great battle in France is now ended. It lasted twenty-six years. . . ."

The price

What had been the cost of this earth-shaking last round of the great battle? When the figures were added up, during the six weeks' fighting German casualties amounted to:

Killed	27,074
Wounded	111,034
Missing	18,384

Thus—despite repeated Allied and neutral reports of hecatombs of German casualties—the overall total of just over 150,000 was equivalent to not much more than a third of the number of men Germany lost at Verdun in 1916, in one single battle of the First World War. During the three decisive weeks up to Dunkirk, German casualties (as claimed by the Wehrmacht) were reported to have totalled approximately what Britain suffered during the first day of the Somme alone. Even the losses of its elite forma-tions which had been in the forefront of the battle were com-paratively light (at least, by First War standards); Rommel's 7th Panzer, for example, lost a total of 2,273 in killed and wounded; the Grossdeutschland Regiment, 1,108 (including 221 killed) out of its complement of 3,900 men; and the losses of one of the most constantly engaged infantry divisions—the 3rd —had totalled no more than 1,649. On the other hand, as the cost of the Wehrmacht's enormously successful doctrine of "leading from the front," a relatively high proportion of the German dead—5 percent—were officers. The strain imposed by the tempo of the campaign also exacted its casualties; one was Colonel Werner, commander of the 31st Panzer Regiment (5th Panzer Division), who died of a heart attack shortly after the armistice.

On the Allied side, French losses during the six weeks' campaign are estimated* at somewhere in the region of 90,000 dead, 200,000 wounded and 1.9 million in prisoners and missing. British total casualties came to 68,111; Belgian 23,350 and Dutch 9,779. While the Luftwaffe lost 1,284 planes, RAF losses amounted to 931, of which 477 were priceless fighters. French losses in the air are difficult to assess. One reasonable French figure puts the number of planes lost in combat at 560, of which 235 were destroyed on the ground. It was months before the victorious Germans could even count up the vast piles of captured war booty of all descriptions. Among the guns taken were some 7,000 French 75s of First War vintage, many of them only brought out of retirement in the last desperate hours of the battle; nevertheless, slightly modified by the Wehrmacht, four summers later they would be used with deadly effect to halt British and American tanks landing on the Normandy beaches.

Tears and celebrations

At 35 minutes past midnight on the 25th, the cannon ceased firing. Something like the silence of the grave descended on France. Already the endless lines of weary, footsore, broken-spirited refugees had begun to retrace their footsteps, to find out what had happened to their homes. Foodstuffs were in seriously short supply, transportation and other public services had broken down; but in some respects, French life reverted—at least temporarily—to normality with surprising speed, just as it had done after the defeat of 1870. The day after the armistice was concluded, a German war correspondent (Stackelberg) lunching in a restaurant in Lyon was astonished to observe a bourgeois French family at the next table going through the important ritual of their Sunday lunch as if nothing had happened in the world. They spent approximately half an hour "bent over the menu, dis-

---

* Because of the confusion of the collapse, there are discrepancies here.

cussing the food, and then at length and with great seriousness discussed city gossip. It struck me as remarkable that their thoughts on this day should not assume other lines, but the meal was something very important for them." Returning to Paris from Compiègne, William Shirer was intrigued to find that along the Seine "the fishermen were dangling their lines from the bank, as always," and thought: "Surely this will go on to the end of Paris, to the end of time." Ilya Ehrenburg also watched Paris coming back to life, in an implausible way: "The Germans bought souvenirs, smutty postcards, pocket dictionaries in the little shops. Notices appeared in restaurants: *'Ici on parle allemand.'* Prostitutes lisped *'Mein Süsser.'*" In the countryside Simone de Beauvoir registered surprise at the conquerors' good behaviour; they

did not cut off children's hands; they paid for their drinks and the eggs they bought on the farms, and spoke politely. . . . As I was reading in a field two soldiers approached me. They spoke a little clumsy French, and assured me of their friendly feelings towards the French people; it was the English and the Jews who had brought us to this sorry pass.

By and large, the German troops appeared to be kind and helpful. The Gestapo, the *Sicherheitsdienst,* and all the apparatus of Nazi terror had yet to arrive.

Meanwhile, in England, once it was apparent that Hitler was not going to follow up Dunkirk with an immediate invasion, the shock of defeat turned to a kind of relief that, somehow, strangely enough, life had at least become simpler. King George VI spoke for many when he wrote to his mother: "Personally, I feel happier now that we have no allies to be polite to and to pamper." There was, after all, something to be said for being "in the finals"—to quote the headline which one Cockney newsvendor chalked up on his stand.

For the victorious German troops in France, the first summer days after the armistice indeed seemed like a halcyon time of insouciant rapture. They clambered up the Eiffel Tower, gazed down at Napoleon's tomb, clicking cameras everywhere, like tourists of any country at any time. On the wreckage-strewn Channel beaches, they kicked off their jackboots to paddle in the warm water, gazing across at a defiant but impotent enemy. As the cease-fire came into force, the ascetic Halder noted from his desk, "Now begins the administrative work." War production was cut back, and there was talk of massive demobilisation of the army. It was also a time of mutual congratulation, and of thanksgiving and celebration, rather than of preparation for any further fighting. Even the icy Molotov—while reaching out with one hand for the Baltic States and the Rumanian province of Bessarabia, as Russia's self-awarded "tip" for her benevolent neutrality— had sent to Hitler "the warmest congratulations of the Soviet Government on the splendid success of the German Wehrmacht." On July 17, the Grossdeutschland paraded in triumph through Paris, to hold a thanksgiving service in Notre-Dame.* The next day in Berlin, a victory parade marched through the Brandenburger Tor—for the first time since 1871. Then, on the 19th, Hitler in a solemn ceremony at the Kroll Opera House promoted twelve of his triumphant generals to the rank of field marshal.† Such an inflation of military pomp had never been seen during the time of the Kaiser; but neither had such victories.

Shadows: The flaws of victory

Yet already there were shadows. As young Lieutenant Mende wrote home: "I feel full of peace within this enemy country, and yet also I feel a certain anxiety about this not entirely finished war." When in the course of the Berlin victory celebrations Hitler remarked to his sober-faced financial wizard, "Well, Herr Schacht, what do you say now?" Schacht, sibyl-like had simply replied, "May God protect you!" Meanwhile, thousands of miles away in Chicago, Roosevelt was being nominated by the Democratic party to run for a third term. For June 28th, the twenty-first anniversary of the signature of the Versailles Treaty, Hitler had planned a further act of humiliation for prostrated France by holding a massive parade in front of the palace, followed by an oration delivered inside the Hall of Mirrors. But it was cancelled;

---

* It subsequently received orders from Keitel banning all such religious services.
† These were: Keitel (the OKW Chief of Staff); Brauchitsch (Army C-in-C); Rundstedt, Bock and Leeb (the three Army Group commanders); Reichenau, List, Kluge, and Witzleben (Army commanders); and Milch, Kesselring and Sperrle from the Luftwaffe. Conspicuously absent from these so honoured was Halder; Shirer, watching the scene, thought him the "saddest figure" there.

there were fears (which even Goering could not allay) that the RAF might also attend. Meanwhile, it was not until June 17th— the day of the Grossdeutschland's thanksgiving ceremony in Notre-Dame—that the OKH issued its first orders for "Operation Sea Lion"—the invasion of England. Then, on July 29th, Jodl gathered together some of the senior OKW staff officers in a rail- way restaurant car, ensured that all windows and doors were closed, and informed them that Hitler had it in mind to attack Russia the following spring.

Soon Hitler's astounding achievements in France would turn to dust as the diamond brilliance of *Sichelschnitt* was shattered by the fatal flaw latent within it. In his appreciation drawn up for the Kaiser, which prepared the ground for the German attack on Verdun in 1916, Falkenhayn, the German Chief of Staff, had recognised Britain to be Germany's principal enemy. By "bleeding white" the French Army at Verdun, he had argued, Britain's "best sword would be knocked out of her hand." The U-boat blockade would do the rest, in due course. Now Hitler had suc- ceeded where Falkenhayn and all the Kaiser's generals had failed. Britain's "best sword" lay shattered on the ground. But Hitler and the planners of genius who had created *Sichelschnitt* had in fact thought no further ahead than Falkenhayn; no contingency plan had been prepared whereby a tottering Britain might be invaded immediately after success had been achieved in France. By mid-July when the first OKH plan was drafted it was already too late. The Germans had missed the bus, as Chamberlain would have said. The two great errors of the otherwise perfect *Sichel- schnitt*—this original fault of high strategy, and the tactical fault of the May 24th Halt Order which allowed the BEF to escape at Dunkirk—in conjunction added up to one thing: Britain would remain at war, inviolate. And as long as Britain was there, it was inevitable that sooner or later the immense power of the United States would be brought in too. But, like so many of his generation of Germans, their vision blinkered by the memories of '14–'18 and the shame of Versailles, Hitler could only see France and "the last decisive contest" which would have to be fought there.

In fact, as one now sees it in the perspective of time, Hitler's astonishing triumph over France was to be directly the source of his greatest disaster. After France, the mighty warrior nation which had defeated Germany in 1918, had been overthrown with such ease, what nation on earth could stand up to the Wehrmacht? So Hitler in 1941 was convinced that—while reducing his war production and demobilising part of his forces, and without furnishing his cohorts with any winter equipment—he could knock out Russia in one lightning campaign. But, although in many ways their doctrine of war may initially have been as faulty as that of the French, the Russians would be able to make a retreat equivalent to a French withdrawal from Sedan across the Pyrenees and down to Saragossa, before launching any major counter-offensive. What might even Gamelin and Weygand have achieved, had they but disposed of such space over which to manoeuvre and behind which to form fresh armies? Even more lethal to the Germans than their self-assurance derived from the easy successes in France was the supreme reliance Hitler now placed in his own infallibility. He saw himself as having been proved right in his audacity over the cautiousness of his professional advisers during the planning of *Sichelschnitt:* and, in retrospect, he saw how wrong had been the strategic assessment in battle of even those like Rundstedt whose judgement he trusted most. (In his unquenchable animosity towards the OKH, he could not admit that it was in fact not he but Halder who—during the campaign—had been right.) So Hitler became less and less inclined to accept the advice of his military experts, and more and more to rely on his own intuition, until finally it led him to the point of no return at Stalingrad.

French post-mortems

For four grim years, France disappears from the stage of war. "The choice is always between Verdun and Dachau," wrote a severe French critic of 1940,* Jean Dutourd. Unable to face the prospects of another Verdun in 1940, it was indeed Dachau that became France's fate. In their hundreds of thousands Frenchmen were shipped off to concentration camps or to slave labour inside the Reich. With superb psychological cunning the Nazis divided the conquered country geographically in two, thereby imposing yet another enduring source of division upon those that already plagued France. In the act of liberation, her old and new Allies

---

* "The Taxis of the Marne."

would inflict at least as much damage upon France's cities and countryside as had the Luftwaffe, and the prostrate nation would have little say in the conduct of its redemption. A proud people could hardly be subjected to greater humiliation. But there were many Frenchmen who did not agree that the final battle to save national "honour," which so obsessed General Weygand, had yet been fought. Using every device and subterfuge they slipped off to join de Gaulle's Free French in England, or the "Normandie-Niemen Squadron" in Russia; later, with Anglo-American support, the Resistance would rekindle the flame of "honour" inside France itself.

Who, and what, were responsible for France's catastrophe? Could the game have been played differently? At what point did disaster become irremediable? The questions are still asked and reasked, and the answers become no simpler with time. But postmortems are irresistible. The Riom Trials, held under the auspices of the Vichy Government in 1942, attempted to saddle the blame for the lost war upon earlier French Governments. The questions asked were loaded; no official record was made of the proceedings; the "trials" were finally adjourned and then dropped. Equally inconclusive and incomplete were the 2,500 pages of the "Serre Report," based on the findings of the French official Commission of Inquiry which sat from 1947 and 1951. It did its best to disculpate the politicians of the period; but it could not even agree as to whether it was the break-through on Corap's or Huntziger's front which precipitated the military break-through on the Meuse. However, as this book has tried to show, more than any individual or set of individuals was to blame. Two doctrines and two philosophies and the past events of a generation were involved. Since the *jour de gloire* of July 14, 1919, almost every throw of the dice had turned out to France's disfavour and Germany's advantage. Upon Hitler's reoccupation of the Rhineland, unchallenged, in 1936, the road to disaster was clearly signposted. Three years later France went reluctantly to war, while she was still herself close to a state of civil war; with morale (as Mandel admitted to Spears during the last days of defeat) "sapped by the feeling of the last twenty years that there would be no war because France could not stand another bleeding like that of 1914"; and—in the words of Weygand—with a French Army of 1918 facing a Wehrmacht of 1939.

Before the decisive battle itself opened, there were two other chronological milestones on France's road to disaster. In August 1939, the signature of the Ribbentrop–Molotov Nonaggression Pact effectively removed any prospect of Germany's military potential being split by a war on two fronts; a month later, this was compounded by France's unwillingness to come to the aid of her solitary Polish ally, by launching an offensive in the west. Thus, from October 1939 onwards, France had no option but to remain on the defensive and wait to be attacked. When the attack came the following May, the preponderance of strength—with all factors taken into account—was immeasurably greater on the German side than at any time during the First World War. Therefore, there is a fatalistic view which regards the Battle of France as having been lost even before it was begun. Might France still have been defeated even if the Germans had not marched to the masterly blueprint of *Sichelschnitt*, if they had simply utilised a crude replay of the Schlieffen Plan of 1914? Possibly.

On the other hand, in war Fate contains many surprises. For all its impressiveness, the Wehrmacht of 1940 was a more fragile instrument, less consistently solid throughout, than the Kaiser's Army of 1914; nor did it have the same weight of resources behind it. On almost every occasion when Allied troops in 1940 came up against the ordinary infantry divisions which comprised the great mass of the Wehrmacht, they held their own. Acutely limited in their fuel supplies, the panzers could not have fought a protracted campaign without a major reorganisation. Then there is the prime consideration of the steadfastness of the German High Command, about which much has already been said. It is always held that the Younger Moltke lost the First War on the Marne because his nerve failed. Yet there were times during both the Norwegian and the French campaign when the German High Command of 1940 revealed itself to be potentially little less impressionable than Moltke. What, then, if the steel tip provided by the few panzer and motorised divisions could have been blunted, the nerves of the German High Command shaken by one sharp reverse? Might the German onslaught have been brought to a temporary halt, perhaps long enough for the Allies to reorganise their forces into a more coherent defence? The impact Rundstedt's Ardennes offensive of 1944 made upon the Allies indeed suggests how even such a last-gasp effort (and against a far greater relative superiority than the Germans possessed in May 1940) can at least win time.

It was *time* that was the vital element which—more than weapons, even perhaps more than morale—France most lacked in 1940. After the battle had been engaged, the afternoon of May 15th—the sixth day of fighting—marks the moment of almost certain military defeat for France. This was the decisive day that saw the failure of the first French counterattacks, to which had been dedicated the main weight of her armoured reserves, and the day on which it was clear that the Germans could not be prevented from breaking out of their Meuse bridgeheads. For the French armour to have concentrated for a blow effective enough to have halted the panzers on the 15th, the necessary dispositions would have had to be decreed by the 12th. But with the essential French reserves dispersed as they were in the line-up for the Dyle-Breda Plan's advance into Belgium, this would have proved virtually impossible. The French ripostes were almost bound to be too late. The speed with which panzer warfare developed in 1940 certainly proved the validity of the dictum of Moltke the Elder: "*One* fault only in the initial deployment of an Army cannot be made good during the whole course of the campaign." On top of this must be added the tremendous significance of the Luftwaffe's supremacy in the air; which (although later in the war the Germans were able to conduct an imposing defence in the teeth of even greater Allied tactical air superiority) constituted a decisive factor at this stage of the Second World War. Apart from the lethal effect of the close-support Stukas, the Luftwaffe's far-ranging medium bombers were what finally denied the French High Command the time it needed to commit its reserves to battle, at the right moment and the right place.

The odds against France's opposing *Sichelschnitt* in 1940 with any successful defence and even allowing for the element of the unexpected—remain enormously high. When all is said and done, the strategic brilliance of the German plan and the tactical skill with which it was executed will always make it one of the classic campaigns of history.

What happened to them? The Germans

So immense were the universal consequences of the Fall of France that one tends to lose sight of the leading actors in the tragedy. On the German side, there were countless thousands of all ranks who, like Rommel's two ace commanders, Rothenburg* and Bismarck,† either fell later in the war or else ended in disgrace with the Nazi hierarchy. Rommel's own subsequent career is well known: the legendary hero of the desert war yields to the disillusioned field marshal conducting a hopeless defence of northern France against the Allied invasion of 1944; and finally to the critic of the regime forced to take poison or be shot by the Gestapo. Curiously enough, of all the commanders of the ten panzer divisions which proved so decisive in France, Rommel alone later rose to great prominence; Kirchner, for instance, who had led the enormously successful 1st Panzer, ended the war as a corps commander. On the other hand, his junior, the tough and ruthless Lieutenant Colonel Hermann Balck, was to become a full general commanding an Army Group in France (1944–45) —one of a handful of Germans to be awarded the highest grade of the Ritterkreuz decoration.‡

Guderian, promoted colonel general in September 1940, was given command of the Second Panzer Army, which he led in the battle for Moscow during the autumn of 1941. After the failure of the campaign, he fell under a shadow and was transferred to the reserve. The strain of the past years had left its mark and in 1942 he began to suffer from heart trouble. Following the bomb *Attentat* of July 1944, Guderian—always politically acceptable to Hitler—was given the job once held by Halder as Chief of the OKH General Staff, until in March 1945 he too was finally dismissed. In poor health in his last years, he died in 1954, aged sixty-six. His portrait still hangs in a place of honour in the barracks of panzer units of the present-day Bundeswehr. Kleist led the First Panzer Army into the Ukraine in 1941, and became another of Hitler's field marshals. Manstein was also promoted field marshal and justly came to be rated as Germany's ablest field commander; he fell into disgrace with the Führer on the same day as Kleist—March 30, 1944. Rundstedt led Army Group South at the start of the Russian campaign in 1941, and it was he who (reluctantly) commanded the last German offensive of the war— the Ardennes offensive of winter 1944–45—over terrain which he

---

* Killed in Russia.
† Killed in the Western Desert, once again fighting under Rommel.
‡ "Knight's Cross with Oak Leaves, Swords and Diamonds."

knew so well from 1940. After the war he was imprisoned in England, but released in 1949. He died, aged seventy-eight, in 1953. Hitler's *bête noire,* Brauchitsch, was sacked after the failure to take Moscow, when Hitler himself took over command of the OKH, thereby ending, once and for all, the independence of the German General Staff. After the war, Brauchitsch was to have been arraigned on war crimes charges but died (in 1948) before a trial could be held. Franz Halder lost his job in 1942, after yet another disagreement with Hitler; implicated with the resistance in the 1944 bomb plot, he was found inside Dachau by the Americans in 1945.

The French

For the French leaders, defeat was followed by long years of frustration or imprisonment, of recrimination by their compatriots and of attempts to justify their own roles in the battle. Many lived to considerable ages. On his replacement by Weygand, Gamelin had rejoined his wife in their "comfortable, modest ground floor flat in the Avenue Foch which we had bought in 1937, in anticipation of the moment of my retirement." As the Germans approached Paris, Gamelin wrote to Weygand informing him that he was leaving for his sister's house in the country; but he would, naturally, be available to return at any instant. He was hurt to receive no acknowledgment from Weygand. After confinement in various châteaux, from 1943 onwards Gamelin found himself in Buchenwald, together with Daladier, Blum, and President Lebrun. All survived, and in 1945 Gamelin threw himself tirelessly into the publication of three hefty volumes of memoirs and apologiae, entitled *Servir.** He died in 1958, aged eighty-six. General Maxime Weygand, after a brief interlude as Minister of National Defence in Pétain's Government, was sent to Algeria as Governor General. Here he acquitted himself with distinction, maintaining the spirit of the army there while keeping the Germans at bay. Later he too was imprisoned by the Germans; and later still by his own countrymen, for a short period. He died in 1965, at the venerable age of ninety-eight, mistrustful of the British and shrewdly alert (though rather deaf) to the very end.

Unlike Gamelin and Weygand, General Georges left no

---

* "To serve."

memoirs. Before vanishing finally into oblivion, he reappeared briefly and contentiously in the intrigue-ridden world of Algiers in 1943; the Allies, having imported him from France, soon came to regard him (in the words of Anthony Eden) as "a reactionary old defeatist" and pensioned him off. The unhappy General Corap also made no attempt to justify himself against the charges made publicly by Reynaud, which led him to a nervous break-down. He was later cleared at the Riom Trials, and died—in silence—at his home in Fontainebleau in 1953. Huntziger, commander on the fatal field of Sedan and leader of the armistice delegation, also had no opportunity to write his side of the battle; he was killed in a plane crash in 1941. Among the French generals taken prisoners of war, General Giraud managed to escape* from Königstein Castle, where he was interned with General Prioux. He too made his way to Algiers and, with American backing, established himself briefly as a rival claimant to de Gaulle for the leadership of the Free French. General Frère died of maltreatment in a concentration camp.

Of the British participants, Lord Gort, although he had succeeded in saving so many of his men, was shattered by what had happened to the BEF. Not favoured by Churchill, he received no further fighting command; whereas his juniors in the BEF—Brooke, Alexander and Montgomery—rose to the highest summits of fame. Probably Churchill was right; Gort was not the man to lead or organise a modern, mechanised army. But no one deserved greater recognition for the incalculable services he had rendered Great Britain and the Allied cause. Wars, however, "are not won by evacuations." Later, Gort was made Governor General of Malta at a time when the island's position seemed hopeless; here, once again, was a challenge for which his tenacious courage was supremely adapted. His career ended as High Commissioner in Palestine at the end of the war, but soon after his appointment his health broke down and he died in 1946, aged sixty.

Reynaud and Pétain

Of all the major figures of this epoch, none seem so closely shrouded in tragedy as the two French premiers, Reynaud and his

---

* He had also escaped from a German POW camp in the previous war.

successor Pétain. A few days after the armistice, there had been a scandal when two emissaries were caught trying to smuggle out to America gold and jewellery belonging to the Comtesse de Portes—apparently unbeknown to Reynaud. On June 28th, Reynaud was driving in the south of France with the woman for whom he had worked so hard, and whose love was now about all that was left to him. To distract him from his misery, she persuaded him to take the wheel. Almost immediately the car swung off the road, into one of the plane trees lining it. A heavy suitcase hurtled forward from the back of the car to strike Hélène de Portes in the neck. She was killed instantly. Reynaud suffered only minor injuries. When he regained consciousness in hospital and was told of her death, he is said to have remarked simply: *"Elle était la France."* The remaining war years Reynaud spent in German prisons, narrowly escaping the fate of his fellow inmate, Georges Mandel. After the war, he re-entered politics, devoting himself to the cause of European unity, and once more became a minister. His first wife having died, he remarried in 1949 (aged seventy-one) and begot three children—the youngest born when he was approaching eighty. Still exercising regularly in the private gymnasium he had constructed in his Paris apartment, Reynaud lived to be eighty-seven. He died in 1966.

Alas for him, Pétain lived to be even older, the receptacle of France's dishonour, abandoned by his colleagues of the generation which should have been in control of the destiny of France, and later condemned by them for allowing members of the defeated nation to be marched to the Nazi slave labour camps. As Paul Baudouin deserted him, the old Marshal said with tears in his eyes: "Pity me. You are going, but I, at eighty-four, must stay and lead this sort of life." Finally, aged ninety-five, he too died in an austere French prison in 1951. By one of the strange quirks of fortune, a few years later Pétain's erstwhile protégé and the man who had gone to continue the fight from England while Pétain capitulated, General de Gaulle, would be summoned back from old age, just like Pétain, to take over the reins of France after younger men had abdicated.

Few indeed of the leaders in May 1940 are alive today. In Germany the survivors are represented, strangely enough, by the two principal architects of *Sichelschnitt*—Halder and Manstein—who live in retirement at opposite ends of the Federal Republic;

while in France Reynaud's adversary, ex-Premier Edouard Daladier, still lives quietly in Paris, after a brief political comeback under the Fourth Republic. All are octogenarians.

Scars of battle

In a way, the physical scars left by these cataclysmic six weeks of 1940 seem not to have lingered on as did those of Verdun. The court at Vincennes which housed Gamelin's *Thébaïde,* though destroyed by the Germans, is now being rebuilt at last; the villages and towns of France seared by the Luftwaffe (and again by the liberating British and Americans) have long since been rebuilt.* At Dinant on the Meuse and Bouillon on the Semois, German and French tourists come in thousands each summer to visit the pseudo-medieval Citadel and Crusader Godefroy de Bouillon's keep, perhaps pausing midway to admire the fantastic panorama from Monthermé's Roch-à-Sept-Heures. But there is little to suggest the events of just thirty summers ago. Noirefontaine, whence Guderian planned his crossing of the Meuse, is now a resting place recommended by the idyllic *Route de Bonheur.* At Sedan itself, the battlefield where France's Third Republic was first engendered and subsequently killed, it is easier now to find reminders of the battle of 1870 than of 1940. There are calvaries celebrating the gallant charge of General Margueritte's cuirassiers and the Maison des Dernières Cartouches at Bazeilles, and there are war memorials and cemeteries dating from 1914–18. But 1940 has left none of the pockmarked, lunar shell fields and the ghost-ridden atmosphere that one feels will characterise Verdun for all time. Down on the Meuse at Sedan, where the heaviest fighting took place, a few concrete bunkers (now used as cow stalls by local farmers) still bear the marks of blows delivered by the German flak and tank guns seeking out their embrasures. But all too many of them reveal little sign of damage; a mute testimony to the fact that Grandsard's "B" reservists did not stand fast like the men of Verdun. In any case the battle did not rest here long enough for the scars to be lasting. At Houx, the weir over which Rommel's motorcyclists crept is still there; the island itself is a camping ground, frequented by young Germans not born in 1940.

---

* Some of the untouched bunkers of the costly Maginot Line are now being auctioned off at between $125 and $1,000 apiece by the French Government as bijou summer retreats.

It is not easy to discover locals who can recount precisely what happened on the Meuse during those glorious May days.

As the revolutionary nightmare of Paris in May 1968 has most recently revealed, the wounds of political self-division—the heritage of the Commune and the Front Populaire, with the schisms of Pétainist-versus-Gaullist now superimposed—linger unhealed in France. But where perhaps the invisible scars lie deepest are in the relations between the former allies, Britain and France. After 1945, disillusion and mistrust at the French performance in 1940 played their part in Britain's determination never again to rely upon other peoples' forces for her own security. She would loyally contribute to the collective security of NATO; but at the same time she would build her own costly Maginot Line of atomic weaponry and call it the "Independent Deterrent." (Fortunately, unlike France's, Britain's "Maginot Line" has been allowed to lapse into graceful obsolescence without ever being put to the test.) Meanwhile, in the irony of history, it was the Germans who pushed Britain out of the continent of Europe in June 1940; but within the Common Market framework of the 1960s, it is France who prevails upon the Germans not to let Britain back in again.* Yet this is no accident of fate, nor just the resentment of the once humiliated towards the superciliousness of the unvanquished. In France, the consequences of Dunkirk do not cease to engender suspicions that, if the going ever gets too tough in Europe—whether in military or economic terms—Britain will always be tempted to pull out—as she did in 1940. Will it ever be said that, in saving the BEF and thus winning the war, Britain perhaps lost the peace for herself?

Though it remains vivid and fresh in the memories of many men now barely middle-aged, historically that May of 1940 now seems to have belonged so much more closely to 1918, to the world of Foch and the Kaiser than the one we live in today. In some respects the figures involved in the great drama of *Sichelschnitt* are seen to march back and forth across a screen almost as dimly distant as that of the Crimea. The weapons they used have become as outdated as the national causes they represented. How many centuries ago can it have been that Vietnamese fought

---

* As a further piece of irony, it is the statesman who first sold to the French government the amazing notion of an "indissoluble union" between Britain and France in the darkest hour of June 1940 who now keeps the door barred.

A TOUS LES FRANÇAIS

La France a perdu une bataille!
Mais la France n'a pas perdu la guerre!

Des gouvernants de rencontre ont pu capituler, cédant à la panique, oubliant l'honneur, livrant le pays a la servitude. Cependant, rien n'est perdu!

Rien n'est perdu, parce que cette guerre est une guerre mondiale. Dans l'univers libre, des forces immenses n'ont pas encore donné. Un jour, ces forces écraseront l'ennemi. Il faut que la France, ce jour-là, soit présente à la victoire. Alors, elle retrouvera sa liberté et sa grandeur. Tel est mon but, mon seul but!

Voilà pourquoi je convie tous les Francais, où qu'ils se trouvent, à s'unir à moi dans l'action, dans le sacrifice et dans l'espérance.

Notre patrie est en péril de mort.
Luttons tous pour la sauver!

VIVE LA FRANCE !

TO ALL FRENCHMEN..

France has lost a battle.
But France has not lost the war!

A makeshift Government may have capitulated, giving way to panic, forgetting honour, delivering their Country into slavery. Yet nothing is lost!

Nothing is lost, because this war is a world war. In the free universe immense forces have not yet been brought into play. Some day these forces will crush the enemy. On that day France must be present at the victory. She will then regain her liberty and her greatness.

That is my aim, my only aim!

That is why I ask all Frenchmen, wherever they may be, to unite with me in action, in sacrifice and in hope.

Our Country is in danger of death. Let us fight to save it.

LONG LIVE FRANCE!

GENERAL DE GAULLE
HEADQUARTERS
4, CARLTON GARDENS

C. de Gaulle

GÉNÉRAL DE GAULLE

QUARTIER-GÉNÉRAL,
4, CARLTON GARDENS,
LONDON, S.W.1.

and died for France at Monthermé, Algerian Tirailleurs at Philippeville, Senegalese at Amiens? How much has changed within these three decades! The French and British Empires have ceased to exist. The German Reich is split into a Soviet satellite and a secondary power. Both emerging from the Second World War as defeated nations, France and Germany have at last discovered a common denominator; in consequence relations between them have become more harmonious over a longer period than at any time since Louis XIV came to the throne. The army of a reconditioned but truncated Germany now provides France (and Britain) with her "best sword" in Europe. In face of a docile Germany, France herself is—in appearance, and temporarily—the continent's most powerful political force west of the Elbe. But all this is irrelevant. In the modern world, the combined influence of the three chief belligerents of 1940 adds up to little when weighed against the might of the two new super-powers which maintained their neutrality, through military impotence, during the Battle of France.

Back and forth through Dinant and Sedan the prosperous, well-fed burghers of the Common Market flock in their Citroëns and their Mercedeses, apparently oblivious to all the misery perpetrated in this tiny blood-sodden corner of France during the past hundred years. Watching them, it is sometimes hard not to wonder—did the First Sedan, the Battle of Verdun, the Second Battle of Sedan *have* to be fought before Germany and France would lower the frontier barriers between their two countries? Perhaps Hitler's blood-curdling prediction in *Mein Kampf* that Germany would have to fight "one last decisive battle" against France has come true in a sense that he indeed could never have foreseen. Certainly this Franco-German battle *must* have been the "last"; the facts of life today are such that one cannot possibly conceive of there being any repeat. At last *finis* seems to have been written to the saga wherein the ancient rivalry between France and Germany set the tempo of world affairs. But at what a cost!

Bibliography

BOOKS

Abetz, Otto. *Das Offene Problem*. Cologne, 1951.

Abshagen, Karl Heinz. *Canaris*. London, 1956.

Accart, J. M. *Chasseurs du Ciel*. Paris, 1945.

Allard, Paul. *L'Énigme de la Meuse: La Verité sur l'Affaire Corap*. Paris, 1941.

Armengaud, A. *Batailles Politiques et Militaires sur l'Europe*. Paris, 1948.

Astier de la Vigérie, François d'. *Le Ciel n'était pas Vide*. Paris, 1952.

Balbaud, René. *Cette Drôle de Guerre*. Oxford, 1941.

Bardies, R. M. *La Campagne de 1939–1940*. Paris, 1947.

Bardoux, Jacques. *Journal* (September 1, 1939–July 15, 1940). Paris, 1957.

Barlone, D. *A French Officer's Diary: August 1939–October 1940*. Cambridge, 1943.

Baudouin, Paul. *Private Diaries: March 1940–January 1941*. London, 1948.

Bauer, E. *Der Panzerkrieg*. Bonn, 1965.

Baumbach, Werner. *Zu Spät*. Munich, 1949.

Bayet, A. *Pétain et la Cinquième Colonne*. Paris, 1944.

Beaufre, Gen. *Le Drame de 1940*. Paris, 1965.

Beauvoir, S. de. *The Prime of Life*. London, 1963.

Bekker, Cajus. *Angriffshöhe 4,000*. Oldenburg, 1964.

Bénoist-Méchin, J. *60 Days That Shook the West*. London, 1956.

Bernard, H. *La Guerre et Son Evolution à travers les Siècles*. Brussels, 1957.

Bloch, Marc. *Strange Defeat*. Oxford, 1949.

Blum, L. (1) *De Munich à la Guerre, 1937–1940*. Paris, 1965.

———. (2) *Mémoires*. Paris, 1955.

Blumentritt, G. *Von Rundstedt: The Soldier and the Man*. London, 1952.

Bois, Élie J. *Truth on the Tragedy of France*. London, 1940.

Bongartz, Heinz. *Luftmacht Deutschland*. Essen, 1939.

Boothe, Clare. *Europe in the Spring*. New York, 1940.

Borchert, Hubert W. *Panzerkampf im Westen*. Berlin, 1940.

Bräck, Hermann. *Als Kampfflieger über Frankreich*. Berlin, 1942.

Brogan, D. W. *The Development of Modern France*. London, 1940.

Bryant, Arthur. *The Turn of the Tide*. London, 1957.

Bucheit, Gert. *Der Deutsche Geheimdienst*. Munich, 1966.

Carron, Lucien. *Fantassins sur l'Aisne*. Paris, 1943.

Chambrun, René Aldebart, Comte de. *I Saw France Fall*. New York, 1940.

Charles-Roux, F. *Cinq Mois Tragiques aux Affaires Étrangères*. Paris, 1949.

Chastenet, Jacques. (1) *Les Années d'Illusions, 1918–31*. Paris, 1960.

———. (2) *Déclin de la Troisième, 1931–38*. Paris, 1962.

———. (3) *Le Drame Finale de la 3ᵉ République, 1938–40*. Paris, 1963.

Chautemps, C. *Cahiers Secrets de l'Armistice, 1939–1940*. Paris, 1963.

Christophe, E. C. *Wir Stossen mit Panzern zum Meer*. Berlin, 1940.

Churchill, W. S. *The Second World War*. Vols. I and II. London, 1948–1949.

Clark, Douglas. *Three Days to Catastrophe*. London, 1966.

Conquet, Gen. *L'Énigme des Blindés*. Paris, 1956.

Conrad, Florence. *Comrades de Combat*. New York, 1941.

de Gaulle, Gen. (1) *Vers l'Armée de Métier*. Paris, 1935.

——. (2) *War Memoirs*. Vol. I: "The Call to Honour, 1940–42." London, 1955.

Dolléans, E. *Histoire du Mouvement Ouvrier*. Paris, 1939.

Douglas, Sholto. *Years of Command*. London, 1966.

Doumenc, Gen. *Histoire de la 9e Armée*. Grenoble, 1945.

Draper, Theodore. *The Six Weeks War, 10th May–25th June*. London, 1946.

Ehrenburg, I. *Eve of War, 1933–41*. London, 1963.

Ellis, Major L. F. *The War in France and Flanders*. London, 1953.

Fabre-Luce, A. *Journal de la France*. (I) Mars 39–Juillet 40. Trévoux, 1940.

Fauvet, Jacques. *Histoire du Parti Communiste Français de la Guerre à la Guerre, 1917–1939*. Paris, 1964.

Fechner, Fritz. *Panzer am Feind*. Gütersloh, 1942.

François-Poncet, André. *The Fateful Years*. London, 1949.

Fuller, Major- Gen. J. F. C. *Decisive Battles of the Western World*. Vol. III. London, 1956.

Galland, Adolf. *Die Ersten und die Letzen*. Darmstadt, 1953.

Gamelin, Gen. *Servir—Les Armées Françaises de 1940*. 3 vols. Paris, 1946.

Gauché, Maurice Henri. *Le Deuxième Bureau au Travail*. Paris, 1953.

Gontaut-Biron, Ch. A. de. *Les Dragons au Combat*. Paris, 1954.

Gorce, P. M. de la. *The French Army*. London, 1963.

Görlitz, Walter. (1) *Der Zweite Weltkrieg, 1939–1945*. 2 vols. Stuttgart, 1951.

——. (2) *The Memoirs of Fieldmarshal Keitel*. London, 1965.

Goutard, Col. A. *The Battle of France, 1940*. London, 1958.

——. *La Guerre des Occasions Perdues*. Paris, 1956.

Grandmougin, Jean. *Histoire Vivante du Front Populaire, 1934–39*. Paris, 1966.

Grandsard, C. *Le 10e Corps d'Armée dans le Bataille 1939/1940*. Paris, 1949.

Greenwall, H. J. *When France Fell*. London, 1958.

Guderian, Heinz. (1) *Achtung—Panzer!* Stuttgart, 1937.

——. (2) *Panzer Leader*. London, 1952.

——. (3) *Mit den Panzern in Ost und West*. Stuttgart, 1942.

Guérin, Daniel. *Front Populaire. Révolution Manquée*. Paris, 1963.

Habe, Hans. *A Thousand Shall Fall*. May–Dec. 1940. London, 1942.

Halder, Franz. *Kriegstagebuch*. 3 vols. Stuttgart, 1962–1964.

Harsch, Joseph C. *Pattern of Conquest*. London, 1942.

Hartog, L. J. *Und Morgen die Ganze Welt*. Gutersloh, 1961.

Hassell, C. A. U. von. *The Von Hassell Diaries, 1938–44*. London, 1948.

Haupt, W. *Sieg ohne Lorbeer*. Holstein, 1965.

Hautecler, G. *Le Combat de Chabrehez, 10 mai 1940*. Brussels, 1955.

Hébrard, J. *25 Années d'Aviation Militaire*. Paris, 1947.

Heinkel, Ernst. *Stürmisches Leben*. Stuttgart, 1953.

Herriot, Édouard. *Episodes, 1940–44*. Paris, 1950.

Heusinger, Gen. A. *Befehl im Widerstreit, Schicksalstunden der Deutschen Armee, 1923–45*. Tübingen, 1950.

Ironside, General Sir E. *The Ironside Diaries*. London, 1962.
Jacobsen, H. A. (1) *Decisive Battles of World War II: The German View*. London, 1965.
——. (2) *Fall Gelb*. Wiesbaden, 1957.
Jamet, Claude. *Carnets de Déroute*. Paris, 1962.
Jong, Louis de. *The German Fifth Column in the Second World War*. London, 1956.
Kammerer, A. *La Vérité sur l'Armistice*. Paris, 1944.
Kielmansegg, Graf. *Panzer zwischen Warschau und Atlantik*. Berlin, 1941.
Klein, Burton H. *Germany's Economic Preparation for War*. Cambridge, Massachusetts, 1959.
Koeltz, Louis. *Comment s'est joué Notre Destin*. Paris, 1957.
Koestler, A. *Scum of the Earth*. London, 1941.
Kosak, Georges. *Belgique et France, 1940*. Paris, 1946.
Laure, Gen. *Pétain*. Paris, 1942.
Lebrun, Albert. *Témoignage*. Paris, 1945.
Lee, Asher. *The German Air Force*. London, 1946.
Lerecouvreux, M. *Huit Mois d'Attente, Un Mois de Guerre*. Paris, 1946.
Leverkuehn, Paul. *German Military Intelligence*. London, 1954.
Lévy, L. *Truth about France*. London, 1941.
Liddell Hart, B. H. (1) *Memoirs*. Vols. I and II. London, 1965.
——. (2) *The Other Side of the Hill*. London, 1948.
——. (3) *The Tanks*. Vol. II (1939–45). London, 1959.
Liss, U. *Westfront, 1939–40*. Neckargemund, 1959.
Lossberg, Gen. von. *Im Wehrmachtführungsstab*. Hamburg, 1950.
Lyet, Pierre. *La Bataille de France*. Paris, 1947.
Maassen, Heinz. *Über die Maas*. Düsseldorf, 1942.
Maine-Lombard, Pierre. *Ceux du Béton*. Paris, 1957.
Manstein, Field Marshal von. *Lost Victories*. London, 1958.
Manteuffel, Gen. Hasso E. V. *Die 7 Panzerdivision im Zweiten Weltkrieg, 1939–1945*. Cologne, 1965.
Maurois, André. *Tragedy in France*. New York, 1940.
Mellenthin, Major-Gen. F. W. von. *Panzer Battles, 1939–45*. London, 1955.
Mende, Karl Heinz. *Briefe aus dem Westen*. Berlin, 1940.
Mendès-France, Pierre. *The Pursuit of Freedom*. London, 1956.
Mengin, Robert. *No Laurels for de Gaulle*. New York, 1966.
Menu, Charles Léon. *Lumière sur les Ruines*. Paris, 1953.
Middleton, Drew. *Our Share of Night*. New York, 1946.
Minart, Col. *P.C. Vincennes. GQG. Sector I*. Paris, 1945.
Montreuil, J. *Histoire du Mouvement Ouvrier en France*. Paris, 1947.
Monzie, A. de. *Ci-devant*. Paris, 1942.
Moulton, J. L. *The Norwegian Campaign of 1940*. London, 1966.
Mueller-Hillebrand, Gen. B. *Das Heer. 1933–45*. Darmstadt, n.d.
Müller, K. J. *Das Ende der Entente Cordiale*. Frankfurt/Main, 1956.
Murawski, Erich. *Der Durchbruch im Westen*. Oldenburg, 1940.
Muray, Jean. *La Ballade des Tordus*. Paris, 1943.
Namier, L. B. *Europe in Decay*. London, 1950.
Narracott, Arthur Henson. *War News Had Wings*. London, 1941.
O'Neill, Robert J. *The German Army and the Nazi Party*. London, 1966.
Osterkamp, Theo. *Durch Höben und Tiefen Jagt ein Herz*. Stuttgart, 1952.
Paquier, Pierre. (1) *L'Aviation de Bombardement Française en 1939–40*. Paris, 1948.
——. (2) *Combats de Chasse*. Paris, 1946.

Pertinax, A. *The Gravediggers of France.* New York, 1944.
Picht, Werner. *Das Ende der Illusionen.* Berlin, 1941.
Prételat, Gen. *Le Destin Tragique de la Ligne Maginot.* Paris, 1950.
Prioux, R. *Souvenirs de Guerre.* Paris, 1947.
Prittie, Terence. *Germans against Hitler.* London, 1964.
Rauschning, H. *Hitler Speaks.* London, 1939.
Reile, Oskar. *Geheime Westfront: Die Abwehr, 1935–45.* Munich, 1962.
Reynaud, Paul. (1) *In the Thick of the Fight, 1939–1945.* London, 1955.
———. (2) *La France a sauvé l'Europe.* Paris, 1947.
———. (3) *Mémoires. Venue de Ma Montagne.* Paris, 1960.
Richards, D. J., and H. St. G. Saunders. *Royal Air Force, 1939–45.* Vol. I: "The Fight at Odds." London, 1953.
Ritter, G. *Carl Goerderer und die Deutsche Widerstandsbewegung.* Stuttgart, 1956.
Rocolle, Lt. Col. *Le Béton a-t-il trahi?* Paris, 1950.
Romains, Jules. *Seven Mysteries of Europe.* New York, 1940.
Rommel, Field Marshal E. *The Rommel Papers.* B. H. Liddell Hart, ed. London, 1951.
Rossi, A. *Une Page d'Histoire. Les Communistes Français pendant la Drôle de Guerre.* Paris, 1951.
Roton, G. *Années Cruciales.* Paris, 1947.
Rowe, Vivian. *The Great Wall of France.* New York, 1959.
Ruby, Gen. Ed. *Sedan, Terre d'Épreuve.* Paris, 1948.
Saint-Exupéry, Antoine de. *Pilote de Guerre.* Paris, 1942.
Salesse, Lt. Col. *L'Aviation de Chasse Française en 1939–40.* Paris, 1955.
Sarraz-Bournet, Colonel. *Témoignage d'un Silencieux G.Q.G. 2ᵉ Bureau.* Paris, 1948.
Schlabrendorff, Fabian von. *The Secret War Against Hitler.* London, 1966.
Seive, Fleury. *L'Aviation d'Assaut dans la Bataille de 19⬤.* Paris, 1948.
Sendtner, K. *Die Vollmacht des Gewissens (Die Deutsche Militäropposition im Ersten Kriegsjahr).* Munich, 1956.
Serre, E. (Rapporteur). *Les Evénements Survenus en France de 1933–45.* 5 vols. Assemblée-Nationale, Paris, 1947.
Serrigny, Gen. *30 Ans avec Pétain.* Paris, 1959.
Seydewitz, Max. *Civil Life in War Time Germany.* New York, 1945.
Sheean, James Vincent. *Between the Thunder and the Sun.* New York, 1943.
Shirer, William L. (1) *Berlin Diary, 1934–1941.* London, 1941.
———. (2) *The Rise and Fall of the Third Reich.* London, 1962.
Spaeter, Helmuth. *Die Geschichte des Panzerkorps Grossdeutschland.* Vol. I. Duisburg-Ruhrort, 1958.
Spears, E. L. *Assignment to Catastrophe.* 2 vols. London, 1954.
Sponeck, (Graf) von. *Mit Schnellen Truppen an 6 Fronten.* Leipzig, 1943.
Stackelberg, K. von. *Ich War Dabei, Ich Sah, Ich Schrieb.* Berlin, 1940.
Starcke, Gerhard. *Die Roten Teufel Sind die Hölle!* Berlin, 1941.
Stoves, Rolf. *1 Panzer Division, 1935–45.* Bad Neuheim, 1961.
Strohmeyer, Kurt. *Stukas.* Berlin, n.d.
Supf, Peter. *Das Buch der Deutschen Fluggeschichte.* Berlin, n.d.
Taylor, A. J. P. (1) *English History, 1914–1945.* Oxford, 1965.
———. (2) *Origins of the Second World War.* London, 1961.
Taylor, Telford. *The March of Conquest.* New York, 1959.
Thompson, Laurence. *1940.* London, 1966.
Tippelskirch, Admiral. *Geschichte des Zweiten Weltkriegs.* Bonn, 1951.
Tissier, P. *The Riom Trial.* London, 1942.

Tournoux, J. R. *Pétain and de Gaulle.* London, 1966.
Tschimpke, Alfred. *Die Gespenster-Division.* Munich, 1940.
U. S. Air Force. *German Air Force Operations in Support of the Army.* Washington, 1962.
Vasselle, Pierre. (1) *La Tragédie d'Amiens, Mai, Juin, 1940.* Amiens, 1952.
——. (2) *La Bataille au Sud d'Amiens, 20 Mai–8 Juin.* Paris, 1948.
Voisin, Pierre. *Ceux de Chars.* Lyon, 1941.
Walter, G. *Histoire du Parti Communiste Français.* Paris, 1948.
Warlimont, Gen. W. *Inside Hitler's Headquarters, 1939–1945.* London, 1964.
Waterfield, Gordon. *What Happened to France.* London, 1940.
Webster, Sir Charles, and Noble Frankland. *The Strategic Air Offensive against Germany, 1939–45.* London, 1961.
Weiss, Wilhelm., ed. *Der Krieg im Westen.* Munich, 1941.
Werth, Alexander. *The Last Days of Paris.* London, 1940.
Westphal, Gen. S. *The German Army in the West.* London, 1951.
Weygand, Gen. M. (1) *Recalled to Service.* London, 1952.
Weygand, J. (2) *The Role of General Weygand.* London, 1948.
Wheeler-Bennett, John W. *The Nemesis of Power.* London, 1953.
Wittek, E., ed. *Die Soldatische Tat. Berichte von Mitkämpfern des Heeres in Westfeldzug, 1940.* hrsg. vom Generalstab des Heeres. Berlin, 1941.
Young, Desmond. *Rommel.* London, 1950.

PERIODICAL ARTICLES

Aschenbrandt, Maj. Gen. Der Einsatz der französischen 4 Panzer-Divisions. *Militär-Wochenblatt,* July 1942.
Cailloux, Col. Campagne de France 1940: La Contre-attaque qui n'eut jamais lieu, 19–25 mai. *Revue Historique de l'Armée,* Vol. 3 (1966).
de Cossé-Brissac, Gen. L'Armée allemande dans la Campagne de 1940. *Revue d'Histoire de la Deuxième Guerre Mondiale,* January 1964.
Dhers, P. Notes on the Comité de Guerre du 25 mai, 1940. *Revue d'Histoire de la Deuxième Guerre Mondiale,* June 1953.
d'Hoop, J. M. La Politique française du réarmament. *Revue d'Histoire de la Deuxième Guerre Mondiale,* April 1954.
d'Ornane, Lt. Col. Le XIX Corps blindé allemand dans les Ardennes en 1940. *Revue Historique de l'Armée,* Vol. 3 (1955).
Ely, Gen. La Leçon qu'il faut tirer des opérations de 1940. *Revue Défense Nationale,* December 1953.
Godet, Maj. Jean. Rommel en Belgique. *L'Armée: La Nation,* July/August 1958.
Grubnau, 1st Lt. Brückenschlag über die Maas westlich Sedan für den Übergang einer Panzer Division. *Militär-Wochenblatt,* January 1941.
Guderian, Gen. La Campagne de France. *Revue Historique de l'Armée,* Vol. 1 (1947).
le Goaster, Lt. Col. L'Action des Forces Aériennes. *Revue Historique de la Deuxième Guerre Mondiale,* June 1953.
Le Goyet, Lt. Col. Le XIᵉ Corps d'Armée dans la Bataille de la Meuse, 10–15 mai, 1940. *Revue Historique de l'Armée,* Vol. 1 (1962).
——. Contre-attaques manquées, Sedan, 13–15 mai, 1940. *Revue Historique de l'Armée,* Vol. 4 (1962).
——. L'Engagement de la 2ᵉ Division Cuirassée Française. *Revue Historique de l'Armée,* Vol. 1 (1964).
——. Rethel 1940. *Revue Historique de l'Armée,* Vol. 4 (1964).

——. La Percée de Sedan, 10–15 mai, 1940. *Revue d'Histoire de la Deuxième Guerre Mondiale,* July 1965.

Liss, Ulrich. Der französische Gegenangriff gegen den deutschen Maasdurchbruch im Mai 1940. *Schweizerische Militär-Zeitschrift,* 1958.

Lyet, Col. P. Témoignages et documents, 1939–40. *Revue Historique de l'Armée,* Vol. 1 (1960).

——. À propos de Sedan, 1940. *Revue Historique de l'Armée,* Vol. 4 (1962).

——. Les Tirailleurs malgaches à Monthermé, mai 1940. *Revue Historique de l'Armée,* Vol. 4 (1963).

Marin, Louis. Gouvernment et Commandement, mai–juin, 1940. *Revue d'Histoire de la Deuxième Guerre Mondiale,* October 1952.

Nyssens, Lt. Gen. Lord Gort avait raison. *L'Armée: La Nation,* May 1953.

Rollot, Gen. La Bataille de Sedan. *Revue d'Histoire de la Deuxième Guerre Mondiale,* October 1958.

——. L'Offensive de Sedan; les rapports Franco-Belges. *Revue d'Histoire de la Deuxième Guerre Mondiale,* April 1960.

Rothe, A. So war die erste grosse Panzer schlacht . . . *Deutschen Soldaten Zeitung,* May 1952.

Schulze, Sgt.-Maj. Erste Einfass vor Sedan. *Militär-Wochenblatt,* April 1941.

Soldan, Lt. Col. Der Durchbruch über die Maas am 13 mai 1940. *Militärwissenschaftliche Rundschau,* November 1940.

Tournoux, Gen. Les Origines de la ligne Maginot. *Revue d'Histoire de la Deuxième Guerre Mondiale,* January 1959.

Über die Maas am 15 mai 1940. *Alte Kameraden,* No. 9 (1959).

Vanwelkenhuyzen, Jean. L'alerte du 10 janvier, 1940. *Revue d'Histoire de la Deuxième Guerre Mondiale,* October 1953.

Villate, R. Le Changement de Commandement de mai, 1940. *Revue d'Histoire de la Deuxième Guerre Mondiale,* January 1952.

Wanty, E. La Défense des Ardennes en 1940. *Revue d'Histoire de la Deuxième Guerre Mondiale,* April 1961.

Willequet, J. La Politique Belge d'Indépendance, 1936–40. *Revue d'Histoire de la Deuxième Guerre Mondiale,* July 1958.

OTHER SOURCES

Contemporary newspapers and magazines.

Federal German Archives, Koblenz; War Diaries of German units.

Supplement to the *London Gazette,* October 10, 1941 (Lord Gort's dispatches).

Reference Notes

THE FOREGOING bibliography contains the principal published works, books, periodicals and unpublished official sources used either to a greater or lesser extent by the author. But it represents only the small visible tip of the iceberg of an immense volume of words which have been written about the Fall of France, in all its aspects. Works relating to the fifth column alone would easily fill several times over the pages allotted to the bibliography in this book.

As far as source material is concerned, the book falls into two fairly independent sections, 1919–1940 (Part I), and the battle itself (Part II). Of the great mass of histories and memoirs covering the interwar period from which I have directly or indirectly benefited, I have not attempted to list the more obvious; the titles appended below refer chiefly to works quoted or specifically alluded to, and which I feel may be of use to a reader desirous of reading further.

For Part II, there are certain works which I have kept by my side throughout, and can recommend for their particular value. One of the best military sources on the campaign from the French side remains Colonel Goutard's account (the English edition, however, is a heavily abridged version of the French), which is fair, generally accurate and critical enough not to have endeared the author to the French military establishment. Less accurate, and more biassed, but of considerable interest in the chronological relation of political events, is Bénoist-Méchin's volume (also reduced in translation, from three volumes to one). On the German side, Werner Haupt's *Sieg ohne Lorbeer,* is one of the best general accounts of the campaign. Another source used extensively throughout is General Roton, who is particularly useful on French High Command decisions; meanwhile, for details of the actions in which they themselves were involved, Rommel and

Guderian (2) are indispensable, and generally trustworthy. Considering the little time that Rommel had to bother with keeping up a diary, as an eyewitness account his remains outstanding. I have also made constant and extensive use of the War Diaries of various German units, now located in the Bundesarchiv in Koblenz. Among the most interesting of these is a bound copy of Rommel's own orders and reports, together with situation maps kept up in his own hand,* which was presented to Frau Rommel by the 7th Panzer and subsequently handed by her to the *Bundesarchiv*. For a pictorial memory of the campaign, I used the numerous illustrated volumes produced on either side, and derived particular value from the official German film, *Sieg im West*, the first of the major wartime documentaries which—despite its propaganda content—contains excellent material.

Much of the mass of battle accounts requires to be treated with suspicion. Many are based, secondhand, on other (secondhand) narrations, and have not necessarily gained accuracy in the retelling. Some written very close to events have the invaluable stamp of the unprocessed, fresh memory—such as Clare Boothe's impressions and William Shirer's *Berlin Diary*. Others inevitably suffer from the distortion of the passions of the moment—such as the bitter post-defeat reminiscences of French writers who tend to see a fifth columnist and a traitor in every *Poste de Commandement,* or the boastful, superman accounts emanating from Nazi Germany and often published for propaganda purposes when the war was going against Hitler. Nevertheless, neither of these categories is without value. For the reasons outlined in the Preface, I have been wary about using unpublished "I was there" material; on the other hand, my researches were helpfully supplemented by the responses to various correspondence and interviews on specific points. I have referred to these below under the general title of "personal correspondence."

On specific and recurrent war topics, there were also certain standard books used consistently. *For fighting on the French Ninth Army front (up to May 16th)*: Doumenc and Menu. *The Second Army front:* Ruby, Grandsard and Menu. *The war in Northern Belgium and Holland:* Prioux, Ellis, Fechner, Christophe. *The war in the air:* d'Astier, Paquier (1), Bekker, Rich-

---

* Geschichte der 7 Panzer-Division im Westfeldzug.

ards (for RAF especially), Seive, Salesse, Tissier, Accart. In the source notes below, therefore, I have not necessarily made repeated allusion to these works each time the relevant topic comes up; and similarly with the general references (e.g. Goutard) mentioned earlier. The following notes list solely the principal source material utilised in each chapter. Works to be found in the bibliography bear the author's name only; where there are more than one by the same author, the appropriate number is given; where a work is not listed in the bibliography the title is given in full.

CHAPTER 1

The 1919 Victory March: *Illustrated London News, Times, Matin, Figaro*. French postwar illusions and stresses: Chastenet (1) and (2), Brogan, Taylor (2), Churchill I.

CHAPTER 2

The French Army; Verdun and the Maginot Line: Rocolle, de Gaulle (1), Beaufre, Prételat, Horne (*The Price of Glory*), Rowe, Rodolphe. State of the Army for 1935: Chastenet (1) and (2), Brogan, Ruby, Beaufre. Armoured doctrine and foreign policy: Conquet, Guderian (1), Taylor (2), Reynaud (1), Liddell Hart (1), Namier. Hitler reoccupies Rhineland: Shirer (1) and (2), Churchill, Armengaud, Taylor (2), Reynaud (1), Grandmougin, Beaufre, Osterkamp, Rocolle.

CHAPTER 3

Hitler rearms: Shirer (1) and (3), Wheeler-Bennett, O'Neill, Klein, Gauché, Demeter (*The German Officer Corps*). Guderian and the Panzerkorps: Guderian (1) and (2), Michael Howard (ed.) (*The Theory and Practice of War*), Rauschning, The revolutionary Wehrmacht: Shirer (1) and (2) Wheeler-Bennett, Taylor (2), O'Neill, Churchill I, Prittie, Guderian (1). Antimilitarism in France: Chastenet (1) and (2), Fauvet, Beauvoir. French political scandals: Chastenet (1) and (2), Grandmougin, Pertinax, Bois. Beginnings of "civil war": Horne (*The Price of Glory* and *The Fall of Paris*), Pertinax, Taylor (1), Chastenet (1) and (2), Brogan, Levy, Fauvet, Montreuil, Grandmougin, Walter, Ehrenburg.

CHAPTER 4

French industrial unrest and the Front Populaire: Montreuil, Walter, Levy, Chastenet (1) and (2), Grandmougin, Fauvet, Beauvoir (*The Blood of Others*), Pertinax. France rearms: Roton, Conquet, Rowe, Serre, Goutard, Pertinax, Reynaud (1), Tissier, Namier, Conquet, Tournoux, de Gaulle (1), Mengin, Gamelin I and II, Beaufre, Grandmougin, Chastenet (2), Gauché. The Luftwaffe: Lee, Galland, Heinkel, Osterkamp, Bongartz, Bekker, Seive, Taylor (1), Douglas, d'Astier, François-Poncet. The French Air Force: d'Astier, Maurois, Brogan, Seive, Churchill I, Tissier, Gamelin I, Armengaud, Paquier, Salesse. Widening political rifts in France; the fifth column: Brogan, Namier, Chastenet (2), Spears I, Pertinax, Levy, Bloch,

Rauschning, Menu, Bayet, Abetz, Bois. Fall of the Front Populaire and rise of the Communists: Chastenet (2), Grandmougin, Levy, Walter, Fauvet, Rossi, Beauvoir, Pertinax. The rush towards war: Taylor (2), Chastenet (2) and (3), Pertinax, Churchill I, Klein, Reynaud (1), Fabre-Luce, Shirer (1).

CHAPTER 5

War begins: Chastenet (3), Fabre-Luce, Shirer (1), Seydewitz, Klein, Harsch, Barlone, Maurois, Pertinax. The Saar "Offensive" and Poland: Allied periodicals, Gamelin III, Goutard, Rowe, Lerecouvreux, Prételat, Rodolphe, Minart, Spears I, Chastenet (3), Guderian (2), Balbaud, Liss, Lossberg, Blumentritt. The Phoney War: Fabre-Luce, Waterfield, Pertinax, Boothe, Sumner Welles (*Time for Decision*), Beauvoir, Koestler. Life at the front; French Army morale: French periodicals (see Bibliography), Fabre-Luce, Pertinax, Barlone, Spears I, Jamet, Sarraz-Bournet, Koestler, Barlone, Lerecouvreux. Impact of Nazi and Communist propaganda: Chastenet (3), Fabre-Luce, Conrad, Greenwall, Spears I, Rossi, Bois, Koestler, Ehrenburg, Pertinax, Bardies, Walter.

CHAPTER 6

Gamelin: Menu, Spears I, Romains, Maurois, Bardies, Bardoux, Gamelin I and II, Pertinax, de Gaulle (2), Minart, Baudouin. French Command and Georges: Goutard, Minart, Roton, Beaufre, Spears I, Sarraz-Bournet, Gauché, Weygand (1), Pertinax, Bardies. Gamelin's strategy: Doumenc, Gamelin I and III, Roton, French periodicals, Jacobsen (1), Ellis, Goutard, Lyet, Reynaud (1), Minart, Draper, Prioux. The Mechelen Incident: Jacobsen (2), Koeltz. French neglect of Polish lessons: Armengaud, Gauché. Finland and other distractions: Taylor (1), Koestler, Bois, Clark, Gamelin III, Bardoux, Ironside, Weygand (1), Pertinax, Beaufre, Fabre-Luce.

CHAPTER 7

Fall Gelb: Jacobsen (1) and (2), Koeltz, Warlimont, Ellis, Westphal, Manstein, Goerlitz (1), Liss, Telford Taylor, Haupt, Blumentritt, Heusinger, Guderian (2). Halder and the "Resistance": Krausnick (*Schicksalfragen der Gegenwart*), O'Neill, Prittie, Görlitz (1), Sendtner, *Von Hassell Diaries*, Namier. Manstein and his Plan: Blumentritt, Westphal, Manstein, O'Neill, Liddell Hart (2), Koeltz, Jacobsen (2). Finalising the *Sichelschnitt* Plan: Jacobsen (2), Koeltz, Liss, Warlimont, Telford Taylor, Guderian (2), Lossberg, Abshagen.

CHAPTER 8

Norway: Moulton, Reynaud (1), Churchill I, Koeltz, Telford Taylor, Taylor (1), Lossberg. Allied government crises: Gamelin III, Boothe, Bois, Fabre-Luce, Baudouin, Chastenet (3), Pertinax, Churchill I. Daladier, Reynaud and Hélène de Portes: Bois, Pertinax, Fabre-Luce, Maurois, Spears I and II, Harold Nicolson *Diaries* II, Baudouin, Chastenet (3), Sheean, Boothe. Strength of opposing forces by May 1940: Goutard, Jacobsen (2), Menu, Conquet, Lyet, Tissier, Bauer, Guderian (2), Roton, Bardies, d'Astier, Gamelin I, Lee. French line-up on the Meuse: Ruby, Menu, Goutard, Allard, Prételat, Gamelin I. French military unpreparedness: Lerecouvreux, Goutard, Maurois, Menu, Grandsard, Ruby, Conquet, French periodicals,

Doumenc, Draper, Bauer, Allard, Gauché, Bernard, Beaufre, Prételat. Allied reconnaissance and German deception: Accart, Salesse, Bauer, Liss, Gauché, Lossberg, Jacobsen (2), Abshagen, Bartz (*Die Tragödie der Deutschen Abwehr*), Leverkuehn. Last days in France and Germany: Boothe, Fabre-Luce, Bardoux, Gontaut-Biron, de Beauvoir, Hassell (op. cit.), Seydewitz, Shirer (1), Warlimont, Halder, German periodicals, Sendtner (op. cit.).

CHAPTER 9

Beginning of the German offensive, May 10th: Stackelberg, Kielmansegg, Flack, Reile, Sponeck, Spaeter, Osterkamp, Bekker, Draper, Liddell Hart (2). German advance into the Ardennes: Stoves, Spaeter, Starcke, Halder, Manteuffel, Lerecouvreux, German "Special Operations," "Brandenburgers," Eben Emael: Leverkuehn, Abshagen, Bucheit, de Jong, Haupt, Strohmeyer, Hartog, Lossberg, Bekker, Telford Taylor, Purnell (*History of the Second World War*). The Allies move into Belgium: Ironside, Minart, Reynaud (1), Boothe, Baudouin, Chastenet (3), Prioux, Bryant, Menu, Kosak, Gontaut-Biron, Ruby, Lerecouvreux.

CHAPTER 10

Fighting in the Ardennes, May 11th: Manteuffel, Kosak, French periodicals, Stoves, Halder, Goutaut-Biron, Guderian (3), Mende. Allied progress in northern Belgium: Lyet, Bardies, Middleton, Roton. French High Command reactions: Draper, Roton, Minart, Goutard, Gamelin I, Weygand (1).

CHAPTER 11

War in Holland and northern Belgium, May 12th: Picht, Ironside, Draper, Bénoist-Méchin. Guderian crosses the Semois: Weiss, Stoves, Christophe, Lerecouvreux, Conrad. Corap withdrawn from the Ardennes: Kosak, Manteuffel, French periodicals. Rommel crosses at Houx: French periodicals, Manteuffel, Tschimpke, Lyet. Huntziger prepares for Guderian's attack at Sedan: Conrad, Lyet, Minart, d'Astier, Gamelin I.

CHAPTER 12

Rommel, background: Young, Rommel, Lossberg, Mellenthin. Corap: Chastenet (3), Allard, Draper, Maurois. Rommel's bridgehead at Dinant: in addition to Rommel himself, Manteuffel, Draper, Borchert, Young, Tschimpke, Minart. Guderian's preparations at Sedan: Spaeter, Stoves, Christophe, Liddell Hart (2), and here as well as later—Grandsard, Ruby, Menu, Goutard. Luftwaffe bombing at Sedan: Lee, Telford Taylor, Bekker, Richards, Goutard, Salesse, d'Astier, Stoves, Guderian (2), German periodicals. The crossings at Sedan: *Sieg im West*, Draper, German periodicals, Guderian (2) and (3), Wittek, Haupt, Spaeter, Mellenthin, Stoves, Weiss, Christophe. The French view: in addition to Roton, Goutard, Menu, Ruby, Grandsard—Lerecouvreux, Gamelin I and III, Conrad, French periodicals, Bardies, Draper, Doumenc. French High Command reactions: Minart, Baudouin, Gamelin I and III, Beaufre, Ironside.

CHAPTER 13

Rommel consolidates his bridgehead: Manteuffel, Tschimpke, Young, Bardies, Allard, Draper, Minart, German periodicals, Wittek. First French counterattacks at Sedan: Spaeter, Mellenthin, Stoves, Guderian (3), German and French periodicals. Guderian decides to swing westwards: Guderian (2), Halder, Stoves. Allied air attack on Sedan bridges: Richards, Haupt, d'Astier, Paquier (1), Kielmansegg, Bekker, Ellis, Tissier, Guderian (3). French 3rd Armoured Division at Stonne: Spaeter, Serre, Lerecouvreux, Roton, French periodicals, Waterfield. Guderian and Kleist at odds: Guderian (2), Halder, German War Diaries. Holland capitulates: Draper, Bekker, Telford Taylor, Sponeck. French High Command reactions: Bardies, Minart, Menu, Spears I, Gamelin I, Reynaud (1), Ironside, Werth.

CHAPTER 14

The French 1st Armoured Division and Rommel's breakout: Serre, d'Astier, Starcke, French periodicals, Bardies, Tschimpke, Borchert, German periodicals, Manteuffel, personal correspondence. Reinhardt breaks out at Monthermé: German periodicals; Guderian (3), Stackelberg. Fighting at Stonne: Spaeter, Wittek, Lemelsen (*Die 29 Infanterie Division*), French periodicals, Serre; 1st Panzer breaks out at Sedan: Guderian (3), Kielmansegg, Stoves, Lemelsen (op. cit.), Draper, French periodicals, Doumenc, Bardies. RAF begins bombing Ruhr, Reynaud asks for more fighters: Paquier (1), Richards, Ellis, d'Astier, Müller, Webster, Narracott, Bräck, Churchill II, Douglas. Kleist's Halt Order of 15th to Guderian: Guderian, Goerlitz (1), Goutard, personal correspondence, French periodicals, Halder.

CHAPTER 15

French High Command actions, May 10th–15th: Gamelin I and III, Bois, Baudouin, Beaufre, Minart, Menu, Bardies, French periodicals, Goutard, Bardoux, Ironside, Churchill II, Reynaud (1), Lyet, Draper, Hartog, Pertinax. Reynaud and Churchill, May 15th–16th: Bois, Baudouin, Bénoist-Méchin, Reynaud (1), Ironside, Churchill II, Gamelin III. French Government actions of May 16th: Baudouin, Herriot, Reynaud (1), Draper, Bois, Monzie, Gamelin III. French censorship: Sheean, Boothe, Chastenet (3), Vasselle (1), Koestler, Waterfield, Bois, Werth. First panic in Paris: Sheean, Mendès-France, Bardoux, Hartog, Werth, Bois, Herriot, Bénoist-Méchin. Churchill in Paris, May 16th: Bénoist-Méchin, Churchill II, Spears I, Chautemps, Baudouin, Reynaud (1), Ironside, General Ismay (*Memoirs*), Ellis, Douglas, Müller, Taylor (1), Richards. French High Command decisions, May 16th: Mellenthin, Minart, Roton, Doumenc, Lyet, French periodicals, Bardies. Guderian's break-through: May 16th: Gontaut-Biron, Lerecouvreux, Ruby, Kielmansegg, Stoves, Spaeter. French 2nd Armoured Division's operations: Serre, Voisin, French periodicals, personal correspondence, Bardies, Roton, Doumenc. Rommel's Avesnes Raid: principally Rommel and Doumenc, Rocolle, Menu, Roton, Borchert, Goutard, German periodicals, Manteuffel.

CHAPTER 16

The German High Command, May 10th–17th: Murawski, Wehrmacht communiqués, Shirer (1), Ettighoffer, P. C. (*44 Tage und Nächte*), Halder, Warlimont, Goutard, Heusinger, Jacobsen (1), German periodicals, Ellis, Guderian (2), Haupt, Telford Taylor, personal correspondence, Blumentritt, Mellenthin, Manteuffel, Kielmansegg. De Gaulle's first counterattack: Serre, de Gaulle (2), Tournoux, d'Astier, Gontaut-Biron, Voisin, Stoves, Kielmansegg, French and German periodicals, Mengin, Bardies, Roton, Bauer. Panzers consolidate: Doumenc, Manteuffel, Kosak, Prioux, Stackelberg, Guderian (2), Haupt, Lemelsen (op. cit.). Waning Allied air effort, effect on land forces: Webster, d'Astier, Richards, Narracott, Balbaud, Paquier (1). Retreat from northern Belgium: Prioux, Ellis, Balbaud, Bryant, Jacobsen (1). French High Command and Government actions: French periodicals, Weygand (1) and (2), Gamelin III, Minart, Doumenc, Baudouin, Bardoux, Roton.

CHAPTER 17

Panzers advance again: Stoves, Churchill II, Draper, Jacobsen (1), Christophe, Manteuffel, Starcke, Haupt, Halder, Murawski, Wehrmacht communiqués. End of Ninth Army and capture of Giraud: Vasselle (1), Habe, Draper, Doumenc, Guderian (2), Ellis, Minart, Middleton, Roton. Fugitives and refugees: Accart, Sarraz-Bournet, Muray, Mendès-France, Bardoux, de Jong, Kosak, Koestler, Waterfield, Maurois, Carron, Beauvoir, Chambrun, Bryant, Kielmansegg, Boothe, Chastenet (3), Bardies, Chautemps, Saint-Exupéry. The fifth column: Barlone, de Jong, Waterfield, Habe, Vilfroy (*The War in the West*), Werth, German archives, Tissier, Spears II, Conrad, Pertinax, Reile, Telford Taylor, Menu, Ruby, Lerecouvreux, Reynaud (1), Rauschning, Shirer (1), Beaufre, personal correspondence, Bayet, Koestler, Gamelin III, French periodicals. French High Command recognises German objective: Minart, Roton, French periodicals, Baudouin, Weygand (1), Voisin, personal correspondence, Baudouin, Gamelin III, Reynaud (1), Bardoux, Spears I, Ironside, Bénoist-Méchin. Operations on May 19th: French and German periodicals, Kielmansegg, d'Astier, de Gaulle (2), Salesse, Voisin, Halder, Gontaut-Biron, Vasselle (1), Wittek, Ellis, Stoves. Fighting on the Maginot Line: Prételat, Rowe, Picht, Bénoist-Méchin. Withdrawal from northern Belgium and rumours of British evacuation intent: Ellis, Roton, Prioux, Reynaud (1), French periodicals, Barlone, Draper, Lyet, Richards, Ironside, Detrez and Chatelle (*Tragédies en Flandres*), Churchill II, Bénoist-Méchin. Instruction No. 12 and end of Gamelin: Minart, French and German periodicals, Roton, Reynaud (1), Gamelin I and III, Beaufre. Weygand takes over: Levy, Reynaud (1), Spears I and II, Greenwall, Werth, Beaufre, Jamet, Bois, Waterfield, Weygand (1) and (2), Baudouin, Minart. The Germans reach the Channel: Manteuffel, d'Astier, Kielmansegg, Stoves, Draper, Bryant, Shirer (1), Telford Taylor, Guderian (3), Lyet.

CHAPTER 18

German "pause" of May 21st: Halder, Goutard, Telford Taylor, Guderian (2). Allied High Command; Ironside's Plan: Reynaud (1), Lyet, Baudouin, Detrez (op. cit.), Bénoist-Méchin, Chambrun, Ellis, Ironside, Weygand (1), French periodicals, Müller, Churchill, Gort's Dispatches. Gort, background: Draper, Thompson, Spears I, Ellis, Maurois, Bryant. The Arras attack: Detrez (op. cit.), d'Astier, Bardies, Bryant, Chambrun, Draper, Ellis, Prioux, Roton, Weygand (2), Telford Taylor, Goutard, Guderian (2), Churchill II, Gort's Dispatches, Reynaud (1), Jacobsen (1), Flack, Halder, Mellenthin, Haupt, Manteuffel, Rommel, Starcke, *Sieg im West*, German archives, personal correspondence. Weygand's visit to Ypres: Baudouin, Churchill II, Weygand (1) and (2), Reynaud (1), French periodicals, Bardies, Ellis, Lyet, Bénoist-Méchin, Beaufre, Goutard, Bauer,

Hartog. Reynaud and Churchill in Paris, May 22nd: Bois, Bardoux, Werth, Goutard, Baudouin, Draper, Roton, Weygand (1), Reynaud (1), Churchill II, Ellis, Ismay (op. cit.), Ironside. German operations, May 22nd: Christophe, Shirer (1), Mende, Stoves, Manteuffel, Ellis. French counter-strokes, May 22nd; Detrez (op. cit.), d'Astier, Bekker, Prioux, Ellis, Lyet, Roton, Weygand (2), Goutard, Gort Dispatches, Bardies, Vasselle (2). Gort withdraws: Ellis, Churchill II, Gort Dispatches, Weygand (1), French periodicals, Draper, Richards, Detrez (op. cit.), Bryant, Prioux, Weygand (2), Telford Taylor, Bardies, Reynaud (1), Ironside.

CHAPTER 19

The German Halt Order of May 24th: Taylor (1), Ellis, Halder, Rommel, Telford Taylor, German periodicals, Guderian (2), Fechner, Haupt, Goutard, Bekker, Blumentritt, Warlimont, Heusinger, Bénoist-Méchin, Churchill II. Growing French despair; rancour among the Allies: Werth, Jamet, Bardoux, Spears I, Koestler, Picht, Sheean, Waterfield, Telford Taylor, Prioux, Draper, Boothe, Baudouin, Bénoist-Méchin. Weygand; beginnings of "separate peace" lobby: Waterfield, Telford Taylor, Draper, Baudouin, Bénoist-Méchin, Müller, Chautemps, Spears I, Reynaud (1). French Cabinet session of May 25th: Müller, Baudouin, Spears I, Reynaud (1), Bénoist-Méchin. Footnote on air strengths: Bauer, Baudouin, Jacobsen (1), Ellis, Paquier (1), Richards. French attacks from south; fading of Weygand Plan: Goutard, Vasselle (1) and (2), Bénoist-Méchin, Weygand (2), Reynaud (1), Baudouin, Draper, Churchill II. Dunkirk: Jacobsen (1) and (2), Bekker, Spears I, Draper, Lyet, Ellis, Weygand (1), Ironside, Richards, Gort Dispatches, d'Astier, Goutard, Bénoist-Méchin, Churchill II.

CHAPTER 20

Operation "Red" begins: Draper, d'Astier, Weygand (1), Warlimont, Spears II, Goutard, Richards, Churchill II, Halder, Reynaud (1), Telford Taylor, Sieg im West, Manteuffel, Rommel, Guderian (2), Bénoist-Méchin. Paris falls: Draper, Shirer (1), Werth, Telford Taylor, Ehrenburg, Waterfield, Maurois, Fabre-Luce, Bénoist-Méchin, Halder. Italy attacks: Reynaud (1), Bénoist-Méchin, Goutard, Richards. Last resistances: Draper, Spears I and II, Chastenet (3), Bénoist-Méchin, Beaufre. Political struggle between "softs" and "hards": Spears I and II, Churchill II, Bénoist-Méchin, Bois, Koestler, Levy, Weygand (1), Reynaud (1), Baudouin, Bénoist-Méchin, Maurois. Reynaud at breaking point; his plea to America: Spears II, Bois, Bénoist-Méchin, Baudouin, Boothe, personal correspondence, Reynaud (1), Churchill II. Reynaud resigns: Reynaud (1), Spears II, Bénoist-Méchin, Churchill II, Baudouin, Shirer (1), Chastenet (3).

CHAPTER 21

The armistice: Shirer (1) and (2), Halder, Mende, Warlimont, Sieg im West, Weygand (1), Bénoist-Méchin. Casualties: Haupt, Manteuffel, Chastenet (3), Werth, Picht, Ellis, Webster, Richards, Tissier, Starcke, Spaeter, personal correspondence. First days after cease-fire: Stackelberg, Halder, Beauvoir, Ehrenburg, Shirer (1), Middleton, Thompson, Spaeter, Mende. Shadows of defeat for Hitler: Mende, Warlimont, Shirer (1) and (2), Telford Taylor, Blumentritt, Dorgelès, Jacobsen (1), Klein, Murawski, Sieg im West, Bauer, Ellis. Post-mortems: French and German periodicals, Spears I, de Jong, Habe, Doumenc, Ellis, Goutard, Telford Taylor,

Koestler, personal correspondence. Subsequent careers of principals: Reynaud (1), Gamelin III, Prioux, Telford Taylor, Baudouin, d'Astier, Bénoist-Méchin, Greenwall, Nicolson (op. cit.), personal correspondence, *The Times, Chambers Encyclopedia, Encyclopaedia Britannica.*

Index